AN AMERICAN PORTRAIT

AN AMERICAN PORTRAIT

Charles Scribner's Sons · New York

A History of the United States

SECOND EDITION ☆ VOLUME 1

DAVID BURNER
SUNY, Stony Brook

ELIZABETH FOX-GENOVESE
SUNY, Binghamton

EUGENE D. GENOVESE
University of Rochester

FORREST McDONALD
University of Alabama

TO SANDY, ERIC, DIANE, AND BOB

Cover Illustration: The Sierra Nevada in California, Albert Bierstadt. Courtesy, National Museum of American Art, Smithsonian Institution. Bequest of Helen Huntington Hull.

Library of Congress Cataloging in Publication Data
Main entry under title:

An American portrait.

Rev. ed. of: The American people / by David Burner, with Eugene D. Genovese, Forrest McDonald. c1980.
Includes bibliographical references and index.
1. United States—History. I. Burner, David, 1937– II. Burner, David, 1937– . American people.
E178.1.A4936 1985 973 84-23476
ISBN 0-02-371260-0
ISBN 0-02-371250-3 (pbk. : v. 1)
ISBN 0-02-371270-8 (pbk. : v. 2)

This book published simultaneously in the United States of America and in Canada—Copyright under the Berne Convention

1 3 5 7 9 11 13 15 17 19 20 18 16 14 12 10 8 6 4 2

Printed in the United States of America

Preface

Textbooks have led generations of students into the comfortable illusion that a single history book can summarize the nation's past. As historians know, it is impossible to resurrect the past exactly. In the reconstruction of events we rely on written records, along with some art objects and physical remains. Yet few occurrences are even recorded in writing. Many documents, morever, are lost, and the historian can never be certain of having seen every manuscript; or the sources may be too voluminous to read exhaustively. A document carries the point of view, or bias, of the person who wrote it and the time in which it was written. To these documents the historian brings his or her own bias.

For these reasons I have asked two eminent historians, the leftist Eugene D. Genovese and the conservative Forrest McDonald, to debate in question and answer form great issues of the American past. Their differences go beyond ideology, and in setting forth distinctive viewpoints these two men may help to crystallize your own thinking. This series of debates will provide material for class discussion or written reports and will demonstrate that there is no fixed truth about the past, which makes it all the more rewarding as an intellectual study. Students in any classroom deserve a challenge; and instructors can employ these verbal interchanges in any way they deem suitable. Another feature of the book is an account of a dramatic historical event at the beginning of each chapter.

The debates will provide theoretical content. But narrative itself is an analytical act. The introductory courses in the other social sciences, so popular and so simple, often fall into easy manipulation of abstract definitions, axioms, dicta, isolated from the facts that might clarify or test them. As fine historians like Samuel Eliot Morison and Allan Nevins have repeatedly demonstrated, a complex readable story is far more sophisticated for its embracing concrete and sometimes contradictory detail. This textbook, in this sense, offers three different interpretations of the American past: Genovese's, McDonald's and Burner's. There are important areas of agreement as well as of argument in the three accounts. There is but one past; there are many ways to illuminate that past. We hope this volume will introduce you to the genuine excitement historians have found in casting their own light on the history of the United States.

For this new edition published by Charles Scribner's Sons, Elizabeth Fox-Genovese has contributed very substantial sections on women's history. Tom West has edited this work with me in a manner that demands prime acknowledgment. John McClymer contributed the Points To Think About that follow each chapter while Pete Seeger chose most of the folk songs that are reprinted in the text. Invaluable assistance came from Robert Marcus for help throughout the book; from Tom McLuen for sections on North American Indians and on Spanish settlement; from Forrest McDonald on the chapters to 1763; from Alan January on the chapters from 1815 to 1860; from James Moore on twentieth-century diplomatic history. Also due thanks are Virginia Bernhard, Hugh Cleland, James Mooney, Gus Seligmann, Jr., Mel Rosenthal, Norm and Emily Rosenberg, Terry Cooney, James Cebula, Alex Holzman of Scribners, and the Sylvis Society.

DAVID BURNER
Stony Brook, New York
June 1984

About the Authors . . . .

DAVID BURNER earned his A.B. at Hamilton College and his Ph.D. at Columbia University. He has published *The Politics of Provincialism: The Democratic Party in Transition, 1918–1932* (1968); *Herbert Hoover: A Public Life* (1979); and *The Torch Is Passed: The Kennedy Brothers and American Liberalism* (1984), coauthored with Tom West. He is currently writing *Breaching the Wall: Religion and American Politics.* A Guggenheim Fellow, Burner teaches at the State University of New York at Stony Brook.

ELIZABETH FOX-GENOVESE teaches American history and women's studies at the State University of New York at Binghamton. She has published *Origins of Physiocracy* and is coauthor of a recently published study of Southern slave holders, and another forthcoming one, with Eugene D. Genovese. Fox-Genovese has received Guggenheim and Rockefeller fellowships and is currently director of the Organization of American Historians' project on women's history compiled for the United States survey course.

EUGENE D. GENOVESE, son of a dockworker, earned his B.A. at Brooklyn College and his Ph.D. at Columbia University. A distinguished leftist historian, he was president of the Organization of American Historians in 1979. His studies of slavery include *The Political Economy of Slavery* (1965), *The World the Slaveholders Made* (1969), *Roll, Jordan, Roll* (1974). With Elizabeth Fox-Genovese, he has published *The Fruits of Merchant Capitalism* (1983). Genovese, a Rockefeller Fellow, teaches at the University of Rochester. His stand against the Vietnam War won him a vituperative attack from Richard Nixon in 1965.

FORREST McDONALD earned his Ph.D. at the University of Texas and is now Distinguished Senior Fellow at the University of Alabama Center for the Study of Southern History and Culture. A Guggenheim Fellow, McDonald has published major works on the founding of the nation and in recent American history, among them *We the People: The Economic Origins of the Constitution* (1958); *Insull* (1962); and *Alexander Hamilton* (1979). A brilliant, prolific, and controversial historian, McDonald served as northeast co-chairman of Citizens for Goldwater in 1964. He is currently writing on political vocabulary in the English-speaking world and on Celtic influences in the South.

Contents

13 Distant Thunder: The 1850s / 327

14 Civil War and Reconstruction / 347

Appendixes / *i*

Index / *xxi*

Chronology

1492-1504 Columbus's four voyages to New World.

1497-98 John Cabot explores Newfoundland, Labrador, and Nova Scotia, and establishes English claim to North America.

1508-9 Sebastian Cabot explores Hudson Bay.

1509-47 Henry VIII.

1513 Balboa discovers Pacific Ocean after crossing Isthmus of Panama.

1513 Ponce de León discovers mainland of Florida.

1519-21 Cortés conquers Mexico.

1523 Verrazano explores coast of North America, establishing French claim.

1528-36 Cabeza de Vaca explores northern Gulf of Mexico, west to Gulf of California.

1532-35 Pizarro conquers Peru.

1534 Cartier's explorations establish French claim to St. Lawrence basin.

1535-39 Spanish conquest of Ecuador, Chile, northern Argentina, and Bolivia.

1539-41 De Soto explores southeastern United States and discovers the Mississippi.

1540-42 Coronado seeks legendary cities of wealth in North American Southwest.

1558-1603 Elizabeth I.

1562-67 Hawkins trades and plunders in Spanish America.

1574 Gilbert leads expedition to Hudson Bay.

1577-80 Drake circumnavigates globe.

1585-87 Raleigh's Roanoke Colony fails.

1603-25 James I.

1603-35 Samuel de Champlain establishes French colonies in Canada.

1607 Virginia Company establishes settlement at Jamestown.

1619 First Africans arrive in Virginia; First representative assembly meets.

1620 Mayflower Compact signed; Pilgrims establish Plymouth Colony.

1621 Dutch West India Company chartered.

1624 Virginia Company charter annulled; English crown takes control of Virginia; First settlements in New Netherlands by Dutch.

1625-49 Charles I.

1629 Massachusetts Bay founded.

1630 Puritan emigration from England begins.

1632 Cecilius Calvert, Lord Baltimore, receives charter for Maryland colony.

1634 First settlements in Maryland.

1635 Roger Williams banished from Bay Colony.

1636 Harvard College founded; First permanent English settlements in Connecticut and Rhode Island.

1638 Anne Hutchinson convicted of heresy in Massachusetts; flees to Rhode Island.

1642-48 Civil war in England.

1643 Confederation of New England.

1644 Rhode Island receives patent.

1647 Law requiring towns to maintain schools passed in Massachusetts Bay Colony.

1649 Charles I beheaded; Maryland Toleration Act.

1660 Restoration of Stuart monarchy (Charles II, 1660-85); Navigation Act passed by Parliament (The Enumeration Act).

1663 New navigation act (Staple Act) passed, channeling colonies' importation of European goods through England; Carolina charter granted to eight proprietors; Rhode Island granted charter.

1664 English take over New Netherlands; Grant of New Jersey to two proprietors.

1670 Settlement of Charleston.

1675-76 King Philip's War in New England.

1676 Bacon's Rebellion.

1677 Culpeper's Rebellion in Carolina.

1680 New Hampshire given royal charter.

1681 Pennsylvania charter granted to William Penn; First settlements in 1682.

1686 Dominion of New England.

1688 Glorious Revolution in England drives out James II (1685-88) in favor of William and Mary.

1689-91 Leisler's Rebellion, New York.

1692 Witchcraft hysteria in Salem, Massachusetts; nineteen "witches" hanged, one pressed to death.

1696 English government establishes Board of Trade and Plantations; passage of comprehensive navigation act, extending admiralty courts to America.

1699 Woolen Act.

1732 Georgia established to furnish buffer against Spanish and as philanthropic effort to relocate England's paupers; Hat Act.

1733 Molasses Act restricts colonial importation of sugar goods from French West Indies.

1734-35 Jonathan Edwards's evangelical revival in Northampton, Massachusetts, and Connecticut River valley.

1735 New York jury acquits John Peter Zenger of charge of seditious libel on ground that printing truth can be no libel.

1739-40 George Whitefield tours America and brings major phase of Great Awakening.

1750 Iron Act, limiting production of finished iron goods in colonies, passed by Parliament.

1751 Currency Act, restricting issuance of paper money in New England colonies, passed by Parliament; Publication of Franklin's *Experiments and Observations on Electricity*.

1754 Albany Congress and Plan of Union.

1754-63 French and Indian War (colonial phase of Europe's Seven Years' War, 1756-63).

1759 Quebec falls to British army.

1760-1820 George III.

1763 Treaty of Paris ends Seven Years' War between Great Britain, and France and Spain; Pontiac's rebellion, uprising of Indians in Ohio Valley; Proclamation line drawn along Appalachians by British forbids settlement in West; Paxton uprising by Scotch-Irish settlers in western Pennsylvania.

1764 Sugar Act; Currency Act prohibits issues of legal-tender currency in the colonies.

1765 Stamp Act; Stamp Act Congress meets in New York; Quartering Act.

1766 Stamp Act repealed by Parliament, which adopts Declaratory Act asserting its authority to bind the colonies "in all cases whatsoever."

1767 Townshend Duties passed; American Board of Customs established; John Dickinson's *Letters from a Farmer in Pennsylvania*.

1768 British troops sent to Boston.

1770 Lord North's ministry; Townshend duties repealed, except for duty on tea; Boston Massacre.

1772 British schooner *Gaspée* burned in Rhode Island; Boston Committee of Correspondence formed.

1773 Tea Act imposed; Boston Tea Party.

1774 Coercive or Intolerable Acts; Continental Congress meets in Philadelphia; Galloway's Plan of Union.

1775 Battle of Lexington and Concord; Fort Ticonderoga taken by American forces; Second Continental Congress meets in Philadelphia; George Washington appointed commander in chief of Continental army; Battle of Bunker Hill; Congress adopts its "Declaration of the Causes and Necessities of Taking Up Arms."

1776 Thomas Paine's *Common Sense;* Declaration of Independence; British troops evacuate Boston; Battle of Long Island, New York; British take New York City; Battle of Trenton.

1777 Battle of Princeton; Battle of Monmouth; Battle of Brandywine, Pennsylvania; British occupy Philadelphia; Battle of Germantown; Burgoyne surrenders at Saratoga; Articles of Confederation adopted by Continental Congress, but not ratified by all states until 1781; Washington retires to Valley Forge for winter.

1778 United States concludes military alliance and commercial treaty with France; British evacuate Philadelphia; Seize Savannah, Georgia.

1779 Spain enters the war against Britain; George Rogers Clark captures Vincennes and ends British rule in Northwest.

1780 Americans surrender 5500 men and the city of Charleston, South Carolina; Battle of Camden, South Carolina; Battle of King's Mountain, South Carolina.

1781 Battle of Cowpens, South Carolina; British under Tarleton defeated by Morgan; Battle of Guilford Courthouse, North Carolina; Cornwallis withdraws to coast; Cornwallis surrenders to Washington at Yorktown, Virginia.

1782 Fall of Lord North's ministry.

1783 Treaty of Paris with Britain signed.

1785 Land Ordinance for Northwest Territory adopted by Congress.

1786 Jay-Gardoqui Treaty rejected by Congress; Virginia Statute for Religious Freedom; Shays's Rebellion in western Massachusetts; Annapolis Convention adopts plan to meet in Philadelphia to revise Articles of Confederation.

1787 Federal Constitutional Convention meets in Philadelphia; Northwest Ordinance enacted by Congress. *The Federalist Papers* by Madison, Hamilton, and Jay.

1788 Ratification of United States Constitution by all states except Rhode Island and North Carolina.

1789 First session of Congress meets; Washington inaugurated as first President; Outbreak of French Revolution.

1790 Hamilton's Report on Public Credit; Father John Carroll made first Roman Catholic bishop of United States.

1791 Bank of the United States established; First ten amendments to Constitution (Bill of Rights) adopted.

1792 Washington reelected.

1793 Citizen Genêt Affair; Samuel Slater erects first cotton mill at Pawtucket, Rhode Island; Eli Whitney applies for patent on cotton gin.

1794 Whiskey Rebellion in western Pennsylvania; Battle of Fallen Timbers, Ohio; General Anthony Wayne defeats Indians.

1795 Jay's Treaty with Britain; Pinckney's Treaty with Spain.

1796 Washington's Farewell Address, warning against foreign entanglements and domestic factions; John Adams elected President.

1798 XYZ Affair reported by Adams to Congress; Quasi-war with France on high seas; Alien and Sedition Acts enacted by Federalists in Congress; Virginia and Kentucky resolutions.

1800 Washington, D.C., becomes capital; Thomas Jefferson elected President.

1801 War with Barbary states; John Marshall becomes chief justice.

1803 *Marbury* v. *Madison,* Supreme Court upholds right of judicial review; Louisiana Purchase; Lewis and Clark expedition begun.

1804 Hamilton killed by Vice-President Aaron Burr in duel; Jefferson reelected.

1807 Embargo Act; Robert Fulton's steamboat travels on Hudson River from Albany to New York in 30 hours.

1808 Congress prohibits Americans from participating in African slave trade; James Madison elected President.

1809 Embargo repealed; Nonintercourse Act passed, prohibiting trade with Britain and France.

1810 Macon's Bill No. 2 passed, restoring trade with Britain and France, but providing for trade restrictions to be reimposed on one of the powers if other should abandon its seizure of American ships.

1811 Madison, believing Napoleon has removed restrictions on American commerce, prohibits trade with Britain; Battle of Tippecanoe, Indiana, in which William Henry Harrison defeats Tecumseh and prevents formation of Indian confederacy.

1812 Congress declares war against Britain; Americans surrender Detroit to British; Madison reelected.

1813 Battle of Lake Erie, Captain Oliver Perry defeats British naval forces; Battle of the Thames; General Harrison defeats British and their Indian allies.

1814 Battle of Horseshoe Bend, Alabama; General Andrew Jackson defeats Creek Indians fighting for British; British burn Washington, D.C.; Commander Thomas Macdonough defeats British fleet on Lake Champlain; invading British turned back at Plattsburgh, New York; Hartford Convention of Federalist delegates from New England; Treaty of Ghent signed between United States and Great Britain.

1815 Battle of New Orleans, Jackson defeats British; *North American Review* founded in Boston.

1816 Second Bank of the United States chartered by Congress; Protective tariff passed; James Monroe elected President.

1818 General Jackson invades Florida to end Seminole War; Rush-Bagot Convention between Britain and United States establishes fishing rights and Canadian boundary.

1819 Depression begins; Adams-Onis Treaty; Spain cedes Florida; *Dartmouth College* Case; *McCulloch* v. *Maryland.*

1820 Missouri Compromise; Relection of James Monroe without opposition, "Era of Good Feelings."

1822 Denmark Vesey's Conspiracy.

1823 President issues Monroe Doctrine.

1824 John Quincy Adams elected President by House of Representatives after failure of any candidate to win electoral majority.

1828 John C. Calhoun's anonymous *South Carolina Exposition and Protest;* Congress passes "Tariff of Abominations"; Election of Andrew Jackson as President brings victory to new Democratic Party.

1829 Mexico abolishes slavery.

1830 Jackson vetoes Maysville Road Bill; Anti-Masonic Party holds first national party convention.

1831 Nat Turner's slave insurrection in Virginia.

1832 Beginning of Jackson's "war" against Second Bank of the United States (BUS); Special convention in South Carolina nullifies new protective tariff; Jackson reelected President.

1833 Congress provides for a gradual lowering

of tariffs, but passes Force Bill authorizing Jackson to enforce federal law in South Carolina.

1836 Jackson's "specie circular"; Martin Van Buren elected President.

1838 Aroostook War.

1840 Congress passes Van Buren's Independent Treasury Act; William H. Harrison elected President; Whigs in power; World anti-slavery convention.

1840 American Female Moral Reform Society organized as first national female reform association.

1841 John Tyler becomes President upon Harrison's death.

1842 Webster-Ashburton Treaty settles disputed U.S.-Canada boundary.

1843 First overland caravans to Oregon.

1844 Senate rejects Calhoun's Texas annexation treaty; James K. Polk elected President; Lowell Female Reform Association organized.

1845 Texas enters Union as slave state; John Slidell's unsuccessful mission to Mexico to negotiate purchase of New Mexico and California; Margaret Fuller publishes *Woman in the Nineteenth Century.*

1846 Beginning of Mexican War; General Zachary Taylor invades Mexico from the North; Treaty with Britain divides Oregon Territory along 49th parallel.

1847 General Winfield Scott captures Vera Cruz and Mexico City.

1848 Gold discovered in California; Van Buren, running for President on Free-Soil ticket, receives 10 percent of popular vote; Zachary Taylor elected President; Treaty of Guadalupe Hidalgo ends Mexican War, establishes Rio Grande as border; First Women's Rights Convention at Seneca Falls, New York; Elizabeth Cady Stanton drafts "Declaration of Sentiments."

1849 California gold rush.

1850 In Congress, sectional debate culminates in Compromise of 1850; Fugitive Slave Law requires federal agents to recover escaped slaves from sanctuaries in the North; Taylor's death makes Millard Fillmore President.

1851 Herman Melville's *Moby Dick.*

1852 Franklin Pierce elected President.

1853 Upsurge of political nativism, the Know-Nothing Party.

1854 Spectacular Know-Nothing election victories; Collapse of Whigs; New Republican Party; Commodore Perry opens Japan to American trade; Kansas-Nebraska Act rekindles sectional controversy over slavery; "Bleeding Kansas."

1856 John Brown's raid at Pottawatomie Creek; James Buchanan elected President.

1857 *Dred Scott* v. *Sanford;* In Kansas, proslavery Lecompton Constitution ratified as free-state men refuse to vote.

1858 Lincoln-Douglas debates.

1859 John Brown's raid on Harpers Ferry.

1860 Democratic Party, deadlocked at Charleston convention, divides along sectional lines at Baltimore; Abraham Lincoln elected President; South Carolina secedes from the Union.

1861 Secession of remaining states of deep South (Texas, Louisiana, Mississippi, Alabama, Georgia, and Florida); Jefferson Davis begins serving as President of the Confederate States of America; Firing on Fort Sumter precipitates war; Secession of Virginia, North Carolina, Tennessee, and Arkansas; Union army routed at first Battle of Bull Run (Manassas); McClellan heads Union Forces; *Trent* affair; Vassar College founded.

1862 Both Union and Confederacy adopt paper money; Union general, U.S. Grant, captures Fort Henry and Fort Donelson; Battle of the ironclads; *Virginia (Merrimack)* vs. *Monitor;* McClellan's Peninsula campaign brings Union army to outskirts of Richmond, the Confederate capital; Robert E. Lee becomes commander of Army of Northern Virginia; Confederate victory at second battle of Bull Run; Stalemate between Lee and McClellan at Antietam; Confederate invasion of Kentucky; Lincoln issues preliminary Emancipation Proclamation; Confederate victory at Fredericksburg.

1863 Lincoln issues final Emancipation Proclamation; Confederates defeat Union army under Hooker at Chancellorsville; Lee's invasion of North checked by Union army under Meade at Gettysburg; Grant captures Vicksburg; Draft riots in the North; Confederate army under Bragg defeats Union forces at Chickamauga; Union victory at Chattanooga (Lookout Mountain and Missionary Ridge); Lincoln offers lenient reconstruction program.

1864 Grant named Union general in chief; Grant's direct advance on Richmond checked at the Wilderness, Spotsylvania, and Cold Harbor; Lincoln reelected President; Sherman marches from Atlanta to the sea.

1865 Sherman pushes northward through South Carolina and North Carolina; Lee gives up Petersburg and Richmond; Lee surrenders at Appomattox; Lincoln assassinated; Andrew Johnson becomes President; Johnson moves for speedy, lenient restoration of Southern states to Union; Thirteenth Amendment ratified.

1866 Johnson breaks with Republican majority in Congress by vetoing Freedman's Bureau bill and Civil Rights bill (passed over his veto); Congress approves Fourteenth Amendment; Ku Klux Klan formed.

1867 Congress passes Military Reconstruction Act over Johnson's veto; Congress passes Tenure of Office Act and Command of Army Act to reduce Johnson's power.

1868 Former Confederate states hold constitutional conventions, for which former slaves are allowed to vote, and adopt new constitutions guaranteeing universal suffrage; President Johnson impeached; escapes conviction by one vote; Republican Ulysses S. Grant elected President.

American Letter for Gerald Murphy

It is a strange thing—to be an American
Neither an old house it is with the air
Tasting of hung herbs and the sun returning
Year after year to the same door and the churn
Making the same sound in the cool of the kitchen
Mother to son's wife, and the place to sit
Marked in the dusk by the worn stone at the wellhead—
That—nor the eyes like each other's eyes and the skull
Shaped to the same fault and the hands' sameness.
Neither a place it is nor a blood name.
America is West and the wind blowing.
America is a great word and the snow,
A way, a white bird, the rain falling,
A shining thing in the mind and the gulls' call.
America is neither a land nor a people,
A word's shape it is, a wind's sweep—
America is alone: many together,
Many of one mouth, of one breath,
Dressed as one—and none brothers among them:
Only the taught speech and the aped tongue.
America is alone and the gulls calling.

It is a strange thing to be an American.
It is strange to live on the high world in the stare
Of the naked sun and the stars as our bones live.
Men in the old lands housed by their rivers.
They built their towns in the vales in the earth's shelter.
We first inhabit the world. We dwell
On the half earth, on the open curve of a continent.
Sea is divided from sea by the day-fall. The dawn
Rides the low east with us many hours;
First are the capes, then are the shorelands, now
The blue Appalachians faint at the day rise;
The willows shudder with light on the long Ohio:
The lakes scatter the low sun: the prairies
Slide out of dark: in the eddy of clean air
The smoke goes up from the high plains of Wyoming:
The steep Sierras arise: the struck foam
Flames at the wind's heel on the far Pacific.
Already the noon leans to the eastern cliff:
The elms darken the door and the dust-heavy lilacs. . . .

This, this is our land, this is our people,
This that is neither a land nor a race. We must reap
The wind here in the grass for our soul's harvest:
Here we must eat our salt or our bones starve.
Here we must live or live only as shadows.
This is our race, we that have none, that have had
Neither the old walls nor the voices around us,
This is our land, this is our ancient ground—
The raw earth, the mixed bloods and the strangers,
The different eyes, the wind, and the heart's change,
These we will not leave though the old call us.
This is our country-earth, our blood, our kind.
Here we will live our years till the earth blind us—

—ARCHIBALD MACLEISH

Columbus—the messenger of the "new heaven and new earth" of the Biblical Apocalypse—planting the cross and giving trinkets to the natives of the New World. *(Courtesy, The Hispanic Society of America, New York)*

CHAPTER 1

Europe and America

CHRISTOPHER COLUMBUS

Son of a Genoese weaver, Columbus was an extraordinary weaver of dreams. The belief in riches and perfection beyond the sunset was strong in the cultures of his landlocked Mediterranean; for the only sea route leading outward—going everywhere and nowhere—was west through the Straits of Gibraltar and beyond the Canary Islands. America was an idea in the mind of Europe, and the writings of Columbus reveal the vividness and extravagance of the idea. It represented the possibility of wealth, freedom, and happiness, the concept of the noble savage, and the beckoning mystery of the wild frontier—elements that would later go into the "American dream." The new Western hemisphere was also primitive and frightening—full of cannibals by Columbus's testimony. On this fresh, unchartered land Europe could stamp its own shifting character and conflicting desires.

Columbus was a great mariner, and an atrocious geographer. Both qualities helped him to sell his enterprise to the monarchs of Spain. He sharply underestimated the circumference of the globe, placing Asia about 2400 miles from the Canaries of the eastern Atlantic: the actual distance is more than 10,000 miles, most of it vast oceans. Possessed of the intellectual certainty of the self-taught (he had first learned to read as a young man), convinced of the mystical significance of his name (after St. Christopher, who had carried the Infant Jesus across the waters), persuaded that the Bible supported his geographical notions and made likely his discovery of lost Christians, Columbus was an effective salesman for his grandiose project. Besieging King Ferdinand of Aragon and Queen Isabel of Castile for more years than they besieged the Alhambra, he finally got his ships, his crews, his promises of riches, and his striking title "Admiral of the Ocean Sea." And so he set out on what would be four earth-changing voyages, a story endlessly told, rich with symbols of a world's transformation.

He first weighed anchor on August 2, 1492, the very day upon which the last Jews who refused to convert to Catholicism had to leave Spain—most of them bound for the more tolerant countries of Islam. "After having turned out all the Jews from all your kingdoms," Columbus records in his first diary entry, "your highness gave orders to me that with a sufficient fleet I should go." The great explorer even gave assurances that he would exclude Jews from any land he discovered. The idea of a new world as a haven for persecuted people would have astonished Columbus. He envisioned himself the messenger of the "new heaven and new earth" of the Biblical Apocalypse—in which Jerusalem is recaptured and the Jews converted—but never admitted he had discovered a new world. Columbus died convinced that he had found the Eastern Indies, the Orient of India, China, and Japan.

On one voyage a tremendous waterspout threatened Columbus's ship. He calmed the waters by reading aloud the account in the Gospel According to St. John of the storm on the Sea of Galilee, tracing a cross in the sky and a circle around the fleet with his sword. On the same journey, marooned and starving in Jamaica, he terrified the local Indians into supplying his crew with food by threatening the divine gesture of removing the light from the moon—his up-to-date almanac correctly predicted a total eclipse of the moon. Such were the methods of this man who was at once a modern scientist, a medieval sailor, and a mystic.

The new world that Columbus never knew he had discovered contained wealth beyond his dreams of the riches of the Indies, and offered an opportunity for the expansion of Christianity far greater than his mystical vision. America would fuel the economy of Europe and offer a haven for millions whose lives his discovery disrupted. Columbus brought back Indian captives, initiating the Atlantic slave trade that would forcibly disrupt the lives of further millions, and it has been suggested that these first transatlantic slaves brought with them their own revenge, carrying in their bloodstreams the bacillus of syphilis—previously unknown to Europe. It was Columbus, too, who began the colonization of the New World, introducing on the island of Hispaniola an imperialist regime and its result: genocide. Columbus Day is not considered a holiday among American Indians.

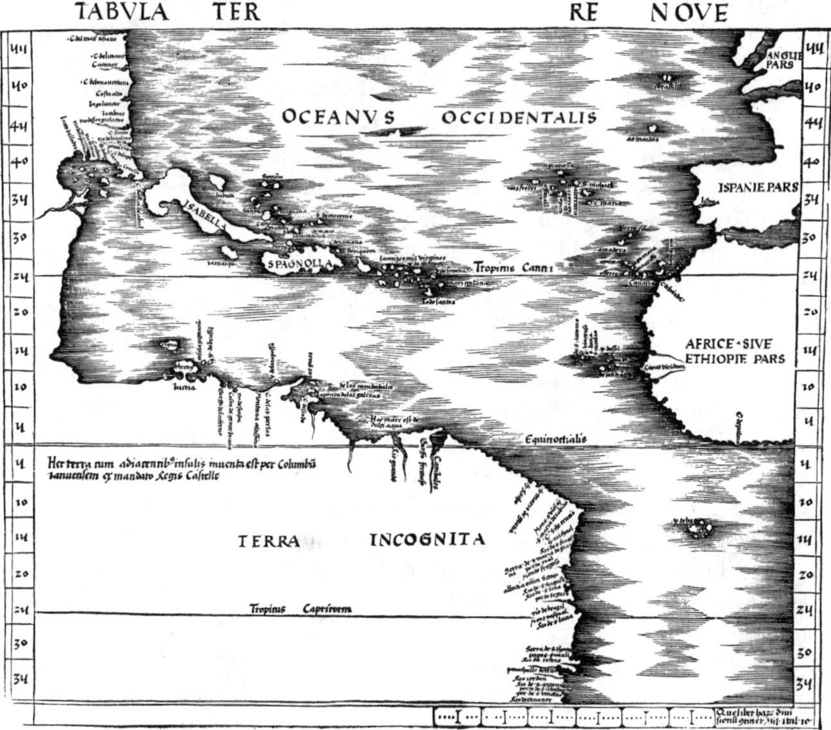

***Tabula Terre Nove*, Map of the New World, 1507–1513.** *(N. Phelps Stokes Collection. Prints Division. The New York Public Library, Astor, Lenox and Tilden Foundations)*

The World Stage

At the time of Columbus's discovery of America, Europe was in a state of unending warfare, Europeans fighting Europeans as well as Africans and Asians. Europeans contended for control of one square mile and another of their subcontinent. Emperors, kings, princes, and dukes laid claims to empires, kingdoms, principalities, and fiefs. Wars in defense of rival claims never ceased. Whatever unity held within European Christendom rested upon the hostility and contempt with which Europeans viewed all other racial, religious, and cultural groups.

The hostility was justified but the contempt was not, for Europe, being one of the least unified, was also one of the most primitive and least potent of the world's great cultures. For some centuries its home territory had been shrinking.

In the twelfth century, the great cultures had arrived at a temporary stalemate. Islam, the most dynamic and aggressive culture on the planet for four centuries, had temporarily spent its force after subduing the Iberian peninsula in Europe, all of North Africa, and Asia Minor as far as northern India. But the territory dominated by Islamic civilization did not diminish appreciably, and the Moslems retained a commanding superiority over the Europeans in science, technology, warfare, and general learning. To the east, the Hindu culture continued to dominate the Indian subcontinent, as it had for a thousand years; but the culture had long since passed its zenith and it was torn by revolution and by warfare among scores of satraps, great and small. In the Orient, the Sung dynasty dominated a vast area and Chinese culture basked in its golden age; but in the 1120s the Sungs lost half their territory through war and rebellion, and before the end of the twelfth century central Asia had spawned a new Mongol Empire that would be the terror of the thirteenth.

The Mongols. Europe so successfully gathered energy during the twelfth century that the ascendance of the West might soon have begun, but for the rise of the Mongols. The French and British in northwest Europe, the Germans in the center, the Swedes and Danes in the North, and the Slavs in the East made enormous strides toward national unity, and gained great strength in the process. Europe as a whole also gained strength, for a rather less obvious reason: enormous amounts of human resources, formerly required to defend hundreds and even thousands of small frontiers, were no longer needed for this purpose, and could be diverted to other ends. And Christendom's new-found energy was invested in enterprises that yielded even more vitality.

Some of this energy went into the Crusades, a series of wars against Islamic territory along the eastern Mediterranean and particularly in the ancient Christian Holy Land. While the Crusades had no lasting military or territorial consequences, they opened up large-scale trade with the East that planted new life in the European economy.

But the thirteenth century belonged to the Mongol hordes. In the space of forty years these terrible warriors swept over three continents, totally subjugating China and pressing the other three major civilizations into portions of their home regions. They overran all of Russia, subdued and ravaged Slavic eastern Europe, and thrust into the Germanic lands. There the onslaught against Europe stopped, for the interior mountains were not suitable to the Mongol style of mounted warfare. Then the hordes swung south to devastate Islamic territory. Western India fell, and then the Near East, and westward the Mongols swept until 1260, when Islamic forces stopped them just short of Egypt. Thenceforth, the Mongols expanded no more; they held on for a century and then, as abruptly as they had risen, they retreated and declined into impotence.

The Mongol occupation quickened Europe's economy and in ways that would have vast consequences. When the Mongols seized land to the east, the wealthiest and most advanced centers in Europe were the great city-states of northern Italy; Venice and Genoa in particular had gained large profits by supplying and transporting the armies of the Crusades, and then established themselves as the principal entrepôts for the importation of spices and other commodities from the Far East. During the Mongol years, trade from the East came overland across Asia to the Byzantine Empire, the easternmost portion of the Christian world, and then by sea to Venice and Genoa. To exploit this trade the Italians, using Portuguese and Italian Jews as intermediaries, borrowed extensively from the technological and scientific storehouse of the Moslems. They learned to use the lateen rigging, which enabled vessels to sail toward the wind, and acquired a knowledge of mathematics, astronomy, and navigation that was far superior to any then current in Europe. Late in the thirteenth century a Venetian, Marco Polo, spent twenty years in the Far East, mostly in the service of the Mongol khan; when he returned he wrote a journal describing his travels. Polo's journal gave Europeans their first direct information about the geography and civilization of the Orient, quickened their curiosity, and introduced them to a host of Chinese technological and scientific advances—including a revolutionary invention, gunpowder. Through such borrowings, and by their own ingenious improvements on them, the Italians started Europe along the way to the technological superiority that would, in time, make Europeans masters of the world.

The Ottoman Turks. But Europe's time was yet to come: for at the beginning of the fourteenth century, just as the menace of the Mongols was abating, the Moslems rose again, this time under the most terrible group of all, the Ottoman Turks. Before this wave of Islamic fury had spent itself, the Moslems would dominate a land mass extending ten thousand miles, from West Africa to Indonesia, and, through their advanced seamanship, would dominate the entire Indian Ocean as well.

This expansion had drastic effects on economic conditions in Europe. Eastern commodities could no longer be carried overland to Constantinople; they now went by water to the Red Sea or the Persian Gulf, and thence overland, through a series of what were in effect toll stations, to Mediterranean ports in Africa and Asia Minor. The price of spices rose greatly, with severe consequences to Europe. Spices were a necessity, not a luxury: to the end of the seventeenth century Europe suffered from a chronic shortage of winter feed for cattle, and the spices were needed as preservatives for the huge amount of livestock slaughtered every autumn. The population of Europe, moreover, began to increase rapidly at this time, which meant that Oriental spices were becoming scarcer and dearer as the demand was becoming greater. By 1453, when Constantinople fell to the Moslems, old trade patterns with the East had been thoroughly disrupted, and Europe's strength was at its lowest in centuries.

Portugal's Crusade by Sea

Europe desperately needed a way of coping with the Moslems and trading with the East. Portugal found it. The people of that tiny kingdom, free for three centuries from Moslem domination but struggling for survival in a rocky and barren land, had turned to the sea, first as fishermen, then as traders. As seagoing traders whose home base was in the southwestern corner of Europe, and on the Atlantic, not the Mediterranean, they understandably thought of an indirect route to the spices that Europe needed. Western Africa below the Sahara had gold and ivory in abundance, and with these Europe could buy spices. Overland, through the Moslem territories of northern Africa, the black kingdoms that ruled western Africa and controlled the ivory and the gold could be reached only through Moslem intermediaries. But if Europeans could find a sea route around Africa to the East, they could bypass the Moslems, establish trade relations with the blacks, and simultaneously edge toward the Orient.

The black peoples Europe was seeking to trade with were impressive. In the area drained by the Senegal and Niger rivers, the rulers of Ghana, Mali, and Songhay had successfully established imperial domains; and in a vast territory extending from the Gulf of Guinea to the savannahs on the edge of the Sahara, and from the Atlantic Ocean deep into the interior, subsidiary kingdoms ruled. Those black kingdoms that had converted to Islam or come under its influence had developed written languages; and all of them possessed most of the other attributes that Europeans regarded as the marks of civilization, including agriculture, metal tools, political organization, professional armies, social stratification, cities, creative arts, and regular international and intercultural trade.

Prince Henry the Navigator. The man who directed Portugal's efforts to take advantage of all this was Prince Henry the Navigator. Henry began his explorations in 1415. He retired from the court and from politics, became governor of the southernmost province of Portugal, and began building a strange settlement there, on Cape St. Vincent—"where endeth land and where beginneth sea." For the next forty years he gathered sailors, astronomers, map makers, instrument makers, and ship builders from all over Europe, and subsidized expeditions to explore the West coast of Africa, seeking a route to India. Overcoming the fears of superstitious sailors that ships would run into boiling hot waters at the equator, Henry's grand and audacious Portuguese undertaking was only temporarily set back by his death in 1460. In 1497 Vasco da Gama made his celebrated voyage to India with a four-vessel fleet, returning two years later with a cargo of pepper and cinnamon. Within twenty more years Henry's dream was fulfilled, for Portugal had established a maritime empire that extended the full breadth of the Indian Ocean.

Other Europeans, inspired by the Portuguese, sought to share in the glory and profit of war and trade in the East. None reckoned that they could overtake Portugal in the race around Africa, but several thought they might find an alternate course. It was reasonably well known that the earth was round. And since America was not known to exist and even knowledgeable Europeans underestimated the earth's circumference, they thought that a daring sailor might easily reach the Orient by sailing west from Europe. The most persistent of seamen who so reasoned was Christopher Columbus, a native of Genoa who had several years' experience on Genoese and Portuguese ships. These voyages profited from Prince Henry's development of a small sailing ship, the caravel. Its hull design, combined with its lateen sail plan, enabled the caravel to sail closer to the wind and therefore faster than earlier ships. Now mariners could go as far as they wished with assurance that they could return. And so Columbus made his spectacular voyages, thinking that he was finding the Orient but in fact discovering a new continent.

The Spanish Empire

The consequence of Columbus's discovery of San Salvador in the West Indies on October 12, 1492, was a flurry of efforts by other Europeans to capitalize on his discovery of new lands. The Portuguese did little, for they were convinced that Columbus had not reached Oriental islands, as he claimed and believed. Other European monarchs, including the kings of England and France, backed voyages upon Columbus's mistaken belief that he had found the Indies, or a passage to them. Henry VII of England sponsored voyages by the Italians John and Sebastian Cabot in 1497 and 1498. The Cabots explored the American coast from Labrador to Chesapeake Bay and discovered vast areas teeming with fish; but they found neither spices nor a passage to India, and Henry's England profited little from these and two additional expeditions. French and Venetian efforts were likewise un-

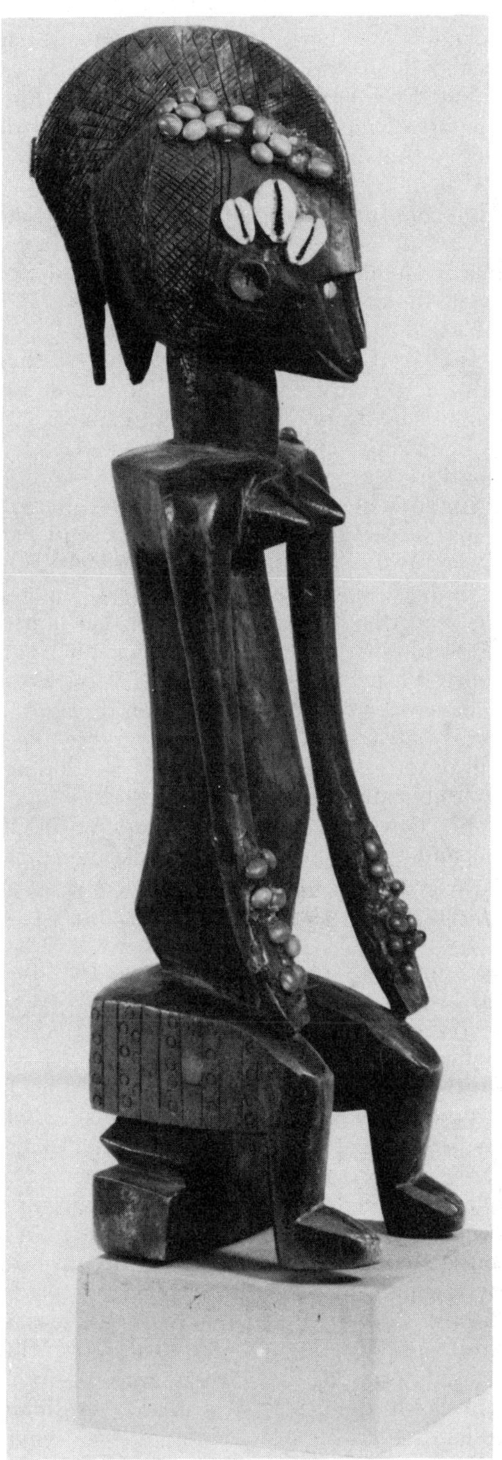

African Art. Figures like this one were sometimes given to tribal girls when they came of age. It is decorated with cowry shells from the Indian Ocean, which were used as currency in many parts of Africa. *(National Museum of Denmark, Department of Ethnography)*

profitable, and both kingdoms had pressing preoccupations, and so they, like England, soon abandoned the search. Hence, for a time Spain had a virtual monopoly on exploration and discovery in the New World.

Explorers for Spain. The greatest of discoverers sailing under the Spanish flag was, of course, Columbus himself. Columbus made four voyages in all (1492–93, 1493–96, 1498–1500, and 1502–04). He discovered most of the major islands of the Caribbean, Trinidad, the Northern coast of South America, and the Central American mainland from Honduras to Panama, and planted colonies in several of these places. In nonmaritime activities, however, he proved inept. He so neglected and mismanaged the colonies that he had to be removed as governor; and when he died in 1506 he was still convinced that what he had explored was part of Asia.

The man who did most to correct that impression was another Italian in the service of Spain, Amerigo Vespucci, for whom the New World was named. Vespucci made four voyages to America between 1497 and 1505 and wrote a series of descriptive letters to friends in Florence. Their publication in 1507 added greatly to European knowledge and understanding of the shape and size of the New World. Henceforth all Europe knew America for what it was, a new continent and a barrier between Europe and Asia.

Nothing of any recognized value had yet been found in America, and so the problem now became one of finding a strait through a landmass of unknown size. A chance discovery of 1513 stimulated the search for a passage to the Orient. Vasco Nuñez de Balboa, a Spanish adventurer, led a band of followers in search of gold in Central America, crossed the Isthmus of Darien, and sighted the Pacific. Spain promptly planted a colony in the vicinity, and explorers, encouraged to learn that the two oceans were separated only by an extremely narrow strip of land, renewed their hopes. After the coast of Central America and Mexico had been fairly thoroughly cruised, the most promise of finding a route lay to the south. And in 1519 Ferdinand Magellan, a Portuguese sailing under Spanish auspices, set out on his monumental voyage. This voyage was completed in 1522 by Sebastian del Cano, a Spanish navigator who succeeded to command after Magellan was killed in the Philippines. As the first circumnavigation of the globe, it added enormously to Europe's knowledge of the world. It demonstrated for all time that it was not feasible for Spain to try to compete with Portugal in the East by sailing west. The route was simply too difficult; and besides, by the time Magellan's vessels reached the Indian Ocean the Portuguese had already established the bases that made them dominant in the entire area. Other nationals, much later, would resume the search for a northwest passage to the Pacific, but from the time of Magellan's voyages Spain had to be content with exploiting what it could in America.

The Aztecs, Incas, and Mayans. The Spanish settlements proved reasonably prosperous, establishing some economies based on cattle raising with Spanish labor and others founded on sugar planting with Indian slave labor. But raising cattle and growing sugar were not the kinds of activities that quickened the imagination or filled the treasuries of the Spanish monarchs. Far more exciting were rumors and information of highly civilized kingdoms in the interiors of Mexico, Central America, and northwestern South America, and of their stores of gold and silver. An expedition set out in 1519 to find, conquer, plunder, and Christianize these kingdoms. Hernando Cortés, a thirty-two-year-old soldier and adventurer, commanded the expedition. The Aztecs under the emperor Montezuma II, who believed himself a god, dominated the valley of Mexico. From their capital city of Tenochtitlán, they sent out war parties to exact tribute from other tribes. In the capital the Aztecs had surgeons and hospitals as advanced as the best in Europe. They also worshiped many gods but particularly Quetzalcoatl, the feathered serpent, and the bloodthirsty Hummingbird, who demanded human sacrifice. In the space of only four days the Aztecs once sacrificed 80,000 human beings at the altar in Tenochtitlán. As news of the Spanish encroachments reached him, Montezuma's astrologers forecast a war of the gods and he stepped up the ritual murders, which understandably weakened the loyalty of his subjects. When the emperor finally realized that the Spanish were not gods, he fought ably and might have defeated them. But during the siege of his city, smallpox decimated the Indian population.

The Aztecs, like the later Indian tribes Europeans encountered in America, had developed no immunity against the perennial European epidemics. Between 1500 and 1600 the native population of New Spain declined incredibly from about twenty-five million to about one million.

In a matter of months Cortés had penetrated

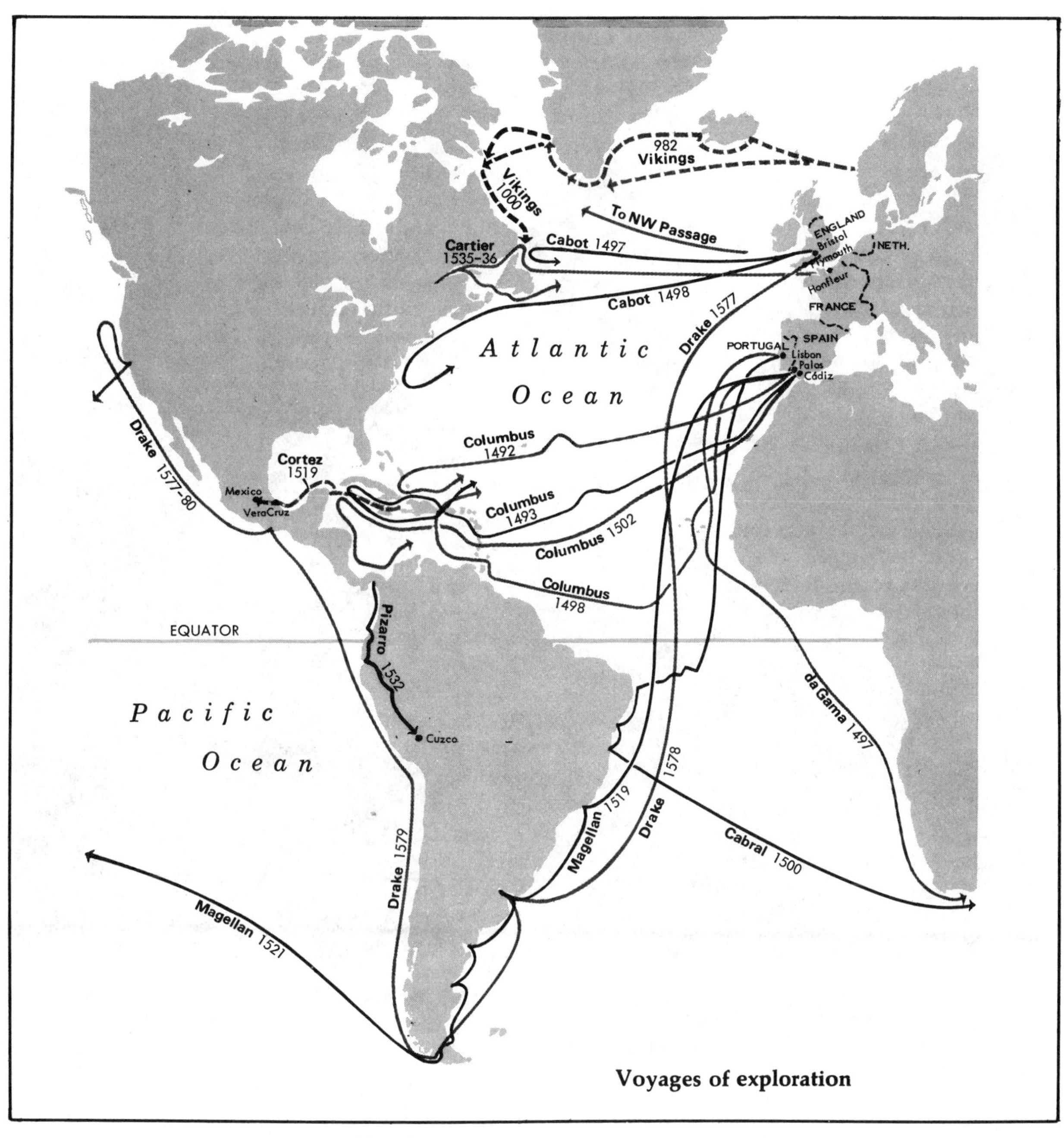

Voyages of exploration

the heart of the Aztec Empire and slain Montezuma, though it took two years to complete the systematic looting and destruction of the Aztec capital (now Mexico City) and the total subjugation of the Aztec people. In the next few years Cortés's lieutenants brutally conquered the Mayan territories of Central America. And in 1532 an obscure adventurer, Francisco Pizarro, led a tiny band into Peru, seized and executed the Incan leader, Atahualpa, and on behalf of the King of Spain placed himself at the head of an empire of about six or eight million souls. Finally, the Mayans of the southwestern Mexican coasts, literate and skilled, were subjugated. Only Brazil, awarded to Portugal by the Treaty of Tordesillas of 1494, remained outside the empire of the Spanish *conquistadores.* In each instance the Spaniards consolidated their conquest with ease, partly because of their superior weapons, cunning, and aggressiveness, and partly be-

Machu Picchu, the mysterious "Lost City of the Incas," 50 miles from Cuzco, Peru. Used by the last Inca ruler as an impregnable refuge from Pizzaro and his conquistadores, it clings to a ridge 2000 feet above the Urubamba Valley. Abandoned after the Spanish conquest, it was unknown for centuries until rediscovery in 1911. ***(Braniff International)***

cause their victims were accustomed to total obedience, and so mastery over them required little more than the defeat of their existing masters. In each instance, the conquerors reaped fantastic wealth in gold and silver.

The first exploration in the southeastern United States occurred in 1513 under the leadership of a Spanish explorer, Juan Ponce de León. He named this area Florida, meaning in Spanish "full of flowers." Another attempt to explore the Southeast occurred in 1528 when a Spaniard, Panfio de Narvaez, lead about 400 men into Florida in search of gold. The explorations of these gold-seekers ended in disaster in the form of shipwrecks. Hernando de Soto landed in the Tampa area in 1539 en route to the Mississippi River. No permanent settlements resulted from any of these early Spanish explorations.

The French, however, in 1564 established a colony, Fort Caroline, near present-day Jacksonville. The French Protestants, called Huguenots, remained in this colony until the Spanish massacred them. In 1565 the Spanish founded St. Augustine, the first permanent settlement in what would one day become part of the United

States. This provided the base from which the Spanish would attempt to teach their way of life to the Florida Indians over the next several hundred years.

In the 1540s de Soto and Francisco Vasquez de Coronado separately explored parts of the present-day United States for gold. De Soto, after landing on the west coast of Florida, led his men into North Carolina, turning westward and finally ending near Memphis, Tennessee, where he died in 1542. Ultimately, over 300 of his followers made their way back to Mexico via the Mississippi River. Coronado moved northward out of Mexico and probably traveled as far as Kansas. When he returned to Mexico he made clear that the fabled "seven Cities of Cibola," cities said to be made of gold, did not exist and that there was little else in the area to attract settlement.

Spanish exploration of the California coast also occurred in the 1540s. In 1542 Juan Rodriguez Cabrillo, a Portuguese explorer in the employ of Spain, hoped to discover the Northwest Passage between the Pacific and Atlantic oceans. He first sailed into San Diego Bay and later went northward, perhaps as far as Oregon. Following Sir Francis Drake's claiming of California for the English, the Spaniards, fearing they might lose the region, sent Sebastian Vizcaino in 1602 to report about California to the Spanish monarch. Vizcaino recommended to the king that Spain establish colonies there, but further Spanish activity along the west coast would await the passing of nearly a century.

Spanish Rule. By 1550, with the major centers of settled population in tropical America under Spanish control, Spain had imposed over the entire area a highly centralized imperial system. The contrast with the later British Empire is intriguing. The Roman Catholic Church, through its missionary orders, vigorously pursued the

Francisco Vasquez de Coronado, one of the earliest Spanish explorers of Mexico and the American Southwest, in a 1905 printing by Frederic Remington. *(Copyright 1905 by P. F. Collier and Son)*

spiritual conquest of the Indians and obtained a considerable measure of power in its own right, more or less independent of the lawyers who ran the imperial administration for the king. The empire had a fairly rigid caste system. At the top were the Spaniards who held most of the political and religious offices; next came the Creoles, or pureblood Spaniards born in America, who held the larger landholdings or *encomiendas*. But the bulk of the population was made up of pure Indians and the *mestizos*, people of mixed Indian and Spanish blood, ultimately the most numerous element in the population. In the Spanish island plantations there was a still lower group, the black slaves. For all its faults, and for all the follies of the Spanish kings, the Spanish Empire thus organized survived for more than two and a half centuries, and for much of the time made Spain the foremost power in the world. The Spanish kings were never able to find anything better to do with the treasure of the New World than to spend it on crusades and conquest in the Old. Then a newer British empire to the north, peopled by vigorous farmers, craftsmen, merchants, and seafarers prospering amidst considerable political freedom, would grow in strength while the hierarchical Spanish empire—its immense boundaries a source of unending trouble—declined.

Yet the Spanish empire endured four hundred years and has left its legacy in the United States in a growing number of Spanish-speaking citizens.

England: The Sceptered Isle

Henry VII. When Henry VII, the first Tudor king, ascended the throne in 1485, the royal treasury had been depleted by a long civil war (the War of the Roses). The throne itself was insecure, a number of ruthless and powerful noble families supporting the claims of various pretenders.

Henry might have been expected to secure his position in the traditional way, allying himself with various groups of nobles and playing them off one against the other. Instead, he built up the independent power of the Crown by taking a number of commoners into the government and launched a direct attack on the nobles who would not support him. As the principal instrument for this attack he created, with the consent of Parliament, the Court of the Star Chamber, through which people could be seized, tried without a jury, and punished by fines so heavy as to be confiscatory. In these early days the Star Chamber functioned and was looked upon as a protector of the common people against the tyranny of the nobles. By its means Henry weakened and divided the nobility, strengthened the Commons—the House of Parliament that was more representative of the people—and won the respect of the populace. To replenish the royal treasury, Henry managed his fiscal affairs efficiently and frugally and made most of his wars economically successful undertakings. He chose his wars carefully, acting only when he was likely not only to win, but also to reap profit from plunder or from ransoming captives. By the time he died in 1509 his dynasty was firmly secured, and the royal treasury was the richest in all Europe.

Henry VIII. His son and successor, Henry VIII, began his reign by dissipating the royal treasury in little more than a decade. By the early 1520s, as a result of his own extravagance and overambitious meddling in Continental politics and wars, the treasury was bare. The problem increased when the first great influx of American gold and silver into Spain inflated European prices.

Just at this time, a number of circumstances coalesced to induce Henry to another radical measure. Of the six children borne by Henry's wife Catherine of Aragon, only one daughter survived and Catherine was unable to have more; and so the Tudor dynasty was in danger of having no successor to the throne. In addition, Henry fell passionately in love with Anne Boleyn, who was willing to marry the king but refused to become his mistress. Henry turned to the Pope with a request for an annulment, which might readily have been granted except that the Pope was virtually a prisoner of King Charles of Spain, Catherine of Aragon's nephew. The request was refused, and in 1529 Henry called Parliament into a historic session that lasted seven years. Before it was dissolved, a new Church of England had cut all ties with Rome.

That opened the way for a solution to Henry's financial problems. He confiscated the property of the church monasteries, which brought him nearly a sixth of all the land in England. Over the years Henry sold most of the land, mainly to the landholding classes on all levels, including many city merchants. A number of the new owners quickly resold their lands to smaller holders, and this somewhat broadened the landholding class. The releasing of land from the control of the Church, the consequent growth in the number of landholders, and the commercial activity that the sale of the lands awakened together modernized the English economy.

The break gained for England the zealous enmity of its traditional ally, Spain. That enmity intensified with the accession of Philip II to the Spanish throne in 1556; for Philip was fanatically dedicated to using all the wealth and power of the Spanish Empire to suppress Protestantism.

Elizabeth I. And so when Queen Elizabeth, Henry VIII's daughter by Anne Boleyn, ascended the throne in 1558—after a turbulent and bloody eleven-year interval in which her half-brother Edward and her Roman Catholic half-sister Mary each occupied the throne for just over five years—England's internal order and external relations had been fundamentally rearranged.

Elizabeth faced spiraling prices and had no more monasteries to confiscate. One solution was for England to obtain a share of Spain's gold and silver through direct trade with Spanish colonies, and for Elizabeth to augment her treasury either by taxing or licensing this trade or by going into secret partnership with the English traders.

For a while such undertakings were entrusted to private enterprise. The first outsider to exploit this market was the Englishman John Hawkins. The two Old World commodities most in demand in Spanish America were cloth and slaves, the first a product of England and the other easily obtainable in Portuguese West Africa. In 1562 Hawkins acquired 300 black slaves and sailed with them to Hispaniola, where he sold them at a handsome profit; he received payment in sugar and hides, which he sold for further profit in Europe. On his second venture the queen and several members of her Privy Council were Hawkins's secret partners, and he again made a whopping profit, this time mainly in silver. Subsequent ventures were handicapped by a Spanish crackdown and by 1569 trade was thoroughly closed to outsiders. Within another four years, more or less open conflict between the Catholic and Protestant countries had begun, the rebellious Dutch having allied themselves with England. For the next thirty years, British and Dutch ships engaged in smuggling to Spanish America and in systematic plunder of Spanish shipping.

The greatest of the English captains in these enterprises was Sir Francis Drake, kinsman of Hawkins. Drake conducted a brilliant and profitable privateering raid in 1573, and launched his most spectacular venture four years later. With secret authorization and an investment from the queen he crossed the Atlantic, passed through the Strait of Magellan, plundered Spanish shipping off South America, captured a shipload of Peruvian silver, explored the Pacific coast of North America, crossed to the East Indies, concluded a treaty with a sultan who was at war with the Portuguese, bought several tons of cloves, and sailed home by the Portuguese route around Africa, returning with considerable glory and incredible treasure. Meanwhile, Elizabeth encouraged Martin Frobisher and John Davis in their exploration of North America for a northwest water passage to Asia, and supported Humphrey Gilbert and his half-brother Walter Raleigh in schemes to colonize North America. When Drake came home from his spectacular circumnavigation of the world in 1581, the queen knighted him on his own quarterdeck and rejected all attempts by Spain to recover the stolen booty.

Open war with Spain soon followed. Spain under Philip II had had more than enough of Elizabethan "sea dogs," and the somber Catholic

Sir Walter Raleigh, encouraged by Queen Elizabeth to colonize North America, explored a new region which the monarch named Virginia in honor of herself. *(Courtesy, N.Y. Public Library, Picture Collection)*

zealot Philip was committed to rewinning England and Calvinist Scotland for the Roman Catholic Church. Naval warfare began in 1584. Elizabeth sent troops to aid Protestant Holland in its long struggle to retain its independence from the Spanish Crown, which had nominal sovereignty over it. Drake set forth with more than twenty men-of-war and a royal commission to attack the Spanish position in America. In the ensuing year Drake wreaked considerable devastation in the West Indies and sacked Santo Domingo. In 1587 he conducted an audacious raid that sank much of the Spanish fleet in its home harbor at Cadiz.

Philip of Spain then ordered the construction of an "Invincible Armada" of 132 vessels carrying 3165 cannon. The British hurriedly prepared for defense by constructing a more numerous though less heavily armed fleet, and one far better suited to fighting in rough seas. The Spanish were handicapped by being required to move on orders from Madrid. The English were bold, swashbuckling, and infinitely more flexible. In a great naval battle in July 1588 the British outmaneuvered the Spanish in the English Channel and defeated the great Armada. Most of the Spanish vessels that escaped fled north hoping to return home by circling the British Isles, only to be destroyed by a storm off the Hebrides.

At the time of Elizabeth's death in 1603, the English people, a scant three million, but proud, aggressive, and prosperous, had gathered the energy that would propel them into virtual domination of the world.

English Colonization. While the Spanish were planting their colonies in the New World, Englishmen had given little energy to colonization. The English at the time of Henry VII as well as in Elizabeth's reign had sent voyages of expedition to North America in search of a northwest passage to the Orient, and Elizabethans had made some effort to colonize; but much of the activity of the English in the Western hemisphere had been in trade with the Spanish colonies, with or without the acquiescence of Spanish authorities, and in plunder of Spanish shipping.

In the late sixteenth and the early seventeenth centuries, however, the idea of colonization found its promoters and publicists. Colonies, it was said, could enrich the investors and the kingdom with wine, precious metals, and naval stores—the products that forests yielded for the maintenance of ships: later, in fact, North America would prove rich in naval stores. Colonization might also attract enough people to ease an overpopulation that some observers thought they were seeing in the kingdom. Actually, England was far from overpopulated; but the poor who were packed into London gave the impression that the whole island was crowded beyond its resources. Publicists for colonization insisted that Christians had a duty to do missionary work among the American Indians. Adventurers hoped that colonization would be profitable in its own right; they hoped also that colonies in North America, which James I recognized as belonging to the Spanish Crown, might provide an occasion for renewed war with Spain and renewed plunder.

The English after 1600 began crossing in large numbers to North America and the West Indies. Some searched for wealth, and some for a modest prosperity in the new lands. Many came for reasons connected with the religious controversies of the seventeenth century. Both the economic and the religious motives would leave their marks on American history.

The First North Americans

Though the English, Spanish, and French languages and cultures ultimately dominated North America, the continent was first the domain of the Indians. The "pre-Columbian" story belongs largely to prehistory, that state of human development preceding adequate written records. And Spanish explorers and conquerors damaged what little written evidence existed in their attempt to weaken Indian beliefs. Our knowledge of early American Indians therefore can be reconstructed only from bits and scraps: tools, bones, pits, pots, graves, weapons, and garbage.

When Columbus landed in the West Indies, the "New World" was new only to the Europeans. Neither Columbus nor the Norsemen who touched Newfoundland and possibly present-day New England centuries before discovered the New World. The ancestors the European explorers came upon had discovered the continent in far prehistoric times. They came from Asia, of an oriental stock, possibly mingled with some traces of European and African blood. The time of their arrival is subject to dispute. Once a thousand mile land bridge, which geographers called Beringia, stretched between Siberia and Alaska. It existed fifty thousand years ago during the early part of the most recent Ice Age, sank below sea level, resurfaced about fifteen or twenty thousand years ago as the last Ice Age made its final surge, and disappeared again about ten thousand years ago. The migration from Asia occurred during one or more of the Beringian periods. Anthropologists and archaeologists agree that humankind reached the continent at least twenty thousand years ago, and that the main migration from Asia to America began about ten thousand years ago.

Early Indians in North America were seed gatherers and game hunters. They formed bands of twenty to fifty people. Some ten thousand years ago, they learned to remove flakes from stone, forming what are called "Folsum points," which made them more efficient hunters, though they continued where possible to drive big game such as mammoths, bison, deer, and antelope off cliffs or into swamps preparatory for the kill. Gradually diets diversified to include raccoons, opossums, shellfish, and sea animals in some areas. As the Ice Age retreated and the continent dried, great forests grew in the east and north of North America; the bow and arrow aided in the kill of small, swift woodland animals. Hooks, nets, and weirs caught fish and snared ducks. Desert Indians relied increasingly on plants, ground seeds, berries, bulbs, and nuts. About seven thousand years ago American natives, like peoples elsewhere around the world, developed agriculture. In comparison with modern technologies, basic agriculture seems simple; but in comparison with hunting and the gathering of wild plants it is a major, sophisticated control of the environment. Efficiency in food growing increased populations and produced more village life. Plant domestication emerged first in the Mexican highlands, and then spread north and south. It probably reached the peoples north of Mexico about three thousands years ago.

The degree to which this agricultural revolution had developed among the North American Indians varied widely at the time of Columbus's arrival. Hundreds of tribes speckled the continent, separated into the linguistic and cultural groups that scholars today define.

The Indians of the Far North, across Canada and Alaska, were few. Divided into two major language groups, Algonquin and Athabascan, they included such tribes as Algonquin, Beaver, Chippewa, Cree, Chowo, and Yellowknife. Since the growing season was too short for agriculture, they gathered berries, plants, and nuts, and hunted caribou, moose, deer, elk, musk-ox, and buffalo. Nomadic Indians used portable tepees; others built sturdy log homes. The Far North Indians appear to have fought rarely.

A unique hunter-gatherer culture existed in the northwest corner of the present-day United States. The Northwest Coast Indians, their pop-

A North Pacific Coast Indian village as depicted in a nineteenth-century painting by Arthur A. Jansson. Indians in this region probably never developed agriculture, relying instead on fishing and hunting for food. *(Courtesy, American Museum of Natural History)*

ulation stretching from Northern California to Southern Alaska, probably never developed agriculture. The Bella Coola, Chinook, Klikitat, Nootka, Quinault, and Tlingit Indians harvested the oceans and rivers, taking salmon, steelhead, inland trout, shellfish, sea lions, sea otters, and whales. In the lush forests, they hunted bear, caribou, deer, elk and moose. Unlike most Indians north of Mexico, these people were not very egalitarian. A few families accumulated wealth in canoes, blankets, or hammered copper sheets. Lavishing wealth brought magical power over others, and these extraordinarily competitive Indians therefore held ceremonial feasts called "Potlatches"; the hosts fed their guests and displayed, gave away, or even destroyed valued possessions. Like the hunter-gatherer Far North Indians, the Northwest coast tribes had no pottery; they used wood for masks, grave markers and utensils. The abundant redwoods, cedars, firs, and pines served as posts, beams, siding, and gables for their homes, and as raw material for the huge sixty-foot seagoing canoes that could carry up to sixty men. The Northwest coasters kept alive the myths surrounding their pantheon of gods by enacting religious dramas.

To the south of the coast tribes lived an Indian culture between the Cascade-Sierra Nevada ranges and the Rockies, in what is now called the Great Basin. Food was not abundant in this semi-arid land. Animals were scarce, and few edible plants could survive the droughts. Small Indian bands often ate rats, snakes, grasshoppers, grubs, and roots. The California Indians had an easier economic life. They lived in villages, hunted small game, fished and gathered wild plants, seeds, and nuts, and handcrafted some of the finest basketry in the world. Interestingly, these Indians greatly feared the spirits of the dead. To prevent the deceased from being summoned back to earth, they burned the corpse and personal belongings and forbade the speaking of the departed's name.

The land between the Mississippi River and the Rocky Mountains belonged to the Plains Indians. Not many lived on the vast grasslands before the Europeans arrived with horses and guns. The Plains Indians preferred a more settled agricultural life in villages near rivers. When the agricultural output was insufficient, they would venture onto the plains and, when possible, stampede buffalo off cliffs. When they stayed in their permanent villages, they built homes of log framing covered with brush and dirt. When they traveled, they lived in portable tepees.

Another combination of hunter-gatherer and settled agrarian culture occupied much of the Southwest. These Southwestern Indians showed remarkable ability to adapt to the arid buttes, mesas, and steep canyons in the northern part of this area and the flatter desert country to the south. The Anasazi, whom the Navaho call "the Ancient Ones," and their descendants, the Pueblos, Hopi, and Zuni, built cliff dwellings, some with as many as 800 units, centering around the point where Colorado, Utah, New Mexico, and Arizona meet. This more advanced agrarian culture developed specialization in work, yet sophistication did not lead to hierarchy: religious and military leaders worked much like anyone else. Pueblos were peaceable, preferring to pull up the ladders to their adobe homes when attacked. When an Anasazi killed someone, even in self-defense, elaborate purification preceded his reentry into the village. This peaceful, advanced culture faded, possibly because of a prolonged thirteenth-century drought and growing population pressures from the north. The chief invaders consisted of the Navaho and Apache, both warlike hunter-gatherers related to the Athabaskan language tribes of Northwestern Canada.

The territory of the Eastern woodland Indians extended from Canada to the Gulf of Mexico and from the Mississippi River to the east coast. They belonged to three major language groups: Algonquin, Iroquian, and Siouan. Two great societies, the Moundbuilders of the Ohio River and the temple-building Mississippians, centering south of modern-day St. Louis, rose and declined well before the first European contacts.

On the eve of European discovery several Indian cultures dominated the Eastern woodland, the third of the continent bordering the Atlantic. The Eastern Algonquins occupied the Atlantic coast from Labrador to present-day North Carolina. Deep in the interior, on the Western Great Lakes, a Northern and Western Algonquin culture shared many of the traits of its Eastern relatives. The Iroquois peopled the area between the two Algonquin cultures, from the Great Lakes to the central Appalachians. They included the Hurons, located north of the lakes; the Five Nations (Cayuga, Onondaga, Oneida, Mohawk, and Seneca) of the Mohawk Valley; and a conglomerate of related tribes including the Cherokee, Tuscarora, Moneton, and Monacan in the central and southern Appalachian Mountains. The Muskogean culture occupied the lowlands of southeastern North America.

The Five Nations confederation numbered

"They have likewise a notable way to catche fishe in their Rivers, for whear as they lack both yron, and steele, they faste unto their Reedes or longe Rodds, the hollowe tayle of a certain fishe like to a sea crabbe in steede of a poynte, wehr with by nighte or day they stricke fishes, and take them opp into their boates."— Harriot (1590). John White, *The Manner of Their Fishing*, drawing 1585. *(Courtesy, British Museum, London)*

perhaps 10,000 people by the year 1600. It emerged by probably the late fifteenth century and its purpose was to eliminate blood feuds and cope with the nagging conflicts with nearby Algonquins (which may have resulted from population growth generated by improved agriculture). The leader credited with solving these problems was Hiawatha, who apparently lost relatives around 1450 and, rather than taking blood revenge, recommended that a ritual bereavement replace the vendetta, that retaliations be forbidden, and that a council of forty-nine chiefs make decisions for all the villages. Thereafter villages were bound together for internal peace and external defense. Communal sharing extended to land use, the hunt, and the home. Although plowed by a family, the land was not "owned," and although one hunter might outdo another, the kill was distributed. Families might live together in one house, but no single family owned it. If one person went hungry, all did.

Women dominated familial lineages and were influential in Iroquois politics. The families included the oldest female and her daughters, immature male children, and sons-in-law. Married men joined the family of their wives. Women initiated divorce by throwing their husbands' belongings outside. In politics women picked replacements for vacancies in the council of forty-nine, and influenced village decisions behind the scenes. The women farmed, controlling the villages, while the men warred, fished, and hunted; women could sometimes veto military expeditions by refusing to supply footwear or food.

Although the Iroquois did compete among themselves in hunting, fishing, and fighting, they employed egalitarian values to raise children. Youngsters were rarely punished physically, and were expected to err as they imitated adults. This freedom continued as the child grew up. Without specialized legal personnel, laws, or jails, acceptable behavior was maintained by the ostracism and consensus that are typical of many small agricultural communities.

Among themselves, then, the Iroquois were civilized people, in some ways more civilized than the Europeans. Yet they do not deserve to be romanticized as a lost, virtuous civilization destroyed by white invaders. Like Europeans and white Americans, they could be as ruthless toward people outside their polity and culture as they were civil to their own kind. Indians such as the Algonquins knew the Iroquois as cruel warriors.

Indians in the Americas had too little technology and were too little united to stop the European newcomers. The very lack of unity among North American natives meant that each group would have to find its own way to accommodate the increasingly numerous and powerful Europeans.

Points To Think About

1. Medieval Christianity supplied little that was helpful to an understanding of a new world being born in the fifteenth through seventeenth centuries. As trade expanded, for example, the need for credit grew apace. Lenders were, as always, being asked to risk their money; but the risks were far higher than today's. Ships were small and fragile. A storm could turn an otherwise successful venture into a total loss. So interest rates—the money charged for credit—were high. Yet any interest at all the medieval church viewed as usury, a sin against the virtue of charity. Nor was medieval Catholicism in step with the emergent individualism of the early modern period. Catholicism taught the individual to seek for meaning, and for salvation, in the community. The Church promoted a corporate, as opposed to an individualist, world view. It urged everyone to find his place in the order of creation, and faithfully fulfill the duties of that station. It provided no guidelines for those who had left their traditional station and were seeking to make their own way in the world.

The various faiths of the Reformation, on the other hand, all began with the notion that each person must find his own way to God. And each must seek to glorify God by succeeding on earth. Each Protestant faith defined morality as the obedience of the individual to his own conscience.

Puritanism, as you will see, made especially great demands on the individual. It called for an enormous self-discipline. The Puritan learned he could control the world only by first controlling himself. He was to love the world as part of God's creation but to love it with "weaned affection." He was to steel himself to accept any reverse, from business losses to the death of loved ones, as part of God's inscrutable Province. And he came to regard success as a sign of God's pleasure.

Such people were to be self-governing in the most literal sense of the term. And, some scholars have argued, it is not surprising that they had developed a politics which also emphasized the ability of people to govern themselves. As Michael Walzer points out, succeeding generations of Americans have continued to believe in popular government, but have abandoned the Puritan emphasis on self-control. Perhaps, as Walzer says, we may find that only those who practice the Puritan virtues of self-control can truly make a success of self-government.

2. Christopher Columbus set sail in the very year that Ferdinand and Isabella succeeded in driving the Moors off the Iberian peninsula, thereby unifying Spain under a strong central government. That 1492 marks both events is no coincidence. Imperialism and the modern nation-state go hand in hand. Spain's early lead in the race for control of the non-European world came exactly because Spain was the first large European state to develop a modern, unified government. France succeeded in doing the same by the last third of the next century, while England did not consolidate its hold over even the British Isles until the end of the sixteenth century. So it is no mystery why

England was a comparatively late entrant in the imperialist sweepstakes.

Imperialism awaited the formation of the centralized, bureaucratic state. This has led some historians to say that empire-building is what marks the transition from medieval to modern history. It is tempting to say still more. Can we say that imperialism is a byproduct of the formation of the modern nation-state? Typically, that formation involved expansion of some kind. In the Spanish case it meant defeating the Moors and uniting, by marriage, the kingdoms of Aragon and Castile. In the French case it meant the defeat, by the monarchy, of various feudal lords as well as the defeat of the English who had, since the time of William of Normandy (called William the Conquerer in English history), claimed various chunks of French territory.

In England the same families that brought Cornwall (England's westernmost province) under the effective control of the Crown, subdued the Irish and joined Scotland and Wales to England also led the earliest colonial adventures. It is tempting therefore to say that colonialism was a direct continuation of this same process, that it was expansionism under a different name.

The same argument can be applied to the nineteenth-century imperial powers. Germany was not unified until the 1860s. German imperial ambitions date from shortly thereafter. In America, continental expansionism was largely over by the 1890s—exactly the time when the United States began to acquire large overseas possessions. If this analysis holds up, then imperialism is one of the key components in the nation-building process.

3. The emergence of England as a modern nation-state involved more than changes in the role of the monarchy or the growth of a centralized bureaucracy. It also involved profound economic and social changes. In the first half of the sixteenth century there was an enormous growth in British exports of woolen goods. This new source of prosperity caused English landlords to shift from farming to sheepgrowing on a wide scale, a change that altered the society as well as the economy of the English countryside. Small farmers, usually tenants, were driven from the land. These people, literally set in motion, wandered from place to place looking for work. Trade also made England more sensitive to fluctuations in the international economy. Downturns in demand for cloth produced wholesale unemployment. Earlier these same people would have had their small farm holdings to cultivate. The Crown sought to control prices and wages in an attempt, largely unsuccessful, to mitigate the resulting distress. The government also passed a number of laws designed to punish vagabonds, robbers, poachers, and others whose distress made them careless of property rights.

Colonies seemed the perfect solution to these new problems. Not only would they lead to increased trade, but they would also provide a place for the surplus population to go in the chartered trading colonies. Thus it can be said that the United States began as a business venture.

Suggested Readings

Any study of the voyages of discovery can begin with Samuel Eliot Morison's works: *The European Discovery of America: The Northern Voyages, A.D. 500-1600* (1971) and *The European Discovery of America: The Southern Voyages, A.D. 1492-1616* (1974). Morison examines in impressive detail, and from an extraordinary number of unpublished sources, the personalities and the routes followed by the great navigators who explored the continents. Volume I documents the coastal discoveries north of Cape Fear; volume II traces the voyages of Columbus, Magellan, Drake, Vespucci, Sebastian Cabot, and many lesser figures. Both works have been abridged into a single volume: *The Great Explorers: The European Discovery of America* (1978). A beautifully illustrated book on the period of discovery is Richard Humble, *The Explorers* (1979). J.A. Williamson's *Sir Francis Drake* (1966) is a stirring biography, and Kenneth Andrews's *Elizabethan Privateering* (1964) is exhaustive. See also Ralph Davis, *The Rise of the Atlantic Economies* (1973), Charles Gibson, *Spain in America* (1966), R.C. Padden, *The Hummingbird and the Hawk* (1967), and Carl Bridenbaugh, *Vexed and Troubled Englishmen, 1590-1642* (1968).

DEBATE

FORREST McDONALD

To talk about causation in history, particularly a phenomenon as complex as Europe's discovery of the New World and expansion over it, is to flirt with oversimplification. Surely greed, power, and religion were involved; but that does not tell us much, for those motives were old long before Columbus set sail. As surely, there are determinants in human history—social habits and norms, institutional structures, technology, history itself—but their effects can vary in response to time, chance, and even the efforts of a single individual. We can, however, understand the way history commonly unfolds if we realize that causes are normally plural, that they overlap and interact, and that circumstances produce different results from one society to another.

Portugal and Spain began their explorations largely for religious reasons. The Iberian Peninsula had been for centuries the front line in the warfare between Christianity and Islam, and the Age of Discovery was but another chapter in that saga. Finding gold and silver in the Americas was a coincidence that spurred further explorations. It was also coincidental that Cortez was conquering Mexico just as the Protestant Reformation was getting under way. The Spanish kings, having expelled the last of the Moors, turned to renewed religious warfare, this time trying to suppress Protestantism; and during the next two hundred years they spent in that futile undertaking most of the treasure they had plundered from the New World.

Other nations of western Europe sent expeditions in search of windfall wealth, but none was successful. Then during the seventeenth century the age of colonization began. When we speak of colonization, however, we really refer to the British. In the Spanish and Portuguese empires the vast majority of subjects were of native descent. The Dutch, Swedish, and Danish colonies were miniscule. France claimed a huge area, but few Frenchmen settled the lands. On the North American continent, small numbers of French occupied military and fur-trading posts and lived among the Indians, often intermarrying with them. On the Caribbean islands a few grew extremely rich from the slave-labor of large numbers of blacks. The French crown was interested in colonies to increase royal revenues and to control political factions at home through the granting of lucrative monopolies. Even stronger was its desire to gain strategic advantage over England.

The reasons the British Crown encouraged emigration differed from the reasons particular individuals or groups emigrated. King James I (1603–1625) actively promoted resettlement to maintain political and religious order at home. England had suffered a long period of poor harvest and was thought to be overpopulated; sending Englishmen abroad was a way of averting the dangers inherent in that combination. But James also believed in colonization as a means of pacifying, Christianizing, and "civilizing" native populations. (He chartered colonies on the Scottish island of Lewis and in Northern Ireland as well as in America.) Charles (1625–1646), seeking to establish religious uniformity, both persecuted dissenters and encouraged them to emigrate. Charles II (1660–1685) dispensed colonial charters as a means of paying his political and monetary debts. Unrestricted emigration persisted until the early nineteenth century simply because no one thought it worth the trouble to stop it.

The reasons for migrating were varied. A sizable number of people went involuntarily: blacks were forcibly transported to the New World, and many Irish and Scots were deported for rebellion or for nonpolitical crimes. The Puritans left largely for religious reasons, though the push of hard times and the pull of opportunity were contributing factors. Quakers also emigrated to escape religious persecution, as did some Catholics. But after 1689, when the greatest emigration took place, most who left were in flight from grinding poverty; and most of these earned their passage by selling themselves into indentured servitude for four to seven years. Others went because changes that were taking place would have made it necessary for them to change their accustomed ways if they had remained. And many went just from a spirit of adventure.

The nature of the emigration helped stamp the American character indelibly. It took initiative, enterprise, and courage to venture to the New World. And thus, though the settlers came mainly from the lower to middle orders of the population, they were a preselected, hardier breed than the kinsmen they left behind. America was blessed from the start.

EUGENE GENOVESE

Of British North America Professor McDonald says, "It took initiative, enterprise, and courage to venture to the New World. And thus, though the settlers came mainly from the lower to middle orders of the population, they were a preselected, hardier breed than the kinsmen they left behind." But why should Professor McDonald limit that description to British North America? It applies nicely, for example, to Brazil; no word need be altered. The Northern colonies of British North America, to be sure, were settled primarily by Europeans of initiative, enterprise, and courage, while Brazil was settled by a much smaller number relative to the African slaves imported to do the work. Those Africans had their share of initiative, enterprise, and courage, but of a different order and necessarily put to different uses, such as slave rebellion. The Southern colonies of British North America and the British West Indies, which for a long time were the most lucrative of colonies, resembled Brazil. But throughout the New World, settlers, both African and European, were well endowed with the virtues Professor McDonald lists.

In what, then, was British North America "blessed," as Professor McDonald says, especially the colonies north of the Potomac? Initiative, courage, and enterprise the British settlers shared with the Spanish, Portuguese, Dutch, and others. But the English had developed and disciplined these qualities in a new kind of society. Long before the industrial revolution the English had come to live among one another in freedom. Their ties to their lords and to the land had been steadily eroded, and with those ties the protection and security supposedly conferred by feudal relations. The great English revolutions of the seventeenth century legally and constitutionally consolidated this historic transformation in social relations. Those who came to North America, however "traditional" they may appear when compared with later generations, were products of this revolutionary new social system. For better or worse they were their own men in a way in which the Spanish and Portuguese, even the haughty aristocrats who defiantly stood on their feudal liberties, were not. The British settlers brought new institutions to match their new sentiments, sensibilities, and ways of thought. Those institutions embodied large concessions to the rights of individuals and would eventually spark a great revolution against Britain, carried out in defense of the British liberties that recent centuries had wrought.

The emerging "modern" personality and "modern" institutions rested on private property—on the right of everyone to own land and other property in a manner as close to absolute as compatible with social order. Those who did not own real property owned property in themselves; they could sell their labor-power to the highest bidder. And, if lucky, they could apply their earnings to the purchase of real property, which itself was increasingly clear of traditional obstacles to sale, and was abundant in the New World.

Private property, as the modern Western world defines it, has been intimately connected with the expansion of freedom, but it can also be the enemy of freedom. My private property intrudes upon your free space, or fences off from you the land or other wealth with which you could have expressed your freedom. The institution of slavery in the new colonies was the clearest instance in which property turned against freedom. But even today, over a century after the end of slavery, the systems of private property that attended the growth of freedom in the West choke off the possibilities for a full development of freedom and justice. When freedom and property landed together on the shores of British North America, they were to begin a long, complex, and tortured relationship.

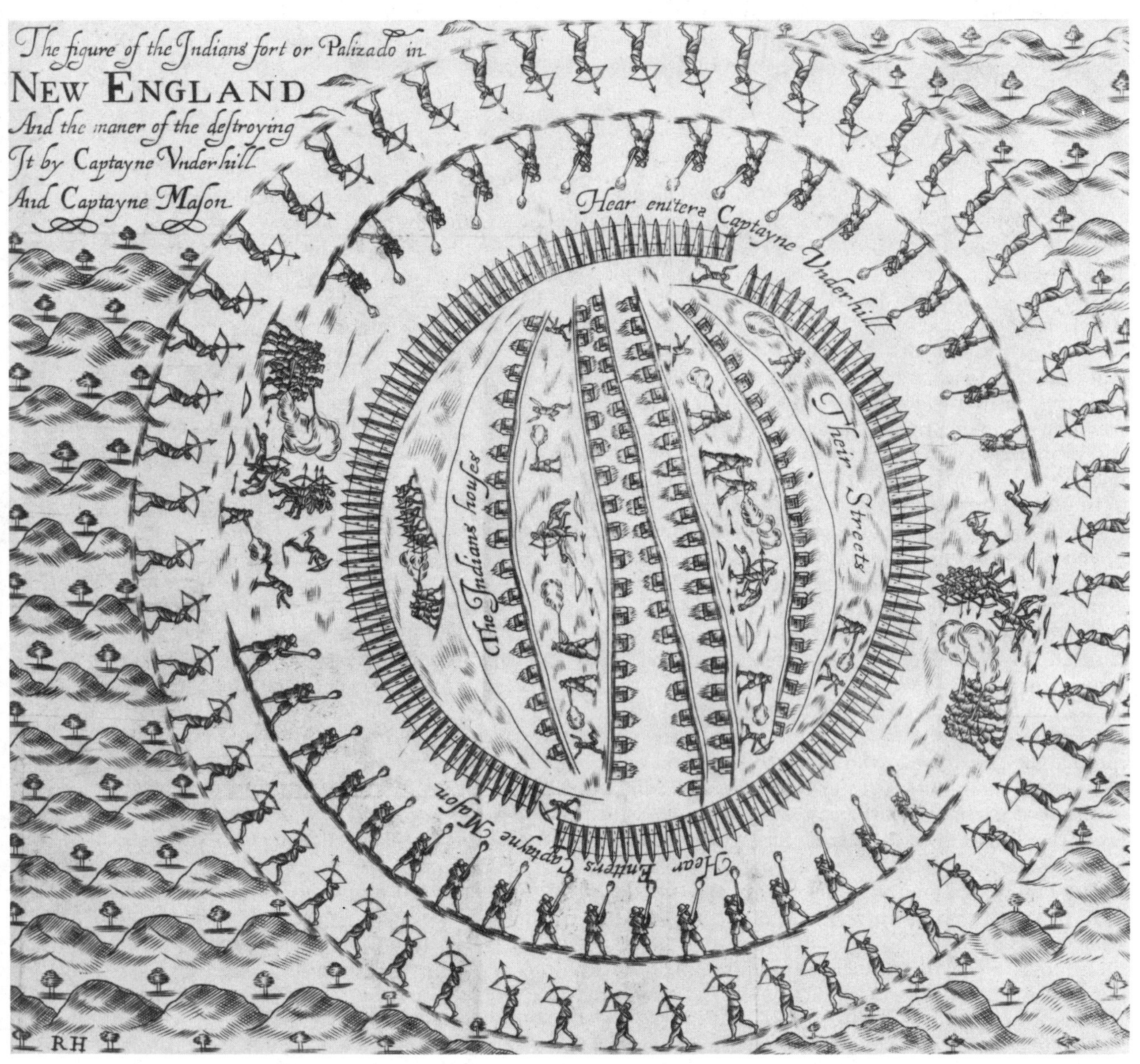

Diagram of the attack on the Pequot Fort on Mystic River. Led by Captains John Mason and John Underhill, the colonial forces set fire to the fort, burning alive between 400 to 700 men, women, and children. From an illustration, artist unknown, accompanying John Underhill's *Newes from America*, London, 1638. *(Courtesy, Rare Book Room, New York Public Library)*

CHAPTER 2

British North America

PURITANS AND PEQUOTS: THE INVASION OF NEW ENGLAND

Disruption and violence marked the history of the region we now call New England in the late sixteenth and early seventeenth century. Shortly before 1600 a powerful and warlike tribe from the upper Hudson had pushed its way into the Connecticut Valley. Originally called Mohegans, they earned by their brutal conquests the name Pequot—"destroyer" in the Algonquin dialects of New England. Soon they dominated the valley, terrorizing and exacting tribute from the Narragansetts to the East, the Montauks to the South on Long Island, the Nipmucs to the North, and the Podunks, Wongunks, Siciaoggs, and other tribes to the West.

New England was a poor, hard, thinly populated land. The total population in 1600 was perhaps 25,000, a population density of about one person per four acres. The various tribes, none larger than 4000 people, lived in relatively settled territories, moving about within them among winter, summer, and autumn quarters to sustain their mixed farming and hunting economy and to escape into more sheltered valleys for the winters. The white man's later image of them as nomadic hunters was as false as William Bradford's sense of their numbers when he spoke of "a hideous and desolate wilderness, full of wild beasts and wild men." Warfare over boundaries, hunting lands, and the like was common enough, but most encounters were no more than skirmishes affecting only a few braves on each side. Diplomacy was as intricate and complex as in Europe: most tribes had traditional rivals as well as slowly shifting alliances.

During the winter of 1616-17 an epidemic of smallpox suddenly decimated many of the tribes. No Indian would have connected this mysterious visitation with the occasional and usually friendly encounters with European fishermen drying their catches on the beaches in summer or trading a few items for furs and skins or food; but they were the source of the disease that wiped out as much as one-third of the area's population. Thousands more would die during the winter of 1633-34 from a similar outbreak. Since these epidemics did not stretch beyond the region, the New England Indians found themselves even less capable than before of withstanding the depredations of the powerful border tribes. But then potential allies—white settlers equipped with modern firearms—suddenly arrived from the East.

Despite the many obvious cultural differences and the language barrier between English settlers and Indians, the Pilgrims and after that the larger Puritan settlement in Massachusetts Bay received a generally friendly welcome. Trade, Indians perceived, made tribes rich and powerful and usually ended with their acquiring firearms. At first the needs of the two cultures seemed compatible. The English settlers understood the basically monarchical structure of most tribal government. They carefully purchased land titles granting the Indians the right to continue to hunt or fish.

Nonetheless, misunderstandings turned into resentments and finally conflict. Neither Puritan governors nor tribal Sachems could control all that occurred in each trading venture or settlement. New England attracted not only well-disciplined Puritans, but many a reckless adventurer seeking fortune and excitement. Thomas Morton, famous for his colony's merriment and frolic about the blasphemous maypole, is less well known for his mistreatment of Indians or for his gunrunning. Yet he was expelled from the colony in part for the "many wrongs hee hath done them [the Indians] from tyme to tyme." Massachusetts court records are full of the colonial fathers's attempts to punish and make restitution for the deception, sharp dealings, kidnappings, and little battles that marked many Indian-white encounters. By the early 1630s the number of English colonists was far larger than that of any single tribe; by mid-decade there were probably as many English as Indians in New England. And as the colony grew in size, the disposition to impose order on Indians as well as whites provoked increasing friction. The colony expanded from lands close to the coast from which Indians had moved into the Connecticut Valley, where the tissue of intertribal diplomacy had been so shredded by Pequots.

An eighteenth-century poet chronicler of the Pequot war blamed the Pequots for provoking war by killing three Englishmen: *"First, helpless Stone! they bade thy bosom bleed,/A guiltless offering at th' infernal shrine;/Then, gallant Norton! the hard fate was thine,/By ruffians butcher'd, and denied a grave;/Thee, generous Oldham! next the doom malign/Arrested; nor could all thy courage save;/Forsaken, plunder'd, cleft, and burried in the wave."*

Since John Stone, the victim, had already been banished from New England under penalty of death for larceny, adultery, and attempted murder of the governor of Plymouth we may wonder if his murder by the Pequot was not, as they claimed, under dire provocation. Norton was in cahoots with Stone; and Oldham, apparently, met his fate at the hands of the Narragansetts—who remained allied to the British—rather than the Pequots. Despite these uncertainties, the Puritans, goaded by their Indian allies and perhaps nervous over the religious schisms occurring in the colony, dispatched ninety men under John Endicott on a mission of destruction. Endicott's orders included putting to death all Indian men on Block Island. When the band of Englishmen with guns was frustrated by the Indians' retreat into swamps, they fired all their wigwams, destroyed all their possessions, then wantonly "destroyed some of their dogs."

The Pequots replied in kind. Ambushing five men near Saybrook, they dispatched three immediately, roasted one alive, and "the other came down drowned to us . . . with an arrow shot into his eye through his head." Similar fates befell about thirty white settlers in the next year before skirmishes and ambushes turned into a full-scale war of extermination, whose genocidal intent was expressed in the Reverend Thomas Hooker's admonition "not to do this work of the Lord's revenge slackly."

The Pequot war was not an early version of cowboys and Indians. There was not a white and an Indian side. The climactic battle pitted Mohegans (who had broken with the Pequots), Narragansetts, and Englishmen against the Pequot fort on Mystic river within which somewhere between 400 and 700 men, women, and children perished by fire, musket ball, or arrow in less than an hour's time on May 26, 1637. God, so the Puritan commander reported, had "laughed his Enemies and the Enemies of his People to Scorn, making them as a fiery Oven. . . . Thus did the Lord judge among the Heathen, filling the Place with dead Bodies."

By 1675 the pattern would be set: in King Philip's War all except Christianized Indians were the enemy. Herman Melville, the great nineteenth-century American novelist, called Captain Ahab's ship in *Moby Dick* the *Pequod*, "the name of a celebrated tribe of Massachusetts Indians; now extinct as the ancient Medes. . . ." But Melville, of course, was not thinking of Indians; he was thinking of all of humanity, doomed to destruction rooting out the evil it sees not in itself, but only in some other, some great white whale.

***The Town of Secota*, by John White, depicts a seventeenth-century Indian village in the Tidewater Virginia area. Europeans in the New World quickly adopted Indian ways as the best means of survival.** *(Courtesy, Virginia State Library)*

The Columbian Exchange

What has come to be called the "Columbian exchange" involved a redistribution of peoples, animals, and plants around the world. By 1500 as many as one hundred million Indians may have lived in the Americas, perhaps ten million of those in what are today the United States and Canada. But European conquest and disease decimated American Indians to about five to ten percent of their earlier numbers. They were replaced by Europeans in three major patterns. The Spanish and Portuguese intermarried with highland Indians and lowland black slaves to form the mestizo, mulatto, and zambo populations that dominate Latin America. The West Indies and the Southeast coast of the present-day United States established an aristocracy over imported black slaves. And in Northeastern North America, whites developed exclusively European communities, largely segregated from Indian villages.

Animal and plant exchanges accompanied Indian-European contact. Domesticated animals—pigs, goats, horses, cattle, and sheep—accompanied Europeans to America, along with wheat, rye, barley, oats, rice, melons, coffee, dandelions, sugar cane, and olives. The plants that American Indians made available to the rest of the world now constitute one-third of the world's food supply: Indian corn, beans, squash, pumpkins, white potatoes (which first went from South America to Europe and finally, through the Scotch-Irish, to North America in the eighteenth century), tomatoes, peppers, and peanuts. Tobacco, drugs such as cocaine, novocaine, and quinine, and the strains of cotton in modern use also entered the world market from the Americas.

Some of the biological exchange also involved microscopic life in the form of diseases. Indians had developed no immunity to measles, chicken pox, smallpox, and whooping cough, from which they had been isolated by three thousand miles of ocean. These diseases devastated American Indians, killing far more than did conquest. And Europeans may have contracted syphilis from Americans. While medical historians cannot definitely attribute the disease to the Indians, circumstantial evidence suggests an American origin. Traces have been found in Indian but not European bones in pre-Columbian times. The first recorded case appeared in Cadiz, Spain, soon after Columbus returned from America. In any event, about ten million Old World people died of syphilis within the next fifteen years.

Following these global human, animal, and plant integrations, life around the globe changed. Central and South American gold and silver enriched European monarchies and stimulated trade and industry. European merchants prospered from the trade in American agricultural raw materials. While European ethnocentricity increased among those who judged superiority on such bases as written languages, military technology, and Christianity, America also provided a storehouse of information in the natural sciences and contributed to the intensification of scientific inquiry. Europeans were captivated by the notion of the "noble savage" and took that mythic creation into their political and moral philosophies. The very idea of a new and open land enlarged the vision of human possibility.

In America, Europeans adopted Indian ways. Beside eating Indian foods, they wore moccasins, snowshoes, ponchos, and parkas, plied rivers and lakes with canoes, and rested in hammocks. They played lacrosse, built homes of adobe, and rode on dogsleds and toboggans. The early European settlers followed Indian trails, smoked native tobacco, and used their medicines. Indian names entered English usage. They would serve for nearly half of the eventual state names—from Connecticut and Alabama to Iowa, Texas, and Wyoming—and were used for many rivers and cities.

Besides declining in numbers, the original Americans underwent enormous cultural changes. Indian lands shrank as the plow, lumbering, cattle, and sheep permanently transformed the Eastern woodlands. Other changes in Indian life were largely a matter of choice. European knives and guns improved hunting. Iron pots replaced pottery and baskets. Sheep made possible the beautiful wool blankets of the Pueblos. The iron hoe and plow increased agricultural productivity, and the metal fish hook enhanced catches. Many natives also responded to the lure of profit from the fur trade. European demand for pelts soon outstripped the animal population near the sea coast, and some tribes had to abandon older settlements in favor of new ones farther inland, eventually depleting animals there, too. The pelts purchased not only European weapons and utensils but also alcohol.

American natives selectively borrowed from the Europeans, but Indian cultures persisted. Material and economic incentives and the need for alliances against other tribes lured Indians, but they never adopted Western political, social, or religious values and customs. No evidence shows that Indians sought to live permanently among whites, although there were a substantial number of "white Indians," whites who lived permanently among Indians. In North America, Indians were not conquered and enslaved to the extent that occurred in Latin America, and so were able to maintain a largely separate racial and cultural existence. They interacted with the whites primarily in trade and war, which could take place outside the villages and without miscegenation. The two cultures failed to assimilate.

Early Southern Settlements

Roanoke. The history of British settlement of North America begins with a tale of mystery. Late in the sixteenth century a group of adventurers, among them the courtiers Sir Humphrey Gilbert and his half-brother, Sir Walter Raleigh, had developed plans for establishing settlements in the new world. An advisor to them was Sir Richard Hakluyt, a propagandist for colonization. He argued that American settlements would spread England's Protestant religion, expand the country's shipbuilding industry and naval fleet, decrease its dependence on foreign sources of supply, provide an outlet for surplus population, and help English explorers discover the Northwest Passage, the dream of a water route north of the American continent going directly to the Orient. Gilbert himself left for the New World in 1583, but after reaching Newfoundland he and two of the expedition's five ships went down during a fierce autumn storm.

Jamestown, founded in 1607, fared better than the Roanoke settlement. Though ravaged by disease and Indian attacks, the settlement survived and became the preeminent Southern colony. *(Courtesy, American Historical Society)*

Raleigh then assumed command. The group sent over one hundred eleven settlers who established themselves in 1585 on Roanoke Island off the coast of what is now North Carolina. In this colony was born Virginia Dare, the first known English child to be born in the present-day United States. For a time the settlement received supplies from British ships. But then war between England and Spain temporarily prevented a further resupply mission. A relief party that did reach the site in 1590 discovered the encampment deserted and letters "CRO" carved on a tree and the word "CROATOAN" on a doorpost. Where had the colonists gone? Perhaps they had abandoned the inhospitable site and sought refuge with the friendly Croatoan Indians or perhaps they had perished. No one has ever found any further trace of the colony.

Jamestown. The mercantile and maritime adventurers of the seventeenth century were of the lusty and aggressive character that had marked the Elizabethans. They were eager to exploit the American continent that Europeans only a few decades earlier had considered no more than an annoying obstacle on the route to the Orient.

In 1606, two groups of investors, one in London and one in Plymouth, formed joint-stock companies and petitioned the king for charters of incorporation for the purpose of colonizing North America. Both companies were chartered, the Plymouth Company for operations in the Northern part of the continent, the London Company in the South; but councils named by the king controlled each of the plantations.

In May 1607 the London Company landed three ships and planted a settlement called Jamestown. The settlers made countless blunders in trying to learn to live in the swampy, mosquito-infested site. "We were constrained," wrote one of them, "to eat dogs, cats, rats, snakes, toadstools, horse-hides and what-not; one man out of the misery endured, killed his wife, powdered her up to eat her, for which he was burned." In fact, the man was exceptional in having his wife with him. The predominance of men in the Jamestown settlement largely accounts for its difficulties. For the male settlers, who had come expecting to find an easy fortune and were loath to do any labor, were especially unwilling—and frequently unable—to perform women's labor. And women's labor included cooking, washing, and other tasks that were essential to survival. But the colonists did remain, and were soon reinforced by more immigrants. The colony was governed by an unwieldy and bickering council, which meant in practice that it was not governed at all; and most settlers took to wandering into the interior to hunt or to search for gold, leaving no one to do the work of building the settlement and making it self-sufficient. One of the settlers, twenty-seven-year-old John Smith, became president of the local council. He took charge, drove and led men to do the necessary work, and ensured the permanence of the settlement, although many had died during the first year.

Back in England a faction in the Company arose, headed by Sir Edwin Sandys, one of the most influential leaders of Parliament. Joining in a scheme to win for the company a monopoly on the sale of tobacco in England, he recruited support from small shareholders in the company, and in 1618 succeeded in overthrowing the old management.

The Sandys group immediately instituted a series of policies, deriving from philanthropic, religious, and ideological motives as well as from the desire for regular profit, and aimed at transforming the company into a permanent colonization enterprise. To attract more investors, more settlers, and more servants, the company liberalized its landholding and land granting rules, providing an elaborate system of bonuses and requiring the payment to the company of moderate annual rents. At its own expense the company undertook to send to Virginia a variety of craftsmen and a number of female settlers, who would make the colony's economy more self-sufficient and its life more tolerable. The company relaxed its governing rules, provided that settlers continue to be governed by English law and have the rights of Englishmen, and gave settlers a voice in the management by allowing planters to send representatives to an assembly that would have an advisory place in company affairs. The first assembly, the House of Burgesses, met in 1619.

Though settlers were going to Virginia, the population remained scanty for some time. In 1624, when more than 5000 immigrants had made the voyage to Virginia, the total population numbered only 1275. Some died of disease; many others died in a disastrous Indian war that broke out in 1622, some years after the powerful Chief Powhatan and his daughter Pocahontas had befriended the newcomers. Relations with the natives so deteriorated that, on one occasion, whites lured a band of peaceful Indians into drinking a toast with poisoned wine.

By the mid-1620s the original Virginia Com-

John Smith, one of the original settlers of Jamestown, wrote a history of the colony. President of the local council, Smith's leadership was a chief factor in the permanence of the settlement.

pany had failed and Virginia became a royal colony, a colony governed directly by the Crown. But by then the colony was exporting in considerable quantity a valuable crop, tobacco, which appealed to Europeans. King James I published an incisive pamphlet that denounced smoking as

> a custom loathsome to the eye, hateful to the nose, harmful to the brain, dangerous to the lungs, and in the black stinking fumes thereof, the nearest resembling the horrible smoke of the pit that is bottomless.

But the King's perception failed to dissuade seventeenth-century smokers. Whatever the eventual impact on European lungs, tobacco ensured a long and prosperous history for the preeminent Southern colony.

The New England Puritans

James I, the first English king of the Stuart monarchy, reigned from 1603 to 1625. James wished to be the undisputed head of the Church of England, sharing no significant authority with Parliament. And the Church he wanted would have more of ritual and hierarchy than suited the consciences of the stricter of English Protestants. Those who resisted James's plans for the Church and aimed to simplify its structure and practice—making it, so they thought, more Protestant—came to be known as Puritans. During James's reign and that of his son and successor, Charles I, supporters of the Church of the Stuart monarchy clashed with Puritans, while an overlapping constitutional controversy took place between champions of royal authority and champions of the rights of Parliament. The arguments between royalists and Puritans would bring on several years of armed warfare, beginning in 1642 and ending in a victory for Parliament and Puritanism, the execution of Charles I in 1649, and the transformation of England into a kingless Puritan Commonwealth that lasted from 1649 until 1660.

Early in his reign, Charles hoped to get Puritans to leave England and to this end maintained a policy of continuous though mild persecution while offering them generous, even lavish, grants for settlement in America. One such grant went to a group of Puritans for settlements in the Leeward Islands of the West Indies, and another went to the Massachusetts Bay Company. Charles also granted a charter to George Calvert, Lord Baltimore, for the establishment of a colony north and east of Virginia, where Roman Catholics would be permitted to settle. In 1620 the Pilgrims—a small group of separatists, religious dissenters who, unlike most New England Puritans, had separated from the Church of England—founded a colony at Plymouth, Massachusetts. Between 1629 and 1642 there followed a great exodus to America.

Boston. The Massachusetts Bay Company, organized in 1628 by a group of well-to-do English Puritans, received from the King a Charter granting it land in present-day New England. Members of the Company signed a document, known as the Cambridge Agreement, to settle with their families in the new land, provided that they be allowed to take the Charter and government of the Company with them. Nothing in the Charter required the Company to

BUNDLING

It was too cold in the parlor for Puritan young people to hug and kiss. A sensible solution, to these sensible people, was to place a hot brick under the bed and take your lady or gentleman friend under the covers. The results were unpredictable.

Whether they must be hugg'd or Kiss'd when sitting by the fire
Or whether they in bed may lay, which doth the Lord require?
In Genesis no knowledge is of this thing to be got,
Whether young men did bundle then, or whether they did not.
The sacred book says wives they took, it don't say how they courted.
Whether that they in bed did lay, or by the fire sported.

Young miss, if this your habit be, I'll teach you now yourself to see:
You plead you're honest, modest too, but such a plea will never do;
For how can modesty consist, with shameful practice such as this?
I'll give your answer to the life: You don't undress, like man and wife.
That is your plea, I'll freely own, but who's your bondsman when alone,
That further rules you will not break, and marriage liberties partake?
But you will say that I'm unfair, that some who bundle take more care,
For some we may in truth suppose, bundle in bed with all their clothes.
But bundler's clothes are no defense, unruly horses push the fence.

maintain headquarters in England, and the transfer was arranged. The Company elected as its governor John Winthrop, a solid country squire. Within the year Winthrop and a dozen or so other members of the Company had set sail for America, a thousand adults and children with them. From the start, the immigration of families distinguished the settlement of New England. The presence of somewhere near as many women as men among the Puritans guaranteed that the settlement would grow in population. Women's presence further guaranteed the accomplishment of basic tasks necessary for survival. By the end of 1630 six settlements had appeared in and around Boston. The organization that the Massachusetts Bay Company possessed for the conduct of its business was now the government of the colony, and Winthrop, the Company governor, was the governor of the colony.

The Massachusetts Bay Company, like other English business corporations of the time, was governed by its voting members, or "freemen." At first the only members were the stockholders, but in 1631 the government of the Company and therefore of the colony admitted to membership more than a hundred adult male settlers. Subsequently all male members of Puritan congregations were admitted as freemen. Like the original governing body, this extended body was constituted on the assumption that men only were fitted for governance and would naturally speak for the women of their families when speaking for themselves. The Charter provided that Company members gather as a "General Court" four times a year, and that between times management be in the hands of a governor, deputy governor, and council of eighteen "assistants," all elected annually by the freemen. As the colony expanded, legislation by the entire body of freemen became unwieldy, and after 1634 they elected annually representatives from each settlement. This general structure of government formed the type for most subsequent governments established in British America.

The Puritan government enacted into law the biblical injunctions against drunkenness, adultery, murder, theft, and violations of the Sabbath, and otherwise attempted to regulate the religion and morality of the people. Yet Massachusetts Bay was not a theocracy: its ministers did not run the government. And as the colony developed in the seventeenth century, it was by no means merely a gray, guilt-ridden, pleasure-denying society. Its members engaged in lively and profitable commerce; they developed a bright if decorous social life and did not prohibit alcohol; and well-educated Puritans read secular as well as religious literature. Government of the church was the domain of the members of the congregation; and the government of the town was also the domain of the members of the local church.

Puritan Theology. There was a flaw in the system. It was a government of, by, and for the orthodox Puritans, and a sizable minority of the Puritans who poured into the colony during the 1630s were of dissenting persuasions. Almost all shared John Calvin's belief in predestination: the belief that those who were to be saved had been so chosen from the beginning of time. Calvin's premise might be taken to mean that there was no need to make any effort to be moral and good since nothing could alter the individual's predestined fate. Not so: orthodox ministers in Massachusetts observed that religious "conversion," a personal experience by which individuals came to know that they were saved, would be attended by a life of good works, and that conviction induced Puritans to lead good lives and thereby demonstrate to themselves that they were among the saved. Such behavior could relieve predestinarians of their greatest discomfort in life, that of agonizing over whether they had been destined for heaven. And while the Puritans were as convinced as all their contemporaries in English society of the superiority of men to women, and the need for men to govern the "weaker sex" firmly, they did hold women accountable for their own souls, and as responsible as men to meet their obligations to God—in a manner appropriate to their sex.

Not all Puritans reasoned the same way from these premises, and not all agreed even on the principle of cooperation among congregations. One who shared none of the Puritans' values was Thomas Morton, an adventurer whose followers enjoyed drinking freely and dancing around a maypole; the Puritans disapproved of his conduct and ejected him from Merrymount. Other settlers were lazy in their faith but were also easy to manage. Those who shared Puritan values but disputed specific points of the colony's religious practices were a good deal more troublesome.

Rhode Island. In 1631 Roger Williams, a saintlike man of great personal gifts and Separatist persuasion, arrived in Massachusetts. He began immediately to point out the numerous defects he saw in the Massachusetts scheme of things, condemned the religious requirements for suffrage, and delivered such seditious doctrines as that no government should have authority over religious matters. Such was Williams's charm that he became minister of the congregation in Salem despite his views; but when large numbers began to share those views the government found it necessary to banish him, lest the foundation for all authority in Massachusetts be undermined. He went to the head of Narragansett Bay, established a settlement he named Providence, and for almost half a century presided as the spiritual head of what became the colony of Rhode Island and Providence Plantations—a haven for religious nonconformists. So close were Williams's views to those of modern libertarians that today he is sometimes mistaken for an early secular liberal. He was not. His opposition to government coercion of conscience was founded in a dense religiosity very much in the seventeenth-century character.

The Rhode Island part of the colony was founded in 1638 by another religious leader, Anne Hutchinson. Having arrived in Boston with her husband and children as prosperous

Roger Williams, banished from Salem for arguing that a government has no authority over religious matters, found Providence. *(Courtesy, Ewing Galloway, New York)*

AN EARLY HARVARD RIOT (1639)

College students have long complained about the quality of food in university dining rooms. If this very first American instance of an incipient food riot is typical, they have good reason for their complaint. Mistress Eaton, the cook and author of this letter, was wife of Harvard's first headmaster, Nathaniel Eaton. Both lost their jobs when students protested the severe discipline that Mr. Eaton dispensed and the atrocious food that his wife served.

For their breakfast, that it was not so well ordered, the flour not so fine as it might, nor so well boiled or stirred, at all times that it was so, it was my sin of neglect, and want of that care that ought to have been in one that the Lord had intrusted with such a work. Concerning their beef, that was allowed them, as they affirm, which, I confess, had been my duty to have seen they had it, and continued to have had it, because it was my husband's command; but truly I must confess, to my shame. I cannot remember that ever they had it, nor that ever it was taken from them. And that they had not so good or so much provision in my husband's absence as presence, I conceive it was because he would call sometimes for butter or cheese, when I conceived there was no need of it; yet, forasmuch as the scholars did otherways apprehend, I desire to see the evil that was in the carriage of that as well as in the other, and to take shame to myself for it. And that they sent down for more, when they had not enough, and the maid should answer, if they had not, they should not, I must confess, that I have denied them cheese, when they sent for it, and it have been in the house; for which I shall humbly beg pardon of them, and own the shame, and confess my sin. And for such provoking words, which my servants have given, I cannot own them, but am sorry any such should be given in my house. And for bad fish, that they had it brought to table, I am sorry there was that cause of offence given them. I acknowledge my sin in it. And for their mackerel, brought to them with their guts in them, and goat's dung in their hasty pudding, it's utterly unknown to me; but I am much ashamed it should be in the family, and not prevented by myself or servants, and I humbly acknowledge my negligence in it. And that they made their beds at any time, were my straits never so great, I am sorry they were ever put to it. For the Moor his lying in Sam. Hough's sheet and pillowbier, it hath a truth in it: he did so one time, and it gave Sam. Hough just cause of offence; and that it was not prevented by my care and watchfulness, I desire [to] take the shame and sorrow for it. And that they eat the Moor's crusts, and the swine and they had share and share alike, and the Moor to have beer, and they denied it, and if they had not enough, for my maid to answer, they should not, I am an utter stranger to these things, and know not the least footsteps for them so to charge me; and if my servants were guilty of such miscarriages, had the boarders complained of it unto myself, I should have thought it my sin, if I had not sharply reproved my servants, and endeavored reform. And for bread made of heated, sour meal, although I know of but once that if was so, since I kept house, yet John Wilson affirms it was twice: and I am truly sorry, that any of it was spent amongst them. For beer and bread, that it was denied them by me betwixt meals, truly I do not remember, that ever I did deny it unto them; John Wilson will affirm, that, generally, the bread and beer was free for the boarders to go unto. And that money was demanded of them for washing the linen, it's true it was propounded to them, but never imposed upon them. And for their pudding being given the last day of the week without butter or suet, and that I said, it was miln of Manchester in Old England, it's true that I did say so, and am sorry, they had any cause of offence given them by having it so. And for their wanting beer, betwixt brewings, a week or half a week together, I am sorry that it was so at any time, and should tremble to have it so, were it in my hands to do again.

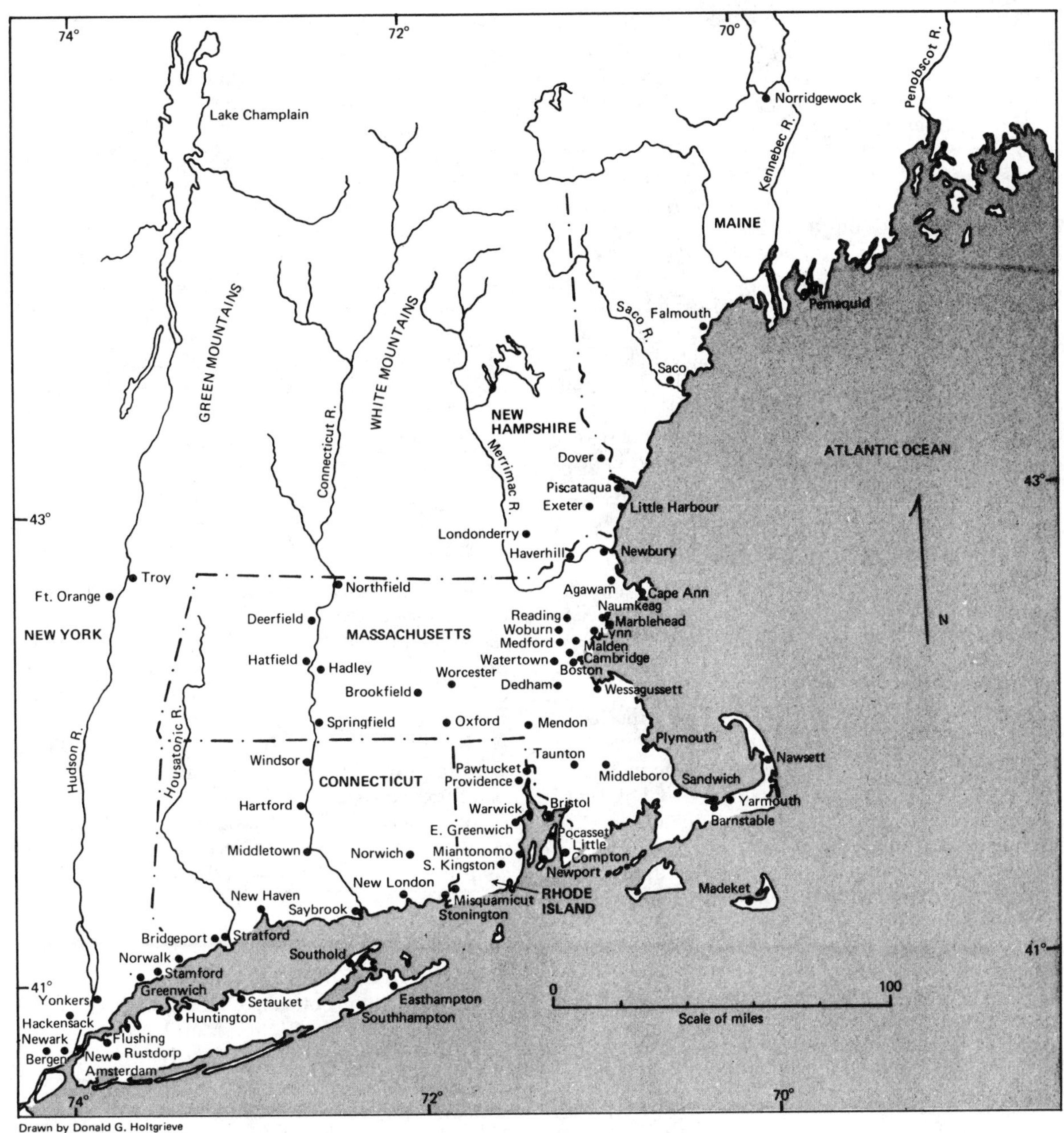

The New England Colonies

and valued additions to the colony, Hutchinson soon emerged as a charismatic amateur theologian, who held informal meetings in her home to discuss the Sunday sermon. Her interpretations favored a radical emphasis on the importance of the individual independent of ascribed status and community ties. This individualism found a receptive audience among some women who were conscious of regularly risking their lives—and confronting eternity—in childbirth, and among those merchants who favored the development of a more mobile and commercial society in the new world. Even the most learned ministers had difficulty in countering the hair-splitting logic of her reasoning. She agreed with the accepted premise that God only granted salvation in accordance with His own designs, not those of mere human beings, but also concluded that good behavior offered no evidence of salvation. If the grace of the Holy Spirit was in a person it was in that person, and if not, not. Such teachings were not only subversive of state-enforced morality, but of state-enforced order as well. As increasing numbers of Bostonians embraced Hutchinson's doctrines, she became even more dangerous to the established authorities than Williams had been. Under the leadership of John Winthrop, they reacted sharply, accusing Hutchinson and her followers not merely of heresy, but of familiarity with the devil. She was condemned by both civil and religious authorities and banished. Like Williams, she then established a settlement of her followers on Narragansett Bay.

Other parts of New England were settled simply out of an urge to have more room to move around in, physically and politically. In 1635 a group settled along the Connecticut River. The Reverend Thomas Hooker of Newton (Cambridge) led his flock west also, to establish Hartford. In 1639 these new towns, choosing to place themselves outside the jurisdiction of Massachusetts, drew up an agreement called the Fundamental Orders. They established their own government, which differed from the one in Massachusetts in a single important feature: suffrage was not confined to church members. In 1638 English immigrants set up the rigid religious community of New Haven.

The Colonies on Their Own

Maryland. The elaborate rituals of Roman Catholicism, far more than those of the Anglican religion of the Stuart monarchy, clashed with the plain worship of Puritans and Separatists. Henrietta Maria, the wife of Charles I, was a Catholic, and in the later years of Charles's reign, attendance at Mass in the queen's Catholic chapel would become popular among some upper-class Englishmen. During the Civil War of 1642-47 between Puritans and Royalists—the supporters of Charles I and the monarchy—many Catholics would fight in the Royalist army. Yet Roman Catholicism was officially a forbidden religion, and Catholics were isolated within an England of Protestants—Anglican, Puritan, and Separatist. Sir George Calvert, Lord Baltimore, wanted to expand his holdings in land. The charter of 1632, by which the Crown granted to his son Cecilius the vast estate that would become the colony of Maryland, constituted the fulfillment of the plans George Calvert had begun.

Maryland was the first proprietary colony, a colony possessed not by a joint-stock company as were Virginia and Massachusetts Bay but by a close-knit group, family, or an individual. Later the Carolinas, New York, New Jersey, Pennsylvania, and Georgia also would begin as proprietary colonies. The powers of Maryland leader Lord Baltimore were modeled after those of a medieval bishop who had administered a section of England's turbulent northern border. He had the authority to set and collect rents, issue legal writs, appoint administrative officials, confirm laws, and supervise the defense of the colony. The only important limitation required the proprietor to make laws "with the advice, assent, and approbation of the freemen of the province," a provision that led Baltimore to establish an elective assembly similar to Virginia's House of Burgesses.

The colony remained small, less than six thousand in 1660. Most heads of families were small planters, cultivating tobacco for export. Prominent rival landholders clashed with the Calvert family over its proprietary privileges, and the assembly became a center of opposition to the family. Roman Catholics never settled in Maryland in large numbers, and Protestants soon sought greater influence. During the 1640s the militant Protestantism of the period of the English Civil War put the Calvert family on the defensive. In 1649 the Maryland assembly adopted an act, framed by Lord Baltimore in response to pressures in England and America and in response to his own conscience, that guaranteed religious toleration to all Christians. And during the 1650s a Protestant faction wrested control away from the proprietor. Lord Baltimore regained authority in 1660. But Maryland never fulfilled his early plans.

"The Beginnings of Salutary Neglect." In 1642 the Puritan Parliament in England began open warfare with the Royalists. Parliament triumphed in 1647, and in 1649 executed Charles I. Then for eleven years a nation without a monarch was given over to experimentation in politics and in the shaping of a virtuous Protestant society. Parliament made the country into a Commonwealth that soon gave way to a Protectorate under Oliver Cromwell. In 1660, not long after the death of Cromwell and the succession of his son to the Protectorate, a Parliament tired of the unsettled times invited a Stuart to resume the monarchy, and Charles II became king after years of exile in Europe.

From the Civil War until the restoration of the Stuarts, England was occupied with argument, war, and experiment, and the colonies were orphaned, virtually independent of the mother country. During these times they hardened institutionally and socially.

New England vs. Virginia. From the beginning the settlers in New England differed fundamentally from those in Virginia. The New Englanders (Rhode Islanders always excepted) had a tight cooperative community, based upon a shared devotion and a shared theology. A spirit of adventure and a quest of private fortune had prompted Virginians, by and large, to move to America. To the extent that they had any common loyalty, it was to the king and his bishops. Natural conditions strongly reinforced the initial tendencies of both groups of settlers. In New England the sharply contoured and heavily forested terrain, intersected by few navigable streams, made movement difficult and thereby encouraged the planting of compact settlements. In Virginia the broad, flat terrain, intersected by swamps and tidal creeks, and the abundance of navigable waterways, made movement easy and thus encouraged settlers to spread out and act on their own. The experience of isolation that resulted from the English Civil War drove the two groups of colonies into remarkably different, and yet remarkably similar, courses of development.

In New England, the Puritan magistrates formally dissolved their connections with the Crown. Various of the colonies, partly to establish more regular and consistent relations with the Indians in the wake of the Pequot War of 1637-8, acted as Indians had learned earlier to act: they formed the New England Confederation, for mutual defense and general cooperation. Rhode Island was excluded, on the ground that it was a sinkhole of depravity and heresy. The sense of a common identity among the members of the Confederation hardened through their isolation from England and their sense of being surrounded by enemies: not only the Rhode Islanders and the squatters, but also hostile Indians, belligerent French trading posts to the north, and prosperous and militarily strong Dutch trading settlements on the Connecticut, the Hudson, and the Delaware. In their mood of self-reliance New Englanders took to the sea, ventured into occasional trading activities with the West Indies, and therein laid the foundations for New England's robust maritime future.

In Virginia the colonial government likewise separated itself from England, but for the opposite reason. Virginia proclaimed its loyalty to Charles I, and when the Puritan Parliamentarians won the Civil War Virginia declared its allegiance to the Stuart heir-in-exile, Charles II. The English Puritan Commonwealth government in 1652 sent four commissioners, two of them Virginians, a fleet, and 600 troops to bring the Southern colony into line, and though the royal governor, Sir William Berkeley, wanted to resist, he was overruled by the council and assembly. The commissioners made few requirements except the election of Puritan governors, and during the remaining years before the restoration of Charles II, Virginia virtually governed itself without interference from the Commonwealth and the Protectorate.

When the Civil War broke out in England the flow of Puritan immigrants to New England stopped, but by the time the war was over in 1647 it had become clear that the population of the colonies was increasing as fast as ever. In New England the increase derived from an extremely high birth rate; in Virginia it sprang from a new immigration, first in trickles and then in waves, of fugitives from Puritanical repression that was unfolding in England.

The first generation of New Englanders, or the more rigorous Puritans within that generation, had come to the new land with singleness of purpose. But before long John Winthrop's vision of the colony as a "cittie upon a hille," a society standing as an example of virtue and piety, was fading. With new people arriving throughout the 1630s there was bound to be contention, even among those who shared the same goals. What was the common law or village custom on a particular point? How should meetings be run? And many new people came seeking material rather than spiritual satisfaction. Villages spread; settlers scattered and became less amenable to central control. Boston, the heart of the Massachusetts Bay Colony, grew most rapidly. Soon there were two, then three churches. Occupations became more diverse and status groupings more complex. The unity of the new settlement shattered.

During the 1640s Massachusetts also suffered a severe depression. The economic trouble of New World Puritans stemmed largely from the success of their brethren in England. When the

***Pilgrims Going to Church*, by George Boughton. The original Massachusetts settlements were governed by and for the Orthodox Puritans, but by the 1660s other settlers and congregations were laying the basis for religious pluralism.** *(Courtesy, New York Historical Society, New York City. From the Robert L. Stuart Collection)*

Puritans came to power there, the migration of Puritans into Massachusetts stopped; the influx of English currency, brought by successive waves of new settlers, ceased to buoy New England's economy. Without a major exportable commodity, the future of the Puritan settlements dimmed.

The location of the Massachusetts Bay Colony proved to be its economic salvation. Good harbors, especially at Boston, provided the foundation for a thriving commerce. The growth of trade and the development of a shipping industry insured the colony's prosperity. After about 1650, New England began to boom. But the quickening of economic activity turned heads away from the Puritan founders' original purpose and attracted profit seekers who remained outside the religious community. And by the 1650s Puritans uneasily noticed that many of their children were not undergoing the conversion experience required for church membership. If the trend continued, Puritans feared, the bulk of the population would soon be outside the church.

In 1662 a meeting of Puritan ministers arrived at a solution to the problem of declining church membership. The ministers agreed to baptize the children of church members and to admit them into partial fellowship even though they could not give evidence of grace. To preserve the church's purity, the ministers excluded these "halfway" members from participation in the sacrament of Holy Communion. This Half-Way Convenant did revive lagging church membership, but it also showed that the Puritans' early dreams were yielding to practicality. The colony of Massachusetts, and even the church itself, was no longer a community of "saints."

Mayflower Compact. New England in its first four decades had established institutions that have profoundly influenced the American perception of democracy. The Mayflower Compact of 1620, the agreement among the Pilgrims aboard the *Mayflower* to bind themselves into a single government, resembles that primitive contract among free individuals that political philosophers in early modern times have imagined as the beginning of all government. And so the Mayflower Compact has existed in the American imagination ever since, as though those early settlers had reenacted the very foundation of government. The granting of the vote in Massachusetts Bay to all male members of

Puritan congregations gave that colony a moderately democratic government. That government granted considerable autonomy to the towns; and the New England towns, with their meetings at which the citizens debated local issues, are distinctive of the region today. In their own church activities, the Separatist and the New England Puritan churches rested power not in bishops—they had no bishops—but in the congregations (English Puritanism and the Presbyterian church, which was strong in Scotland, favored a more hierarchical structure). But although each represented an adaptation of inherited traditions to new purposes the needs of adaptation were never taken to justify overthrowing traditional notions of hierarchy that subordinated women to men, children to parents, and servants to masters. Nevertheless, Americans since then have pointed to those early churches, as much as to colonial governments, as nurturing the American democratic spirit.

It is easy, and in part correct, to trace American democracy to those early New England institutions. But neither the Mayflower Compact nor the government of Massachusetts Bay nor church polity of the New England congregations sprang from anything close to a conscious modern democratic theory. Each of the three came out of its own special circumstances and needs.

The Mayflower Compact was in the form of the covenant of a Separatist church. Its signers, indeed, were a Separatist congregation, deciding in the Mayflower Compact to govern themselves in their secular lives, just as they had previously agreed to form a church for their spiritual good. But the Compact had little in the way of a philosophical basis. It was the act of a group of immigrants who would soon put up a settlement in a wilderness thousands of ocean miles away from English law. To agree among themselves to have a government was a simple, necessary act. And the Compact did not project an independent government: it specifically declared allegiance to the king of England.

The Puritan and the Separatist congregations made an absolute distinction between people who were of the faith and those who were not. The New England Puritan congregations admitted to membership only individuals who could convincingly claim that they had undergone an experience that revealed that they were of the "elect." Within the Puritan and the Separatist congregations, members were spiritual equals, of a sort. While women could be of the elect and therefore could be full members of congregations, they could not be ministers or members of the governing body of the church. And that concept of equality derived from the doctrine, which no modern democrat would accept, that they belonged to the special, chosen assembly, selected for salvation from the beginning of time. Members were spiritual equals, but only because there can be no inequality among saints.

The suffrage in Massachusetts Bay represented the fusion of the organization of a business company with that of the New England Puritan congregations. That English joint-stock companies gave a vote to each shareholder for the conduct of business was, of course, not theoretical democracy but a practical arrangement among people who had chosen to pool their resources for some enterprise. The decision on the part of the company to turn itself into a colony had historical precedents. Several centuries earlier, English companies of merchants had set themselves up as semi-military colonies in enclaves within European cities, where they would govern themselves while managing some flow of commerce between the natives and England. In making all male members of Puritan congregations voting freemen of the Massachusetts Bay Company and therefore voting freemen of the colony, the government of Massachusetts Bay was in effect basing itself in the congregations. It was acting in a practical manner to hold settlers who might otherwise have refused to live within the reach of the colony.

Yet even if the early institutions of New England did not derive from any philosophical notions of equality or democracy, they deserve a place in the history of American democracy. The manner of their formation represents the way in which many of the nation's political and social institutions came into being—neither by theory nor by ancient custom but by matter-of-fact response to conditions and needs.

New Colonies

The division of British North America into colonies had been on a patchwork basis. In 1660, when England abandoned the Puritan government and returned the throne to the Stuart family, some settlements had no official sanction. The new king Charles II had to give these some legal status. His government and that of his successor James II also proceeded to provide for further colonization.

Earlier in the century lands lying within the present states of New Hampshire and Maine had gone to individual proprietors receiving authority from the Crown, but that authority was shadowy and from time to time Massachusetts Bay had extended its government to settlers there. During the reigns of the last two Stuarts, the question of what was to be the legal government of New Hampshire remained unanswered. In later years New Hampshire would receive a separate government, while Maine stayed with Massachusetts until 1820.

Connecticut and Rhode Island were quickly provided for. In 1662 the towns in the Connecticut valley received a charter from Charles. The charter, to the displeasure of New Havenites, placed the strict Puritan town of New Haven within the same colony as the more liberal settlements of the Connecticut valley. The Puritan government of England had granted some recognition to Rhode Island. In 1663 Charles granted a charter to that democratic collection of towns. The grant confirmed the policy of religious freedom that had made Rhode Island a haven for religious dissenters. Their charters gave to Connecticut and Rhode Island the privilege of governing themselves. Therein appeared a colonial form, the charter colony, taking its place alongside the proprietary colony such as Maryland, owned by a single individual or small group, and the colony owned by a business company. Before long the British American mainland would contain more royal colonies, with governors appointed by the Crown.

New York. Since earlier in the century the Dutch West India Company had owned New Netherland, the territory that is now the state of New York. By the 1660s the colony had no single character or purpose. New Englanders and Dutch had settled on Long Island. A collection of Dutch, English, and other European peoples dwelt in the little village of New Amsterdam, which lived off the fur and land trade and whatever other commerce the colony could offer. Farther up the Hudson were the beginnings of a system that would leave its mark on New York society for two centuries and more, in which patroons—the word suggests the English "patron,

The Bogardus farm looking southwards towards New Amsterdam, ca. 1679, province of the Duke of York. *(Courtesy, New York Public Library, Picture Collection)*

patrician," or aristocrat—presided over huge farming estates and their workers. The Dutch West India Company had extended over New Netherland a loose control under directors-general and provided local self-government and freedom of religion. The company was not able to turn a profit from the fees, taxes, and duties it imposed on the colony, and in 1654 it went bankrupt.

The restored Stuart monarch, continuing the commercial conflict with the Netherlands that the Puritan Commonwealth had entered, in 1664 seized New Netherland bloodlessly, the famed and magnificent temper of Peter Stuyvesant proving to have some mixture of prudence. (The Dutch would briefly retake the colony in the 1670s.) Charles II gave the province to his brother James, the Duke of York, and it became New York; the town of New Amsterdam also took that name. James's lieutenant in the colony proceeded to work out a set of laws. The scheme gave the freeholders—in essence, the landholders—of the colony the vote for town officials, but insured that the Duke would hold ultimate power. There was to be freedom of religion, though each town was required to sustain a church. To two royalists, Lord Berkeley and Sir George Carteret, the Duke transferred the conquered Dutch territory that received the name New Jersey, so named in honor of Carteret's earlier defense of the English Channel island of Jersey against the Puritans. Berkeley and Carteret then offered freedom of religion and granted to the freeholders the right to elect representatives who, along with a governor and council appointed by the proprietors, would legislate for the colony; the proprietors retained the authority to annul the laws.

The Carolinas. In 1663 a group that included Berkeley and Carteret became the proprietors of Carolina. In a charter of 1665, wherein Charles extended the boundaries of Carolina, the king affirmed the right of the inhabitants to liberty of religion. The proprietors provided for a legislature elected by the freeholders, but retained the right to revoke laws. In 1669 Lord Ashley, one of the proprietors, and his secretary, the political philosopher John Locke, designed "The Fundamental Constitutions of Carolina," conceiving an elaborate and fanciful scheme for the colony. Toward the end of the century Carolina was centered in two unconnected locations: in the North, benefiting from migration from Virginia, a society of small farmers; and around the seaport of Charles Town (Charleston) in the South, a cluster of Virginians, migrants from the Northern colonies, English immigrants, Scots, French Protestants called Huguenots, farmers from the British West Indies. The economy of the Southern part of Carolina subsisted in part on the fur trade with the Indians. The West Indians were familiar with slavery, and the settlers around Charles Town were beginning to grow rice with slave labor. North and South each possessed self-government under ultimate proprietary control, and early in the eighteenth century each would become a royal colony, its governor appointed by the Crown.

Pennsylvania. In 1681 an upper-class Quaker, William Penn, received from Charles II a proprietary grant to "Pennsylvania." Penn had already joined other Quakers in purchasing from Carteret the proprietary rights to part of New Jersey.

The intimate friendship between the dissolute Charles and the devout Penn seems highly improbable. It derived in part from the earlier friendship between Charles and Penn's father; Charles owed Penn £16,000 for services rendered by the father, an admiral, and the grant was made in payment of that debt. And Penn was as delightful a companion as any courtier in the kingdom: he was witty, high spirited, and an excellent swordsman. His religious convictions were actually an advantage, not a handicap, in his relationship with the king. He was a Quaker. Wildly eccentric, governed only by their own "Inner Light," the early Quakers had heard voices, appeared nude in church, and thrived on persecution to the extent of deliberately seeking martyrdom. But Penn was not of that early fanatical generation. And as a member of an extreme sect outside of orthodox English Protestantism, he had something in common with Charles II, whose high church religion also diverged from that orthodoxy, though in a different direction.

The charter to Pennsylvania required that Penn enforce British trading acts, permit appeals from Pennsylvania courts to the king, submit all Pennsylvania laws to the king for approval, and upon request from twenty colonists, provide an Anglican minister—a minister of the established Church of England. The king reserved the power to impose taxes "by act of Parliament." In all other respects Penn was free to govern his colony as he pleased.

Penn provided, in an elaborate *Frame of Government* (1682), that the governorship of the col-

***Penn's Treaty with the Indians*, by Benjamin West. The Quaker William Penn's historic treaty with the Delaware Indians in 1682 created a peaceful settlement in Pennsylvania.** *(Courtesy, Pennsylvania Academy of Fine Arts)*

ony would go to the proprietor or his deputy, and that legislative power would be vested in a council and an assembly, both elected by the freeholders of the colony. He proposed to earn an income from his colony by collecting rents from the settlers, and to attract the settlers by advertising widely the good land, free government and religious liberty available in the colony. The campaign was an immediate success. Quakers flocked to Pennsylvania from England, Holland, Germany, Wales, and Ireland. Many non-Quakers went as well, for in the wake of the reestablishment of the Stuart monarchy, a new wave of refugees poured out of England; and a group of German Mennonites, driven from their homes by the continental religious wars, also emigrated to Pennsylvania.

Penn also possessed deeds to what is now Delaware, though the grounds of his legal claim to govern "the Territories," as the lower region was called for a while, were unclear. In the first decade of the eighteenth century Delaware, settled in part by Swedes, in effect would separate from Pennsylvania, though both colonies continued to have the same governor.

The Colonies vs. London

The Navigation Acts and Mercantilism. In 1651 the government of the Commonwealth had passed a Navigation Act aimed at building up the shipping of England and the empire. The government was particularly interested in excluding from English and colonial posts the ships of the fellow Protestant nation of the Netherlands, with which the Commonwealth was in close economic competition. The Act provided that no ships except those belonging to the people of England or her colonies could import Asian, African, or American goods into England or the colonies, and that European goods could be imported only in English ships or ships of the country producing the merchandise.

After Charles II reestablished the English

monarchy in 1660, his ministers and Parliament, building on principles established by the Navigation Act of 1651, enacted a broad program designed to stimulate England's economic growth and to transform the scattered American settlements and East Indian trading posts into a world empire. The primary aim of the "mercantilist" program was to make England and its overseas colonies a vast, closed trading area, as self-sufficient as possible, protected by an enlarged navy, and serviced by an expanded merchant fleet. Each part of the empire was supposed to specialize in supplying the products and services for which it was best suited, and thereby contribute to the well-being of all the other parts and to the strength of the whole. The colonies would produce goods that England could not produce economically—such commodities as lumber, naval stores, fish, tobacco, indigo, and West Indian sugar—and would be discouraged from competing with the manufacturing activities of the mother country. The colonial products would be sent only to Britain, but would have a monopoly on the English market. Insofar as was feasible, the colonies would buy their finished goods from England, even if the goods were originally produced in continental Europe. All products would be subject to customs duties and would be carried only in English or colonial ships.

Two major acts laid the legal foundations of the system: the Navigation Act of 1660 and the Staple Act of 1663. The Navigation Act restricted all colonial trade to vessels owned and manned primarily by Englishmen or British colonists, and required that certain enumerated articles produced in the colonies—tobacco, sugar, indigo, and ginger—be shipped only to Britain or to another English colony. The Staple Act required that most goods imported into the colonies, whether they originated in Britain or in foreign parts, must be shipped from a British port. The Staple Act aimed to benefit the Crown by increasing the customs revenues on exports from England; to help English exporters by giving them a monopoly of the colonial market (even as the Navigation Act gave colonial producers a monopoly of the English market); and to protect the colonists by confining their trade to shipping lanes that could be patrolled and protected by the English navy.

For all the laxity of its enforcement, the new commercial system was an immediate success. English commerce boomed and the merchant fleet became the largest and most profitable the nation had yet known. This was not surprising. Simply by virtue of establishing the system England took exclusive possession of a large and growing colonial trade. The colonies also prospered under this new system. The West Indies, booming with the rapid expansion of sugar production, welcomed the naval protection afforded by the new system, for the Caribbean was teeming with pirates. The tobacco colonies, Virginia and Maryland, paid perhaps a bit more for freight than they had before, and tobacco prices continued to decline, but the establishment of a great central marketing system in England facilitated an enormous increase in production that in the long run more than compensated. By 1672 the two colonies were exporting seventeen million pounds of tobacco a year. The New England colonies, being free to elect their own governors, were also free to ignore the Acts of Trade when it was to their advantage. Thus they profited from trade with the enclosed imperial market as well as from the protection of the English navy, and otherwise did as they pleased. Consequently, the merchant fleet of New England, built by a burgeoning new local industry, grew even faster than that of Old England.

Another Restoration policy, the resumption of discrimination against those who dissented from the Church of England, also promoted New England's prosperity. Another wave of dissenters went to America in flight from this policy, and in the 1660s the population of New England increased from about 33,000 to about 52,000.

During the Restoration the colonies cultivated that independence that they had already enjoyed in the days of the Commonwealth. The Massachusetts Bay Colony led the way.

Massachusetts: Resistance to the Crown. From the outset of the Restoration Massachusetts was troublesome. It secretly harbored two of the men condemned to death for the execution of Charles I; it ignored the Navigation Acts; and it violated its charter by retaining on its statute books a number of laws, particularly those concerning religion, contrary to the laws of England. Very early, Charles sent orders commanding Massachusetts to make its laws conform to those of England. The colony did temporarily stop persecuting the Quakers and did modify its laws concerning suffrage, but neither action was taken in response to the king's orders, which the colonial assembly flatly ignored. And so, when the British mission to seize New Netherland from the Dutch—that colony would subsequently become New York—was dispatched in 1664, Charles sent four commissioners along to investigate the New England governments.

The Thirteen Original Colonies

Name	*Founded by*	*Year*	*Made Royal*	*Status at Revolutionary War*
1. Virginia	London Company	1607	1624	Royal
2. New Hampshire	John Mason and others	1623	1679	Royal
3. Massachusetts	Separatists and Puritans	1620-30	1691	Royal
4. Maryland	Lord Baltimore	1634	———	Proprietary (controlled by proprietor)
5. Connecticut	Emigrants from Massachusetts	1635	———	governing
6. Rhode Island	Roger Williams	1636	———	Self-governing
7. North Carolina	Virginians	1653	1729	Royal (separated informally from S.C., 1691)
8. New York	Dutch	c.1613		
	Duke of York	1664	1685	Royal
9. New Jersey	Berkeley and Cartaret	1664	1702	Royal
10. South Carolina	Eight nobles	1670	1729	Royal
11. Pennsylvania	William Penn	1681	———	Proprietary
12. Delaware	Swedes	1638	———	Proprietary
13. Georgia	George Oglethorpe	1733	1752	Royal

The commissioners encountered no difficulty in Plymouth, Connecticut, or Rhode Island, but when they arrived in Boston they met with a reception that was at once icy and bold. The magistrates referred the commissioners to the Massachusetts Bay Charter of 1629, refused to submit to investigation, and publicly forbade the citizens to offer any testimony. The commissioners returned to England, and three of them recommended to the king that the Charter be revoked. The open defiance might have provoked not only a revocation of the charter, but armed suppression of the colony as well. But the confrontation came just at the time England was suffering from a triple disaster of the London plague, a great fire in that city, and military reverses abroad. For the next six years Massachusetts, together with the other colonies, was largely ignored, and could take advantage of the situation.

Massachusetts did so. The price of tobacco fell in 1667 to about half a penny per pound. Under normal circumstances, about half the tobacco shipped to London was reexported to the Continent through Holland, and though the English market had vanished the European market continued to exist. So the merchants of New England, ignoring the Acts of Trade, carried tobacco directly from Virginia to Holland, and from 1667 to 1672 reaped considerable profits for themselves and improved Virginia's tobacco prices in the bargain.

Virginia, the most Royalist of all settlements, and New England, the least, had become equally disenchanted with the government in London. And in the late summer of 1675, both colonies were subjected to difficulties that would have strained any loyalties.

Renewed Conflicts with Indians. The difficulties in both places resulted from the renewal of Indian hostilities, and the ultimate wellspring of the trouble was the ambitions of France. Since the 1630s the Indians had gradually and peacefully retreated to the interior rather than face the devastating fire of English muskets. But in the late 1660s the French adopted a broad strategy of encircling the English colonies with settlements along the St. Lawrence, the Great Lakes, and the Mississippi, and forged alliances with the Indians between their own settlements and those of the English. The five Iroquois nations of New York had for long been enemies of the French and their Indian allies. Hence the new French policy forced the Iroquois back. They, in turn, pushed back the Algonquin tribes of New England and the Susquehannocks of what is now Pennsylvania, with the result that in the 1670s they clashed with the whites to the east, and the Susquehannocks engaged in hostilities with the whites to the south.

In New England the fighting was known as King Philip's War. Philip's tribe, already hemmed in between rival governments and land speculators in Rhode Island and Massachusetts, was pressed to the point of desperation by the Iroquois drive; and just at that time the Massachusetts government ordered the Indians to disarm. They responded in the only way they could, by attacking the white settlements. The Indians did not fight according to the rules of formal territorial warfare, European-style: a contest in which the only combatants and subjects of attack were uniformed armies, and in which both sides campaigned until one or the other surrendered. The Indians fought only intermittently, and regarded all whites, women and children included, as fair prey. There was considerable barbarism on both sides. But the whites had the advantage of superior arms and superior organization. The New England Confederation mobilized about a thousand men and conducted a ruthless, systematic, relentless campaign, and by 1676 the Indians had been thoroughly defeated. King Philip's War cost the white settlers about a sixth of their adult males and the destruction of about twenty towns. During the entire campaign, the English sent no help.

Instead of help, a special agent of Charles II, Edward Randolph, arrived in Boston to convey new royal instructions and to investigate the enforcement of the Navigation Acts. After a less than cordial reception and a cursory investigation, Randolph submitted two reports to the Crown. He charged Massachusetts with refusing to comply with the Navigation Act, executing English subjects for their religious faith, denying appeals to the king's Privy Council, and refusing to take the oath of allegiance.

Massachusetts continued to be obstinate. The General Court refused to recognize Randolph as customs officer, set up its own customs office, and imprisoned the deputies Randolph had appointed. Randolph reported on the conduct of the colony. When Massachusetts did not satisfactorily reform its behavior, court proceedings began against the colony. In 1684 the Massachusetts Bay Company lost its charter and Massachusetts became a royal colony.

Royalism in Virginia. In Virginia bands of Susquehannock Indians, fleeing the Iroquois, crossed the Potomac in the summer of 1675. Relations between the outland Indians and the Virginia planters deteriorated until a planter was killed over a fur transaction, several Indians (including five Susquehannock chiefs under a flag of truce) were killed in retaliation, and the whole Potomac frontier erupted in raids and counterraids. The royal governor of Virginia, William Berkeley, sought to stop the outbreak, but he did so from premises and with policies that were certain to alienate the frontiersmen.

A staunch, pigheaded royalism guided Berkeley's policy. He had been royal governor from 1642 to 1652, had suffered humiliation and exile under the Commonwealth, and had been restored with the Stuarts in 1660; thereafter, he would not yield an inch of the royal prerogative. Indeed Charles, in his gratitude for such loyalty, rashly proclaimed Virginia as one of his kingdoms, coequal with England, Scotland, and Wales. As part of the restored royal authority, according to Berkeley, Indians became subjects of the king, on an equal footing with whites, and were therefore entitled to the protection of royal justice. No warfare upon the Indians was to be tolerated, despite the Indian attacks—which Berkeley regarded as minor frontier incidents. Berkeley met the crisis by raising funds to rebuild the frontier forts and to pay and equip a band of mounted rangers, and by prohibiting fur trade by any but a handful of traders whom he himself licensed. The new tax was ill calculated to please the frontiersmen, and the new trade regulations threatened the ambitions of a number of frontier fur traders, land seekers, and border barons.

The malcontents soon raised a leader who was willing to defy the governor: Nathaniel Bacon, the governor's nephew, recent settler in the interior of Virginia, artful demagogue, unscrupulous Royalist adventurer and lawyer who had been trained at the Inns of Court in London. Bacon held that the Indians were not subjects of the Crown but were outside the law and could be attacked by any Englishman so disposed. In May 1676, without a commission from the governor, Bacon marched at the head of an expedition that descended upon the Roanoke River to destroy a Susquehannock village. He was promptly accused of treason, but the governor pardoned him when he acknowledged his offense.

Meanwhile Bacon, along with a goodly number of other radicals, was elected to the House of Burgesses. They proceeded to push through a series of enactments, collectively known as "Bacon's laws," which reversed most of Berkeley's Restoration policies by liberalizing voting, tax, and religious regulations. Bacon himself had little or nothing to do with all this. Instead, he took up his military career again. He raised an army of 500 men, marched on the colonial capital at Jamestown, forced Berkeley to commission him as a militia captain, and set about looking for more Indians to kill.

And now the tobacco planters demonstrated what recent royal and parliamentary policies had accomplished. The planters professed no allegiance at all to Parliament, and their loyalty to the Crown had become only formal, devoid of any personal commitment. When Governor Berkeley again declared Bacon a rebel, the planters swore their allegiance to Bacon. In 1676, they held to their oath, enabling Bacon to drive Berkeley's forces out of Jamestown and burn the village to the ground. Order was restored in the ensuing months, largely as a result of Bacon's death in October.

The Dominion of New England

With the death of Charles II in 1685, his brother James became king. James II soon suppressed a rebellion led by a pretender to the throne supported by a faction of Whigs. Thereupon James proceeded to try to establish absolute rule by the Crown and to bring back Roman Catholicism. But the most ambitious project for the establishment of royal rule, and for bringing some coherence to the government of the colonies, was the Dominion of New England. New Hampshire, Massachusetts, Plymouth (not yet absorbed into Massachusetts), Connecticut, Rhode Island, New York, and the Jerseys were all to be governed by one governor and his council, without the interference of representative assemblies. As governor of the dominion James appointed Sir Edmund Andros, a former governor of New York, who arrived in Boston during 1686.

Sir Edmund Andros. The new system made a great deal of administrative sense. For the first and only time in the history of the English empire in America, England had a system that was,

William Andros, Governor of the Dominion of New England, from 1686–1688, being taken prisoner in Boston. Though this was triggered by rumors of a Popish Plot, opposition to Andros stemmed from the colonists' belief that he was limiting local self-government.

at least on paper, as efficient as those of France and Spain. Andros's administration was in many respects both shrewd and enlightened. He left most of the existing laws in force. He respected the established churches and schools—though in his attempts to provide for the Church of England he antagonized Puritans, and his observance of Christmas, which Puritanism rejected for savoring of ritual and Catholicism, drew the indignant notice of Samuel Sewall, the famous diarist. For the most part Andros left the towns in control of their own local affairs—and the town and congregation constituted the primary unit of government in New England. He governed with a strong hand; for example, he offered the merchants of his dominion the protection of the Royal Navy if they cooperated with him and threatened them with its great destructive power if they refused. Andros tempered his unpopular measures skillfully.

Thus, while he antagonized the merchants of Boston, Newport, and New York by insisting on enforcement of the Navigation Acts, he also reversed his earlier policy and stopped offering pirates haven in these principal ports; this meant that he may have reduced the merchants' profits though he reduced their risks as well. Again, Andros provoked considerable grumbling by declaring that the Massachusetts Bay government had proceeded illegally in granting land for town settlements.

The grumbling was aggravated when he ordered all landholders, present and prospective, to obtain land titles from the governor and pay quitrents as well. But virtually everyone was confirmed in his title to the land he already possessed, the rents proved to be nominal and were not collected, and it turned out to be far easier to obtain land from the new governor than it had been from the Puritan government. Andros also levied taxes without legislative approval, but they were no larger than they had been when duly elected representatives levied them. Andros further encroached upon the principle of local self-government by ordering that town meetings be held no more than once a year and that control of the militia be vested in the governor; but the towns customarily met officially only once a year anyway (they met once a week at church congregations, and that Andros did not change), and as it happened Andros never had occasion to call out the militia.

In short, Andros's innovations directly challenged the professed principles of the New Englanders, but altered the daily lives of most of them precious little. It is uncertain whether this experiment in enlightened despotism would have won over New Englanders inclined to hostility toward outside rule, and more especially rule by a communicant of the Church of England. It was never put to the full test, for it failed in England. James's undoing came in 1688 after he had alienated his strongest supporters by attempting to go too far, too fast, in his efforts to restore Roman Catholicism. Even the Tories, the party more sympathetic to the privileges of the Crown, were antagonists. Rich country gentry, who made up much of the strength of the Tories, were wedded to the Church of England; and some of them feared that full restoration of the Roman Church might include restoration of its lands, which happened now to belong to them. Even then, James might have prevailed but for a sudden change in the prospects for the succession.

The Glorious Revolution. James was in his fifties and his only children were two daughters, Mary and Anne, both by his first wife and both devoutly Protestant; his second wife, an Italian princess and a Catholic, had borne him no children. Most Englishmen, however much they despised the king, therefore thought it better to wait out the Papist storm as they had the Puritan, on the theory that little permanent harm could be done before James died and the Crown passed to a Protestant. But in June of 1688 the queen had a son, and that opened the possibility of a permanent Catholic succession. It seemed to be now or never for English Protestantism; and so seven prominent Englishmen, supported by a vast conspiracy, invited William of Orange of Holland, husband of James's daughter Mary, to rescue England from Catholic tyranny. William accepted and on November 5 landed with a force of about 14,000 at Torbay, in southwestern England. General John Churchill and Colonel Percy Kirke led a carefully planned desertion of great numbers of royal troops, and much of the remainder of James's army refused to obey their Catholic commanders. James was left defenseless, and in December he fled to the continent. Eight weeks later William and Mary became joint sovereigns of England.

Governor Andros was in Maine when he got news of William's landing, and he returned to Boston to prevent an anti-royalist reaction. But he had neither army nor police, and rioting broke out in response not to James's removal but to rumors of a Popish plot. Andros fled to the local fort, but before the end of the day he and the other royal officials surrendered and were jailed. A Puritan oligarchy governed the colony for two months, until a new General Court could be elected. In July Andros was ordered to return to England.

As soon as the news of Boston's uprising reached New York that colony too was swept with a great fear of a Popish plot, and three of its counties, those populated mainly by Congregationalist Puritans, threw out the royal officials and elected their own. In the city, Jacob Leisler, a successful German trader, led a group that ousted Andros's deputy governor and established a provisional government with Dutch support. At first Leisler had little support outside the city, but soon French-inspired Indian raids in the upper part of the colony lent gruesome reinforcement to the rumors of a Papist-Indian campaign to massacre Protestants. Leisler offered firmness, discipline, order, and military strength, and became in fact governor of the entire colony.

The Jerseys and Pennsylvania adjusted to the new state of affairs with little drama. In Maryland a group of colonists calling themselves the Protestant Association forced the resignation of the governor appointed by the Catholic proprietor, Lord Baltimore, brought back the assembly, which had been dissolved, and petitioned the Crown to take over the colony. In Virginia the dominant planters announced their support of William and Mary and their confidence that James's governor would be removed, which soon happened. Settlers in Northern Carolina turned on the proprietary governor, who fled to Charles Town and temporarily set up a government there. Soon afterward the proprietors suspended him.

John Locke. The philosopher of the English revolution (and the American Revolution) was John Locke. At the behest of various champions of the revolution, Locke published in 1689 and 1690 several essays, notably the *Second Treatise on Civil Government* and *An Essay Concerning Human Understanding*. Locke argued that man is born innocent, capable of good or evil, a creature whom conditions will mold. Locke reasoned that man had once lived in a state of nature, in accordance with the laws of nature (or of God), which endowed man with rights to life, personal freedom, and the property that he accumulated through honest labor. But in the natural state the strong prey upon the weak, and so men had formed societies and created governments. Governments existed by virtue of voluntary agreements, or contracts, between the governed and governors, and their function was to protect the individual's natural rights to life, liberty, and property. The government of James II, founded upon such a contract, had been legitimate until the king broke the contract by depriving people of their natural rights, in effect declaring war upon his subjects. The people therefore had no recourse but to overthrow James's government and to establish a new contract with a new sovereign who seemed more likely to abide by his agreements, William of Orange.

To make legitimate the Glorious Revolution, a Convention Parliament proclaimed early in 1689 what a formal Parliament enacted and William and Mary approved later the same year, the Declaration of Rights. The Declaration and subsequent Bill of Rights established, for all time, limits upon the English monarchy and judiciary. The Crown could no longer make or suspend laws, levy taxes, or maintain standing armies without the consent of Parliament, which was guaranteed frequent meetings, free elections, and free debate. Some ecclesiastical courts were eliminated and others had their powers reduced, and in all courts every person was guaranteed trial by jury and protected from excessive bails and forfeiture of estates before conviction.

Equally important was a series of steps taken to regularize, modernize, and render more flexible the system of public finance, which had previously occasioned such destructive conflict between the Crown and Parliament. Henceforth Parliament did not merely grant monies, but controlled their expenditure as well. To that end, it began to make specific appropriations for specific purposes, and to require estimates and accounts of expenditures.

As a part of the process of putting things in order, Crown and Parliament again attempted to bring order to affairs in America.

England Tries Again: The Navigation Act of 1696. The colonists had taken advantage of England's military preoccupations to profit from illegal trade. It had been possible to do so largely because enforcement of the earlier Navigation Acts had depended more upon private morality, supplemented by generous rewards to informers, than upon efficient administrative machinery. The new Navigation Act of 1696 sought to change that. Colonial governors were now held responsible, on penalty of forfeiture of office, for violations of the law. Regular customs officers were now appointed for each colony, whereas previously there had been only a few officers who had moved about from one colony to another. The new officers were authorized to obtain from local courts "writs of assistance" permitting them to enter buildings in random searches for smuggled goods—a far more potent device than mere search warrants, which had to specify the particular items searched for. Trials for violations of the law were to be in admiralty courts, where proceedings were not encumbered by juries.

But the new system could not overcome the physical circumstances in English America, which were not conducive to efficient supervision of trade. Effective customs operations require concentration of shipping, and in much of America such concentration was not feasible. Tobacco, for example, which was by far the most valuable product of the mainland colonies, was normally loaded on ships directly at the plantations along the rivers of Virginia and Maryland and on Chesapeake Bay. Short of placing customs officers on every plantation or stationing armed ships at every river and inlet, it was virtually impossible to prevent masters of local, New England, or foreign vessels from carrying tobacco anywhere they pleased.

Another difficulty was institutional. England had, as yet, no tradition of civil service, royal or parliamentary, in the colonies or at home. Posts were filled through influence, bribery, or other corrupt means more commonly than through regard for honest and efficient administration. Colonial service attracted the least savory of a generally unsavory lot, not only because life in the colonies was far from desirable to most courtiers, but also because the rewards for legitimate service there were small. In all the colonies except Virginia and Barbados the governor was dependent upon the local assembly for his salary, and the customs officers were paid out of fees and fines, not the royal treasury. Accordingly, many of those who filled imperial positions were quite amenable to bribes, offered in exchange for looking the other way when colonials proposed to trade outside the rules established by the Navigation Acts.

By and large, the imperial commercial system worked when it was to the mutual advantage of the colonies and the mother country to abide by it; which is to say, it worked for about three-quarters of the trade affected by the Navigation Acts. Otherwise it was generally ignored, except when the Royal Navy was not engaged in war and had nothing better do do than police the seas against pirates and smugglers.

In the years following the Glorious Revolution of 1688-89 colonial governments underwent a reorganization that replaced the absolute rule the monarchy under James II had tried to maintain over several of the colonies—but gave the Crown a tighter control than had been the case for much of the seventeenth century. Connecticut and Rhode Island retained their self-government, and the Penn family, after losing the original charter to Pennsylvania, regained the proprietorship of that colony. In 1691 the Crown took over Maryland, though the Calvert family retained property rights there. But then the Calvert family converted from Roman Catholicism to the Church of England, and in 1715 it was given back its proprietary rights to the government of Maryland. In that colony that had been founded as a refuge for Roman Catholics, people of that faith now lost the right to vote and their right to worship was limited. Virginia, Massachusetts, and New Hampshire were now royal instead of proprietary colonies. In 1702 New Jersey too became a Crown colony, and in 1729 North Carolina and South Carolina each became a separate Crown colony.

Within a few years after the Glorious Revolution, then, British North America had the kind of government and the relationships to Great Britain that would determine its course until the American Revolution. At a time when in England power was going increasingly to parliament, government in the Crown colonies was in effect being unintentionally divided. In the eighteenth century governors and councils appointed by the monarch would often clash with elected assemblies that alone had the authority to tax the colonists, and therefore had the authority to withhold money from a governor in the pursuit of his policies. The navigation system, with further legislation in the eighteenth century, would in time lead to major conflict with the government in Great Britain. The foundations had been laid for a grand but restless empire.

The Settlements Become a Society

The new continent was rich beyond anything that a settler of ordinary means could have attained in the Old World. The forests were thick with fine timber for ships' masts and other uses. The soils of Virginia and the Carolinas hungered to be planted with the South's cash crops. The New England seacoasts invited the forming of a great merchant and seafaring culture, and nearby were the teeming fish banks of Newfoundland. And everywhere there was land: land to plant with American corn and other subsistence foods, land to test for the possibility of new commercial crops, land to flee into, away from civilization and its troubles, land to settle with religious communities that Europe would not tolerate.

Take today's crowd at a Yankee Stadium double-header and scatter it along the East coast, and you will have the entire population of this land in 1660. Though the death rate in Virginia in the earliest times had been terrible, the population of the colonies was growing, by births in some regions and elsewhere by immigration. Throughout the colonies, stable, self-perpetuating growth depended upon the presence of women in their child-bearing years who could marry the male settlers. Where the ratio of men to women remained very high—3 to 1 in the Chesapeake, and as many as 9 to 1 in the fishing settlements in Newfoundland—it took considerable time for the settler population to establish self-reproduction. Even at the end of the century the European population was a sprinkling of people at the Eastern edge of the American continent. The British government, when it thought about this land at all, saw it as part of a commercial and territorial empire, and granted chunks of it to courtier proprietors, or legislated for it with the Navigation Acts, or otherwise tried to control it. Colonists were keenly aware of their place within that empire, and such things as the Navigation Acts and the Dominion of New England reminded them of it. They were meanwhile forming societies of their own, establishing ways of life that did not subordinate themselves to the needs and programs of the empire. But colonial societies did not simply develop spontaneously within the rich land and opportunities of the continent; they took much of their shape from the societies of the Old World.

Meeting House, Plymouth, Massachusetts, built in 1683. The system of New England towns meetings begun in the first settlements, in which local citizens decide on local affairs, persists to this day. *(Courtesy, Colonial Society of Massachusetts, Boston)*

New England Towns. The early New England settlers gathered into villages that duplicated something of the physical arrangement of the English communities they had known. A family did not live in isolation on the land it worked. Homes were close together in the village, and each family worked plots of the surrounding lands. The system was well suited to the needs of the first generation in New England. On a stubborn soil in a harsh winter climate and under threat of Indian attack, that generation sought to establish a stable and comfortable life. For several generations thereafter in Massachusetts, attendance at church was required of everyone, including nonmembers; and the centrality of the churches in the life of the colony was further reason for the colonists to cluster into villages. By the eighteenth century the agricultural population was scattering into the countryside on individual farms. But the village pattern that had developed in the early years left its permanent stamp on New England: and the system of town meetings, in which local citizens directly make decisions that elsewhere in the country are left to elected or appointed officials, persists to this day.

Even in the seventeenth century New England, at least in its most settled portions, was a remarkably well-educated region, possibly one of the most civilized places in the English world. The government of Massachusetts Bay had the towns provide free elementary schools—although girls were not expected to benefit from them and women's literacy lagged far behind that of men. Scholars have rejected the notion that New Englanders were black-clad haters of life, the world, and pleasure. Most New Englanders did not even wear black, although they would have been happy to do it. Black was the color not of grimness but of wealth and prominence. The diarist Samuel Sewell and others like him might grumble at Edmund Andros for celebrating Christmas. But Sewell himself wrote in fluent, lively prose; New England sermons could employ an imagery beautiful in its homespun simplicity and educated New Englanders

Tobacco quickly became a commercial staple in Virginia and the need for labor on the tobacco plantations gradually led to the use of black slaves.

enjoyed not only religious but secular literature written in the language of everyday life. Men's sermons and history dominated colonial reading, but there was also an audience for women's writings that ran from Anne Bradstreet's poetry to Mary Rowlandson's wildly popular narrative of her captivity among the Narragansett Indians.

New England settlers also imported English class distinctions. Yet here as in other matters the land and conditions of the New World modified the institutions of the old. Class distinction in New England meant not the presence of a powerful aristocracy but a somewhat milder component of the English system of class, a deference on the part of the majority toward people of greater wealth, schooling, and political position.

Southern Plantations. The upper South, unlike New England, had land suitable for the growth of a great commercial staple crop. And since the leadership was not interested in setting up villages with churches as the focus of their life, society in Virginia spread out into tobacco plantations of various sizes. A portion of the English social system that easily adapted itself to the tobacco plantations was the gentry, a class of substantial landholders, without aristocratic titles who possessed great local power, official and informal. Members of the gentry could administer the law locally. In Virginia the larger tobacco planters stood for election to the colonial assembly, sat in the local court, and served in the vestry that provided some lay management of the established Anglican church.

In the seventeenth century the tobacco colonies were badly in need of labor. The major solution was to import undentured servants. In exchange for passage money to America, servants were obliged to work for a number of years for the employer—usually four years, perhaps six or seven. The paper on which the agreement was written would then be torn in two, the servant receiving one piece and the master the other. Each thereby had evidence that he or she had been a party to that specific agreement, for the jagged indentations along the tear line of one piece would fit exactly into those on the other. Such servitude existed throughout the colonies, but it was most pronounced in the South. Only gradually in the seventeenth century did black slavery appear.

In the colonies as a whole, the institutions of the Old World were neither disappearing nor remaining intact, but instead were accommodating themselves to the opportunities the American continent offered. Customs and institutions became more open. The availability of property, and the tasks of settlement, brought women more into the management of property than was the case in Britain. The Northern and middle colonies provided civil marriage as an alternative to ecclesiastical marriage, and in civil marriage the woman was something of an independent party to a contract. Indentured servants could look forward to freedom and perhaps to entry into the propertied classes. A large part of the population could vote or otherwise engage in local government. And yet, while so much of British civilization was becoming freer in North America, the new land had begun to cultivate the institution of slavery, unknown in Britain for centuries. Freedom and slavery were growing up together.

Points To Think About

1. The New World was not new to the Indians. Neither was it a wilderness. Nor did they incline to the view that Providence had reserved it for reformed Christians. The various tribes had their own visions of America, which they attempted to preserve in spite of the continuing incursions of Europeans.

The first and most important effect of European settlement was the spread of European diseases to Indians who had no immunities against them. The resulting epidemics enormously weakened the Indians' ability to defend their land. Initially, however, Europeans needed little land and they were too few to pose any immediate military threat. Nonetheless their coming did upset the Indian balance of power since those tribes which traded with the Europeans acquired firearms in exchange. These new weapons encouraged their possessors to attack other tribes—a development which, in the long run, could only weaken the Indians and strengthen the Europeans.

Rapid population growth caused colonists to encroach upon Indian lands within a generation of first settlement. Indians would resist, often with some initial success, but the superiority of European arms coupled with tribal rivalries would, in the end, lead to Indian defeat. The badge of defeat was a treaty which would guarantee to the Indians permanent rights to their remaining land. The treaty would be observed until population pressures brought new white settlers into Indian lands. Then the cycle would repeat itself.

2. The American colonists of the seventeenth century faced the challenge of developing new political institutions. So, of course, did the nations of Europe. But while Europeans were solving their problems by centralizing power and developing bureaucratic procedures, the colonists found themselves practicing a decentralized politics. While Europeans, furthermore, were strengthening the executive, colonists were again moving in the opposite direction. They were coming to rely increasingly on the legislative branch of government. Finally, while European nations—with the partial exception of England—were becoming more autocratic, Americans were opening their political system to ever wider levels of participation.

Why were the colonists exceptions to these general European rules? The reason, at first, had little to do with political philosophy. The early colonists were eager to transplant European institutions and practices. But the need to work out solutions to pressing local concerns forced them to perfect the arts of local government. Similarly, the executive in colonial government had sweeping powers in theory but little knowledge of local needs. So colonists turned to the popularly elected lower house of their legislatures for leadership.

Political participation widened not only because property ownership was widespread. Also widespread was the experience of social mobility. Because it was possible for those who began with little or nothing to rise to a decent competence there seemed little need to restrict political participation unduly. Colonial practice, in other words, came before theory; and Americans ever since have tended to believe that practice should take precedence over theory.

3. Societies, it would seem, sooner or later develop a sense of their special mission or role in history. In the Russia of the Tsars, for example, Moscow

was thought to be the "Third Rome"—the successor to Rome and Constantinople as the capital of true Christianity. France, during its revolutionary era, proclaimed itself the carrier of political freedom to the rest of the world. China and Japan have also developed distinctive notions of their special historical destiny.

So there is nothing very surprising in that Americans also developed an ideology of their special place in history. As early as 1630 John Winthrop was reminding the first Puritans of their mission:

> Wee must consider that wee shall be as a cittie upon a hille. The eyes of all people are uppon us. Soe that if wee shall deale falsely with our God in this worke wee haue undertaken, and soe cause him to withdraw his present help from us, wee shall be made a story and a byword through the world.

As Winthrop's words suggest, this idea that America was to be an example to the other nations of the world derived in large part from his Puritan conviction that the Reformation was a continuing process and that God had saved America for settlement by adherents of reformed churches. Americans, Puritans and other Protestants believed, were a chosen people—latter day Jews—just as America was to be a new Israel.

Reinforcing this religious interpretation was the secular belief that whoever controlled this vast continent would necessarily, in time, play a leading role in world affairs. America was, after all, a new world. So however small the first beginnings, they were immediately enhanced by this vision (largely borne out) that they were the start of a vast new chapter in human history.

Americans found congenial this notion of themselves as a model of mankind, and not only because it was so flattering. The first colonists were people whose lives contained more than a full measure of upheaval, danger, suffering, and uncertainty. They needed to ask themselves why they were making the sacrifices involved in leaving the unfamiliar scenes of home; they needed a heroic vision of themselves, and the notion of America as a "city upon a hill" provided one.

Suggested Readings

The most important new book on American Indians is William Cronon's *Changes in the Land: Indians, Colonists, and the Ecology of New England* (1984). *The Columbian Exchange* (1972) by Alfred W. Crosby, Jr., shows how ways of life were altered in both hemispheres. In his examination of how white Americans perceived the Indian, *The White Man's Indian: Images of the American Indian from Columbus to the Present* (1978), Robert Berkhofer, Jr., continues his practice of applying to the study of history analytical devices developed in anthropology and the behavioral sciences. Elizabeth A. H. John, in *Storms Brewed in Other Men's Worlds: The Confrontation of Indians, Spanish, and French in the Southwest, 1540–1795* (1975), tells the shockingly neglected story of the settlement of the Southwest. On white-Indian relations, see also Gary Nash, *Red, White, and Black* (1974).

New England continues to inspire excellent scholarship: Kenneth Lockridge, *A New England Town: The First Hundred Years* (1970), John Demos, *A Little Commonwealth: Family Life in Plymouth Colony* (1970), Sumner Chilton Powell, *Puritan Village* (1966), Robert Middlekauff, *The Mathers: Three Generations of Puritan Intellectuals* (1971), and Sacvan Bercovitch, *The American Jeremiad* (1978) add to the earlier work of Perry Miller. See Miller's brief *Errand into the Wilderness* (1956) for a distillation of parts of *The New England Mind: From Colony to Province* (1953).

Edmund S. Morgan wrote the brilliant *American Slavery, American Freedom* (1975), which serves as a fine introduction to colonial Virginia. See also Richard Morton, *Colonial Virginia* (1960). Alden Vaughan illuminates the early history of the colony in *Captain John Smith and the Founding of Virginia* (1975). Michael Walzer, in *The Revolution of the Saints* (1965) depicts an English Calvinism transformed by the American wilderness while Peter Laslett, *The World We Have Lost* third edition, (1984) tells of the highly stratified world of preindustrial England.

DEBATE

FORREST McDONALD

The Puritans endowed the future republic with much that is good. They bequeathed us what were once known as the middle-class virtues, or what Professor Fox-Genovese may call bourgeois values. They taught us to believe that people justify their existence by the work they do; that every man is responsible for the welfare of himself and his family; and that the community is obliged to care for the needy, but only if misfortune has made them unable to care for themselves. The Puritans taught cleanliness, honesty, and thrift, obedience to law, involvement in the affairs of the community, respect for learning, deference toward elders and those in authority, and above all reverence toward God. To the extent that Americans still treasure such values, they have enriched us.

But the Puritans also implanted defects in the American character. Puritanism had much in common with two ancient, perverse Christian heresies, Gnosticism and Manichaeism. "Gnostic" stems from the Greek word *gnostikos,* meaning to know; the gnostics regarded themselves as having "knowledge of the divine mysteries reserved to an elite." The Puritan counterpart was the "elect": the chosen few whom God has predestined for eternal salvation and incidentally for blessings in this life. As a theology this doctrine became unfashionable, but its psychological substance has endured. Partly it persists as what Albert Camus called a nostalgia for the absolute—a craving for knowledge of absolute truth that is a mark of the ideologue. Partly it persists in an attitude of superiority: he who is chosen "knows" absolutely and this knowledge entitles him to invade, regulate, and direct the lives of the non-elect—for their own good, of course.

Manichaeism, a species of gnosticism, was the belief in two gods, a God of Light and pure goodness and a God of Darkness and pure evil. The Puritan equivalent of Manichaeism was the inability to distinguish among gradations of good and evil, the belief that things were all one or the other, which in turn led to an inability to compromise, to accommodate, or to accept things as they are. Evil became something external rather than something carried in the heart of every man.

Puritanism was therefore a contradictory force. During hard times its ethic of work, frugality, and self-reliance was constructive, and during such times Puritans were too busy trying to keep their heads above water to cause any mischief. But they could not stand success: in times of general prosperity nearly everyone enjoyed material abundance, which was inherently sinful and also contrary to the belief that only a few were chosen.

The Puritan responded to sinfully prosperous circumstances in one of two characteristic ways, both destructive. One was to pronounce the whole of society hopelessly corrupt and to drop out, to join with a few like-minded souls and to make a world apart. Countless variants of dropping out have occurred throughout American history and are with us today.

Another response was not to leave the world but to cleanse it of its evil, and this usually meant isolating a single, external source of all evil and seeking to exorcise it. During the seventeenth century the source was identified as supernatural: the devil seduced women and made them witches. Later the demons became secularized, but to the Puritan and his intellectual descendents they did not go away. In the eighteenth century the demons were the ministers of George III; in the nineteenth they were variously alcohol, the slaveocracy, and the plutocracy; in the twentieth they have ranged from the immigrant hordes to the communist conspiracy to the military-industrial complex to simply the "system." In all of its forms the urge to cleanse the world of evil reflects a primitive fear of the God of Darkness.

Do We Need Puritan Virtues?

ELIZABETH FOX-GENOVESE

Yes, I do call Puritan values bourgeois, a term difficult to define but suggestive of a people hardworking, thrifty, smug, complacent, conventional, and greedy for money. I agree with Professor McDonald that at least some of the bourgeois values are a great legacy to modern civilization. I also agree with his eloquent testimony to the contributions of the Puritans and with his sober estimates of the good and bad effects of Puritanism on our national character and personality as Puritanism became secularized, democratized, and absorbed by later generations whose ethnic and social origins were far removed from Puritan Britain.

I would also caution that those values intentionally spoke in the male voice and for men's purposes. Puritanism did insist upon doctrines that seemed to promise equality among individual souls, but in practice mainstream Puritanism never fully divorced souls from the bodies they inhabited. And it largely accepted the assumptions of the day that men should dominate women, should govern households and families, should speak in churches. Within Puritanism lay a temptation, which most Puritans resisted, to turn away from all outward laws and teachings and rely instead on emotions and impulses that the believer could identify with divine grace. This antinomianism, as it is sometimes called, could imply that all social distinctions are false, impudently discarding grace and instead exalting human virtues or learning or wealth or ancestry. The more radical Puritans spoke of the equality between men and women, criticized the institution of marriage, occasionally favored free love, and frequently encouraged women's prophecy.

But even the radicals did not always seriously question the natural relations of dominance and dependence between men and women: female prophets often captured an audience precisely because they were seen to be transcending women's normal roles. The very irregularity of their behavior was accepted as proof of their special relations with God. Yet irregular behavior sometimes got women in trouble; it could be seen as proof that they were witches. And when, in the early years of the Bay Colony, Anne Hutchinson claimed to challenge the authority of John Winthrop and other Puritan fathers in the name of family beliefs in general and the special needs of women and merchants in particular, she was first publicly tried and censured for behavior unbecoming a woman and for beliefs incompatible with Puritan orthodoxy, and then banished.

Hutchinson's case reveals a deep contradiction in Puritan thought between the egalitarian spiritual ideology and the acceptance of unequal relations in the world, a contradiction that would plague the legacy of Puritanism to our own time. The Puritans do not stand alone in their failure to implement the more radical implications of their beliefs, but in questioning hierarchy in theory while continuing to accept manifestations of it in practice, they allowed Puritan belief and practice to be invoked for contradictory purposes. It could be used to justify rebellion as the legitimate expression of conscience in the English and American revolutions or it could be used to condemn rebellion as an illegitimate attack on the social order and the individual's place in it, as in the cases of Anne Hutchinson and Roger Williams. The confusion for both the Puritans and their heirs is one of the ironies of American history.

Gallow's Hill, Salem, Massachusetts, where the witches were hanged.

CHAPTER 3

The Developing Colonies

THE WITCHES OF SALEM

The Devil in 1692 assaulted the seaport town of Salem, Massachusetts, with an unparalleled fury. This village of a few hundred people was invaded by over one hundred witches and wizards, men and women who had leagued with the Devil to make mischief, to drive little children mad, to sicken and kill livestock and people. One witch, it seemed, had killed fourteen members of a single family. The jails of nearby Boston bulged with over a hundred prisoners awaiting trial including a four-year-old child bound for nine months in heavy iron chains. Twenty-seven people eventually came to trial: the court hanged nineteen as witches. Having refused to enter a plea, Giles Cory suffered *peine forte et dure*: heavy weights were laid on his body until, still refusing the plea, he was pressed to death.

The trouble had begun with a craze for the occult that had swept across Massachusetts toward the end of 1691. "Conjuration with sieves and keys, and peas, and nails, and horseshoes" at first seemed harmless activities with which to pass the New England winter. But these games turned serious when grim-visaged adults tried to discover what was causing their children's "fits" and "distempers." Salem Village's minister, Samuel Parris, was the first father to react. His nine-year-old daughter, Betty, and her eleven-year-old cousin, Abigail Williams, had fallen into "odd postures" and "foolish, ridiculous speeches." The concerned father called in a local doctor who, diagnosing no physical illness, raised suspicions of the "Evil Hand"—witchcraft.

This was a reasonable supposition. Everyone knew about witchcraft. Just as those who were saved covenanted together to form a church, so too some of those who were damned convenanted with the Devil. They "wrote in his book," joining his legions for the thrill of conjurations, midnight frolics, obscure or perhaps obscene rituals, and the power to harm their neighbors. Waves of witchcraft had swept across Europe for the past two centuries as the Reformation had inspired a direct struggle between Christ and the Devil. Do not "suffer a witch to live," the Bible commanded, and tens of thousands, mostly women but many men as well, had been burned or hanged as the Evil One's followers.

Before 1692, the Devil had paid small attention to New England, except through the incursions of his New World minions, the Indians. A handful of cases, a few hangings, no burnings—such was the entire history of New England witchcraft before Betty and Abigail's malady spread to seven or eight adolescent girls in Salem Village. Under intense questioning, and responding to this attention with yet further manifestations of demoniac possession, the girls named three women as the source of their sufferings. These were likely candidates. Sarah Good, daughter of a well-to-do innkeeper, had steadily tumbled down the social ladder; she was in 1692 a surly, pipe-smoking beggar whose "muttering and scolding" seemed to cause cows to die. Sarah Osborne's name swirled in contention and scandal: her battle with her own sons for control of her first husband's estate, her liaison with the Irish indentured servant who became her second husband. And Tituba, the slave woman who had introduced Betty and Abigail to the practices of voodoo she had learned in the West Indies, at the pre-trial examination readily and noisily told the audience of townspeople and "possessed" girls what they wanted to hear. For three days, she regaled them with stories of her comportings with the Devil and with witches Sarah Good and Sarah Osborne, of midnight sabbaths and rides through the air with Satan, whom she described as "a thing all over hairy, all the face hairy, and a long nose." She had seen the Devil's "book" and although she could not read, she had counted nine names in it. Nine names! There were more witches: soon the girls, shrieking, contorting, sobbing hysterically, dredged up still more names. Not all were outcasts like Sarah Good, Sarah Osborne, and Tituba; not all were from Salem. The jails groaned; the gallows rope snapped. The girls' madness, for the better part of a year, infected a whole society until the hysteria subsided as mysteriously as it had risen. Reason returned; probing questions were asked; the jailed were sent home and pardoned.

The girls' part in it is easiest to explain. The life of young girls in Massachusetts Bay was dull in the best of times. In the winter it must have been torturous. Puritans did not consider children "innocent." They were "willful" little creatures whose animal spirits had to be "broken," "beaten down." They had to be taught piety, responsibility, and habits of work. "I am not fond," wrote Cotton Mather, foremost Puritan minister, "of proposing *Play* to children, as a Reward of any diligent Application to learn what is good; lest they should think *Diversion* to be a better and nobler Thing than *Diligence.*" Mather, like other Puritan parents, preferred to "awe them." (Cotton Mather would have his moment when, to combat a popular fear of the new medical practice of inoculation for smallpox, he allowed his son to be inoculated.) While young men, taught to pray and work, could at least look forward to the adventure of choosing careers, girls could do little more than wonder "what trade their sweethearts should be of." It is hardly surprising that when the little girls dabbled in magic with Tituba, their slightly older friends and relatives joined the only excitement midwinter had to offer. (Many teen-aged girls—including most of the afflicted ones—did not live at home where parents might spoil them, but were sent to relatives' or neighbors' houses to learn their adult roles and to be evenly disciplined.) Once the adults began to fuss over their fits, how could the young resist pursuing their adventure and showing their power over the adult community, particularly over the married women who laid on endless chores and discipline? Even these antics would have been relatively harmless had not the adults panicked. It is their role, not the children's, that cries out for explanation. Two generations later, when children in Northampton behaved the same way, their minister, Jonathan Edwards, read the cues differently and perhaps it was their contortions, sobbing, and fits that, under his counseling, fueled the start of a great religious revival.

The witchcraft epidemic had fed upon Salem's local conflicts as people from different political and clerical factions hurled accusations back and forth. For Salem was an angry place. Town and countryside were sharply diverging. Conservative back country farmers smarted under the growth of commercial capitalism and its accompanying secular style. Sons coming of age found difficulty establishing themselves as land became increasingly scarce. The values of Puritanism itself seemed more and more in question as ministers bemoaned the "declension" from the high ideals of the colony's founders three generations before. Nearly every adult must have been startled at a changing world crowding in on what had been for two generations a largely fixed culture. Men and women who were supposed to practice Christian unity engaged year after year in lawsuits over boundaries and legacies. Like the witches, they were at war with their neighbors, disrupting the church and government, bursting the old molds. Were they too possessed? How much easier it must have been to blame everything on the literal bewitchment of enemies rather than on their own bewitchment with the new and perhaps dubious values and goals that were transforming Puritans into Yankees.

So historians and sociologists will reason. But there is a simpler explanation for both the witchcraft and the trials. For all the learning, the sobriety, the orderliness, the industry that New England Calvinism could muster there was within it from the beginning something close to hysteria. The hysteria would break out again, though with less lethal form, when the scholarly Jonathan Edwards would lead the Great Awakening in the 1730s. And it was not until Puritans had turned completely into Yankees that New England was free at last.

The New England Colonies

As a condition of survival, the Yankees found it necessary to buy large quantities of manufactured goods from England. New England was almost entirely dependent upon England for clothing or at least for the material from which clothing could be made, for almost all tools beyond the most primitive, for muskets and other firearms, and for clocks, compasses, and a host of other instruments. The New Englanders drank oceans of tea and used considerable quantities of spices, which could be legally obtained only through the East India Company in London; and despite recurring waves of puritanical hostility toward the consumption of luxuries, the Yankees sought and bought the finer things of life when they were able. And since New Englanders could not grow staples, such as Virginia's tobacco or the sugar of the West Indies, that would pay the mother county for imports, the region's balance of trade with Great Britain was invariably unfavorable.

Prosperity. And yet the years from about 1715 to 1755 were ones of great prosperity, for the unfavorable balance of direct trade with England was more than compensated for through a more complex system of trade. It is not true that, as myth once had it, New England's commercial success was based upon hauling freight or upon the slave trade. The colonial Yankees were never more than marginally engaged in either of these maritime activities. The key to the New Englanders' system was the great sugar plantations of the West Indies. These were not self-sufficient, for it was uneconomical to waste the labor of slaves on growing staple food when it could be bought so cheaply and land was so valuable. The sugar islands were also deficient in timber suitable for providing the bare necessity of wood products, even including staves for making containers in which to ship their sugar. By supplying the West Indies the Yankees made enough profit not only to pay what they owed for imports, but to provide employment for their whole population.

New England farmers produced fruit, beef, pork, butter, and cheese for the West Indian market, and many also raised cattle, horses, and chickens for live export. During the seventeenth century the farmers generally supplied forest

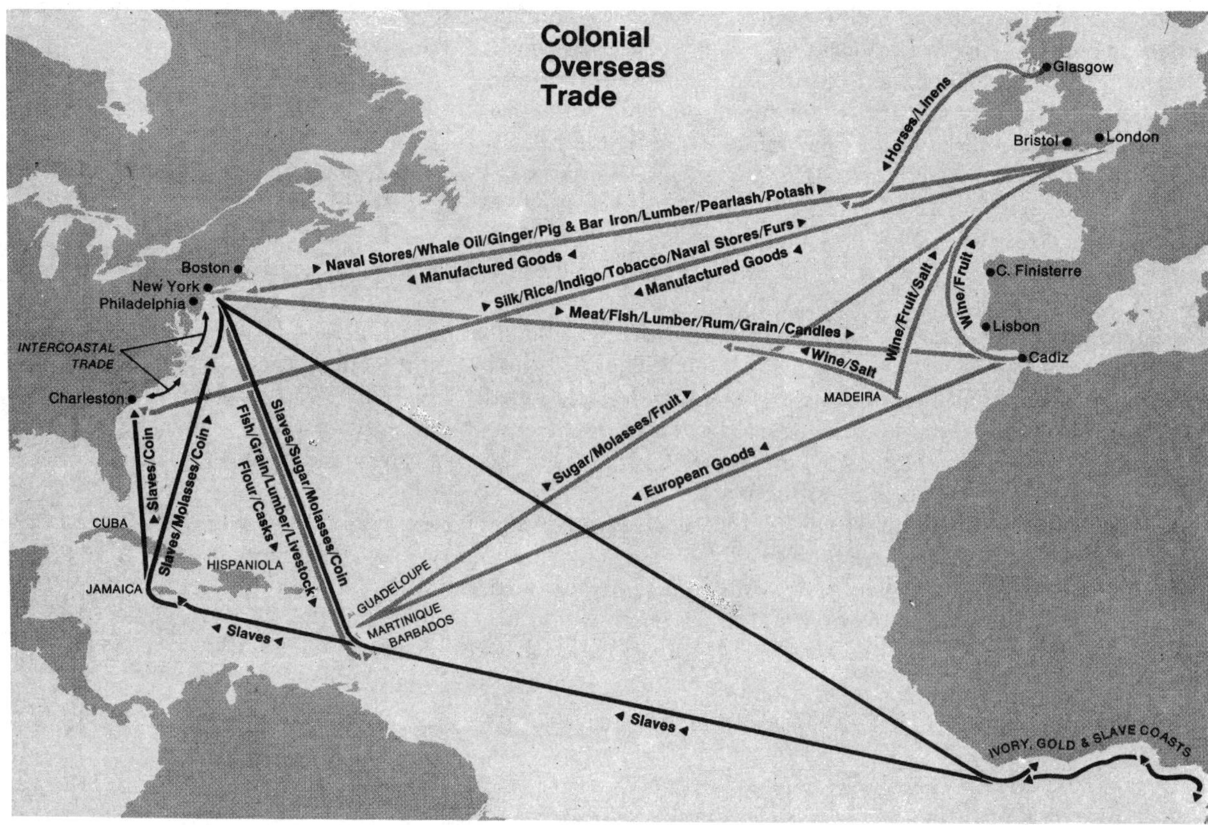

products as well. Fishing expanded enormously and became highly commercialized after 1715. By the 1730s as many as 150 new fishing vessels were being built annually, and the number of people employed in the fisheries was more than 5000. Whaling developed as an additional specialty in some places, notably Nantucket, where it was even more valuable than fishing.

In the early days, when settlements were concentrated along the seacoast and immediately to the interior from Boston and the other ports, farmers produced marketable timber from the trees they felled to clear their lands for the plow. But timber is a bulky commodity and the only practical way to transport it is by river; and south of Salem the Massachusetts coast was almost entirely devoid of streams that extended as much as five miles into the interior. New settlers in towns beyond that distance developed the practice of burning the trees they felled and making the ashes into potash and pearlash; these could easily be carried to port towns for merchants who found a ready market for them in England. But the change also meant that the supply of lumber from Massachusetts and Connecticut dwindled just at the time the demand for lumber products in the West Indies was expanding rapidly. For this expanding market, a commercial lumber industry was developed after about 1720 in New Hampshire and the province of Maine, where there were magnificent stands of white pine and the river systems afforded convenient transportation.

The merchants of New England secured their provisions for the West Indies from the local farmers by selling them goods imported from England, but the owners of fishing fleets and lumber camps and their employees consumed little of such commodities. The fishermen and lumber workers did, however, consume one thing abundantly, and that was rum. Accordingly, New England merchants made a practice of importing West Indian molasses for part of the goods they sold in the islands; the molasses was then manufactured into rum with which to buy more lumber or fish.

Payment of the duty on molasses that the British government imposed in 1733 would have been detrimental to New York and Pennsylvania and ruinous to New England. So the merchants in those places did what American businessmen would do ever after when the law ran counter to their interests: they simply ignored the law. It was easy enough to do so, for Britain's machinery for collecting customs and preventing smuggling in America was as yet primitive, and many customs officials were amenable to bribery. The passage of the Sugar Act of 1733, therefore, in no way altered the course of New England's economic growth, except to place the entire economy upon illegal foundations.

The Middle Colonies

The middle colonies of New York, Pennsylvania, New Jersey, and Delaware contained by the mid-eighteenth century a varying mix of population. People of Dutch ancestry in New York were retaining their ethnic identity, Scotch-Irish and Germans had settled in Pennsylvania west of the Quakers, and there were Swedes to their south. Philadelphia was a principal landing place for immigrants who in the eighteenth century moved to British America by the hundreds of thousands. Each successive wave of immigrants sought land for settlement in the immediate vicinity, until all the cheaply available land in the middle colonies was taken up and it became necessary to push toward the interior and toward the back country of the South.

German Immigrants. Many if not most German immigrants came as redemptioners, paying for their passage by binding themselves to serve as laborers for five to ten (normally seven) years before becoming freemen and ordinary settlers. Then, migrating to the back country, they settled in a broad area extending twenty to a hundred miles west of the Delaware River. They picked the choicest lands, especially those in the limestone valleys, cleared their farms slowly but thoroughly, and built solid buildings upon them. Because of the care with which they proceeded, by the time they were able to produce for market they were able to bring in regular and bountiful harvests. Their principal crop, as long as they remained in the middle colonies, was wheat, which became the second great staple (or third, if New England fish be counted) to be produced in British North America. Virginia tobacco of course was the first.

The Germans continued to arrive at a steady rate, about 2000 a year, from 1717 until about 1750. By the 1730s they were beginning to overflow the middle colonies. Thenceforth, they proceeded to the Pennsylvania back country and headed south, settling the Cumberland Valley in Pennsylvania and Maryland and much of the Shenandoah Valley of Virginia.

By and large, wherever they went the Germans kept to themselves, retaining their own ways and making no effort to become involved in the political or social life of the colonies they inhabited. They tended to cluster in groups that had little to do even with one another. They represented a wide variety of religious sects, Reformed, Scots, Mennonite, Dunker, Moravian Brethren, Schwenkfelder, and even Roman Catholic. Considerably more numerous and far more disruptive were the descendants of the Scottish Protestants who had settled in Ulster in the North of Ireland. The total number of Scotch-Irish immigrants was around 250,000.

The Scotch-Irish. The first wave headed for New England. The Ulstermen, like the Yankees, were Calvinist, but the congregation-based church polity of New England was incompatible with the Scotch-Irish polity, with its more centralized Presbyterian church structure. Besides, the New Englanders were exclusive almost by instinct, welcoming no foreigners. What was more, Boston and its vicinity had no excess land and no shortage of labor; the inhabitants feared that immigrants would become just so many paupers to feed from the resources of their stingy land; and New Englanders generally regarded the Ulstermen as illiterate, slovenly, and filthy. A few thousand immigrants of the first wave landed in Boston and, with difficulty, founded settlements around Worcester and along the Merrimack Valley of New Hampshire, but irate mobs greeted subsequent boatloads at the docks and refused to let them land.

The remainder of the first wave of Ulstermen and the overwhelming majority of future shiploads headed for Philadelphia, along with the Germans. The Scotch-Irish also followed the same routes to the interior, but there the resemblance between them and the Germans ends. For reasons of preference as well as circumstance, the two groups of immigrants did not mix. The pattern of settlement, all the way down through the Virginia valley, was that the German firstcomers farmed staples on the rich bottom lands and the Ulstermen who came later

The Middle Colonies.

raised cattle and corn on the hillsides and poorer lands. And whereas almost all the Germans could be expected to be industrious, frugal, orderly, and peaceful, many of the Scotch-Irish worked by fits, drank prodigiously, and were quick-tempered, impetuous, and likely to pick up stakes and move for no apparent reason. And yet, having a zeal for education deriving from their Presbyterianism, the Scotch-Irish founded schools and colleges on a scale that no other group of Americans ever approached. They loved freedom, by which they meant the right to be left alone to be themselves, and were quick to fight for it. In constant friction with the

Indians, Scotch-Irish often did not hesitate to slaughter them or involve colonial authorities in wars with them. They became avid politicians, skillful and disputatious, and regularly demanded a voice in the lawmaking process when the law affected their way of life, but they totally disregarded the law when it did not suit them. By the late 1730s Ulstermen were filling the Shenandoah Valley of Virginia; by the late 1740s they were spilling out over the Piedmont Plateau of southern Virginia and central North Carolina; and a decade later they were invading the uplands of South Carolina.

Amidst enormous growth in population—from around 75,000 in 1715 to 400,000 by the 1750s—the economic and political life of the middle colonies developed rapidly. The economy grew even faster than the population and, as had been the way in New England and the tobacco colonies, proceeded along two lines: development of small-scale production of tools and other equipment for the expanding population, and development of production for trade in international markets.

The middle colonies differed from the colonies to the north and south in the business of supplying newcomers. Elsewhere, by far the biggest portion of the business was selling land, but in the four middle colonies, for different reasons in each, the population at large could not participate in this lucrative enterprise. In New York the governors and assemblies continued the policy, originated by the Dutch, of granting land only in huge tracts—and only to themselves and their friends and relations. The great patroons, as the Dutch called them, who received the grants were more often interested in leasing the lands than in selling them. In Pennsylvania and Delaware the land belonged originally to the Penn family as proprietors, and all proceeds from sales and rentals went to them. In New Jersey, too, the land belonged to small groups of proprietors, and though the system of land disposition was always complex the profits from land sales went to these small groups.

Philadelphia. The supply of craftsmen, the abundance of raw materials, and the insatiable market combined in the middle colonies to breed a thriving industry in farm implements, other hardware, clocks, locks, guns, flints, glass, stoneware, paper, nails, and woodwork. The port of Philadelphia burgeoned: by the mid-1730s several hundred vessels were entering and clearing the port every year. At first most of these vessels belonged to others, but then Philadelphians began to acquire their own ships, and with this development came another, the establishment of a shipbuilding industry and such linked activities as importing and processing naval stores and manufacturing ropes, anchors, and sails.

By the 1730s, Philadelphia (like New York City to a lesser extent) had begun to emerge as a major export and import center. Among the exports were beef and pork, which, along with the livestock, were produced mainly by the Scotch-Irish. These products found ready markets on the sugar plantations of the West Indies. More important were wheat and flour, produced by the industrious Germans and the scores of mills that sprung up along the Delaware and

ESTIMATED POPULATION OF AMERICAN COLONIES: 1630 TO 1750

	1630	1650	1670	1690	1730	1750
White						
New England	1,796	22,452	51,521	86,011	211,233	349,029
Middle Colonies	340	3,786	6,664	32,369	135,298	275,723
Southern Colonies	2,450	22,530	49,215	75,263	191,893	309,588
Black						
New England	0	380	375	950	6,118	10,982
Middle Colonies	10	515	790	2,472	11,683	20,736
Southern Colonies	50	705	3,370	13,307	73,220	204,702
Total White	4,586	48,768	107,400	193,643	538,424	934,340
Total Black	60	1,600	4,535	16,729	91,021	236,420

Schuylkill rivers. The Navigation Acts did not confine colonial wheat and flour to the English market. Some went to the West Indies and much to the European continent, where Philadelphia merchants could acquire bills of exchange and goods for trade in England. This made Philadelphia a principal importing center for English manufactures in North America.

By mid-century, Philadelphia was fast becoming America's richest and largest city. In another decade or two it would be the second largest city and second busiest port in the entire English-speaking world. New York port also thrived, though it developed much more slowly. Because of the colony's restrictive immigration and land policies, New York lacked Philadelphia's business of transporting and supplying newcomers, and it also had a smaller productive base for its international trade. But the Iroquois Indians in New York's interior did trap some furs themselves and also served as middlemen between the Albany traders and many of the western Indians, who trapped furs in enormous quantities and were eager to sell them. The fur trade was profitable, and so for a time New York's prosperity matched that of Philadelphia, although its population grew more slowly.

Quaker Influences. William Penn's plans late in the seventeenth century for Pennsylvania had been ambitious. The colony would be a place of love and harmony. Penn had established friendly relations with the Indians. The very act of establishing a government that could back up its laws with force meant that whether or not Penn, like other Quakers, would oppose all wars among nations, he was not prepared to practice a Quakerism of total nonresistance at home. But one of his schemes provided that imprisonment would be humane and seek the reformation of criminals. For a short period Pennsylvania actually attempted a system of imprisonment for reform of criminals—an experiment that prefigured the modern penitentiary. The earliest Quakers had been given to fits of emotionalism accompanied by disruptive behavior. Penn prized more sober virtues and conduct; an account that he wrote of Pennsylvania, translated into German, Dutch, and French and published on the European continent as well as in Britain, invited solid, industrious farmers and craftsmen to settle in the colony. His Quakerism, then, cherished the compound of spirituality and virtuous worldliness that have been characteristic of the Society of Friends ever since.

In Penn's lifetime political disputes broke out in Pennsylvania. And in the years after his death the colony took shape as something considerably different from the harmonious commonwealth he had envisioned. The presence of the Scotch-Irish on the frontier guaranteed that the Indians would receive something other than the treatment Penn would have wanted for them. The tide of immigration made the Quakers a minority in the colony, though a wealthy and powerful one, and Quakers lost favor with the proprietors when the sons of William Penn left the Society of Friends for the Church of England. To promote and protect their interests in the face of these reversals, the Quakers gathered allies and formed a political faction called variously the Quaker party and the Anti-Proprietary party. Their wealth and influence normally gave them control of the elections to the Assembly from Philadelphia and its environs and, through an alliance with Germans in surrounding counties, they could usually dominate the Assembly. Arrayed against them in the Proprietary party were the Scotch-Irish (who were perhaps America's least peaceful people), most frontiersmen, and a considerable number of non-pacifist Germans.

The South East Prospect of the City of Philadelphia, **by Peter Cooper. By mid-century Philadelphia was fast becoming America's richest and largest city.** *(Courtesy, The Library Company of Philadelphia)*

In contrast to the popularly based politics of Pennsylvania, politics in New York was aristocratic. The colony did have numerous and vociferous lower elements, fighting one another as well as the upper classes and clamoring for a voice in government: but the lower classes largely canceled one another out in antipathies among Scotch-Irish and New Englanders and older Yorkers, among Presbyterians and Congregationalists and Dutch Calvinists, among tenant farmers and squatters and the plain folk of the city. Such of these inhabitants as could vote were normally easy for the landed aristocrats to manage, for they voted orally, in public, and were therefore amenable to bribery and pressure when mere deference failed to secure their vote.

The Southern Colonies

Slavery. Black slavery had existed in the colonies of Spain and Portugal since the early sixteenth century, and for an even longer time in Africa. But it was not until the eighteenth century that it became entrenched on a large scale in British North America.

Through most of the seventeenth century slavery had not been of major importance on the American mainland. There was a perpetual shortage of labor in the colonies, but as long as the farm unit remained small and was worked by the owner alongside his family and such indentured servants as he could afford, servants who spoke English were preferred to others. Even large planters shunned slaves as expensive and subject to a high mortality in a new land. The black population in the English colonies grew very slowly. The first blacks in the English colonies had arrived in Virginia in 1619, but in 1641 only about 250 lived in the colony, and as late as 1680 there were still no more than 3000 in Virginia and fewer than 7000 in all the mainland colonies combined. English common law had no concept of slavery, and for a time slaves may have been in a legal position somewhat like that of indentured servants. Records in the middle of the seventeenth century referred to slaves as "servants for life."

But then in the 1680s and the following decades a series of developments combined to establish slavery firmly, though still on a modest scale, in the tobacco-growing colonies of Virginia and Maryland. One was a change in the laws of both colonies that finally made it legal and even easy to buy land in large tracts. Another was that, despite a rapid increase in production, tobacco prices remained fairly high from about 1684 to about 1703. In these circumstances small farm units began to give way to sizable plantations, where workers could be employed efficiently in gangs. At just this time, the Royal Africa Company and other groups of English merchants were beginning to dominate the African slave trade and were looking for markets. Competition between slave traders of several nations, moreover, temporarily reduced the profits of supplying blacks for West Indian sugar plantations, so the English were willing to sell slaves in Virginia and Maryland at bargain prices.

And so, using colonial law (mainly as enacted in the 1660s) rather than English law as their legal justification, Virginia and Maryland imported thousands of African slaves and laid the foundation for the plantation system of Southern agriculture. Slavery acquired a sharper legal definition. By 1710 there were well over 30,000 slaves in the two colonies, whose total population was about 120,000. Most of the blacks came from west Africa, a settled area in which agriculture, mining, and handicraft were well established, and they adapted easily to work on American farms and plantations. They soon lost their native languages and many other elements of their original culture, taking readily to European ways, and had it not been for their legal enslavement, they might have merged into the polyglot colonial society along with the Germans, the Ulstermen, and other non-English groups. Slavery, however, made a crucial difference, and the blacks, no matter how talented and capable as individuals, were denied any opportunity for social advancement.

Few whites protested the use of slaves. Quaker meetings in and around Philadelphia regularly denounced slavery, but many Quakers themselves acquired slaves. A pamphlet denouncing slavery, Samuel Sewall's *The Selling of Joseph*, was published in Boston in 1701, but the theologian Cotton Mather piously informed a group of blacks that slavery was "what God will have to be the thing appointed for you."

Even so, the expansion of slavery in the tobacco colonies slowed and almost stopped early in the eighteenth century, and was not renewed until the mid-1730s. One reason was that tobacco started on another long cycle of depressed prices.

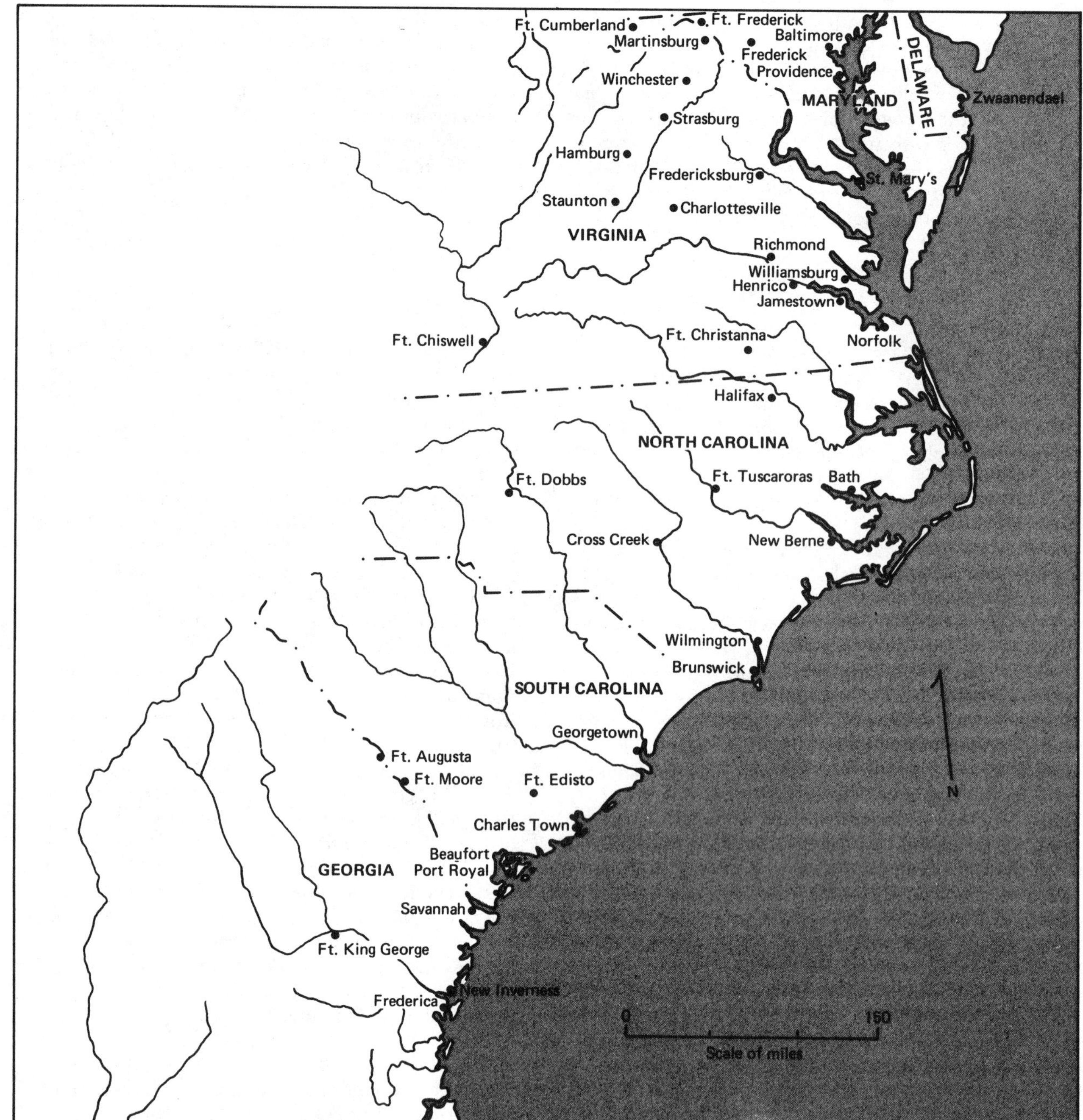

The Southern Colonies.

But while slavery was stagnating in the tobacco colonies, it was rapidly spreading in another quarter, on the rice plantations of South Carolina (and, a little later, of Georgia). Slavery was a part of life in South Carolina almost as soon as the colony passed beyond its primitive frontier stage, for many of the early settlers were immigrants from Barbados, where slavery had long been firmly established, and they brought their slaves with them. Of the roughly 3900 inhabitants of the colony in 1690, about 1500 were slaves. Then, in the early decades of the eighteenth century the South Carolinians began large-scale rice cultivation in the coastal swamps, and with a phenomenal increase in rice production, slavery increased apace. South Carolina exported 394,000 pounds of rice in 1700, 1,600,000 pounds in 1710, 6,400,000 in 1720,

18,700,000 in 1730, and 43,000,000 in 1740; in the same years the number of slaves in the colony increased from 2400 to 30,000. From 1720 onward, slaves outnumbered whites about two to one.

Planters in Virginia and Maryland had developed slavery only after their institutions had become pretty well established. Perhaps also their claim to being seventeenth-century gentlemen gave them some sense of noblesse oblige, of the obligations of the upper classes toward the rest of the human race. They never, in any event, became quite as callous about their human chattel as did the South Carolinians, whose very origins on the sugar plantations of the West Indies hardened their feelings on the subject. These distinctions in attitudes were reinforced by physical and climatic differences between the upper and the lower South.

On a tobacco plantation the atmosphere was generally healthy and the labor to be done, though fussy and tedious, was not back-breaking. It was both possible and profitable for a plantation owner to encourage both breeding and some semblance of family life among his slaves. Since tobacco was a commodity that fluctuated in price, often falling below the margin of profit, it was not economical to buy everything the slaves required for their sustenance. Accordingly, slaves learned crafts, grew much of their own food, and otherwise formed a more or less self-sufficient community. The system was not drastically different from the village-and-manor land system that prevailed in most of England and continental Europe, except that the European peasant's prospects for bettering his lot were merely almost hopeless, while those of most black American slaves were absolutely so. Perhaps a majority of the slaves in the tobacco colonies were not on large plantations but belonged to smaller farmers, each owning only a few and many of them working alongside their slaves.

In the Northeast, where at about the middle of the eighteenth century a small but substantial portion of the populations of Boston, Philadelphia, and New York City were slaves, most worked as craftsmen, laborers, or personal servants rather than as field workers. In Rhode Island, New Jersey, New York, Pennsylvania, and Delaware, however, slaves worked for commercial farmers or in some places for small manufacturers.

The Carolinas and Georgia. No gentle village-and-manor system developed in South Carolina. Rice was grown in the coastal swamps, where the climate was hot and humid and teemed with malaria and other disease. The work was possible only for strong young adult males, and even many of these normally died from overwork and disease within five to seven years. For the few slaves, most of them women and children, who lived in or near the master's house and worked as menial servants, life was tolerable and could even be pleasant, but for the field hands it was hell. Whereas flights for freedom were rare in the tobacco colonies, they were common in South Carolina. Many a Carolina slave escaped from his master and found refuge among the Creek and Seminole Indians to the south, despite a law permitting any white to shoot on sight a slave who left his plantation without a written pass from his owner. There were isolated uprisings, and in 1739 slaves on several plantations rose in a rebellion that was not put down until twenty-one whites and forty-four blacks had been killed and scores more of both races had been wounded.

North Carolina rapidly became even more separate socially and economically. Plantation slavery was slow to take root, for the colony was covered with thick pine forests, was too dry to permit rice cultivation, and lacked the access to the sea necessary to the growth of tobacco plantations. Until well into the eighteenth century North Carolina's principal products were the naval stores that could be extracted from the pines: tar, pitch, rosin, turpentine, and masts and spars. After 1705, the British government subsidized the production of all these commodities.

Georgia, the last British colony to be established in America, developed slowly until the 1760s. James Oglethorpe, a Tory member of Parliament, received a charter to plant the colony in 1732. He conceived of it as a refuge for paupers and debtors, and as a laboratory for experiments in social and religious reform; but for the first twenty years of its existence the colony served mainly as a buffer between South Carolina and the hostile Indians to the immediate south and the Spanish colony further south in Florida. Thereafter, Georgia began to develop on a more permanent basis, largely through the establishment of a rice plantation system much like that of South Carolina.

Developments in Virginia. In the early 1730s there began a remarkable economic boom in Virginia. Before it had ended the entire area from Pennsylvania to South Carolina had been transformed.

Part of the boom was in tobacco prices. They snapped back from the depressed levels that had

***A Carolina Rice Plantation of the Fifties*, by Alice R. Huger Smith. Slavery was especially harsh on the rice plantations that flourished in the Carolinas.** *(Courtesy, William Morrow and Co., Inc., N.Y.)*

long prevailed, and despite a great increase in production that soon followed, prices remained high enough to make tobacco planting profitable for most of the next three decades. The plantation system spread rapidly, and slavery spread with it. An enormous volume of importations as well as natural increase doubled the number of slaves in Virginia to 60,000 in 1740, pushed it past 100,000 in 1750, and took it to 140,000 in 1760.

Meanwhile, land sales surged in Virginia. When the Penn family in the 1730s raised the prices and rents on Pennsylvania lands, Scotch-Irish and German immigrants flooded to the West and South. As they poured southward down the great valley of Virginia, North Carolina and Virginia both promised freedom of worship for Presbyterians, and Virginia and Maryland liberalized their land policies. These policies stimulated a thriving sale of land, and Virginia in particular moved to capitalize on it. Planters and other influential inhabitants of the old tidewater settlements began to realize that there was as much money to be made from selling land as from selling tobacco, and perhaps a great deal more. The members of the House of Burgesses, in collaboration with the governor and his council, began to grant large blocks of interior lands to themselves: sometimes for nominal sums, sometimes for nothing, sometimes in exchange for their services in attracting new settlers to the colony.

In mid-century the Southern colonies, like the middle colonies, were thriving, and their growth and prosperity were largely a function of the arrival, on a grand scale, of newcomers of non-English stock. For a variety of reasons, however, the immigrants (or rather the white immigrants) had much less of an effect on the social and political life of the South, except in the back country.

The system that evolved in Virginia was designed to insure the primacy of a class that can best be termed gentry. The gentry were not of the same class as the royal officials, and did not possess the wealth of the largest planters and land speculators. But by education and the size of their lands they stood apart from their neighbors and from the Scotch-Irish and Germans of the backwoods. Their position of leadership came in large part of the willingness of their humbler neighbors to grant it to them, a habit of deference on the part of the lowly toward people of education and political training. That deference was easily and happily given, for the gentry were generous and pleasant. No great social or economic gulf, in fact, separated the gentry from other white Virginians. In a generation or two, a family might acquire the land, the schooling, and the sense of its social responsibility that would place it in the gentry class.

The social preeminence of the Virginia gentry was reinforced by the rules governing politics. Institutional power was concentrated into three overlapping organizations: the vestrymen (lay administrators) of the local parishes of the established Church of England, the justices of the peace who constituted the county courts, and the popular branch or lower house of the colonial legislative assembly, the House of Burgesses. The electorate, those who chose the rulers on all levels, consisted of free white adult males, members of the Church of England, who owned at least twenty-five acres of improved land and a house or fifty acres of unimproved land, or a town lot in the county in which they voted or stood for office. Almost everyone who was not a tenant or a slave could vote, and for legislators the Virginia voters respectfully selected members of the gentry.

The Great Awakening and the Enlightenment

A new enthusiasm for religion and moral reform appeared almost simultaneously in continental Europe, Great Britain, and the colonies. In the 1730s, a fervent new religious movement—Pietism on the Continent, Wesleyanism in Britain, and the Great Awakening in America—began to infect the ministry and to spread rapidly everywhere. The message of the new religion was essentially the same, whatever its form: that the way to salvation lay not in faithful performance of sacraments and rituals as the Catholics and Anglicans had always maintained, or a life of good works, but simply in opening the heart to God through prayer. A simple and total act of faith in God's goodness and mercy would bring to the faithful an unspeakably profound experience of personal conversion and salvation.

Any such doctrine is potentially dangerous to an established social order, for it implicitly vests in the individual alone the capacity to judge the moral rectitude of his own behavior. The new pietist faith of Anglo-America was disruptive. It rejected leadership by any but fellow converts, advocated the separation of converts from others and their formation into small groups, and aimed at the immediate reform and the final transformation of all of man's ways—to serve the coming of the Kingdom of Heaven on earth.

George Whitefield. Various French, German, and Dutch ministers were associated with the movement, and John and Charles Wesley were the most important figures involved in England. The most influential of all in British America was George Whitefield. After receiving some training at Oxford, Whitefield had persuaded the Bishop to ordain him before he was of canonical age, and preached his first sermon. In his maiden sermon, this restless, charismatic preacher raved and exhorted, sang and shouted, wept and thundered and, it is said, drove fifteen people mad.

Whitefield made his first evangelical tour to America in 1739, preaching under the open air and converting hundreds in Georgia, and returned two years later to conduct a great revival

The powerful British minister George Whitefield fueled the Great Awakening on several evangelical tours to New England. *(Courtesy, National Portrait Gallery)*

SINNERS IN THE HANDS OF AN ANGRY GOD *by Jonathan Edwards*

Among the preachers associated with the Great Awakening, Edwards is the most famous. His sermons embodied the tremendous emotionalism of a powerful religious revival.

The God that holds you over the pit of hell, much as one holds a spider, or some loathsome insect, over the fire, abhors you, and you, and is dreadfully provoked; his wrath towards you burns like fire; he looks upon you as worthy of nothing else, but to be cast into the fire; he is of purer eyes than to bear to have you in his sight; you are ten thousand times so abominable in his eyes, as the most hateful and venomous serpent is in ours. You have offended him infinitely more than ever a stubborn rebel did his prince: and yet it is nothing but his hand that holds you from falling into the fire every moment: it is ascribed to nothing else, that you did not go to hell the last night; that you was suffered to awake again in this world, after you closed your eyes to sleep; and there is no other reason to be given, why you have not dropped into hell since you arose in the morning, but that God's hand has held you up: there is no other reason to be given why you have not gone to hell, since you have sat here in the house of God, provoking his pure eyes by your sinful wicked manner of attending his solemn worship: yea, there is nothing else that is to be given as a reason why you do not this very moment drop down into hell. . . .

How dreadful is the state of those that are daily and hourly in danger of this great wrath and infinite misery! But this is the dismal case of every soul in this congregation that has not been born again, however moral and strict, sober and religious, they may otherwise be. . . . There is reason to think, that there are many in this congregation now hearing this discourse, that will actually be the subjects of this very misery to all eternity. We know not who they are, or in what seats they sit, or what thoughts they now have. . . . It would be no wonder if some persons, that now sit here in some seats of this meeting-house in health, and quiet and secure, should be there in hell before tomorrow morning.

---

in New England. The New England mid-Atlantic tour was the greatest triumph of Whitefield's career, though he made several successful trips to America during the next thirty years. In 1740 the populace was ready for him, if only out of restlessness, boredom, or economic troubles. A brief religious revival that Jonathan Edwards had conducted five years earlier in Northampton, Massachusetts, had already primed New England. Edwards had carried the right message, and with Whitefield's personal magnetism and style might have set the region aflame himself. The clergy of New England was at first also energetic in support of the crusade by Whitefield and his followers and imitators, in the understandable if mistaken belief that a new outburst of religious zeal would reinvigorate and thereby preserve a church that had lately lost much of its following. So Whitefield infused New England, along with most of the other British colonies, with enthusiastic piety that matched any that Americans had ever experienced.

"Enthusiastic" Religion. But the impact of the Great Awakening was not quite what the ministry that had welcomed Whitefield expected. The number of active participants in church affairs doubled, trebled, and quadrupled, and for the first time in years religion attracted the enthusiasm of the young; but the effect was to divide the church everywhere. Much of New England, for example, became divided into fiercely hostile camps of "Old Lights," or defenders of the existing order, and "New Lights," who embraced the new piety.

The Great Awakening had its philosophical connections with more sober forms of Protestantism that preceded it. Puritans, like other Protestants, had taken the conversion experience very seriously, and even after the Half-Way Covenant it had been a requirement for admission to full church membership among New England Puritans. But the Puritan congregations had not demanded the violent outpourings of emotion that revivalism sometimes identifies with religious experience. The Great Awakening

George Whitefield and John Wesley promised salvation to those who opened their hearts to God through prayer. To them was offered eternal life in the New Jerusalem depicted in this drawing; to others the door to hell stood open.

was the earliest large instance of a revivalism that has become a recurrent phenomenon in American Protestantism. Like the Great Awakening, moreover, American religion since has emphasized the experiential component of religion. In breaking open churches that had been stable and undivided, the Awakening is suggestive of the tendency within Protestantism to multiply churches and sects. And the Awakening introduced America to a movement that John and Charles Wesley were spreading within the Church of England and therefore prepared the way for the later growth of Methodism, a faith that has stressed both religious feeling and a morality of self-discipline and industriousness. In the nineteenth century the Methodist and Baptist churches, well adapted in structure, practice, and belief to spread to the frontier and the back country, would become one of the largest denominations both in cities and the countryside and a notable influence on American ideas of morality.

The Enlightenment. The energies of revivalism were directed against reason, or at least the cool, detached reason that opposed bursts of emotion. But there began in Europe around the middle of the eighteenth century a movement called the Enlightenment—some Europeans thought themselves to be living in the Age of Reason; and the Enlightenment, with its confidence in reason, reached American shores.

In its European continental form, the Enlightenment practiced an abstract kind of thinking known as deductive logic, a reasoning that begins with general principles and then applies these to particular cases or details. Philosophers of the Enlightenment, for example, abstractly defined large, general "laws of nature," which could be laws governing the material world or natural laws fixed in human beings; and having determined the laws of nature that applied to human beings, Enlightenment thinkers considered what particular kind of government would best serve or express these laws. The European

Enlightenment would make for great advances in science; and its political thought, much of which presumed that the laws of nature make all human beings equal in rights, contributed to the modern political revolutions seeking freedom and legal equality.

Numbers of American writers later in the century were much under the influence of the political as well as the scientific Enlightenment in Europe, talked of the "laws of nature," and argued in the language of the Enlightenment for liberty and equality. But some historians have identified a difference in emphasis between the European Enlightenment and its American counterpart. Americans tended more than European philosophers of the time to follow not deductive reasoning but a kind of thought that is now called empiricism, a reasoning that begins with the observation of particular details rather than with speculation about general principles. American thinkers confined much of their work to looking at plants and animals, to experimenting with practical gadgets, or to solving concrete practical problems of government.

The Wren Building (1695) designed by Sir Christopher Wren at the College of William and Mary, Williamsburg, Virginia.

Empiricism produced early and important scientific studies in America. Late in the seventeenth and early in the eighteenth century the New Englanders Thomas Brattle and Thomas Robie made a number of astronomical observations that proved useful to Newton and other Europeans, and the Royal Society in London published papers by John Banister, Cotton Mather, and Paul Dudley on American flora and fauna. Eliza Lucas Pinkney's observations pioneered the cultivation of indigo, which led to its widespread adoption as a new cash crop. Mathematical observations of note came from John Winthrop IV, Ezra Stiles, and David Rittenhouse. Perhaps the crowning American scientific achievements were Benjamin Franklin's experiments in electricity, particularly his demonstration that lightning is electrical. Perhaps as important as these scientific discoveries were the mediums through which scientific knowledge was introduced and spread.

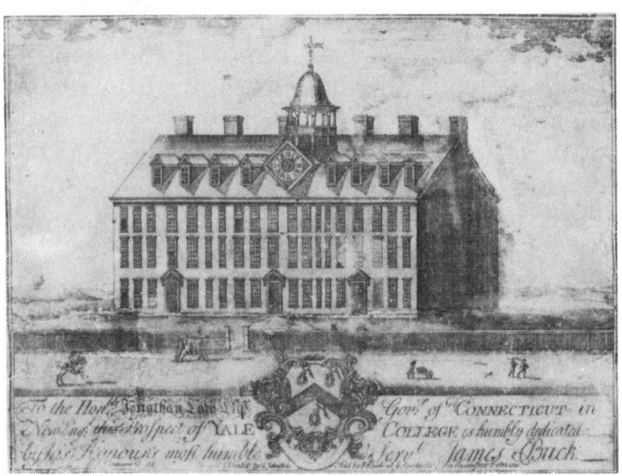

The first building at Yale College, New Haven, Connecticut. The college founded in 1701.

The most advanced were the colleges, along with philosophical and scientific societies, the most important being the American Philosophical Society, established in Philadelphia in 1743. Most colleges started during the colonial period were founded by religious groups. Harvard (1636) and Yale (1701) were Congregationalist, the term that came to be used for New England Puritanism, with its placement of church government in the hands of the congregation. Dartmouth became a college in 1769 after having been established much earlier as an Indian missionary school. William and Mary (1693) and King's College (1754, later renamed Columbia) were founded by Anglicans. Rhode Island College (1764, later Brown) was Baptist, Queen's College (1766, later Rutgers) was Dutch Reformed, and the College of New Jersey (1746, later Princeton) was Presbyterian. The only nonsectarian college founded in the colonial period was Franklin's Academy, established in 1751, which became the University of Pennsylvania in 1791. King's and Franklin's introduced practical courses in agriculture, navigation, and astronomy.

Higher education was available to a much wider spectrum of classes in the colonies than in England. The prestigious institutions of higher learning were reserved for males. During the eighteenth century, a few private academies for women were founded, but systematic attempts to provide even for the education of upper-class girls would not emerge until after the Revolution. The colonies did produce some well-educated and even learned women, but these women had invariably benefited from private instruction from tutors who had been hired for their brothers or cousins. In general, female literacy continued to lag behind male literacy, and even such an intelligent and privileged woman as Abigail Adams could suffer from embarrassment at her own spelling mistakes.

The Press. On the popular level, scientific and other information was spread mainly through newspapers. Law in Massachusetts and Connecticut had required every town to provide a school at which children could learn reading and writing. Elementary schools, established most zealously by Congregationalists and Presbyterians, gave America a much higher literary rate than Europe possessed: ninety percent or more could sign their names in New England, fifty to sixty percent in Virginia, and somewhere between these figures among the Scotch-Irish. Before 1704 there was little for ordinary Americans to read except the Bible (which they did read, avidly), but in that year the first newspaper, the *Boston News-Letter*, was established. It was followed two decades later by *The New-England Courant*, published by James Franklin and his younger brother Benjamin. In 1725 the British mainland colonies still had only five newspapers. Then along with the rapid expansion of commerce and land settlement came a proliferation of newspapers: by 1765 there were twenty-five. Four-page weeklies were filled with advertisements, notices of arrivals and departures of ships, and reprints of news that had appeared months earlier in European journals. But as time went by the colonial newspapers printed more and more articles, written by their readers, in which the nature of man, society, and government was endlessly explored, and so it was largely through the newspapers that Americans formed their opinions of themselves and their world. Following the English lead, the colonies also began to produce a few journals such as the *Lady's Magazine* and the *Gentleman's and Lady's Town and Country Magazine* that catered to the female members of polite society.

Colonial America provided an important incident in the development of freedom of the press. In 1735 Peter Zenger faced a charge of libel for publishing in his newspaper an attack by the former chief justice of New York on actions of the governor of the colony. The counsel for Zenger argued that since the statements printed in the paper were true they were not libelous. The jury agreed, and returned a verdict of not guilty. The effect of the verdict was to establish the principle that only false statements are libelous, and thereby to free newspapers to widen the range of their commentary and criticism.

America in 1750

The Colonies and the Empire. By the middle of the eighteenth century thirteen contiguous British colonies were clustered on the North American mainland. Together they contained well over a million inhabitants. Rhode Island and Connecticut existed by virtue of corporation charters that vested the power of government in the body of freemen. The Penns' Pennsylvania and Delaware and the Calverts' Maryland were proprietary colonies, whose administration had fallen to the heirs of the original proprietors. The proprietors had the title to all the land, and the nominal power of government, though as a result of various charters and agreements they actually appointed or served as the executive branch; the legislative power resided in the inhabitants. In 1752, when Oglethorpe's proprietorship was terminated, Georgia became a royal colony. None of the seven other provinces of the Crown had begun as royal colonies. Virginia and Massachusetts had been the possessions of business companies; others had been proprietary colonies; for a time there was no one clearly official government for New Hampshire. In the royal colonies the executive branch, consisting of a governor and a council that in some colonies also functioned as an upper house of the legislature, was appointed by the king, as were some of the colonial judges.

The Board of Trade, a fifteen-member agency of the Crown, exercised general supervisory power over the entire overseas empire. It selected most royal officials for the colonies and reviewed all legislation passed by the colonial assemblies; of about 8500 colonial laws passed in the entire period prior to 1776, all were at least nominally reviewed and 469 were rejected. The Board had established vice-admiralty courts in five mainland colonies, with jurisdiction over the acts of Parliament and the various orders concerning trade, other maritime activity, and the conservation of timber for the Royal Navy. Appeals from these courts went to the High Court of Admiralty in London until 1748, after which the Admiralty court shared jurisdiction with the Board of Trade. Appeals from colonial courts on all other matters went to the king's Privy Council, some of whose members also sat on the Board of Trade; all told, something like 1500 court decisions were appealed prior to 1776. This jerry-built structure, cumbersome enough in theory, was doubly so in practice, for officials were generally slipshod, inefficient, and negligent in executing their duties. That left the royal governors as the principal instruments of the royal will in the colonies, but since the governors normally received their salaries from the local legislatures they were prone to identify themselves less with the Crown than with the richer and more powerful colonials.

The informal adhesives of the empire were somewhat stronger than the formal. The colonies and the mother country had common enemies, France and Spain, and that alone was enough to hold the empire together. They were also bound by economic interest: Britain and the colonies alike profited from the maintenance of a vast, enclosed common market, and when colonials wanted or needed to trade outside the empire, lax law enforcement usually made it possible to do so. Beyond such tangible considerations were common language, customs, constitutional and legal institutions, and above all pride in a heritage of freedom, of sharing the celebrated "rights of Englishmen." Even so, Americans were well on their way to becoming recognizably a new breed, and many Europeans who encountered them remarked on their distinctiveness.

The American Character. British Americans, for example, were energetic or at least busy; or rather, enough of them were that way to give the impression that busyness was a central attribute of American life. Having vast quantities of good unoccupied land at their disposal and having accepted population explosion as a social norm, they had become eager and avaricious speculators in land: the fever for land, for seizing the main chance and growing wealthy through big land deals, reached epidemic proportions. Americans seemed ambitious, optimistic, presumptuous, and—compared to Europeans and despite having developed their own forms of social deference—egalitarian. Europeans were inclined to view them as bumpkins for those reasons and because all but a few lacked the finer social graces; they were in fact quite cosmopolitan, for their daily existence and their very survival depended upon keeping abreast of events all over the Atlantic world. So, at least, they believed. And, having a higher literacy rate than perhaps any nation of Europe, they read newspapers and exchanged letters avidly. But there was also some social timidity, a fear of provincialism in their attitude toward Europe, which Americans have never completely lost. Their fear of being isolated from Europe led them to slavish imitation of the London fads and styles in clothing, architecture, and entertainment. Americans drank coffee and tea incessantly, but the most common form of release among men was alcohol; they consumed prodigious quantities of wine and rum, and many of them drank whiskey, gin, and beer as well. Women of Nantucket Island in Massachusetts were addicted to opium, and it is not unlikely that opium and other drugs were in common use among women elsewhere, for many experienced great pain through prolific childbearing without medical care. It is also possible that the black slaves knew (as their masters apparently did not) the anesthetizing joy of smoking hemp, for Africans had cultivated and used marijuana and hashish for ten centuries and more, and hemp was fairly widely grown in the South, for use in rope making.

But the most important generalization applicable to these early Americans is that they defied generalization, for heterogeneity was their very essence. Americans were pluralistic in other than their ethnic and religious backgrounds.

Multiple forms of social stratification, for instance, existed in the colonies. Each local community—the town in New England, the manor in New York, the county or parish elsewhere—had its own hierarchy, which sometimes did and sometimes did not correspond to the gradations of power and status in the colony as a whole. The most common determinants of social rank were wealth, occupation, and ethnic stock, but the most important determinant involved connections and sponsors, especially with officials or families of high station in England.

The distinction between male and female remained a fundamental determinant of an individual's social opportunities, but in any given instance wealth, inherited social status, and family membership could outweigh it. The familial, or dynastic, character of colonial politics cast women as pawns in the use of successful marriages as a base for alliances, but family connections could also permit women, either married or single, to play significant political roles in exceptional circumstances. In 1647 Margaret Brent administered Maryland as the executrix of Governor Leonard Calvert's estate, although her subsequent request for two seats in the Maryland legislature—one as executor, the other on the basis of her own holdings—was denied. Most women, however, spent their lives firmly under the governance of their fathers, husbands, and male kin to whom they were considered constitutionally, intellectually, and often morally inferior.

An equally important division of American society was between interests and attitudes that decades later, in the early days of the United States, would have as their spokesman Alexander Hamilton and Thomas Jefferson respectively. This was a division between town dwellers and country dwellers, between merchants and farmers, between planters who were wholly dependent on commerce and those whose plantation units were largely self-sufficient as well as commercial. It was a difference in attitude between those who accepted the expansive commercialism of the eighteenth century and those who rejected it, adhering to slower and less acquisitive ways. This line of division cut across all others and defies precise definition by place and group.

Political Theory. Among the differing political ideas available to the eighteenth-century British and Americans was the notion that the British constitution, as a collection of laws and customs that make up the British system is called, had achieved a fine balance among three forms of government. These forms are monarchy, or rule by the one; aristocracy, or rule by the few; and democracy, or rule by the many. Each needs to be restrained, or it will degenerate into an evil: monarchy will fall into tyranny, aristocracy into selfish domination by the wealthy and powerful, democracy into mob rule. The British government, according to this concept, contained an element of each of the three forms. The Crown represented rule by the one;

By 1752 Baltimore was an important city in the proprietary colony of Maryland. *(Courtesy, New York Public Library)*

the House of Lords represented the titled aristocracy, the privileged few; the House of Commons represented the democracy. In the British system, the theory went, each of the three was properly restrained by the other two.

The idea was not an accurate reading of the British constitution. The House of Commons did represent, directly or indirectly, a considerable range of British public opinion. But it was not democratic. For the most part only the propertied classes, and not all individuals within these, had the privilege of voting for members of the Commons. And the Commons did not balance neatly against the Lords. Interests represented in the House of Commons could be as hostile to one another as to the aristocracy. The monarchy in the later years of the century did wield much power. But it was no longer able to rule by sheer sovereign will and command. Its strength now lay in its ability to influence Parliament through the appointments and other royal favors at its disposal. It was closer to being the leader of a political party then to being an independent branch of government balancing and restraining the rest. Eighteenth-century observers, in fact, perceived the politics of their time as a corruption of a system that had once been pure. It was not until the nineteenth century, when the Crown had lost almost all of its remaining power, that it would become fully the object of loyalty and affection that it is today. The belief that government should combine the three elements, and that the British system had once possessed the right combination, was to persist into the early days of the independent United States and to offer an explanation for the scheme of the Constitution, claiming that the President provided government by the one, the Senate—for which the Constitution did not require popular elections—provided rule by the few, and the House of Representatives supplied rule by the many.

By 1750 the governments of the royal colonies—all the colonies except Rhode Island and Connecticut—appeared to reflect the structure of the British government. The governor, appointed by the Crown, had the authority to veto legislation passed by the colonial assembly and to call or dissolve the assembly. The governors' powers in the colonies were not identical to those of the monarch in Britain, but the governors, like the king, could be described as providing government by the one. While some governors were upper-class Americans, the Crown more often appointed someone from Britain. A council, drawn for the most part from among the wealthier or more distinguished colonists and in most royal colonies appointed by the governor, could amend or reject legislation by the more popular branch of the colonial legislature and served as the highest court in the colony. A political theorist might have described the council as supplying government by the few. The other branch of the legislature, called in most colonies the assembly, did have a wide representation. Throughout British America between fifty and seventy-five percent of adult white males possessed enough property to vote according to the laws of the colonies.

How Much Democracy? Why were the colonies so much more nearly democratic politically than Great Britain? No passionate commitment to the idea of universal equality had moved proprietors, companies, and colonial leaders to provide for broad distribution of the right to vote, or led kings and the rest of the British government to accept the arrangement. But while only a small portion of the British population voted for members of Parliament, the British were learning to think of it as representing the wishes of the British nation as those wishes expressed themselves in the vote of the enfranchised. And so a certain respect for the vote, as an institution firmly grounded in the British constitution, would have predisposed the founders of colonies to provide it to numbers of settlers. Expediency must also have had something to do with the granting of the franchise to large numbers of colonists. Colonial leaders, and British entrepreneurs with a financial or other interest in North America, wanted fast settlement, and offering prospective settlers a share in local government would have been a way of enticing them. But another reason for granting the vote to colonists would be that the settlers, and those elements in the British and European populations most likely to move to America, were the kind of people whom the founders and leaders of colonies would be comfortable with as voters. Farmers holding land, hard-working and property-owning craftsmen, British and Europeans with the ambition and energy to have started up a life across the ocean: such people would look worthy of being entrusted with the vote. One concept favored among the politically minded in Britain was that property gives the holders a stake in society, firmly planting them in that society and providing them a self-interested reason to work for its orderly well-being. Much of the colonial populace would meet that test. And, in any event, giving colonists the vote signified in most cases not an idea of what is the proper government for all human beings but a practical choice of an arrangement that would allow colonists to work efficiently together for their common concerns. And so much of colonial British America enjoyed a democracy that had little ideology to it, and represented instead something of British tradition and much of the realities of colonial life.

Still, the colonies were not democratic by the standards that the egalitarian beliefs of the nineteenth and twentieth centuries would demand. In nearly all the colonies governors not chosen by the people could veto legislation. Common colonists were untroubled at the presence of gentries and elites since, being democratic by circumstance rather than by ideology, they had no philosophical reason to be troubled at it; and they were prepared to offer to people of wealth and standing a certain deference. Virginia is a notable example. The gentry there provided most of the colony's leaders. Their humbler neighbors gave them respect, and received it in turn. On election day a candidate might treat his neighbors with drink, and each vote was cast orally and in public, which must have strengthened the personal bond between the candidate and the common voters who could make this public expression of loyalty to him. In areas within the colony of New York patroons presided over the tenants who worked their large estates. By no means all white American males could vote. There were laborers and seamen with almost no property, and paupers with none. In Philadelphia on election day in 1742 some sailors without the vote rioted in anger at the unwillingness of the Quaker-dominated assembly to provide measures for military defense—a common complaint also among the Scotch-Irish voters on the Pennsylvania frontier. The incident gives witness both that a disfranchised class existed and that it was prepared to make its own political mark. As a general rule, women were similarly disfranchised, but there is no record of their having protested their condition. Since in principle married women could own no property without very special legal arrangements, and since officially no women performed military service, they could not claim the two main justifications for a vote. Colonists of both genders widely shared the basic assumption of their society that public affairs were the business of men. And finally, throughout British America the institution of slavery mocked whatever of democracy white Americans practiced.

So democracy in British America was incomplete and only imperfectly aware, if at all, that its existence was remarkable. But in a few years the American Revolution and the agitations leading to it were to call forth a more explicit and philosophical discussion of the virtues of equality and popular government. American democracy became somewhat conscious of itself, 72and therefore conscious of its own incompleteness; and the American nation was launched on a long career of perfecting an equality that had begun with the practical, limited measures of proprietors, British government, and colonial leaders.

The Imperial System. The system of imperial regulation that the colonies followed or evaded as expediency demanded was not an effort to build up the prosperity of the mother country at the expense of the colonies. It aimed at protecting the empire as a whole and encouraging each part to do what it could do best. The Navigation Acts gave a monopoly of the carrying trade within the empire to ships of England and the colonies, with crews made up mostly of colonists or Englishmen.

The acts not only protected the American carrying trade but stimulated the shipbuilding industry in British America. Another measure of the imperial system gave the tobacco colonies a monopoly for their product. The Wool Act of 1699, the Hat Act of 1732, and the Iron Act of 1750 did shield producers in the home country against potential competition from American makers of these goods. But at the moment there was not enough colonial production of wool, hats, or iron to make them competitive with British producers. The Molasses Act did injure the colonial manufacture of rum, or would have done so if colonists had obeyed it, but its object was to protect other colonists, those of the British West Indies, against foreign competition. The imperial system, then, was designed to nourish the whole empire and each of its parts, and the scheme was intelligent within the understanding available to statesmen at that time. By the eighteenth century, not long after the Navigation Acts, an economic concept, centuries long in development, known as mercantilism had gained full expression. It held that a nation or empire should increase its wealth, measured in gold, by policies that insure it will sell more abroad than it imports. By that standard much of the imperial system could claim to be sound economics. Not until a little later would economists be arguing extensively for free trade among nations, unhindered by protective legislation, as the best means of enriching each of the traders. But to colonists aware that the imperial system was the work of a government in which they had no direct voice, every item of the system that seemed to clash with their interests could turn them suspicious of the motives of the mother country.

Women and the Family

The Status of Women. According to the Puritan leader John Winthrop, a woman's husband "is her lord, and she is subjected to him, yet in a way of liberty, not of bondage: and a true wife accounts her subjection her honor and freedom." Puritans could reconcile the apparent opposites of subjection and freedom, for their religion, particularly the doctrine of predestination, taught that freedom resulted from obedience to the law of God. But the Puritans also meant something more when they spoke of the subjection of wives to their husbands. The Puritans, and other English settlers, were heirs to the doctrine of patriarchalism that prevailed among many Englishmen in the early seventeenth century. It viewed all sovereignty—or authority to govern—as equivalent to the absolute authority of fathers over families. The political events of the seventeenth century in England, like the Puritans' own resistance to the absolute power of monarchs, would challenge patriarchalism as a political doctrine. By 1688, the dominant opinion in England would look to property-holding individuals as the source of sovereignty. But the fading of patriarchalism—the rule of fathers—as a justification for government did not change attitudes toward the relation between men and women, especially within the family. They were supposed to be subject to their husbands in all matters. Women when they married normally lost whatever property rights they might have had. As the eighteenth-century jurist William Blackstone would put it: "Husband and wife are one and that one is the husband." Husbands were expected to govern their wives with gentleness and love whenever possible, but an unruly wife required stronger measures.

The laws of the Bay Colony differed from those of England in restricting the husband's right to correction. Wife-beating with a stick that was larger than one inch in diameter was prohibited, but even the gentler laws of the new world did not interfere with "corrections" or "chastisements" administered with switches of the proper size. And the Puritan emphasis on the responsibility of the individual to God did not encourage women's equality in religious institutions; Puritan fathers were especially fond of St. Paul's dictum: "Women, keep silent in the churches." By the end of the seventeenth century, women usually outnumbered men in church congregations, a tendency marking the beginning of the "feminization of religion" that would become overwhelming in the nineteenth century. But it did not open to women the role of minister or church leader. Among American congregations, only the Quakers permitted women to preach. And women were almost entirely excluded from all forms of politics. The subordination of women to men within the family was accompanied by their exclusion from positions of authority in the public spheres of church and state.

The inferiority of women to men, like women's necessary subordination to men, was the dominant view of gender relations and one of the most widely shared assumptions throughout

Puritan women in their Sunday best. Some wore masks to protect themselves from wind and sun.

the colonies. It has, nonetheless, been argued that women enjoyed a better position in the new world than they had—or than their sisters did—in the old. This view rests on the assumption that since women remained in short supply throughout the seventeenth century they were especially valued. But there is little evidence to suggest that simply because the authorities tried very hard to encourage women to imigrate to the colonies the reigning idea of women's nature and worth actually changed very much. The incentives offered to women had more to do with improving their social and economic position among other women than improving the status of women relative to men. It is possible that new world conditions did, at least initially, bring women somewhat greater freedom in their daily lives—and perhaps even somewhat greater respect as individuals. But when women strayed out of their assigned roles they were rapidly accused of insubordination, of defying the order of God and man, and even of familiarity with the Devil.

If free white women in colonial America were assigned a subordinate status, female indentured servants were doubly subordinate. Indentured women were seldom allowed to marry until their servitude was fulfilled, and most masters reserved the right to lengthen the period of service if the woman became pregnant. The possibility of marrying better than they might have married in England offered the main incentive to single female immigrants, and delaying marriage for the normal minimum of the seven years of indenture meant that the female servant might only marry after many of her child-bearing years had passed and after brutal work in a harsh climate had perhaps undermined her health. Those who did get pregnant during their term of indenture were very likely to have been the victims of the sexual exploitation of the same masters who then punished them for their pregnancy. And although masters justified extension of service on the grounds that pregnancy reduced the woman's capacity to work, in most cases extension far exceeded the time missed. A poem speaks in the voice of an indentured servant who, after recalling her happier days and more attractive appearance in England, laments her condition in the New World:

In weeding Corn or feeding Swine,
I spend my melancholy Time,
Kidnap'd and Fool'd, I thither fled,
And to my cost already find,
Worse Plagues than those I left behind.

The hardships that weighed on female indentured servants weighed even more heavily on slave women who lacked the minimal rights and promise of eventual freedom that masters accorded to indentured servants. Initially, slave women were as scarce relative to slave men as indentured females were relative to indentured men. Apparently, African societies placed a high value on women, or at least on their productive and reproductive abilities, and so African slave-traders withheld women from the slave trade. Those women who were transported to the New World might easily have been separated from their families; those who made the crossing with children who might or might not survive or be separated from their mothers upon arrival. Slave women certainly resisted enslavement and transportation as desperately as slave men, and many participated in revolts aboard slave ships. In the colonies a slave woman might not survive the harshness of her labor or the adaptation to the new climate and new diseases. In the early years of slavery in the colonies, conditions were too harsh and the ratio of men to women was too high for the newly enslaved population to reproduce itself; those slave women who did survive might form attachments to American In-

***Jersey Nanny*, by John Greenwood. The opportunities open to women in the colonies were limited.** *(Courtesy, Museum of Fine Arts, Boston)*

dian men or to white men. Only toward the end of the seventeenth century did a community of slaves begin to take shape in the Chesapeake colonies and South Carolina. By then, some slave women were forming stable unions with slave men and bearing their children. Slaveholders frequently encouraged their slaves to have children, who would also become the property of their masters. But the legality of slave marriages was never recognized at law. And slave women, even more than indentured females, lacked any resources to oppose the sexual exploitation of the master or other white males. Most slave colonies forbade interracial fornication, but enough black women bore mulatto children—either because they had been raped, or because they had established a relation with a man who was not black—to make the status of mulatto children a pressing legal question. In most Latin American slaveholding countries many masters acknowledged their mulatto offspring and often freed them, so a distinct class of free mulattoes emerged. In English America, such acknowledgments and manumissions were less common: there were many mulatto slaves, and free mulattoes simply joined the class of free blacks. All slave children inherited the status of their mother; no child born of a slave mother, whoever its father, could escape slavery without formal manumission.

Legal Rights. The law severely circumscribed the status of most women. The general presumption that all women should come under the authority of some man governed their lives whether their status be slave, indentured, or free. Only adult single or widowed free women could act in their own name or hold or dispose of property for themselves. These legal barriers to all forms of female independence derived primarily from the English common law, which assigned all minor children to the authority of their fathers and viewed all married women as "femmes coverts"—or, literally, covered women. New World practice apparently modified the severity of this legal doctrine; some married women signed contracts with their husbands-to-be prior to marriage and thus preserved control of their own property. Women were also known to act in a legal capacity on their own or their family's behalf. Wills reveal that at least some women did bequeath property to heirs of their own choosing. But all of these solutions presupposed the existence of some property worth controlling, some education, and some knowledge of the legal possibilities—that is, a comfortable social and economic position. Law in some colonies such as Massachusetts and Connecticut also permitted women somewhat easier access to divorce than they had in England, and the records reveal that at least some women took advantage of the opportunity. But formal divorce was never common and some states, notably South Carolina, prohibited it absolutely except by act of the legislature. And, in a predominantly rural society, most women had few opportunities to live comfortably on their own. Men had difficulty managing an agricultural household without a woman; women alone faced even greater obstacles. In cities women enjoyed greater opportunities to take a furnished room or preside over their own households. By the eighteenth century, single and widowed women were occasionally running small businesses, managing shops, or otherwise supporting themselves and perhaps their children. The ranks of independent women included women of a variety of social origins and free black women.

Whatever the limitations imposed by the law, in practice married free women probably enjoyed considerable feelings of importance to the survival of their households. Their work was as necessary to the survival and solvency of those households as was that of their men. Most white women who survived their child-bearing years—normally from marriage in their early twenties until their early forties—bore about eight children. Some bore more, and many lost one or more in childbirth or infancy. In addition to this vital contribution, most women shouldered a significant portion of the labor necessary to the household. They were responsible for food processing and preparation, for the making of many household necessities such as candles and soap, for washing, for sewing, and frequently for making clothes. This labor could include heavy tasks such as carrying the water for cooking and washing from streams or wells to a house. Women also usually assumed responsibility for certain kinds of agricultural labor, such as milking cows, tending vegetable gardens, keeping chickens, and collecting eggs. When circumstances required, especially at harvest time, they worked in the fields beside men. But the indispensability of women's labor to colonial society did not necessarily result in any permanent improvement either in women's status, or in the general view of women's position in society. The women themselves recognized the importance of their contributions. But it is doubtful if many colonial women gave any thought to equality with men, or if many colonial women aspired to male status. Many, however, doubtless aspired to lives of greater ease.

The woman of the day who enjoyed the greatest freedom was not the one who worked equally alongside her husband, but the one who could enjoy the more leisured life of the colonial aristocracy. She was the woman who enjoyed freedom from calluses on her hands and from legs swollen after a lifetime of standing and bending. She was the one who might acquire something of the more serious education provided for her brothers. By the eighteenth century, she was likely to have silver instead of pewter, an ample supply of linen sheets, nice clothing, looking glasses, furniture from Europe, books, periodicals, and more. But the comfort of her life depended upon the labor of other women—slaves or servants—who performed the tasks from which wealth had liberated her.

***Alice Mason*, 1670. Artist unknown. Alice is not a child as we would think of one today but a miniature adult fully responsible for her moral behavior.** *(National Park Service, Adams National Historic Site, Quincy, Massachusetts)*

Children. In a land where labor was scarce, children also contributed to the livelihood of the family. Colonial Americans had no concept of "adolescence." But if familial responsibilities came early, the opportunities of a new land also provoked tensions within the family, frequently pulling children away from home.

The apparent disruption of family life in the New World was a frequent source of complaint and worry. The president of King's College, Samuel Johnson, bemoaned that

> it is obvious that our youth are apace running headlong into all sorts of debauchery and uncontolled (*sic*) indulgences, which I doubt not is... chiefly owing to the fond indulgence of their parents.

Shortly after founding, every colony passed laws demanding obedience from children; the potential punishment for disobedience in Massachusetts and Connecticut was nothing less than death. Records do not reveal that any court ever resorted to such extreme punishment. In fact, by permitting a child to present a case in court, such laws guarded against parental abuse at the same time that they sought to curb recalcitrant children. Colonial law reflected the belief that the community, acting through the courts, had an interest in maintaining order within individual families.

A few Northern communities also assumed the burden of providing formal education. A famous Massachusetts statute of 1642 anticipated the nineteenth-century community provision of schooling for all members of society. And as society became more secular, so did education; the inculcation of civic virtue and good citizenship took priority over religious instruction. History became important in a child's studies because, as Benjamin Franklin once explained,

> history will...give occasion to expatiate on the advantage of civil orders and constitutions; how men and their properties are protected by joining in societies and establishing government.... Thus may the first principles of sound politics be fixed in the minds of youth.

Yet most young people learned pedagogical and vocational skills within their families. If a son did not want to learn his father's trade, then he might be apprenticed into another family for study under the direction of the master. Whatever young colonials failed to absorb from elders they had to learn on their own. Colonial newspapers and almanacs, such as Ben Franklin's *Poor Richard's Almanac*, served as early home study guides.

Courtship. Particularly in the cities, customs changed rapidly, disturbing the older generation, shocking rural visitors, and even surprising foreign observers. A young man described a party he went to in Quaker Philadelphia: "Seven sleighs with two ladies and two men in each, preceded by fiddlers on horseback," rode to a public house where "we danced, sung, and romped and ate and drank, and kicked away care from morning till night, and finished our frolic in two or three sideboxes at the play." A British traveler in Virginia in 1755 reported that "dancing is the chief diversion here," and another was shocked at the widespread dancing of "jigs." Claiming that the dance was borrowed from the slaves, the proper Englishman found it "without method or regularity: a gentleman and lady stand up, and dance about the room, one of them retiring, the other pursuing, then perhaps meeting, in an irregular fantastical manner." Serenading under the window of a favored lady also came into vogue during the late colonial period. Sometimes the gentlemen first lubricated their throats at a local tavern, yet women reportedly considered the midnight visitation and inevitable disharmony a high compliment.

Like folk songs everywhere, those of colonial America revolved around courtship, unrequited love affairs, or doomed lovers. Many American ballads came from Britain; "Greensleeves" was one of the most popular and graceful tunes, and it provided the melody for about eighty different sets of lyrics. Compare the lyricism of the English "Greensleeves" ("Alas, my love/You do me wrong/To cast me off/Discourteously...") with the blunter expression of the native song "Springfield Mountain," the first popular folk song known to be native to the colonies in both words and music:

On Springfield Mountain there did dwell
A lovelie youth I knowed him well....
He had scarce mowed half round the field
When a poison serpent bit at his heel....
They took him home to Mollie dear,
Which made him feel so verie queer....
She also had a rotten tooth
And so the poison killed them both.

The song describes a true incident.

The French and Indian War

Since the last years of the seventeenth century Britain and France had been rivals in Europe and wherever their empires clashed. The War of the League of Augsburg, waged from 1689 to 1697, had led to skirmishes in North America that British colonists called King William's War. The War of the Spanish Succession, from 1702 to 1713, again had produced its small counterpart in America, Queen Anne's War. So far the colonial fighting had been border raids between British and French colonists, sometimes employing their Indian allies. The American phase of the War of the Austrian succession, which took place from 1740 to 1748, was called King George's War. New England troops won an important victory in the capital of Louisburg, which guarded the entrance to the St. Lawrence River. Colonists were disappointed when Britain returned Louisburg in the Treaty of Aix-la-Chapelle. Then in 1756 Britain and France began a seven-year world war for empire. The fighting in North America became known as the French and Indian War. The victory of Britain more than doubled the territorial extent of an overseas domain it had been building for a century and a half. And then, as an indirect result of the same war, it lost almost all of its old empire in a decade and a half.

Though they had claimed and occupied much of North America for more than a hundred years, the French had by no means settled it. During the seventeenth century explorers such as René La Salle pushed down the St. Lawrence River into the center of North America and down the Mississippi River. The vast area of New France, comprising most of present-day Canada, the Ohio Valley, the Mississippi, and lands to its west, constituted a serious threat to the English colonies. France established a brisk fur trade with Algonquin-speaking Indian tribes and introduced guns to their Indian allies. As French traders moved along the St. Lawrence and into the Great Lakes region, they established Indian Alliances that would later aid them in fighting the English. But there were only about 55,000 French settlers in North America, the overwhelming majority in the far Northeast and along the St. Lawrence River and the remainder distributed in widely scattered trading posts on the Great Lakes and the Ohio and Mississippi rivers. Quebec and Montreal were the only towns of consequence on the St. Lawrence, and New Orleans the only one of importance on the Mississippi. As buffers between their own settlements and those of the aggressive, coastbound British Americans, the French had long depended upon the friendly but subject Indians. A sudden establishment of favorable relations between the British Americans and the Indians upset all balances and jeopardized the entire French position in North America, for the greedy and land-hungry British Americans outnumbered the French Americans by almost thirty to one.

Skirmishes in the Ohio Valley. The new governor of Virginia, Robert Dinwiddie, had instructions to promote the interests of the Ohio Company, a business interested in the Ohio Valley lands, but to do so without antagonizing the French. Accordingly he dispatched a seven-man mission, which included a twenty-one-year-old Virginian named George Washington, to urge the French to respect British rights in the area. The mission was politely received and, with equal politeness, informed that the construction

A view of Fort Ticonderoga on Lake Champlain, New York. This was a strategic battleground in several wars. *(The Crown Collection in the British Museum)*

of Fort Duquesne would begin in the spring. The place where the fort was to be located, the site of present-day Pittsburgh, was in territory that had not yet been clearly assigned to Pennsylvania rather than Virginia. Upon being told of the French intention, Governor Dinwiddie rushed a work force to the area with instructions to build a British fort on the spot. To protect the workers young Washington followed with troops a little later, quite unaware that the French had expelled the work force almost immediately upon its arrival. In May 1754 Washington was encamped at Great Meadows on the Monongahela when he learned of the existence of a small French force a few miles ahead. He ordered a precipitous night march and attacked the French, capturing twenty-one and killing ten. Then he pushed on until he learned that the French were about to attack him in force. He retreated and hastily threw up a stockade, imaginatively called Fort Necessity. In June his force of 150 grew by 200 more men, and on July 3 he was attacked by 500 French and 400 Indians. After a nine-day siege Washington surrendered. The French and Indian War had begun.

It took European statesmen two years to complete the necessary formalities of choosing up sides (France and Austria, later joined by Spain, against Great Britain and Prussia) and reaching a state of official hostility. Meanwhile, French and English Americans were busily engaged in killing one another, or in discussing plans for enlisting the aid of various Indian tribes.

Albany Plan of Union. Even before Washington's abortive expedition, the Board of Trade had ordered a conference of colonial officials, and even as Washington was blundering in the wilderness a congress was in session in Albany, New York, attended by delegates from all colonies north of the Potomac save New Jersey and Delaware. Schemes for uniting the colonies were afloat at the congress. The Pennsylvania delegation, led by Benjamin Franklin (who had long since abandoned his native Boston to go into newspaper printing in Philadelphia), proposed what is known as the Albany Plan of Union. The plan called for a president-general for the British colonies, to be chosen and supported by the Crown, and a grand council, representing the several colonies in proportion to their contributions to the colonial treasury. This agency was to have general legislative and taxing powers for the purpose of defense and Indian relations. The delegates approved the plan with modifications, but the colonies rejected it; so the first effort to establish an American union was stillborn. The colonial legislatures had been jealous above all of sharing their power to tax; that jealousy would be an impelling force toward the American Revolution.

General Edward Braddock. It remained obvious that unless the British were willing to forfeit their newfound opportunities, some sort of plan would have to be devised for coping with the French in America. Though eminent Londoners were preoccupied with the gaming tables, court intrigues, and other pressing pursuits, someone in the capital did come up with a vague plan of action. Official British policy was to engage in what, at a later day, would be called limited warfare. One British army, manned primarily by colonial militiamen, would march up from Virginia and capture Fort Duquesne. Another and similar force, to be gathered in New England and New York, would seize Crown Point on Lake Ticonderoga and Fort Niagara. General Edward Braddock was put in charge of the campaign.

Braddock arrived in Virginia early in that year, delegated responsibility for raising troops for the multiple attack, and chose Washington as his aide-de-camp. In June he started over the mountains with a force of 2500 men. In an open space near Fort Duquesne on July 9 he received fire from the enemy forces, many of them Indians fighting from behind cover. Some of the Virginia troops abandoned the tight, conventional eighteenth-century military formation and tried to fight in the frontier manner, which meant using cover; and some of Braddock's British regular troops attempted the same thing. But they were all ordered back into line, where they were slashed by enemy fire until they broke. By the next evening Braddock's forces had been destroyed: General Braddock himself was killed. The planned expedition on Fort Niagara, directed by Governor William Shirley of Massachusetts, got as far as Oswego, half the distance, before being defeated. The campaign to take Crown Point, led by William Johnson, brought great accolades to the British commander but not a single victory to the British troops.

Attack on Canada. By the middle of 1756 the French had taken the offensive, and throughout 1757 French forces won victory after victory. Then a new expedition, commanded by General John Forbes and composed of 6000 men, began in the fall of 1758 to cut its way through the forests of western Pennsylvania tow-

French troops being reviewed in Quebec, an almost impregnable fortress commanded by Louis Joseph Montcalm. *(Courtesy, William H. Coverdale Collection, and the Canada Steamship Lines Limited, Montreal, Canada.)*

ard the forks of the Ohio. The French defenders of Fort Duquesne, deserted by their Indian allies as Forbes's army drew near, blew up their stronghold and fled to Canada in November of 1759. Forbes immediately began to reconstruct the defenses, rechristened Fort Pitt—hence the later city of Pittsburgh—and settlers began to pour into the area, despite British orders. A second expedition, commanded by William Johnson, directed a force of 3500 Americans, 2500 British regulars, and 1000 Indians against Fort Niagara, with the aim of cutting Montreal and Quebec off from the Great Lakes region. The expedition marched in the spring of 1759 and achieved total victory. A third expedition, commanded by Sir Jeffrey Amherst, was directed to move north from New York City, clear the French posts on Lake Champlain, bypass Montreal, and lay siege to Quebec from the southwest. A fourth expedition, under General James Wolfe, was ordered to move with a combined army and naval force up the St. Lawrence and attack Quebec from the other side. Amherst's expedition took both Ticonderoga and Crown Point, but was so slow in the doing that it was forced to stop on Lake Champlain for the winter of 1759-60. That left Wolfe to attack Quebec alone, and Quebec was protected by a high rock cliff that made it the most formidable natural fortress in America. The French commander at Quebec, Louis Joseph Montcalm, remained inside the fortress, confident that high cliffs would prevent any attack on Quebec from the southwest by way of the Plains of Abraham. It was a momentous occasion for the future of North America.

Points To Think About

1. The most significant fact about the Salem witchcraft trials is that they were the only outburst of their kind in colonial America. Similar episodes had been relatively commonplace in England and Europe during the seventeenth and early eighteenth centuries. So, important as it is to ascertain why the trials occurred, it is even more important to determine why there were no other Salems. This is the kind of question historians rarely ask and one they are not particularly well suited to answer. Their whole training is directed to explaining what did happen.

One way of approaching the question is to isolate the features of Salem village life that set it apart from other colonial American communities. Perhaps these peculiarities answer not only "why Salem village" but also "why not elsewhere?" But we find that there was little in the community's economic situation, or its ethnic or religious makeup, that set it apart from other New England towns. The strains introduced by the growth of a market economy, for example, were felt in many other places. What Salem village conspicuously lacked were social and governmental mechanisms for resolving conflict. The village had originally been part of the town of Salem and continued to look to the town for leadership. When, for example, villagers found themselves at odds over the choice of the minister, they turned to the town for guidance. The minister was expected to provide moral leadership. Disputes between neighbors or family members were routinely referred to him. And, normally, the minister's moral authority was sufficient to cause the disputants to accept his advice. But this could never work in Salem village where the minister's authority had never been accepted by the entire town. As a result, grievances persisted, and old resentments festered. The sorts of normal social pressures that the average community had managed to deal with built up to the flash point in Salem village.

The witchcraft outburst can be seen as testimony of a sort to the effectiveness of colonial social arrangements elsewhere. Every community had its own problems, of course, but normally colonists could feel confident that they would be solved in an effective and legitimate way. Only in Salem village did they seem *devilishly* recalcitrant.

2. Prior to the Awakening New Englanders had thought of conversion as an individual experience that often lasted for months. It became, under the ministrations of the "New Light" ministers, a communal event which lasted but a few days or even hours. The New Light preachers appealed to the hearts of their listeners. While some, like Jonathan Edwards, maintained a dignified tone, others thundered forth. And all used emotionally charged and dramatic images (see the excerpt in the text from Edwards's "Sinners In The Hands Of An Angry God" for a famous example) designed to bring their hearers to an immediate awareness of their needs for salvation.

In seeking after conversion in their sermons, the "New Lights" took what had been an intensely private experience and made it public. In so doing they created an emotional atmosphere at their meetings unlike anything that had come before. People cried out—presumably under the conviction of sin. They wept, they groaned, they fell to their knees. Some lost consciousness. And, most critically, the excitement was contagious. Whole gatherings experienced the drama of conversion together.

Those used to the old ways, called "Old Lights," were horrified. This was not religion, they thought. It was mass frenzy. And so the first of several battlelines over the Awakening was drawn. Established congregational churches often split. New Lights refused to heed a minister they regarded as cold or lifeless or spiritually dead; the Old Lights roundly condemned the excesses of the Awakening.

Several important questions were at stake. One was the authority of the established clergy. The Awakening led many to challenge or even condemn them. Another was the traditional deference paid to learning. The New Lights encouraged lay men and, sometimes, lay women, to lead prayers and even, on occasion, to preach. Their lack of training was no handicap, said New Light ministers. Instead it was an advantage. New Lights spoke straight from the heart. Their sentiments were not filtered through so much useless learning.

In these ways, the Awakening proved a disruptive experience in much of colonial America. It led to a proliferation of churches, divided religious authority, and enabled ordinary men and women to challenge their betters.

3. At first brush, the dominant religious and intellectual currents of mid-eighteenth century America seem out of phase with each other. The emotional intensity of the Awakening seems a far cry from the cautious appeal to trial-and-error which characterized the American mind of this time. And, of course, the contrast is quite real—as it nearly always is between the "heart" and the "head." Yet there are also elements common to the nation's level-headed empiricism and its fervent pietism.

Both religion and thought acknowledged the primacy of experience. This is obviously the case with empiricism. It consists of an inductive approach to knowledge, each piece of evidence being weighed and carefully added to the total. It is less obvious but equally true that the New Lights also rested their case on an appeal to experience. What, after all, was conversion? It was the single most overpowering experience an individual could undergo. And, when challenged by Old Lights over their use of new methods in preaching, the New Lights rested their defense on an appeal to the results. The new methods, they said, worked. They might seem unorthodox or strange, but they worked. They brought people to God.

Both New Lights and empiricists distrusted appeals to abstract learning. We have already noted the New Lights' disdain for formal theological learning as irrelevant to the business of salvation. Religion was, for them, a matter of the emotions because it was an experience. So too empiricists found abstract, deductive arguments unpersuasive. They could only be persuaded by facts. And facts, for them, had to involve real, tangible things. This is at the root of the famous American preference for practical applications over pure theory in science, a preference which lasted well into the twentieth century.

4. The rapid growth of the British colonies during the eighteenth century convinced many contemporaries that the Americans would in time be independent or that the seat of empire, as Benjamin Franklin once prophesied, would move to their side of the Atlantic. The sheer size of British North America, the rapid growth of its population, and the wealth of its resources all plainly forecast its ultimate preeminence or independence. Yet these facts do not explain the reasons why the revolution took place when it did. Nor do they explain why the revolution took the form that it did. To address those questions, we need to examine the patterns of colonial government.

The colonies had long benefited from what is often called "salutary neglect." Imperial control had been intermittent at best. This meant that the colonists had grown used to regulating most of their affairs. Furthermore, they had experienced little difficulty in evading those few imperial regulations they did find bothersome. This happy state of affairs encouraged Americans to think of themselves as partners in the British imperial enterprise. They thought of possessing all "the rights of Englishmen," for example. And they engaged in numerous wars with France as patriotic Englishmen. They saw an identity of interest between themselves and the mother country.

The colonists, often without fully realizing it, had embraced one vision of mercantilism while the British government embraced another. Mercantilism taught that there was a limited amount of wealth and power and that the various nations of the globe were engaged in an unending struggle to get their shares. Colonies were intended to secure a larger share. But while the colonists thought of themselves as equal partners and believed that only those common policies that benefited the two should be adopted, successive governments in England thought of the colonies not as partners but as subordinates, existing to benefit the mother country through whatever policies she designed.

Suggested Readings

Paul Boyer and Stephen Nissenbaum attribute the witchcraft hysteria in Salem to a rift in the social structure ultimately traceable to an emergent mercantile capitalism. See *Salem Possessed: The Social Origins of Witchcraft* (1974) and three volumes, *The Salem Witchcraft Papers: Verbatim Transcripts of the Salem Witch-craft Outbreak of 1692* (1977). John Demos's excellent 1983 study, *Entertaining Satan*, offers a broader view of the episode.

People of Paradox (1980) is Michael Kammen's venture onto the perilous ground of national character; he finds the hallmark of American society to be contradictions ("biformities") and tensions within colonial life that contributed to the formation of a peculiar American style reconciling a European sense of order with a New World thirst for freedom. A good brief view of the early American economy is Gary M. Walton and James P. Shepherd, *The Economic Rise of Early America* (1979). The early history of blacks in America is brilliantly analyzed in David Brion Davis, *The Problem of Slavery in Western Culture* (1966) and Winthrop Jordan, *White Over Black* (1968).

Richard Hofstadter's *America at 1750* is a social history of the thirteen colonies; the late author's lucid, crisp style freezes a moment in history for close scrutiny and ready understanding. Michael Kammen carefully covers *Colonial New York* (1975) while Edwin Bronner has written *William Penn's Holy Experiment* (1962).

FORREST McDONALD

It is fashionable to accuse the white man of every manner of crime against the American Indians. They are generally depicted as simple, peaceful, happy, and free people who were perfectly attuned to nature and had wondrous things to teach the whites. The invaders burst into this paradise of the "noble savage," plundering, slaughtering, and stealing land. Of all the burdens of guilt that white Americans must bear, we are frequently told, that the injustices committed against the Indians is among the heaviest.

It is a bum rap. The doom of the Indians was sealed the moment outsiders began to set foot in America, and would have been if the invaders had been saints or had come from Africa or Asia. The people of the Old World had developed immunities to a wide variety of diseases the native Americans had not. As soon as Europeans and Indians made contact, Indians started to die in epidemic proportions. During the first fifty years after the Spanish arrived, well over nine-tenths of the roughly six million inhabitants of the Aztec and Incan empires died of smallpox. Measles and other infectious diseases took additional droves. Gradually, as contacts spread over the two Americas, nearly ninety-five percent of the remaining Indians died in epidemics. Later, diseases such as malaria and yellow-fever, brought over from Africa, resulted in more deaths. No question of morality is involved: nothing the newcomers did, apart from simply being there, had anything to do with the demise of the red man. (There is an object lesson in humility here, namely that it is presumptuous if indeed not blasphemous to blame ourselves for things that are entirely beyond human control.)

As for the idea of the noble savage, the portrait is grossly overdrawn. Mexico and Peru were highly civilized, but the vast majority of the people there were for practical purposes slaves of their rulers. By far most of the Indians elsewhere were by European standards dirty, treacherous, ignorant, and superstitious. Tribal warfare—which routinely included theft, arson, rape, and torture as well as the indiscriminate slaughter of women, children, and the aged—was almost continuous. For most of the Indians, as for Thomas Hobbes's man in a "state of nature," life was "poor, nasty, brutish, and short."

The question of Indian lands is a complex one. The lands did not belong to the Indians, for they had no conception of private ownership of property in land. It is true that various tribes occupied hunting grounds that they considered the collective possession of the tribe; but there was nothing sacrosanct about such possession, for neighboring tribes were wont to seize control of the lands whenever it struck their fancy and they had the chance to do so. British Americans regularly purchased titles to Indian lands they occupied. This must have struck the Indians as a humorously fair bargain, being paid for something that was not theirs to sell and that other Indians would have taken by force.

One special aspect of relations between whites and Indians requires brief notice. The English had been hardened by a long history of dealing with the Irish, the Highland Scots, and the Welsh. They had regarded these tribal Celtic peoples as a dangerous nuisance, as contemptible savages whose periodic attacks (often in alliance with France or Spain) led to costly wars, as an almost subhuman species who occupied but did little farming on land that Englishmen could put to profitable use. English settlers in America consciously saw the Indians as being replicas of the "wild Irish" and were disposed to treat them accordingly. This meant, among other things, that they rarely intermingled with Indians and almost never married them. Anglo-Americans did not face the problem of assimilating or Europeanizing the natives and did not change their own ways to accommodate the ways of the Indians. That made the experience of Englishmen in America radically different from that of their Spanish, French, and Portuguese counterparts.

Were the Indians Victims? ☆

EUGENE GENOVESE

I have some sympathy for Professor McDonald's outburst against the silly moralizing that tries to make Americans out to be premature Nazis. Those who find Americans especially wicked, either absolutely or relative to the Third World peoples, might profitably study the Mongol conquests; Muslim slave-trading in Africa; slaughters of Hindus and Muslims in India; the career of the Zulus before the Europeans did unto them what they had been doing unto other black Africans; the periodic and often sadistic butchering of peasants by German, Japanese, Russian, and many other ruling classes across the globe. Cortez could not have conquered the great Aztec empire without the support of the "Indian" peoples whom the Aztecs had conquered, exploited, oppressed, terrorized, and tortured.

I do not, however, find helpful a substitution of conservative cant for liberal cant. The forcible reorganization of the native economy and the destruction of much of traditional social and cultural life are brutal, however much hostility the old culture may have contained. And the story of the European conquest of the American Indians will not be complete without some account of the slaughters and the enslavement of the subject peoples.

If the Indians were "by European standards, dirty, treacherous, ignorant, and superstitious," they were indeed a bad lot. Let us start with "dirty." The Europeans who landed on the African coast, looking for gold and slaves, sickened the natives by their stench and filth. The Africans could not believe that human beings could be as filthy as the Europeans were. Could the Indians really have outdone them? Treacherous. Toward whom? About what? Did the United States government ever make a treaty with the Indians that it did not break? Were the Indians more treacherous than the princes of Renaissance Italy, those much admired benefactors of the early modern world? More treacherous than the Borgia Pope Alexander VI or his famous daughter Lucrezia? More treacherous than the British in Ireland . . . than Francis II of France toward his fellow Catholics during the religious wars? This charge, like that of "ignorant," is offensive primarily for being meaningless. Of "superstitious" I shall say little. Since Protestants have always denounced Catholics for being superstitious, we should hardly expect them to treat with respect the religious beliefs of Indians, Africans, or Hindus.

The question of Indian land is more serious. Professor McDonald employs the concept of "private property" as though such property, in its modern form, has always existed. But in fact private property as an absolute possession of an individual or business corporation is a recent legal and social event. Even under late European feudalism, property was in some sense collective, not individual or "absolute." What Europeans did to the Indians, as to the Africans and others, was to swindle them, either by the simple device of imposing on the transactions that were being made their own harshly modern idea of property, or by making deals with corrupt leaders who were alienating common property without legal or moral authority.

Let these matters pass, and with them any attempt to do justice to the culture of the Indian peoples. Yet even from a Eurocentric perspective the conquest of the continent from the Indians—their expulsion as well as their slaughter—had fearful consequences. It contributed mightily to the deepening, broadening, and hardening of a racist arrogance and inhumanity that would extend, in even more virulent form, to the black people who were being brought in as slaves. That racism, to which the war on the Indians contributed so much, has poisoned American life. Even those who are disposed to take lightly the treatment of the Indians—to excuse it, to explain it, to place it in tendentious perspective—ought to be willing to ponder the cost our nation has been paying.

***The Death of Wolfe*, by Benjamin West. Though Wolfe was killed in action at Quebec, the British victory there marked a turning point in the French and Indian War.** *(Courtesy, National Gallery of Canada)*

CHAPTER 4

An Independent Spirit 1763–1776

THE PLAINS OF ABRAHAM

At 2 a.m. on September 13, 1759, the English major General James Wolfe ordered two lanterns raised to the maintop shrouds of his flagship, the *Sutherland,* anchored on the St. Lawrence River. It was the signal to attack the French fortress of Quebec, which lay on the heights 175 feet above the dark river.

The attack had been long delayed. Wolfe and his army of redcoats, Scottish highlanders, and American rangers had arrived before the French stronghold the previous June and had fought a score of skirmishes with the French-Canadian militia, their Indian allies, and the crack French regulars of the Guyenne, Royal Roussillon, Bearn, La Reine, and La Sarre regiments. By now the brief Canadian summer was nearly spent, and the bitter Northern winter would soon descend. The British naval commander, faced with the prospect of being trapped by ice, was threatening to sail home with his fleet.

Wolfe and his men were confident. They were fewer than the French, but what they lacked in numbers they made up in morale and experience. In the boat taking him to the French side Wolfe himself, as though with some premonition of what was about to happen to him, recited Gray's "Elegy in a Country Churchyard." It contained the line "The paths of glory lead but to the grave."

As the small boats carrying the British troops edged along the darkened north bank of the St. Lawrence a French sentry shouted: "what regiment?" A highland officer responded in fluent French: "the Queen's." The boats were allowed to pass. Soon after, they touched the bank close to where Wolfe some days before had spied a zig-zag path up the steep cliff that separated the river from the plain stretching before Quebec city. Twenty-four volunteers leaped out and, grabbing trees and bushes, pulled themselves up the plateau. Hundreds more followed.

The invaders spied a small French encampment. They immediately attacked, captured two of the French soldiers, and put the rest to flight. Hearing the triumphant shouts of his men above, Wolfe and his remaining force disembarked and scaled the cliff by way of the path to join the advance party. As morning broke with clouds and threatening rain, 3500 British troops drew themselves up in battle order on the Plains of Abraham a mile west of Quebec, the center of French power in America.

In the walled city itself, news of the British move provoked great alarm. For many weeks the *Quebecois* had endured bombardment from the British fleet and army. Much of the city was in ruins, although it was packed with refugees from the countryside who jammed into every remaining dwelling and spilled over into the town's hospitals, convents, and public buildings. Worse than the physical devastation and discomfort was the political confusion in the city. The military commander was Louis de Montcalm, a forty-four-year-old veteran of France's wars who had been pulled from retirement to command His Majesty's troops in distant Canada. The civilian leader was Pierre de Rigaud, the Marquis de Vaudreuil, a Canadian-born son of a previous governor of Canada. The two men did not get along, and their lack of rapport would hurt France in the hours ahead.

As news spread of the British success in scaling the heights, the French and Canadians poured out of the town to assemble on the plain outside the walls. Montcalm asked the city commander to send him big guns from the palace battery, but was given only three on the plea that the rest were needed to defend the town itself. Montcalm might have waited for troops from Vaudreuil, but the governor too held back, fearing, apparently, to be part of any defeat while at the same time reserving the right to arrive in time to claim credit for any victory. As his men formed ranks, Montcalm rode back and forth along his lines brandishing his sword and urging his troops to show their mettle for France and for the King.

At 10 a.m. the French, with the white-clad regulars in the center and the Canadians at either end, started forward against the double-ranked British, firing and shouting. The redcoats and highlanders advanced a few yards and then stopped. When the two lines were within forty paces the British commander ordered his men to fire. Two precise volleys rang out like single shots, and then a ragged clatter followed as the men reloaded and fired at will. When the smoke lifted, it was clear that the battle was over. As far as the eye could see, the field was covered with French dead and wounded. The French troops still on their feet had stopped short and were milling around in a confused mob. The British officers now gave the order to charge. The cheering redcoats ran forward with their bayonets poised. The highlanders dashed ahead yelling in Gaelic and brandishing their broadswords. Leading the charge of the Louisburg Grenadiers was Wolfe himself. At that moment of triumph the British general was struck in the chest by a French bullet and was carried to the rear. A few minutes later he died.

By now the French were fleeing pell-mell to the safety of Quebec's walls. Borne along with the human tide was Montcalm, still mounted. Close to the walls a British shot hit him in the thigh and passed along it to lodge in his stomach. The French commander was escorted through the city gate by three soldiers and brought to the military surgeon. But nothing could be done, and he died the next day.

Meanwhile the timid Vaudreuil, despite the urging of his senior officer, refused to move his large remaining force against the exhausted British. When reinforcements arrived under the Chevalier de Levis several days later, it was too late: Montcalm's successor at Quebec had already surrendered the city to Brigadier General James Murray.

Nonetheless, fighting continued for some time before French Canada was completely subdued. In early spring 1760 the French tried to retake Quebec from the British, but were beaten. That summer British troops from three directions descended on Montreal, the last remaining French strong point in Canada. On September 8 Vaudreuil surrendered all of French Canada to the British.

The great war between France and Britain went on officially for three and a half more years before the negotiators at Paris signed a peace treaty in 1763. In reality, it had ended on the cloudy battlefield before Quebec, where both brave commanders surrendered their lives.

Imperial Reform

Treaty of Paris (1763). News of Wolfe's victory deeply affected the North American public. The young hero had given his life to save Protestant America from Catholic France and his sacrifice took on epic proportions. Grateful for the victory and moved by the young general's death, thousands of King George's subjects sang the words to Gray's "Elegy" in taverns all over the colonies.

The French and Indian War as a whole was an invigorating experience for Americans. They had fought well in a score of battles from Canada to the Caribbean. After 1763 they would exhibit a new confidence and a new pride in what they, mere provincials before, could accomplish.

The elimination of France as a major power in North America enhanced this new spirit. For a century New France and then Louisiana, representing absolutism and clericalism, had hung like a sword over Anglo-America, forcing the colonists to acknowledge dependence on the British army and navy. The Treaty of Paris of 1763 changed all this. To Great Britain, which had already won Canada by the surrender of Montreal in 1760, France now relinquished all claims to America east of the Mississippi. Spain, an ally of France, turned over Florida to the British. In compensation for Spanish losses, the French gave Spain New Orleans and all their possessions west of the Mississippi. Now that the most dangerous foreign power had been removed, the colonists were free to reassess their relationship with the mother country.

The British were aware of the possibility of change in the colonial temperament. During the negotiations at Paris the Duke of Bedford spoke for returning Canada to France to prevent Americans from growing too mighty and asserting their independence. Bedford's views were overruled, but in later years there would be those who believed that the conquest of New France had been a mistake. During the fierce debate between the colonies and Britain that preceded independence, the loyalist governor of Massachusetts, Thomas Hutchinson, noted: "Before the peace of 1763 I thought nothing so much to be desired as the cession of Canada. I am now convinced that if it had remained to the French none of the spirit of opposition to the Mother Country would have yet appeared and I think the effects of it worse than all we had to fear from the French or Indians."

Renewed Conflict with Indians. By the war's end, moreover, it had begun to look as if Britain would have to maintain a permanent and expensive military force in America. France was down but not out. Unreconciled to Britain's triumph, the French were reported to be rebuilding their navy in preparation for further war. More immediately, the Indian tribes in the West were becoming a problem. During the war American settlers and Indian traders had flooded into the trans-Appalachian region in the wake of British victories over the French. The newcomers were often unscrupulous. Many plied the Indians with rum and then "bought" their lands for a few cheap goods and rifles and powder. It seemed that these difficulties would become worse once the Americans poured across the mountains in force after 1763. Troops clearly would be needed in the West to hold down the tribes and assure a rational policy of Western development.

Even before the British could formally announce their Western policy the Indian frontier exploded. Indian discontent took the form of the first pan-Indian movement. One of the leaders was the Delaware, Prophet, a visionary and seer who assured his followers that if they rejected the white man's ways, they would regain their former strength and former lands. The other, the Ottawa chief, Pontiac, led his warriors in May 1763 against the British fort at Detroit and came close to taking it. Pontiac's attack commenced a massive Indian uprising all along the Northern frontier; by June only three major British military posts remained.

The British quickly struck back. Two columns went to the relief of the surviving posts. One, led by Colonel Henry Bouquet, forced Pontiac to accept a truce. Soon after, Pontiac's chief allies made peace with the English, and before long Pontiac himself "smoked the calumet" with the white men. During the strife, not all Western frontiersmen had distinguished themselves. On the Pennsylvania frontier a band known as the Paxton Boys had attacked some peaceful Indians and then, marching on Philadelphia with a demand for greater protection, spent their time fighting the colonial assembly instead of the hostile Indians. Benjamin Franklin persuaded them to petition the assembly instead of invading the city.

The End of "Salutary Neglect." The French and Indian War had forced the British government to focus attention on American affairs as never before and the experience had been an eye-opener. As British officials saw it, the Americans had behaved badly. Their illegal trade with the enemy had profited them and made the war more costly in men and money. The war, meanwhile, had burdened Great Britain with huge debt. The mother country had chosen to govern the colonies by an easy and benign policy of "salutary neglect"; now, it was argued, this would have to be replaced by a tighter, more rational, and financially sounder system. Colonists were not unaware of this British perception of them. Spokesmen pointed to heavy local taxation for the repayment of the colonial war debt. Colonists were also prepared to argue that the commercial laws worked to pull wealth from the colonies into Britain. Since the dispute was over money, each side was inclined to feel itself the victim.

The chief advocate of the British position was George Grenville, Chancellor of the Exchequer and King George III's chief minister following the retirement of William Pitt, the great wartime leader. Grenville was a man of limited vision who treated the empire as if it were a business concern. As a contemporary noted, Grenville judged "a national saving of two inches of candle . . . a greater triumph than all Pitt's victories." He soon initiated measures to reduce British expenses and to generate income for the mother country.

Grenville first took aim at policy toward the West and the Indians. To generate orderly settlement and to prevent further Indian wars caused by land-hungry settlers, the Proclamation of 1763 set the limit of white settlement at the crest of the Appalachians. All colonists west of that line must "forthwith . . . remove themselves." British military authorities would now be in charge of all Indian territory west of the mountains; all traders in Indian territory would have to be licensed, and they could trade only at designated points under British military supervision. The Proclamation was soon followed by a flurry of measures designed to raise revenue in America when the colonists refused to provide for their own defense.

The intention of the Revenue Act of 1764, a renewal and revision of the Sugar Act of 1733, was to increase the low receipts of the British customs service in America. The law added a dozen items to the list of "enumerated" American articles that must go first to Britain to be taxed before they could be sent elsewhere. The law also established a new set of taxes for goods imported into the colonies and set up new admiralty courts with power to enforce their collection with the aid of general search warrants called "writs of assistance." The most important change affected the trade between the mainland colonies and the West Indies. Molasses was the chief raw material in the making of rum, a major New England industry. For many years American merchants had relied on the French and Dutch Caribbean islands for this product, which was cheaper there than in the British Caribbean islands. By smuggling, the colonists had evaded the high tax Britain had imposed on foreign-produced molasses. Because the Molasses Act of 1733 imposing a six-pence-a-gallon duty on the foreign product had been uncollectable, the British now cut the duty in half but determined to collect the money.

John Singleton Copley's portrait of Paul Revere remembers him as a silversmith and craftsman. He also cast cannon for the army and designed the state seal still used by Massachusetts. *(Courtesy, Museum of Fine Arts, Boston)*

A second measure of 1764, the Currency Act,

struck at the practice of issuing legal tender paper money. The colonials believed paper to be an indispensable medium of exchange in a chronically coin-poor community. British merchants had long complained, however, that the paper issued under the colonial legal-tender laws was a cheap and flimsy currency. Its use by Americans, especially Southern planters, in payment of their debts to British creditors, amounted to a scaling down of the debt. The right to issue legal tenders had already been forbidden the New England colonies. Now, the prohibition would extend to the middle and Southern colonies as well.

Americans did not take these new measures lightly. The Proclamation threatened the ambitions of land speculators, Indian traders, and would-be settlers in the West alike. For the moment, the reaction was comparatively mild. Americans interested in Western development simply ignored British policy and went ahead with their own plans. As George Washington wrote a fellow land speculator: "any person who . . . neglects the present opportunity of hunting out good Lands and in some measure marking and distinguishing them for his own . . . will never regain it." Reaction to the Revenue and Currency Acts was more vigorous. A Boston town meeting had listened to James Otis's impassioned attack on writs of assistance as violating God's "natural law" (and hence illegal), and condemned the Revenue Act as taxation without representation. A group of Boston merchants, joined by the city's artisans, resolved to boycott several items imported from Britain. By the end of 1764 a limited boycott of British goods had spread to several other colonies.

The Stamp Act Crisis

Trouble awaited the Grenville program. But few people could have anticipated the full extent of American hostility to British policy. Then came the Stamp Act—the first attempt to impose an internal tax on American colonists, a tax on their activities within their own localities. Previous taxes had been external; they had applied to American commerce with the outside world.

Grenville must have realized the danger in the new policy, for when he asked for a tax on colonial documents and other articles that would apply directly to transactions in America rather than to overseas trade, he promised to consider other means of raising revenue in the colonies if Americans objected. But he gave the colonial legislatures little time to respond and when their agents in London tried to induce Grenville to withdraw the stamp act tax proposal he refused.

In February 1765 the Chancellor of the Exchequer introduced the fatal measure to a poorly attended session of the House of Commons. The debate, though brief, was significant as an expression of the different views of the colonies that were then current among Englishmen.

Speaking for Grenville, Charles ("Champagne Charlie") Townshend gave voice to a widespread condescension toward Americans that would poison relations between the two peoples. Townshend called Americans "children planted by our care." They had been "nourished up" by British "indulgence" and protected by British arms. Would "they grudge to contribute their mite" to relieve the British people from "the heavy burdens" they suffered?

Townshend's remarks offended Colonel Isaac Barré, an officer who had fought under Wolfe and unlike other upper-class Englishmen argued for relaxing the bonds of empire. Townshend was seriously mistaken, Barré declared. The Americans had been planted not by British care, but rather by British oppression which had driven so many refugees to the New World. Nor were they nurtured by British indulgence. Rather they "grew by your . . . neglect of 'em." Indeed, these "sons of liberty" had suffered under greedy British officials for many years. Nor had they been protected by British arms; they had nobly fought for themselves.

Americans would cheer Barré's words, and "patriot" organizations would soon adopt "Sons of Liberty" as their name. But Parliament was unmoved. On March 22, 1765, it passed the Stamp Act, taxing newspapers, almanacs, pamphlets, legal documents, insurance policies, dice, playing cards, and other items. These taxes would be paid in the form of a stamp, purchasable from collectors to be chosen from among Americans residing in the colonies, and placed on the specified documents. Grenville expected

The TIMES are Dreadful, Difmal Doleful Dolorous, and DOLLAR-LESS.

An Emblem of the Effects of the STAMP. O! the fatal Stamp.

Adieu, Adieu to the LIBERTY of the PRESS.

Thurſday, *October* 31, 1765. THE NUMB. 1195.

PENNSYLVANIA JOURNAL; AND WEEKLY ADVERTISER.

EXPIRING: In Hopes of a Reſurrection to LIFE again.

I AM ſorry to be obliged to acquaint my Readers, that as The STAMP-ACT, is fear'd to be obligatory upon us after the *First of November* enſuing, (the *fatal To-morrow*) the Publiſher of this Paper unable to bear the Burthen, has thought it expedient TO STOP a while, in order to deliberate, whether any Methods can be found to elude the Chains forged for us, and eſcape the inſupportable Slavery; which it is hoped, from the laſt Repreſentations now made againſt that Act, may be effected. Mean while, I muſt earneſtly Requeſt every Individual of my Subſcribers, many of whom have been long behind Hand, that they would immediately Diſcharge their reſpective Arrears, that I may be able, not only to ſupport myſelf during the Interval, but be better prepared to proceed again with this Paper, whenever an opening for that Purpoſe appears, which I hope will be ſoon.

WILLIAM BRADFORD.

Reaction to the Stamp Act by the *Pennsylvania Journal*, "The Times are Dreadful, Dismal, Doleful, Dolorous and Dollar-Less," reflected the widespread anger among the colonists.

the law to raise £60,000 of the £300,000 needed to maintain the British military establishment in North America.

News of the Stamp Act's passage reached America in mid-April. Consternation was immediate and almost universal. By this "single stroke," wrote the conservative jurist William Smith of New York, Britain had "lost . . . the affection of all her colonies." In the Virginia House of Burgesses at Williamsburg the young lawyer Patrick Henry denounced George III as a tyrant and implied that like all tyrants he might have to be overthrown. Although some conservatives reproached Henry for his rash remarks, the delegates at Williamsburg adopted resolutions attacking the Act and declaring that the right to tax rested in the people themselves or their chosen representatives. Soon almost all the other colonies had adopted similar resolutions. When the Massachusetts General Court proposed that representatives of all the colonies meet in New York in October to consider joint action against the detested measure, most of the colonies quickly accepted the invitation.

Violence

By the time the Stamp Act Congress assembled, Americans had resorted to more than words to express their indignation.

Sons of Liberty. In Boston the newly formed Sons of Liberty hanged in effigy the man who was to be the new tax commissioner, Andrew Oliver. Oliver was a brother-in-law of Lieutenant Governor Andrew Hutchinson, a descendant of the Anne Hutchinson who had clashed with the Puritan ministers of Massachusetts Bay more than a century earlier. Later a mob tore down a house that Oliver had allegedly built to serve as his tax office. They next marched on Oliver's home and broke all the windows. The following day a delegation of respectable citizens called on Oliver and asked him to resign his tax commission. Although he had not yet received either official confirmation of his appointment or his stamps, the terrified Oliver agreed to write to England declining his commission.

The Boston Sons of Liberty next attacked the house of William Story, deputy register of the admiralty court, smashed down the doors, and burned Story's public and private papers. Another contingent sacked the home of the comptroller of customs, carried away his records, and pillaged his wine cellar. A few days later a mob targeted Hutchinson's own home. They battered down the walls, burned the furniture, destroyed the library, tore windows and doors from their frames, and cut down the trees in the Hutchinson yard. They also stole £900 in cash, and walked off with the family silver. Hutchinson, in fact, had opposed both the Revenue Act and the Stamp Act.

The mob's fury appalled even such committed Boston patriots as John Adams and Josiah Quincy. The Boston town meeting condemned the rioting, and the authorities issued a warrant for the arrest of the Sons of Liberty leader, Ebenezer McIntosh.

In Newport, Rhode Island, a mob burned and sacked the homes of "Tory" defenders of British power and forced the Stamp Act collector to resign. Connecticut patriots conducted a mock trial of stamp distributors. New York Sons of Liberty vented their fury on the house of the British military commander. In the words of one observer of the attack, "The Beds they cut open, and threw the Feathers abroad, broke all the Glasses, China, Tables, Chairs, Desks, Trucks, Chests." They then started a fire, threw all the remaining furnishings into it, "drank or destroyed all the Liquor," and left the major's garden in ruins. In Charleston, capital of South Carolina, a mob attacked the house of the prominent merchant Henry Laurens, whom they suspected of being the future stamp collector. Only Laurens's bold denials kept the irate patriots from doing harm to him and his property.

So it went from colony to colony. Everywhere Tories were intimidated, and collectors forced to surrender their commissions. When the stamps finally arrived, there was no one to sell them or to see that they were affixed to the designated documents.

Mobs like those that controlled the streets during the Stamp Act crisis would appear in later confrontations between colonists and the British government. They were, in fact, a feature of eighteenth-century politics. Across the Atlantic, the London mob was a menacing presence to the government. And by the end of the eighteenth century, the Paris mobs of the French Revolution would enter history.

Stamp Act Congress. In early October 1765, twenty-seven delegates from nine colonies convened in New York to consider united action against the detested law. This Stamp Act Congress was relatively conservative, but its Declaration of Rights and Grievances effectively summed up most of the colonists' complaints. Taxation, the Declaration asserted, could be imposed only by the people's consent, "given personally, or by their representatives." Moreover, trial by jury, ignored by the new admiralty courts, was an inherent right of Englishmen. The Stamp Act as well as the other recent measures restricting American commerce, the Congress declared, must be repealed.

Demonstrations erupted throughout the colonies in response to "taxation without representation." In New England, Tories were hanged in effigy.

Far more effective than the words of the Stamp Act Congress were the actions of businessmen in the major American port cities. Two hundred New York merchants agreed to make all new orders for British goods contingent on repeal of the Stamp Act. They were joined by the traders of Philadelphia, Boston, Salem, and other ports. Meanwhile, November 1, the date when the Act was supposed to take effect, rolled around. For a while business was disrupted, since very little could be done legally without the stamps. Slowly it resumed without them. The law was dead.

The British government could not ignore the American response to the Stamp Act. Some Englishmen were outraged at American defiance. Dr. Samuel Johnson, the critic, diarist, and lexicographer, called the opponents of the Act "incendiaries" and "fractious demagogues." But others, particularly merchants who found their American business dwindling, sympathized with the Americans and bombarded Parliament with petitions for repeal of the measure. In Manchester, Leeds, Nottingham, and other English industrial towns thousands of workingmen lost their jobs as the workshops and mills dependent on the American market slowed and then stopped.

A teapot celebrating Parliament's repeal of the Stamp Act in March 1766. *(Courtesy, Essex Institute, Salem, Massachusetts)*

The man who now had to face the uproar was the Marquis of Rockingham, who had succeeded Grenville as prime minister in July 1765. Rockingham's group drew its support largely from the merchants and manufacturers and was particularly sensitive to their plight. Leading the battle for repeal in Parliament was William Pitt, the great wartime prime minister. Pitt eloquently defended the colonists' rights. "The Americans," he declared, "are the sons, not the bastards of England." The Stamp Act must "be REPEALED ABSOLUTELY, TOTALLY, IMMEDIATELY. . . ." In March 1766 Parliament complied. But at the same time, to satisfy its more conservative members, it passed the so-called Declaratory Act, asserting its power to make laws binding the American colonies "in all cases whatsoever."

Few Americans took note of the Declaratory Act amid general rejoicing at the end of the detested stamp tax. Merchants immediately abandoned their nonimportation agreements and placed large orders with British suppliers. Several towns voted to erect statues to Pitt. The ordinary people greeted the news with special exuberance, ringing church bells, placing lighted candles in their windows, and firing off guns. The Boston Sons of Liberty built "a magnificent pyramid, illuminated with 280 Lamps," on Boston Common. Crowning the pile was a box of fireworks which went off at dusk producing a magnificent effect.

In the words of a crude popular song, written for the great occasion:

> In spite of each parasite, each cringing
> slave,
> Each cautious dastard, each oppressive
> knave,
> Each gibing ass, that reptile of an hour,
> The supercilious pimp of abject slaves in
> power,
> We are met to celebrate in festive mirth,
> The day that gave our freedom second
> birth,
> That tells us, British Grenville never more
> Shall dare usurp unjust, illegal power,
> Or threaten America's free sons with
> chains,
> While the least spark of ancient fire
> remains.

Not Yet Americans. The colonial protest over the Stamp Act indicates little thought of denying that Parliament had the right to legislate for the empire. A reason why spokesmen for the protest seemed willing to acknowledge the legitimacy of external taxes in the form of duties on trade with foreign nations was that such taxes could be defined not as taxation at all but as a way of regulating trade, which colonists in 1765 were still willing to perceive as within the authority of Parliament. That many Americans were quite prepared to evade those duties is another matter.

Noteworthy also is that the protesters proudly identified themselves as British, entitled to the right of Englishmen to be free of any taxation except such as they had consented to. British history provided sources for the distinction that colonists continued at least for a short time to make between taxation, which must be by the consent of those being taxed, and laws that did not require popular consent. In past centuries English monarchs had needed money for essentially private projects, such as wars on foreign soil for the extension of their personal domains. For these and other objectives they would call Parliaments representing the various classes of the kingdom and ask for money to be raised by taxes. And so the idea formed that taxes are a gift from the people to the sovereign, and as a gift must of course be given freely rather than by coercion. Law, on the other hand, is according to this theory an act of sovereignty, an expression of the will of the monarchy, and can apply even to a population that has not agreed to it. Actually, by the eighteenth century the real power to make law in Britain was almost wholly in the hands of Parliament, and so the distinction was nearly irrelevant there. But the colonies were in another situation. They had assemblies, elected by a considerable portion of the people, that made local laws and raised local taxes.

Even angry colonists, then, still saw themselves as part of the empire, subjects of the king, honoring the authority of Parliament, sharing in the rights that belonged to the British nation and history. But recent events had made them touchy; they were developing a habit of asking large questions about the legitimacy of the actions of the British government; and they had gained experience in confronting Great Britain not as Virginians or people of Massachusetts but as united colonists, as Americans. Soon political theorists in the colonies would be abandoning the distinction between internal and external taxation, denying the validity of both. Then they would question the thesis that Parliament had the right to legislate for the colonies. And that would leave them with little to accept in the empire as it then existed.

Blunder Again

Americans did not rejoice for long. In 1765 Parliament, in an attempt to reduce expenses associated with the colonies' defense, passed the Quartering Act. It required the colonies to provide the king's troops with barracks and furnish them with "candles, firing, bedding, cooking utensils, salt and vinegar, and five pints of small beer or cider, or a gill of rum per man, per diem." For a year or two the colonies complied. Then, in 1767, the New York assembly, believing the colony overburdened, refused. In retaliation, Parliament suspended all acts of the New York provincial legislature until it should vote money for the army.

Townshend Duties. Many British leaders still wanted colonials to pay a larger share of colonial administrative and military costs. In early 1767, Charles Townshend, chancellor of the exchequer in yet another ministry, unveiled his program. The colonies had successfully resisted the Stamp Act, which had taxed their internal business without their consent. But since the colonials themselves had not yet challenged Parliament's right to tax their external commerce, Parliament might still impose an import tax. Capitalizing therefore on the distinction between "internal" and "external" taxation, Townshend proposed taxing a wide range of colonial imports including glass, paper, lead, and tea. These duties, he argued, would raise badly needed funds and also teach the disruptive colonials that Parliament had the authority to tax them. He further proposed creation of a new American customs service as well as a crackdown on New York's continually defiant assembly. After Parliament enacted all these potentially explosive measures, the ministry indicated its determination to enforce the trade laws. It appointed several unpopular officials to the new customs board and established the body's headquarters in Boston, the center of opposition to stricter commercial regulation.

In some areas, enforcement of commercial

regulations broke down almost completely. A Boston ship's captain, Daniel Malcolm, drew a pistol on two revenue agents searching for illegal wine in his basement. Returning with the sheriff and a search warrant, the agents discovered the captain's house surrounded by a crowd of his friends, and the harried sheriff avoided a direct confrontation only by stalling for time until the search warrant expired. After the disgusted officials departed, Captain Malcom treated his protectors to buckets of smuggled wine. Such cases were not infrequent. Investigating past enforcement, Townshend's customs board discovered only six seizures and one smuggling conviction in all of New England during two and one half years. Mobs had rescued three of the seized ships, and colonial juries had acquitted two other defendants. Initially the new customs officials fared little better, enforcing restrictions only enough to enrage colonial merchants. The same Captain Malcom brought an entire load of illegal wine into Boston on small boats during the night and then boldly sailed his empty ship into port the next day. The vessel's water line clearly revealed his subterfuge, but enraged customs officers could find no Bostonian who would testify against him. Malcom's friend and fellow smuggler, John Hancock, was less fortunate; the customs board seized his ship *Liberty* in 1768. But the violent popular reaction forced most of the board's members temporarily to flee the city.

Colonists feared that authority was being shifted across the Atlantic to London. Americans thinking of settling in the West or of speculating in Western lands chafed at the Proclamation line as the limit of settlement. Yeoman farmers who cherished the relatively egalitarian social and economic system of America worried that the tightening of empire would bring feudal privilege and a more aristocratic society. In Puritan New England laymen and Congregational clergymen worried that the new bonds of imperial control implied Anglican bishops for America.

Another Boycott. Americans were therefore sensitive about any further extension of British power, and an outcry greeted the Townshend Duties. That the duties did not constitute an internal tax made slight difference. This time, though, leading merchants and lawyers kept dissent under control. In each colony, the Sons of Liberty and the merchants adopted strict non-importation agreements. In South Carolina, the legislature resolved that until the colonies were restored to their former freedom by repeal of the Townshend Duties the people of the colony would encourage the use of American manufactures and refuse to import any of the manufactures of Great Britain. South Carolinians would practice the "utmost economy in our persons, houses, and furniture, particularly that we will give no mourning, or gloves, or scarves at funerals."

Colonial leaders fully recognized that they could not expect to enforce non-importation without the fullest possible cooperation of all members of society, notably women. For women, in accordance with their role as suppliers of food to their families, had become the principal purchasers of those foods and beverages that were not produced by the household. Numerous newspaper writers vehemently urged women to refrain patriotically from purchasing tea. And many women apparently welcomed this appeal to contribute to the defense of colonial interests. Certainly non-importation could not have been as successful as it was without their cooperation. In 1774 John Adams would encounter a landlady who refused to serve him any tea even though he had requested smuggled tea on which no duties had been paid.

By early 1769 non-importation was in force in every colony. Some Americans were either still pro-British or so lukewarm toward the patriot cause that they were unwilling to deprive themselves of British goods to promote it. Still, the boycott was effective. And it brought American leaders together to an even greater extent than the Stamp Act crisis. It was at this time that the General Court of Massachusetts initiated a practice of sending "circular letters" among the various colonial legislatures, laying out British misdeeds and suggesting united continental action to counter them.

The Townshend Duties also encouraged a great deal of pamphleteering advocating a new imperial relationship with more freedom for the colonists—or, rather, with the liberties of Englishmen that they claimed already to possess by right. The most effective and eloquent of these statements was John Dickinson's *Letters from a Farmer in Pennsylvania* (1768). Posing as a simple Pennsylvania yeoman, Dickinson cautioned against violence and expressed an affection for "mother Britain" that foreshadowed his later refusal to sign the Declaration of Independence. But on the question of British taxation he was adamant. "Let these words be indelibly impressed on our minds," he concluded "—that we cannot be free without being secure in our property—that we cannot be secure in our property if without our consent others may as by right take it away—that taxes imposed on us by Parliament do thus take it away." And Dickinson meant all taxation, taxes on imports as well as on internal business.

Lord North. In June 1768 a British customs official was locked into the cabin of John Hancock's sloop *Liberty* while the crew unloaded untaxed madeira wine. When customs officials promptly seized the vessel, patriots forced them to flee to the British garrison at Castle William. Royal officials reacted angrily at this latest instance of mob defiance. They ordered the governor of Massachusetts to demand that the General Court either rescind its circular letter attacking British policy or face dissolution. Instead, the legislature asked that Governor Bernard be recalled. Bernard in turn called on British authorities for troops to restore order in unruly Boston and prevent a repetition of the *Liberty* incident. The new British prime minister, Lord Frederick North, ordered two regiments of redcoats from Ireland to the rebellious Massachusetts capital.

Meanwhile, despite the tough line they were taking, North and his colleagues were having second thoughts about the Townshend Duties. Widely evaded, they brought in virtually no revenue. Particularly galling was the smuggling of untaxed Dutch tea into the colonies. And non-importation agreements had reduced annual exports to America from £42.4 million in 1768 to £41.6 million in 1769. The British government was in a quandary: repealing the duties would end non-importation, but it would also be the second time the British government had backed down.

In the end, the North ministry yielded to American pressure, but in a grudging and halfhearted way that only highlighted British weakness without calling forth American gratitude. In 1770 Parliament allowed the Quartering Act to expire and rescinded the taxes on glass, paper, and painters' colors; it also reduced the tea tax from twelve to three pence a pound, but did not repeal it.

This partial repeal ended the boycott. It did little to end resentment of Britain—as one American merchant remarked about the repeal: "Doing things by Halves of all others [was] the worst Method." Many fundamental disagreements with Britain persisted. The whole question of the constitutional relationship between mother country and colonies was still unsettled. What body, colonists asked, was the ultimate source of authority in America, the colonial legislatures or Parliament? By now some colonists were advocating an American relationship with Great Britain resembling that of the later British dominions within the British Commonwealth: the King of England would also be King of Massachusetts, New York, Virginia, and so forth, but each American colony would be autonomous in all its domestic affairs. Few, if any, as yet endorsed complete independence. Americans remained proud of their British heritage and of the rights of "free-born Britons," and even the most ardent patriots still insisted that they merely wished to preserve these rights from the arrogant usurpers who had gathered around the king. Three years later, however, a further reduction of the tea tax combined with new enforcement efforts generated a fresh challenge to the British Empire.

The Boston Massacre

Quartering British Troops. In the months following repeal of the Townshend Duties, resentment toward Britain remained particularly strong in Boston. Aside from the long-standing grievances the Boston townspeople shared with other communities, there was the question of the recently arrived troops. Even when, as in the late war with France, professional soldiers had come to protect the civilian population from an enemy, they had been an affliction. How much worse would they be now, when they were coming to intimidate the Americans?

Before the British regiments arrived, the Boston town meeting called upon the people of the city to arm themselves, and demanded that the governor call a meeting of the General Court, which he had dissolved in June. When Bernard refused, the patriot leaders called an assembly of the colony's towns as a substitute for the General Court. This "convention" helped to acquaint the citizens of smaller communities with the view of the radical leaders of the capital, and it demonstrated that John Hancock, John Adams, his cousin Samuel Adams, an effective

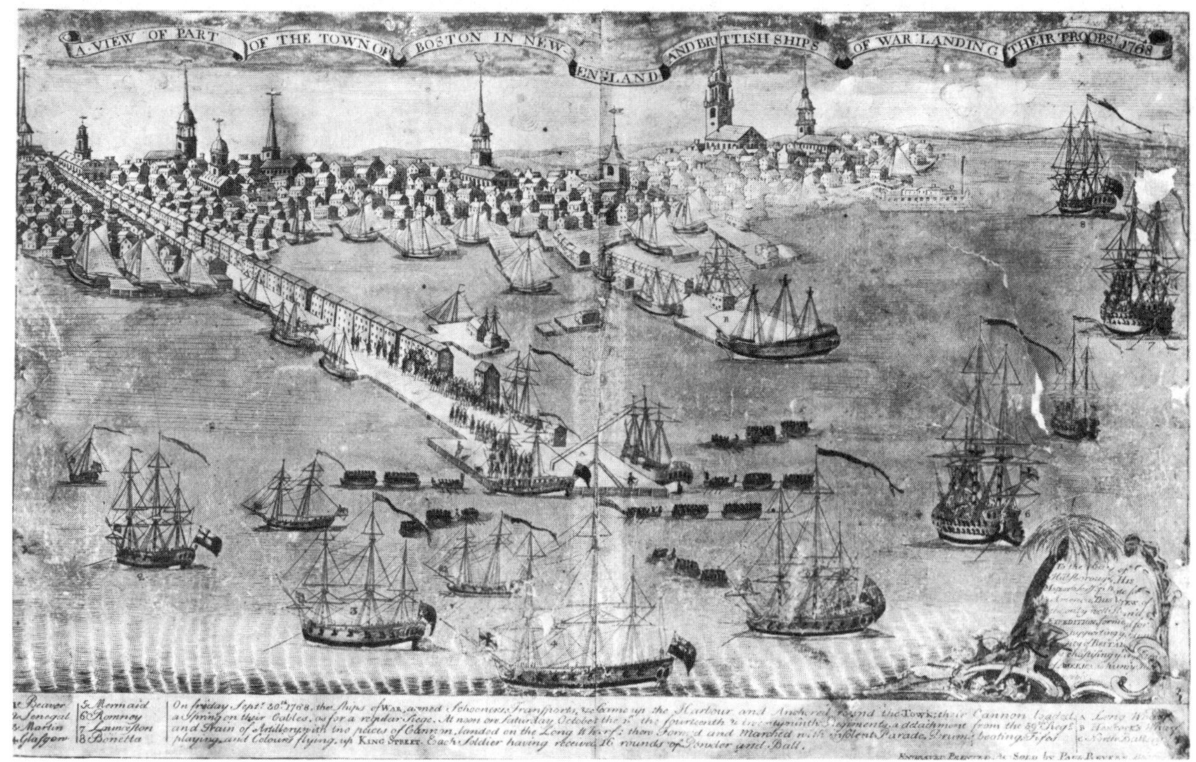

Engraving by Paul Revere depicting Friday, September 30th, 1768, when British "Ships of War, armed Schooners, Transports, etc., came up the Harbour and Anchored round the Town; their Cannon loaded." *(Courtesy, The I. N. Phelps Stokes Collection, The New York Public Library)*

writer of popular political literature, and the rest spoke for a large part of the colony's yeomanry, not just for the merchants and artisans of the metropolis.

The day the convention adjourned, the British troops dispatched by North arrived in Boston harbor, protected by guns of British men-of-war. While the city's dubious citizens looked on, the soldiers debarked at the Long Wharf and marched up King Street to the music of drums and fifes. It was a moving sight, even for the most ardent patriots. The men's red tunics, criss-crossed by white straps and topped by black three-cornered hats, were far more colorful than modern uniforms. Towering over the regular troops were the grenadiers, chosen for their height, a feature emphasized by their tall, mitre-shaped bearskin caps. The grenadier officers wore crimson sashes and carried swords at their sides.

Boston's pleasure at the bright display soon faded, however, and the troops found it no pleasure to be quartered among a hostile populace. While their officers had no difficulty finding good lodgings with wealthy Tories, the troops were refused barracks by the city council, and had to be scattered around the town at whatever empty buildings, generally workshops and warehouses, the British commander could rent.

"Lobsterbacks." Before long, the patriots' worst fears were realized. The bored troops turned for solace to Boston's cheap rum and loose women. To get money for their dissipations, many engaged in petty theft. Inevitably they got into fights, especially with sailors in the local taverns. When winter came many soldiers deserted, and although the citizens of the Massachusetts countryside had little reason to love the "lobsterbacks," they also refused to help the military authorities return them to duty. The colonists saw the redcoats as an army of occupation.

On Friday, March 2, 1770, a civilian ropemaker, William Green, asked a soldier passing by, Patrick Walker of the Twenty-ninth Regiment, if he wanted work. Such part-time jobs were permitted to off-duty soldiers, and Walker said yes. Green responded: "Then go clean my shithouse." Walker retorted in kind and left, threatening to come back with some friends. Soon afterward he appeared with forty of his mates, led by a tall, black regimental drummer. The soldiers, armed with clubs, sailed into Green and his friends, who defended themselves with sticks. When other civilians joined in, the soldiers retreated.

All that weekend rumors circulated that the soldiers intended revenge. And so they did. On the night of Monday the 5th, bands both of soldiers and of citizens roved the icy streets of Boston looking for trouble. It came at Private White's sentry post adjacent to the Custom House, when a wigmaker's apprentice baited White until the sentry hit him with the butt of his gun. When the apprentice fled, a British sergeant pursued him, brandishing his musket.

News of the fight spread quickly, and a half-dozen young men descended on the sentry post screaming "Lousy rascal! Lobster son of bitch!" Soon the swelling crowd pelted White with snowballs and jagged chunks of ice, crying "Kill him, kill him, knock him down." Finally Captain Thomas Preston, officer of the day, decided he must save White even at the risk of a serious confrontation. With six grenadiers he marched on the beleaguered sentry post and surrounded White. But with angry civilians pressing on him from every direction, Preston now found that he could not return to the safety of the barracks. He tried to persuade the crowd to disperse, but they responded by daring the soldiers to shoot. At this point someone struck one of the redcoats with a club, knocking him off his feet. The soldier fired, forcing the crowd back. Now another British soldier fired, this time hitting Sam Gray in the head. A third pulled the trigger of his musket and hit Crispus Attucks, a black man, in the chest. By the time the shooting stopped, three Bostonians lay dead and others were mortally wounded.

The whole city might then and there have erupted in a bloody rebellion. But Lieutenant Governor Hutchinson intervened, and by promising a quick investigation and punishment of

"The Bloody Massacre perpetrated in King Street, Boston on March 5th, 1770, by a party of the 29th Reg [iment]." Engrav'd, Printed and Sold by Paul Revere, Boston.

the guilty parties prevented a blow-up. That morning, Preston and his men were arrested and confined to jail pending trial. The trial itself was conducted with propriety and fairness. Captain Preston hired as counsel two prominent Boston patriots, John Adams and Josiah Quincy, who took the case out of a combined concern for the colony's and their own good names. Patriots wished to avoid any suspicion that the Massachusetts courts would not give the accused a fair trial.

In the end, Preston and his men were acquitted. Adams demolished the charge that Preston had given the order to fire. He and Quincy appealed for fairness. "The eyes of all are upon you," Quincy told the jurors. It is "of high importance to your country, that nothing should appear on this trial to impeach our justice or stain our humanity." The two defense lawyers called witnesses who demonstrated that the soldiers had been taunted and abused beyond bearing. Some soldiers were convicted of manslaughter but punishments were light. Massachusetts justice had been vindicated.

The trial eased angers in Boston and the colonies as a whole. It was followed by a period of relative calm in relations between Britain and the colonies. During these months the non-importation agreements totally collapsed, despite the attempts of more radical patriots to continue them until tea too was exempted from duty. Actually, little had happened to settle fundamental differences, but for a time both Americans and Englishmen chose to believe that reason had prevailed.

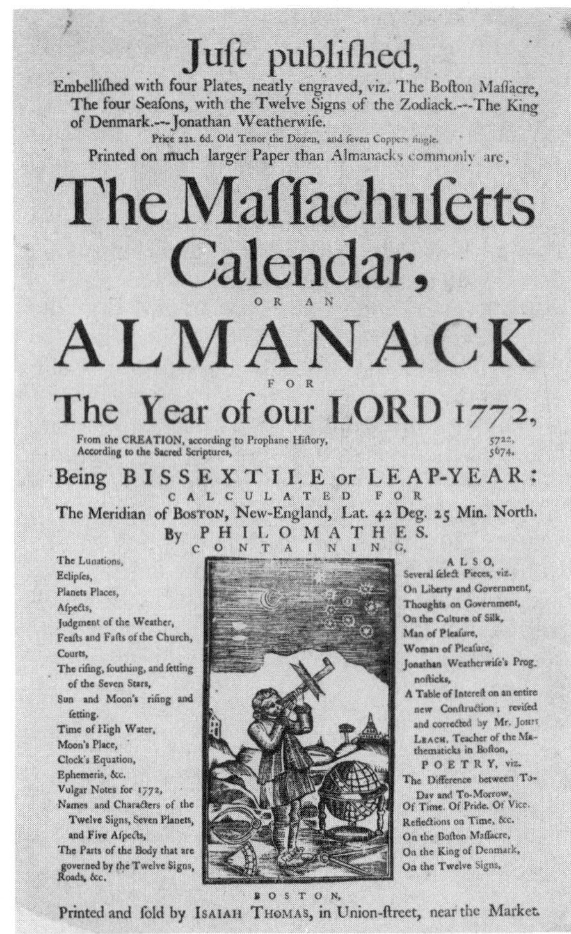

Juſt publiſhed,

Embelliſhed with four Plates, neatly engraved, viz. The Boſton Maſſacre, The four Seaſons, with the Twelve Signs of the Zodiack.---The King of Denmark.---Jonathan Weatherwiſe.

Price 22s. 6d. Old Tenor the Dozen, and ſeven Coppers ſingle.

Printed on much larger Paper than Almanacks commonly are,

The Maſſachuſetts Calendar,

OR AN

ALMANACK

FOR

The Year of our LORD 1772,

From the CREATION, according to Prophane Hiſtory, 5722,
According to the Sacred Scriptures, 5674.

Being BISSEXTILE or LEAP-YEAR:

CALCULATED FOR

The Meridian of BOSTON, New-England, Lat. 42 Deg. 25 Min. North.

By PHILOMATHES.

CONTAINING,

The Lunations,
Eclipſes,
Planets Places,
Aſpects,
Judgment of the Weather,
Feaſts and Faſts of the Church,
Courts,
The riſing, ſouthing, and ſetting of the Seven Stars,
Sun and Moon's riſing and ſetting.
Time of High Water,
Moon's Place,
Clock's Equation,
Ephemeris, &c.
Vulgar Notes for 1772,
Names and Characters of the Twelve Signs, Seven Planets, and Five Aſpects,
The Parts of the Body that are governed by the Twelve Signs,
Roads, &c.

ALSO,
Several ſelect Pieces, viz.
On Liberty and Government,
Thoughts on Government,
On the Culture of Silk,
Man of Pleaſure,
Woman of Pleaſure,
Jonathan Weatherwiſe's Prognoſticks,
A Table of Intereſt on an entire new Conſtruction; reviſed and corrected by Mr. JOHN LEACH, Teacher of the Mathematicks in Boſton,
POETRY, viz.
The Difference between To-Day and To-Morrow,
Of Time. Of Pride. Of Vice.
Reflections on Time, &c.
On the Boſton Maſſacre,
On the King of Denmark,
On the Twelve Signs,

BOSTON,

Printed and ſold by ISAIAH THOMAS, in Union-ſtreet, near the Market.

The Massachusetts Calendar or an Almanack **of 1772 included "reflections" on worldly affairs—the Boston Massacre—as well as other-worldly concerns—the signs of the Zodiac.** *(Courtesy, American Antiquarian Society)*

The *Gaspée* Affair

Then in June 1772 came the *Gaspée* affair. Rhode Island, one of the two self-governing colonies (Connecticut was the other), had long been notorious for ignoring imperial trade laws. For years, its many coves and inlets had sheltered smugglers, who defied the customs authorities with impunity. To stop the traffic, the British authorities finally dispatched the ship *Gaspée* to Narragansett Bay. Tricky tides ran the ship onto a sandbar near Providence. That night a band of Rhode Island Sons of Liberty boarded the stranded *Gaspée*, overwhelmed its captain and crew, and burned the vessel to the waterline.

The British were outraged. Civilians had attacked one of the King's naval vessels in performance of its lawful duties. British authorities immediately appointed a commission of inquiry, with power to send suspects to England for trial. The commission—stymied by the refusal of witnesses to testify against the culprits, many of them substantial citizens of the colony—adjourned without fulfilling its mission.

The *Gaspée* affair had important consequences. British officials concluded that the patriots would stop at nothing, and resolved to take a harder line. The patriots themselves were angered by the authorities' intention to drag men off to England to stand trial for crimes committed in America. It violated one of the elementary "rights of Englishmen," and they determined to prevent it from taking place.

The instrument of this newly revived patriotic spirit was the committees of correspondence, consisting of men in each colony who dedicated themselves to sending and receiving communications of mutual concern. Before long, these men began to form a network of responsible patriots who would remain leaders of the struggle against Britain for the next decade.

The Boston Tea Party

The East India Company. Another brief period of calm followed the *Gaspée* affair. Then came swift events that ripped apart the old empire. The shock came from an unexpected source. In 1773 the East India Company was on the verge of financial collapse. Since the seventeenth century the company had exploited India as its private corporate enterprise. Many company officials had become rich through bribery and special privileges, but the company itself had suffered. One of its few remaining assets, seventeen million pounds of tea held in its London warehouses, remained unsold because of the American boycott, and also because heavy

---

THE TEA TAX

We are used to thinking of revolutions as events of grim slogans and ideological absolutes. This ballad suggests that Americans could perceive political events, even revolutionary events, with shrewdness, lightness, and humor. The song was written some years after the event.

And t'other day we Yankee folks were mad about the taxes,
And so we went, like Indians dress'd, to split Tea chests with axes,
I mean, 'twas done in seventy-five, an' we were real gritty,
The Mayor he would have led the gang, but Boston warn't a City.

Ye see Yankees didn't care a pin for wealth or booty,
And so in State street we agreed we'd never pay the duty,
That is, in State street 'twould have been, but 'twas King street, they call'd it then,
And tax on Tea, it was so bad, the women wouldn't scald it then.

To Charlestown Bridge we all went down to see the thing corrected,
That is, we would have gone there, but the Bridge it warn't erected;
The Tea perhaps was very good, Bohea, Schouchong or Hyson,
But drinking Tea it warn't the rage, the duty made it poison.

And then we went aboard the ships, our vengeance to administer,
And didn't car a tarnal curse, for any King or minister;
We made a plaguy mess o'Tea, in one of the biggest dishes,
I mean, we steeped it in the Sea, and treated all the fishes.

And then you see, we were all found out, a thing we hadn't dreaded,
The leaders were to London sent and instantly beheaded,
That is, I mean, they would have been if ever they'd been taken,
But the leaders they were never cotch'd, and so they saved their bacon.

Now Heaven bless the President and all this goodly nation,
And doubly bless our Boston Mayor and all the corporation;
And may all those who are our foes, or at our praise have falter'd,
Soon have a change, that is, I mean many all of 'em get haltered.

---

taxes made it too expensive in Britain itself. Why not, Lord North asked, drastically reduce the English tax? With only three pence per pound to be paid on arrival in America, the tea would become so cheap that it would undersell smuggled Dutch tea. The tea would sell widely and the East India Company would be saved from ruin. This plan received legislative form in the Tea Act of 1773.

What North did not foresee was that Americans would perceive this scheme as an insulting bribe. To make matters worse, he consigned the East India Company tea exclusively to Tory merchants who favored British policies and obeyed the trade laws. The British government, the colonists decided, was clearly determined to destroy economically those whom it disliked. If tea, why not wine, spices, and other goods, until all those who resisted British oppression had been forced into bankruptcy?

A wiser leader would have seen the consequences of the Tea Act. But North, though witty and energetic, was a hard-liner on America who had supported the Stamp Act and opposed its repeal, and had endorsed the Townshend Duties. Such a man could not have anticipated what would now take place.

News of the new British affront enraged Americans. In New York City, most of the merchants resolved that the tea would not be sold, and local Tories feared mob violence when the tea was nonetheless put on sale. The patriot citizens of Philadelphia met and adopted resolutions declaring that since "the duty imposed by Parliament upon tea landed in America is a tax on the Americans, or levying contributions on them without their consent, it is the duty of every American to oppose this attempt." Along the Delaware River, ship pilots learned that anyone who helped guide tea-carrying vessels into port would be tarred and feathered. In Charleston, patriot pressure also frightened off tea importers. But, as usual, Boston responded more violently than any other town.

Governor Hutchinson warned the British authorities soon after the Tea Act passed that "at and near Boston the people seem regardless of all consequences. To enforce the Act appears beyond all comparison more difficult than I ever before imagined." If Hutchinson had allowed this perception to guide him, disaster might have been avoided. But, though he was American born, his Tory prejudices blinded him, and when three tea-carrying cargo ships arrived in Boston harbor he determined that they must unload, come what may.

The Boston Tea Party. Hutchinson had accurately judged his fellow Bostonians. On the evening of December 16, 1773, on a signal from Sam Adams at the close of a town meeting, a band of men disguised as Mohawk Indians rushed down Milk Street to Griffin's Wharf. Three companies of these "Indians" rowed out to the anchored tea ships, boarded them, split open the tea chests, and dumped their massive contents into the waters of the harbor. Their mission accomplished, the men quickly and quietly dispersed.

The British saw the Boston Tea party as an outrage and they determined not to let it go unpunished. In Parliament William Pitt and the eloquent Irish member Edmund Burke warned that punitive measures would lead to revolt. Burke urged the government to let Americans tax themselves, and not worry about whether they were legally required to obey Parliament. But the Burkes and the Pitts were a minority. Other politically influential Englishmen believed, as one expressed it, "that the town of Boston ought to be knocked about their ears and destroyed."

Determined to prevent "the haughty American Republicans" from ending all parliamentary control, North introduced the Boston Port Bill. Until Massachusetts had paid for the tea destroyed, a naval force would close Boston Harbor to shipping. Troops withdrawn from the town to Castle William following the Boston Massacre would reenter the city.

Fury in Boston itself was predictable, but indignation swept the colonies. Messages of sympathy for Boston's plight poured in from every colony. In Virginia, George Washington urged his fellow patriots to support the Bostonians. We must not "suffer ourselves to be sacrificed by piece meals," he wrote. The Virginia House of Burgesses convened in the Raleigh Tavern in Williamsburg after the Tory governor refused to let it sit at the capitol, and there it called for a continental congress to meet to consider united action. Similar calls came from New York, Providence, and Philadelphia. Everywhere Americans recognized that a final crisis had been reached, and in North Carolina patriot groups began to arm and drill in preparation for combat.

The closing of the port of Boston was the first in a series of parliamentary measures of 1774, known collectively as the Coercive or Intolerable Acts. The Administration of Justice Act declared that if any royal official were sued for carrying out his official duties, he could have his trial transferred out of unfriendly Massachusetts to Britain, where he would face a more favorable jury. The Massachusetts Government Act struck a severe blow at self-government by taking away from the provincial legislature many of its powers of appointment and giving them to the royal governor. Henceforth juries were to be summoned by sheriffs rather than elected by the town meetings, and the town meetings themselves could be called only by the governor, who would also dictate their agendas.

Another measure passed in 1774, the Quebec Act, was not intended as punishment, but so offended the colonists that it is often included among the Intolerable Acts. This law established a permanent government for the conquered province of Canada that provided few of the rights the English colonists enjoyed. It also extended toleration to the predominant religion of Quebec's inhabitants, Roman Catholicism. And the law extended the boundaries of Quebec south to the Ohio River into a region claimed by Virginia, Connecticut, and Massachusetts.

The First Continental Congress. The First Continental Congress assembled in Carpenter's Hall, Philadelphia, early in September 1774, in response to what many colonists perceived as Parliament's oppression. Twelve colonies were represented at Philadelphia—Georgia patriots had tried to pass a resolution to send a delegation, but had been dissuaded by the popular royal governor. Of the fifty-six delegates, twenty-two were lawyers, and most of the others were planters or merchants. Almost all had been prominent in the affairs of their individual colonies, and many had belonged to the committees of correspondence.

The delegates did not all agree on the best course. Some held it sufficient to petition the king informing him of wrongs done the colonists and asking that he intervene. The Massachusetts delegates, led by John and Sam Adams, along with Christopher Gadsden of South Carolina, Charles Thomson of Pennsylvania, and Patrick Henry and Richard Henry Lee of Virginia, favored retaliatory measures such as a new nonimportation agreement and a blunt refusal to pay for the tea dumped at Boston.

The delegates quickly demonstrated an emerging sense of continental unity and shared nationality. Patrick Henry, in a sample of his famous oratory, sounded the new note. "The distinctions between Virginians, Pennsylvanians, New Yorkers, and New Englanders," he declared, "are no more. I am not a Virginian, but an American." All imperial government, he continued, was at an end. "All Distinctions are thrown down. All America is thrown into one mass." Henry was exaggerating, but the Congress would help to create a new feeling that Americans all shared a common distinctive destiny.

It was a radicals' convention. In the midst of the debates and deliberations the delegates received a set of resolutions adopted by a convention recently held in Suffolk County, Massachusetts. These declared that Americans should not obey any of the Coercive Acts, attacked the Quebec Act as dangerous to Protestantism and American liberties, and demanded that all imports from Britain and all exports to it cease, pending repeal of the offensive measures. Over the strong objections of conservatives, the Congress endorsed the "Suffolk Resolves."

When it came to passing resolutions of their own, the delegates disagreed. On one side was Joseph Galloway of Pennsylvania and his supporters, who proposed a "Plan of Union" that would establish an overall government for the colonies with a president-general appointed by the king. This official would exercise authority over a grand council selected by the various colonial assemblies. Together the president-general and the grand council would constitute an "inferior branch" of the British Parliament. Radicals in the Congress, correctly perceiving this as a scheme to freeze into law the colonies' political subordination to Britain, defeated it. The radicals' own plan—which was the one adopted—denounced the Coercive Acts as cruel and unconstitutional and condemned the various revenue measures Parliament had passed since 1763, the maintaining of a British standing army in America, and the dissolution of colonial assemblies by British authorities. The Congress also adopted a stringent set of regulations virtually cutting off all commercial relations with Britain until American grievances had been redressed. A final resolution called for a second Congress to meet on May 10, 1775, if by that time Britain still refused to yield.

Toward Lexington

The work of the Congress pleased many colonists. Following adjournment the Pennsylvania Assembly gave the delegates a dinner at the City Tavern, where their work was toasted and praised. Patriots throughout the American community congratulated Congress for its efforts. Tories were dismayed and depressed by what had transpired in Philadelphia. Governor William Franklin of New Jersey, Benjamin Franklin's Tory son, noted that the Congress had left Britain "no other alternative than either to consent to what must appear humiliating in the eyes of all Europe, or to compel obedience to her laws by a military force." A Massachusetts Tory insisted that the men at Philadelphia had made the "breach with the parent state a thousand times more irreparable than it was before." A New York loyalist charged that the Congress had "*erected itself into the supreme legislature of North America.*"

In England itself, high officials were thunderstruck. British merchants once more became a voice for conciliation. So did Pitt and Burke. But the North government refused to budge.

Lexington and Concord. In Boston, events moved toward a showdown. For months the army commander there, General Thomas Gage, had been reinforcing the British garrison so that by the end of 1774 there were eleven battalions of redcoats, some four thousand men, in the city and at Castle William. Patriots armed and drilled. Outside the city, bands of militia calling themselves "minutemen" patrolled the countryside and made it dangerous for British troops to leave the city even on official business. Before long, Gage began to feel as though he were under siege and fortified Boston Neck against the time when he might actually be attacked. Elsewhere in New England armed patriot militia seized British military supplies and arms. To English officials and American Tories, the patriots' insistence that they were still loyal to the king by now seemed rank hypocrisy. A patriot called the redcoats "debauched Weavers' 'prentices,' and fops who would not, and indeed could not, fight." Those who had fought beside the British in the French and Indian War claimed that "lobsterbacks" would be no match for hardy American yeomen in a straight fight.

At the Battle of Lexington, April 19, 1775, British troops quickly overwhelmed the small band of minutemen. *(Courtesy, The I. M. Phelps Stokes Collection, The New York Public Library)*

Following their rout at Lexington, farmers and minutemen surprised the British at the North Bridge in Concord and sent them into retreat to Boston.

Why, the British scarcely knew how to shoot a gun!

Relations between Boston patriots and British authorities reached the flash point early in 1775. First, there was a brawl between butchers and redcoats at the public market. The anniversary of the Boston Massacre in March became a second occasion for friction when some British officers heckled the patriot leader Joseph Warren as he was delivering a commemorative oration.

At about this time spies for the British informed Gage that the minutemen were collecting arms and ammunition at Concord, a few miles outside of Boston. In addition, the Massachusetts legislature, in defiance of Gage's orders, was holding meetings at Concord. Why not, Gage thought, capture the arms and, perhaps, seize some of the rebellious patriot leaders?

On the evening of April 18, 1775, a force of seven hundred redcoats set out for Concord. Patriots in the city quickly learned of the move and dispatched William Dawes and Paul Revere, a patriot silversmith, to alert the minutemen and the patriot leaders that the British were coming. Although Revere was captured and Dawes turned back, another rider conveyed the news to the patriots at Concord in time. When the British reached nearby Lexington after marching most of the night, they discovered seventy armed minutemen lined up on the town commons shivering in the early morning chill. The British commanding officer, Major John Pitcairn, immediately rode toward them shouting: "Ye villains, ye rebels, disperse! Lay down your arms!" At the same time the British light infantry began to run forward to intercept the Americans, who retreated to a stone wall at the edge of the field. No one knows which side fired first, but at the wall the minutemen stopped and fired off a ragged volley, wounding one redcoat and Major Pitcairn's horse. The British replied more effectively, killing ten of the Americans and wounding nine others.

As the British reassembled to move on Concord, the Massachusetts countryside rose in fury. By the time the redcoats had arrived at their destination, a large force of armed and angry farmers had collected to intercept them. When the Americans began to advance on their enemy, the British tried to withdraw. At this point the minutemen fired, killing and wounding several of the redcoats.

Now began a long, dismal, and bloody retreat from Concord all the way back to the safety of Boston. As they plodded back, the British took a withering barrage from behind hedges, trees, houses, and stone walls. A British lieutenant, seeking to explain the debacle, reported that his men had been attacked "from all sides but mostly from the rear, where people had hid themselves in houses till we had passed, and then fired." At Lexington the original British force picked up reinforcements that had come out from Boston. After a short wait to rest the exhausted Concord contingent, the combined force resumed the retreat to Boston choked by dust, the heavy woolen uniforms sweat-drenched. Once again, the British came under devastating fire. Many were hit. Occasionally detachments broke off from the main body to charge a knot of Americans or even to loot the houses along the road. Despite their contempt for amateur soldiers the British had to admit that the colonists' fire was often deadly.

The British arrived back in Charlestown in the evening and counted their losses. Of the eighteen hundred men who had been sent to Concord, some seventy-three had been killed and two hundred wounded. Only by the sheerest good luck had the Americans been prevented from cutting off the whole force and capturing it. Although complete disaster had been averted, the Americans had won a victory against the finest troops of Europe.

Concord and Lexington marked the beginning of the Revolution. After April 19, 1775, there was no turning back. General Gage warned the British government: "These people are now spirited up by a rage and enthusiasm as great as ever People were possessed of, and you must proceed in earnest or give the Business up." Yet in the ensuing months thousands of native-born Americans would become "loyalists" (or "Tories"), partisans of the king. Loyalism would prove especially strong among certain classes of Americans. Natives like Thomas Hutchinson who had close ties to the British government were natural loyalists. Anglican ministers who recognized the king as head of the Church of England also tended to take the British side, as did many Anglican laymen, especially in New England, where they formed an unpopular minority.

Loyalists were not invariably rich with a large property stake in society. Besides loyalist merchants, officials, and planters, there were also loyalist mechanics, farmers, and small shopkeepers. In the western Carolinas, where small farmers known as "regulators" had rebelled against low-country domination in the 1760s and early 1770s, there was a good deal of loyalist sentiment. Angry at the seaboard Carolina gentry for denying them representation in the colonial assemblies and for crushing their rebellion by force of arms, some of the Western farmers chose the king's side after 1775, if only because the low-country Carolina planters and merchants had chosen the opposite side. There were even slave loyalists. In Virginia, especially, the royal governor would appeal to the slaves to help the Crown against its enemies among the planters, and many would respond.

Like the loyalists, patriots or "rebels" came in different shapes and sizes. If many Anglican clergymen chose the king, almost all Congregational and many other dissenting ministers chose Congress. In the major port towns—Boston, Newport, New York, Philadelphia, and Charleston—artisans, apprentices, and laborers were rebels. But so were the merchants, especially those who felt threatened by the trade regulations that had been piled on top of the existing navigation acts since 1763. The landed gentry of New York split. Families such as the Delanceys took the king's side; the Schuylers and the Livingstons, equally wealthy and aristocratic, supported Congress. In Virginia and the Carolinas, the patriot leaders were almost all Anglican gentlemen, many of them owners of large estates and scores of black slaves. Indeed, men such as George Washington, Henry Laurens, and Robert Morris were among the wealthiest Americans of their day.

"Bunker Hill" and the Drift Toward Independence

The response of patriot leaders to the events in Massachusetts was prompt and vigorous. In Massachusetts the Provincial Congress, as the illegal colonial legislature was called, authorized the raising of troops and appealed to the other colonies for aid. Before long, several thousand militia from Rhode Island, Connecticut, and New Hampshire, along with contingents of Stockbridge and Mohawk Indians, were pouring into the colony and assembling in a ring around Boston, where Gage's troops were ensconced. The American general in charge was Artemus

Ward; his subordinates included the talented Nathanael Greene and Israel Putnam.

In some ways the besiegers of Boston were in worse shape than the besieged. The men lived without sufficient tents and amidst filth. Unused to the standards of hygiene necessary where men lived together in masses, they refused to take precautions. Before long, disease invaded the American camp. The British in Boston, on the other hand, seemed to be living off the fat of the land, well housed and well supplied with food and necessities. At the end of May 1775, Gage was joined by three other high-ranking British officers, Sir William Howe, Sir Henry Clinton, and John Burgoyne. Howe took over command from Gage, who remained as civilian governor of the colony.

"Bunker Hill." Sooner or later, in any event, Howe would have had to attack the Americans ringing the city, but they forced his hand by fortifying Breed's Hill, across the Charles River from Boston and within cannon range of the city. On June 17 the British navy began to bombard the American positions. Confident that the untried amateur soldiers under Colonel William Prescott's command could not stand up against redcoats in a regular battle, Howe and his fellow officers decided to make a direct attack on the entrenched Americans. Troops of grenadiers and light infantry, with packs containing three days' rations, were being ferried across the Charles to Charlestown peninsula.

As the British troops landed on the beach, the Americans waited silently. When the redcoats prepared to charge, Prescott gave the order to fire. There was a great crash and a cloud of smoke; scores of Welsh Fusiliers fell. In seconds the light infantry regiment was fleeing in panic, leaving behind its wounded, its dead, and most of its equipment. Meanwhile the tall grenadiers were advancing on the Americans atop Breed's Hill in well-dressed lines. When the redcoats

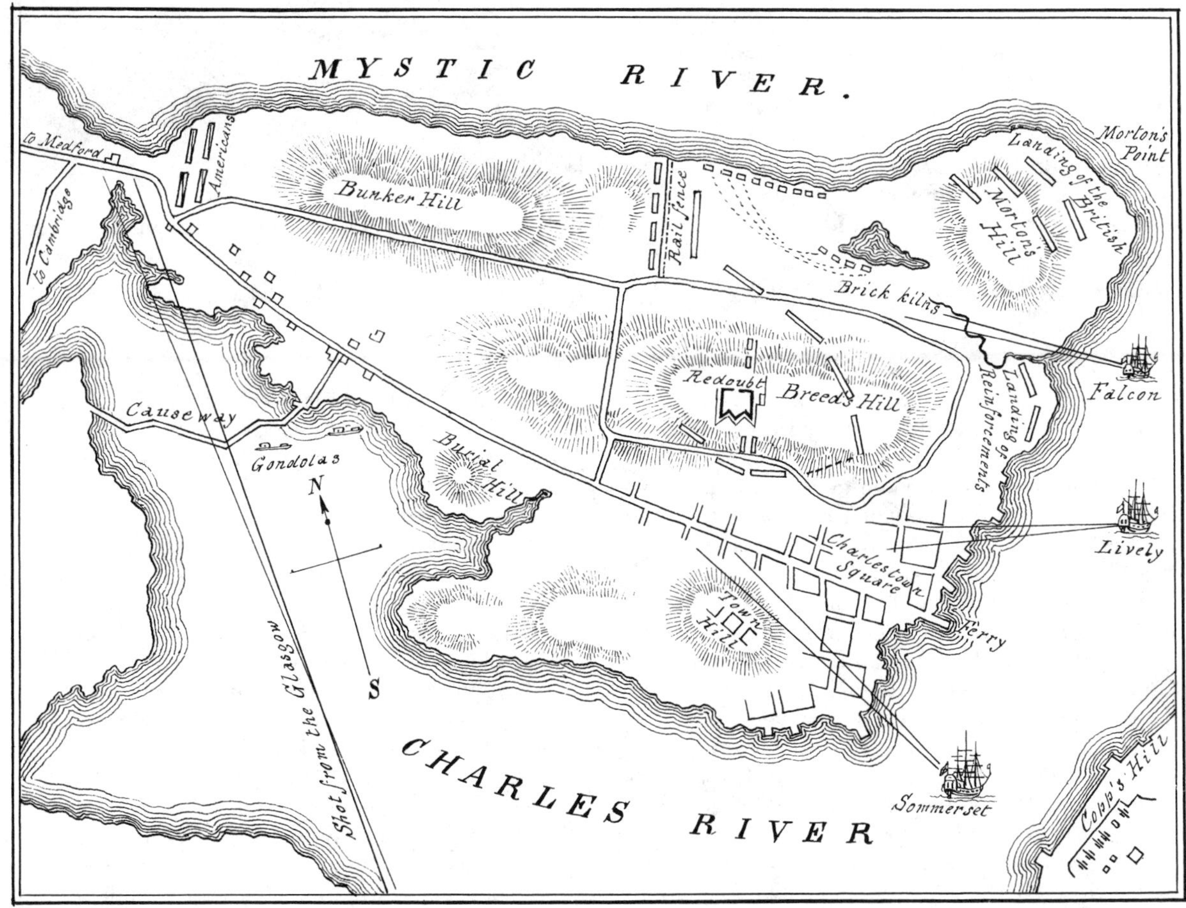

The Battle of Bunker Hill (actually Breed's Hill), June 17, 1775. The British won but suffered a great number of casualties. For the Americans it was a moral victory.

were within twenty yards of the American position a volley rang out, knocking down scores. The grenadiers, unlike the Welsh Fusiliers, continued to advance, their bayonets fixed. The Americans, now almost within spitting range, continued to fire away. Finally grenadiers too broke ranks and fled.

Howe was not finished. Once more he ordered his men against the American position. Once more they were mowed down and retreated. Again Howe ordered his men to attack, this time without their heavy packs. By now the Americans were low in ammunition. Assuming the battle was over, many had disobeyed their officers and had begun to leave for home. Despite heavy casualties, this time the redcoats drove the Americans off the hill and took possession of the Charlestown peninsula.

The British had won, but at what a price! Over a thousand redcoat casualties, with over two hundred killed. Almost fifty percent of the British troops engaged were either dead or wounded. As Howe commented: "A dear bought victory, another such would have ruined us."

The battle, misnamed "Bunker Hill," was of vast symbolic importance. To Americans, it was a great moral triumph. Combined with Lexington and Concord, it had demonstrated that American militia could stand up to the best the British could throw against them. In reality, the Americans, with fifteen thousand men encamped around Boston, should have done much better. Far too many had been insubordinate; some had been cowards. The Americans' staff work and supply services had been poor. Finally, American success had been due as much to British errors in using a frontal assault as to their own planning. Still, they had reason to be proud and to look to the future with some hope.

Washington Takes Command. Meanwhile, the Second Continental Congress had assembled in Philadelphia, as scheduled, in early May. Among its first acts was the choice of an overall commander for the Continental army who would take charge of the troops around Boston. Following the advice of John Adams, it appointed George Washington of Virginia on June 15, just days before Bunker Hill. It also voted to raise six companies of riflemen from the middle colonies and the South to join the New Englanders at Boston and decided to issue bills of credit to support the accelerating rebellion.

Despite the outbreak of hostilities, Congress resisted a final political break with Britain. There were those at Philadelphia who favored a bold declaration of American independence.

The Second Continental Congress appointed George Washington commander of the Continental army, filling him with "inexpressible concern." *(Courtesy, The Pennsylvania Academy of the Fine Arts)*

John Adams urged his fellow delegates to accept the advice of Massachusetts and endorse the formation of new constitutions for each colony to break the tie with England. These independent states, he believed, would ally themselves in a continental league that would be equivalent to an independent nation. But even this oblique road to independence did not please most of the delegates, who still hoped for British conciliation. Adams's proposals were ignored.

George Washington's appointment filled him with "inexpressible concern." He arrived in the Boston area after Bunker Hill to find the largely New England army a disappointment. The Yankees, he complained, were "an exceedingly nasty and dirty people," excessively concerned with money. Other observers found the troops enterprising, though highly individualistic, and unwilling to submit to discipline or even call their officers by official titles. The new commander in chief had his work cut out for him in seeking to turn this ragged collection of farmers and mechanics into an army and to combine it smoothly with the regiments of Virginians, Marylanders, and Pennsylvanians who began to arrive at Cambridge.

In these months of 1775, and virtually all through the war, one of the general's chief problems was simply to keep his force intact. Few Americans considered military service a full-time occupation. Farm boys were willing to enlist for a few months, especially in the winter or after the crops had been planted. But when needed at home, or when confronted with long stretches of idleness, they grew restless. Some simply deserted. Others waited until their term of enlistment had ended and, regardless of the military situation, went home.

Early Fighting. While the commander in chief was trying to construct a Continental army out of fifteen thousand individualists encamped outside Boston, the war was not marking time elsewhere. In May a force of Massachusetts men and Vermonters under Ethan Allen and Benedict Arnold had attacked and captured the small British garrison at Fort Ticonderoga on Lake Champlain. The Americans acquired valuable military supplies, including one hundred cannons. In August the captured British post became the jumping-off point for an attack on Canada led by General Philip Schuyler of New York and the British-born Richard Montgomery. On November 13, 1775, Montgomery captured Montreal. Meanwhile, Arnold, with one thousand volunteers from Washington's force, set out across Maine heading toward Quebec City. He reached the British fortress in November and was joined by Montgomery and his men. The combined little army attacked the city in a howling snowstorm. In the battle Montgomery was killed and Arnold wounded. A hundred Americans were killed and four hundred captured. With his pitiful remnant Arnold continued to besiege the town all through the winter. In the spring he gave up the siege and returned home.

During these early months of the Revolution the fighting was not confined to the North. In Virginia the royal governor, the Earl of Dunmore, had gathered the colony's loyalists together at Norfolk, formed them into a small army, and set them to destroying patriot-owned plantations. In November, Dunmore issued a proclamation establishing martial law and calling on all citizens to support the king. He also offered freedom to all slaves who would desert their patriot masters and join his forces. This proved to be a mistake. Dunmore's little army did attract some runaway slaves. But white Virginians feared nothing more than a rising of slaves, and Dunmore's proclamation may have pushed many of the undecided into the patriot camp. When Dunmore sallied out of Norfolk with his mixed band of loyalists and blacks, he was defeated. Soon after, he loaded his blacks and loyalists aboard ships and abandoned Norfolk to the Americans. In February 1776 he returned and set fire to the city.

While Americans and Englishmen were sporadically killing one another in the fields and forests of North America, efforts were being made to bring the two sides together. In July 1775 Congress adopted the Olive Branch Petition announcing continued American attachment to the king and asking him to desist from further hostile acts until some scheme of reconciliation had been arranged. It also adopted a "Declaration of the Causes and Necessities of Taking Up Arms." This document did not proclaim independence, but pronounced American determination to refuse submission. Several weeks later, Congress rejected Lord North's proposals of February, by which the British government offered to forgo parliamentary taxes on any colony that would agree to tax itself for defense and to pay its own expenses.

Congress adjourned in August 1775, but reconvened in mid-September with a full representation from all thirteen colonies. In early November, members learned that the king had rejected the Olive Branch Petition and declared the colonies in open rebellion. On December 6 Congress responded to the king's declaration by disavowing American allegiance to Parliament, but acknowledging continued allegiance to George III.

As these proposals and counterproposals flew back and forth across the Atlantic, Americans were moving rapidly toward practical self-government. Congress established a Continental army. It appointed commissioners to deal with the Indian tribes and set up a Post Office Department. In October 1775 it organized a navy. Its most momentous act was to appoint in November a five-man Committee of Secret Correspondence to negotiate with potential allies abroad. In December the Committee made contact with a French agent, who informed them that France would aid the colonists against the British. Soon after, the French Foreign Minister, Comte de Vergennes, consulted his Spanish counterpart regarding joint action to aid the Americans. When the Spanish gave their approval, Vergennes ordered a large amount of

Common Sense *by Tom Paine*
Paine's rousing pamphlets circulated by the tens of thousands and galvanized sentiment against England.

The sun never shined on a cause of greater worth. 'Tis not the affair of a city, a county, a province, or a kingdom; but of a continent—of at least one-eighth part of the habitable globe. 'Tis not the concern of a day, a year, or an age; posterity are virtually involved in the contest, and will be more or less affected even to the end of time by the proceedings now. Now is the seedtime of continental union, faith, and honor. The least fracture now will be like a name engraved with the point of a pin on the tender rind of a young oak; the wound would enlarge with the tree, and posterity read it in full grown characters. . . .

Small islands not capable of protecting themselves are the proper objects for government to take under their care; but there is something absurd in supposing a continent to be perpetually governed by an island. In no instance hath nature made the satellite larger than its primary planet; and as England and America, with respect to each other, reverse the common order of nature, it is evident that they belong to different systems. England to Europe: America to itself. . . .

O ye that love mankind! Ye that dare oppose not only the tyranny but the tyrant, stand forth! Every spot of the old world is overrun with oppression. Freedom hath been hunted round the globe. Asia and Africa have long expelled her. Europe regards her like a stranger, and England hath given her warning to depart. O receive the fugitive, and prepare in time an asylum for mankind.

munitions to be sent to the Americans through a "front" company, Hortalez et Companie. In April 1776 Congress responded to these French moves by opening American ports to the commerce of all nations except Britain.

Common Sense and The Declaration of Independence

A final wrench to the remaining ties of empire came with the publication of *Common Sense*, a hundred-page pamphlet composed by a recently arrived Englishman, Thomas Paine. Written with extraordinary passion and eloquence, *Common Sense* denounced the institution of hereditary kingship. "For all men being originally equals, no *one* by *birth* could have a right to set up his own family in perpetual preference to all others forever," Paine declared. George was a "royal brute," not the generous father of his people, and Americans had no reason to continue to obey him or remain his subjects. George III was not a royal brute. But *Common Sense* was an important document in the modern rejection of the whole system of hereditary rule.

The pamphlet had an electrifying effect. Perhaps a million Americans read it as it passed from hand to hand, and were profoundly affected by its message. Washington noted that it was "working a powerful change in the minds of men." After reading it, he himself ceased to toast the King, as he had done till now through thick and thin.

The Declaration of Independence. On April 12, 1776, the North Carolina Convention authorized the colony's delegates in Congress to vote for independence. The Virginia legislature followed soon after. On June 7 Richard Henry Lee, responding to the House of Burgesses, offered a motion in Congress that "these United Colonies are, and of a right ought to be, free and independent states, and that all political connection between them and the state of Britain is, and ought to be, totally dissolved."

Congress responded by appointing to frame a statement of independence a five-man committee consisting of Thomas Jefferson, John Adams, Benjamin Franklin, Roger Sherman, and Robert Livingston. Jefferson was made chairman. At thirty-three the tall Virginian was one of the youngest members of Congress. But he was also a man of great charm and eloquence, with a reputation as a scholar. Still, if anyone had then realized how important the document would be, the choice of chief author would undoubtedly have fallen on either of two better-known members, Adams or Franklin.

Jefferson's Declaration of Independence is one of the most eloquent and moving endorsements of human freedom and equality ever composed. With simplicity and directness the document captures the essence of the ideas that numbers of American political philosophers had articulated, among them the seventeenth-century English Whigs who had overthrown James II and helped establish England's constitutional monarchy. The document announces that "all men are created equal" and "endowed by their Creator with certain unalienable Rights," more especially "to Life, Liberty and the pursuit of Happiness." Governments exist only to "secure these rights." When a government becomes "destructive of these ends," it is "the Right of the People to alter or abolish it" and establish a new one that will respect them.

Americans today do not have to be reminded tha the framers of the Declaration of Independence did not intend "people" to refer to all members of their society. Slaves and women were to enjoy the benefits of independence only as dispensed by the husbands and masters who retained control over them. A few months previous to the signing of the Declaration, Abigail Adams had written to her husband, John Adams, who was a member of the Continental Congress, that she longed "to hear that you have declared an independency." And, she added, for the new code of laws "which I suppose it will be necessary for you to make I desire you would Remember the Ladies, and be more generous and favourable to them than your ancestors." Abigail Adams was not claiming citizenship or equal political rights for women. She sought only that the lawmakers "not put such unlimited power into the hands of the Husbands." For, she reminded her husband, "all Men would be tyrants if they could." Abigail Adams marvelously adapted the revolutionary vocabulary of her day to the women's situation as she understood it. She accepted women's domestic role, but sought to introduce greater freedom for women into the domestic sphere. Should men fail to reduce their own domestic tyranny, she warned, the ladies would surely foment their own "Rebellion."

The rest of the Declaration was a detailed—and not altogether fair—indictment of the British government for general attitudes and specific acts designed to establish "an absolute Tyranny" over America. Here Jefferson marshaled virtually every American grievance, both immediate and of long standing, against Britain and defended the actions of the colonists during the years since 1763. All pointed toward one inescapable end: "these United Colonies are, and of Right ought to be, Free and Independent States." "With firm reliance on the Protection of Divine Providence," the Declaration concluded, "we mutually pledge to each other our Lives, our Fortunes and our sacred Honor."

The Declaration of Independence, signed on July 4, 1776, celebrated by the American artist John Trumbull. *(Courtesy, Yale University Art Gallery)*

Adams and Franklin suggested a number of changes, primarily stylistic. Congress as a body, when it received the draft, struck out several phrases and clauses. On July 4, 1776, all fifty-five members present, except John Dickinson, signed it.

In the next few days the Declaration was read to large gatherings of Americans throughout the self-proclaimed independent country. In Philadelphia John Nixon, head of the city guard, read the document to a large audience in the State House yard. When he finished, the crowd cheered. In New York, the officers of the Continental army, after hearing the Declaration read, all "went to a Publick House to testify to

. . . their joy at the happy news of independence." Bostonians celebrated by removing the plaque bearing the King's coat of arms from the State House wall and burning it.

The United States dates its independence as a nation from July 4, 1776. But as many contemporaries knew, there was a long distance between signing a document and winning actual freedom on the battlefield. Now there could be no turning back. Victory would mean that the efforts at Philadelphia had not been in vain. Defeat might well mean the surrender of lives, fortunes, and sacred honor. The die was cast.

Windsor chair, reputed to be the sort used by Thomas Jefferson while he wrote the Declaration of Independence, probably made in New England, mid-eighteenth century. *(Courtesy, Index of American Design)*

Points To Think About

1. The Stamp Act crisis was in several senses, as Edmund S. Morgan points out, the "prologue to the Revolution." It set the stage for future conflicts, not only by providing a dress rehearsal for the various constitutional arguments but also by providing each side with a terrifying glimpse into the other's true motives.

The arguments confirmed the extent of Parliament's authority to regulate colonial affairs. And the intensity with which these arguments were advanced has given the American Revolution a peculiarly intellectual character. The colonists, that is, objected not simply to the particular exercise of power (which, however ill-advised, was anything but tyrannical), but to what it boded for the future. Americans of the revolutionary generation had a positive genius for searching out the farthermost implications of every British action. Hence they devoted their most vigorous condemnations not to the Stamp Act but to the principles it embodied. The British were equally sensitive to questions of principle. For them, too, the Stamp Act quickly ceased to be a mere means of raising revenue and became instead a test of parliamentary authority.

Why did two peoples—both reputed to be intensely practical and uninterested in theoretical issues—see every disagreement over colonial policy as involving critical questions of principle? The answer, in large measure, rests in each side's reading of the other's intentions. The colonists saw the Stamp Act as only the first step in an elaborate plot to deprive them of their rights and reduce them to a state of slavery. The British government saw American resistance to the act as signifying disregard for its authority.

Both sets of suspicions were initially mistaken. Parliament did not wish to enslave America. It wished merely to oblige the colonists to pay a larger share of the expenses of running the empire. The colonists did not wish to be independent. They wished simply not to be taxed internally without their consent. But the intense suspiciousness both sides displayed meant that their expectations, however wrong initially, quickly became self-fulfilling prophecies. Colonial intransigence provoked ever sterner measures from Parliament, culminating in the attempt to abolish the Massachusetts colonial assembly. Meanwhile, the colonists advanced ever greater claims to home rule, culminating in the Declaration of Independence.

2. The American colonists after 1763 were, on the one hand, deeply suspicious of every parliamentary act and, on the other, avowed admirers of the

British constitution as the finest form of government ever wrought by the hand of man. Both the suspicion and the admiration were sincere. For Americans believed that the British constitution was being systematically undermined. The term they used was "corruption" and they meant by it more than simple venality.

The genius of the British constitution, all agreed, lay in its exquisite balance. Under it the king ruled, but ruled in Parliament. Both houses had to consent to all decrees. The House of Lords was composed of the hereditary nobility. Its role was to temper the popular enthusiasms of the Commons on the one side, and the tendencies of the Crown on the other to be tyrannical. The Commons represented the "people," an undifferentiated term applied to all who were not of noble birth. It represented the ruled; yet as the Commons grew more important throughout the century, supplying the Crown with ministers to oversee the management of the realm, it began to take on more and more executive functions. Americans, in their own constitution, reinstituted the distinction between the legislature and the executive that had marked seventeenth-century British practice, a distinction that they believed had guarded against corruption.

Corruption arose out of two sources. One was this gradual merger of executive and legislative functions. The king's ability to appoint to high office members of Parliament or their relatives enabled him to forge a working majority in the House of Commons. This, to American colonists, was a clear perversion of the British constitution. Moreover, this political corruption seemed, in colonial eyes, to mirror the larger social corruption of Georgian England. It seemed to them a land given to luxury and pleasure, and London appeared to be a capital of vice. Americans contrasted the "simplicity" of their own society with the imperial pomp they found in England. This distrust of elaborate ceremonials, luxurious dress, and highly polished manners persisted well past the revolutionary era in the cult of republican simplicity.

3. In the eighteenth century the popularly elected lower houses of the legislatures in the royal colonies protested against whatever they found to be heavy handed in imperial policy or in the conduct of governors. In time the lower houses came to argue that since colonists were entitled to "the rights of Englishmen," they were entitled to representation in any body that governed them. The full implication of this argument, which it took a generation or more to realize, was that, since colonists were not properly represented in Parliament, only the lower colonial houses could legitimately pass laws for British America.

Some British defenders of the existing arrangement argued that the colonists were already "virtually" represented in Parliament and needed no other voice in the imperial government. A member of Parliament, so the concept of virtual representation argued, spoke not only for his own constituency but for other constituencies with similar interests. This reasoning would hold that a member of Parliament from a seaport town in England also represented Boston or New Yorkers. It made a certain sense to the English because the franchise in Britain was severely limited. But virtual representation made no sense on the other side of the Atlantic. Most male Americans were accustomed to voting directly for their representatives.

Suggested Readings

Bernard Bailyn's *The Ideological Origins of the American Revolution* (1967) and Morton White's *The Philosophy of the American Revolution* (1978) are readable intellectual histories of the revolutionary era. Changes in social history during the period are treated in J. H. Huston and S. F. Kurtz, *Essays on the American Revolution* (1973) while Gary Nash studies the importance of cities in *The Urban Crucible: Social Change, Political Consciousness, and the Origins of the American Revolution* (1979). Pauline Maier traces the rise of popular hostility to England in *From Resistance to Revolution* (1972) while David Ammerman's *In Common Cause* (1974) analyzes the Coercive, or Intolerable, Acts. Esmond Wright provides a British view in *Fabric of Freedom, 1763-1800* (1961). Lexington and Concord are beautifully studied in Thomas Fleming's *The First Strike* (1978). See also Robert Gross, *The Minutemen and Their World* (1976).

FORREST McDONALD

Revolutions, we customarily think, are born amidst the poor and oppressed. The crowds call for bread and for release of political prisoners whose bodies are broken with torture. In the American Revolution the colonists were indeed reacting in anger. The King, wrote Thomas Jefferson in the Declaration of Independence, had "sent hither swarms of officers to harass our people, and eat out their substance. . . . He has plundered our seas, ravaged our coasts, burnt our towns, and destroyed the lives of our people." But the anger in America was not about torture or the extremes of poverty.

We also expect revolutions to make for violent change—the destruction of a ruling class, the overthrow of political institutions, and even the coming of a revolutionary style of dress and behavior. The French Revolution popularized short hair, mustaches, and modern trousers, and revolutionists addressed one another as "Citizen," as Russian Communists would later call one another "Comrade."

By such measures as these, the American Revolution was no revolution at all. Rather, it was an attempt by all classes of Americans to conserve what they already had. The leaders of the American Revolution did not come from some oppressed lower class and certainly did not speak for any such class. They were people of wealth and more particularly wealth in land. Though it was far easier in the colonies than in any part of Europe to move upward in property and social position, the gates to wealth and power had been steadily closing for a generation by the time of the Revolution. Everywhere in the colonies a relative handful of large landholding or merchant families dominated society as well as government. Intent on preserving their privileges against British attempts to rule the colonies more closely, these families might talk loudly in favor of the rights of the people, but they were not eager to share their power with the lower orders.

Yet the small farmers, the frontiersmen, and the craftsmen who supported the Revolution did not resent the leadership of these powerful families, or at any rate not enough to turn against them. Here a family of the common people could obtain a slice of land; or if it lived in one of the young American cities, it could do well in a craft or trade or perhaps rise into the prosperous mercantile class. As conservatives, well satisfied with their basic condition, common people joined with the wealthy in resisting the efforts of the British to impose change on the colonies.

Britain, the colonists believed, had once been a virtuous agricultural nation, with a balanced government, honest labor on the land and craftsmanship in the cities, and direct honest trade among individuals—it had been, in effect, a society much like their own. But Britain, so they decided, had now sunk into corruption, enslaved to money that brought monopolies, standing armies, and vicious government hungry for tax revenues. Britain had actually given birth to a modern, dynamic, expanding economy that would greatly improve the well-being of its inhabitants. This the Americans were too hidebound perhaps to see. They learned to believe only the worst, and to fear that, soon or late, the British would attempt to impose their sinister system upon the colonies. As the imperial crisis deepened in the 1760s and 1770s, that fear grew into a widespread conviction that just such a thing was happening, and then into something approaching a delusion. Finally, the Americans saw no way of preserving their own agricultural paradise except to declare their independence. In this sense the American Revolution was a conservative crusade against the forces of modernism.

The American Revolution, then, was culturally, politically, socially, and economically a conservative movement. But there were ironies in the colonists' successful defense of their established ways. Their victory brought great change. The new states found themselves unable to deal with their problems, and soon they had to create a central government with far greater powers than any that Parliament had dared to exercise. Though elements of the old colonial aristocracy remained, it had been weakened through the departure of some aristocratic Loyalists, the quick rise of some businessmen and politicians, and a general relaxation of social restraints. And financing the war had created an enormous public debt—which would provide the basis for governmental policies in the new American republic as economically dynamic as any that the Americans had detested on the part of the British government.

What Kind of Revolution 

EUGENE GENOVESE

Was the American Revolution a conservative movement that somehow produced unintended radical results? No, it was truly radical. Where in the world have conservatives reacted with anything short of hostility to slogans like "All men are created equal—the slogans under which Americans took up arms? Who else except European radicals welcomed the direct participation of the common people in rebellion, or in any major political action? Where else before the French Revolution did a national movement bring about a republic, surely the most radical political experiment since Cromwell's Puritan government in England over a century earlier?

While many leaders of the American Revolution were indeed wealthy and even aristocratic the Revolution meant the triumph not of an aristocracy but of people who owned only small amounts of property. Professor McDonald speaks of the satisfaction the colonists took in their prosperous circumstances, and he is right. They had reason to be satisfied. The natural richness of the continent had made possible a wide distribution of property. Americans rose in anger against British taxes imposed on their property without their consent and against restraints on the trade that their property provided for. And it was precisely in being a victory of independent owners of small property that the Revolution was radical rather than conservative. It represented the furthest point of social transformation that the European world had so far achieved. The old order in Europe was a society of great families, and of peasants who worked but did not own the land. Only in European cities did there exist a class of small, self-reliant, property owners somewhat like Americans. And as the French Revolution would make clear, the class threatened the aristocracy.

The fledgling American republic threw down the gauntlet to monarchical and aristocratic Europe. In breaking with the theory and practice of established hierarchy, it challenged not merely the ruling classes of Europe but all old ideas of rank and privilege. Creating a large republic shorn of king or nobles constituted a radical act of the first order. European political theory at the time assumed that only an Athenian city state or a small territory like that of the Netherlands could exist without a hereditary monarch. It is no wonder that conservatives feared and hated the new American nation.

The property holders who fought and won the American Revolution had already been enjoying a personal independence greater than that which their ancestors had possessed. The young nation had to seek new laws and institutions that would provide the social unity that older customs had once provided. To have to invent more democratic institutions is to engage in a radical act.

The equality that the Declaration of Independence enshrined was not total nor was it intended to be. The reservations, however, did not amount to limits on the notion of equality. The founders of our nation said what they meant and meant what they said: in fundamental human and political respects all men are created equal. The politics of the new nation excluded women, children, servants, blacks in general, and slaves in particular, but this was understood not to qualify the principle of equality among men but to qualify the definition of "men." Only free adult males, according to the beliefs that then prevailed, were full and equal members of the political process. And while the victors in the Revolution did have hopes that slavery might one day disappear, they did not desire much more in the way of further change. But the language of the Declaration and the ideal of equality had a power to press far beyond all that, and in the course of the nation's history to awaken demands for a real social and political equality that would include all races, women as well as men, the poor along with the prosperous.

The economy of small independent property-owning that triumphed in the Revolution, moreover, contained the conditions for its own eventual destruction. That economy made possible the accumulation of wealth by mercantile and industrial capitalists. And capitalism, for all its beliefs in the rights of property, does not make for a society of individual property holders. To the contrary, it turns the population into wage earners who receive their subsistence from the hands of employers. And in the years to come, economic inequality, like the inequalities of race and sex, would collide politically with the egalitarian morality that the Revolution had fixed in the nation's conscience.

The Death of Jane McCrea, **by John Vanderlyn. McCrea's murder by Indian allies of the British aroused the entire region against Burgoyne and his troops.** *(Courtesy, The Wadsworth Atheneum)*

CHAPTER 5

Revolution and Independence 1776–1787

VICTORY AT SARATOGA

Of all the generals sent by Great Britain to subdue the American rebels, the one the colonials most enjoyed hating was "Gentleman Johnny" Burgoyne. To a generation bred on tales of English decadence, corruption, and arrogance, he was the ideal enemy to defeat in the critical battle of the Revolutionary War—the Battle of Saratoga, New York (1777). "Sir Jack Brag" (as one song called him) was rumored to have told the king that "with one regiment he could march triumphantly through all the American colonies."

Burgoyne initiated his campaign in 1777 with an infuriating proclamation denouncing "the present unnatural Rebellion" as "the compleatest System of Tyranny that ever God, in his Displeasure, suffered, for a Time, to be exercised over a froword *(sic)* and stubborn Generation." He threatened the rebels with "the Indian forces under my direction—and they amount to thousands."

Burgoyne's pomposity offered rich opportunity for parody. But the campaign that he directed was no joke. Colonial leaders had long worried that the British might become "masters of the Hudson River," which would "divide our strength, and enfeeble every effort for our common preservation and security." As originally planned, one army of British, Hessian, and Indian troops would march down from Montreal, while a second came from the West through the Mohawk Valley, and a third up the Hudson from New York City, all to converge on Albany. Along a line from New York to Montreal they would create a chain of forts to cut off New England—the heartland of rebellion.

The campaign began with a signal British victory on July 6, 1777, the capture of Fort Ticonderoga, key to the lake route to Albany. King George III is said to have shouted on receiving the news: "I have beat them! I have beat the Americans." Alexander Hamilton was a better prophet than the king: "I am in hope," he wrote, "that Burgoigne's success will precipitate him into measures that will prove his ruin. The enterprising spirit he has credit for, I suspect may easily be fanned by his vanity into rashness."

Burgoyne immediately blundered. Deciding that he now had ample time to move his army a mere seventy miles to Albany, he set out through the woods rather than following Lake George. Hauling fifty-two cannon, his enormous wardrobe and wine cellar, and a female entourage through forests cluttered by thousands of trees that the Americans had felled, Burgoyne covered twenty-three miles in twenty-four days and became lost in the woods while the patriots gathered strength. Then, at Oriskany and Fort Stanwix in the Mohawk Valley, in tough hand-to-hand fighting, they soundly defeated the British army advancing from the West. Meanwhile the murder and scalping of Jane McCrea by Indian allies of Burgoyne had set the citizens of the upper Hudson Valley into a fury at the British, who had been paying Indians for the scalps of revolutionists.

"Miss McCrea," wrote patriot commander Horatio Gates to Burgoyne, "a young lady lovely to the sight, of virtuous character and amiable disposition, engaged to be married to an officer in your Army, was with other women and children taken out of a house near Fort Edward, carried into the woods, and there scalped and mangled in a most shocking manner. . . . The miserable fate of Miss McCrea was particularly aggravated by her being dressed to receive her promised husband, but met her murderer employed by you."

Burgoyne, fearing mass desertion by his Indian allies, refused to execute her murderer and thereby aroused the entire region: for one of the few times in the war, militiamen and volunteers came and stayed to fight. When Burgoyne sent out a force to gather supplies in Vermont, two thousand minutemen from Vermont, New Hampshire, and Massachusetts threw the British back with heavy losses.

Short of troops, hungry for supplies, and facing a large and capable continental army well supported by local militia, Burgoyne was now in serious trouble. Nonetheless, as Hamilton had predicted, his vanity drove him to fight. Crossing the Hudson he stood at Saratoga facing Gates's army, which held a commanding position behind powerful fortifications built at the direction of a Polish engineer, Thaddeus Kosciusko. On September 19, Burgoyne threw his troops into action against Gates at Freeman's Farm. The battle sapped British strength while Gates easily reinforced his army. With supplies running low, Burgoyne had to decide whether to fight again or retreat. Of course he fought and on October 7, in the second battle of Saratoga, again suffered heavy losses. His position completely untenable—only the women in his company, whom the chivalrous Americans would not shoot, could get water from the nearby river—Burgoyne surrendered. A popular topical verse said it all:

Burgoyne, alas! unknowing future fates,
Could force his way through woods,
but not through GATES.

The Armies

The King's Army. A soldier of the Revolution who overheard talk in the ranks of the king's troops might have caught the sound of various accents from the British Isles, or American accents, for there were several loyalist regiments among the Crown troops. And it is likely that he would have heard German. In the eighteenth century a nation might rent whole military units from such rulers as were willing to go into the business, and in the course of the war the British rented nearly 30,000 troops from German princes, including the Hessians from the principality of Hesse-Cassel. The regular British army also contained many Germans recruited by contractors. The "patriot" army, like the troops that were to fight for the Union in the

Civil War nearly a century later, was itself a little congress of nations and ethnic groups, as were the rebellious colonies. (The word "patriot" as applied here to the revolutionists is a useful but somewhat arbitrary convention among historians; loyalists too were patriots, faithful to an America under Crown and Parliament.) New England Yankees, descendants of German and Scotch-Irish immigrants, and Southerners of varied ancestry in the British Isles were prominent. The Continental army, like the loyalist forces in Virginia, contained black recruits.

In the American navy, which preyed on British commerce, the *Bonne Homme Richard* can exemplify the diversity of the ethnic and national strains that could collect under a single flag. This ship, the conqueror in 1779 of the British warship the *Serapis*, had been supplied by France. It was under the command of John Paul Jones, a Scotsman who had gone to America not long before the war. Only a minority on board were clearly definable by residence as American. By their side were seamen from Scotland and Ireland, Scandinavians, Portuguese, and a French unit of marines. In the course of the war there were deserters from the patriot to the king's troops, and from the king's to the patriot, which could add to the diversity in both armies. One source of confusion in the determination of ethnic identity is that the word "Irish" in eighteenth-century American usage applied not only to Irish from the Roman Catholic South of Ireland but more particularly to people we would call Scotch-Irish, descendants of the Protestant Scottish settlers in the North of Ireland.

Uniforms of the armies reflected the relative positions of the warring nations. Left: A British sentry in full regalia. Center and right, the less formal colonial uniforms—for those who had them. *(Courtesy, The New York Public Library, Astor, Lenox and Tilden Foundations)*

Types of Warfare. The British were not scrupulous in their methods of recruitment. British prisons yielded some materials for the army, and strict enforcement of the vagrancy laws helped, for enlistment was a way to avoid prison. But British military discipline turned the recruits into a superior army. European battles required a set, formal way of arranging the forces. The officers of each army would march the troops as close to the enemy as possible. The soldiers, placed in several parallel ranks, one behind the other, would fire in unison—not having taken careful aim, for the troops on the other side were also closely packed. The troops might thereupon have time to reload and fire at will, as the British had done on the Plains of Abraham against the French defending Quebec. But reloading was a lengthy process, and in place of a second volley the soldiers might charge with bayonets, which in the eighteenth century were a major weapon. What a European army needed from the bulk of its troops, then, was not literacy, technical or administrative skills, or initiative in the performance of a job, the properties that twentieth-century armies demand, but the ability to go through the formal operations of eighteenth-century war: to stand or kneel in rank and not break under fire, to shoot or to charge at the proper time. The disposition of troops in a battle, one rank behind another, had as one of its objects to prevent the front ranks from fleeing. British discipline produced an army that could endure much enemy fire without breaking. But under sufficiently heavy fire, the best of soldiers could break.

"Patriot" Troops. The patriot forces contained both state militias and the Continental army. Congress had no power to conscript troops, and so it had to assign quotas to the states for the Continental army and let each state decide how to fill them. Congress, also lacking the authority to tax, even had to requisition money from the states and hope that they would fulfill their obligations. Some of those who joined the Continental army were volunteers who fought not only for the bounty but because they were committed to the patriot cause. More effective, perhaps, were the bounties that states offered, which later in the war were supplemented with a draft. A state, in turn, might impose quotas on towns, and they could pay men to enlist. States also raised their own militias, in which discipline was likely to be light. After Washington took command outside Boston, he induced about 10,000 militiamen to join the Continental army. The army of the Revolution was a foreshadowing of something more modern than the king's troops: it represented the beginnings of a citizens' army, like those that have fought in the major wars since the French Revolution; and like citizens' armies since then, it had to find ways of dealing with the reluctance of citizens to join.

As the patriot troops differed from the Crown forces in their recruitment, they differed at least somewhat in methods of fighting. At the beginning of the war outside Boston soldiers had been electing their own officers, and it was some time before the practice was ended. The Continental army had to instill discipline, which must have been difficult among soldiers who had no thought of becoming long-term military professionals. The Baron von Steuben, who worked to train them, was among the Europeans who made important contributions to the War for Independence. The patriot forces did not remain consistent or predictable in size. And citizen soldiers, committed more to their families than to army life—many of them were farmers who knew that the year's crop depended on the accomplishment of seasonal tasks—might decide to go home to plow, returning to the army if and when they felt like returning. It is perhaps to be expected that soldiers so averse to military discipline and the formalities of eighteenth-century battle should become known for fighting as individuals, firing from behind cover rather than in ranks, and taking aim. Some Americans were expert marksmen and used the Pennsylvania rifle, which was accurate at longer distances than the smoothbore musket. The method of fighting from cover was close to that of the Indians and appropriate to fighting them. In this, as in constituting a citizen army, the patriot troops seem more modern than their British and Hessian opponents. Lord Percy, a British survivor of Concord, remarked of the Americans of the area:

> Whoever looks upon them as an irregular mob will find himself much mistaken. They have men amongst them . . . who know very well what they are about, having been employed as Rangers against the Indians and Canadians, and this country being much covered with woods, and hilly, is very advantageous for their method of fighting.

But the picture that comes down to us of the American crouched behind a stone fence and picking off soldiers in the bewildered British ranks may owe much to the work of the Massachusetts farmers during the British retreat from Concord and to other incidents. During much of

Midshipman Augustus Brine, 1782, by John Singleton Copley. *(Courtesy, The Metropolitan Museum of Art)*

the war, Americans fought on the open field, managing as much of conventional warfare as training could teach them and their inclinations allowed.

And in the course of the fighting, the Continental army developed a pride in itself as a seasoned and knowledgeable fighting force. If few of its troops wanted to become permanent professionals, if most of them like citizen soldiers in other wars wanted a quick return to their homes, they were nonetheless more than farmers or artisans who had picked up a gun for a scrap or two with the British; they were now real soldiers of a trained and national army. That means that they were a major embodiment of the new nation itself.

The American army embodied the new nation in other ways as well. Like other eighteenth-century armies, the American army drew upon the services of many who were not officially soldiers. Women accompanied it in many capacities. Only officers were provided with quarters that could accommodate their wives, but other women frequently accompanied the army as camp-followers, laundresses, nurses, cooks, and provisioners. Wives might also accompany husbands to the actual field of battle and assist them by such tasks as fetching the water required to keep the cannon functioning. It is not certain that the legendary Molly Pitcher actually existed, but many women did what has been attributed to her: they brought their husbands water for the cannon, and then took over firing it themselves after their husbands had been wounded. Other women, notably Deborah Sampson Gannett, actually disguised themselves as men and fought, undetected, for long periods. Other women were able to capitalize on their femininity to serve successfully as spies and messengers.

The many American women who did not participate in battle or accompany the armies also frequently provided important services that today would be the responsibility of the military authorities. They provided lodging for officers, allowed their homes to be turned into prisons and hospitals, and a vast network of women emerged to make shirts for the American soldiers. Nothing better illustrates the impact of the war on American society than the extensive participation of women. The war effort mobilized society in the full sense.

The Course of Battle

The Critical Battles, 1776–1778. Against the rebels Britain massed an overwhelming force. Only days after Congress proclaimed independence on July 4, 1776, a huge British fleet—a "forest of masts"—sailed into New York harbor: 32,000 soldiers with 11,000 sailors manning thirty major ships of the line and dozens of transports. The commanders, General William Howe and his brother Admiral Richard Howe, aimed at establishing a principal base in New York, isolating New England from the other states, and providing easy communication between New York and Canada. One British force would descend from Canada by way of Lake Champlain and the Hudson River; the main force would strike New York City from the sea. Meanwhile, the British fleet's blockade of the coastline would deprive the Americans of both income and supplies from trade. The "revolting colonies," Lord North, the British prime minister thought, "cannot last long."

The upstate campaign was never effective. The brilliant tactics of Benedict Arnold in his courageous stand against a superior enemy fleet on Lake Champlain delayed a British thrust southward for a year. The strike against New York City, on the other hand, was child's play. Washington unwisely divided his makeshift army, sending about half of his troops to Long Island while the rest stayed on Manhattan. English ships slipped around both islands to block retreat, while Howe's soldiers attacked Brooklyn Heights, inflicting heavy losses. Realizing his mistake, Washington skillfully retreated across both islands into New Jersey, although his army was now demoralized and in disarray. It was, Washington lamented, a "disgraceful and dastardly" flight.

Wishing to negotiate with the revolutionists, not destroy them, Howe pursued them only as far as the Delaware River. Washington used this pause to regroup his armies, and on Christmas night of 1776 returned to the attack. After a polished military maneuver across the frozen Delaware, his army pounced on a camp of Hessian mercenaries at an outpost in Trenton, New Jersey. The Hessians, who had gone to bed drunk and confident that no army would attack on such a hallowed occasion, were quickly overwhelmed. Nearly a thousand were captured. A week later Washington struck again, outmaneuvering a British force at Princeton and driving them back to the Hudson before both armies went into hibernation. Washington took up winter quarters in the hills of western New Jersey; Howe diverted himself in New York "in feasting, banquetting, and in the arms of Mrs. Loving. . . ." He had fumbled a chance to end the war quickly.

In 1777 Britain renewed its efforts to occupy major coastal cities and isolate New England. In July General Howe embarked from New York with 15,000 men, sailed around to land at the head of Chesapeake Bay, and began fighting his way north toward Philadelphia. Washington and his troops scurried overland to meet the British, but could not turn them back. By September 26 Washington had lost a fifth of his total force and Howe had occupied Philadelphia—forcing Congress to flee to the Pennsylvania interior. On October 4, at the Battle of Germantown, Washington executed a series of intricate maneuvers

***Washington Crossing the Delaware*, by Emanuel Leutze. On Christmas Eve, 1776, General George Washington led his troops across the icy Delaware River, a maneuver that surprised the Hessian troops at Trenton and led to a much-needed American victory.** *(Courtesy, The Metropolitan Museum of Art)*

that placed him in a position to destroy Howe's main encampment, but the American troops became lost in a heavy fog and at one point even fired on one another. Only General Nathanael Greene's skillful retreat prevented disorder. Humiliated, Washington's remnant of an army was forced to spend a half-frozen and half-starved winter near Valley Forge, one of the few iron foundries still in patriot hands.

The victory of the United States at Saratoga (see introduction to this chapter) in October 1777 more than made up for any losses. It revived patriot morale, secured a crucial European ally, and transformed the war.

The French Alliance. As early as 1775, the Continental Congress had sent agents to France. Some, like Silas Deane and Arthur Lee, had arranged a trickle of loans and shipments of military supplies. The small Dutch island of St. Eustatius in the Caribbean served as a transit point: French ships unloaded munitions there, and patriots picked them up. Late in 1776, Congress sent Benjamin Franklin to Paris to negotiate an alliance. But King Louis XVI hesitated. His government was nearly bankrupt; his Spanish allies feared that the example of the Revolution might encourage revolution among their own colonies; the armies of the United States seemed weak. It seemed enough to have the secret trade in military hardware supporting the patriot armies, accomplishing French objectives by tying Britain down in a protracted war. However much Franklin's republican wit and easy charm captivated courtiers at Versailles, diplomatic grace could not, by itself, gloss over hard realities. For two years, Franklin moved through France, winning many friends for the new nation and establishing his own formidable reputation. But for the time being the king avoided any overt alliance.

Nonetheless, France and Spain did see opportunities. King Louis yearned for revenge against an old enemy, while Spanish courtiers in Madrid feared the mushrooming British empire in the New World. After the Battle of Saratoga opponents of the war in Britain persuaded Parliament to open peace negotiations, and by early spring 1778 a delegation under the Earl of Carlisle was on its way to the colonies with an offer

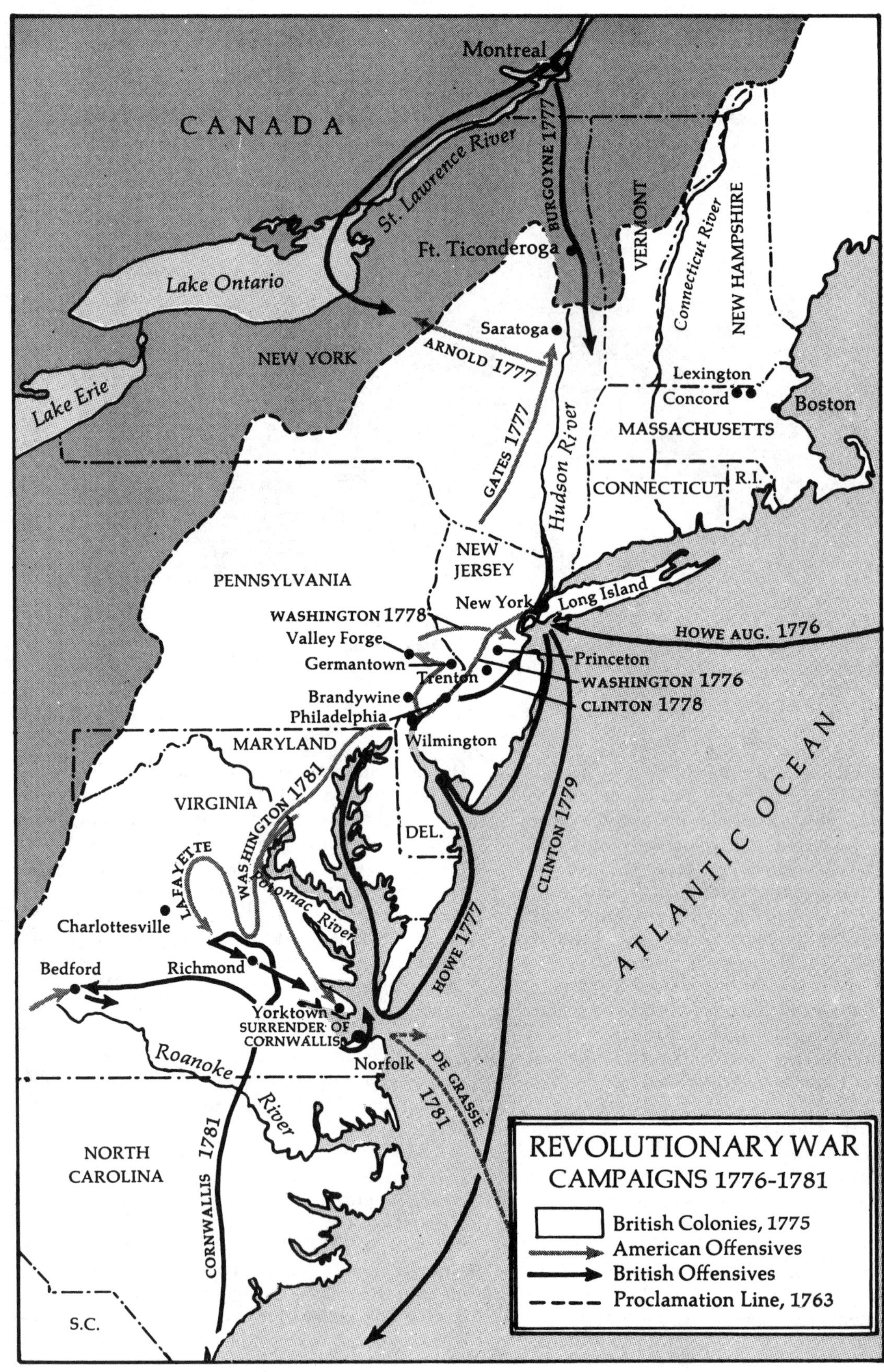

Montreal
CANADA
St. Lawrence River
BURGOYNE 1777
Ft. Ticonderoga
Lake Ontario
Saratoga
ARNOLD 1777
NEW YORK
Lake Erie
GATES 1777
Hudson River
VERMONT
Connecticut River
NEW HAMPSHIRE
Lexington
Concord
Boston
MASSACHUSETTS
CONNECTICUT
R.I.
NEW JERSEY
PENNSYLVANIA
New York
Long Island
WASHINGTON 1778
HOWE AUG. 1776
Valley Forge
Germantown
Princeton
Trenton
WASHINGTON 1776
Brandywine
Philadelphia
CLINTON 1778
MARYLAND
Wilmington
WASHINGTON 1781
VIRGINIA
DEL.
CLINTON 1779
LAFAYETTE
Potomac River
Charlottesville
Bedford
Richmond
HOWE 1777
ATLANTIC OCEAN
Yorktown
SURRENDER OF CORNWALLIS
Norfolk
Roanoke River
DE GRASSE 1781
NORTH CAROLINA
CORNWALLIS 1781
S.C.
REVOLUTIONARY WAR CAMPAIGNS 1776-1781
British Colonies, 1775
American Offensives
British Offensives
Proclamation Line, 1763

of limited autonomy within the British empire. Fears that the Americans might accept such terms, along with the encouragement that the victory at Saratoga gave to France, finally prompted Louis XVI and his foreign minister to offer Congress a formal alliance. The patriots ratified the bargain on May 4, 1778, only weeks before the Carlisle commissioners arrived in Philadelphia. With the entry of France into the conflict, the American Revolution became a world war.

In the dark and drifting time from 1778 to 1780, when the United States could not find a winning strategy, British generals could not defeat Washington's army or control the countryside. One major difficulty for the British was the sheer vastness of the country. The redcoats fought at the end of long lines of supply; small, slow-moving wooden ships would not maintain large land armies. Americans attacked like guerrillas and then easily escaped across rivers into forests. Short of occupying the whole country—a physical impossibility—His Majesty's generals would find no way to strike some final, decisive blow that would crush the rebellion once and for all. Nor did the British have the ruthlessness to destroy the morale of the revolutionists. Fighting to bring the rebels back into the empire, British generals did not scorch the earth or brutalize the population. Lord Dunmore, the last royal governor of Virginia, had offered freedom to slaves who fled or fought the rebels, but most remained with their owners. As British strategy failed to divide the states or to quell the rebellion, Parliament grew increasingly restless with the war.

A Passive Strategy. American strategy played upon British weakness. Unable to dislodge the redcoats from major seaport cities or confront their superior numbers in pitched battles, Washington adopted a policy of "watchful waiting." Patriot forces often conducted guerrilla warfare against isolated British units or their supply columns. Washington hoped to wear down the resolve of the British to continue the war or to force them into a situation in which he could make a decisive strike.

Washington needed time, and yet the new nation found even this passive strategy difficult to execute. Most men shunned enlistment in the Continental army, especially as patriotic fervor subsided after 1776. Farming required the most work in spring and early fall, precisely those times most favorable for eighteenth-century warfare. With the habit of nationalism not yet firmly established state governors maintained tight control over their local militias, sometimes not letting them leave the state. Many Americans, fearful of military authority and centralized power, refused to pay taxes to support Washington's troops, and so the regular army lacked not only soldiers but also arms and equipment. The national government, too, lacked sufficient revenue; unable to levy taxes itself, it was dependent on inadequate state contributions. To finance the war the Continental Congress printed millions of paper dollars popularly called "continentals." This flood of currency drove up prices mercilessly. After the French alliance Congress, unwisely assuming that France would pay its bills, printed still more paper money. By 1780 few merchants or farmers would accept "continentals" in payment for supplies. Washington had to resort to impressment—forced sales on credit—to provision his troops. Localism hampered Congress in other ways, too. It could not act without unanimous consent from all thirteen states, a rule that allowed the smaller states to intrigue for large gains as the price of their consent. And the government conducted the war through cumbersome committees. A serious lack of manpower and money, compounded by provincialism and defects in organization, hampered the new nation's effort to survive.

During the war some Americans deplored frivolity as wasteful of money and energy, and at odds with the sobriety needed in a time of national crisis. In the interest of economy, Congress had officially condemned balls and entertainments. A while later it condemned plays put on by officers and men of the Continental Army stationed in Philadelphia as "disagreeable to the sober inhabitants" of the Quaker city. Moralists condemned the growing "licentiousness"—gambling, cockfighting, and wenching—that developed whenever large numbers of young men congregated together in barracks and military encampments.

The moralism of the early wartime years did not last. As the conflict dragged on, standards relaxed. To relieve the tedium of sacrifice and offset the general gloom, urban Americans sought out amusement and pleasure. In British-occupied New York, officers of the military and naval forces opened the "Theater Royal" and sold hundreds of tickets for benefit performances to succor "the Widows and orphans of those who have lost their lives in his majesty's service." Patriots, too, organized theatricals. These, despite congressional disapproval, were popular with officers of the Continental army and attracted many well-dressed ladies and gentlemen.

By 1779 the war had reached a stalemate. Both sides reduced the scale and intensity of the fighting in North America as skirmishes there simply became part of an international war. Now forced to defend as well their possessions in India and the Caribbean, the British withdrew ships and men from America. France, benefiting from England's distress, was slow to aid the revolutionists. Washington's beleagured army mounted no major offensive for a year after the unsuccessful Battle of Monmouth, New Jersey, in June 1778. Civilian morale sagged; unrest mounted in the army. On New Year's Day 1781, Pennsylvania troops mutinied and marched on Philadelphia to seek redress from Congress, which had reassembled there following the British departure. Only promises of quick relief persuaded them to return to camp. It was in this period of despair that General Benedict Arnold began treasonable negotiations with the British to turn over West Point. When his activities were discovered he fled to the British.

Then the war turned in favor of the revolutionists. In Congress a group favoring energetic national government took control. They centralized the administrative departments and enacted a new financial program under the direction of Robert Morris. Supplies were soon flowing to the army again. Meanwhile French money and manpower finally began to arrive in significant amounts. And on the military front Washington at last had a chance to strike.

In the winter of 1778-79 the new British commander-in-chief in America, General Henry Clinton, lacking sufficient troops to pacify the North, had shifted British operations to the South, where he anticipated aid from the large loyalist population. Washington, unable to mount a two-front war, remained encamped outside British-occupied New York City. The British took Savannah and Charleston and encouraged the loyalists to make war on their patriot neighbors. In these circumstances the war in the back country became uncharacteristically savage. At Waxham Creek, South Carolina, in May 1780, Colonel Bonastre Tarleton's Tory Legion massacred a Virginia regiment that had surrendered. According to an eyewitness,

> Not a man was spared . . . and for fifteen minutes after every man was prostrate [the Tories] went over the ground plunging their

---

CORNWALLIS COUNTRY DANCE

The General Cornwallis's retreat and advance across Carolina and Virginia in 1781 reminded an American Balladeer of the contemporary "contre" dance, where two facing lines move back and forth. The English dance tune to which the ballad is set became popular in early nineteenth-century music halls as "Pop Goes the Weasel."

Cornwallis led a country dance the like was never seen, Sir,
Much retrograde and much advance, and all with general Green, Sir.
They rambled up, they rambled down, joined hands, and off they run, Sir,
of General Green to Charlestown, the Earl to Wilmington, Sir.

Quoth he, my guards are weary grown with doing country dances.
They never at St. James had shown at capers, kicks, or prances.
No men so gallant there were seen while saunt'ring on parade, Sir,
or dancing o'er the park so green, or at the masquerades, Sir.

Good Washington, Columbia's sons, whom easy nature taught, Sir,
Now hand in hand they circle round in ev'ry dancing mood, Sir,
The gentle movement soon confounds, the Earl's day draws near, Sir,
the gentle movement soon confounds, the Earl's day draws near, Sir.

His music soon forgets to play; his feet can't move no more, Sir,
And all his men now curse the day they jigged to our shore, Sir.
Now, Tories all, what can you say . . . Cornwallis is no griper,
But while your hopes are danced away, it's you that pay the piper.

The victory at Yorktown, while a serious blow, did not cripple Britain militarily, but it soured British public opinion on the war to such a great extent that George III had to relent and grant the colonies independence.

> bayonets into everyone that exhibited any signs of life, and in some instances, where several had fallen one over the other, these monsters were seen forcing their steel through several bodies at once.

The term "Tarleton's Quarter" became a rallying cry among Southern patriots.

Yorktown. Believing that the South had been subdued, Clinton returned to New York in June 1780, leaving General Charles Cornwallis to complete mopping up operations. A year later, harassed by guerrillas and "tired out marching about the country in quest of adventures," Cornwallis marched his army north toward Virginia for the purpose of cutting rebel communications between North and South. Counting on protection and supplies from the seemingly invincible Royal Navy, he repeatedly violated one of the cardinal rules of warfare: never let your forces be backed up to the sea, where retreat is impossible. Marching up into Virginia, the British army, fooled by Washington's clever feint toward New York, crossed narrow peninsulas again and again along the way.

General Washington seized his opportunity, joined forces with the French, and began moving south. His men, well-fed and well-clothed for a change and sensing the coming climax, fairly trembled with excitement. In September 1780, by secret arrangement with Washington, a French fleet attacked the British fleet off the Virginia Capes; and though the outcome was indecisive the British admiral, not suspecting what was happening on land, sailed away after the battle to New York for repairs, leaving the coast unguarded. Then Cornwallis made the fatal blunder: he moved his army onto a narrow peninsula between the York and James rivers, near Yorktown, and encamped there. The French navy was at his back and a combined force of 9000 Americans and 7800 French suddenly began to besiege him by land. Hopelessly trapped, he fought for three weeks before surrendering his whole army on October 19, 1781. That same day a relief force under Clinton reached the Capes—too late to help.

Diplomacy Wins Independence

The defeat at Yorktown was by no means a military disaster for the British, since they still held America's major seaports. But what Yorktown did accomplish was to dramatize how slender were the possibilities for eventual British victory against the combination of American armies and guerrillas and French power. Another vital consideration was that an end to the fighting in North America would free badly needed fleets and armies to fight in the West Indies and India. Early in 1782, Parliament forced Prime Minister North out of office and demanded negotiations with the United States. Although George III disagreed, most of his subjects thought that a generous peace might conciliate the former colonists, and even draw them back into the British orbit.

The Peacemaking. The Americans, too, were ready to end the war. The Continental Congress was near collapse, and local loyalties and interests were continuing to strain against the national purpose. The victory at Yorktown, however welcome, was more lucky circumstance than a triumph of superior military power or skill. Chances for a large territorial settlement and the prospect of better relations with Britain, a dangerous adversary for any nation so exposed to attack from the sea, understandably attracted many Americans. In fact, the Congress authorized its negotiating team, headed by Benjamin Franklin, to accept almost any treaty that included independence and a withdrawal of British troops. With their mutual interests so aligned, the two enemies seemed likely to conclude a quick agreement.

Yet, negotiations dragged on for nearly two years. The Franco-American alliance of 1778 bound the United States not to make a separate peace. In turn, Louis XVI and his minister Vergennes, in order to gain Spanish support, had promised ministers in Madrid much British territory as booty, especially strategic Gibraltar. The Spanish, moreover, wanted to confine the United States to the area east of the Appalachian Mountains. Although Spain could expect few concessions from Great Britain, it could still hold up indefinitely a settlement between Britain and the United States. In short, America now had more to lose from its friends than from its enemies.

At last, Franklin broke the diplomatic logjam by violating the terms of the alliance with France and opening separate negotiations with English agents. (The French, themselves weakened by a long and costly conflict, were not much upset, for Franklin in effect rescued them from an embarrassingly democratic ally.) Once started, talks progressed steadily. The series of treaties that ended the war, collectively known as the Treaty of Paris, was signed on September 3, 1783. England granted independence and promised to withdraw all of its troops from the colonies. The new nation acquired a huge dowry of land: from the Atlantic seacoast to the Mississippi River. Its boundaries in the north with Canada remained vague, and redcoats still occupied forts south of the Great Lakes. The Gulf coast was ceded to Spain, although both Americans and Englishmen were guaranteed navigation rights on the Mississippi. Britain successfully demanded that "no unlawful impediment" block the collection of prewar debts owed by Americans to British merchants. The treaties also pledged the United States to make restitution to loyalists who had suffered financially during the Revolution. British merchants did succeed in closing the Americans out of imperial commerce, a serious loss for the young nation. Despite these concessions and the lack of adequate enforcement procedures, the Americans had benefited handsomely from European rivalries. War and diplomacy created a new nation with boundaries generous enough to insure future growth and prosperity.

The Revolution at Home

The excitement of warfare obscured important changes within American society. The long struggle for independence accelerated forces and trends already apparent in the colonies before it began. The Revolution strengthened the possibilities of rearranging relationships among classes. Certainly there was, as one historian later wrote, "a struggle not only for home rule, but also over who should rule at home." The colonial elite aimed at preserving much of the old order so beneficial to them. Laborers, artisans, and small farmers often challenged, sometimes successfully, traditional prerogatives. Yet revolution in America involved no wholesale redistribution of property or wealth, no long-term change in the control of government. The War for Independence stopped short of creating an egalitarian society; it is doubtful that most patriot leaders really wanted one. Most people simply yearned for the restoration of harmony and for economic advancement. The colonists, now citizens, wanted to build, not destroy.

Prosperity and Inflation. Eight years of warfare not only profited many individuals but also pushed the overall economy upward. An immense amount of money in circulation raised the prices of nearly everything. The Continental Congress and state governments spent nearly $200 million in hard money, followed by many more millions in paper currency. British soldiers and purchasing agents poured another $50 million into the economy. All this money created an extraordinary demand for commodities and, of course, persistent inflation. Yet few Americans suffered economically. War stimulated production, almost ending unemployment. The need for uniforms and arms, for example, produced rapid growth in the textile and iron industries. Merchants' inventories and farmers' crops grew in value. Bankers lent at high rates of interest to importers and privateers—goods brought through the British blockade commanded enormous profits. State and local governments often imposed price and wage controls, a device used since the Middle Ages to control inflation. Congress regulated monopolies and prevented exports of crucial raw materials. More and more local economies were coming together into a broad national market.

Despite occasionally rigorous local efforts at regulation, the pressures of wartime inflation produced extensive black markets. Shopkeepers and small farmers preferred to deal with Englishmen and private citizens who spent silver and gold coin. An indignant Pennsylvanian angrily refused to sell his grain to one of Washington's agents, saying, "Your money's not worth a damn continental." The phrase caught on. Throughout most of the war, America itself prospered while its government and army suffered penury and hardship. This paradox so angered Washington that he proposed hanging all profiteers.

Land and Slavery, Freedom and Religion. Major changes occurred in the pattern of land ownership. Probably a quarter of the population was loyal to the British Crown, either openly or secretly. Self-interest, an older patriotism that identified the colonies with the Crown, and fear of the mob all combined to give force to loyalist sentiment. By 1778 all thirteen states had confiscated the property of those who "took refuge with the British tyrant." Some 100,000 already had left the country, most for Canada or England, and their estates were sold for money to support the patriot cause. The con-

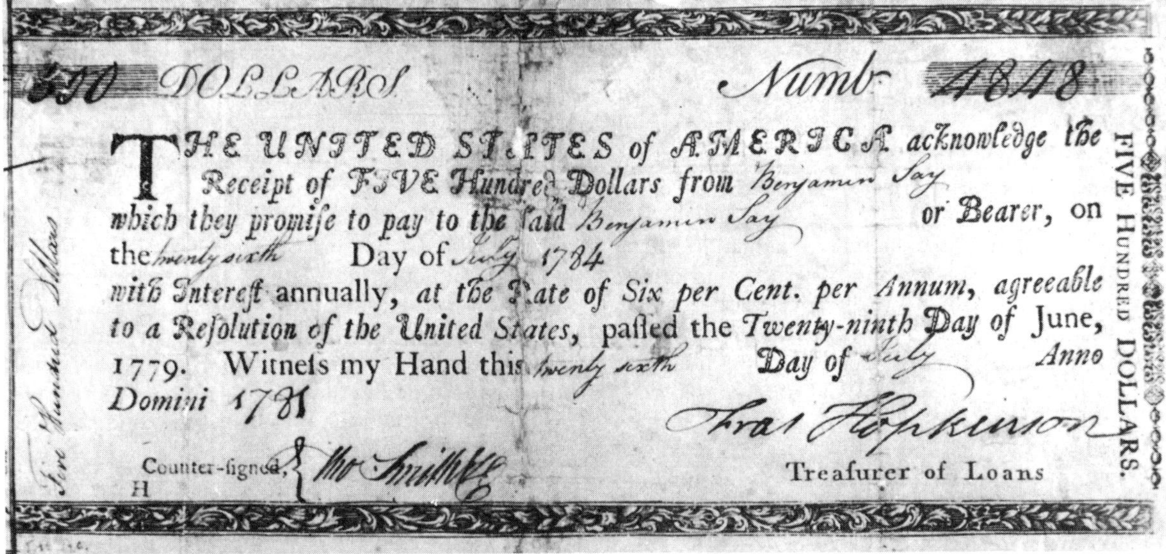
500 DOLLARS Numb 4848

THE UNITED STATES of AMERICA acknowledge the Receipt of FIVE Hundred Dollars from Benjamin Say which they promise to pay to the said Benjamin Say or Bearer, on the twenty sixth Day of July 1784 with Interest annually, at the Rate of Six per Cent. per Annum, agreeable to a Resolution of the United States, passed the Twenty-ninth Day of June, 1779. Witness my Hand this twenty sixth Day of July Anno Domini 1781

Fras Hopkinson
Treasurer of Loans

Counter-signed, Tho Smith
H

Five Hundred Dollars

FIVE HUNDRED DOLLARS.

Bonds paying 6% per year were sold to finance the Revolution. The inflation rate was much higher. *(Courtesy, Chase Bank Collection of Moneys of the World, New York)* fiscated lands were usually bought up by rich speculators or other large landowners, not by tenants and small farmers, who rarely had enough money to buy in places already settled. Instead, they and their children looked westward to the mountains and beyond. Even before the war ended, thousands had moved into Tennessee and Kentucky, northern New England and northern New York. This was one important reason why there was no major attack against property—so much was available elsewhere. Colonial elites fattened themselves on loyalist estates, while smaller farmers moved toward the frontier.

The Revolution made for a rhetoric of liberty that stumbled against the reality of human bondage. "How is it," chided the crusty British writer Samuel Johnson, "that we hear the loudest yelps for liberty among the drivers of Negroes?" Over 5000 blacks served in the American army and navy. Several states granted freedom to slaves who served in the military. Soon a voluble antislavery movement emerged. In most Northern states, slavery was not a large part of the economy, and patriot leaders struck decisively at the institution. Slavery was outlawed in Massachusetts and Vermont, while New York and Pennsylvania adopted plans for gradual emancipation. After the war Congress prohibited slavery in the Old Northwest, that is, north of the Ohio River. But along that part of the Eastern seaboard south of the Mason-Dixon line, antislavery proposals foundered. Leaders there, mostly plantation owners like Washington and Jefferson, granted that slavery was immoral and violated the republican spirit, but accepted it as a "necessary evil."

The Revolution also affected colonial institutions of religion. Patriots drove from their pulpits Anglican ministers, many of whom were strong loyalists. Most states "disestablished" churches, ending the special privileges or civil functions of particular sects. Only Massachusetts and Connecticut still collected taxes to fund a state church; the other states viewed competing religions as equal in the eyes of the law. Tolerance did not extend to atheists, however, and most state legislatures established a religious test (aimed against Jews and Catholics) for holding public office. Blasphemy remained a crime punishable by imprisonment.

Documents like Thomas Jefferson's Statute of Religious Freedom in Virginia, finally enacted by the Virginia legislature in 1786, granted tolerance for the free practice of religion, not a guarantee of rights for non-believers. If narrow by twentieth-century standards, the Statute was for its time a model, proclaimed to the rest of the world as a showpiece of America's new freedom.

How Revolutionary? Historians have argued fiercely about whether or not American society became more open, more fostering of upward mobility, during the Revolutionary era. Certainly some older marks of privilege did disappear. In feudal times European law, seeking to keep intact the property of the upper classes, had enforced the principle of entail, that such property could be passed on only within the same family, and the rule of primogeniture, that it could not be divided in inheritance but must go to the eldest son. Such rules had survived in some colonial laws, applying at least in cases in which a landowner had not provided otherwise in a will. These laws were now swept aside as relics of an age of artificial privilege and inequality. Citizens abandoned titles like "Esquire" or "Colonel" or "Your Excellency," and instead addressed one another simply as "Mr." or "Mrs." Class distinctions based on dress waned; Franklin, for example, insisted upon wearing a simple republican black coat when he appeared in the gaily outfitted courts of Europe. The emigration of thousands of loyalists left many local political offices vacant and created new opportunities.

Yet America remained firmly under the control of an elite class, although that group occasionally shifted in membership. Revolutionary ardor hardly touched the traditional "politics of deference" south of Pennsylvania: local plantation owners there kept control over tidewater society and local government, partly because they received genuine respect from their less affluent neighbors. These wealthy country gentlemen had little trouble beating back challenges to their power from small farmers in the highlands. In Philadelphia, New York, and Boston, long occupied by the British, a coalition of lawyers, merchants, and landowners dominated the cities after the war, much as it had before. The rich held disproportionate power in the Continental Congress. Robert Morris, for example, a merchant and speculator who served in the early 1780s as the nation's chief treasury official, possessed an $8 million fortune.

American political rhetoric, in the heady days that followed revolution, exalted liberty and equality. Yet the kind of freedom, and the kind of equality, that Americans who thought of such things had in mind would be of a stable sort, among farmers, artisans, shopkeepers, and large landowners secure in their lives and possessions. Upper-class Americans who worried that politics might turn into an attack upon wealth had little grounds for concern. Patriot leaders, even the more democratic ones, had no taste for leading mobs against property.

The American Revolution and its aftermath, then, presented no scenes of revolutionary crowds pitted against a besieged upper class. What happened instead was a rational application of the principle, pronounced in the Declaration of Independence, that governments derive "their just Powers from the consent of the governed." Many states liberalized voting qualifications, most of them by substituting taxpaying for a property requirement. Reapportioned legislatures welcomed representatives from backcountry areas; the "middling ranks" of society—small farmers, local businessmen, and artisans—came to occupy office more frequently; and bills of rights prefaced many new state constitutions. Everywhere governors lost power: elected assemblies gained control of patronage and tax matters, while governors in every state but Rhode Island no longer had the power to veto legislation. Legislators stood for election each year. In Pennsylvania, a new constitution abolished altogether the legislature's upper house, traditionally the bastion of the wealthy.

Some less democratic practices lingered. High political office still required the ownership of large amounts of land. Upper chambers of most state legislatures could block the demands of the majority, and unfairly apportioned assemblies mocked the popular will in South Carolina, Virginia, and Georgia. In Georgia, for example, the piedmont—the inland region toward the mountains—contained three-fourths of the population yet received only one-fourth of the seats in the assembly, which was still rigidly dominated by tidewater plantation owners. Nonetheless, throughout the colonies government officials were elected, lower houses had most of the power, and state officials proved extremely susceptible to public opinion. Many people never before interested in politics had discovered their voice.

Even before the Revolution, street protests and intercolonial organizations had begun to bring together working-class people and tenant farmers for common action. Public meetings might be flamboyant exchanges among artisans and sailors. Individuals of every class found themselves taking part in a democracy of public discussion and common action, which is more basic than the formal democracy of the vote. The Revolution must have sustained that sense of being a participant in a public drama. It is fitting that the years of discussion, protest, and revolution resulted in the establishment of a national republic—a continental public that would have a continuing life of discussion, argument, and cooperative action.

Women and the War. The war also affected the lives, and perhaps the self-image, of women. Many had participated in the war effort, either at the front or on the homefront. Many more had become accustomed to discussing politics and military news. Some few, like Mercy Otis Warren, who first wrote anti-British plays and then a history of the Revolution, engaged directly in propaganda. Still others, and Abigail Adams offers a good example, in the absence of husbands and fathers took over the management of farms and businesses about which they had previously known little. In this sense, the war years offered many women an education in independent action. Few, if any, translated that experience into a demand for political rights or equality with men. But many must have emerged from those years with greatly increased confidence in their own abilities, and some even with views like those of Abigail Adams about reducing the tyrannical powers of husbands. Those women who had worked together in the Ladies Association that organized a national fund drive to collect money for the American troops had also experienced the power and satisfaction of women's collective action. That experience would be multiplied in the many women's voluntary associations that emerged in the early nineteenth century.

By and large, women did not gain independence from the Revolution in the same sense that most free men gained it. During the final decades of the eighteenth century single, property-holding women were allowed to vote in New Jersey, but that was not typical of the states, and New Jersey rescinded this limited suffrage at the beginning of the nineteenth century. Few Americans of either gender seriously contemplated political rights for women. Some historians have even argued that some women actually lost independence during the revolutionary period. It appears that by 1800, independent businesswomen were declining in numbers. Certainly the Revolution did not noticeably improve married women's standing in law in general, or their right to hold property in particular. Yet the historian Linda Kerber has argued that in one respect the Revolution brought significant improvement in the status of women—the ideal of virtuous "Republican motherhood." That ideal corresponds quite closely to Abigail Adams's goals. For the ideal of republican motherhood suggested that women deserved a special kind of independence and dignity within the domestic sphere so that they could contribute their special qualities of nurture to the raising of young republicans to ensure the future of the new nation. In this respect as in so many others the slim advantages gained by free white women did not extend to black slave women, whose experience looked more like a grim caricature than an extension of the sanctity and dignity of motherhood.

The Articles of Confederation

The New Government. The same Second Continental Congress that had convened in May 1775 managed the domestic and foreign affairs of the United States for many months following the battles at Concord and Lexington. During this wrenching and momentous period Congress operated effectively as a government. It raised an army and appointed its commander in chief, negotiated with the enemy, authorized a navy, and sent agents and commissioners to France, Spain, Prussia, Austria, and Tuscany. It issued millions of dollars of paper money. And that Congress, meeting within the red brick walls of the Pennsylvania State House, declared that "these United Colonies are, and of Right ought to be, Free and Independent States."

But however effective as a provisional government, the Second Continental Congress could not be a permanent instrument for managing the affairs of a free and independent nation. In June 1776, almost simultaneously with the resolution that led to the Declaration of Independence, Richard Henry Lee proposed a permanent new government to represent all the states. In July, John Dickinson of Pennsylvania, chairman of the committee appointed to draw up the plan of government, submitted his proposals. The Dickinson scheme contained several controversial features. The new Congress was to have broad powers, including the right to establish state boundaries and to dispose of unoccupied Western lands. Each state would have one vote, regardless of its population and the number of representatives it actually sent to Congress.

The Dickinson proposals came under immediate attack in open Congress. The large and influential state of Virginia, which claimed much of the trans-Appalachian West, opposed granting the new government sweeping powers over lands. Many of Virginia's most prominent leaders had for years anticipated selling Western lands to the farmers whom they expected to pour over the mountains when peace returned. On the other hand, delegates from states such as Maryland and Pennsylvania, owning no Western lands as far inland as Virginia claimed, wanted the United States as a whole to acquire the lands toward the Mississippi. Only in this way, they insisted, could Americans from all parts of the new nation benefit from these millions of fertile acres. The delegates also fought over the voting provision. Large states wanted voting by population size. The small states supported the Dickinson proposal. By their reasoning, allotting one vote to each state meant that the new government was a league of sovereign states, while apportioning representation to the states on the basis of their population would suggest, they thought, that the power of the new government flowed directly from the American people, bypassing the states. But some members of Congress objected to the absence in the Dickinson document of any provision reserving specific powers to the states.

The Articles. For almost a year and a half, amidst the smoke and flames of war, Congress debated the issues. Opponents of the original proposal succeeded in adding to it a provision that Congress could exercise only those powers specifically delegated to it by the states. Another change was a victory for Virginia. Under strong pressure from that land-rich state, the delegates at Philadelphia agreed to drop the provision that Congress would control the new nation's Western lands. With these modifications accepted, Congress in November 1777 adopted the Articles of Confederation and sent the new frame of national government to the states for ratification.

Twelve states swiftly ratified the Articles. Maryland, however, held out for the original proposal that Congress control Western lands and refused to ratify until it was restored. A number of prominent Virginians, including Thomas Jefferson, had a grander vision of the West than merely as a mammoth, overgrown Virginia. The great interior valley of North America, they believed, should be carved into

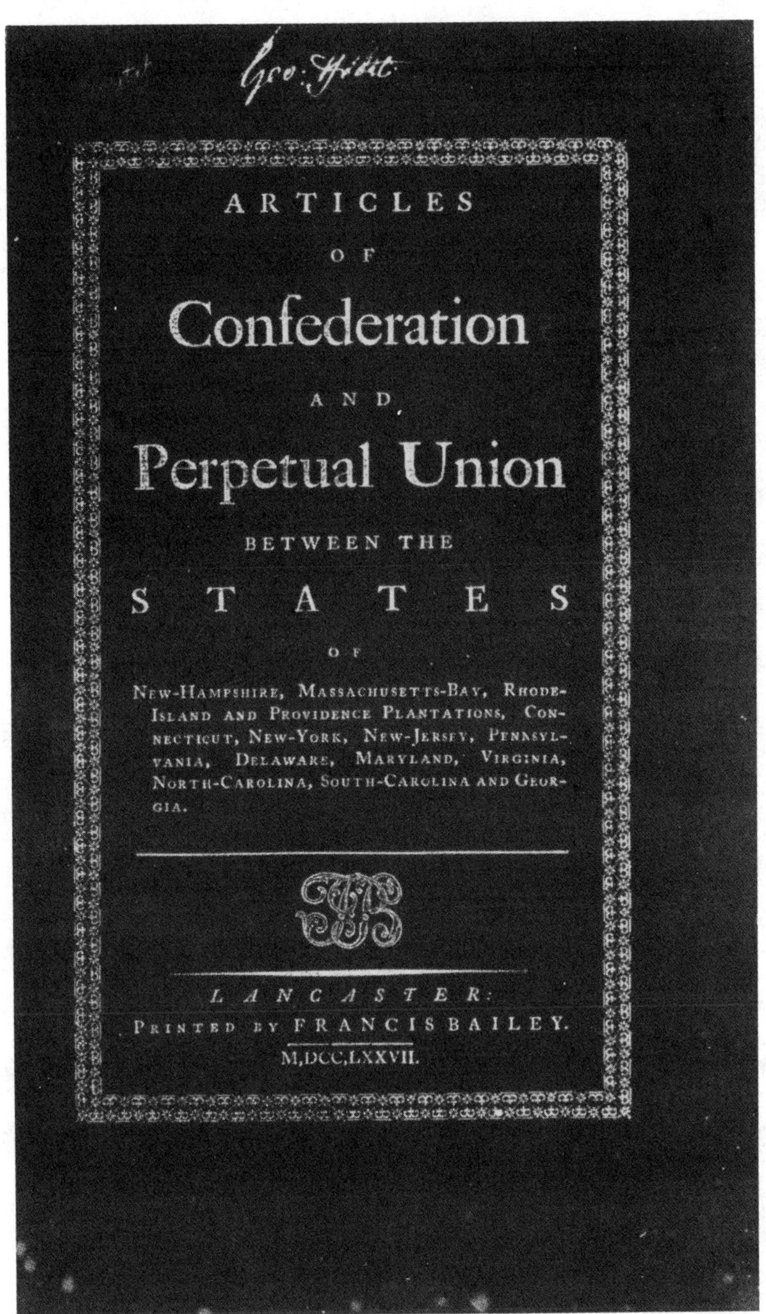

Geo: Hiatt

ARTICLES OF Confederation AND Perpetual Union BETWEEN THE STATES OF NEW-HAMPSHIRE, MASSACHUSETTS-BAY, RHODE-ISLAND AND PROVIDENCE PLANTATIONS, CONNECTICUT, NEW-YORK, NEW-JERSEY, PENNSYLVANIA, DELAWARE, MARYLAND, VIRGINIA, NORTH-CAROLINA, SOUTH-CAROLINA AND GEORGIA.

LANCASTER:
PRINTED BY FRANCIS BAILEY.
M,DCC,LXXVII.

***The Articles of Confederation and Perpetual Uni Between the States*, signed in 1784, pledged the thirteen states to "a firm league of friendship" with one another but failed to create a strong national government.**

new, self-governing states, rather than remain colonies of the seaboard. For the good of the whole nation they were willing to surrender their own state's claims. Under their influence, Virginia ceded its Western lands to Congress. In 1781 the United States had its first constitution. The agreement pledged all the states to "a firm league of friendship" with one another, and committed them to mutual support against attack. It gave to Congress sole power over foreign affairs and over the issues of war and peace. Congress would also deal with the Indians, and the states agreed to surrender to one another all escaped criminals and to give "full faith and credit" to court orders, sentences, and other judicial decisions of other states.

Artillery, both land-based and aboard vessels in the harbor, boomed out a salute to the new government. On the evening of ratification Philadelphia's citizens enjoyed an opulent "collation" presided over by Congress's chief executive officer and a brilliant display of fireworks. The *Pennsylvania Packet*, a Philadelphia newspaper, rhapsodized over the momentous event: "Thus has the union, begun by necessity, been indissolubly cemented. Thus America, like a well constructed arch . . . is growing up in war into greatness and consequence among the nations."

The *Packet's* editor spoke too soon. From the very first, the Articles proved inadequate as a basis for dealing with the difficulties of a new nation. The Confederation amounted to a league of virtually independent sovereign states, not a modern nation. The new government lacked many vital powers. Congress could not tax and had to depend on contributions from the states. Nor could it regulate trade and commerce either among the states or between the United States and other countries. Any attempt to change or modify the Articles required a unanimous vote of all the state legislatures. There was no national judiciary. Under this instrument of government, however weak, Americans did succeed in bringing the war to a successful conclusion. But the Confederation's authority would be too feeble to garner the fruits of victory and manage demobilization successfully.

The "Critical Period"

Yorktown in October 1781 was the war's last important clash of arms. Soon afterward the Lord North ministry in Britain fell, and peace negotiations began in Paris. British and American representatives signed the peace treaty at the end of November 1782. The following April, Congress ratified the treaty. The war was over; the United States was an independent nation.

Debt Problems. During the months following Yorktown, the strains of nationhood, no longer obscured by military events, became painfully apparent. By early 1783 discontent plagued the army stationed at Newburgh, New York. Officers protested Congress's failure to establish a promised pension system for discharged veterans. In early March a group of officers at Newburgh threatened that if Congress did not abide by its pledge, the army would defy the government. Washington calmed the soldiers who were threatening a military coup. When Congress found the means to provide the officers with five years of full pay in lieu of the pensions, the near-revolt was over.

The rank-and-file soldiers still had not received their pay. Congress simply could not raise the money. Some politicians wanted the individual states to make good the back pay, but that would have kept the men in service for many months, a discontented standing army with nothing to do. In the end, Congress discharged most of the troops without meeting their just demands. Most of them rushed back to civilian life with little fuss, but several hundred marched to Philadelphia protesting their shabby treatment. The legislators did not respond bravely. Unable to meet the soldiers' demands and terrified by the angry troops, they fled first to Princeton, then to Annapolis, and finally came to rest in New York, which remained the national capital for several years.

Patriots despaired over the pitiful state of the national government. Congress could pay neither its troops nor its creditors. The war had been financed by a combination of loans, paper money, and, in the case of several states, some taxes. The paper money had seriously depreciated; in 1781 Congress announced that it would not give in exchange to holders of paper currency the hard, coin money that in those days was considered to be the only real and reliable money. But other sizable obligations remained. Congress had borrowed directly from its own citizens, issuing IOU's in exchange for supplies, food, services, and cash. It had also borrowed from Dutch bankers. The states had similar problems. Massachusetts and a few others imposed high taxes to pay their debts; most were content to default like the Confederation government. These unpaid public debts cast a pall over the nation in the years after the war. How could such a country not be an object of scorn in the eyes of the whole world?

The national government was powerless in foreign affairs. That offended both those whose specific interests were hurt and others who merely grieved for the state of their country.

Trouble with Spain. Spain controlled both Florida and the lower reaches of the Mississippi, including the all-important port of New Orleans. By the end of the Revolution 50,000 American farmers lived on the "Western waters" in Kentucky and Tennessee, and many more American husbandmen were eagerly awaiting the opportunity to cross the mountains to the fertile lands of the Mississippi Valley. If these people were not to remain subsistence farmers, they would need outlets for their wheat, pork, beef, corn, and forest products. The route over the mountains was too difficult for the shipping of bulky products, but the great river that flowed to the Gulf of Mexico was a cheap and safe natural highway. Raft-like flatboats could be constructed of local lumber and loaded with barrels of pickled beef, pork, and grain to float with the current to New Orleans. There the rafts could be broken up and sold for lumber, and the barrels reloaded on ocean-going vessels to be carried to the Atlantic coast ports, the Caribbean islands, or Europe. The farmer could then buy some horses and return to Kentucky with some cash in his pocket and manufactured goods in his saddlebags. Control of New Orleans, then, gave Spain a strong hand in dealing with the United States.

In 1784 the Spanish government announced that it was closing the Mississippi to American commerce. Now only Spanish subjects could use the river and the port of New Orleans. All others would be arrested.

Westerners threatened to raise ten thousand troops to march on New Orleans. Some listened to British agents who promised protection if they would reunite with Great Britain. Washington, seriously worried at the prospect of national dismemberment, reported after a long journey through the frontier that "the western settlers . . . stand as it were upon a pivot. The touch of a feather would turn them any way."

America's diplomatic weakness was soon confirmed. Negotiations began in 1785 between Spain and America over the "right of deposit" at New Orleans—in effect, the right to use the port there for foreign trade. Dour, tight-lipped John Jay, Congress's Secretary for Foreign Affairs, met with the suave and charming Don Diego de Gardoqui, Spain's negotiator. The Spanish emissary knew that the powerless Americans were in no position to threaten Spain, and refused to grant the major American demand, the right of deposit, although he was willing to make minor boundary adjustments along the West Florida border and allow some American trade within the Spanish empire. Congress refused to accept the treaty, and it died. New Orleans remained a tight cork bottling up the mouth of the Mississippi.

Trouble with Britain. The British, who could make more trouble for the new nation than Spain, had no reason to wish the Americans well. The rebels had gotten the independence they wanted, and they could jolly well accept its burdens. In 1783 Lord Sheffield, a prominent member of Parliament, published a pamphlet urging the British government to deny the Americans the trading rights within the empire that they had enjoyed before 1776. The "American states," Sheffield noted, could not "act as a nation," and so were "not to be feared as such by us." The pamphlet struck a receptive chord.

The all-important port of New Orleans became a point of conflict between Spain and America. *(Courtesy, The I. N. Phelps Stokes Collection, The New York Public Library)*

In July 1783 the English Privy Council issued an order that closed the British West Indies to most American commerce.

This order dismayed farmers of the Northern states, who had long sent their surplus provisions to Jamaica, Barbados, and the other British islands. It also hurt the New England fishing industry, which had supplied the sugar plantations with dried cod and mackerel, and the merchants of New York, Philadelphia, Salem, and Boston who had carried these goods. The shipping industry employed hundreds of seamen, and thousands more in such related occupations as shipbuilding and the making of sail and rope. The British Caribbean planters connived at the smuggling of needed products, but this scarcely made up for the damage to American interests.

The Americans were in no position to retaliate. The British, of course, needed the American market for their manufactured goods. In the immediate postwar period, in fact, British goods flooded the United States, causing severe distress among American artisans and manufacturers who could not compete with the cheaper English commodities. Paying for imports from Britain also drained gold and silver coin from the nation. Had Congress been able to impose a tariff on British imports, it might have stemmed the inward flow of English manufactured goods, encouraged native production, and forced the British to reconsider their exclusion of American agricultural products from the West Indies. Several states, urged on by mass meetings of artisans and craftsmen, did impose duties on foreign goods. But then the British found ways of sending their product through adjacent states that had no such taxes. Efforts to erect trade barriers between states created bad feeling among neighbors. Merchants of New London, Connecticut, boycotted New York; New Jersey taxed the New York lighthouse at Sandy Hook.

Under the peace treaty ending the war, the British had granted the United States all the territory south of the Great Lakes and north of the Spanish possessions—all the way to the Mississippi River—and had promised to give up their military posts in the Northwest "with all convenient speed." For many months, however, they refused to remove the garrisons. The British did not wish to abandon their Indian allies and were reluctant to surrender the rich fur trade. They justified their delay by citing two provisions of the peace treaty: the promise that the Americans would do nothing to prevent British creditors from collecting millions of pounds in prewar debts, and the assurance that Congress would try to get the states to compensate loyalists for their wartime losses. The states had not yet fulfilled either of these promises, and Congress was powerless to compel compliance. The governments of Virginia and Maryland, dominated by planters, wrote off about £2,000,000 in private debts that their citizens owed to British merchants.

The Confederation tried to achieve a settlement of these issues. John Adams, the American minister to England, threatened, pleaded, and cajoled, in an effort to persuade the British to relent on trade and meet their obligations under the peace treaty. But British officials presumed the weakness of the United States and dug in their heels.

Barbary Pirates. One final confrontation came close to being the most humiliating of all. For many years the deys and pashas of the Barbary Coast states of North Africa, Algiers, Tunis, Tripoli, and Morocco had preyed on European commerce. Most European nations either paid blackmail to these corsairs or provided naval protection for their own commerce. So long as the Americans were dependents of Great Britain, the British navy and treasury had covered them as well as Englishmen. After independence this protection ceased. In 1785 the New England ship *Maria* was captured by Algerians, who stole its merchandise, stripped the crew of all their clothes and possessions, and then sold them into North African slavery. American merchants demanded that Congress respond to such ruthless attacks. But without a navy or the means to create one, the Confederation government could do nothing to overawe the Barbary pirates. Congress did manage to raise $80,000 to buy exemption from the deys, but this was so little that only the Moroccan leader would conclude a treaty. In a few years, under the administration of John Adams, the American navy would so punish the pirates as to free the country from further trouble with them. It would be one of the most assertive acts of the new nation.

Paper Money. Creditors of the new government, whether original holders of Congress's securities or speculators in them, had no more reason to respect the new government than did foreign nations. They had little hope of ever being paid. Farmers who had supplied commodities to the British West Indies and southern Europe, merchants who had traded with these regions, and all those in the port towns who had relied on this trade for a living saw their economic horizon shrink. Equally aggrieved were craftsmen and artisans in the towns who found their businesses and jobs wiped out by the deluge of cheap British goods.

Debtors, too, found times hard and sought to offset the difficulties they encountered. One favorite scheme of debtor groups to counteract the postwar deflation was state-issued paper money. When paper money is in circulation a unit of money tends to decline in value more quickly than when the only currency is in "hard" money of gold or silver. That is because the quantity of gold and silver is limited while paper can be printed in any amount a government chooses. Even when the understanding is that the government will give gold or silver to any holder of paper money who demands the exchange, the government can print more paper than it possesses in gold and silver hoping that it will never be asked to exchange all the paper for metallic coin. The more paper money a government prints, or even the greater the public expectation that the government will flood the economy with paper, the less will be the value of any single unit of currency. A paper currency would therefore be to the advantage of debtors, for they would be able to pay their debts with units of money cheaper than those they had borrowed. Once it had been said that only farmers favored such paper-money schemes, but in Maryland indebted planters supported them and in Pennsylvania and South Carolina merchants endorsed them. Not only were planters and merchants often in debt themselves, but many believed that the lack of a circulating medium made all business hard to conduct and contributed to the depressed state of the economy. Where state paper money issues were kept under control, even the richer and more conservative had few objections. In a number of states, however, paper money became in effect a way of confiscating a part of creditors' property.

In North Carolina, Georgia, and New Jersey the paper money issues authorized by the state legislatures quickly depreciated, yet creditors were forced to take it at face value. The most notorious case occurred in Rhode Island. In 1786 that maverick little state issued an avalanche of paper money. These notes were legal tender, so if any creditor refused to accept them the bills could be deposited with a judge and the debt legally canceled. Many Rhode Island merchants closed their doors rather than accept the notes. Creditors fled the state to escape debtors anxious to pay them in depreciated paper. Social and economic conservatives found this situation just another example of the anarchy that was inevitable when there was no strong central body to restrain abuses.

Daily Life

It would be a mistake to paint too dark a picture of the so-called "Critical Period," the years between Yorktown and the meeting of the Constitutional Convention at Philadelphia during the summer of 1787. Most ordinary Americans went about their daily affairs without too much thought to the problems that beset their nation. The vast majority of the 2.8 million Americans of 1780—say, eighty percent—were farmers or members of farm families. The people who worked the soil were by no means all alike. Some 600,000, virtually all living south of Pennsylvania, were black slaves. Another considerable group was made up of white tenants or indentured white servants. A few thousand, also mostly in the South—though some were to be found in the Hudson Valley and a few other spots as well—were owners of great estates worked by slaves, tenants, or servants. In between was the largest group, perhaps sixty percent: these were free farmers who owned their own land.

Social and Economic Classes. Among such varied groups there was inevitably a wide range of habits, customs, and conditions. Slaves who worked in the fields wore rough cotton trousers, shirts, or dresses. They went barefoot in summer and put on crude leather shoes in winter. Their workday was long, typically from dawn to dusk. They ate corn in various forms—hominy, corn bread, roasting ears—and consumed some pork, fish, and poultry, as well as vegetables raised in their own small gardens. Some slaves were skilled craftsmen or house servants who dressed better, ate better, and had more freedom of movement and more privacy than field hands. But this privileged group was a small minority of the total, perhaps ten percent.

The day-to-day lot of indentured servants was not much better than that of slaves. But there were several crucial differences between them and black bondsmen. They were not subject to race prejudice and after a prescribed number of years—usually from four to seven—they were

***Head of a Negro*, by John Singleton Copley. By 1780, some 600,000 slaves worked the lands of the south.** *(Copyright © 1983, Founders Society, Detroit Institute of Arts)*

free and could, with luck and enterprise, rise on the social scale. A number did. Several signers of the Declaration of Independence, for example, had been indentured servants. We think of indentured servitude as primarily a colonial institution, but many such servants continued to come well after independence and even into the nineteenth century.

White tenant farmers lived more comfortably than either slaves or white servants. Many enjoyed full citizenship rights and could vote. Their actual lot depended a great deal on special circumstances.

Yeoman farmers who owned their hundred to two hundred acres of land outright were the backbone of the country. They were especially numerous in New England, Pennsylvania, New Jersey, and the back-country and mountain areas of the Southern states. Those who lived close to cities or connected to them by good roads or navigable rivers produced crops not only for themselves and their families but also perhaps for distant markets in the West Indies, the Mediterranean, or Newfoundland. These farmers were by no means rich; the trade provided the means to buy a few luxuries and goods they could not themselves produce. Farmers distant from markets had to make do with what they and their wives and children alone could make. This accounts for the extraordinary range of household manufactures common in this period. The farmer or his wife spun cotton, linen, or wool yarn and wove it into cloth. They made shoes and clothing of skins and leather. They produced candles, beer, cheese, preserves, and pickled meats. They built their own houses with the help of neighbors and perhaps a local skilled carpenter. Families were generally large, and children helped. Their labors created modest comfort and a rough abundance of food, clothing, and shelter even among the subsistence farmers. By comparison with the lot of a European peasant, that of an American farming family was enviable.

A few got rich cultivating the soil: the growers of tobacco in Maryland and Virginia, the planters who raised rice and the dye indigo in South Carolina and Georgia, the Hudson Valley landlords who grew grain and raised livestock. The traveler in Confederation America encountered many mansions through the Hudson Valley, along the streams and inlets of the Chesapeake region, and in the Carolina and Georgia sea islands and coastal lowlands. Most of those built since the 1740s were of brick with plaster trim, designed in the gracious Georgian style with evenly spaced windows and classical cornices and moldings over windows and doors. With large ballrooms, imported English furniture, and many bedrooms, these structures attested to growing affluence and sophistication.

Merchants and Townspeople. Maritime merchants of the port cities constituted another wealthy class. In Boston the average merchant left $5000 in real estate and personal property to his heirs. A few were fabulously rich. Sharing in the prosperity in about equal measure were lawyers and doctors, especially those who practiced in the larger communities. Instead of country homes the urban rich had large townhouses surrounded by gardens. They too ate elaborate meals, dressed in silk and fine broadcloth, wore wigs or powdered their hair, and traveled by coach or on horseback.

The towns were busy with the work of shopkeepers, innkeepers, clerks, seamen, laborers, and artisans. Few of the day laborers earned more than two shillings a day. This was sufficient to keep a young man in modest comfort, but it was not enough to marry and raise a family. Porters, pick-and-shovel workers, and the like could marry only if their wives were to work as seamstresses, laundresses, or servants of some sort. Skilled craftsmen, on the other hand,

***Pat Lyon at the Forge*, by John Neagle. Skilled craftsmen often owned their shops and had little trouble earning a good living.** *(Courtesy, Museum of Fine Arts, Boston)*

had little trouble earning a good living. Carpenters, blacksmiths, shipwrights, tailors, cordwainers, barrelmakers, masons, printers, and other artisans often owned their own shops and so were small businessmen. The typical urban artisan family ate well. Daily clothing was often of leather or coarse wool, but each member had a good outfit for Sunday. The father often owned his own small house. The family ate off pewter, rather than silver. Some craftsmen became fairly prosperous. The tailor Ephraim Copeland had a house and land worth $1130, a silver pocket watch, silver buckles for his shoes, two gold rings, six silver spoons, and furniture and household goods worth $375.

Churches. Sunday was a day of rest not only in Congregational New England, but also in the middle states and the South, where there were many Baptists, Methodists, and Presbyterians, as well as more easygoing Episcopalians. For the Sabbath each member of a family reserved one suit of clothes of good wool or corduroy that might last through a person's lifetime and be handed down to children. Religious observances were more than a quest for solace in an uncertain world, or traditional observances imposed by community pressure. They were also social events. Young people dressed up not only for the minister but for one another. The church was one of the few meeting places for young men and women and many a courtship began in church under the watchful eyes of parents and older brothers and sisters. Many older Americans enjoyed the ministers' sermons although these often droned on for two hours or more at a stretch. They enjoyed meeting neighbors and liked to sing hymns.

Members of the new evangelical sects, such as the Baptists, Methodists, and "new light" Presbyterians, found deep emotions in church attendance and did not confine their religious participation to the weekly meeting. Beginning in the 1780s, great revivals swept the back country, especially in the South. Many of these were held in churches; others took place at temporary encampments in open places where hundreds of pious people came for several days, well provided with provisions, to listen to eloquent preachers exhort sinners to repent their evil ways, turn to God, and find everlasting salvation. More sedate people despised these camp meetings; they sneered at the "ranting" preachers and expressed horror at the shrieks, jerks, and groans of the listeners caught up in the emotions of the event. Critics also claimed that these camp meetings were opportunities for the nubile young to indulge their awakening sexual appetites. But however unseemly or disreputable, the camp meeting provided an important emotional release for rural Americans whose lives otherwise were largely bound up in a round of monotonous toil.

Amusements. The ten percent or so of Americans who dwelt in substantial towns or cities enjoyed more varied lives. Cities brought people together daily and offered great opportunities for amusement.

A popular urban pastime was the street celebration or pageant. During and after the war the anniversary of the signing of the Declaration of Independence became a general occasion for bonfires, fireworks, and noisy parades. In Philadelphia, news of the treaty of peace set off a surge of revelry so boisterous that prudent citizens feared for the safety of their property.

Then, as today, Americans were susceptible to fads and crazes. A peculiar one of the Confederation period concerned balloons, the first of which, inflated with hot air, had recently been launched in France. The idea of men finally freeing themselves from the force of gravity seized the public's imagination. By midsummer 1784 it was said that nothing attracted attention unless it had the word "balloon" attached to it. Fashionable people wore "balloon" ornaments and a farmer hawking his vegetables in town sold them as "fine balloon string beans." Perhaps the fad was no more explicable than other popular fancies, but it would not be an exaggeration to say that release from earthly limits had a special appeal to newly independent Americans.

Progress Under the Confederation

Not all Americans found the "Critical Period" to be a time of distress. Some had reason to see it as one of progress. If businessmen engaged in the Caribbean and Mediterranean trades were hurt, others trading with France, northern Europe, and non-European parts of the world made clear gains.

Expanding Commerce. With the break from England, American merchants ceased to be hindered by Parliament's navigation acts and began direct trade with parts of Europe from which they had been virtually excluded. Soon American vessels were showing up regularly in the harbors of Sweden, Holland, and Denmark, and even faraway Russia.

Still more interesting was the new trade with the Far East. In 1784 Robert Morris and some partners fitted out the 360-ton *Empress of China* with a cargo containing the root ginseng, which the Chinese believed increased sexual potency. The vessel sailed for Canton around the Cape of Good Hope. It returned to New York the following year with its hold stuffed with tea, silk, chinaware, cotton cloth, and other goods that earned a profit for the promoters of almost $40,000. In a few years American ships were rounding Cape Horn, scudding up the Pacific coast to the region north of California, picking up the beautiful otter skins of the Pacific Northwest, and sailing on across the Pacific to Canton. On one such voyage in 1792, Captain Robert Gray discovered the mighty Columbia River. These voyages provided a much-needed outlet for American commodities, and at the same time created a taste for Chinese furniture, housewares, and textile patterns, as well as an interest in Chinese civilization.

The New Land. The peace treaty of 1783 had left the United States with a princely landed domain. Between the Appalachians and the Mississippi, stretching from Canada in the North to the Spanish possessions in the South, lay enough unoccupied real estate to provide every free American family of 1775 with a tract of 750 acres, over a square mile of land. A dense level forest of hardwoods and pines, interrupted by occasional clearings and a few rolling hills, the region remained formidable. Mosquitoes and biting flies swarmed everywhere in summer. Winters were bitter. The Indians of the region, especially the Shawnee, Wyandot, Iroquois, and Miami in the North, and the Cherokee, Choctaw, and Chickasaw to the South, claimed millions of acres as their hunting grounds; most stood ready to resist any white settlers who would come to occupy their lands. Isolated settlements of French farmers and merchants were still scattered through the region, at Vincennes in present-day Indiana and at Kaskaskia, now within the state of Illinois.

The legal claims to this magnificent region were ambiguous. Virginia, with the broadest claims, had ceded its lands to the Confederation government. But other states tried to hold substantial portions of the West, a number of them awarding some of this land to their war veterans. Bit by bit, the states gave up their claims in favor of the nation, retaining in most cases only small parcels. For many years, however, state and federal claims overlapped.

Some Americans, especially Easterners who feared the political eclipse of their own part of the country, wanted the new region to remain secondary to the older states, with new settlers denied full representation in Congress. Others, more liberal in outlook, hoped to see equal states carved out of the region. Supporters in the older states saw the public domain as a source of federal revenue. One obvious maneuver was to sell the land at high prices—for immediate returns, large wholesale parcels could be sold to land speculators, who in turn could profit by retail sales to settlers. Pioneer farmers urged to the contrary that cheap land be available for all Americans, and felt less concern for the Confederation government's need for money.

A tray from the late eighteenth or early nineteenth century, depicting the rare sight of a black minister preaching to the flock. *(Rhode Island School of Design)*

Still another disagreement arose between those who favored the New England mode of settlement, in which after survey the land would be settled in small, tight-knit communities, and those who preferred the Southern system, in which an individual could buy a land warrant to a certain number of acres and then simply stake out settlers' land. The first system would be slow but orderly; the second promised to work faster, but would be likely to lead to overlapping claims and confusion.

The Land Ordinance of 1785 was one of two measures in which the Confederation government laid down its basic policy toward the West and the public domain. It provided first for a careful survey of the land and then its division into townships six-miles square, these to be divided into thirty-six sections, each of one square mile, or 640 acres. Half the township might be sold as a unit; the other half would be offered on the market only in single sections. Actual sales at auction to the highest bidder started with a minimum price of a dollar an acre. Congress reserved four sections of each 36-section township for later use and kept one to sell for revenue to maintain local schools.

The Land Ordinance did not please everyone. It provided in effect for slow, orderly settlement, and its minimum price and prescribed plot size meant that a pioneer farmer needed at least $640 to acquire a farm—in those days, a hefty sum. At the same time, it favored the establishment of family farms over speculation, however imperfectly. Congress soon violated its own principles, however, by also selling almost two million acres of land to a group of speculators organized under the name of the Ohio Company, granting them an option on an addi-

In 1785 the federal government built Fort Harmar on the Ohio, providing the opening wedge of settlement in what was established as the Northwest Territory two years later. *(Courtesy, The New York Public Library)*

tional five million—all for well under a dollar an acre.

The Northwest Ordinance. Before long, Congress also reached a decision on the political organization of part of the trans-Appalachian area—the region bounded by Pennsylvania on the East, the Great Lakes to the North, the Mississippi on the West, and on the South the Ohio River. The Northwest Ordinance of 1787 was a milestone in the progress of Americans across the continent. This ordinance, along with the Land Ordinance, represented one triumph of statesmanship for the weak and faltering Confederation Congress. Borrowing from an earlier plan proposed by Jefferson, the Ordinance laid out the process by which the Northwest might eventually become a group of self-governing states, equal in all respects to the original thirteen. In time the area would be carved into between three and five territories, governed initially by officials appointed by Congress. When a territory acquired a population of five thousand adult males, it would be allowed to elect an assembly and could send a non-voting delegate to Congress. With a population of sixty thousand free inhabitants, the territory became eligible to apply for admission as a fully equal, self-governing state. The final section of the Ordinance of 1787 reflected the most liberal spirit of the Revolutionary era. All residents of a territory would enjoy complete freedom of worship, full representation in the territorial assembly in proportion to their numbers, trial by jury, and other fundamental protections to both persons and property. In a provision that would later take on great significance, slavery was forbidden in the whole of the vast region.

There remained an important Western problem that the Confederation government could not solve: what to do with the Indians. In 1784 Congress had sent five commissioners to meet with the tribes of the Northwest in an effort to open the eastern portion of the region to white settlement. At Fort Stanwix the commissioners got the Iroquois to surrender their claims for a few trinkets. Next, they coerced the Chippewa, Ottawa, Wyandot, Shawnee, and Delaware into giving up most of their Ohio lands. The resentful tribesmen quickly repudiated these agreements and were soon trading blows with the frontiersmen now pouring into the Ohio country in advance of survey. The government sought to pacify the irate Indians by promising them additional gifts, while at the same time it strengthened the army garrisons in the West. But the Indians were not at peace with the settlers.

Points To Think About

1. The war had advanced the unity of English America and helped create a sense of shared nationality. Thirteen separate political and social entities in 1775, these communities had learned much about cooperation between 1763 and 1783. But were they truly a nation? Previous republics had always been small, homogeneous city-states. Never had one been so large in extent. Could this unusual creation called the United States, with its 900,000 square miles and 3 million people, survive as an independent republic?

2. Another way of thinking about the Revolution was available to American statesmen and writers. Educated people knew the history of the ancient city republics and Rome. They looked into history for examples of republican virtue: patriotism, honesty, simplicity, the rejection of wealth and luxury. It must have been natural for Americans to suppose that the ancient republican spirit might have a rebirth on the American continent amid a free and industrious people uncorrupted by the vices of older civilizations. The idea of virtuous republican simplicity survived into the early years of the United States, expressing itself particularly in Jeffersonian politics. It was not until much later that Americans would become fully committed to the tasks and virtues appropriate not to a simple republic but to a modern, urban, industrial nation.

Suggested Readings

Garry Wills, *Inventing America: Jefferson's Declaration of Independence* (1978) is a readable and engaging study of the intellectual background of America's first national document. Gordon Wood's *The Creation of the American Republic, 1776-1787* (1969) explores the relationship between ideology and social and political reality. In *We the People: The Economic Origins of the Constitution* (1958) and *E Pluribus Unum: The Formation of the American Republic, 1776-1789* (rev., 1979), Forrest McDonald presents the Founding Fathers not as the self-interested businessmen an earlier twentieth-century generation of scholars had described but as statesmen committed to the founding of a secure republic. Jackson Turner Main stresses class and sectional differences in *The Social Structure of Revolutionary America* (1956) and subsequent studies. Other important studies are Mary Beth Norton, *Liberty's Daughters: The Revolutionary Experience of American Women* (1980) and Rhys Isaac, *The Transformation of Virginia* (1982). A nationalist account of the confederation era is J. N. Raskove, *The Beginnings of National Politics* (1979).

☆ ☆ DEBATE ☆ ☆ ☆

ELIZABETH FOX-GENOVESE

Was the American Revolution, whether conservative or radical for men, a revolution at all for women? The previous debate between McDonald and Genovese scarcely touches the question. Presumably the two gentlemen assume that women, confined as they should be to the custody of their husbands and fathers, experienced the Revolution as members of families and social classes. Women gained or lost as their men gained or lost. Their independent political rights were not an issue.

In practice, the experience and opportunities of most women did depend on the position of the men of their families. Most women lived the large part of their lives within households that were directed and politically represented by men. But that does not exhaust the debate. As members of revolutionary or loyalist families and communities, women participated extensively in the events of the revolutionary period, including the fighting. And after the smoke had cleared and peace was restored, women faced the future as members of a new country—the United States. Most of the laws that resulted from the Revolution, especially the Constitution, did not directly address women's position and rights in society. And those few that did derive from the English common law largely retained by United States courts. But the consolidation of the new national government did bring increasing standardization in women's experience. The definition and implementation of men's rights inexorably led to the eradication of all the quirks and anomalies that had permitted women to act independently in public. The more American laws and institutions defined men as citizens and individuals, the more they defined women as domestic beings, as non-citizens, as dependents.

It never occurred to any of the revolutionary leaders that there was any reason to modify the prevailing relations between men and women. When Abigail Adams wrote to her husband that he should "remember the ladies," she was asking that the domestic powers of husbands be reduced and, above all, that they cease behaving like tyrants within the household, but she was not asking that women be allowed to participate in government. During the second half of the eighteenth century advanced advocates of women's rights were insisting on women's capacity for an essentially female excellence, but not asking that women be recognized as functionally interchangeable with men.

In effect, the American Revolution strengthened gender as a form of social classification. If previously women had been able to relate to the polity—or at least the public area—as delegates of families on occasion when family and class membership superseded gender membership, then after the Revolution they related to the polity as women first and members of families or classes second. This intensification of gender as a form of social classification has led historians to argue that women actually lost opportunities as a result of the Revolution.

Others contend that women gained through their heightened identification with other women, through the emergence of a recognizable "women's sphere" within which they forged tight bonds of sisterhood. But neither ties the short-term changes of the Revolution very closely to the long-term changes in society. So the question remains: If the Revolution did not result in women's inclusion in the polity, if the new republic did not welcome women as citizens, what did the specific political transformations offer women?

What changed was that the view of women as women—what it meant to be a woman—improved. Previously seen as potentially dangerous and deviant, as possible witches or probable shrews, women were suddenly seen as the mothers of citizens and the republic. Where they had previously been bound to labor under the direction of the male heads of their households, they now were ascribed governance of the home. The ties that bound women to their gender tightened, but their gender gained status. The belief that women had a particular feminine sensibility legitimated their demands for education, though a different education from that for men; the conviction that they were capable of superior moral purity and had special insights into the human condition legitimated their concern with social problems, though not with the political wrangling over those problems; the respect and self-respect that they had won legitimated their quest for excellence within their own sphere.

The record then leaves us with a paradox. The most important results of the Revolution were political and resolutely excluded women. The indirect results were social and ideological and attempted to circumscribe and control women. But in contributing to a clearer definition of women as women, these results also undercut the time-honored vision of women as inferior or lesser men. By proposing that women should aspire to excellence in their own sphere, they allowed that women *could* be excellent. Once that possibility had been granted, it remained only a matter of time until women would begin to claim that they could be excellent citizens.

Women and the Revolution 

FORREST McDONALD

The Revolution was even more of an all-male phenomenon than Professor Fox-Genovese imagines. Prior to 1775 Americans were monarchists who regarded England's "mixed" form of government—partly monarchical, partly aristocratic, partly democratic—as the source of their liberty. They respected and loved their king, and during the imperial crisis they repeatedly petitioned him to use the royal prerogative to prevent Parliament from encroaching upon American rights and naively hoped he would do so. When, instead, he declared them to be in rebellion and sent troops to suppress them, they were convinced of betrayal: fully three-quarters of the Declaration of Independence consists of angry charges against George III.

In their reaction Americans committed themselves irrevocably to a republican form of government. Republicanism had not been common in Europe for many centuries, but ancient Greece and Rome furnished models, and a variety of modern political philosophers theorized about republics. The principles of republican theory were familiar even to the common man in America, and Americans had fashioned their state constitutions upon those principles. What does all this have to do with the role of women in the Revolution? Republicanism totally and expressly excluded them.

The word "republic" derives from the Latin *res publica*, meaning the public thing or that which is of concern to the public. "Public," in turn, comes from the same Latin root as pubic, meaning maturity or manhood. Women were necessarily excluded, as were children, slaves, and the propertyless; for all these descriptions of people were dependent, which was regarded as incompatible with the full status of manhood. (Unlike "public," the "people" and "popular" were terms that included everybody).

It was universally agreed that the activating principle of a republic was and must be public virtue. This did not mean benevolence, kindness, thoughtfulness, or any of the other attributes associated with the idea of Christian charity. Rather, "virtue" stemmed from the Latin *virtus*, meaning manliness; it connoted courage, strength, virility, self-sufficiency. To say that public virtue must activate the republic, then, is almost to be redundant: it means that manly men must attend to those matters which are of concern to men. The opposite of virtue, in eighteenth-century usage, was "effeminacy," which was used interchangeably with "vice" and "luxury."

John Adams had a great deal to say on the subject. When the principles of a republic were pure, he wrote, it was "productive of everything, which is great and excellent among Men." But "there must be a positive Passion for the public good, the public interest, Honor, Power, and Glory." This public passion "must be Superior to all private Passions. Men must be ready, they must pride themselves, and be happy to sacrifice their private Pleasures, Passions, and Interests, nay, their private Friendships and dearest Connections, when they stand in Competition with the Rights of Society." As for women, "their delicacy renders them unfit for practice and experience in the great business of life, and the hardy enterprise of war, as well as the arduous cares of state."

A less rigorous form of republican theory, popular among Americans outside of New England also had little place for women. Agrarian republicanism, formulated by the seventeenth-century English political theorist James Harrington, held that ownership and cultivation of the land bred independence and manly virtue, and contended that if most of the people did own and cultivate their own land the supply of public virtue would always be adequate for the support of the republic. The great mass of the white adult males in America were in fact owners and cultivators of the soil, but the consequence for women was to deprive them of part of the limited role that Professor Fox-Genovese depicts them as having had in the early republic. They could be mothers of the sons of the republic, it is true, but they could not have the dominant role in child rearing. The menfolk were physically present almost all the time in the vast majority of American households; female children were required to be dutifully submissive to them, males to be respectfully imitative of them. In other words, after the first few years mothers were normally excluded from the shaping of the characters of their sons. Not for another generation, when increasing numbers of men began to go into manufacturing, commerce, and other urban pursuits that kept them away from home all day, did women begin to take over the rearing of their sons.

As a postscript, it should be noted that there was one significant exception to the exclusion of women from public affairs. Quite a few wives of printers outlived their husbands and continued to publish their newspapers after becoming widows. Because the press was the only medium for making an appreciable impact on public opinion in a large and thinly populated nation, such women as the widows of Benjamin Franklin Bache and Thomas Greenleaf were potentially more influential than any males except those in the highest echelons of government and business.

Alexander Hamilton, by John Trumbull. Hamilton seized on the Whiskey Rebellion as an opportunity to establish the authority of the new constitutional government. *(Courtesy, Yale University Art Gallery)*

CHAPTER 6

We the People 1787–1800

THE WHISKEY REBELLION

The United States in 1794 was an insecure young nation. Although the federal government now possessed augmented powers under the new Constitution and the prestige that the national hero, George Washington, brought as its president, it was nonetheless a most fragile polity beset by enormous pressures. No one was certain what to expect from a "republic." History told of dangers from mob rule, and the contemporary revolution in France seemed to be confirming to many that view of the mob as a frightening drama. Renewed war between France and Great Britain pointed up American weakness. The British Navy disrupted American trade, seized American cargoes, and impressed American sailors—forcibly took them into service. At the same time, the French interfered boldly in American affairs, encouraging the organization of pro-French democratic societies and commissioning privateers from American ports to prey on British shipping. Different American regions, political subdivisions, and ethnic groups had their own interests, and looming over all were the diverging concerns of the rich and the poor, the agrarians and the developing commercial elites, the varying class and economic groups making up a sprawling land.

The new government's great initiative to unite this variegated republic was Secretary of the Treasury Alexander Hamilton's financial plan, which sought to use the federal government and the national debt to give the developing commercial classes a direct fiscal stake in the success of the new government. One cornerstone of that policy was an excise tax on alcoholic beverages. This would provide revenues to fund the national debt and to finance the government—including, many feared, its military capacity.

Whiskey was the cash crop of Western Pennsylvania. Readily transportable and salable, it stored much better than the grain whence it came. It gurgled and jostled in jugs and barrels swaying across the mountains on the backs of mules to slake the thirst of Easterners with coins in their pockets. Westerners, even when they hungered for the word of God, continued to thirst for the "old Monongahela rye."

The evangelical religion so strong in Western Pennsylvania had not yet come out against the drinking cup. A local historian writes of the back country habits:

> The use of whiskey was universal. The quality was good, the taste pleasant, its effect agreeable. Storekeepers kept liquor on their counters and sold it in their stores, and the women customers used it as well as the men. Farmers kept barrels of it in their cellars. . . . It was good for fevers, it was good for a decline, it was good for ague [malaria], it was good for snake-bites. It made one warm in winter and cool in summer. It was used at all gatherings. Bottles of it were set out on the table at christenings and wakes. . . . Ministers drank it. . . . Rev. Father McGirr's drink was whiskey-punch, of which it is said he could drink with any of his day without giving scandal.

Westerners did not like the excise tax. They objected, as one petition phrased it, to "a duty for drinking our grain more than eating it." They objected to the appointment of excisemen with their right of entering private property and inspecting stills. And they especially objected to the trying in federal court of cases against those who refused to pay the exciseman's levy. These trials required expensive and disruptive jaunts across the mountains to federal court at Philadelphia. The West, cut off from the Mississippi trade by the Spanish, and from most trade other than in alcohol by the expense of carrying goods over the mountains, was desperately short of currency. The drain of excise payments was a burden on the region's economy. Pennsylvanians had to wonder why the government in Philadelphia (then the nation's capital) could not open the Mississippi to them rather than spending its time and effort on collecting this hugely unpopular tax.

The backcountry was not strong on being governed. These Western farmers, particularly the Scotch-Irish Presbyterians, had little faith in anyone's governance but their own. They were soon passing resolutions not merely calling for an end to the tax, but overtly threatening excisemen and even those who cooperated with them by paying the tax. Soon barns began to be fired, gristmills damaged, excisemen attacked. "Tom the Tinker's men," it was claimed, were everywhere "mending" stills. This became the local expression for shooting holes in stills whose owners had paid the tax.

The West was not united on the issue. Battle spread between the small and the large whiskey producers, as the more prosperous distillers began to realize that this specie-draining tax would eventually drive the small producers out of business, leaving the more substantial men with a lucrative monopoly. Men of large property feared as well that this excise rebellion could ignite into a war against property. In 1794 this almost came true, as the backwoods farmers marched on Pittsburgh, threatening to burn to the ground that symbol of the advance of commercial capitalism. Only adroit maneuverings by several Pittsburgh leaders persuaded the farmers that they ran too large a risk of retribution if they fired the city.

Something had to be done about the sporadic rioting in the West. A finding that the courts had been obstructed in carrying out the excise law provided the federal government with grounds for intervention. Hamilton, eager for a show of force that would establish the precedent of federal military power, led the administration in a vast overreaction. Washington himself for a time directed a larger force than he had ever at one time commanded during the Revolution. Disorganized militia, about thirteen hundred strong, slogged through endless mud during a rainy November in search of a rebellion. Hamilton marched with the army from start to finish but was not away from his desk overly long; the army remained in the West about three weeks before arresting a few men and marching back to Philadelphia for heroes' welcomes. A grand jury in 1795 indicted over thirty men for treason. Of these but two were convicted. Both were mentally incompetent, and Washington pardoned them.

Despite the element of comedy within the rebellion—a sense that it had perhaps resulted from a bit too much of the spirits at issue—the episode possesses considerable importance for the political and constitutional development of the United States. A direct result of the insurrection was the forcing out of the last Jeffersonian, Edmund Randolph, who had succeeded Jefferson as secretary of state. Never again, except in moments of wartime emergency and then as a deliberate departure from the norm, would any president strive for a nonpartisan rather than a party government. The events of the rebellion had brought successes for both sides in the quarrel. The precedent of national power that Hamilton and Washington considered necessary for the future success of the American experiment was firmly established: without firing a shot, they had won something they had succeeded in defining as a war. What the farmers failed to achieve by rioting they got from the political activity that followed: in 1802 the new Jeffersonian government repealed the hated excise tax. Americans remained by all accounts the hardest drinking people in the world for two more generations until a new wave of evangelism from the West brought fundamental changes in American values, and millions of Americans forgot the "old Monongahela rye" and denounced "Demon rum."

In the summer of 1786, farmers' discontent over taxes broke into rebellion when Daniel Shays and his band attacked state troops at Springfield, Massachusetts, an action that was soon quelled. *(Drawing by Howard Pyle, Courtesy, The Library of Congress)*

***The Constitution*, mural by Barry Faulkner, showing James Madison presenting the Constitution to Washington and the Convention.** *(Courtesy, The National Archives, Washington, D.C.)*

The Drive Toward the Constitution

The move to convert the Confederation government into a more effective political instrument began when the war ended. In 1783 nationalists devised a scheme to grant Congress the right to collect duties on imported liquors, sugar, tea, coffee, cocoa, molasses, and pepper; each state would collect the duties at its own ports and then remit them to the Confederation treasury. This plan was submitted as an amendment to the Articles, and so required a unanimous vote of all the states. New York, however, refused to accept it.

As Congress declined to little more than a sleepy debating society, the future of national affairs passed into the hands of men who thought, as Alexander Hamilton of New York put it, "continentally." In early 1785, commissioners from Virginia and Maryland met at Washington's home, Mount Vernon, to discuss common problems concerning navigation of the Potomac River, which separated the two states. So successful was this meeeting that it led to calls by both state legislatures for a larger conference on commercial cooperation to meet at Annapolis the following year. Only twelve delegates from five states turned up at Annapolis, however, and so consideration of the planned agenda was postponed. Instead the delegates, led by Hamilton, drew up a proposal for a new convention, to meet at Philadelphia in May 1787, to discuss every issue necessary "to render the constitution of the Federal Government adequate to the exigencies of the Union." Congress received this proposal and cautiously endorsed it.

By the time of the Philadelphia meeting, all

doubts moderate Americans may have entertained about the need for a stronger central government had been shattered by the farmers of western Massachusetts. One state that took its wartime debt seriously, Massachusetts, had imposed heavy taxation on its citizens to meet this obligation. At the same time, farm prices declined. There were efforts to relieve by issues of paper money the distress of farmers who had gotten into debt. But in Massachusetts creditor groups defeated the attempts to issue paper currency. In the Berkshire hills of western Massachusetts, where few farmers had ready cash, many lost their land for non-payment of debts or taxes. The troubles that followed made it look as though anarchy threatened at least a portion of the new republic.

Shays's Rebellion. The farmers' wrath focused on the courts, where judges were busily ordering forced sales of land to pay taxes and reimburse creditors. In August 1786, 1500 farmers of Hampshire County prevented the meeting of its Court of Common Pleas. A few weeks later, at Worcester, a hundred men armed with swords, muskets, and clubs blocked the judge from entering the courthouse. The insurgency quickly spread throughout the western part of the state, and the rebels acquired a leader in Daniel Shays, a former captain in the Continental Army. Although Shays condoned the attacks against the courts, he did seek to restrain his followers from committing personal violence against judges and the militia.

Eventually Governor James Bowdoin, urged on by the more conservative citizens of the state's commercial center, sent a force of 4400 men against the rebels. At Springfield, Shays and his men attacked the state troops, but when the trained soldiers fired, the insurgents fled. A few days later, Shays and his small remaining force were taken prisoner. Disorders continued for some weeks thereafter, but by the spring of 1787 Shays's Rebellion was over. Shays and several other rebel leaders were sentenced to death, but a reaction set in against this harshness. The governor met defeat when he ran for reelection, and his successor pardoned the condemned Shaysites and reduced taxes.

Yet the uprising alarmed many Americans. In a letter to a friend Washington could have been speaking for many who had fought for their independence. "I am mortified beyond expression," he wrote, "that in the moment of our independence we should by our conduct render ourselves ridiculous and contemptible in the eyes of all Europe." Henry Lee of Virginia declared: "We are all in dire apprehension that a beginning of anarchy with all its calamitys has approached, and have no means to stop the dreadful work." The rebellion was an argument for Washington's conviction: "I do not conceive we can exist long as a nation without lodging, somewhere, a power which will pervade the whole Union in as energetic a manner as the authority of the state governments extends over the several states."

The Constitutional Convention

All eyes now turned to Philadelphia and the coming conference. With its forty thousand inhabitants, the city was the largest in the United States. During the postwar period, it had suffered like other ports from the decline of foreign trade. Nonetheless, it remained a bustling, neat, tree-lined community that reflected the original orderly plan of its founder, William Penn, and the sobriety as well as the prosperity of its Quaker elite. The delegates who gathered in 1787 in Independence Hall were a mixed lot. Several men of great intellectual force and ability were prominent national leaders; still others scarcely contributed at all to the deliberations and disappeared from history after their brief day at the convention. Together this group of delegates from a geographical fringe of Western civilization were to produce one of the most remarkable political schemes in Western history.

The Founding Fathers. The presiding officer, George Washington, richly honored as the commander in chief of the Continental forces that had defeated the British and made independence possible, enjoyed enormous prestige throughout the nation. His opening appeal to "raise a standard to which the wise and the honest can repair" set the tone for the solemn deliberations that followed. Nearly as eminent was Benjamin Franklin, fresh from the triumphs he had won as minister to France and chief negotiator of the peace treaty. Though now aged and infirm, Franklin could still inspire confidence and rally support. Both men favored a stronger central government.

Yet a short and lively Virginian, James Madison, proved more important at the Convention than either of these two commanding figures. A close friend of Jefferson, a man of wide reading and deep reflection, Madison would be the major architect of the Constitution. A few of the more able men present at Philadelphia during the spring and summer of 1787—Robert Yates of New York, Luther Martin of Maryland, and George Mason of Virginia, for example—remained defenders of local power against expanded federal authority. Most of the delegates, however, were strong nationalists who wished and expected to remake the federal government into an effective instrument of the national will. Perhaps the convention's most extreme nationalist was New York's Alexander Hamilton, who had scant use for the states at all and would prefer to see them reduced to little more than administrative units.

All through the humid heat of the Pennsylvania summer the fifty-five delegates argued, negotiated, maneuvered, and deliberated. Nearly all of them lawyers and educated men, they drew on their knowledge of history, especially the experience of the ancient Roman Republic. They also culled ideas from the political thinkers of modern times, most notably Montesquieu, Harrington, and Blackstone. But ultimately their own common sense, their experience of government, and the interests of their states and their sections guided their decisions. Historians once argued that most of the delegates were either public creditors or representatives of commercial interests, and that the chief consideration determining their actions was their desire to protect their own wealth and that of fellow businessmen. But public creditors and merchants were not the only Americans who had deplored what they saw around them between 1781 and 1787. Almost all occupational groups throughout the country had reason for discontent during the Critical Period. Above all, most of the delegates thought as patriots whose task it was to save the country from the humiliations that the feeble Confederation government had to endure.

Federalism

The new government must be strong without being oppressive. The delegates kept striving to balance liberty and order. The Constitution represents a series of compromises between strong government and government limited in the interests of freedom, between national and local authority, and between the interests of the large states and those of the small ones.

Virginia and New Jersey Plans. As debate opened Edmund Randolph of Virginia presented a proposal by his friend Madison. The Virginia Plan, as it would come to be called, recommended a new national legislature that would represent not the states, as the Confederation Congress did, but the people. The new body would have two houses. The numbers that each state would have in both houses was to be proportionate either to the state's population or to its wealth. The voters of each state would choose directly their representatives to the lower house, and that state's delegation would select the state's delegates to the upper house. On other matters delegates in both houses would vote as individuals, not as members of separate state delegations. The new Congress could define the powers of the federal government and overrule the states, appoint a national executive, and choose a new national judiciary.

The Virginia Plan came under immediate attack. Many delegates believed that it veered too far toward nationalism, practically obliterating the states as governing units except in relation to minor local issues. It also smacked of favoritism: the largest and richest states such as Virginia, Massachusetts, or Pennsylvania would have many more delegates in the new Congress than the smaller and poorer states such as New Hampshire, Georgia, or Rhode Island.

Opponents of the Virginia Plan countered with a scheme submitted by William Paterson of New Jersey. The New Jersey Plan granted to a new, single-chamber legislative body powers expanded beyond those in the Articles of Confederation. Congress would regulate foreign and interstate commerce, levy tariffs on imports, and raise various internal taxes. It would also choose the executive and judicial branches. But all those powers not specified were to remain with the states. Congress, as in the Articles, would represent the states—all equally; members would vote by whole state delegations, the decision of each state delegation counting as a single vote in Congress. Thus the government would remain a league of states as before, though a more effective one.

For many weeks, debate swirled around these two proposals. Attacks on the Paterson proposal pointed out the injustice of allowing, say, the voice of a few thousand New Jerseyites to equal the voice of many more Virginians. The small-state people complained that under the Virginia Plan the three largest states could outvote virtually all the others together. The Randolph scheme raised another difficulty: who were to be counted as "population"? Should slaves, who could not vote, be considered the equals of freemen for purposes of representation? If so, the Southern states, with their many slaves, would have many more delegates in proportion to their voting population than the Northern states.

A Balanced Government. Eventually, a set of compromises was hammered out. The major compromise, sometimes referred to as the Connecticut Plan, established a two-house national legislature. In the lower, the House of Representatives, the people of each state would be directly represented in proportion to population. In the upper, the Senate, each state legislature would elect two members regardless of population. A later arrangement determined that slaves would each be treated, in effect, as three-fifths of a person for the purpose of calculating representation in the House of Representatives. The new Congress was given broad powers over foreign and interstate commerce, permitted to levy taxes directly on citizens, and awarded the sole right to coin money and regulate its value.

Borrowing from the French political philosopher Montesquieu a system of "checks and balances" that would reconcile strong government and private freedom, the delegates set alongside Congress two other equal branches of government, the executive and the judicial, to be selected separately from Congress. The president, or executive, could be chosen by a group of "electors" in each state, the electors being in turn selected by any method each given state legislature deemed best. The judicial branch, headed by a Supreme Court, would be selected by the president with the approval of the Senate. To insure their independence from political pressure, the Convention provided that judges would serve for life and could not have their salaries reduced. The president, too, would be independent of Congress. His term of office would last four years regardless of what Congress thought of him, and he could be reelected.

Each branch of government, the executive,

legislative, and judicial, was empowered to check the others, so that no one branch could become tyrannical. The president held the power of veto over laws enacted by Congress, although this veto could be overridden by a two-thirds vote in both houses. He would choose all federal judges, ambassadors, and high officials of executive departments, including what would later come to be called his "cabinet." But most of these appointments had to be confirmed by a two-thirds vote of the Senate. The Supreme Court also exerted a brake. Not only would it deal with violations of federal laws and suits between citizens of different states, but it held the power to decide whether a measure passed in Congress and signed by the president was "constitutional," or in accord with the Constitution. This responsibility, though not explicit in the Constitution, was assumed by the delegates at Philadelphia and was soon accepted in practice. Congress could put on trial and remove from office for bad conduct both the president and members of the judiciary.

Congress itself had a built-in check. The delegates at Philadelphia expected the House of Representatives to be the branch more responsive to the people as were the lower houses of the state legislatures. Under the original terms of the Constitution, members of the Senate were to be elected by the state legislatures rather than directly by the people of each state. The upper house would accordingly, the delegates believed, tend to be above public whims. Since any measure would have to pass both chambers to become law, the Senate could check the House. Likewise, the House could stop any effort by the Senate to pass an unpopular measure. As a means (it was hoped) of assuring protection against excessive taxation, it was provided that all money bills would have to start out in the House.

By September the new Constitution had assumed its essential form. At times the debate had grown as heated as the weather. Franklin had proposed that a chaplain open each session with a prayer for divine guidance. At least three delegates objected so strenuously to what the majority had wrought that they left Philadelphia in disgust. Many of those who stayed were not much happier. A substantial number continued to object that the Constitution conferred too much power on the federal government; at least one delegate, Alexander Hamilton, believed it created too weak a government for America's needs.

The Convention finished its task in September 1787. Soon after, Gouverneur Morris of Pennsylvania wrote a preamble to the document. On September 17, with only three members abstaining, the delegates affixed their signatures to this great work and commended it to Congress and to the people.

Ratification

On September 20, 1787, the Confederation Congress received in New York the Constitution composed in Philadelphia. A few members protested, but the majority agreed to transmit it to the states for ratification or rejection through special state conventions. For over a year, national political discussion would revolve about whether to accept the new frame of government or continue with the Articles.

By early 1788, five states, either unanimously or by overwhelming majorities, had ratified the Constitution. Not until the debate commenced in Massachusetts did serious opposition develop. In that state, resistance arose among popular leaders who believed that the new frame of government offered insufficient protection from tyranny. What these men wanted was a "bill of rights" that would defend personal freedoms against federal power. Eventually that state's leaders gave the Constitution their support and the convention ratified it, but the ratification contained the proviso that amendments be added to the document protecting the citizen's rights against encroachment by the federal government.

Political scientist Cecilia Kenyon has given the anti-federalists, the opponents of the Constitution, the label "men of little faith." Her point was that beneath their specific objections to one or another provision of the new constitution lay a deep-seated distrust of all government no matter what form it might take. Governments are dangerous because they are composed of men, and men are corrupted by the exercise of power. Anti-federalists sought to limit the power of government. The less power a government has, the less harm it can do when—as in time it must—it becomes tyrannical. Or so reasoned the anti-federalists. In the same spirit they believed that terms of office should be brief (usually this meant annual elections) so that the people can speedily turn out oppressive officials. And, of

A silk banner carried by the Society of Pewterers of New York City in the Federal Procession, July, 1788, celebrating the impending ratification of the Constitution. *(Courtesy, The New-York Historical Society, New York City)*

course, they opposed appointive offices. The obligation to run for office would itself, they thought, partially restrain tyrannical office-holders.

The paradox of anti-federalist thought, as James Madison pointed out in *The Federalist Papers,* is that the same human weakness that makes government dangerous also makes it necessary. Were men angels, Madison observed, government would be unnecessary. But they are not.

In actuality, the paradox cut both ways. The federalists were themselves men of little faith. They shared with their political opponents the same dour view of human nature. The difference was that they feared government less and people more. Hence they were eager to shield much of the government from direct popular control. Only the House of Representatives would be directly answerable to the people, and then only once every two years. The Senate would be elected by the state legislatures, the president by the electoral college. The Judiciary would be appointed, and would hold office indefinitely. Each branch of the government would balance the others so that no one individual or party could work its will. So the federalists shared much of the anti-federalist fear that all government tends to become tyrannical, but rejected their solution, which was to make the government weak and dependent on popular support.

In March 1788 the federalists received their first setback when feisty Rhode Island rejected the Constitution. As the state where the battle during the Critical Period between debtors and creditors had been the most intense, Rhode Island represented the one clear case of a division along economic lines. The merchants and professional men, smelling certain defeat, boycotted the referendum, and their absence gave the anti-federalists a margin of ten to one. But federalist victories by large majorities soon followed in Maryland and South Carolina.

On June 21, New Hampshire became the ninth state to ratify and, by the terms of its own ratification provision, the new Constitution was now technically in effect for the nine states that had accepted it. Yet two very important states, New York and Virginia, had not yet acted, and without them the new union would be like the limbs of a tree lacking a trunk. The federalists would have to win the two big states.

In Virginia the formidable Patrick Henry, James Monroe, and George Mason led the anti-federalists. Favoring the Constitution were James Madison, Edmund Randolph, and, above all, George Washington. The expectation that the state's most revered statesman would be the first President of the Republic made the federalists difficult to stop. In the end Virginia ratified, but like Massachusetts requested a bill of rights.

The Federalist Papers and The Bill of Rights. Now the struggle shifted to New York. The inclusion of that state, with its great port and strategic mid-continental location, was essential if the union was to work. But for a while it seemed as if New York would refuse to enter the new union. The convention that assembled in Poughkeepsie was under the control of the state's violently anti-federalist governor, George Clinton. Arrayed against Clinton and his supporters, however, were John Jay, the Confederation Secretary of Foreign Affairs, and the strong-willed Hamilton. Soon the two New York federalists, joined by James Madison, were engaged in a war of words with their anti-federalist opponents. Day after day the *Independent Gazeteer* carried the short, pithy articles in which the three men, writing under the common name "Publius," explained the virtues and necessity of the new Constitution. Dealing both with immediate concerns and universal political values, these eighty-five pieces—in later years published under the collective title *The Federalist Papers*—constitute a classic commentary on the nature and purposes of government. Publius's articles helped change the minds of the Poughkeepsie delegates. Equally important was pressure from New York City, where merchants and artisans threatened that if New York State did not join the Union, New York City would. On July 25, 1788, after an impassioned personal address to the delegates by Hamilton, the state ratified the new frame of government.

The battle, in effect, was over. Rhode Island and North Carolina were still outside the new Union, but they did not seem essential. After setting up electoral procedures, the old Congress then quietly passed out of existence. When the body of electors—called the "electoral college"—assembled, every presidential vote cast went for Washington, with John Adams of Massachusetts receiving the vice-presidency. On April 14, 1789, Washington received formal notice of his election and departed from his beloved Mount Vernon to take up the duties of president in the nation's temporary capital, New York. There, on April 30, he was sworn into office and delivered his first inaugural address. The celebration in New York when Washington came to the city for his presidential inauguration exceeded anything previously seen. The barge that brought the General across New York harbor from New Jersey was surrounded by large and small vessels of every sort full of cheering New Yorkers. Debarking at Murray's wharf, where he was greeted by Governor Clinton and other officials and escorted to the house where he was to stay, he made his way through streets lined with cheering citizens. At night the city was illuminated with bonfires, and happy celebrants crowded the city's thoroughfares and coffeehouses.

The next few months were busy ones. In the fall, Congress debated and then passed ten amendments to the Constitution, known collectively as the Bill of Rights, which the prescribed three-fourths of the states quickly ratified. The first eight amendments placed certain fundamental restraints on the power of the federal government over ordinary citizens. Congress could not limit free speech, interfere with religion, deny to the people the right to carry arms for militia services, require the quartering of troops in private homes, or allow homes to be searched by federal authorities without search warrants. Persons accused of crimes could not be made to testify against themselves, nor could the federal government deny the citizens trial by jury or deprive them of life, liberty, or property "without due process of law." The central government could not impose excessive bail or "cruel and unusual punishments." Amendment Nine ordained that the rights included in the earlier list did not exclude others; the Tenth Amendment provided that those powers not given to the federal government or denied the states should belong solely to the states or the people.

Never before had any single document enumerated so clearly and emphatically the rights of private citizens. The Bill of Rights became, accordingly, a landmark in the history of human liberty. But the Bill applied to the federal government only. It was recognized that most of the states had similar provisions in their own constitutions. But what if a state chose to violate fundamental human rights; would a citizen have any official or agency to turn to? Not until the Fourteenth Amendment that followed the Union victory in the Civil War would this issue be clarified.

The Hamiltonian Program

On March 4, 1789, the first Congress under the new Constitution assembled in New York City. Federal Hall, the former city hall, was still being remodeled and the new Senators and Representatives took their seats amidst the carpenters' noise and flying sawdust. The confusion and disorder caused little harm. Only eight Senators and thirteen Representatives had slashed their way through the muddy roads of spring to take their oaths of office that opening day.

The New Government. Friends of the Constitution composed most of Congress. Many members had been present at Philadelphia during the momentous summer of 1787 to write the new frame of government, and the majority hoped to carry out the purposes of the nationalists: to make the United States a going concern and create respect for the republic among the older nations of the world.

Yet the first deliberations were nearly farcical. For three weeks the members debated the proper title of address for the president. Vice President John Adams insisted that without some such title as "His Elective Highness" or "His Excellency," the president might be mistaken for the head of a volunteer fire company or leader of a cricket club. His opponents believed any such title would be unrepublican, ill-suited to the new nation. They thought ridiculous the pudgy vice president's serious concern, and they took to calling him "His Rotundity." Washington himself settled the momentous issue. Though protective of his dignity on all occasions, he preferred to avoid "monarchical" trappings. He did travel through the streets in a gilded coach and held "levees," formal receptions for visitors and guests. He also insisted on reading his annual message to Congress in person and, like the British King, he asked for a formal congressional response. But he would not accept a title of any sort, and remained "Mr. President."

From the beginning Washington's command-

April 30, 1789, New York. George Washington taking the oath of office as first president of the United States.

ing presence lent the new government some badly needed respect and dignity. Occasionally, however, the president overstepped his bounds. Early in his administration Washington, taking literally his power to "make treaties" with "the advice and consent of the Senate," appeared before the Senators to explain an Indian treaty. After an awkward debate a Senator proposed referring the treaty to committee. The President, offended by this snub, walked out, saying that he would "be damned" if he would ever come back. He did return once, but no other President has attempted to discuss treaties personally with the entire Senate.

In November 1789 North Carolina officially ratified the Constitution and entered the Union. Reluctant Rhode Island joined at last in 1790. Meanwhile, Congress had set up three major executive departments, State, War, and Treasury, and appointed a Postmaster General. In 1789, it passed the Federal Judiciary Act, which specified that the Supreme Court was to consist of a chief justice with five associates. It also established a system of inferior federal courts and created the office of Attorney General as the government's chief law officer.

In response to one of the new government's most pressing concerns, that of providing itself with revenues, Congress passed the nation's first tariff, setting low duties on a host of imported goods. Congress now had the means to pay the army and official salaries, and to begin to meet its debts. But those debts were still troublesome. By 1789 they amounted to about $52 million—$40 million owed to Americans, and $12 million due foreigners. In addition to these obligations of the federal government, there were also the still-unpaid state debts, amounting to about $25 million.

Few people doubted that the foreign debt must be paid in full. Otherwise, the United States would not earn the respect of foreign powers or be able to borrow abroad again. But what about the domestic debt? Speculators had bought Continental IOU's for a song from those who had actually given the wartime Congress money or supplies to fight the British. Should these speculators alone benefit by the improved credit of the national government, or should the original holders also get something? And what about the state debts? Many Southern states had already paid off these obligations while many Northern states had not. If the government were to "assume" or take over these obligations, the residents of the middle states and New England would benefit at the expense of those south of Pennsylvania. Congress turned over to Alexander Hamilton, Washington's Secretary of the Treasury, the problem of how to handle the debt as well as other pending financial questions.

Alexander Hamilton. A young man of thirty-five, Hamilton was a former aide-de-camp to Washington who had married into the prominent Schuyler family of New York. Able, handsome, and well-connected, he had risen high in New York political life after his army service despite his West Indies origin and his illegitimate birth.

Hamilton was a nationalist, lacking the emotional attachment that men like Jefferson and Madison felt for the local community. Like many other veterans of the Continental Army, he recalled bitterly the petty jealousies and selfishness of the states during the Revolutionary War. He had so little respect for the states that at the Constitutional Convention he had proposed their virtual elimination. He prized banking, trade, and manufacturing, and believed that the United States could not afford to remain an agricultural nation, producing raw materials for Europe. Britain, rapidly becoming the industrial workshop of the world, must be America's example, he claimed. This required a vigorous central government commanding its citizens' loyalty. Hamilton was skeptical of human nature. Men of the Enlightenment, such as Jefferson, tended to believe that human beings were inherently more good than evil, social and political evil being the result largely of evil institutions. Freed of these, mankind would flourish. Hamilton, on the other hand, believed that the people tended to be "ambitious, vindictive, and rapacious." He wrote, ". . . they seldom judge or determine right."

Congress's problem was Hamilton's opportunity. The new Secretary of the Treasury seized the occasion to advance some of his fondest political and economic hopes. In three great *Reports* he embedded his solution to several immediate problems in his larger plans for American society.

Hamilton Reports. The *Report Relative to Public Credit* boldly proposed that the national debt be paid in full through a complicated process know as "funding." Current holders would exchange their IOU's at par for interest-bearing bonds. Hamilton asserted in this *Report* that the public debt would prove a "public blessing." His *Report on a National Bank* early in 1791 explained why. The nation's economic development required stronger currency and banking facilities. Hamilton proposed a new federally chartered banking corporation, drawing its capital both from the Treasury and from private investors. The new "Bank of the United States," governed by privately elected directors and ones chosen by the government, would serve both public and private needs. It would stimulate commerce and manufactures by lending money to private businessmen. The bank would as well hold the government's deposits, pay its bills, and accept its receipts. The institution's most important service would be to issue the paper money of the nation. The Bank was to use the paper to make payments in business transactions. In itself, paper money was considered a cheap, untrustworthy currency. But the Bank's paper would have something solid to back it up. Its holders could, if they so wished, have the government give them in place of it an equivalent amount in the securities that were part of the new funding scheme. And the public's knowledge that the currency would be so exchanged would make for willingness to use it. Gold-poor America would thereby convert the national debt into a powerful engine for mobilizing its economy.

Later that same year Hamilton issued the last of the major *Reports*, on manufactures. The Secretary acknowledged that agriculture was currently the most important single economic activity. But he saw no conflict between agriculture and industry. The two complemented each other; both together would benefit the nation. Noting the beginnings of the factory system in Britain, Hamilton observed that the new system of manufacture employed every class of people in productive labor, even women and children. Hamilton, in fact, especially favored the employment of women in factories, believing that in a predominantly agricultural society men would be needed, and would prefer, to work the land. He viewed women as the most readily available pool of wage labor. America with its magnificent resources was potentially a great industrial nation, but to compete with other nations would require government aid. To protect "infant industries" until they could compete successfully, the government must impose high tariffs that would raise the price of foreign manufactures. It should also offer premiums for the production of needed goods and new inventions. Above all, the proposed Bank must lend capital to entrepreneurs.

These three great *Reports* together outlined an economic revolution. Through the positive use of the national government, the country might be transformed: bustling cities, humming factories, and busy arteries of communication and transport would erupt from the quiet American landscape of prosperous farms and brooding forests.

Hamilton's friends submitted bills to Congress implementing the recommendations of his reports. But the program, so bold in its projections, aroused fierce opposition. Hamilton's vision threatened to violate the character of the nation as some Americans saw it, a land of small farms and the simple social relations of the countryside. Many also feared the expansion of federal powers his program required. They imagined that Hamilton's schemes would create an all-powerful centralized government that would become the source of graft and corruption. In America, as in Britain, liberty and republican virtue would then degenerate into tyranny and licentiousness. Especially fearful were the Virginia leaders—James Madison, now a leading member of the House of Representatives, and Thomas Jefferson, Washington's Secretary of State.

Jefferson deplored the industrial and urban society that Hamilton eagerly anticipated. Having witnessed European urban life, Jefferson was convinced that "the mobs of great cities" were "sores" on the social body, and that when people "get piled up one upon another as in Europe, they shall become corrupt as in Europe." Farmers, he insisted, were God's "Chosen People, if ever he had a chosen people," and they alone could be relied on to support the common good. The Virginia leaders also believed that Hamilton and his supporters wanted to create a plutocracy, a government of the rich.

Hamilton's bill to fund the public debt aroused Madison, who quickly became the leader of the forces arrayed against Hamilton. Madison spoke as a Southerner, aware that four-fifths of the unpaid securities and state debts were Northern. Yet his attack was a principled one. He did not oppose funding in itself, he declared; rather, he believed that Hamilton's scheme unduly benefited speculators. Under Hamilton's plan these people would receive the full face value of their holdings, while original possessors would get nothing. Even now, Madison and his supporters asserted, advance news that the government would assume the state debts had been leaked by people in high places, and speculators were traveling through the South buying up securities from gullible farmers.

For many weeks the funding bill remained blocked. The particular sticking point was the provision that the federal government would assume the payment of the states' debts. Then one morning in July, Jefferson bumped into Hamilton on the steps of the president's house. The Secretary of the Treasury told the Secretary of State that the deadlock in Congress was endangering the Union. Could Jefferson do anything to help? The next day the two cabinet officers met with Madison, and a deal was arranged. The national capital would be moved from New York to Philadelphia. Then, in ten years, it would be permanently located in the South between Virginia and Maryland. In return, Madison and his friends would cease to oppose assumption. The following month the funding measure passed Congress.

Next on the agenda was a national bank. The bill would charter a Bank of the United States for twenty years with a capital of $10 million, one-fifth to be subscribed by the federal government and the remainder by private investors. The Bank could issue banknotes that the government would accept in payment of taxes. Philadelphia was to be the Bank's home office, but it might establish branches in other cities.

Over the opposition of Madison, Congress passed the bill chartering the Bank and sent it to the president for his signature. Washington was stumped. His fellow Virginian, Madison, had raised doubts in his mind as to whether the Constitution allowed Congress to charter such a bank. Might this not be an unwarranted extension of federal powers? The president asked for the opinions of his Cabinet. Both Jefferson and Attorney General Edmund Randolph replied that by no stretch of its meaning did the Constitution authorize a federally chartered bank. Hamilton took the opposite view. In a masterly application of what came to be called the principle of "broad construction" of the Constitution, he argued that since a bank was necessary to the collecting of taxes, the regulating of trade, and other functions explicitly conferred on Congress in that great document, its constitutionality was "implied," if not specified. Convinced by Hamilton's logic, Washington signed the bill into law. On July 4, 1791, the stock of the Bank was put up for sale. In a few hours the whole $8 million reserved to private investors was sold out and hundreds of eager capitalists had to be turned down.

The third of Hamilton's major *Reports* was not enacted into law in his own day. It stood, however, as an eloquent defense of a high tariff that would become an inspiration to later generations of "protectionists." Meanwhile, other items of Hamiltonian legislation also became law. In 1791 Congress passed the Whiskey Tax, imposing an excise on distilled liquors to help pay interest on the funded debt. In 1792 it passed the Coinage Act, establishing the dollar as the United States currency unit, dividing it into dimes and cents, and making it equivalent to a specified amount of gold or silver.

The mint at Philadelphia was established after Congress passed the Coinage Act in 1792. *(Courtesy, New York Public Library Picture Collection)*

Hamiltonians vs. Jeffersonians. As Congress and the American people debated the Hamiltonian program, two distinct and conflicting positions began to emerge. One had as its principal spokesmen Jefferson and his chief congressional lieutenant, Madison. On the other side were Hamilton and his followers, including John Adams, and, increasingly, President Washington himself.

The Jeffersonians favored state over national power and agriculture over industry, trade, and banking. They believed that limited government and "strict construction" of the Constitution were best for the nation and the American people. They claimed to have faith in the people and to distrust the rich and powerful. Many were Southerners, deeply attached to their local communities, which they did not want to come under the domination of a powerful central government. But the Jeffersonian party would also win support among the farmers of the middle and New England states and the artisans of the towns. Increasingly this group took on the name Republican, a label they adopted to contrast their political views with the supposedly more "monarchical" ones of their opponents.

Calling themselves Federalists, the Hamiltonians favored an ever stronger federal government, if necessary at the expense of the states. They believed that America's future lay in industry, not in agriculture alone. Generally speaking, they accepted "republicanism" as best suited to the American "genius," but they did not trust majority rule as much as did their opponents, and they hoped to attract the support of the rich and the powerful to the new national government by making their interests coincide with those of the government. The Federalists could count on strong support within the major commercial towns, including such Southern ports as Charleston. As defenders of order and stability they could also count on those people who were by temperament conservative. One group that often favored the Federalist position was the defenders of the established Congregational church in New England. On the other side were to be found the Baptists, Methodists, and other dissenting groups, which tended to be Republican.

It is somewhat curious that American political vocabulary often defines Hamiltonians as conservatives. For they were radicals in their plans for reconstructing the American economy, and the economic future they desired would be progressive and dynamic rather than placid and agricultural like that of the Jeffersonians.

Foreign Affairs

The French Revolution (1789). No sooner had the new government under the Constitution begun its work in New York than Europe went into a colossal political convulsion. In France, our ally in the war for independence, the American struggle for liberty had been deeply influential. "Enlightened" men and women recognized a larger significance in the event, and it strengthened their resolve to reform the Bourbon monarchy, custodian of the privilege and inequality that for centuries had shackled the French people. In August 1788 the French king, faced with a severe financial crisis partly induced by France's recent aid to America, called into session the Estates General, representative of the clergy, nobility, and middle class, expecting that body to give him the taxes he needed, and then adjourn. But instead groups of reformers quickly took over the Estates. In a matter of a few months they had converted the Estates General into a revolutionary body that began to replace the entire old regime and convert the nation into a constitutional monarchy based on respect for human rights and on wide popular political participation. On July 14, 1789, a Paris mob attacked the Bastille, the prison that had become a notorious symbol of oppression, tore down the walls, and freed the prisoners.

The early response in America to the electrifying events in France was almost universally favorable. When the Marquis de Lafayette, who had helped lead the early stages of the Revolution, sent Washington the key to the Bastille, the president hung the key prominently in the presidential mansion. He later wrote Gouverneur Morris that he hoped the disorders in France would "terminate very much in favor of the rights of man." If such a reserved and inherently conservative man as Washington could applaud the French uprising, the followers of Jefferson were certain to be still more enthusiastic. Many Republicans, in imitation of French egalitarianism, adopted the title "Citizen" or "Citizeness" in place of "Mister" or "Miss." Others began to abandon knee breeches and adopt the long trousers worn by the Paris artisans and

French reformers. Republicans considered the French Revolution the beginning of a new age. As Jefferson wrote, "the liberty of the whole earth" depended on the contest in France.

In time the initial consensus among Americans disintegrated. Increasingly the French radical leaders, called Jacobins, denounced the church and organized religion. In 1791 the King fled Paris with his family, but was caught and thrown into prison. By this time many enemies of the Revolution, including a large part of the French clergy and nobility, had been either driven from the country or hustled off to jail. Soon after, the Revolutionary leaders began a reign of terror against all opponents of their policies, even the moderate reformers. In 1793 a revolutionary tribunal pronounced the death sentence on Louis XVI, and the sentence was promptly carried out. In October his queen, Marie Antoinette, was also sent to the guillotine. The excesses of the French revolutionaries shocked many Americans. Still, if the Revolution had been contained within France its effects on the United States would have been limited. But the radical French leaders proclaimed a crusade against conservative regimes elsewhere in Europe in the name of "liberty, equality, fraternity." Before long, France was at war with Austria, England, Prussia, and Spain.

Surrounded as it was with enemies, France sought aid from its ally, the United States. Under the Treaty of 1778 the Americans were bound to protect France's West Indies colonies against any enemy. With England certain to use her powerful fleet to blockade and, if possible, take these possessions, the United States now faced the serious prospect of war with Great Britain.

Many Americans would have welcomed such a war. Britain still limited American commerce with her own West Indies possessions. She still occupied the Western garrisons on American soil. She still stirred up the Indians of the Northwest to discourage American settlement west of the mountains. Now that Britain was locked in combat with revolutionary France, she seemed the special enemy of liberty and freedom. And in 1793 the British began to seize American vessels engaged in trade with the French West Indies and to throw their crews into foul dungeons.

Among the followers of Hamilton, however, France represented all that was chaotic, disorderly, irreligious. That country, exclaimed Fisher Ames, was "an open hell, still ringing with agonies and blasphemies, still smoking with sufferings and crimes." Britain the Hamiltonians perceived as a bulwark of sanity and moderation, and they thought her victory in the struggle to be essential for world order. Another consideration weighed heavily in Federalist calculations. The whole Hamiltonian fiscal program depended on international trade, and in 1793 the United States, like the colonies for over a century before, traded primarily with Britain. Any wartime disruption of this trade would dry up revenues, injure the new national government, and thwart the Federalist economic program.

Citizen Genêt. Meanwhile, the French Republic had dispatched Citizen Edmond Genêt as diplomatic minister to the United States to do what he could to make trouble for Great Britain. Arriving in Charleston early in 1793, Genêt immediately set to work recruiting Americans in his nation's cause. Even before presenting his formal credentials to Washington and Secretary of State Jefferson in Philadelphia, he had commissioned Americans as privateers to prey on British commerce, and opened negotiations with

Citizen Genêt, who came to America to stir up controversy against Britain, remained to live as a country gentleman in Orange County, New York. *(From the Emmet Collection, Manuscript Division, New York Public Library)*

several American frontier leaders to attack Spanish Florida and Louisiana. Despite these high-handed actions, American friends of France cheered Genêt as he made a triumphal procession to the Capitol.

By this time Washington, supported by Hamilton and Jefferson, had decided to proclaim American neutrality. Genêt learned of this seeming repudiation of the 1778 treaty but, convinced by his recent experience that Americans were fervent partisans of the French, he determined to ignore it. Though at first a hero of the Jeffersonians, Genêt finally offended even the friends of the French Republic. So outrageous were his actions that Jefferson wrote Madison that the French minister would "sink the Republican interest" if the Republicans did not "abandon him." Finally, after Genêt threatened to appeal to the American people over the head of Washington, the administration decided it had had enough. By this time the Jacobins were in power. Genêt, who did not belong to this group, most certainly would have been beheaded had he been forced to return to France. The administration allowed him to stay in the United States, but refused to deal with him any further. He soon married the daughter of New York governor De Witt Clinton and settled into the quiet life of a country gentleman.

Settlement with Great Britain

While Americans rioted in the streets for or against Genêt, the United States was moving toward a settlement of sorts with Great Britain. Early in 1794 Washington sent Chief Justice John Jay to England as special envoy. Jay, a staunch Federalist, knew that it would be difficult to get an agreement with Great Britain that would be popular. He was right.

The Jay Treaty (1795). The British made much of the American emissary. He in turn bowed to the Queen and kissed her hand, an act that outraged ardent Republicans. The British did not want war with the United States, but neither did they want to adopt any policy that promised to weaken their war effort against France. They drove a hard bargain. In the agreement that Jay carried back from London, the British promised finally to surrender the military posts they had illegally occupied since 1783. Other disagreements, including disputes over the pre-Revolutionary debts owed Englishmen, a boundary dispute with Canada in the Northwest, and the recent British ship seizures, were referred to British-American arbitration commissions. This device of an arbitration commission was an important diplomatic innovation, and in future years the two countries would make much use of it. Left unsettled were such longstanding American complaints as British incitements of Indians in the West and restrictive trade practices in the British West Indies colonies. On the question of British right to limit neutral trade in wartime, Jay retreated from the original American principle "free ships make free goods"—that a nation at war could not seize the goods carried in a neutral ship trading with the enemy nation—and agreed that the British could seize French or other enemy property found aboard American ships.

Jay returned to the United States to find his fellow Americans in no mood to swallow this un-

***John Jay*, by Gilbert Stuart. Jay's Treaty of 1795 settled most of the disputes with Britain left over from the Confederation period, but was very unpopular at home.** *(Courtesy, National Gallery of Art, Washington, D.C. Lent by Mrs. Peter Jay)*

generous agreement. General Anthony Wayne had smashed the Indians at the Battle of Fallen Timbers in northwestern Ohio. "Mad Anthony" forced the tribes to sign the Treaty of Greenville surrendering all of Ohio and a large part of Indiana to the white man. This victory ended the menace on the Northwest frontier despite the recent British efforts to stir up the Indians. The government's bold action against the whiskey rebels gave some Americans greater confidence in the strength of their new government and this left them even less inclined than before to give way to Britain. When Jay arrived back in the United States, he was greeted everywhere with outrage. One ardent Republican, unable to contain his feelings, inscribed on his fence: "Damn John Jay! damn every one that won't damn John Jay!! damn every one that won't put lights in his windows and sit up all night damning John Jay!!!" Jay himself ruefully remarked that he could have traveled across the nation by the light of his burning effigies.

Hamilton and other Federalists nonetheless marshaled their forces and wrote articles supporting the agreement as the best that could be obtained. Washington put his prestige behind the Treaty, earning for his efforts the contempt of the Republicans. Jefferson himself even remarked: "Curse on his virtues; they have undone the country." But in June 1795 the Senate by a close vote confirmed the Treaty.

Whatever its inadequacies, the Jay Treaty settled most of the disputes with Britain left over from the Confederation period. But difficulties with Spain remained. Then, in 1795, the Spanish government and the United States signed the Pinckney Treaty. This agreement granted Americans rights of free navigation on the Mississippi, restraints on the Florida Indians, and the "right of deposit" for their goods in New Orleans for a period of three years. Although the three-year provision implied possible trouble for the future, the nation greeted the Pinckney Treaty with great enthusiasm and the Senate ratified it unanimously. The Treaty ended temporarily the threat that Western regions of the United States, dependent on unimpeded use of the Mississippi River, might secede from the Union.

John Adams's Presidency

Political Parties. In 1796 the nation faced its first disputed presidential election campaign. By this time American voters had become divided into two distinct parties. As yet, little of the machinery of party politics or campaigns had appeared, but throughout the nation people had begun to call themselves either Federalists or Republicans and their opponents by stronger and ruder names.

The division of the country into these two opposing political camps disturbed many Americans. The founders of the Republic, including the authors of the Constitution, had not envisioned political parties. The voters, they believed, should choose for office the best, most public-spirited men. Only a few people understood that parties could perform valuable functions in a republic: formulating alternative policies, presenting them to the electorate, and implementing programs supported by a majority of citizens. Partisan organizations appeared to be dangerous instruments of selfish men that impeded, rather than advanced, expression of the general will. Many Americans of the 1790s regarded parties as symptomatic of a disease within the body politic. Even the ambitious men engaged in creating the factions thought that they were, at best, necessary evils. "If I could not go to heaven but with a party," Jefferson once wrote, "I would not go there at all."

Such fears were, in part, the legacy of revolutionary thought, particularly the tendency to see an embattled republic surrounded by foreign foes and beset with domestic dangers. Histories of previous republics, Americans believed, revealed that disintegration came from foreign wars and domestic political disputes. Might not the difficulties of the 1790s indicate that the American republic was about to suffer the same unhappy fate?

These beliefs actually contributed to the party spirit and the frenzied political temper of the 1790s. The distrust of party, the belief that party politics expressed corruption and conspiracy, made Americans of each faction look on the other side as polluting the virtuous republic: and so each faction deepened its own partisan emotion. Public men, Jefferson wrote a friend, no longer seemed "to separate political and personal differences. Men who have been intimate all their lives, cross the street to avoid meeting, and turn their heads another way, lest they should be obliged to touch their hats." Name-calling and violence became commonplace, es-

Washington retired to his home in Mt. Vernon, Virginia, where he was buried upon his death on December 14, 1799. *(Courtesy, New York Public Library, Ashton, Lenox and Tilden Foundations)*

pecially in the newly emerged party press. The extreme Federalist William Cobbett described Republicans as "cut-throats who walk in rags and sleep amidst filth and vermin." Some New Yorkers threw stones at Alexander Hamilton. Even Washington himself became the target of vicious remarks; in Virginia his opponents toasted "a speedy death to President Washington."

Washington's official family felt the strains. Within the Cabinet Jefferson, the arch-Republican, had ceased to talk to Hamilton, the arch-Federalist. In 1793 Jefferson resigned as Secretary of State and returned to his Virginia estates. Hamilton, too, left official life and went back to the practice of law in New York. Neither man, however, abandoned politics. From Monticello, his handsome classical mansion on a hill overlooking the Blue Ridge Mountains, Jefferson continued to advise by letter his friends and political allies in Philadelphia and around the nation. Hamilton also remained active politically and, indeed, would exert great influence in the administration that followed Washington's.

Washington, no doubt, could have held the presidency for life had he so desired. But he was weary of politics and anxious to return to Mount Vernon; he looked forward, he said, to sitting down to dinner alone with his wife, Martha. He refused to accept a third term, and with the help of Jay and Hamilton he prepared a final address to his fellow citizens.

Washington's Farewell Address devoted more attention to domestic than to foreign matters. The retiring president deplored the state of political conflict that had arisen and warned Americans against disunity, whether sectional or political. He also cautioned the nation to be wary of "entangling alliances." He did not advocate isolation of the United States from international affairs. He merely recommended that the coun-

***President John Adams,* by E. F. Andrews. Washington's vice-president won a close election in 1796 to become America's second president.** *(Courtesy, The New-York Historical Society, New York City)*

try be guided by its own interests and not become too closely tied to those of others.

As the "Father of His Country" prepared to return to Virginia, political conflict remained fierce. As yet there were no national nominating conventions as we now know them. Instead, both Federalist and Republican leaders merely agreed among themselves on who should run.

The Election of 1796. The choice of the Federalists was Vice-President John Adams. Less extreme than the "high Federalists" such as Hamilton, he was, nevertheless, peppery and opinionated, as well as learned and public-spirited. Adams had been in the forefront of America's struggle for nationhood ever since the 1770s. Now he considered France the chief threat to America's freedom. The Republicans turned to their acknowledged chief, Jefferson. Tall, loose-jointed, red-haired, the former Secretary of State was as anti-British and pro-French as ever. Britain, he believed, was determined to subjugate the United States economically and he thought that under Hamilton's auspices the British had come to dominate the American government.

The campaign lasted into 1797. Although in many states adult male citizens could vote for presidential electors, it was these electors themselves who chose the President and Vice-President. Not until the members of the electoral college actually cast their ballots in January were the results known. During this time the intrigues, the maneuverings, the libels and attacks were numerous.

The Republican press assailed Adams as a monarchist who, if elected, would enslave the American people. The Federalist press accused Jefferson of being a lackey of the French and claimed that as governor of Virginia during the Revolution he had fled his capital in a "cowardly" escape from the British. A particularly unpleasant incident of the campaign was the airing of a scandal involving Hamilton.

In 1791 the Secretary of the Treasury had begun a liaison with Maria Reynolds, the estranged wife of James Reynolds, an unscrupulous speculator and political fixer. Soon after his meetings with Mrs. Reynolds her husband appeared, claimed that his heart was "Burst with Greef," and demanded money to repair it. Over the next few months the Secretary gave Reynolds a thousand dollars to shut him up.

But Reynolds would not be quiet. In 1792 he told all to a group of Republican Congressmen, including James Monroe, and in addition he claimed that Hamilton had made money by swindling the government. The shocked congressmen confronted the Secretary with their information. Hamilton confessed to the romance, but denied any financial wrongdoing. The congressmen seemed satisfied, and pledged to keep the Reynolds matter to themselves.

They did not. In 1796 the story leaked to John Beckley, a man who held the same role in the Republican Party as the chairman of a national political committee does today. Beckley had the story published as a pamphlet in time to provide some edifying reading for the voters.

Meanwhile, the new French Minister in the United States, Citizen Adet, was angry at the Federalist administration for coming to terms with the British and he joined the fracas. In November 1796 he published in the American newspapers a set of proclamations announcing that France would suspend diplomatic relations with the United States and come down hard on neutral shipping. The blame for this new policy, he declared, lay with the Federalists' pro-British policies.

In the end, all the attacks, intrigues, scandals, and dissensions—Hamilton did not get along with Adams—could not stop the voters and electors from keeping the Federalists in power. But the results were close. When the electors' ballots were counted, Adams had seventy-one votes to Jefferson's sixty-eight, with Thomas Pinckney—an ally of Hamilton—coming in third. Under the existing provisions of the Constitution, John Adams became the second president of the United States, and Jefferson the vice-president. The new Chief Executive would face a complex set of problems, especially in foreign relations.

Troubles with Britain. The United States by now had become a major international trader, its ships calling in virtually every port in the world. The reason for this growth was the great European war. As the British Royal Navy swept French and Spanish vessels off the high seas, France and her allies depended increasingly on the most important maritime neutral, the United States, to carry goods to and from their colonies. By 1796 American merchants were bringing in millions of dollars' worth of molasses, rum, sugar, and other products from French and Spanish possessions in the New World, landing them at New York, Baltimore, Charleston, or Philadelphia and then sending them, marked as American exports, to France, Spain, or some other part of continental Europe. They were also pouring into the French and Spanish colonies European goods that Britain's enemies feared to carry on their own vessels.

This wartime trade rained dollars, pounds, doubloons, and gilders on American merchants. Great mansions arose in Salem, Boston, Newburyport, Charleston, and the other centers of foreign trade. Every harbor along the Atlantic coast was dotted with the white sails and black hulls of the brigs, sloops, barges, and full-rigged ships engaged in world trade, while on the shore the streets were crowded with clerks, stevedores, porters, teamsters, and jack-tars hurrying about their business of moving the world's goods and making money.

The British looked on aghast. America's good fortune clearly came at their expense. Not only were the Americans helping their enemies evade the British blockade of Europe and of French and Spanish America, but they were also taking over business formerly handled by British merchants. And the expanding American merchant marine was luring many of Britain's best seamen. Hundreds of experienced British merchant seamen preferred the high wages and clean ships of the Americans to their own, and were deserting. At Norfolk, Virginia, the entire crew of a British merchant vessel quit in a body and signed on a departing American ship. Even sailors from the Royal Navy were escaping its harsh discipline to join the American merchant fleet. The Yankees were profiting marvelously by England's troubles.

For a while after the Jay Treaty, the British left American ships and seamen alone. But then, in 1796, when marine manpower shortages began to hurt, they resorted to impressment. Whenever a British man-of-war stopped an American merchant vessel to inspect her cargo for goods going to France, a British naval officer lined the men up on deck. Back and forth he went, asking each to speak up and identify himself. Often anyone with an English, Irish, or Scottish accent was assumed to be a British subject and removed to serve in the Royal Navy. "Some of these unfortunate people," wrote one angry ship captain, "are American born, and have wives and children, whose existence, perhaps, depends on the welfare of a husband in slavery—a father in chains!"

Trouble with France. The French were no better. The French Directory, as the ruling body was called between 1795 and 1799, considered Adams's victory an unfriendly act on the part of the American people. In 1797 the French government ordered that every impressed United States citizen captured aboard a British vessel be hanged; if any single item of British make was found aboard an American ship, the vessel was to be confiscated. The French gave the United States Minister his walking papers, in effect cutting off diplomatic relations.

The American government responded aggressively to the French challenge. Knowing that the United States was ill prepared to go to war, Adams decided to negotiate and appointed three commissioners, Elbridge Gerry, Charles Cotesworth Pinckney, and John Marshall, to go to Paris to seek a settlement. At the same time, the administration asked Congress for money to build naval vessels and expand the army. The Republicans fought the administration's request for defense funds. Representative Albert Gallatin of Pennsylvania declared that paying the public debt would be "a much more effective way of securing the respect of foreign nations than . . . building a Navy." Feelings between the two parties grew so bitter that one hot-tempered Republican, an Irish-born Congressman from Vermont, Matthew Lyon, spat in the eye of his Federalist colleague, Roger Griswold of Connecticut. A few days later Griswold attacked the Vermonter with a cane. Lyon defended himself with a pair of fire tongs and wrestled his assailant to the floor before other members of Congress separated them. Threatened with expulsion, Lyon cried, "Let me have at him!"

The X, Y, Z Affair. In October 1797 the three American emissaries arrived in Paris prepared to negotiate with the French foreign minister, Tallyrand. Over several weeks they were forced to talk to three French officials whom they later identified as X, Y, and Z. The Americans, these gentlemen informed Marshall, Gerry, and Pinckney, would have to apologize for some recent anti-French statements of President Adams; they would have to promise a loan to France; and they must privately pay money to Tallyrand and members of the Directory. The American envoys were not naive about how diplomacy was conducted in Europe, but they refused to pay bribes before the French agreed to a settlement, and broke off the talks. Soon after, they reported to Adams on what had transpired during their mission.

In 1798 the American government published the entire "X, Y, Z" correspondence. Whatever the worldly American emissaries felt, the American people were shocked by the French government's seeming contempt for the United States. Overnight all but the most ardent Republicans became anti-French. In theaters, taverns, concert halls, Americans sang patriotic songs and demanded to hear "Yankee Doodle" and the "President's March." They drowned out with hisses and groans any attempt by die-hard Republicans to respond to this with the French revolutionary anthem, "The Marseillaise." One Federalist wrote a new chorus to the patriotic favorite "Yankee Doodle":

> *Yankee Doodle, mind the tune,*
> *Yankee Doodle dandy,*
> *If French men come with naked bun,*
> *We'll strike 'em hard and handy.*

Congress appropriated money for forty naval vessels, and for trebling the size of the army. Congress also ended commerce with France, ordered the suspension of the Franco-American treaty of 1778, and created the Navy Department. Shortly thereafter, a full-scale though undeclared naval war broke out on the Atlantic, with American frigates and French vessels exchanging broadside volleys and French privateers attacking United States merchant vessels within sight of the American coast.

Alien and Sedition Acts (1798). In this time of intense political excitement, Federalists found it impossible to regard their opponents' views as legitimate expressions of dissent. As yet, few Americans fully accepted the legitimacy of a party system and so Federalists (like Republicans) found the opposing party to be treacherous by its very existence. And the French Revolution went so far beyond our own Revolution in attacking traditional social institutions that conservative Americans saw chaos, anarchy, and atheism in it and feared its slightest presence in this country. In this mood a Federalist-dominated Congress passed four measures, called collectively the Alien and Sedition Acts of 1798, designed to curb opposition and prevent internal subversion.

The Naturalization Act extended from five to fourteen years the period of residence required for citizenship. The Alien Act gave the president the power to deport any alien suspected of

In the undeclared naval war with France, the American frigate *Constellation* captured the French ship *L'Insurgent*, February, 1799. *(Courtesy, The Peabody Museum of Salem)*

"treasonable or secret" intentions. The Alien Enemies Act gave him the authority in time of war to arrest or banish from the country any citizen of an enemy power.

These first measures were all aimed at foreigners. The Sedition Act was directed at native Americans, and especially at opponents of the administration. Under its terms any resident of the United States who sought to prevent the execution of federal law, to stop a federal official from performing his duties, or to start any riot, "insurrection," or "unlawful assembly" could be fined or imprisoned. Anyone convicted of publishing "any false, scandalous and malicious writing" against Congress, the president, or the government could be fined or sentenced to prison for two years.

Using his powers under the Alien and Sedition Acts, Secretary of State Timothy Pickering began a series of prosecutions of Republican newspaper editors and political leaders. The owners of four leading Republican newspapers were indicted and three Republican editors were convicted of violating the Sedition Act. Pickering also charged "Spitting Lyon," the excitable Congressman from Vermont, with libel against President Adams. Lyon was convicted, fined a thousand dollars, and hustled off to jail for four months. Faced with the possibility of a hot reception when they arrived, many foreigners called off plans to leave for America.

The prosecutions under the Sedition Act damaged Adams badly. Many fair-minded Americans considered them violations of the freedom of speech and press guaranteed by the Bill of Rights. Others saw them as totally unwarranted at a time when the country was not in mortal danger. Before long, opponents of the measures and the prosecutions were holding meetings throughout the middle states, the South, and the West and sending petitions of protest to Congress. Great rolls of paper containing thousands of names were soon deposited on the desks of the House and Senate clerks. A mass meeting in Woodford County, Kentucky, declared: "That for the servants of the people to tell those who created them that they shall not, at their peril, examine into the conduct of [their] servants for the abuse of power is tyranny!"

Kentucky and Virginia Resolutions. Few Americans were as disturbed by the Federalist repressions as the leaders of the Republican Party, Jefferson and Madison. Both regarded the Alien and Sedition Acts not only as a violation of freedom, but also as granting excessive power to the federal government over the states. They secretly drafted two sets of resolutions that friends steered through the Virginia and Kentucky legislatures. The Kentucky Resolution, written by Jefferson, and that of Virginia, composed by Madison, stated that the federal government was a compact of states for certain limited purposes. Under the Constitution the national government did not possess the sort of powers it was seeking to exercise under the Alien and Sedition Acts. Such measures were, accordingly, "altogether void and of no force." The two Republican leaders then attacked the Sedition Act as contrary to the Bill of Rights.

In later years Americans would remember the Resolutions primarily as assertions of states' rights in opposition to federal power, but in their own day they seemed manifestos of freedom. Yet, though followed by a new wave of meetings and petitions from around the country, they accomplished little. The Federalists were too well entrenched in Congress, and a committee of the House rejected the complaints. The Alien and Sedition Acts, the committee majority declared, were both wise and constitutional. When Albert Gallatin and other Republicans attacked the committee report, Federalists drowned them out by loud talking, laughter, hissing, and coughing.

Adams Compromises with France. Despite his loss of popularity, Adams and his party were still in firm control, and the president could have gotten Congress to declare war on France. Hamilton and the "high Federalists" were in a warlike mood and deplored any attempt to negotiate differences with the French. Adams, however, was unwilling to accept Hamilton's lead. By now the president had learned that he had blundered badly in keeping Washington's Cabinet intact. His closest advisers, he had discovered, had scant respect for him and instead looked to Hamilton for advice and guidance. In 1799, without consulting the Cabinet, Adams announced that he intended to send another mission to France to resume negotiations of outstanding differences.

When the American delegation arrived in Paris, they encountered a changed situation. The leader of France now was First Consul Napoleon Bonaparte. His brilliant generalship had reversed sagging French military fortunes. Now, flushed with new victories, the French were reluctant to grant the Americans the indemnities they wanted for "spoliations" of their commerce. But Napoleon was not entirely unreasonable. He agreed to end the naval war and attacks on American commerce; he also agreed to release the United States from its obligations to France under the Treaty of 1778. The American envoys were disappointed, but seeing no possibility of better terms accepted this convention of 1800. Many Federalists called it a cowardly surrender. The president disagreed—the negotiations, he believed, were "the most disinterested, the most determined, and the most successful" of his whole career. Adams no doubt exaggerated, but his defiance of the extremists of his own party was a courageous and constructive act.

The Election of 1800

The political campaign of 1800 was one of the most momentous in the nation's history and in the evolution of modern political democracy. For the first time power passed peaceably and constitutionally from one political party to another.

The rhetoric was by no means peaceable. The Republicans attacked the president once again as pro-British, a monarchist, a spendthrift who had burdened the country with enormous debts. Jefferson, the Federalist press charged, was an atheist who placed scientific reason above the teachings of the Bible. Elect him president and religion would vanish and infidelity flourish. The man was a "voluptuary" who, it was alleged, had fathered mulatto children by his female slaves. If the American people elevated such a man to the nation's highest office, it could expect "the just vengeance of heaven." The nation would suffer every calamity: "dwellings in flames, hoary hairs bathed in blood, female chastity violated, children writhing on the pike and halberd."

A split among the Federalists seriously undermined the party's prospects. By this time, Adams had concluded that he must get rid of Hamilton's influence within his official family, and in 1800 he fired Secretary of State Pickering and

Secretary of War James McHenry. Hamilton considered this a declaration of war. By now Washington was dead and the New Yorker no longer felt obliged to preserve the party. Before long he was scheming with other high Federalists to replace Adams with Charles Cotesworth Pinckney of South Carolina, one of the three emissaries to France in the X, Y, Z affair. Adams remained the party's candidate, but a much weakened one.

The New Capital. One item in the Republican indictment of their opponents was the extravagant cost of the new national capital under construction on the Potomac River. Actually, by the time the government moved from Philadelphia, the "Federal City" was still more a plan than a reality. The scheme drawn up by a Frenchman, Major Pierre L'Enfant, was magnificent in its broad streets, its malls, plazas, and circles; but it had given place to a more modest and achievable plan. The government had begun construction of the president's house in 1792, and shortly thereafter the Capitol began to rise. The third building to appear was a tavern.

The first government officials arrived from Philadelphia in June 1800. On November 1, President Adams and his family moved into the president's house. The new city was little more than a paper community. Besides the Capitol, the tavern, and the building that would later be called the White House, it consisted of some boarding houses, a few huts for construction workers, and not much else. Streets had been laid out, but these muddy or dusty tracks were

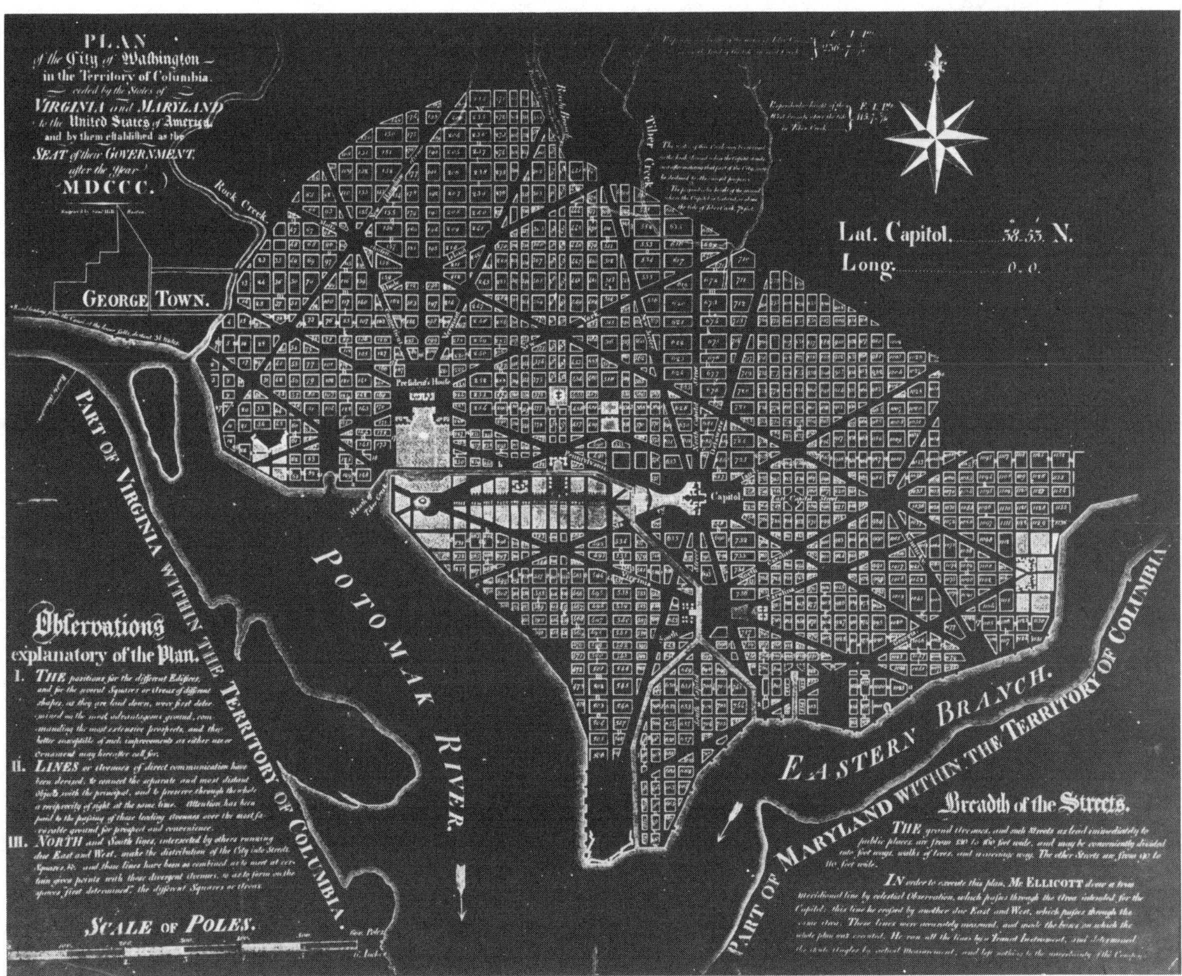

Pierre L'Enfant's plan for the city of Washington. The basic plan with its circles and broad converging streets was retained. *(Courtesy, Stokes Collection The New York Public Library)*

lined, not with residences or stores, but with virgin forest. Even the President's new home was only half complete. The First Lady, Abigail Adams, found the plastering unfinished and, in the absence of a proper laundry room, hung the family wash in the East Room. Nothing was lacking in the new Federal City, Gouverneur Morris observed, but "houses, cellars, kitchens, well informed men, amiable women, and other little trifles of this kind."

Aaron Burr. Under the existing provisions of the Constitution, the electors who would place a president and vice-president in this raw new city did not vote separately for each office. Every elector cast two ballots, and the person with the highest vote total was declared president while the runner-up became vice-president. The Republican caucus in Congress had designated Jefferson as the party's presidential and Aaron Burr as its vice-presidential candidates, but in the actual voting all the Republican electors voted for both equally. When the votes were counted, therefore, Jefferson and Burr were tied for first place. This situation threw the choice of president into the House of Representatives, where the members of each state would cast a single collective vote and for election a candidate needed the vote of a majority of states.

The nation now faced a peculiar problem. The Federalists did not control enough states to re-elect President Adams, but they could deny the presidency to anyone else. It was not likely that they would block a choice, since that would paralyze the nation, but they were capable of excluding Jefferson and substituting Burr.

The Federalists found Burr preferable to Jefferson. The New Yorker was an aristocrat, a friend of banks and Hamiltonian funding, and a believer in a strong executive. He also had the reputation of being corrupt, ambitious, cynical, and unscrupulous, but under the circumstances that appeared to the good: he could be counted on to make whatever arrangements with the Federalists they desired. The choice of Burr would also be sure to upset and confound the enemy party.

The Federalist leaders nonetheless recoiled from this choice. Hamilton despised Burr, who, he believed would "employ the rogues of all parties to overrule the good men of all parties." Jefferson, though "tinctured with fanaticism nor even mindful of truth," had some "pretension to character." Hamilton advised voting for the Virginian if he would give the Federalists guarantees that he would uphold the Federalist fiscal system, remove no Federalist from office except those of Cabinet rank, sustain the Army and Navy intact, and maintain the principles of neutrality in foreign affairs established by the two Federalist presidents. Burr was meanwhile refusing to treat directly with the Federalists, since that would have so outraged his fellow Republicans that they would have denied him all support and so the election was deadlocked.

In the end, Jefferson gave the Federalists some indirect assurances and he was declared elected. The nation could now resume as a going political concern.

The Revolution of 1800. Jefferson would call his victory the "revolution of 1800." The apprehensive Federalists would not have disagreed. They had not only lost the presidency; they had also been swept from power in Congress. What would follow the advent of the "Jacobins"? There was still hope—the judiciary might be saved; and hours before leaving office President Adams appointed a flock of Federalists to new judgeships and other legal posts created by the Judiciary Act of 1801. These "midnight judges" might be able to stop the Republicans from upsetting the economic and political arrangements of the country.

Adams also appointed John Marshall to be Chief Justice of the United States. The president did not rank this appointment as one of the contributions of his administration, yet it would turn out to be the most significant of all.

Still, from the Federalist viewpoint, the future looked ominous. Would the whole structure so painfully created in the previous twelve years be destroyed? Despite the agreement with France, could the United States avoid becoming a French satellite?

Points To Think About

1. Students of government have credited the American parties with making the constitutional system work. It is therefore no small irony that the Founding Fathers detested the very idea of political parties and hoped to create a political system in which the "spirit of party" would wither away. Their feelings go back to pre-revolutionary days. As colonists, Americans had come to associate British parties with corruption. Eighteenth-century British parties, in fact, often were corrupt. They were organized by

means of family ties and patronage. And the Crown, because of the vast number of political offices at its disposal, was frequently able to use the "spirit of party" to control Parliament. Colonists, in turn, often blamed their own troubles on these same corrupt parties.

Madison in particular hoped that the great diversity of interest groups in the new country would prevent the formation of large parties. In fact, it did not. Diversity did, however, help determine the character of the parties that did arise. The need to achieve a majority in the electoral college forced American parties to become broad coalitions which could then appeal to a broad range of interests. So America got her parties, but they were very different from the more ideologically cohesive parties that developed in nineteenth-century Europe.

2. The Alien and Sedition Laws of 1798 seriously jeopardized the Bill of Rights. They were in fact an incident in the unending struggle to reconcile the nation's legitimate need to protect itself with its commitment to safeguarding the rights of citizens—rights which include that of altering the forms of government itself if they so desire. The Alien and Sedition Laws, furthermore, provoked—in the Virginia and Kentucky Resolutions—a political reaction which, in the long run, proved just as dangerous to the safety of the constitutional system. The Resolutions opened a mare's nest of disputation about the rights of states in the federal union. Federalists at the Hartford Convention and, still later, secessionists in the South would repeat the arguments first put forward in the Resolutions.

The American constitutional system is based on the idea of balance. It seeks to balance the states against the national government, the branches of government against each other, the rights of the individual against the power of the government. Push it too far in any one direction, and the response may be an extreme motion in some other direction.

3. What happened to the Federalists once their party disintegrated? Some remained in office, especially in Connecticut and Massachusetts. Others, like John Quincy Adams, went to the Republicans and continued in public life. Still others folded their tents and stole away, reappearing occasionally in sulky memoirs.

Among the most interesting of the Federalists are those who sought nongovernmental means of furthering their social and political goals. Clyde Griffen has written a fascinating account of this last group who became *Their Brother's Keeper* by establishing a series of benevolent societies. Their societies, like the American Bible Society, the American Tract Society, and the American Anti-Slavery Society, formed a "benevolent empire." The goal was to shore up the social order, temper the excesses of democracy, and raise the moral tone of the nation. The societies, which quickly became very large, encouraged people to observe the Sabbath, avoid drunkenness and unseemly language, attend church regularly and practice the other traditional Christian virtues. They organized Sunday Schools, financed ministers in the developing West, distributed millions of pamphlets and tracts, opposed the delivery of mail on Sundays, and otherwise sought to raise the moral tone of society.

The benevolent empire was, as should be obvious, highly conservative. All of its enterprises aimed at promoting an orderly society. But it was largely apolitical. It did not endorse candidates or push legislation. Instead it tried, with some success, to regulate daily behavior by appealing to millions of ordinary Americans directly.

Suggested Readings

In *Securing the Revolution: Ideology in American Politics, 1789-1815* (1972), Richard Buel, Jr., studies the efforts of revolutionary leaders to consolidate their achievements after the adoption of the Constitution. James Thomas Flexner has abridged his four-volume biography into one: *Washington: The Indispensable Man* (1974). See also Marcus Cunliffe's *George Washington* (1958). Forrest McDonald's *Alexander Hamilton* (1979) is an admiring and penetrating work. American legal history has been enhanced by Morton J. Horwitz's *The Transformation of American Law, 1780-1860* (1977); he traces the evolution of law from rigidity in the eighteenth century to a dynamic state in the nineteenth. Alexander DeConde is standard on *The Quasi-War: Politics and Diplomacy of the Undeclared War with France, 1797-1801* (1966). Leonard D. White's *The Federalists* (1948) stresses the administrative achievements of the new government. Like everything that Richard Hofstadter wrote, *The Idea of a Party System* (1973) is illuminating and graceful.

FORREST McDONALD

The political loyalties of countless Americans, having been fixed during colonial days upon individual colonies, had been transferred after the Revolution to specific states. Virginians remained loyal to Virginia; the people of Massachusetts continued to identify themselves with that New England commonwealth. Americans, moreover, believed that their economic interests would be best served by the governments closest and most familiar to them. It was, after all, out of fear of centralized power, and particularly of centralized taxing power, that Americans had rebelled against the government of Great Britain. In establishing the Constitution, which greatly strengthened the central government of the United States, the Founding Fathers therefore had to overcome a good deal of popular suspicion.

There were also serious problems in political theory to be overcome. When the Americans declared their independence from Britain, they had committed themselves to a republican form of government—a government in which there are no hereditary rulers and all power is derived from "the public." This does not mean they believed in democracy. They thought that democracy always led to mob rule, instability, and tyranny; indeed, though in most states only white adult property-holding males could vote and had full legal rights, the Founders thought the existing American political forms, as established by the Revolutionary state constitutions, were already too democratic. Their remedy was to set up a central government strong enough to check the power of the state governments, and thus to turn the United States into a single large republic containing the smaller state republics. But in doing this they were acting against much of the political theory of the time. Eighteenth-century political theory held that governmental power could not be divided; yet they proposed to divide it between the federal and state governments. Theory held that republics could succeed only in small territories; yet the United States was an enormous country. It was assumed that republics could work only if their people were virtuous; yet the Founding Fathers believed that individuals were, for the most part, not virtuous but selfish. And it was generally believed that republics could exist only if property were fairly evenly distributed; yet the Founders knew that inequality of wealth naturally develops in any free society. Their decision to establish a huge federal republic was bold in its departure from conventional political thinking.

What the Founding Fathers did was to accept the fact of human selfishness—the appetite for power and the appetite for property—and to set up a political system in which selfishness would cancel out selfishness. The Constitution gave the central government enough powers to prevent individual states from pursuing policies harmful to the rest of the country. The states retained enough strength to prevent the central government from becoming dictatorial. This "federal" system, together with the division of power at the national level among president, Congress, and the courts, would make it difficult for any one interest group in the country to seize control of the whole machinery of government for its own selfish purposes. The very size of the national republic would be advantageous, for it would include so many different groups of people that no single group could impose its will on all others.

The Constitution established the nation's governmental system, but it left open the question of what kind of economic system the country would have. The Founders took human greed for granted and regarded private property rights as sacred, but that did not mean that they advocated the development of capitalism. The essence of capitalism is a particular attitude toward private property: that it should be put to work for the creation of more property, and that to allow it to lie idle is wasteful, even sinful. This was not the attitude of most Americans. Property, as they saw it, was to be used for comfort, enjoyment, and a livelihood. The distinction can be illustrated with a personal example. I own twenty-odd acres of land, a truck, and a tractor. If I used that property to produce crops for market, it would be capital. Instead, I use it for my personal pleasure, and thus it is not capital. Though Americans did raise crops or animals for market, the attitudes of most were closer to mine than to those of a capitalist.

EUGENE GENOVESE

Could a republic survive over so large a territory, with no ancient government and institutions to hold it together, and with so many of its citizens inclined to give their loyalty not to the nation but to states and localities? Its survival required that its central government be strong enough to impose some measure of will against state and local communities. Such a government the Articles of Confederation did not provide. The Constitution did so. The Articles may have pleased those who, however democratic and noble in spirit, wished for nothing more than a collection of free, placid, small communities. For Americans who wanted to see how much a vast, energetic, and unified republic could do toward building up its economy, its culture, and its civic life, and exploring the possibilities of freedom, only the stronger government that the Constitution established would do.

Politics in the early years of the republic was marked by violence of words that would suggest that the harshest class struggle was taking place. Followers of Jefferson accused the Federalists of monarchism, of arrogance, of planning through Hamilton's policies to set up a monied aristocracy; Hamiltonians accused the party of Jefferson of anarchism, atheism, a taste for rule by the mob.

It was in considerable measure the agricultural policies of the Jeffersonians—policies consistent with a vision of free and equal farmers—that aided the growth of American business and industry. Jefferson's purchase of the Louisiana territory opened a gigantic land for settlement. The Jeffersonian commitment to holding land prices low contributed to the rapid settling of the West by farmers in the decades that followed. Many of these farmers, as it turned out, would have something more in mind than living a simple virtuous life on their own homesteads, growing food only for their own subsistence. They would want to grow big crops for sale and profit—in other words, to be capitalists. And as they filled the West, they provided a vast market that encouraged the textile industry in the Eastern states, the manufacture there of agricultural implements and machinery, and the production of a widening array of other goods; and the commerce between the regions brought roads, canals, railroads, and marketing facilities. American business owed much to the creation of this home market, the greatest in world history, which itself arose on the basis of democratic landholding and would have been unthinkable without a democratic politics.

The Jeffersonians and their successors, however, included one element whose relation to capitalism was uneasy. Southern slaveholders were engaged like other Americans in the production of crops for profit on the market. But capitalism supposes a market of workers free to sell their labor-power. The slave system shaped a deeply reactionary ruling class with a world view radically different from that of the developing business civilization of the North. Before long, the Northern business classes would face a struggle to the knife with unyielding slaveowners, the most formidable class enemy that had yet confronted American capitalism.

Lewis and Clark holding a council with the Indians. Their expedition was prompted by President Jefferson's vision of an America stretching from "the Western ocean . . . to the Atlantic."

CHAPTER 7

Independence Confirmed 1800–1816

THE LEWIS AND CLARK EXPEDITION

The mind of Thomas Jefferson was bountiful of projects and dreams, some of which actually brought new worlds into existence. He wrote eloquently of independence, religious liberty, the education of a free people—as had other men; but Jefferson's words inspired a new nation, a bill of rights, a system of education. The expedition of Meriwether Lewis and William Clark from 1804 to 1806, exploring the Missouri River, the Rocky Mountains, and the Columbus River basin was a bold Jeffersonian vision become a great historical event.

Jefferson's vision of the West was even grander and more complex than Columbus's had been. Like the great Genoese, he saw the westward passage as a way to the riches of the East. Commerce might move "possibly with single portage, from the Western ocean . . . to the Atlantic." To this ancient dream he added the prospect of more immediate riches: the "great supplies of furs and pelts" that were then flowing only into English, not American coffers. It meant even more to Jefferson's philosophy that much of the West could become a vast, peaceful garden filling with the sturdy yeomen he expected to be the embodiments of republican virtue. The West could also be a garden for Indians weaned from their hunting ways by the advance of trade that would "place within their reach those things which will contribute more to their domestic comfort than the possession of extensive, but uncultivated wilds." The more rugged West of the great rivers and mountains would exhibit treasures of natural history. Mammoths, Jefferson suspected, might still roam the lands farther West. Perhaps the llama ranged this far north. For years, Jefferson had encouraged all who would listen to explore the great West for science, for country, for riches.

Except for slightly underestimating the number of men who would be needed (thirty to fifty in various stages of the expedition), and with no idea that an Indian woman, her infant son, and a giant Newfoundland dog named Scammon would go along as well, Jefferson got exactly the expedition and the results he had envisioned. The exploration extended his Indian diplomacy, his commercial policies, and his diplomatic goals while furiously gathering together every piece of information about geography, plants, animals, and minerals that could be gained by observation or collection of specimens and fossils. Seven men kept diaries; every moment when they were not exploring, negotiating, or being ill the two leaders spent in taking detailed field notes and reworking them into coherent accounts, complete with drawings, maps, and lexicons for Thomas Jefferson and the world.

Meriwether Lewis and William Clark were—like Jefferson—amateurs. Though soldiers, neither had been a professional military man, Lewis being on leave from the army to serve as Jefferson's secretary and Clark having resigned some time before. Nor were they professional scientists or explorers: once Jefferson appointed them, they had to scramble for a rapid education in geography and mapmaking, celestial navigation, mineralogy, and medicine to keep an expedition alive for two years. Lewis sought the counsel of America's most distinguished physician, Dr. Benjamin Rush of Philadelphia, who supplied him with a little information and a large supply of "Rush's Thunderbolts," his famous, violently purgative pills, which Lewis and Clark used for all ailments.

The expedition went from St. Louis to the mouth of the Columbia River and back, through incredibly difficult country, with elementary equipment. The first leg, up the Missouri with a winter's stop in a Mandan Indian village, was brutally hard work: poling, pulling, and portaging a string of boats up a huge river whose powerful current undermined banks at each bend, created mudslides, and sent vast jams of tree trunks cascading downriver to knock over the expedition's boats. The second leg, over the mountaintops through high barren badlands, was the hardest part of all. The trip down the Columbia River system was least eventful. The explorers eventually realized that they had gone the long way around and correctly plotted the shortest and fastest route home through the mountains. On the return trip they proved that there was no route, even with portages, where small boats could practically be carried over the Continental divide and relaunched on the Western rivers. Rather, there was a set of mountains and valleys between, which required a substantial trans-shipment. The way west would not be direct or easy: the three-century-old hope of finding a "Northwest Passage" had to be forgotten, at least for a time.

The expedition studied dozens of Indian tribes, arranging trade agreements, asserting the government's influence, presenting gifts, recording manners and customs, seeking geographical information. Lewis and Clark identified 300 new plant and animal species or subspecies, collecting bones, fossils, and seeds. The homely names they gave the new species—since neither man knew Latin—have not survived in the naturalist literature; but creatures like *Salmo clarkii*, the beautiful cutthroat trout named for Clark, and *Asyndesmus lesis*, Lewis's woodpecker, attest to a more learned fraternity's appreciation of their works. The *Notebooks* and *Journals* of the expedition have been fundamental sources for naturalists, geographers, anthropologists, and historians.

The rigors of the journey produced much illness and hardship, yet only one man lost his life—from a ruptured appendix that in those days would have killed him even had he been in Philadelphia. The only serious injury was to Lewis himself, when one of his own men accidentally shot him in the backside. (Lewis made few mistakes, but going hunting for food with a one-eyed sergeant was certainly one of them.) There were only one or two small scrapes with Indians, although it took firm diplomacy and carefully manned swivel guns (small portable cannons) to prevent a few rough encounters from becoming dangerous. Clark's slave, York, the one black on the expedition, was the wonder of dozens of Indian tribes. The Indians would actually pay to touch his hair or run their fingers over his skin to see whether the dark color would come off. One of the interpreters—a Frenchman named Charbonneau who had been hired in St. Louis because he knew the Sioux dialects—

persuaded Lewis to allow him to take his Indian wife, Sacajawea, and their two-month-old baby on the roughest part of the trip from the upper Missouri over the mountains to the Pacific. Apparently, her knowledge of the Shoshonean dialects, which none of the other interpreters (including her husband) commanded, persuaded the captain to agree. When they finally made contact with the mountain Indians, the first party of braves they met had as its chief her brother, whom she had not seen since she had been abducted from his hunting party as a small child. No novelist could have gotten away with such an unlikely plot.

Jefferson had made his proposal for the expedition to Congress before Talleyrand offered to sell the United States the Louisiana Territory; the President had planned to grasp the trade of the West with stations on territory both unknown and unowned. By the time the expedition set out from St. Louis, Louisiana was American territory. But the Oregon country beyond the Great Divide was not. It belonged perhaps to Great Britain or maybe to Spain. Yet Lewis, once back at St. Louis, wrote of "possessions" west of the mountains, and Jefferson himself by January 1807 was referring to "our country, from the Missisipi [*sic*] to the Pacific." Jefferson supported John Jacob Astor's efforts to create an American fur empire that would crowd the British out of the market. In the ensuing race for the strategic mouth of the Columbia River, Astor moved his men across the trail that Lewis and Clark had blazed, while the British pushed southwest from Canada. In July 1811, when the great British explorer and entrepreneur David Thompson pushed his way to the Columbia and canoed to its mouth, he beheld the American flag flying from the parapets of four-month-old Fort Astoria. Lewis and Clark's expedition would, in the end, make Jefferson's largest vision—a continental United States—the future.

Jefferson's Inauguration

At noon on a blustery March day, Jefferson took the oath of office and became the third president of the United States. He had come to Washington the previous November and had spent the winter at Conrad and McMunn's boardinghouse, where for $15 a week he dined and roomed unostentatiously. The inauguration ceremonies were brief and austere, as befitted a party that made a point of republican simplicity. Jefferson's expensive velvet suit failed to arrive, and he walked in plain garb to the still uncompleted Capitol. In the crowded Senate chamber, he swore to defend the Constitution and faithfully discharge the duties of his office. Then, almost inaudibly, he delivered his inaugural address.

Thomas Jefferson, inaugurated as third president of the United States in March 1801. *(Portrait by Rembrandt Peale, 1800. White House Collection)*

Jefferson's address expressed the philosophy of the men who had fought the Federalists for over a decade. It confirmed the Republicans' dedication to freedom of religion and the press. It endorsed the encouragement of agriculture, and of commerce as its handmaid. The federal government, the new president declared, must conduct its business economically and attempt to pay off its debts. The state governments, he said, were "the surest bulwarks against anti-republican tendencies." But besides making these predictable Republican pronouncements, Jefferson sought to calm the fears of Federalists. The nation, he declared, must avoid "entangling alliances": this was a signal that the Republicans would accept the recent termination of the 1778 French alliance. They would also avoid extreme partisanship. Now that the great contest of 1800 was over, all Americans "will, of course, arrange themselves under the will of the law, and unite in common efforts for the common good." Minority rights would be protected, and no one would suffer persecution: "We are all Republicans, we are all Federalists. . . . Let us, then, with courage and confidence pursue our own Federal and Republican principles, our attachment to union and representative government."

So softly did the fresh-minted Chief Executive speak that few in the crowded room could hear what he said. But printed copies of the speech were available, and ushers distributed these to the assembled dignitaries. That evening, the president returned to Conrad and McMunn's to dine as usual. When he entered the dining room, a lady among the paying guests offered him a chair. Jefferson declined the offer and went to his usual place at the foot of the table, far from the warming fire. A simpler age of American manners had begun.

The United States in 1801

The People. This year 1801 was a time of new manners, a new politics, almost a new republic. Yet in many ways the nation had not changed since the clash at Lexington Common on April 19, 1775. In the twenty-five years since the opening gun of the Revolution America's population had grown from about 2.5 to 5.3 million; but the nation's white population remained overwhelmingly British in origin and Protestant in religion. Germans were found in eastern Pennsylvania, in the Shenandoah Valley, and along the Mohawk River in New York. The Hudson Valley contained many Dutchmen, and the guttural sound of Dutch could still be heard in Albany. Scattered here and there, primarily in the towns, were small enclaves of Jews and Huguenot French, as well as a handful of Irish Catholics. The largest non-British group by far was the blacks, who numbered over a million, almost all south of Pennsylvania and almost all slaves. But the Revolution and difficulties of postwar readjustment had discouraged both immigration and the slave trade. The vast majority of the slaves were native-born Americans.

Americans were a young people. Half the population was under seventeen years old. Households were large; almost one-fourth of all families had seven or more people living under one roof. This placed a heavy burden on families, and especially on women, who spent many of their best, most vigorous years bearing and rearing children.

The United States in 1801 was a nation of farms and villages. Only 300,000 Americans lived in communities of even 2500 people—fewer than seven percent of the total. Perhaps only a dozen places in the whole country deserved the label of "city."

The Cities. Of these, the largest, the most cosmopolitan, and most gracious was Philadelphia, with almost 70,000 inhabitants. Penn's town was also the most modern in the nation. Most American city-dwellers drew their water from wells or cisterns or bought it from vendors. They relied on hogs to consume the garbage dumped on the street. They were forced to tramp streets usually ankle-deep in either dust or mud, depending on the season. Not so Philadelphians: the city of Brotherly Love, after the cholera and yellow fever epidemics of the 1790s, piped water from the Schuylkill River; its streets, paved with cobblestones, were regularly cleaned.

Boston, with 25,000 inhabitants, had fallen behind New York and Baltimore in population since colonial days. Nevertheless, it remained the commercial, financial, and intellectual capital of New England. With its narrow streets and crowded wharves, it had not much changed since the 1770s. The city government was still the same as in the seventeenth century: its affairs were in the hands of "selectmen" chosen at the town meeting. Although Boston's elite was no longer composed of dour Puritan gentlemen, the Federalist merchants, ministers, and lawyers who now formed the town's upper crust retained much of the old Puritan self-confidence and respect for learning. The Bostonian George Cabot was expressing the unshakable conviction of his class when he declared that his native city possessed "more wisdom and virtues than any other part of the world."

Two hundred miles to the south of Boston was New York, on Manhattan Island. In 1801 the city was still partly Dutch. Many houses sat gable-end to the street, as in Amsterdam, and were faced with the characteristically Dutch yellow brick. Even more than Boston and Philadelphia, New York thrived on commerce; most of its 60,000 inhabitants were crowded into the southeastern corner of the island, adjacent to the docks and warehouses.

Baltimore was a comparatively new city that had not acquired official municipal status until 1797. The outlet for much of the Chesapeake tobacco crop, it also tapped the flour, wheat, and farming provisions of the Pennsylvania backcountry through the Susquehanna River. The city's aggressive merchants had pioneered a lucrative trade to Bremen, Germany, and had attracted in return a substantial number of German artisans.

Charleston, the capital of South Carolina, was in some ways the most colorful of all. It was both a major port and a summer resort where rice planters from the malaria-ridden coastal lowlands went during the "fever season" to protect their health. Built in brick and stone, the city was ruled by a planter-merchant elite who combined republican principles with the aristocratic arts of good living, polite letters, fine manners, and elegant hospitality. These avowed republicans could not live without slaves. Of the eighteen thousand people who packed the little port, six thousand were blacks; they helped keep its streets clean, its markets stocked, and its wharves busy.

Any observer of Charleston between 1790 and 1800 would have noticed a particularly promising development: a new crop, cotton, was being loaded aboard ships in the harbor by black stevedores. With the invention of the cotton gin by the Connecticut Yankee Eli Whitney, greenseed cotton had become a profitable crop in the interior of the Carolinas and Georgia. The South's one major Atlantic port was feeling the invigorating economic effects of the thousands of bales it shipped to Liverpool and Glasgow to feed the new textile factories of Great Britain.

All the nation's cities were coastal communities; only overseas trade employed enough people to create cities. The one potential exception in view was the small town of Pittsburgh, situated where the Allegheny and Monongahela rivers join to form the great Ohio. With about two thousand inhabitants in 1800, it had become a supplier of manufactured goods to the burgeoning West, producing iron, glass, textiles, and vessels for the river trade. As early as 1800 an English visitor reported the town covered with a pall of smoke from the numerous coal fires that fueled the iron foundries and glassworks. By 1810 one expert estimated Pittsburgh's trade at $1 million a year.

The Farms. The great majority of Americans were not urban in any sense. They depended for their livelihood in some fashion on the soil. A few thousand belonged to the great landed families, many of them living in the coastal regions of the Chesapeake, the Carolinas, and Georgia, or in the Hudson Valley of New York. Many were either tenants or slaves of such families. The overwhelming majority of the nation's million-odd blacks in 1800 were slaves cultivating rice, tobacco, or corn, and now cotton as well. A majority of white male Americans owned the ground they tilled.

A typical American yeoman and his family worked hard for what they had. In the better-settled regions, the daily and yearly rounds were hard enough. Animals had to be watered, their stables cleaned. Plowing in the spring, weeding and cultivating in the summer, and harvesting in fall all required heavy labor. The women cooked, cleaned, spun, made preserves, and took care of flocks of young children. Clearing new land on the frontier required the backbreaking labor of girdling trees, clearing underbrush, and breaking virgin sod. The pioneer farmer of Vermont, western New York, or the newly opened Ohio or Alabama country was lucky if he could add more than four or five usable acres to his farm a year. Even then it took many years before the frontier farmer's land was fully cleared of stumps and he could plow a straight furrow. Meanwhile, his family lived in a primitive one-room log house with a sleeping attic above. Techniques of planting and harvesting had not advanced much beyond medieval practices. American plows in 1800 were heavy wooden contraptions pulled by oxen or mules. Farmers still used the scythe to harvest grain and threshed it with a hand flail made of two sticks joined by a leather thong.

Yet the yeoman family enjoyed a rough abundance. Since the soil was rich, the American farm family ate well and produced more than it consumed. Travelers through the nation's rural regions remarked on signs of prosperity. One Englishman reported of the Connecticut countryside during Jefferson's presidency that it "had the appearance of wealth, numerous broods of poultry straying about, with sheep and cattle grazing in great numbers in the fields." Travelers who accepted the hospitality of local yeomen, rather than brave the fare of notoriously bad country inns, reported on the abundance of

Thomas Jefferson's home, Monticello, which he designed and built near Charlottesville, Virginia. *(Virginia State Travel Service)*

everything served. Breakfast tables were loaded down with boiled fish, beefsteak, ham sausages, hotbreads, and cheese. Many Europeans complained at how badly these foods were prepared, and even American physicians warned that their countrymen's diets contained too many greasy foods. But no one denied the plenty of the American country table.

The typical farm family was an isolated social unit. Except in southern New England, where the imprint of the old "town" system of colonial days remained, the rural American lived in a house widely separated by fields and virgin forest from his nearest neighbor. Poor roads, widespread illiteracy, and high postal rates cut rural people off from the more genteel manners and tastes of the towns and cities.

Yeoman women suffered acutely from the isolation of their lives. They frequently lacked the close network of female kin and friends from which New England women drew comfort and companionship. It is likely that among the yeomanry, as on the frontier, the power of the husband within the family remained greater than in the more settled regions of the Northeast, if only because family life and household production remained pretty much one and the same and the husband assumed the leadership of both. Yeoman women also found themselves further removed from the comforts and distractions that the growing markets of the Northeast could provide women as consumers. Ribbons and mirrors remained rare; cookstoves and shoes might have to be ordered from New England. And although husbands and wives frequently worked as close collaborators in daily life—bringing in the harvest, or even delivering children—the lines between male and female spheres remained tightly drawn. When men got together to raise a house or enjoy fights, the women would likely work together to produce meals for a large throng or they would quilt.

When rural Americans did get together with neighbors and friends, it was often to engage in rough-and-tumble sports that could turn brutal. Wrestling included kicking, biting, punching, and eye-gouging. "I saw more than one man, who wanted an eye," noted an Easterner as he crossed the border into Kentucky. Country people, especially on the frontier, "baited" bulls and bears—that is, set large dogs to attack them while rooting for either attacker or defender—or they bet on the outcome of cockfights. Whether at taverns or religious camp meetings, at dances and "hoedowns" or in the home, Americans consumed vast quantities of whiskey, rum, and brandy. Women drank punch or "toddies" made of these. A ditty went:

Hail Columbia, happy land,
If you ain't drunk, I'll be damned.

Foreign travelers often noted that the New Englanders, especially, were more mannerly and "steady" than Westerners and Southerners. In every section there were sober, well-bred, well-informed men and women who read books and newspapers, displayed elegant manners, enjoyed themselves sedately playing cricket or attending sewing and husking bees. Nevertheless, it would take years of good roads, steady cultivation of the land, and growth of towns before the rudeness of the country lessened along with its isolation. America was yet to become the land of Hamilton's dreams; it still held to the Jeffersonian vision.

The Republicans in Power

Thomas Jefferson. Jefferson, the new president, was informal in manners and dress to an extent that shocked strait-laced contemporaries. Senator William Plumer of New Hampshire, calling at the presidential mansion, mistook him for a servant. Other visitors, noting his carelessly tied long red hair, his less-than-immaculate linen, his toeless carpet slippers, and his tall, loose-jointed frame, believed that he lacked the dignity required of his office.

Yet the new Chief Executive was one of the most cultivated men of his day. He read French, Italian, Latin, and Greek, played the violin skillfully, corresponded with many of the outstanding thinkers of Europe, was an imaginative and creative architect and inventor, and in science had considerable talent and range.

The combination of informality and restless intellect represents not only Jefferson's private taste and style but his idea of what the citizen of an enlightened republic should be: free of artificialities of manner, free to cultivate talent and put it to public service. Citizenship of this kind, so Jeffersonianism supposed, could best express itself in a relatively simple and stable environment: a farm, a city without poverty, a nation without dictatorial government. And so Jefferson set out to cut and simplify.

He simplified the manners of his office. In place of the formal receptions of the era of Washington and Adams, he substituted gatherings where scholars, scientists, and interesting men of affairs exchanged ideas over madeira and nuts. He dropped his predecessors' practice of appearing before Congress to present his State of the Union addresses, and sent written messages instead.

Limited Government. Jefferson simplified the government. He and his Treasury Secretary Albert Gallatin opposed any rise in the federal debt, and they managed to cut military spending to a third of what it had been under the Federalists. The army was reduced to just 3000 regulars and 172 officers. The five frigates built during Adams's administration were all rendered inactive; in their place the Jeffersonians created a navy of gunboats fit only for coastal service. The president also closed the American legations in Holland and Prussia. The new administration could not abolish the Bank of the United States before its charter expired in 1811, but under Gallatin the government sold its Bank stock at a profit and ceased to play any further banking role.

If government as Jefferson conceived of it had little business regulating finances, and little use for a large military establishment, it certainly had no taste for enforcing political loyalty. He allowed the Sedition Act to lapse; there would be no more criminal prosecutions for attacking the government.

Jefferson's republic would have a virtuous simplicity. He would have shuddered at the size and scope of twentieth-century governments; but he would have shuddered also at twentieth-century business or twentieth-century cities. It is curious that the Federalists, less egalitarian than Jefferson, actually had a concept that comes closer to the reality of modern democratic societies. They planned for a more active economy than Jefferson seems to have envisioned, and their government policies would draw the country's labor and resources more closely together and put them more vigorously to work for the increase of prosperity.

Jefferson advocated the very sort of limited government that Hamilton in *The Federalist* had warned against: "a government at a distance and out of sight." The national government, Jefferson declared in his first message to Congress, was "charged with the external and mutual relations only of these states." It was the states that had "principal care of our persons, our property, and our reputation." The national government had become "too complicated, too expensive"; offices and officers had "multiplied unnecessarily and sometimes injuriously to the service they were meant to promote." As means to his goal, Jefferson's administration sought economy, limited federal powers, and decentralization.

More immediately Jefferson sought to weed out of the federal bureaucracy those Federalists who had taken too partisan a role in the political battles preceding 1801. Most of these were officeholders whom the president could remove at will; but at least one, Supreme Court Justice Chase, had life tenure and could be gotten rid of only by a process of impeachment by the House and trial and conviction by the Senate. In 1805 a Republican House of Representatives did impeach Chase on charges of high crimes and misdemeanors, but the Senate failed to remove him from office.

***Marbury* v. *Madison*.** Far more significant in its ultimate result was the Jefferson Administration's attempt to undo the effects of the 1801 Judiciary Act. Under that measure Adams, just before leaving office, had appointed a flock of Federalist judges and law officials with lifetime tenure; his purpose had clearly been to retain Federalist control in at least one branch of government and, as the Republicans saw it, prevent the new administration from carrying out the will of the people. Hoping to frustrate this goal, Secretary of State Madison refused to deliver several newly appointed officials their commissions. One of these, William Marbury, sued the Secretary, charging that his action was illegal under the Judiciary Act of 1789. By the provisions of that measure, Marbury's lawyers argued, the Supreme Court could compel a federal official to issue a commission whether he wished to or not.

In 1803 the case came before the United States Supreme Court, Chief Justice John Marshall presiding. Marshall was a Virginian, but not of the political stamp of his fellow Virginians Jefferson and Madison. A Federalist, he deplored the Republican preference for a small national government. He also wanted a strong Supreme Court. Yet Marshall and the Court held, in *Marbury* v *Madison*, that the Court could not compel Madison to deliver a commission to Marbury, since that portion of the Judiciary Act of 1789 that would have made Madison issue the commission was unconstitutional and therefore unenforceable. The Supreme Court, it seems, was surrendering a little power that it might have claimed and exercised. But it was doing so at great gain. *Marbury* v. *Madison* immeasurably strengthened the Supreme Court, for it announced and won wide acceptance of the principle of judicial review, the principle that the Court could decide whether a piece of federal legislation was constitutional. Although the idea of judicial review had been asserted before *Marbury* v. *Madison*, that case provided the first occasion for the Supreme Court to define and exercise the right.

The Louisiana Purchase. In 1803 the United States acquired the province of Louisiana from France and thereby almost doubled its size. Louisiana was a gigantic wedge of territory stretching from the Gulf of Mexico in the South to somewhere in the present-day Dakotas in the North, and from the Mississippi in the East to the Rocky Mountains in the West. Its exact boundaries were unclear, its richness and strategic value unquestioned.

Spain had owned the province until ceding it to France in 1801. Tentative reports of the transfer alarmed Jefferson. The president looked forward to an "empire for liberty" consisting of American farmlands stretching over much of North America. So long as weak Spain controlled the sparsely settled province, he could afford to wait until it dropped into the American lap. But if powerful France now possessed it,

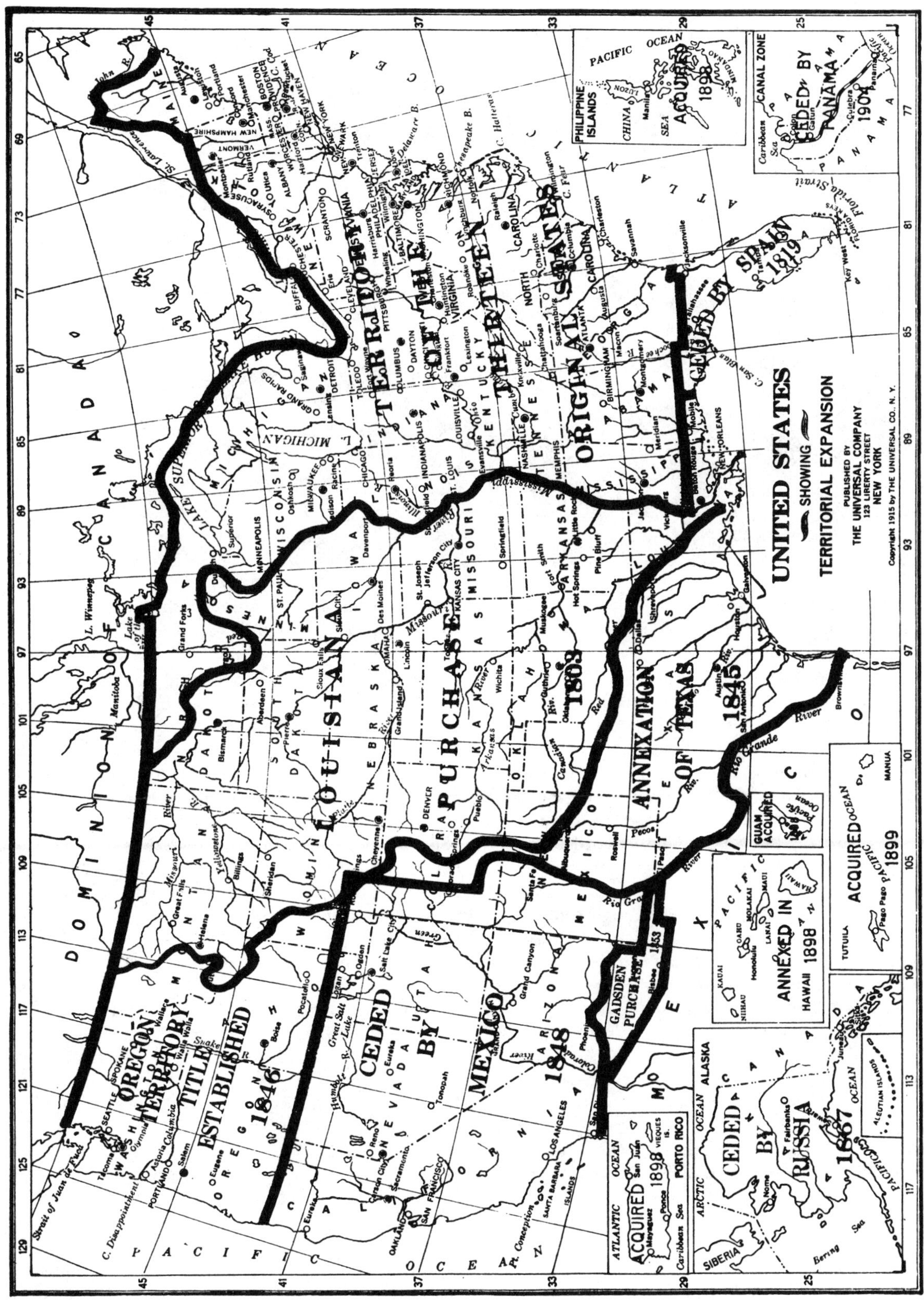
UNITED STATES
SHOWING
TERRITORIAL EXPANSION
PUBLISHED BY
THE UNIVERSAL COMPANY
123 LIBERTY STREET
NEW YORK
Copyright 1915 by THE UNIVERSAL CO. N. Y.
TERRITORY OF THE THIRTEEN ORIGINAL STATES
LOUISIANA PURCHASE 1803
CEDED BY SPAIN 1819
ANNEXATION OF TEXAS 1845
OREGON TERRITORY TITLE ESTABLISHED 1846
CEDED BY MEXICO 1848
GADSDEN PURCHASE 1853
CEDED BY RUSSIA 1867
ANNEXED IN 1898 HAWAII
ACQUIRED 1898 PORTO RICO
ACQUIRED 1898 PHILIPPINE ISLANDS
GUAM ACQUIRED 1898
ACQUIRED 1899 TUTUILA
CEDED BY PANAMA 1904 CANAL ZONE
DOMINION OF CANADA
MEXICO
PACIFIC OCEAN
ATLANTIC OCEAN

View of Council Bluffs, Iowa, on the Missouri River, part of the vast territory acquired in the Louisiana Purchase. *(Courtesy, The New York Public Library, Astor, Lenox, and Tilden Foundations)*

who knew whether the United States would ever be able to absorb it? Besides, Louisiana included the port of New Orleans. Whoever controlled this port controlled the trade and commercial outlet for much of the western United States. Hoping to prevent final consummation of the arrangement between Spain and France or at least to acquire some port on the Gulf coast, Jefferson dispatched Robert R. Livingston to Paris.

Meanwhile, the French were beginning to lose interest in the territory. For a time Napoleon had hoped to fit Louisiana into a great French colonial empire that would also include the valuable Caribbean sugar island of Hispaniola. He first had to recapture the Western part of Hispaniola from the blacks who in the 1790s had risen up against French masters there and established the Republic of Haiti. Napoleon sent an army of thirty thousand men, headed by his brother-in-law, to subdue the Haitians under their brilliant leader Toussaint L'Ouverture. The task was impossible. Eventually the French captured L'Ouverture by treachery, but not before their army had been virtually wiped out by a combination of enemy action and tropical disease. Napoleon decided to abandon his entire dream of a restored French empire in the New World.

It was this new situation that Livingston confronted when he arrived in Paris. France no longer cared much about Louisiana; and Napoleon, facing the prospect of a renewed war in Europe, was certain that he could not keep it from falling into British hands. On the American side, the situation had also changed. In October 1802 Spain, still in legal possession of New Orleans, decided to withdraw the right of deposit the Pinckney Treaty of 1795 had granted to Americans. Once more, the whole American interior was bottled up and this time, so it seemed, France was behind it.

Jefferson now dispatched James Monroe to France with new orders. He should try to get New Orleans from the French, or at least to acquire from Spain part of the Gulf Coast panhandle of West Florida. Either would give the United States an outlet for Southern trade. Two days after Monroe joined Livingston in the French capital, they learned a prodigious piece of news: Napoleon would sell not only New Orleans but all of Louisiana! The price: 60 million francs, and up to 20 million francs in settlement of all American claims against France for the "spoliations" of the 1790s. The offer flabbergasted the envoys. They were not authorized to negotiate such an arrangement, but it was far too good to turn down, and they eagerly accepted. In short order, the signed document was on its way to Washington for Congress and the president to confirm.

It may seem surprising that any American should have questioned such an extraordinary bargain, but many did. One prominent Federalist denounced the purchase as "a miserable calamitous business"—the new nation would now be so gigantic that it would fall apart. Other Federalists were unhappy that the United States had promised to grant citizenship to all the French and Spanish inhabitants of Louisiana. Even Jefferson worried that by buying Louisiana he had exceeded the authority of the federal government under the Constitution, and for a while he supported a constitutional amendment authorizing the purchase. In the end neither side's scruples or reservations could compete with the reality of the most successful land deal in history. On October 20, 1803, the Senate confirmed the treaty, and two months later the United States took formal possession of the province. For a total of $15 million the United States had acquired a region almost equal in area to the whole of western Europe.

Lewis and Clark did immensely valuable work on their expedition to the new territory. They established friendly relations with many Indian tribes. They learned of valuable beaver streams and of many fur-bearing animals. They discovered several usable passes through the Rockies, which they recorded on a map published in 1814. Jefferson sent several other expeditions to the West, the most successful being that led by Lieutenant Zebulon Pike. That explorer traveled the Colorado country, where he gave his name to a high peak of the Rockies west of present-day Denver, and crossed over into Spanish-held New Mexico. His report, published long before that of Lewis and Clark, made him famous and helped to open up the Rocky Mountains to fur trappers.

To the West and the North the vast domain touched Spanish and British territory, but exactly where nobody really knew. The Spaniards suspected that the United States had designs on their possessions in New Mexico and Texas. Years before, they had secretly entered into a financial arrangement with James Wilkinson, a Kentucky adventurer, to act as their spy and agent in the American camp. Wilkinson remained in their pay while rising to brigadier general in the United States Army and to the post of military commander of the new Louisiana Territory. In this strategic position he advised his employers how to thwart American plans. At one point he even suggested that they arrest Lewis and Clark. Another prominent American, Vice-President Aaron Burr, was fishing in the same troubled Western waters.

Burr Again. Burr was a complex man. Witty, charming, and intelligent, he was also ambitious and devious; this son of a Presbyterian minister, this former theology student became a notorious womanizer. John Quincy Adams, the future president, noted of Burr that with his "ambition of military fame, ambition of conquest over female virtue was the duplicate ruling passion of his life." In 1804 he killed Alexander Hamilton in a duel at Weehawken, New Jersey, thereby destroying whatever reputation he had retained. The duel was the culmination of long-standing animosity between the two men.

A year later, Burr, according to Wilkinson, was deeply involved in a scheme to detach Louisiana from the United States, join it together with Texas and other parts of Spanish Mexico, and create a new nation. But Wilkinson decided in the end that it was more profitable to stay in Spain's employ than to continue with this chancy venture. In November 1806 he wrote to Jefferson, warning that Burr intended to detach the West from the United States. At the same time he asked the Spanish Viceroy in Mexico to

Aaron Burr's schemes to detach the West from the United States lead to indictments for treason, charges which he managed to escape. *(Courtesy, The New-York Historical Society, New York City)*

send him $200,000 in appreciation of his refusal to join Burr in dismembering New Spain.

Jefferson ordered Burr's arrest. Burr quickly set out for Pensacola in Spanish Florida, probably intending to escape to Europe. But he was captured and brought to Richmond, Virginia, where he was tried for treason, with Wilkinson serving as an important witness against him. The prosecution produced much damaging evidence against Burr. But the former vice-president had the support of the presiding judge, Chief Justice Marshall; when the jury returned the verdict of "not proved," Marshall changed it to "not guilty."

The government refused to drop the matter. Soon after, it obtained Burr's indictment on another treason charge. This time Marshall granted him bail pending trial and rather than face another legal battle, Burr fled to Europe. He remained abroad for four years, and then returned to live a scandalous life in New York City. In his seventies he fathered two illegitimate children, and at the age of eighty he was sued for divorce on the grounds of adultery.

France and England—Again

European Entanglements. In early 1802 England and France ended their long, exhausting war. It now looked as if the American people would be spared the ordeal they had faced ever since war between the world's two most powerful nations had erupted in 1793. No longer would American commerce be the defenseless prey both of the Royal Navy and of French revenue cutters and port officials. Peace lasted all of fourteen months. By May 1803 Britain was once more at war with France. Austria, Russia, and Sweden soon joined Britain, while Spain allied itself to imperial France. And, once again, America found itself caught between the British hammer and the French anvil.

The Royal Navy immediately resumed its practice of impressing seamen aboard American vessels, claiming that they were deserters from the British fleet. The procedure itself was an insult to American honor; and the British in fact seized numbers of American citizens and forced them into the Royal Navy. Outside American harbors, British ships waited for American merchant vessels, stopped them, sent an officer aboard, and took crewmen. Britain also reversed its former policy and refused any longer to allow Americans the "broken voyage," a practice by which Americans had brought French goods under the protection of American neutrality by transshipping them through American ports. Britain's primary purpose was not to injure American commerce, but to hurt the French economy and frustrate the French war effort.

Responding to the British blockade of the French-held continent of Europe, Napoleon issued in 1806 the Berlin Decree, ordering the seizure of any vessel carrying British goods. The following year he directed French privateers to stop all ships, including neutral ones, suspected of carrying enemy cargo. The Berlin Decree set off a round of British countermeasures, followed by still further French retaliation. It began to seem that no American ship would be able to leave port or approach European shores without facing certain confiscation.

The American response to these indignities and harassments was mixed. Since Britain was now violating American sovereign rights even more flagrantly than France, Britain was the object of an enraged American patriotism. Continuing problems with the Indian tribes in the Northwest further aggravated anti-British feeling. Not all Americans, however, agreed that strong measures were called for. Especially in the Atlantic ports, many citizens were willing to accept harassment. For despite it, American commerce was flourishing in a war-stricken world. So pressing was the need for shipping space that ocean freight rates shot upward. Insurance costs were also high and there was always the risk of confiscation, but profits were unprecedented. Between 1803 and 1807 American exports, much of them in tropical goods from the French and Spanish New World colonies, leaped from $56 million to $108 million, and the American merchant marine grew from 950,000 tons to almost 1.3 million. Why not accept the situation, asked the merchants of Boston, Salem, Providence, New York, Philadelphia, and other ports?

Pressures for War. Still, even the most materialistic citizens could forget their immediate interests in the heat of anger at some indignity committed by the British or French. One such incident took place in the early summer of 1807.

On June 22, the *Chesapeake*, a brand-new Navy frigate commanded by Commodore James Barron, left Norfolk, Virginia, for a Mediterranean cruise. Aboard were several deserters from the Royal Navy. When the *Chesapeake* was only a few miles at sea, it was overtaken by H.M.S. *Leopard*, part of the British squadron patrolling off Hampton Roads. The British captain ordered Barron to heave to and allow a naval party to board to look for deserters. This was the first time the British had attempted impressment off an American man-of-war, and Barron refused. But the *Chesapeake's* guns were not yet mounted, and the ship could not defend itself. After repeated murderous broadsides from the *Leopard*, Barron struck his colors; the British removed four deserters and departed. The *Chesapeake* limped back to port with three dead, eighteen wounded, and a tale certain to inflame every American patriot.

The American public screamed for war against "perfidious Albion." "The country," Jefferson noted, "had never been in such a state of excitement since the battle of Lexington." But the president, although he could undoubtedly have obtained a declaration of war from Congress, wished to avoid armed conflict. He was not a pacifist, but he deplored the expensive armies and navies war required; armies and navies and big treasury budgets were Federalist, not Republican, playthings. In accordance with his distaste for a large military, Jefferson had so reduced American forces that war was virtually out of the question. And the United States, he believed, still had at its disposal some powerful unused weapons short of war.

Diplomatic pressure was one of these, and Jefferson immediately dispatched a message to Britain demanding disavowal of the attack, reparations for lives lost and damage inflicted, the recall of the British admiral responsible for the *Leopard's* action, and an end to the impressment policy. He also ordered all British ships out of United States territorial waters and

The attack on the U.S.S. *Chesapeake* by H.M.S. *Leopard* on June 22, 1807, set off a furor among Americans, but Jefferson avoided armed conflict through diplomacy and passage of the Embargo Act. *(Courtesy, The Mariners Museum, Newport News, Virginia)*

stepped up preparations for defense in case the British forced the nation's hand.

The British response to American diplomatic demands was unsatisfactory. The Foreign Secretary, George Canning, attacked Jefferson for his retaliatory acts and quibbled about reparations for American losses. He also defended the British admiral responsible for the *Leopard's* attack, although he agreed to remove him.

Jefferson now invoked his last peaceable weapon. American trade, the president believed, was essential to both the major belligerents. Both needed American wheat, provisions, and lumber, and the French relied on the United States to carry their Caribbean products. During the imperial crisis before 1775, Americans had forced Britain to back down by boycotting British goods. In all likelihood, Jefferson thought, they would once more yield to commercial pressure if it were applied firmly. In any case, it should be tried before more drastic measures.

The Embargo and Non-Intercourse Acts. Under the president's prodding, Congress passed the Embargo Act of 1807. The law prohibited American ships from sailing for foreign ports. Coastal vessels would have to post bond that would insure that they did not turn east and cross the open sea to Europe, or south to the West Indies. Only ships engaged in public business were to be exempted from the export embargo.

The Embargo Act was temporarily popular in the South and the West. But to the trading centers of the Northeast it seemed a disaster. Almost overnight the glittering trade bubble that had lasted since 1793 burst. Ships rode at anchor, their sails furled, while worms riddled their wooden hulls. Once-busy waterfront streets stood emptied of their milling crowds of seamen, teamsters, tavern-keepers, and stevedores. One ditty went:

Our ships all in motion once
whitened the ocean,
They sailed and returned with a cargo;
Now doomed to decay, they have fallen a prey
To Jefferson—worms—and embargo.

New Yorkers and New Englanders did what they could to evade the new law. Many coastal traders, once out of sight of land, crossed the Atlantic. Jefferson had given the state governors the right to issue special permits for specific reasons. Now the merchants prevailed on the governors to grant permits for almost any excuse. Many New England merchants faced with ruin chose more legal and constructive alternatives: during this period many transferred large amounts of capital from overseas trade to domestic manufactures.

When New England farmers tried to transport their produce across the border to Canada, Jefferson declared them in rebellion and ordered troops to the scene. Pitched battles followed between farmers and militia. Republicans in Congress subsequently passed a series of enforcement acts every bit as repressive as the Alien and Sedition Acts.

Overall, the embargo did not have much effect on the European belligerents. It hurt British workingmen and French colonists, but the ruling classes in both Britain and France were scarcely affected. British manufacturers, meanwhile, could continue to send their goods in their own vessels to compete with American products in America. "It was," wrote a critic of the embargo, "as if a flea had tried to stop a dog-fight by threatening suicide." At home the embargo produced economic hardship and bitterness. In demanding the subordination of economic self-interest to peace, Jefferson had overestimated the patience and patriotism of his fellow citizens.

So loud became the domestic outcry against the Embargo Act that Congress in 1809 replaced it with the Non-Intercourse Act, permitting exports to every nation except England and France. These two offenders could now neither buy from the United States nor sell to her. If either of the two powers reversed its hostile policies toward the United States, this country could resume trade with it. The man who would administer the new law was not Jefferson but his successor, James Madison.

James Madison Takes Over

No one else had been so instrumental as Madison in fostering and shaping the federal Constitution. After the inauguration of the national government, it had been Madison who led the forces against Hamilton and, in alliance with his good friend Thomas Jefferson, helped to create

James Madison, inaugurated as president in 1809, faced growing pressure from the "War Hawks" and others to act against Britain and finally declared war in June 1812. *(Portrait by Gilbert Stuart, Courtesy, Bowdoin College Museum of Fine Arts, Brunswick, Maine)*

the Republican Party. In 1801, Jefferson had selected him as his Secretary of State and he had served with distinction in that office.

Many Republicans viewed Madison as Jefferson's natural successor—but not all. Opposed to him was a group of militant Republicans called the "Tertium Quids," who considered both Jefferson and Madison to be too friendly to Federalist principles. The leading voice of the Quids was John Randolph of Roanoke, an eloquent defender of lost causes and an irresponsible verbal brawler. The Quids tried to deny Madison the nomination, but with Jefferson's support the party caucus in Congress endorsed him. The Federalists were now clearly the minority party, and Madison easily defeated their candidate, Charles Cotesworth Pinckney of "X, Y, Z" fame.

Physically, the new president was not a commanding figure. Small and wizened, he spoke in a barely audible voice and often seemed bored. The First Lady, the former Dolly Todd, helped to offset her husband's dour demeanor. Buxom, pink-cheeked, and charming, Mrs. Madison was a vivacious hostess whose parties and receptions seemed to the social set a vast improvement over the widowed Jefferson's bachelor dinners. Washington was still a city of magnificent distances, as an early observer of its raw, unfilled spaces called it; the presidential mansion was still not complete. But at least the capital now had a social focus it had lacked before.

The new Non-Intercourse Act created difficulties for Madison. Ships leaving American ports were not supposed to touch at French or British ports, but it quickly became clear that there was no way of guaranteeing they would obey the law. The British, in particular, scorned it; it promised to cause them little harm, and they could see little reason to settle the pending *Chesapeake* claims or satisfy American commercial demands.

Not every Englishman took a hard line against the United States. The British minister in Washington, David Erskine, wanted to placate the Americans and told Madison that the British intended to modify their harsh policy toward American trade. On this basis, the president issued a proclamation reopening trade with Great Britain while retaining the restrictions on France. Soon after, Foreign Secretary Canning learned of his minister's indiscretion and disavowed it. The president thereupon reimposed the Non-Intercourse arrangement on Britain.

Macon's Bill No. 2. Dissatisfaction with the Non-Intercourse Act forced Congress into a new tack against the belligerents. In May 1810 it passed Macon's Bill No. 2. This measure was surely one of the most devious in American history. It allowed the president to reopen trade immediately with both Britain and France. In the event that either of the two warring powers modified its trade policies toward the United States before March 1811, the president might reimpose the trade prohibition upon the other. In effect, the United States was offering to ally itself economically against whichever nation was the slower in according it its commercial rights.

An embarrassing and costly blunder was soon forthcoming. In August of 1810, when Napoleon learned of the terms of Macon's Bill, he instructed his foreign minister, de Cadore, to inform the Americans that his commercial decrees would be revoked as of November 1, provided that the United States invoke nonintercourse against the British. (Napoleon had larceny in his heart: even as he issued these instructions he prepared to seize any American vessels that might appear in France.) Cadore, in a manner reminiscent of Erskine, took the liberty of informing the United States that the French decrees had actually been cancelled. Once again, Madison responded without checking: he reopened trade with France and declared that trade with Britain would be closed the following February, unless Britain should revoke its Orders in Council before that time. The British replied by once again stationing their warships outside New York harbor and stepping up their campaign of impressing American seamen. Those vessels that eluded British capture were confiscated by Napoleon as soon as they reached France.

The War Hawks. The 1810 elections sent a group of young men to Congress mostly from the West and South, who were unwilling to temporize. These "War Hawks" were led by Henry Clay of Kentucky, a young Congressman with a rare eloquence and an unusual power to charm voters and fellow politicians alike. Although this was his first term in the House of Representatives, the magnetic Clay was elected Speaker. He quickly placed young men of like mind in key House posts. Peter Porter of western New York became chairman of the Foreign Relations Committee, where he had the support of such fellow War Hawks as John C. Calhoun of South Carolina, Felix Grundy of Tennessee, and Joseph Desha of Kentucky.

The War Hawks felt keenly the British-inflicted indignities, a feeling unmodified by coastal New England and Northeastern concern for profitable transatlantic commerce. England's "aggression, and her injuries and insults to us," proclaimed Clay, were "atrocious"—far more so than those of France. Besides, British assaults on American shipping were responsible for low crop prices in the West since they interfered with sales of these crops abroad. Many Westerners, moreover, blamed the British for recent Indian troubles; the uprising of the Shawnee chief Tecumseh and his brother, "the Prophet," was

Support for the war was by no means unanimous, and aggravated both party and sectional differences. *(Courtesy, Prints Division, New York Public Library)*

instigated by British agents. On November 7, 1811, General William Henry Harrison beat off Tecumseh's braves at Tippecanoe.

The War Hawks also had an appetite for land. For years the United States had disputed with Spain the boundary of West Florida. That narrow province stretched westward along the Gulf coast from the main Florida peninsula, cutting off much of the American Southwest from the sea. Spain, now an ally of England, held the province loosely. If war broke out, it could certainly be wrenched easily from her feeble hands. And there was Canada. Might not it welcome the opportunity to join the American republic?

While the War Hawks and their supporters naturally thought of attacking and taking the exposed colonies of both Spain and England in the event of war, conquest was not their chief purpose. They were nationalists and patriots of the Revolution's memory who hated British arrogance and yearned to avenge the humiliations Britain had recently inflicted. For twenty years, they argued, Britain had refused to treat the United States as a sovereign nation. The effort to preserve peace at any price was making America once more a British colony. "What are we not to lose by peace?" Clay asked rhetorically. His answer: "commerce, character, a nation's best treasure, honor!"

Madison was soon adopting a tougher policy toward England. In 1811 he asked Congress to vote money to build up the Army and Navy. In the spring of that year, the U.S.S. *President* encountered the British sloop-of-war *Little Belt.* Although the results were actually inconclusive—the powerful *President* gave the *Little Belt* a drubbing, but failed to sink the weaker British vessel—Americans considered the results ample revenge for the *Chesapeake* attack of four years before.

For months in early 1812 the prospect of war hovered while both the Chief Executive and Congress dithered. The Republicans had by now come to assume that war was inevitable, but when it came to voting money in preparation for it, their fear of extravagance got in the way of their common sense. Little had been done to authorize the building of new ships, and appropriations for the army remained inadequate. How the country intended to defend its commerce, and pursue an aggressive policy toward Florida and Canada, nobody made clear.

In the end, war came by mistake. Early in 1812, the British finally decided to modify their commercial policies. On June 23 the British government announced that the notorious Orders in Council that had so offended the United States would be lifted. It was too late. Before the news arrived, Madison impatiently had asked for a declaration of war. On June 4, the House voted in favor by 79 to 49; two weeks later the Senate followed, 19 to 13. The vote revealed a disunited nation. If the way congressmen voted is taken as indicative, southern New England, as well as much of New York, New Jersey, and Maryland, opposed the war. Would they continue to resist once the fighting had begun?

The War of 1812

"Mr. Madison's War." By almost any measure, the War of 1812 was mismanaged. The government that was making war had done little to prepare for it, and for three years the Americans lumbered from one encounter to another. One of the government's chief problems was the financing of such an expensive enterprise. Unready for heavy taxes, Americans expected to pay for the war through borrowing. Yet in 1811 the Republicans had refused to recharter the Bank of the United States, and it had died.

The country presented a logistical nightmare. To move troops and supplies over such enormous distances would be next to impossible. Roads were few and poor. The steamboat had been introduced on the Hudson in 1807, but steamboat travel on the Mississippi and the Great Lakes was in its infancy in 1812. The armed forces were unready. Only 7,000 men were immediately available for service, and most of these were scattered in small frontier posts. The state militias were a potential pool of manpower, but most militiamen were poorly trained and led. The best of the state forces were those of New England, but the Yankee governors refused to allow them to be called into federal service unless their own states were threatened with invasion.

And the country was disunited. Many Federalists thought the war a mistake. It was "Mr. Madison's war," a Republican venture, not a national one. Particularly in New England, the home of High Federalism, the war also seemed likely to produce a commercial disaster. Inevitably, Yankees said, it would be their commerce that would be swept off the seas by the Royal Navy.

Strong leadership might have overcome many of these difficulties, but Madison was a better philosopher and congressional manager than war leader. Almost all the high military officers were elderly gentlemen who had not commanded troops against a trained European army since the Revolution.

Canadian Campaigns. Oblivious to these weaknesses, the Americans began the fighting with an invasion of Canada led by General William Hull, commanding 2,000 regulars. Launched from Detroit, far to the west of Canada's chief population centers, the invasion was seriously misconceived. It required extended supply lines, and to protect these long lines the Americans had to control Lake Erie. But without a naval force on the lake they could not do so.

Nevertheless, the campaign at first seemed to be succeeding. Hull crossed the Detroit River into Canada unopposed. He immediately issued a proclamation that if the Canadian militia remained at home they had nothing to fear from the Americans. In a matter of days half of them had deserted the British and returned to their farms.

The British now expected an immediate attack across the river from Detroit on Fort Malden, which was garrisoned by only a few hundred regulars, some Indians, and the remaining militia. But the Americans delayed. By the time Hull's forces mounted their guns against the British, the American garrison at Michilimackinac to the east had surrendered. Certain that his supply lines were now endangered, Hull withdrew across the river and locked himself up in Detroit. On August 17 he surrendered to the British commander.

Prospects of taking Canada now appeared bleak. If the American invasion prong in the West, where the people were enthusiastic supporters of the war, had failed, what could be expected in the hostile East?

From New York State, a part of the American militia crossed the Niagara to attack the British and Canadian forces. They scored some early successes, but then were pinned down. They could have been rescued and the operation saved, but the remaining New York militia refused to cross the Niagara. Without reinforcements, 900 Americans were captured at Queenston Heights.

The third prong of the American invasion was no more successful than the first two. This attack, aimed at Montreal, was at least strategically sound. That city was the heart of British power in North America, and its capture would have been a disaster to England. But the Americans delayed their operations and gave the British many months to prepare. By the time the militia moved northward against a well-entrenched enemy, the autumn was far advanced. The ill-equipped American troops slogged their way through mud and drenching cold rain, sleeping without tents on the soggy ground with dripping blankets. When the American troops reached the Canadian border, many refused to cross. After fighting a few skirmishes, their commander ordered a retreat to Plattsburg, New York. There the militia made camp amid mud and snow; many contracted pneumonia. "The very woods," an army surgeon reported, "[rang] with coughing and groaning." Shortly afterward the invasion force dispersed. Eighteen-twelve had ended with Canada still firmly in British hands and American morale in the cellar.

The Naval War. The naval war was going better. Although the British far outmanned and outgunned the Americans at sea, they were also stretched thin, and suffered from overconfidence. The Americans, they were certain, could not match the Royal Navy in battle or do serious damage to their merchant shipping. They were wrong. Many American merchant captains had secured "letters of marque" commissioning their vessels as privateers. Over the next two and a half years, these ships attacked British commerce in the West Indies, off the east coast of the United States, and even in the waters around the British Isles. While many privateers were captured, others took rich prizes. The success of the small American navy, though less significant in material terms, was important for national morale. The American frigates proved to be remarkably effective in single-ship combat.

In August 1812 the U.S.S. *Constitution*, commanded by Isaac Hull, sighted the British frigate *Guerrière* in the mid-North Atlantic. The *Guerrière* was a slightly smaller vessel with a lighter broadside; part of her crew, moreover, consisted of impressed Americans who had to be allowed to go below rather than fight their own countrymen. The British captain tried evasive maneuvers, but Hull was able to bring his ship within fifty yards of the enemy. For two hours he poured deadly broadsides into the British ship, leaving it a wreck. The *Guerrière* struck her colors. Both sides had fought well and bravely, but the performance of the inexperienced Americans was exceptional. American sailors had fought with greater spirit than American infantry.

This victory was only the first of several such single-ship combats that helped redeem the honor of American arms. Several weeks later the *United States*, under Stephen Decatur, encountered H.M.S. *Macedonian* and in a bloody battle sank her. At the end of the year the *Constitution* defeated H.M.S. *Java* in a two-hour engagement.

Chagrined by their losses, the British began to reinforce their American squadron by drawing off vessels needed elsewhere. The British Navy began to improve its performance. Bit by bit its blockade of the American Atlantic coast became tighter and more effective, confirming all the fears of Northeasterners that war would destroy American commerce. The Americans soon lost control of their own coasts and shortly would be unable to repel British troop landings when they came.

Further Defeats in Canada. Another major attack on Canada came in 1813. In April, 8500 Americans gathered at the eastern end of Lake Ontario under the command of the Henry Dearborn. On April 25, 1700 men of this force sailed off to attack the Canadians at the western end of the lake and two days later arrived before York (now Toronto). The town was defended by only 800 soldiers and some Indians. The British had prepared a surprise in the form of a giant underground mine jammed with high explosives, but the mine went off at the wrong time, killing as many British troops as Americans. Dismayed and outnumbered, the British commander now withdrew. After occupying York for four days, the Americans looted it and burned the parliament buildings—acts for which their country would pay dearly the following year. American troops then departed for the mouth of the Niagara to attack Fort George. By this time the aging Dearborn was too exhausted to lead the expedition, and he turned his command over to the vigorous Winfield Scott. Soon to join the expedition was an equally aggressive young naval officer, Oliver Hazard Perry.

The American force was transported across Lake Ontario, and successfully completed a difficult amphibious landing before Fort George. The Americans, led by Scott and Perry, scrambled ashore with their heavy equipment and secured a foothold while still more men came ashore. Supported by the guns of the American flotilla, the invasion force drove off the British counterattack. The British commander now withdrew from Fort George and retreated to Beaver Dams. Scott was all for pursuing the enemy and destroying his army completely, but was overruled by his superior in the Niagara theater of operations. When the Americans were finally allowed to set off after the defeated British, Scott remained behind. The results were disastrous. The British commander surprised the Americans in their sleep, captured their leaders, and drove them back to Beaver Dams.

The British had now regained the initiative, and advanced on the American base with their small force of Indians and redcoats. The Indian auxiliaries encountered a large group of Americans under Lieutenant Colonel Charles Boerstler, and attacked. Boerstler held the Indians off until a party of British regulars approached under a flag of truce. Lieutenant James Fitzgibbon, the young British officer in charge, told the American commander that he was being closely followed by the main British army of fifteen hundred regulars and seven hundred Indians. The Americans, Fitzgibbon argued, could not possibly withstand the attack of this force, and in all likelihood the British would not then be able to restrain the bloodthirsty red men; the American commander should surrender now and save his men from massacre. Boerstler accepted the lieutenant's advice, laid down his arms, and waited for the main British party to arrive. It never did. Boerstler had surrendered his unit of 500 men to a force only half its size.

The setback on the Niagara frontier was matched by a major defeat before Montreal. Advancing on the Canadian city, the Americans ran into stiff opposition and abandoned the invasion. Soon afterward, the British captured Fort Niagara. They also took Buffalo and burned the city to the ground.

The Battle of Lake Erie. Two victories lightened the gloom. In September, Captain Perry and a small, locally built fleet encountered a British flotilla at Put-in-Bay on Lake Erie and defeated it after a bloody three-hour battle. Americans were greatly cheered at Perry's dispatch to General Harrison: "We have met the enemy and they are ours." Lake Erie was now in American hands, and the British were forced to abandon Detroit. A month later, Harrison overtook a retreating party of British and Indians and at the Battle of the Thames in Canada defeated them decisively. The chieftain Tecum-

We have met the enemy and they are ours:
Two Ships, two Brigs one
Schooner & one Sloop.
Yours, with great respect and esteem
O H Perry.

Oliver Hazard Perry's dispatch to General Harrison on his victory at Lake Erie reflected the pride of the Americans on finally winning a naval battle.

seh was one of those who fell on the British side. Soon afterward, Tecumseh's federation of tribes collapsed and most of Britain's Indian allies deserted her cause.

By 1814 the British navy had established a clear superiority in the Atlantic and in American coastal waters. The Royal Navy could with impunity sail up the Chesapeake Bay, attack merchant ships, and bombard strategic towns and military positions.

Amplifying British successes were American disunity and the Madison Administration's blunders. Hard-pressed New England was riddled with disloyalty. Yankees had not wanted war and felt little inducement to support it now that it was proving so expensive. Hoping to rescue something from the calamity, they became the chief suppliers of commodities to the British army in Canada. Madison sought to cut off this dangerous trade and induced Congress to pass an embargo bill in December 1813 restricting all exports from the United States. The effects were disastrous. American exports plummeted and prices increased sharply. The Treasury found that it could not borrow the money it needed to for military operations, and was forced to the edge of bankruptcy. In April 1814 Congress repealed this measure.

Meanwhile the gloomy military situation promised to get worse. In the spring of 1814, Napoleon's empire collapsed and the conqueror of Europe went into exile on the island of Elba. Until then, the British had been conducting a series of holding operations in America on both land and sea. Now, with France out of the war, all the vast resources of the Royal Navy and the seasoned veterans of the European fighting would be free to teach the pesky Americans a lesson.

In early May, the first detachments of British troops began to arrive in Quebec from Europe. Their mission, as explained in orders to the British commandant in Canada, Sir George Prevost, would be to drive the troops of the American republic out of Canada and recover the American Northwest, and thereby to secure Canada's safety.

Winfield Scott attacked first. At Chippewa and Lundy's Lane, American regular troops fought effectively and gallantly against the best the British had to offer. The campaign ended in a draw, but Scott and Brown had frustrated British goals in the Northwest.

British Offensives. The British soon resumed the offensive. In late summer they set out for Plattsburgh, New York, near Lake Champlain. The British plan, as during the Revolution, was to split the United States in two along the line of Lake Champlain and the Hudson Valley. By September Prevost's army, the largest yet seen in America, was at Plattsburgh's gates. There, however, the American commander was the scrappy John Wool. Though outnumbered almost three to one, Wool put up such a fight along the approaches to Plattsburgh that Prevost paused and called on Captain George Downie, in command of the British fleet on the lake, to come to his aid: together the navy and army would pound the Americans into submission and advance on New York City to complete their mission.

It was not to be. Standing between Prevost and the fulfillment of his scheme was the United

States naval squadron commanded by Captain Thomas Macdonough. Macdonough's little fleet consisted of four moderate-sized vessels and ten tiny gunboats, but in firepower it just about matched Downie's squadron.

Downie attacked the Americans. His first shot hit the deck of Macdonough's flagship, the *Saratoga*, and destroyed the coop of the sailors' champion gamecock. The bird was unhurt and immediately flew to a gun carriage where, its feathers ruffled, it crowed defiance at the enemy. The men laughed and cheered; it seemed a good omen.

For over two hours the opposing fleets poured solid and grapeshot into each other. Macdonough himself was knocked unconscious three times. At last the British surrendered. Macdonough brought the defeated British officers aboard the *Saratoga*, complimented them on their bravery, and refused to accept their swords. Shortly afterward he dispatched a message to the Secretary of the Navy that "the Almighty has been pleased to grant us a signal victory on Lake Champlain."

And a signal victory it was. When Prevost learned of Macdonough's triumph, he decided he could not continue; with the enemy in command on the water, his flanks were exposed. Instead of resuming the assault, he marched his men back to Canada. Another invasion threat was over.

The Burning of Washington. A second British invasion prong was meeting with greater success. On August 19, 1814, Sir George Cockburn landed with 4,000 men between Baltimore and Washington, and set out for the nation's capital. A hastily organized defense force of militia, sailors, and a few regulars sought to stop the British at Bladensburg, but the inexperienced Americans could not hold against seasoned veterans and many fell into British hands. Later that afternoon, after learning of the defeat, Madison and his Cabinet left the city to avoid capture. His wife, the resourceful Dolly, had already removed the sterling silver and other valuables from the presidential mansion. At 8 PM the British entered the city. At the White House they ate the president's dinner. The next morning they burned the public buildings, including the president's house, the Capitol, the Treasury, and the War Office. The following day they left the smoldering capital, having avenged the burning of York.

In early September the British, arriving by land and sea, moved on Baltimore. They broke through the Americans' first line of defense and drew to within a mile and a half of the city. At this point the British commander decided to call on the British flotilla offshore to bombard the city, to help soften it up for his final assault. All through the day and night of September 13 the British fired rockets, big guns, and mortars at

In August 1814, the British captured and burned the city of Washington, including the president's house, the Capitol, the Treasury, and the War Office. *(Courtesy, The New-York Historical Society, New York City)*

Forts McHenry and Covington, but could not silence them. Watching the attack was a Baltimore lawyer, Francis Scott Key. Deeply moved by the defenders' stout resistance, he wrote a poem, "The Star-Spangled Banner," commemorating the event. The British failure to reduce the harbor defenses discouraged further action, and they withdrew. The city was safe.

Baltimore's escape was, of course, a welcome event, but it could not wipe out the memory of Washington's capture and the general ineptness of the American war effort. In the wake of the Chesapeake invasions defeatism swept across the nation.

The fall and winter of 1814-15 was also a time of political crisis. Massachusetts elected representatives to meet with delegates from other New England states at Hartford, Connecticut, to consider defense problems and to discuss the possibility of revising the federal Constitution. Behind this action were the profound disgust of New Englanders with the war and their feeling that their section was suffering unduly in the conflict. At Hartford the militants intended to consider either seceding from the war or seceding from the Union itself, but by the time the convention met in December they were outnumbered. New Hampshire and Vermont refused to send delegations at all; and the delegates from Connecticut and Rhode Island proved to be more moderate than anyone expected. The Convention did not call for dissolution of the Union. It urged amendments to the Constitution that would reduce the power of the West and the South and require that declarations of war, non-intercourse acts, and admission of new states all receive a two-thirds vote of Congress to be adopted. But the resolutions in the end amounted to little more than a protest.

The Treaty of Ghent. As early as November 1813 the British and American governments, partly at the urging of the Russian Czar, had agreed to meet to discuss peace terms. Neither government was happy about the war both had sought to avoid; now, even while fighting continued, they began to arrange for its end.

Negotiations conducted at Ghent in Belgium moved slowly. The British hoped that before long their armies would occupy large stretches of the United States and they could use this territory as leverage for extracting favorable terms. Perhaps they might even get their long-held wish to create an Indian state in the Northwest, cutting the Americans off from the interior of the continent. The American negotiators, Henry Clay, John Quincy Adams, and Albert Gallatin, rejected any scheme to slice up their country and insisted on the abandonment of the impressment of sailors from American ships.

At first, neither side would budge. During the last half of 1814 the British began to realize that, though they could win victories, they could not count on totally defeating the stubborn Americans. Then, too, Britain and Russia began to clash at the Congress of Vienna called to sort out the complex affairs of Europe after Napoleon's defeat. Under the circumstances, war with the United States now seemed an unimportant sideshow that should be ended as soon as possible. The Americans, too, were anxious to bring matters to a conclusion, and abandoned their demand for an explicit elimination of impressment.

On Christmas eve 1814, the commissioners at Ghent finally signed a peace treaty. This agreement merely restored the situation as it had existed before the war. Commissioners from both nations would meet to settle the dispute over the boundary between the United States and Canada, a dispute that had resulted from imperfections in the geographical knowledge available in 1783. The war had been pointless.

New Orleans

Yet the war went on. News of the Treaty of Ghent did not reach the United States for many weeks, and by that time hundreds of men had died in unnecessary battles. The greatest of these was the Battle of New Orleans, which created a national hero, helped destroy the Federalist Party, and restored the nation's battered self-respect. The hero was General Andrew Jackson of Tennessee, a roughhewn, self-made planter, lawyer, and soldier.

General Andrew Jackson. Born in South Carolina, Jackson had gone to Tennessee when that state was still the western district of North Carolina. He had served his adopted state in Congress and as a judge. In 1813-14 he led the

Tennessee militia against the Creek Indians in Mississippi Territory following the massacre of 250 whites at Fort Mims. At Horseshoe Bend, Jackson surprised the Creeks and defeated them in a fierce battle. For his services the government made him a major general in the army and commander of the Seventh Military District with headquarters at Mobile.

While at Mobile, Jackson learned that the British, as part of their final push to crush the Americans, intended to attack New Orleans with another army of European veterans. Though weak with fatigue and dysentery, "Old Hickory" hurried to the city to prepare its defenses. A flood of directives—to obstruct the roads and bayous leading to the city, to build fortifications, and to strengthen the existing ones—flowed from his headquarters. Militia and volunteers from Kentucky, Tennessee, and Mississippi made up the core of Jackson's army, and he recruited additional troops from among the Creoles (people of French or Spanish origin) and black freemen of New Orleans. He also agreed to accept the services of a group of river pirates led by Jean Lafitte, a colorful rogue in trouble with the governor of Louisiana.

On the morning of December 23, 1814, redcoats newly arrived from the West Indies began to disembark fifteen miles southeast of New Orleans, after a cold trip across Lake Borgne in open boats. Jackson quickly learned of the landings. A more cautious general might have waited to see whether this was the main attack or a mere feint. But Jackson immediately turned to his officers and declared: "Gentlemen, the British are below; we must fight them tonight!"

With 2,000 men he advanced on the British force of some 1,600 that was waiting for further reinforcements before advancing against the city. Jackson achieved complete surprise and gave the redcoats a serious drubbing. The British line held, however, and Jackson withdrew to a line between the river and a swamp.

Here, just as the commissioners were signing the peace treaty at Ghent, Jackson and his men prepared to face the British assault behind breastworks of cotton bales and earth. Both sides were being reinforced. The British were also getting a new commander: Sir Edward Pakenham, brother-in-law of the Duke of Wellington and an experienced officer of the Peninsular War in Spain.

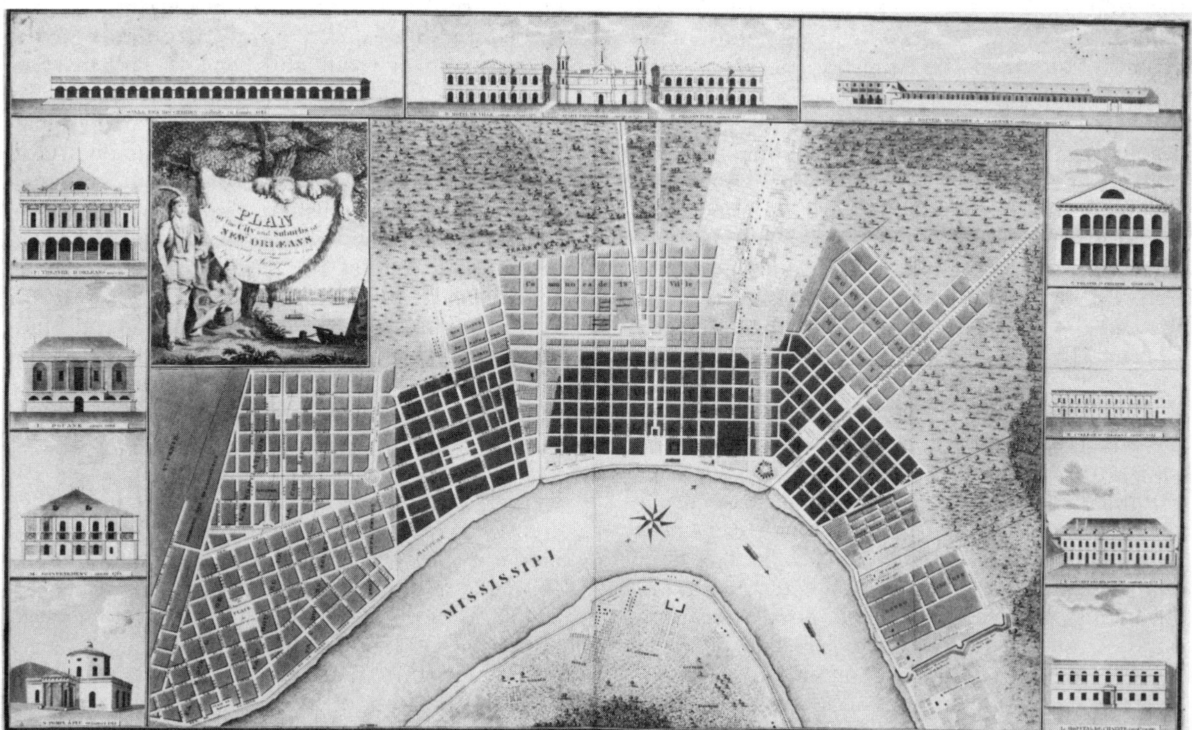

Plan of the City of New Orleans, 1815, where General Andrew Jackson defeated the British. Neither side knew that the treaty ending the war had already been signed. *(Courtesy, The I. N. Phelps Stokes Collection, The New York Public Library)*

Pakenham moved his army to within a few hundred yards of Jackson's force in preparation for a morning assault. All night long, American raiders made sorties against the British, doing little harm, but keeping the redcoats from getting any sleep. The next morning, with the battlefield enveloped in ground fog, the British advanced on Jackson's men hidden behind their breastworks. For a while they made headway against the firearms and artillery to their front, but shelling on their flank by the U.S.S. *Louisiana* from the river proved more than flesh could bear, and the advance stopped.

For the next three days the two armies confronted each other across a field strewn with dead and dying. On the morning of December 31, the British attacked again and the battle became an artillery duel, with Lafitte's pirates doing especially effective work with their big guns. For almost five hours the cannon boomed, until the discouraged British ceased their attack. Once more both sides brought up reinforcements. When Pakenham was ready to resume the attempt to reach New Orleans, he had close to 10,000 men, far more than Jackson.

On the morning of January 8, 1815, Pakenham asked his veterans for the last time to brave the American defenses. Once more, the attack failed. As the redcoats trudged across the ground in front of the American position, their ranks were shredded by grapeshot and arms fire. Some reached the American lines, but then a counterattack threw them back. Many British officers were hit, and Pakenham himself died on the field. Before dying, the British general ordered a subordinate, General John Lambert, to throw in reserves for a final push; but seeing the hopelessness of the situation, Lambert refused. Instead, he ordered his men to fall back to Lake Borgne. The battle was over.

Victory after Defeat. The victory was amazing. Over 2,000 British troops had died or been wounded, it was said, against American casualties of twenty-one. Soon after the smoke cleared, Jackson and his jubilant staff passed along the lines of cheering troops to the stirring strains of "Hail Columbia" played by the army band. Even if it had all been a mistake, it was a glorious moment for the young nation.

A mismanaged war that had humiliated Americans now became a matter of great national pride. Overnight new confidence suffused the nation. Americans had taken on the greatest power in the world, and in the end had defeated the best it could throw at them. No longer would the nations of Europe treat the United States with the contempt they had formerly shown. American nationalists managed the incredible feat of puffing a disastrous war into an epic victory. The country had finally and unquestionably confirmed the formal independence achieved in 1783.

The war had momentous political consequences. The Federalists had bet on the wrong side, Britain. If not for New Orleans and the exhilaration that made a bungled national enterprise seem a triumph, Federalist opposition to the war might have been rewarded with public favor, but Jackson's victory placed the stigma of traitor on every Federalist who had praised England and attacked the administration. In the presidential contest of 1816, the Republican James Monroe overwhelmed the Federalist candidate, Rufus King of New York, carrying every state in the Union except Massachusetts, Connecticut, and Delaware. Thereafter, although they continued to muster some isolated support, the Federalists were finished.

Meanwhile, a strange thing happened: the Republicans became Federalists. In his annual message in 1815, Madison asked Congress to pass a protective tariff, charter a second Bank of the United States, and appropriate funds for the construction of roads and canals—"internal improvements," as they came to be known. Led by Clay, Calhoun, and other converts to nationalism, Congress obliged. In 1816 it passed a tariff affording at least modest protection to American industry, and established the Second Bank of the United States with an even larger capitalization than that of the First. Madison, having changed his mind, vetoed the bill for internal improvements on the grounds that federal funding of them was of dubious constitutionality; but his immediate successors thought differently and thereafter federal subsidies would help the nation overcome its vast distances.

Finally, there was Andrew Jackson. New Orleans had created America's first folk hero since George Washington. Congress struck a gold medal in Jackson's honor and confirmed his rank of major general with the munificent salary of $2400 a year. Before long, a biographer was busy writing a life of the General for an eager public. Another man might have been content with the plaudits of his fellow citizens and easy life at the Hermitage, Jackson's gracious estate near Nashville. But not Old Hickory. Before many months had passed, Americans would hear from him again.

Points To Think About

1. The Hartford Convention, an ill-fated endeavor to advance federalist ideas, showed how short-lived a political principle can be. The New England Federalists had been, so long as their own party was in power, among the most fervent advocates of a strong central government. Once power passed to their political opponents, however, their devotion to "federalist" principles began to wane. By 1814, Jeffersonian policies—from the Embargo and Non-Intercourse Acts to the declaration of war against England—had convinced them of the merits of the states' rights position which Jefferson had propounded in the Kentucky Resolution. Meanwhile, of course, Jefferson and Madison had become staunch advocates of national authority.

So the arguments over the powers of the national government vis à vis the states continued, but the Jeffersonians and Federalists had switched sides. This state of affairs invites cynicism, but there is an element of reason in it. While it does tend to show that many stands defended on principle are really dictated by expediency, it also illustrates the important fact that the legitimacy of power always rests in part upon who is exercising it. Power is always dangerous. Naturally enough, it is those who happen to be not in power who recognize the dangers clearly. That awareness gradually fades as they begin to exercise it themselves. And it is then given to their opponents to ring the alarm.

2. As Federalists explored states' rights, the Republicans underwent a kind of "conversion" to federalist principles. The Louisiana Purchase far exceeded the proper limits of national authority by Jefferson's own admission. Nonetheless he went through with it. Then the war convinced the Republicans of the need for a national bank, for a sound military establishment, and even for a tariff high enough to protect American industry.

Republicans learned most of these lessons the hard way. They had to see just how dangerous it was to conduct governmental finance without a bank, or challenge a powerful foe without an adequate army or navy. The Republicans had combined two antithetical passions. They distrusted government and wished to limit its scope as much as possible, but they were also intense nationalists who wished to see their country grown and become more and more powerful. Their nationalism proved the stronger of the two passions.

Suggested Readings

On Lewis and Clark read the geographer John Logan Allen, *Passage Through the Garden: Lewis and Clark and the Image of the American Northwest* (1968). Dumas Malone presents *Jefferson and His Times* (1948–1981) in six magnificent volumes. Merrill Peterson's is a one-volume biography, *Thomas Jefferson and the New Nation* (1970). Forrest McDonald's *The Presidency of Thomas Jefferson* (1976) complements Fawn M. Brodie's *Thomas Jefferson: An Intimate History* (1974). Gore Vidal's *Burr: A Novel* (1973) presents the controversial Aaron as a gentleman and portrays the vulgarities and hypocrisies of the society that surrounded him. Also sympathetic is Milton Lomask's biography, *Aaron Burr* (1983).

Lance Banning emphasizes Whig ideology in *The Jeffersonian Persuasion* (1978). Also useful on politics are Noble E. Cunningham, Jr., *The Process of Government under Jefferson* (1978), Marshall Smelser, *The Democratic Republic, 1800–1815* (1968), David Hackett Fischer, *Revolution of American Conservatism* (1965), and James M. Banner, *To The Hartford Convention: The Federalists and the Origins of Party Politics in Massachusetts, 1789–1815* (1970).

Alexander DeConde surveys the Louisiana Purchase in *This Affair of Louisiana* (1976) while Reginald Horsman fights *The War of 1812* (1969). James Sterling Young draws a superb picture of *The Washington Community* (1968).

FORREST McDONALD

The most striking achievement of the United States during its early history was that both the country and its form of government survived. Under the circumstances, those were by no means trivial feats. The western world—Europe and the Americas—was almost continually at war throughout the period, and most nations lost their identity through conquest at least once. And of the score and more of nations that came into existence in what has been called the Age of Democratic Revolutions, the United States alone produced a stable constitutional government. Forming such a government was not a simple task. Yet the Constitution strengthened the national republic and Alexander Hamilton's realistic policies would promote that strength and enhance the national wealth despite destructive planter-led agrarianism. When the War of 1812 taught the Republican Party the value of Hamilton's policies, the nation's economic future was secure.

Hamilton wanted the United States to become a great nation, but believed that was impossible so long as Americans retained their local loyalties and their lack of ambition. Americans, he said, worked less than any other people on earth. What was necessary was to use the power of the federal government to cause money, rather than land and family connections, to become the measure of the value of things. For money is the greatest of equalizers, being blind to class, color, religion, and inherited social position. If Americans became accustomed to measuring achievement in dollars and cents, the nation would suddenly bustle with energy, and the United States would be on its way to becoming the richest, freest, and most powerful nation in the history of the world. That was the Hamiltonian vision for America.

As the first Secretary of the Treasury, Hamilton proposed a series of measures that transformed the Revolutionary War debts from a crushing burden into a means of stimulating the entire economy. With Hamilton's urging Congress provided that the debt be "paid" in government bonds. These, amounting to perhaps a quarter as much as that of all the farm land in this nation of farmers, furnished most of the country's money supply, for they could pass from hand to hand like any other currency. The bonds were also used for financing a huge expansion of commercial, banking, and manufacturing activity.

But an older America of small farms and Southern slaveholders remained. Many Americans could fear the Hamiltonian program for reasons of self-interest. They could also cling on principle to that conservatism that had brought about the Revolution, the moral conviction that the slow and self-sufficient ways of farmers are preferable to the more energetic programs of ambitious governments. Jefferson was a conservative of this sort, however radical he was in his egalitarianism and in his faith in reason as an instrument of progress. Jefferson would later refer to his election and the triumph of his party as the Revolution of 1800, but in a sense it was more properly counterrevolutionary. The Republicans tried hard to do away with the system of Hamilton and the Federalists. They established policies that would ultimately pay off the federal debt, for it was the existence of the debt that had been Hamilton's justification for the government bonds with which he had stimulated the development of capitalism. The Republicans also abolished domestic taxes, reduced the army and navy to shadow forces, and cut back on the size and authority of the federal government the Hamiltonians had expanded. To do all that was to defy precedent. It was not in the nature of government to pay its debts, lessen taxes, restrict its power to coerce, reduce its authority. Rather, the tendency had always been the other way around.

The Republicans might have succeeded but for their unrealistic attitude toward the French Revolution. Following the course that violent revolutions almost invariably follow, it led to anarchy and bloodshed and ultimately to a military dictatorship and far more bloodshed. In those circumstances, both principle and self-interest demanded that the United States be at least moderately favorable toward the British. But the Jeffersonians could never bring themselves to take such a stand. The results were nothing less than nightmarish.

How Much Democracy?  

EUGENE D. GENOVESE

Hamiltonian Federalists had neither world enough nor time. Their grand scheme could not be consolidated without a long period in power, and their opponents increasingly had the votes. (It as not for nothing that Federalist conservatives had no use for democracy and swallowed it choking on every bit.) The election of 1800 was no revolution. But power did pass from one party to another without bloodshed, policies were overturned, and the people did firmly decide that American development was to follow a more rather than less democratic path. Those were not trivial matters.

Professor McDonald claims that Jeffersonians began as agrarians, as the particular defenders of agricultural work and life. He is wrong. In a nation almost entirely rural, it would have been even beyond the reach of political paranoia to argue for the rural life as though it were endangered. Jefferson does at one point in his *Notes on Virginia* describe city mobs as "sores" on the body politic, but his remark is not aimed against cities in themselves: the very same passage observes with pride that in American towns citizens have sufficient property to maintain their independence and virtue. What Jeffersonians did argue for was democracy—not absolute social or political equality but at least a widespread distribution of rights, privileges, and power. When they lauded the virtues and stood by the rights of the small farmer, they were merely standing by the common American citizen in his usual role, which was that of a farm worker. Professor McDonald is right in asserting that Jeffersonians were ready to buy into capitalism. But this meant no betrayal of agrarianism, a doctrine that they had never adhered to anyway. Business, industry, cities did not especially disturb them, and so neither did capitalism disturb them so long as capital acculumlation was not monopolistic and the result of special favors of the government. But that is the problem, and the Jeffersonians recognized it at the time. Money is not the equalizer that Professor McDonald claims it to be, as the merest glance at monied societies with their enormous spread of wealth and poverty will reveal. When the Jeffersonians first fought the Hamiltonian program, they did so recognizing that its implications were profoundly inegalitarian. When they came around to Hamiltonian measures, correctly perceiving that the country needed the more energetic economy that only the federal government could evoke, they were surrendering something of their democratic principles in the face of an immediate national need.

Professor McDonald correctly makes much of the lesson the Republicans learned from the War of 1812. The war proved "sorry enough" and "a disgrace" for the United States, which clearly got beaten. (And so the claim that the United States had never lost a war—fed to generations of Americans until the end of the war in Vietnam—has been not only a silly boast but untrue.) The nation's miserable performance in the war demonstrated the need for a stronger government and more energetic policies than the Republicans had previously been willing to accept. But if the Jeffersonians had represented millions of farmers determined to have nothing to do with capitalist enterprise, not even to tolerate its existence, and wishing nothing more for their country than that the United States be a simple land of small farms and graceful plantations, it would have taken more than a blundering war to turn things around.

Westward expansion, begun after about 1785, resulted in five new states between 1816 and 1821: Indiana, Mississippi, Illinois, Alabama, and Missouri. *(Courtesy, Indiana Historical Society)*

CHAPTER 8

Nationalism and Sectionalism 1816–1828

THE WESTWARD MOVEMENT

For almost 200 years American society had grown in the corridor between the Atlantic Ocean and the Appalachian Mountains. Mountain ranges, Indian tribes, and conflict among European powers for the great, unsettled Western lands discouraged Americans from pushing into the West. Even those who crossed some of the eastern mountains found the inviting valleys angling south through Pennsylvania, Virginia, and the Carolinas far more tempting than scaling the next ridges toward an uncertain domicile in the Western plains. Then, after about 1795, with the Revolution won, the Indian tribes dispersed, the European grasp on the West weakened, and the price of good Eastern land mounting, a vast folk migration began; only briefly interrupted by wars and depressions, it relentlessly populated the continent. The land seemed suddenly and permanently to have tilted, shaking its human burden westward in a long rough tumble toward the Pacific.

The return of peace on the frontier after the War of 1812, and rising prices worldwide for agricultural products, set the migration. The continent lay before Americans, writes Henry Adams, "like an uncovered ore bed." In 1810 only one American in seven lived west of the Appalachians; in 1820 it was one in four. Before the land fever subsided, five new states had entered the Union—Indiana (1816), Mississippi (1817), Illinois (1818), Alabama (1819), Missouri (1821)—and they made the West a new force to be reckoned with in national affairs.

Settlers traveled by wagon, flatboat, horse, even on foot. The road west was often scarcely a road at all, but a slightly widened trail full of ruts and stumps so that for a passenger in the unsprung wagons "the pain of riding exceeded the fatigue of walking." No wonder Americans of the early nineteenth century were so hungry for internal improvements, for turnpikes, canals, and finally railroads.

A modern American, in a land of motels, fast-food stands, and gas stations, cannot easily imagine the world that the early traveler encountered west of the Appalachians. Often they saw all around them nothing but a forest of tall hardwood trees, dark, sinister, and gloomy. Settlers gloated over the mighty fires that followed a boisterous log-rolling, when perhaps hundreds of trees, felled after back-breaking labor, vanished into smoke, fire, and ash.

Yet the farmers preferred the forests to the prairies, endless meadows of tall grass sweeping across northern Indiana and Illinois. Americans, much as they might curse the trees they had to girdle, cut, and burn, hard as they might work to let in sunshine so that crops could grow, believed that hardwood forests indicated fertile soil. The prairies (actually richer soil where thick grass strangled most other vegetation) evoked, as one traveler noted, "a certain indescribable sensation of loneliness." Rich as prairie soil was, settlers discovered that to farm this land meant first to break the thick, endless sod. In the early part of the century, when plows were still small and primitive, it was murderous labor.

In addition to doing back-breaking agricultural labor, a man with implements no more sophisticated than an axe and chisel would make "gates, carts, barrows, plow frames, ox yokes, wooden shovels, hay forks, troughs, benches, woodhorses, tool handles, stirring paddles, rakes, mortars, flails, cradles for mowing, swingling knives, flax brakes, and many other articles." More talented woodworkers frequently made their own wagons and furniture as well. And of course everyone, with neighbors helping to raise the logs, built his own house.

Women worked equally hard or harder, raising vegetables and herbs, manufacturing soap, butter, and other household articles, and carrying out every step of the making of clothing, from spinning to sewing. This labor, combined with housekeeping tasks and especially childbearing, tolled heavily. Many women appeared old at thirty, and men widowed two and three times were common.

Homes in the West were far from comfortable or healthy. Clouds of flies and mosquitoes, drafty cabins, primitive sanitation, and animal waste around most cabins were probably more hazardous to life than the better-known dangers of hostile Indians or prairie fires. New Englanders traveled west singing:

Come all ye Yankee farmers who wish to change your lot,
Who've spunk enough to travel beyond your native spot,
And leave behind the village where Ma and Pa do stay,
Come follow me and settle in Michigania.

But others who had been there chanted:

Don't go to Michigan, that land of ills;
The word means ague [*malaria*], *fever, and chills.*

The reward was worth the travail. At the end of the journey and the settlement lay independence and wealth as nineteenth-century Americans understood it: the ownership of productive agricultural land. The true pioneer stage passed rapidly; mills, towns, canals, newspapers, churches, cloth imported from the East, hardware, glass, even pianos eased and elevated the crude life of the frontier, and families rapidly moved from the backwoods to the front pews.

But for a moment, and only for a moment, the frontier was just what legend says it was. One observer caught the flavor of raw Western politics:

> I have just witnessed a strange thing—a Kentucky election—and am disposed to give you an account of it. An election in Kentucky lasts three days, and during that period whisky and apple toddy flow through our cities and villages like the Euphrates through ancient Babylon. I must do Lexington the justice to say that matters were conducted here with tolerable propriety; but in Frankfort, a place which I had the curiosity to visit on the last day of the election, Jacksonism and drunkenness stalked triumphant—"an unclean pair of

Contestoga wagons brought many settlers from east to west. A journey of 600 miles took about 90 days.

> lubberly giants." A number of runners, each with a whisky bottle poking its long neck from his pocket, were busily employed bribing voters, and each party kept half a dozen bullies under pay, genuine specimens of Kentucky alligatorism, to flog every poor fellow who should attempt to vote illegally. A half a hundred of mortar would scarcely fill up the chinks of the skulls that were broken on that occasion. I barely escaped myself.

And a frontier imagination spoke in words attributed to Davy Crockett of Western Tennessee. "I'm fresh from the backwoods," he is said to have boasted, "half alligator, a little touched with the snapping turtle; can wade the Mississippi, leap the Ohio, ride upon a streak of lightning . . . hug a bear too close for comfort and eat any man opposed by Jackson."

Postwar Nationalism

With the end of the War of 1812, Americans turned their attention not only westward but also to pressing national problems.

Era of "Good Feelings." After many years of political bickering, an interlude of one-party politics followed the war. However divisive the War of 1812 had been, its ending brought a general sentiment of partriotism along with an awareness of weaknesses that had made the conduct of the war so difficult. A consensus grew in favor of some unified political solution to the nation's problems. For a time it was common for voters to call themselves Jeffersonian Republicans, and politics became no more than a contest of personalities within a politics of national harmony. To a people brought up with an eighteenth-century view of political parties as self-serving, divisive instruments, this actually seemed healthy. The "demon of party," a newspaper editor noted in 1817, had been exorcised for good.

To preside over this superficially placid era, voters in 1816 elected James Monroe as president. Like his Virginia predecessors, he had spent his life serving his country. At eighteen he had been wounded in the Revolutionary War. He later served as Minister to France, governor of Virginia, Minister to England, and Secretary of State. (From 1813 to 1815 he frequently doubled as Secretary of War.) Monroe was sixty years old when he became president. Dignified in appearance, cautious in manner, he provided a link with the heroic past. At a time when most men wore trousers, he still dressed in old-fashioned knee breeches and long silk stockings. On ceremonial occasions he wore a faded Revolutionary uniform—a fitting costume for the last Revolutionary veteran in the White House.

James Monroe, elected in 1816, sought to unify the states and parties, and established an "Era of Good Feelings." *(Portrait by Gilbert Stuart, Courtesy, The Metropolitan Museum of Art, Bequest of Seth Low, 1929)*

President Monroe's Grand Tour. As president, Monroe sought to create "a union of parties in support of our republican government." His choice of cabinet members reflected this goal: he tried to pick Republicans from every section of the country. The Secretary of State, John Quincy Adams, was a New Englander. Georgian William H. Crawford stayed on in the Treasury Department. Unable to find a Westerner for Secretary of War, Monroe finally picked young John C. Calhoun of South Carolina for the post. William Wirt, a Baltimore lawyer, became Attorney General. Restrained by their loyalty to the president, these political rivals served Monroe well. He also worked hard to gain the confidence of prominent Federalists. Harrison Gray Otis was deeply touched when the "Old Sachem" not only invited him to the White House for dinner, but "drank a glass of wine with me to make friends."

In pursuit of national unity, Monroe set out shortly after his election on a tour of the Northern and Eastern states. Paying his own traveling costs, he followed the seaboard north to Portland, Maine, then headed westward, going as far as Detroit—a three-and-one-half month journey by carriage and steamboat. It was a triumphal procession. Everywhere crowds gathered to honor this "last of the Revolutionary farmers." The high point came at Boston, where over forty thousand turned out to welcome the president. At a public dinner, local Federalists and Republicans sat down together for the first time in years. Monroe's visit, a staunch Federalist editor reported, had established an "Era of Good Feelings." Newspapers throughout the country soon picked up the phrase. For a time, despite bickering on the state and local levels, it seemed appropriate. Overall during this period, before economic crisis in 1819, the country was peaceful and prosperous. In 1820 Monroe was reelected without opposition; only one negative vote in the electoral college prevented his election from being, like Washington's, unanimous.

Government and the Economy

Monroe's presidency expressed the nationalism of sentiment that followed the end of the War of 1812. It was also a time of economic nationalism. Instructed perhaps by his flight from Washington that the country could not get by with the strictly limited central government that the Republican Party had once favored, President Madison in 1815 had recommended an energetic governmental program for the nurturing of the economy. At the very time the Federalist Party was withering, the Republicans were adopting the policy the Federalists had once championed. Congress responded by rechartering a national bank, voting funds for internal improvements, and enacting a protective tariff.

Transportation—"Let us conquer space." During the War of 1812, the nation's transportation network had proved no more adequate to wartime demands than its banking system. With coastal shipping choked off by the British blockade and canals still in their infancy, the burden fell almost entirely on the roads. In a few places in the East turnpikes had been built, but they deteriorated quickly under heavy use. Most roads were hardly more than broad country paths through the forest, filled with ruts and stumps, impassable in wet weather. In one case, it took a wagon drawn by four horses seventy-five days to travel from Massachusetts to South Carolina. Such delays produced serious food shortages in some cities.

Poor roads had severely hampered the American military effort. General William Henry Harrison reported in 1812 that his advance on Detroit could not begin "until the frost shall become so severe as to enable us to use the rivers and the margins of . . . Lake [Erie] for the transportation of the baggage and artillery upon the ice. To get them forward through a swampy wilderness of near two hundred miles in wagons or on pack horses . . . is absolutely impossible." Harrison estimated that overland hauls required "two wagons with forage [for the horses] for each one that it loaded with provisions and other articles."

Recognition that the country needed a better transportation system was one element in the governmental and economic nationalism to which President Madison turned from his earlier philosophy of limited government. He called for a system of roads and canals "executed under national authority." He recommended a constitutional amendment that would eliminate continuing doubts over the federal government's authority to finance such projects. Representative John C. Calhoun of South Carolina, then a vigorous young nationalist, brushed aside constitutional objections. Sheer size and poor communication, he warned the House—in words that would later haunt him—exposed the country to that "greatest of all calamities," disunion. "Let us, then, bind the Republic together with a perfect system of roads and canals. Let us conquer space." Calhoun proposed to set aside, as a fund for internal improvements, the government's share of the profits from the new Bank of the United States. In 1817 Congress narrowly approved Calhoun's plan, only to have Madison veto it on constitutional grounds. The states and private enterprise would have to finance most internal improvements.

Manufacturers. American manufacturers found their most severe trial not during wartime but with the return of peace. Before 1807 Americans had imported most manufactured goods from Europe, but Jefferson's embargo and the war had stimulated the growth of domestic industries. In New England and the Carolinas,

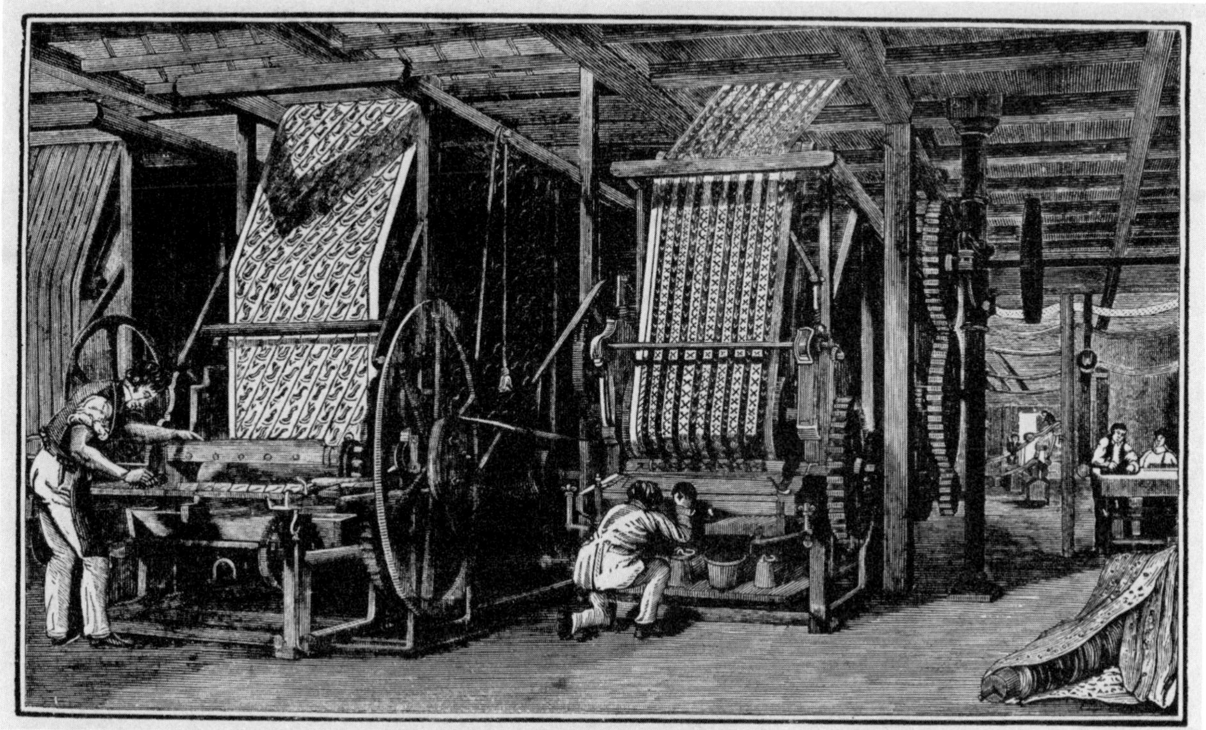

After Samuel Slater began the use of power-driven spinning machines around 1790, spinning and weaving mills rapidly spread in New England and the Carolinas.

mills were spinning and weaving cotton; a new iron industry flourished at Pittsburgh; Kentuckians began making local hemp into bagging. British manufacturers moved quickly in 1816 to crush these new rivals. They dumped vast quantities of goods on the American market at cut-rate prices, in order, a spokesman explained, "to stifle in the cradle those rising manufacturers in the United States, which war had forced into existence, contrary to the natural course of things." To protect these "infant" industries, President Madison proposed increased tariff duties on competing imports, which would push up their price. Congress was receptive, since nearly every section of the country had an interest to be protected. Southerners, who had the least to gain, supported higher duties on political and patriotic grounds. Within a few years, a series of threatening events would cause many Southerners to reexamine their jubilant support of economic nationalism.

The Bank of the United States. When the charter of the first Bank of the United States expired in 1811, the state banks had gone wild. The number increased from eighty-eight to over 200. In making loans and paying debts, they issued huge quantities of bank notes, which thereupon circulated as regular currency. A bank note was, in effect, a piece of paper carrying a bank's promise that upon request the bank would give to the bearer of the note an amount of money in specie (gold or silver) equal in value to the sum printed on the note. A holder of a bank note for, say, $1.00 could believe that while the note was not itself a real dollar, it was virtually an equivalent since it could be exchanged for a specie dollar: and so storekeepers and other merchants were willing to accept bank notes from customers.

As long as there was plenty of reliable specie in the banks—enough to cover a comfortable portion if not all of the bank notes in circulation in case many holders of notes got hungry for metallic money—the notes were a useful currency. A bank's ability to issue them allowed it to make more loans, pay more debts, and in general nourish more business than it could do if its activities were restricted to what its holdings in specie alone could accomplish. But if the bank notes got far out of proportion to the specie on which they were supposed to be based, the public would cease to trust them as currency, they would depreciate in value, and business would suffer from the uncertainty. And that is what happened as the state banks multiplied and carried out their transactions with no national bank to steady them. The mass of confusing, depreciated paper money worried businessmen and pleased counterfeiters. The lack of a national currency such as a Bank of the United States could have provided made it difficult to carry on business among different parts of the country.

Then wartime borrowing overwhelmed this shaky system. By the summer of 1814 every bank outside of New England had suspended the practice of paying specie to holders of notes who demanded it. The country's credit had practically vanished. And after the war the federal government, to accommodate settlers in the West, offered for sale vast tracts of public land. The government's terms were generous: the minimum purchase was 160 acres, and the purchaser had four years to complete payment. Much of the land was purchased with credit supplied by state banks. Land sales, then, were inviting more bad currency into circulation.

In response to the crisis in banking, Congress in 1816 chartered a second Bank of the United States, with headquarters at Philadelphia. It was capitalized at $35 million, of which the government put up $5 million. The president was to appoint five "government directors," and the the domestic stockholders were to elect the other members of the twenty-five member board: foreign stockholders were not allowed to vote. The Bank was to serve as a repository of government funds and could establish branches as the directors saw fit. It could issue its own bank notes and thereby provide a more stable currency than the state banks were issuing. And it had the informal power to regulate the activities of state banks. A decision to be cautious in lending to them, or to refuse weak notes in payment of debts owed to the national bank, could force the state banks to act more cautiously themselves.

Judicial Nationalism: The Marshall Court

During the years 1819-24, the Supreme Court, in a series of important cases decided under Chief Justice John Marshall, aided in strengthening the constitutional authority of the federal government, which had already been strengthening its political presence through its postwar

John Marshall. As chief justice of the Supreme Court, Marshall's decisions helped strengthen the federal government. *(Portrait by J. W. Jarvis, Courtesy, Richard Coke Marshall Collection, Frick Art Reference Library)*

economic policies. The Court also shrank the power of the states over corporations, institutions that, along with the federal government, would assume a larger and larger role in the development of the American economy.

Leading Constitutional Decisions. In *Dartmouth College v. Woodward* (1819) the Court ruled that Article I, Section 10, of the Constitution—"no state shall pass any law impairing the obligation of contracts"—protected charters of incorporation from legislative interference. Dartmouth College had been granted a charter in 1769 by King George III. In 1816 the New Hampshire legislature, in an effort to make the college more democratic, tried to replace the self-governing trustees with a board appointed by the state governor. The trustees retained Daniel Webster to fight their case. Webster's theatrics ("It is . . . a small college," he plaintively told the Justices, "and yet there are those who love it") and his arguments proved effective. Dartmouth's charter, wrote Marshall, was a contractual relationship between the Crown and the College. The state of New Hampshire was a continuation of the Crown; the obligations of contract remained unchanged. So long as the trustees did not abuse their powers, the state could not interfere without violating the contract clause. Coming at a time when private corporations were rapidly gaining favor in transportation, finance, and manufacturing, this defense of contracts made it more difficult for the states to control corporate activity.

In *McCulloch v. Maryland* (1819) the Court confirmed the broad construction of the Constitution that Alexander Hamilton had defended thirty years before during arguments over the first Bank of the United States. This case dealt with assaults on the second Bank, which through careless management and its favoritism to big business had aroused bitter opposition. Several states, Maryland among them, had placed high taxes on the Bank's branches within their borders. The cashier of the Baltimore branch, James McCulloch, refused to pay the tax and Maryland brought suit. In his opinion, Marshall upheld the constitutionality of the Bank. The creation of such an institution, he admitted, was not among the powers listed in the Constitution. But Congress also possessed "incidental or implied powers." "Let the end be legitimate," wrote Marshall, "let it be within the scope of the Constitution, and all means which are appropriate, which are plainly adapted to that end, which are not prohibited, but consistent with the letter and spirit of the Constitution, are constitutional." He found that the financial powers of the national legislature gave it the implied power to charter a national bank that would aid Congress in exercising its authority over finance. Maryland's tax, which attempted to destroy a lawful agency of the federal government, was therefore unconstitutional: "the power to tax . . . is the power to destroy." Champions of states' rights angrily denounced this opinion, which would stretch the Constitution beyond its literal statements and have it implicitly grant large powers to the federal government.

Marshall's opinion two years later in *Cohens v. Virginia* further distressed states' rights advocates. At issue here was the right of a state to limit appeals to the United States Supreme Court from its own courts. The Cohens had been convicted of selling lottery tickets under a Virginia law that prohibited appeals from such a conviction. Asserting that the case involved a "federal question," they turned to the Supreme Court for relief. Counsel for Virginia denied the Court's right of judicial review, citing state sovereignty. The Chief Justice disagreed. He maintained that Virginia had surrendered some of her powers when she joined the Union. The right of the Supreme Court to review cases involving "federal questions" was absolutely essential if the operation of the Constitution was to be uniform throughout the country. Otherwise, the federal government would be prostrate "at the feet of every state in the Union." With this opinion Marshall solidly fixed the Supreme Court as the final arbiter of all constitutional questions.

Gibbons v. Ogden (1824), Marshall's last great decision, gave force to the clauses of the Constitution that had empowered Congress "to regulate commerce with foreign nations, and among the several states." Early in the nineteenth century a number of states had begun awarding monopolies to the operators of the new steamboats. In 1808 New York gave Robert Fulton and Robert Livingston an exclusive right to operate steamboats on the state's waters. It also awarded Aaron Ogden an exclusive franchise to run steamboats on the Hudson River between New York and New Jersey. When Thomas Gibbons began a rival service on this route (the captain of his boat was a young man named Cornelius Vanderbilt), Ogden brought suit to restrain his competitor. When the New York courts upheld the monopoly, Gibbons appealed to the Supreme Court. Once again Marshall championed federal supremacy. A narrow construction of the Constitution, he declared at the outset, "would cripple the government, and render it unequal to the objects for which it is declared to be instituted, and to which the powers given, as fairly understood, render it competent." New York's law was unconstitutional because it conflicted with a 1793 act of Congress regulating the coastwise trade. Congress's power to regulate commerce, "like all others vested in Congress, is complete in itself, may be exercised to its utmost extent, and acknowledges no limitations, other than those prescribed in the Constitution."

For once the public sided with Marshall. New Yorkers, who detested the steamboat monopolies, hailed the Chief Justice's decision. "Yesterday," a newspaper reported, "the steamboat *United States*, Capt. Bunker, from New Haven, entered New York in triumph, with streamers flying, and a large company of passengers exulting in the decision . . . against the New York monopoly. She fired a salute which was loudly returned by huzzas from the wharves." In a few years steamboat navigation spread to lakes and rivers throughout the country.

Marshall could not prevent the removal of the Cherokee Indians from Georgia. He also ducked a case involving the rights of free Negroes. Yet his nationalism ultimately helped to free the slaves. For over thirty years Marshall had argued that the United States was a consolidated nation rather than merely a compact of sovereign states. In 1861, when Abraham Lincoln called for troops, thousands of young men took up arms to defend the national Union Marshall's decisions had done so much to define.

The Panic of 1819

By 1820, even as the Marshall Court was formulating its nationalist constitutional theory, the good feelings of the postwar years had begun to wear thin. As the memory of war faded and the Republican Party, lacking the discipline of electoral competition, declined as a national organization, the various sections of the country began looking to their own interests. Among the reasons for the end of the harmony of the postwar years were a resurgence of jealousies among the sections and a revival of slavery that would put slave owners to quarreling with opponents of the institution and its expansion into the Western territories. An early agent in disrupting the smooth politics of the time was the Panic of 1819, a financial collapse of the greatest magnitude the nation had yet known. The panic was the result of a buoyant but unhealthy expansion of the American economy during the years immediately after the wars, an expansion that economic dislocations in Europe had encouraged.

In 1816 and 1817 Europe had suffered widespread crop failures. These created a large and high-priced market for American rice, corn, wheat, and meat. British cotton textile manufacturers, moreover, having done without American cotton for three years, had accumulated a great backlog of demand for it. The price of cotton, which had fluctuated around fifteen cents a pound before the war, now rose to twenty-five and thirty cents.

Americans responded to this boom in typical American fashion. On the one hand, they grossly overexpanded production, especially of cotton: in the years 1816-1819 annual production of cotton more than doubled over that of 1814.

The production of other American staples likewise increased rapidly, though not so spectacularly as that of cotton. On the other hand, Americans by the thousand succumbed in these prosperous times to what had been, since colonial days, practically a national disease: speculation in land.

Speculation and Collapse. Instead of paying attention first to farming and profiting from the inflation while they could, vast numbers of people put every spare cent into land. To accommodate demand, the federal government after the war threw vast tracts of public land on the market. Auctions at the district land offices attracted eager crowds, including squatters hoping to buy the lots they already occupied and speculators seeking choice tracts for resale at inflated prices. In spite of efforts by speculators to stifle competitive bidding, prices at the sales frequently soared well above the minimum $2 an acre (reduced to $1.25 in 1820). Fertile bottom land near Huntsville, Alabama, brought $70 to $78 an acre in the spring of 1818. Total annual sales of public land rose from less than $3 million in 1815 to over $13 million in 1818. Much of this land was purchased with credit supplied by the steadily increasing numbers of state banks, of which Hezekiah Niles wrote in 1816, "Wherever there is a church, a blacksmith's shop and a tavern seems a proper site for one of them." By 1818 the buyers of public land owed the government over $21 million.

The new Bank of the United States not only made little effort at first to check this speculation, but itself proved a major source of credit expansion. For a while it exchanged Bank stock for IOU's instead of specie. Supervision over Bank branches was notoriously lax. Those in the South and West greatly overexpanded their loans and their issues of bank notes. The officers of the Baltimore branch engaged in embezzlement. By 1818 the Bank had loaned out over $41 million. Some of it was invested in canals, turnpikes, and farm improvements; much more, however, went for speculative ventures in urban real estate, cotton futures, and Western land. Indebtedness mounted, but as long as prices and rents increased, farmers and speculators would hope to meet their obligations.

Suddenly the economy collapsed. With the return of good harvests abroad in the fall of 1818, demand for American grain fell sharply. At the same time, British manufacturers finally reduced their imports of American cotton: prices for the South's great staple dropped by over one half in 1819. Planters and farmers who had borrowed heavily to expand production could not repay their loans.

This reversal left the Bank of the United States in desperate straits. Its liabilities exceeded its specie reserves by a ratio of ten to one—double the limit allowed by law. The Bank then called in the loans of state banks, which forced them in turn to call in their loans. A wave of bank failures followed, most of them in the South and West; money disappeared and credit dried up, spreading economic distress throughout the country. Speculators who had purchased public land were stuck with it. Agricultural prices sank so low that many farmers resorted to barter. Merchants sold their stock at high losses or declared bankruptcy. In Philadelphia County alone, over 1800 people went to prison for debt during 1819. Thousands were thrown out of work: in Pittsburgh, thirty percent of the population went back to the country. Americans for the first time confronted a nationwide depression—the "panic of 1819."

The Causes of the Panic of 1819. The economic crisis provoked a heated debate over both the causes of the depression and appropriate measures of relief. Stephen Girard, a Philadelphia capitalist, blamed the state banks, which "with their fictitious capital have acted imprudently." The state banks, anxious to conceal their own shortcomings, criticized the national Bank. Many, including President James Monroe, lamented the postwar spirit of extravagance and speculation, and called for a return to spartan ways. Advocates of a protective tariff pointed to our dependence on European trade, and urged Americans to produce more of the manufactured goods they consumed. Congress rejected a higher tariff and a bill to abolish federal imprisonment for debt, but did agree in 1821 to allow poeple who had purchased public lands on credit additional time to pay. Real debtor relief came mainly from the states. Several passed "stay" laws delaying foreclosure for debt. Cities set up soup kitchens, and churches collected funds for the relief of paupers.

Out of the confused debate on the depression, the Bank of the United States emerged as the chief scapegoat. Charges of fraud and mismanagement filled the air. The old Southern agrarians, Thomas Jefferson among them, condemned the Bank and the federal government for creating a "paper bubble" and hoped the shock of depression would restore the country to a sound, paper-free past. These critics likened the

Bank to a monster, foreclosing everything in its path. "I know towns, yea cities," charged Senator Thomas Hart Benton of Missouri,

> where this bank already appears as an engrossing proprietor. All the flourishing cities of the West are mortgaged to this money power? . . . they are in the jaws of a monster! A lump of butter in the mouth of a dog! One gulp, one swallow, and all is gone!

Many of these accusations were unfair. Fraud and mismanagement there had been, but the Bank was not responsible for fluctuations in the world market or for the public's compulsion for speculation. If the Bank had been inconsistent in dealing with the state banks, so had politicians and the public. But these considerations made little impression on a people mired in debt and depression. The economy recovered in the early 1820s, but by this time the reputation of the Bank among certain constituencies had deteriorated beyond repair. It is ironic that the recovery would owe much to the Bank and its new president, Nicholas Biddle.

A Resurgent Sectionalism

The changing interests of different parts of the nation soon expressed themselves in disputes over the tariff, internal improvements, and land policy. The South produced cotton for export, obtaining manufactured goods from the North and West as well as from Europe. The tariff pushed up the retail price of European products in this country and thereby allowed Northern manufacturers to raise their prices, too, or forced foreign products out of the American market. Compelled to purchase at higher prices, Southern planters feared also that Europe would retaliate against our tariffs by putting high duties on Southern agricultural goods. Southerners quickly regretted their support for the Tariff of 1816. The disastrous decline in cotton prices after 1819, which cut the planters' purchasing power, made the tariff still more burdensome. In 1820 Southerners in Congress barely defeated a bid to raise import duties again.

Internal Improvements. Sectional jealousies thwarted plans for a national system of internal improvements. New England, with the country's best road system, had no liking for building roads that, by connecting rival ports with the West, would injure Boston. New York and Pennsylvania longed for the national government to construct such routes; but finally, having put extravagant sums into their own roads and canals, they lost their enthusiasm for federal projects. Southern support for federal improvements faded rapidly. Such expenditures, increasing the need for revenue, would justify the hated tariff, and federal internal improvements implied a broad construction of the Constitution which could as easily allow the federal government to interfere with slavery.

Only the West consistently demanded a federal system of internal improvements. A shortage of capital and a vast expanse of territory made that section perpetually hungry for government assistance. Several times Congress responded by appropriating funds for Western roads, but a series of presidential vetoes blocked these expenditures, and this forced state governments and private corporations in the Northwest to join in financing an extensive network of turnpikes and canals.

Public Land Policy. The older sections also differed from the West on public land policy. Land sales were a major source of federal revenues and the seaboard states favored high prices. Northern manufacturers also hoped that such prices would discourage their workingmen from going West. Carolina planters feared that their worn-out cotton lands could not compete with the virgin soil of the Southwest.

The West craved cheap land. Spokesmen like Thomas Hart Benton believed that low prices would encourage "a race of virtuous and independent farmers, the true supporters of their country." These noble freeholders would carry America and its democracy across the continent.

On this issue, sectional rivalries worked in the Westerners' favor: the South usually voted for cheap land to gain Western support for its own special interests. In 1820 Congress reduced the minimum purchasable tract from 160 to 80 acres and the minimum price from $2 to $1.25 an acre. An act of 1830 gave special rights to the "squatter" who occupied public land he did not own; he could now purchase "his" tract prior to public sale at the minimum price, regardless of its market value. The potential for control over westward expansion, which federal ownership of Western land made possible, almost vanished. And the older sections turned to dangerous debates over whether slavery should be restricted in the Western lands that were not yet states.

The Revival of Slavery

In the North the libertarian ideology of the American Revolution, along with the larger drift of the eighteenth century toward rationalism and humanitarianism, had led numbers of Americans to believe slavery was in decline. Beginning with Pennsylvania in 1780, the Northern states had provided for the gradual abolition of slavery. In 1787 Congress decided to prohibit slavery in the vast region of the Northwest Territory. Even in the South, humanitarian sentiments weakened the institution. Virginia and North Carolina passed laws easing the way for slaveholders to free their human property. A Southern president, Thomas Jefferson, urged Congress in 1806 to withdraw American citizens "from all further participation in those violations of human rights which have been so long continued upon the unoffending inhabitants of Africa."

The South's depressed economy in the years after the American Revolution reinforced the ideological objections to slavery. Soil exhaustion and a glutted world market injured Virginia's and Maryland's tobacco economy. Many planters switched to wheat, a crop that required fewer slaves to cultivate. Indigo, an important slave-grown crop in upland South Carolina and Georgia, ceased to be profitable when Britain withdrew her bounty to producers during the Revolution. Prices for slaves generally declined, and the wartime ban on slave imports continued in most states.

Cotton Gins. Planters anxiously experimented with new crops, especially cotton. Samuel Crompton's spinning-mule, James Hargreave's spinning-jenny, and Richard Arkwright's spinning-frame and water-frame, as well as other innovations in manufacturing, had dramatically lowered the cost of spinning and weaving cotton fiber into cloth, stimulating a worldwide demand for cotton goods. The appetites of English manufacturers for raw cotton became insatiable. As early as 1786 planters in lowland South Carolina and Georgia began to experiment with growing the silky, long-fibered sea-island cotton. It proved much superior to the short-staple upland variety that had been produced in small quantities for many years. When the cotton bolls were passed between two close-set rollers, the smooth black seeds of the sea-island variety popped right out; the same roller gin crushed the sticky green seeds of the upland variety, making it unmarketable. But sea-island cotton would grow only in the warm, humid lowlands of the coast. Large-scale cotton cultivation awaited a successful process to remove the seeds from upland cotton.

Eli Whitney. A Connecticut Yankee came to the South's rescue. In 1793 young Eli Whitney, fresh out of Yale and unemployed, came South to work as a tutor. On the way this nimble son of a three-hundred-pound Scots peddler stopped to see his friend Phineas Miller, the overseer at "Mulberry Grove" near Savannah, the plantation of Catherine Greene, widow of General Nathanael Greene. There he turned to inventing a machine to clean upland cotton of its seed. In just six months he had perfected his "absurdly simple contrivance." The cotton was fed into a hopper. A toothed roller caught the fibers of the cotton boll and pulled them through a slotted iron guard, its slits wide enough to admit the teeth and the cotton fibers caught on them, but too narrow to let the seeds through. A revolving brush then swept the cotton from the roller's teeth. One man could operate a small gin; larger ones could operate by horse or water power. Whitney and his friend quickly formed a partnership to manufacture their gins. "It makes the labor fifty times less," the inventor observed proudly, "without throwing any class of people out of business."

Eli Whitney's cotton gin created a cotton boom in the South—and a doubling of the number of slaves by 1820. *(Courtesy, The Smithsonian Institution)*

Whitney's statement hid a cruel irony. The agricultural depression, by throwing slaves out of work, might ultimately have ended slavery. The cotton gin fastened slavery on the South. Rival manufacturers and local artisans quickly copied Whitney's design. Cotton cultivation spread rapidly through upland South Carolina and Georgia. By 1820 the United States was producing 335,000 bales of cotton (a bale weighed about 500 pounds), as opposed to 10,000 bales in 1793. The opening of the rich "Black Belt" of Alabama and Mississippi after the War of 1812 pushed the crop above one million bales by 1835. The cotton boom created an unprecedented demand for slaves. In 1803 South Carolina reopened its foreign slave trade. Before the federal ban went into effect in 1808, nearly 40,000 African forced immigrants had entered Charleston. A thriving trade developed between the older seaboard states like Virginia, which had a surplus of black labor, and the slave-hungry states in the Southwest. Between 1790 and 1820 the slave population of the South more than doubled, from 657,000 to more than 1,509,000. Such a massive growth would have political repercussions.

The career of Eli Whitney held another irony for the South. This imaginative inventor went from the cotton gin to the manufacture of arms, and in that line he was instrumental in developing the principle of interchangeable parts. The principle was a major contribution to the industrial revolution. And it was industrialism, so it can be argued, that met the South on the battlefields of the Civil War and defeated the slave system the cotton gin had revived.

Mississippi River Plantation Scene. **The opening of the fertile "Black Belt" in Alabama and Mississippi after the War of 1812 increased both cotton production and the need for slaves.** *(Courtesy, Minnesota Historical Society)*

The Missouri Controversy

The Tallmadge Amendment (1819). Saturday, February 13, 1819, was a dull day in Washington. The Senate was not meeting and the House was occupied with a proposal to reduce the number of officers in the Army. Late in the day the Representatives took up a routine bill for Missouri statehood. Without warning, James Tallmadge, Jr., of New York, offered an amendment to prohibit the further introduction of slavery into Missouri and gradually to emancipate slave children born there. An "interesting and pretty wide debate" on Tallmadge's amendment began at once. For the next two and a half years the question of slavery in Missouri—which Thomas Jefferson likened to "a fire bell in the night"—convulsed Congress.

Prior to 1819 new states had entered the Union without much controversy over slavery. The Northwest Ordinance had prohibited slavery in the territory north of the Ohio River. North Carolina and Georgia had ceded to the federal government most of the area south of the Ohio, with the stipulation that slavery should be permitted. Before 1820 new free and slave states entered in equal numbers: Louisiana, Mississippi, and Alabama balanced Ohio, Indiana, and Illinois. In 1819 there were eleven slave and eleven free states. The admission of Missouri threatened to upset this delicate balance.

New Englanders had watched with dismay the march of settlement westward; some hoped to preserve their section's influence by checking the expansion of slavery into new territory, and thereby making it their economic and political ally. Federalists had long attributed the triumph of the Republican Party to "slave representation," charging that the Constitution's "three-fifths" clause gave the slave states a disproportionate influence in national politics. Advocates of the tariff and internal improvements looked increasingly on slaveholders as the opponents of their special interests. Humanitarian opposition to slavery was also stirring throughout the North. If the growth of slavery were to be halted, said a New Hampshire Congressman, it would be necessary "to fight the first battle at the water's edge."

Federalist leaders such as Senator Rufus King of New York aimed at reinvigorating their party with an appeal against slavery expansion. They allied with a faction of Northern Republicans under Governor De Witt Clinton of New York, who resented the Southern leadership of the party. Antislavery activists like former Chief Justice John Jay added their support. For a time congressional politics took on a distinct sectional alignment, pitting North against South as morality, politics, and self-interest intersected after Tallmadge introduced his amendment.

The House passed Tallmadge's amendment during 1819, but the Senate rejected it. Congress adjourned without reaching an agreement, and Missouri remained a territory. A year later, when a bill for Missouri statehood was again introduced in the House, Congressman John W. Taylor of New York offered an amendment excluding slavery from the new state. The bill, with Taylor's amendment, easily passed the House, where the North had a sizable majority. But once again the Senate said no. Antislavery forces branded slavery a "monstrous institution" and accused slaveholders of seeking to turn the country west of the Mississippi into a market for human flesh. Southerners talked openly of disunion if the amendment should pass. Missourians threatened to organize a state government without congressional approval.

The Missouri Compromise. At this point a compromise emerged. Massachusetts had agreed to the creation of a new state, Maine, out of her Northern counties, provided Congress acted by March 4, 1820. The free states hoped to admit Maine before the deadline. The Senate decided to tie Maine to Missouri. It added to the Maine statehood bill then before Congress a section admitting Missouri without restrictions on slavery. In order to make this bill more acceptable to the Northern-dominated House, Senator Jesse B. Thomas of Illinois offered his famous amendment prohibiting slavery "forever" in the rest of the Louisiana Purchase territory north of latitude 36° 30′ (the Southern boundary of Missouri). In this form the Maine-Missouri bill went to the House, where, after much wrangling, Speaker Henry Clay secured its passage on March 2. On the key question of excluding slavery in Missouri the vote was extremely close—the motion lost by 90 to 87, with four Northern Congressmen absent.

In the summer of 1820 a convention met at St. Louis and drew up a constitution for Missouri. As expected, this document sanctioned slavery. It also required the legislature to pass laws "to prevent free Negroes and mulattoes from coming to, and settling in, this state." In November 1820, when the Missouri constitution went before Congress for approval, Northerners objected to this clause. They pointed out that the United States Constitution stated that "the Citizens of each State shall be entitled to all Privileges and Immunities of Citizens in the several States." A number of Northern states recognized Negroes as citizens. This clause would prevent them from settling or even traveling in Missouri. This complicated issue of Negro citizenship precipitated another lengthy debate over Missouri's admission to the Union.

Missourians were upset over this latest setback. Whatever the constitutionality of the exclusion clause, they pointed out, several states—North and South—had similar laws. Once again Henry Clay arranged a compromise. He proposed a resolution admitting Missouri on an equal footing with the original states, upon the "Fundamental condition" that the objectionable clause should never be construed to authorize the passage of any law denying to the citizens of any state the privileges and immunities to which they were entitled under the Constitution. In 1821 Congress agreed to this empty resolution. Missouri made the meaningless promise and officially entered the Union. The state legislature in 1825 and in 1847 violated the agreement by enacting laws that barred free Negroes from entering the state.

Denmark Vesey. In the summer of 1822 the white South was shaken by the discovery of an alleged conspiracy led by Denmark Vesey, a free black carpenter who had closely followed the Missouri debates. It was said that he had recruited hundreds of slaves in Charleston, South Carolina, to rise up at midnight, kill the whites, and fire the city. A slave revealed the plot to authorities only a few days before the apparent time of the uprising, and a special court sentenced thirty-five Negroes to death. The executions were a public spectacle: at a mass hanging on July 26 several of the condemned twisted in an "agony of strangulation," because of "some bad arrangement in preparing the ropes—some of which were too long, others not properly adjusted so as to choke effectually the sufferers to death, but so as to give them the power of utterance, whilst their feet could touch the ground. . . ." Afterward, the authorities left the bodies dangling for hours as an example to other blacks.

Slaves and slaveholders everywhere trembled. The court report noted Vesey's careful reading of the Missouri debates. The involvement of so many trusted family servants was especially disturbing to whites. South Carolina Governor Thomas Bennett had often left his family in the care of Rolla, his beloved personal slave. Yet Rolla was listed among the arch-conspirators.

Southern lawmakers moved at once to prevent a repetition of the Vesey Conspiracy. They tightened their slave codes and outlawed the distribution of antislavery propaganda. Southerners resisted all further discussion of slavery in the United States Congress. The South Carolina legislature forbade the entry of free blacks into the state. Free black seamen who violated the law were jailed until their ships left port. When the British government protested these detentions and a federal judge ruled the law unconstitutional, the South Carolina Senate defiantly replied that "the duty of the state to guard against insubordination or insurrection" was "paramount to all *laws*, all *treaties*, all *constitutions*. It arises from the supreme and permanent law of nature, the law of self-preservation; and will never by this state be renounced, compromised, controlled or participated with any power whatever." Neighboring states quickly passed similar statutes. Henceforth, the South bristled at every criticism of its "peculiar institution."

In the period that followed the angry arguments over Missouri, the period of reaction to the Vesey Conspiracy, criticism of slavery virtually ceased in the South. In 1831 and 1832 the Virginia legislature did debate the abolition of slavery in the state, but that was almost the last instance of substantial open questioning in the South. Proslavery theorists, who might earlier have labeled slavery a "necessary evil," began to defend it as a "positive good." Blacks, they contended, could not prosper as freedmen, and the South would be abandoned without black labor to work the cotton fields and rice swamps. Protected by benevolent masters from the burdens of sickness, unemployment, and old age, the slaves were better off than industrial workers in the North or in Europe.

Viewing the growing intransigence of the South on slavery as well as the hardening antislavery feeling in the North, most politicians resolved to mute the slavery issue in the future. For a time they succeeded, in part because the division of the Louisiana Purchase territory into slave and free soil removed the question of slavery expansion from national politics for twenty-five years. Beginning in 1846, with the acquisition of new territory, the furious political struggle over slavery revived. Just as John Quincy Adams had predicted, the Missouri Controversy turned out to be "a mere preamble—a title-page to a great tragic volume."

Exit Monroe. The Monroe administration had attempted to drift with the apparently calm current of nationalism that followed the return of peace in 1815. Monroe's every gesture, from the diverse cabinet he selected to the fading Revolutionary War uniform he wore for ceremonial occasions, aimed at continuing the easy flow of an "Era of Good Feeling." But instead of overcoming the divisiveness of party competition, Monroe found himself presiding over the breakup of the old Republican Party. In the 1824 election, four candidates would take the field. Sectional interests tore apart the facade of national unity and the Missouri debates raised the question of the survival of the Union.

The belief that political parties were incompatible with a republican government was incorrect. The country needed not some bland national unity but articulate argument, a political system that would allow the open expression of all the passions and uncertainties that the rapid alteration of American life called forth. And the country needed not only argument but the whole business of logrolling "pork-barreling" compromise. The Monroe administration, in domestic politics at least, was a noble failure in its attempt to sustain a politics without party conflict. In foreign affairs it achieved remarkable success.

John Quincy Adams and American Continentalism

For the United States, a fortunate feature of the Louisiana Purchase was that no one knew the exact boundaries. When Robert Livingston, one of the American negotiators, pressed the French minister Talleyrand on this point, he replied: "I can give you no direction; you have made a noble bargain for yourselves, and I suppose you will make the most of it." John Quincy Adams, President Monroe's secretary of state, did just that. In important boundary treaties Adams expanded the nation's frontiers into a continental realm.

Few men have been better equipped to guide American diplomacy than John Quincy Adams. In 1778, at age eleven, he had accompanied his father, John Adams, to France. By the time he was thirty he had served as American minister to the Netherlands and to Prussia. Then, in 1801, Massachusetts elected him to the United States Senate as a Federalist. To the distress of his party, Adams proceeded to side frequently with the rival Jeffersonians. When he voted for the hated Embargo, the Federalist-dominated state legislature evicted the "scoundrel" from his seat. Under President Madison he acted as American minister to Russia and to England, and helped negotiate the Treaty of Ghent. In 1817 Monroe named him secretary of state.

Expansionism. Adams took great pride in his country's military and diplomatic victories during these years. The law of nature had intended "our proper dominion to be the continent of North America." It was our national mission to expand westward to the Pacific and north and south as well. Adams disliked European colonialism, with its commercial monopolies and its pretentious claims to "fragments of territory . . . fifteen hundred miles beyond sea, worthless and burdensome to their owners. . . ." As Secretary of State, Adams deliberately sought to make an "American Continental Empire."

Controversy lingered with Britain over the Northwest boundary. The treaty of 1783 had described the boundary line as running from the northwesternmost point of the Lake of the Woods due west to the Mississippi River—an impossible line, since the Mississippi actually rose 150 miles south of the Lake of the Woods. The Louisiana Purchase had compounded the error by creating a Northern boundary running all the way to the Rocky Mountains. Britain had repeatedly sought to set the boundary far enough south to gain access to the Mississippi.

Captain Robert Gray had first claimed the Oregon country for the United States in 1792, when he discovered the Columbia River. The explorations of Lewis and Clark had fired American interest in the area; John Jacob Astor's company established a fur-trading post there in 1811. The United States, Great Britain, Spain, and Russia each had claims in this region. During the War of 1812 British forces had seized Astor's post, which they renamed Fort George. Britain retained this fort until 1818, when Lord Castlereagh, the Foreign Secretary, ordered it returned to the United States.

The Treaty of 1818 with Britain. Castlereagh intended this conciliatory gesture as looking to a reconciliation between Britain and the United States. Britain, absorbed by

As Secretary of State under Monroe, John Quincy Adams negotiated key treaties in seeking to build an "American Continental Empire." *(Stuart and Sully Portrait, Courtesy, Fogg Art Museum, Harvard University)*

events in Europe, dared not risk a further quarrel with the United States. The War of 1812, moreover, had shown clearly how exposed was Canada's position—only American military blundering had saved it. Canada had become a hostage for Anglo-American peace. Castlereagh next invited the United States to send commissioners to London for the purpose of settling all the differences between the two countries. At these negotiations the American envoys, acting under Adams's instructions, secured important gains for the United States. The Treaty of 1818—which one expert has called the most important treaty in the history of Canadian-American relations—granted Americans permanent rights to fish off the coasts of Newfoundland and Labrador. On the Northwest boundary the United States refused to budge, and Britain agreed to draw it at 49° north latitude (approximately the line of 1783) as far as the Rocky Mountains. Adams's stubbornness had saved for the United States a strip of land containing the rich Mesabi iron range of Northern Michigan and Minnesota. West of the Rockies, neither side would yield its claim. As a stopgap, they agreed to joint occupation of the Oregon country, a compromise that lasted until the 1840s.

The Treaty of 1819 with Spain. Adams inherited an even more complicated set of problems with Spain. The Spanish government had never accepted the American claim that West Florida was part of the Louisiana Purchase, nor had the border between Louisiana and Texas ever been determined. Beyond Texas, the Western boundary of the Louisiana Purchase remained undefined. Spain still hoped to salvage part of this vast area, and to retain its claim to the Oregon country. The biggest dispute concerned East Florida (the present state of Florida).

The United States had tried for years to acquire this strategic area, which stood out on the map like a pistol, pointing at New Orleans, the vital outlet for the Mississippi River. Spain steadfastly refused to part with Florida; yet Spanish authorities there were too weak either to curb the repeated raids by Florida Indians into Georgia and Alabama or to return fugitive slaves. Spain's grasp on the peninsula steadily loosened after the War of 1812. The Napoleonic conflict in Europe and revolutions in Spanish America had exhausted its strength. Privateers and pirates sailed forth from Amelia Island near Jacksonville to prey on passing ships. When President Monroe ordered American forces to occupy Amelia Island, Spain in 1817 decided to offer Florida to the United States in return for a favorable boundary west of the Mississippi and an American pledge not to recognize the provinces of Spanish America that had revolted.

The two sides were still far apart in negotiations at Washington when General Jackson took matters into his own hands. Old Hickory had been sent to the Florida frontier with orders to adopt all "necessary measures" to halt Indian raids into American territory. Jackson, interpreting his orders broadly, advanced into Florida in 1818 with 3,000 soldiers, pushed back the Seminole Indians, and seized the towns of St. Marks and Pensacola. For good measure, he tried and executed two British subjects who had been inciting the Indians. Jackson's acts embarrassed the Monroe Administration; several cabinet members urged the president to disavow the General and to restore the occupied areas to Spain at once. But Adams defended Jackson's conduct on grounds of necessity and urged that the occupation of the towns continue until Spain should send a force sufficient to pacify the Indians. Monroe agreed, and Spain received an ultimatum: either place a force in Florida adequate to maintain order or cede it to the United States.

These bold strokes got the negotiations moving. After weeks of hard bargaining, the two sides agreed on the Treaty of 1819. Spain ceded Florida to the United States. Each side renounced all damage claims against the other, and the United States agreed to assume the claims of its citizens against Spain to a total of $5 million. Nothing was said about the recognition of the rebellious Spanish colonies. In return for fixing the Texas boundary at the Sabine River, Adams secured a magnificent transcontinental settlement from Spain, including title to all Spanish territory north of latitude 42° between the Continental Divide and the Pacific Ocean. Adams reckoned that the four nay votes on the treaty in the Senate included two Clay men, one enemy of Jackson, and one suffering from "some maggot in his brain." With this treaty Adams had at last achieved his "Continental Empire," and a place in history as a brilliant secretary of state.

The Monroe Doctrine

The boldest assertion of American nationalism in this period came from President James Monroe. His annual message in December 1823 laid down two important principles: that "the American continents, by the free and independent condition which they have assumed and maintain, are henceforth not to be considered as subjects for future colonization by any European power"; and that the United States would consider any attempt by the European powers "to extend their political system to any portion of this hemisphere as dangerous to our peace and safety." In later years these two maxims, known as "non-colonization" and "non-interference," came to be called together the Monroe Doctrine. No other presidential statement, with the possible exception of Washington's Farewell Address, has won such universal acceptance from the American people. On the hundredth anniversary of Monroe's message, Mary Baker Eddy spoke for millions when she said: "I believe in the Monroe Doctrine, in our Constitution, and in the laws of God."

The principles Monroe expounded in 1823 were not original. From the first Americans had sought refuge in the New World in order to escape the Old. Out of the Revolutionary experience inevitably flowed the belief that the New World should isolate itself from the alliances, the quarrels, and the colonizing schemes of the European powers. Washington gave this idea its classic expression in his Farewell Address, and Jefferson echoed it in his warning against subordinating our affairs to those of Europe. Monroe and Secretary of State John Quincy Adams shaped these broad beliefs into an official statement.

Adams had for years sought an excuse to forbid further European colonization in the Western Hemisphere. Russia unexpectedly gave him the opportunity. Russian explorers had long before laid claim to the northwest coast of America. By 1812 the Russian-American Company had extended its trading operations southward within only a few miles of San Francisco. Suddenly, in 1821, Czar Alexander I issued an imperial decree conferring upon this company exclusive trading rights down to 51° north latitude and forbidding all foreign vessels to come near the coast. In July 1823 Adams flatly told the Russian minister at Washington that the United States would assert the principle "that the American continents are no longer subjects for *any* new European colonial establishments." Here was the genesis of the Monroe Doctrine; the president inserted almost these very words into his annual message six months later.

The warning against European interference within the hemisphere attacked a more fundamental European threat to American interests. In 1815 at the Congress of Vienna, the victors over Napoleon—Russia, Prussia, Austria, and England—had joined in a Quadruple Alliance to crush the spirit of revolution forever. They restored the Bourbon dynasty to the French throne and agreed to meet again whenever European "repose and prosperity" were in political danger. In the summer of 1823, the statesmen of the Alliance (from which Britain had now withdrawn) began to talk of sending French troops to assist Spain in recovering her lost American colonies.

Spain's colonies had been struggling for independence for some time. When Spain tried to regain her American provinces by force, full-scale war broke out. For six years, beginning in 1814, the revolutionists, led by Simon Bolivar and "José" San Martin, liberated one colony after another. The United States sympathized with these heroic struggles and granted belligerent status to the revolted colonies, enabling them to buy supplies in this country. But Monroe, and especially Adams, hesitated to recognize the new revolutionary governments until Britain did. The British government twice refused American invitations to do this jointly. Finally, the United States decided to act alone, extending formal recognition in 1822 to Mexico, Colombia, Chile, Peru, and the Provinces of Rio de la Plata (Argentina). Having taken this bold step, the Monroe Administration was naturally alarmed at the prospect of intervention by the Quadruple Alliance.

Great Britain shared this concern, for the Spanish-American revolts had opened a whole continent to British trade. When rumors of possible intervention by the Continental powers reached George Canning, the British Foreign Secretary, in 1823, he decided to seek American cooperation in opposing such a scheme. Canning proposed a treaty or exchange of notes between the two countries expressing joint opposition to any attempt to restore Spain's lost colonies by force; he still refused, however, to agree to immediate British recognition of the former colonies.

Monroe almost accepted Canning's offer. Former Presidents Jefferson and Madison both advised acceptance, as did all the cabinet—except the Secretary of State. "It would be more candid as well as more dignified," Adams argued, "to avow our principles explicitly . . . , than to come in as a cock-boat in the wake of the British man-of-war." At this point in 1823 Monroe drafted the famous declaration in his annual message opposing further intervention by the European powers in the Western Hemisphere. At Adams's insistence, Monroe inserted a statement disavowing American interference "in the wars of the European powers in matters relating to themselves." And Adams publicly admitted that it was the power of the British navy that had enabled the United States to throw down its audacious challenge to the Quadruple Alliance.

Americans cheered the president's message. The young republic's challenge to the "crowned conspirators" of Europe, boasted one newspaper editor, would be read with "a revolting stare of astonishment." Europe scoffed at the message, labeling it "blustering," "haughty," "arrogant." It had little effect on the actions of the Continental powers. Russia—a major object of the non-colonization clause—had already decided to limit its territorial claims in North America to the area north of latitude 54° 40′. Late in 1823 Canning, tired of waiting for American agreement on a joint statement, had served an ultimatum on France. In reply, the French assured Canning that they had no intention of using force against the former Spanish colonies. By the time Monroe issued his warning, the immediate danger of interference had already vanished. During the next twenty years Britain and France both violated the Doctrine with impunity. Not until the late nineteenth century, when the United States had become a major power, did the Old World respect the new hemisphere.

Yet Monroe's message had an important future. Against an Old World order founded on a doctrine asserting the absolute rights of sovereigns and empires, Monroe championed a new order founded on the right of peoples to determine their own destiny. Only later, by a series of corollaries, did Monroe's successors turn his Doctrine into an instrument for United States meddling in Latin American affairs. "From a candid but commendable United States gesture against European interference," a Mexican diplomat observed bitterly, "the Doctrine was turned into a ruthless axiom utilized by Washington administrations to suit the interests of . . . *'Yankee Imperialism.'* "

The Election of 1824

From 1796 to 1816 meetings of the congressional members of each party had nominated their own presidential candidates. In 1820, when President Monroe ran unopposed, the Republicans did not even bother with a caucus nomination. By 1824 that party, lacking an organized opposition, had dissolved into a series of warring factions. President Monroe wisely declined to pick his successor from among the several Republicans battling for the nomination.

The "Old Republicans," devoted to states' rights and economy, pushed William H. Craw-

In the election of 1824, Henry Clay's program called the "American System" was, in effect, the nation's first campaign platform.

ford of Georgia as their candidate for president. Crawford is an obscure figure today, but to his contemporaries he was a "plain *giant* of a man." Like many young men of his day, he had parlayed a successful law practice into a distinguished career. He married a wealthy heiress, spent a few years in the state legislature, and then went to Washington as a Senator. Crawford later served as minister to France and secretary of war, and had, since 1816, been secretary of the treasury. He used this last post to pack government offices with his supporters. In 1823, just when his position seemed impregnable, illness struck him. Medical experts bled him twenty-three times within three weeks. Crawford never fully recovered, but his partisans continued to put his name forward. They called a caucus of congressional Republicans, and with only a third of the eligible members present, nominated Crawford for the presidency. The other candidates promptly repudiated the caucus as undemocratic, and accused Crawford of trying "to ride into power on 'King Caucus.' " The nomination ruined any chances Crawford may have had.

As an alternative to the congressional caucus, the other candidates accepted nominations from state legislatures and public meetings. A Tennessee newspaper likened the process to a horse race, with each state entering its own "nag."

Several New England states endorsed John Quincy Adams, Monroe's capable secretary of state. South Carolina had supported John C. Calhoun, but he dropped out when Pennsylvania Republicans failed to nominate him. The young Carolinian accepted the vice-presidential spot instead.

Henry Clay's American System. Henry Clay had been charting a course toward the White House for a decade. Born in Virginia, he had migrated to Kentucky, where he became a highly successful criminal lawyer—so successful, according to legend, that no person who hired Clay to defend him was ever hanged. After a stint in the state legislature he went on to Congress, a perfect environment then for a man with his quick mind, engaging personality, and fondness for drinking and gambling. In 1811 his colleagues made him Speaker of the House. After the war Clay became a vigorous advocate of internal improvements, a national bank, and a protective tariff. He hoped that this program, which he called the "American System," would win support in every part of the country. This was, for practical purposes, the nation's first campaign platform. Clay had not anticipated rising sectional jealousies. "I will be opposed," he wrote gloomily before the election, "because I think that the interests of all parts of the Union should be taken care of. . . ."

Clay's rival for the Western vote was Andrew Jackson, a latecomer to the race. Jackson's victories over the Creek Indians at Horseshoe Bend and the British at New Orleans had made him a national hero. His arrogant conduct during the Seminole campaign in 1818 only increased his popularity. In spite of brief terms in both houses of Congress, Old Hickory was not associated in the public mind with the grimy politics of Washington; he was a "plain farmer," his backers claimed, fresh from the people. In the uncertain politics of the time, his lack of experience in public affairs probably worked to his advantage. While the other candidates discussed the tariff or internal improvements, the Jackson people, observed John Quincy Adams resentfully, had only to shout "8th of January and the Battle of New Orleans" to win votes.

When the ballots were counted in November, the Old Hero had received by far the largest popular count—43 percent against 31 for Adams, his closest rival. But none of the candidates had a clear majority in the electoral college; there were 99 votes for Jackson, 84 for Adams, 41 for Crawford, and 37 for Clay. As the Constitution provides, the House of Representatives was required to select the chief executive from among the three men with the largest number of electoral votes. Each state would cast one ballot, determined by majority vote of its delegation.

Everyone now looked to Clay, whose fourth-place finish had eliminated him from the contest. As Speaker he had enormous influence in the House, and the managers and friends of the three candidates besieged him with arguments and deals. Clay considered their words—and his own political fortunes—carefully before making up his mind. He easily eliminated Crawford; the Georgian was physically unfit to assume the burden of the presidency. Clay was inclined to dismiss Jackson as a "military chieftain" with no qualifications "for the various, difficult, and complicated duties of the chief magistracy." And the Hero was a dangerous rival for the Western vote; it was to Clay's future political advantage to exclude him from the contest. This left John Quincy Adams. The two men had quarreled in the past, but Adams was unquestionably qualified for the presidency, and he alone shared Clay's faith in a strong national government. After consulting with friends, Clay threw all his support behind the Secretary of State. By a bare majority, John Quincy Adams was elected president.

At first Jackson took the news of his defeat gracefully. Then, three days after the election, Adams announced his intention to appoint Clay as secretary of state. The cry of "corrupt bargain" went up at once. "So you see," wrote Jackson bitterly, "the *Judas* of the West has closed the contract and will receive the thirty pieces of silver." Had there been a deal? No evidence, then or later, has ever clarified the matter. Ad-

The House of Representatives, 1821. As provided in the Constitution, the House elected John Quincy Adams president in 1824 after none of the four candidates had received a majority in the electoral college. *(Courtesy, Library of Congress)*

ams insisted that the Kentuckian was the best man for the job. Clay presumably could have made the same deal with any of the other candidates. Politically, however, the appointment was extremely unwise. It drove the Jacksonians and the Calhoun men into immediate opposition, and put the new administration on the defensive. Jackson, heretofore a reluctant candidate, set out for Tennessee in full cry: "The people have been cheated," he charged. ". . . The corruptions and intrigues at Washington [have] defeated the will of the people." The campaign of 1828 was underway before John Quincy Adams had settled into the White House.

The Second President Adams

John Quincy Adams, a biographer once remarked, "was not among America's more lovable figures." By his own description, he was reserved, stubborn, and independent. "It is a question," an observer wondered, "whether he ever laughed in his life." A reporter at the Ghent peace conference termed him "a bulldog among spaniels." When he was secretary of state, these qualities served Adams well; once he was in the White House, they quickly became his undoing.

Instead of seeking to overcome his liabilities by building a political machine in the federal bureaucracy and developing a popular program, Adams did precisely the reverse. In the interest of conciliation, he appointed political opponents to his cabinet and retained outspoken critics in government offices instead of making room for his own backers. Above all, he scorned public opinion. The great object of government, Adams believed, was to improve the condition of mankind. It was the president's duty to give direction to the national government, and the people's to follow. Even when proposing a popular measure, he made no effort to dramatize it: instead of making a straightforward statement urging Congress to pass a federal bankruptcy law, Adams recommended "the amelioration in some form or modification of the diversified and often oppressive codes relating to insolvency." In 1828 the Jacksonians revived a popular campaign slogan: "John Quincy Adams who can write and Andrew Jackson who can fight."

Adams spelled out a nationalistic program for the country. Now that America's independence had been secured and her borders enlarged, he would strengthen the country internally with a nationally planned and financed system of roads and canals, a national university, a naval academy, government-supported astronomical observatories and expeditions to map the country, and a department of the interior to regulate the use of natural resources. Adams expected to finance this program by selling public lands.

It was not the right time for a nationalist in the White House, particularly one lacking the political skill to rally support. Westerners wanted free public land, not sales at high prices for revenue. Southerners increasingly feared that a powerful federal government would interfere with slavery. The Old Republicans accused the president of trying to revive the Federalist policies of his father. "The cub," John Randolph remarked, "is a greater bear than the old one." The Jacksonian press derided Adams's proposals: his reference to astronomical observatories as "light-houses of the skies" became a national joke. Congress rejected every one of the president's recommendations.

At every turn, Adams's integrity and his belief in national authority landed him in trouble. In 1825, for example, he refused to enforce a fraudulent treaty dispossessing the Creek Indians of their tribal lands in Georgia. Governor George Troup of Georgia, anxious to open these rich cotton lands to settlement, sent surveyors into the Indian country anyway. A confrontation between the United States and Georgia threatened. A new treaty averted a clash: the Creeks agreed to cede all their lands and move west. Adams's stand had been honorable, but unpopular. Southerners condemned his challenge to state sovereignty; Westerners objected to his defense of the Indians.

The failure of Adams's domestic program had profound consequences for the country. A vast system of roads and canals, coming at a time when the forces of sectionalism were gaining strength, might have tied the nation together and prevented the disintegration of the Union. Instead, as Adams predicted, "the clanking chain of the slave" was riveted "into perpetuity" and "the invaluable inheritance of the public lands" was wasted "in boundless bribery to the West."

The Panama Congress

Adams's presidency was never to reward with success the skills and brilliance he brought to it. His chief effort in foreign policy went no farther than his domestic programs.

In 1824, Simon Bolivar, the "Liberator" of Spanish America, proposed a conference to be held in Panama. He hoped to bind the former Spanish colonies into a confederation to protect the hemisphere against Europe's Quadruple Alliance. Mexico and Colombia, rebuffed in earlier efforts to obtain individual treaties of alliance with the United States, added the Republic of the North to the list of participants. All hoped to bring the United States into a hemispheric alliance that would make the Monroe Doctrine Pan-American. Their invitations reached Washington early in 1825, just as John Quincy Adams was entering the White House.

Pan-Americanism. Secretary of State Henry Clay welcomed the idea of an inter-American conference. He had ardently supported the cause of Latin American independence. Clay envisioned an "American System" of republics, led by the United States, standing against the despotism of the Old World. Adams himself, as Monroe's Secretary of State, had rejected all proposals for collective security with the Latin American republics. At Clay's urging, however, he asked Congress to confirm the appointment of two delegates to the Panama meeting. Now was the time, he decided, to extend "the most cordial feelings of fraternal friendship" to our sister republics. Adams hoped to advance fundamental principles of commercial reciprocity, neutral rights, freedom of the seas, and noncolonization throughout the hemisphere.

Adams's request met unexpected opposition in Congress. The emerging Democrats—led by vice-president Calhoun and supporters of Andrew Jackson—vigorously attacked the administration. They accused Adams and Clay of seeking to fasten the United States to a hemispheric alliance, in plain violation of President Washington's warning against foreign entanglements. Opposition Senators bombarded the President with questions and requests for additional documents. The debates soon turned ugly. At one point John Randolph of Roanoke insinuated that Clay had procured the American invitation to further his own interests: "This Panama mission is a Kentucky cuckoo's egg, laid in a Spanish-American nest," he told the Senate. The hot-tempered Clay challenged the Virginian to a duel. Americans were soon treated to the spectacle of the Secretary of State defending the administration's honor with a gun. No one was hurt. Southerners had a further objection to the Panama meeting. Delegates from Haiti were expected at the conference, and the question of recognizing the black republic might arise. Recognition of Haiti, warned a Georgia Senator, would "strengthen and invigorate" the determination of these black revolutionaries, whose hands still reeked "in the blood" of their murdered masters, "to spread the doctrines of insurrection" to the United States.

Adams defended his proposal. Times and circumstances, he argued, had changed since Washington's day; the United States had trebled its territory, population, and wealth and must act with a breadth of vision befitting a great nation, said this devoted nationalist. After months of debate and delay, Congress finally approved the president's choice of delegates and appropriated funds for the mission. Adams had scored a major triumph—the only one of his presidency.

The triumph was empty. One of the American delegates died on his way to the conference; the other arrived too late. The meeting itself was a fiasco. Only four Latin American nations sent representatives. They signed a treaty of mutual defense and alliance, and quickly adjourned from fever-ridden Panama City, planning to meet again in Mexico early in 1827. By that time Bolivar had lost interest in the idea of a hemispheric confederation, and the conference never reconvened.

The Panama Congress benefited no one, except perhaps Great Britain. The British government, anxious to deflate Latin American enthusiasm for the Monroe Doctrine, sent an observer to Panama. In the absence of any spokesman from the Adams Administration, the British agent had no trouble sowing distrust of the United States among the delegates. At home, the issue of Haiti quickened the sectional controversy that had flared in the debates over the Missouri Compromise. Southerners once again envisioned the federal government moving against their "peculiar institution." Adams's proposal gave his political enemies their first opportunity to attack the president and his secretary of state. Once again John Quincy Adams was ahead of his time; the American people in 1826 were looking West, not South. Not for another fifty years would the United States take an interest in the concept of Pan-Americanism.

His administration a failure in both domestic and foreign affairs, Adams gave up all hope of reelection. His subsequent career was unique for an American president: he served several terms in the House of Representatives, where he was a model of integrity.

Points To Think About

1. Prior to 1820, many prominent Southerners, such as Thomas Jefferson and Henry Clay, had maintained that gradual emancipation was both necessary and desirable. Slavery, many in the South believed, was a positive evil. Even its staunchest defenders tended to argue merely that the evil was a necessary one.

After 1820 the white Southern climate of opinion started to shift dramatically. Gradual emancipation began to have difficulty obtaining a hearing. And defenders of slavery shifted to the offensive. Slavery was good, they held, for both slaveholders and the slave. It was a school in which Africans learned Christianity, English, and civilized manners. It benefited the slave. Eighteen twenty also marked the beginning of the end of the free discussion of the issue in the South. And this may have been the worst "positive evil" of the "positive good" argument. It had the effect of cutting the South off from the rest of the nation.

The "positive good" argument went with a growing sectionalism in the white South. White Southerners began to contrast their section's needs with those of the rest of the country. One result was a sort of neo-Jeffersonianism. Southerners like John C. Calhoun became apostles of limited government and states' rights. What Calhoun and his colleagues abandoned were Jefferson's insistence on equality, his fervent nationalism, and his commitment to civil liberties. The Jeffersonian legacy in the South, in short, was unraveling. Calhoun took only those strands which were of use in defending slavery, his section's "peculiar institution."

2. The rise of sectionalism affected the Northeast as well as the South. But, and it is a crucial but, New Englanders and representatives of the middle Atlantic states could pass their sectionalism off as nationalism. The issue of internal improvements provides a clear case in point. The Northeast and middle Atlantic states shared with the Middle Western states a desire for improved roads and canals, and later for railroads. To pay for them they advocated high tariffs (not so coincidently the tariffs would also protect Northern manufacturing interests even as the internal improvements would bind West and Northeast ever closer). The South consistently stood in the way. It was a comparatively simple matter for Northerners to cast their proposals in language thick with references to future national glory and to castigate Southerners with putting narrow sectional interests before the nation's good. Southerners could contest the rhetoric, but to little avail.

Over the long run, this state of affairs gave the North a distinct rhetorical and, ultimately, a moral advantage over the South.

Suggested Readings

See the *History of the Westward Movement* (1978) by Frederick W. Merk and Ray Allen Billington's *Westward Expansion* (rev. 1974). On population shifts, there are Richard H. Easterlin, *Population, Labor Force, and Long Swings in Economic Growth* (1968), and Robert Riegel and R. G. Athearn, *America Moves West* (1964). A beautiful new book on the American frontier is Annette Kolodny's *The Land Before Her: Fantasy and Experience on the American Frontiers* (1984). Good books on politics and diplomacy are Harry Ammon, *James Madison* (1971), Dexter Perkins, *A History of the Monroe Doctrine* (1955), Samuel F. Bemis, *John Quincy Adams and the Union* (1956), and Glover Moore, *The Missouri Compromise* (1953). Leonard Baker depicts *John Marshall: A Life in Law* (1974).

FORREST McDONALD

The leading public entertainment in America is politics, but it is a form of entertainment that we tend to confuse with reality. Accordingly, we are often inclined to regard past political events as the measure of what was then happening. Seen in that light, the 1820s were a rather humdrum time: a noisy to-do over slavery, a couple of fairly interesting presidential elections, a few Supreme Court decisions of note, a great deal of talk about tariffs, and otherwise ho-hum. But in actuality profound and decisive changes were taking place outside the political arena that would promote increasing sectional conflicts.

The most obvious of the changes were technological and economic. The proliferation of steamboats on inland waterways, in conjunction with the construction of many miles of canals and turnpike roads, set off a transportation revolution that would be an endlessly repeated feature of American life. The transportation revolution, in turn, drastically reduced shipping costs for farmers in the interior and redirected the attention of merchants and producers on the northeastern seaboard away from Europe and toward the hinterland. The South alone would continue to be dependent upon European markets.

The polarization of interests was intensified by the emergence, in the late twenties, of capitalistic manufacturing in New England, namely the production of textiles in mechanized, steam-powered factories. Earlier, textiles had been produced by hand in the home and in small shops. On that basis, slave labor was far cheaper than free labor; under the factory system it was the other way around. This was particularly ominous to slaveholders in the upper South, for there were more slaves there than could be profitably employed in raising tobacco, and none of the other great staple crops could be grown in the region. When manufacturing as an alternative outlet for slave labor ceased to be viable, the economic decay of the area became inevitable.

Less visible and less tangible but not less important political changes were taking place as well. There was a changing of the guard, dramatically symbolized by the death on July 4, 1826—the fiftieth anniversary of the Declaration of Independence—of John Adams and Thomas Jefferson. The Revolutionary generation and its successor had been a race of giants, men who were intensely practical but also immensely learned. Steeped in the Greek and Roman classics, versed in Renaissance humanism, learned in English legal and constitutional history, enriched by the Scottish Enlightenment, they represented a continuum and in some ways the climax of the best in a tradition that had extended over the course of two thousand years. They were the products of a unique set of circumstances, and American society had now become so vulgarized that it would never be able to produce their likes again. The ablest of the public men in the era after the 1820s—John Marshall, Henry Clay, John C. Calhoun, John Quincy Adams, Daniel Webster, Joseph Story, Nicholas Biddle—were towering figures compared to their contemporaries, but apart from Adams and Marshall, who were long-lived holdovers from the earlier era, not even these rare men were on a par with the Founders; and the public arena was soon to be overrun by pygmies. Indeed, the very unattractiveness of political life after the 1820s provided powerful stimulus to economic development, for it diverted the ablest Americans away from government and into private economic activity. Contrary to Professor Genovese's praise of the political system, this decline in the quality of leadership was as important in shaping the American destiny as any of the great technological and economic changes.

Nationalism or Sectionalism?

EUGENE D. GENOVESE

From the first days of the Republic, if not well before, American society encompassed an assortment of geographically grounded differences that nonetheless pointed toward national unity: settled, older regions against newer ones; cities against the countryside; capital-lending areas against debtor regions; manufacturing districts against agricultural. These divisions gave rise to conflicts of interest, to local, state, or regional pride and prejudices, to suspicions and hostilities. But in the North, these conflicts rested upon the solid foundations of a property system and constitutional polity that well represented the common interests of a coalescing nation. And they took place within a developing economy that steadily integrated the parts into the whole by the extension of markets and a superb system of transportation.

The South was another matter. It too had its sections and its sectionalisms: upper South and lower; black belt and upcountry; pro-tariff hemp and sugar areas and anti-tariff cotton areas; genteel tidewater communities and rough-and-tumble frontier communities; economically dynamic regions and economically stagnant or declining regions; and more. But slave property distinguished the entire South. The nonslaveholding majority of whites were caught in the web of the larger social system of slavery. Hence, while the South fought out internal sectional battles within each state and between states and regions, it increasingly closed ranks against the threat to its social system that was being mounted from without and, in muted ways, even from within.

The sectionalism that divided free from slave society had a much different character from the sectionalism that existed within the North. Differences among Northerners were never likely to provoke war. The division between the Northern and the Southern property systems, to the contrary, was likely to provoke war no matter how sensible and restrained the men on either side tried to be.

The republic, then, was from its earliest days dividing itself into distinct sections, but Professor McDonald speaks as though the sections, their economies, their mutual antagonism just happened, each section developing out of its own pre-established nature. He does not recognize how intensely political and ideological the whole process was. Hamiltonianism was possibly an inevitable expression of nascent capitalism and industrialism, but it was also certainly a conscious stimulant to those components of the American economy and for a time Hamiltonianism had to argue against its politically powerful Jeffersonian opponent. Southern slaveholding culture was intensely aware of itself, intensely determined to give itself a satisfying ideology and character—it even tried to import medieval tournaments—and its defensive political assault against Northern politicians was not merely a spasm reflex but a very deliberate attempt to define itself further. And politics, which had so much to do with shaping each of the sections and putting them at verbal war with each other, did a remarkable job of staving off actual war. From the Constitutional compact to the Missouri Compromise, then to the nullification crisis and beyond, Congress, the executive, and the courts, as well as the political parties and their leaders, prevented the issue from being joined. But each compromise proved more fragile than the one before, as two socities, one slave and one free, expanded at a quickening rate within a single nation-state that could not reconcile them.

Professor McDonald's denigration of politics and exultation of economics is an instance of that peculiar contradictory "conservatism" that he presents with considerable eloquence throughout these debates. Like others in his political camp, he perceives of the industrious, hardworking entrepreneur as a being full of will and freedom capable or remaking the world. But then Professor McDonald and his fellow conservatives will not grant to this American society, so plenteous in imagination and will, the ability to impose any measure of social and economic justice though the instrumentality of government.

Asher Durand conveys Andrew Jackson's willfulness by giving attention to his angular nose and jaw; even his swept-back hair stands at attention. *(Historical Pictures Service, Chicago)*

CHAPTER 9

The Jacksonian Era 1828–1840

ANDREW JACKSON'S INAUGURAL

Washington, D.C., was a cheerless place in the winter of 1828-29, after Andrew Jackson's presidential victory. Even the victors were gloomy: Rachel, the president's wife, had just died, and with their leader in mourning, Democrats avoided putting on too boisterous a display of pleasure over their triumph. The weather was dreadful: "snow storm after snow storm—the river frozen up, and the poor suffering the extremity of cold and hunger," wrote Margaret Bayard Smith, a resident who has left us the most vivid account of Washington in the winter of Jackson's inauguration.

One Washingtonian suggested in a letter to the local newspaper that celebrants make the inaugural ball "a means of producing a fund for the relief of the poor [by] dispensing with the usual decorations and expensive accompaniments of such a fete." In response to reports that people had frozen to death, Congress did authorize giving fifty cords of wood to the poor.

Jackson decreed a sober and dignified inauguration: he would have no military parades, no pre-inaugural festivities. Like Jefferson, he would walk to the Capitol to take the oath, then proceed to the White House on horseback. Margaret Smith approved Jackson's "avoidance of all parade—it is *true* greatness, which needs not the aid of ornament and pomp," but wished that "the good old gentleman might indulge himself with a carriage." But thousands of people of every class and from every section of the country flooded into the Capitol to witness the inauguration of the "people's president."

The sun finally shone on March 4th, and tens of thousands of citizens gathered for the oath-taking. The spectacle reflected the fondest hopes of ardent Democrats. People "without distinction of rank" stood "silent, orderly and tranquil" to glimpse Jackson—who could be picked out from the crowd around him because he alone wore no hat—a servant of the sovereign people:

"There, there, that is he," exclaimed different voices. "Which?" asked others. "He with the white head," was the reply. "Ah," exclaimed others, "there is the old man and his gray hair, there is the old veteran, there is Jackson."

Jackson, in a low voice that only a handful of the massed thousands could have heard, delivered his inaugural address, which John Quincy Adams described as "short, written with some eloquence, and remarkable chiefly for a significant threat of reform." Then, in a scramble of people that suggested to some the mobs of the French Revolution, but to a modern observer would seem reasonably orderly, farmers, politicians, women, children, carts, wagons, horses, and carriages followed the silver-haired hero down Pennsylvania Avenue to the White House. Once there they jammed inside hoping to pump the president's hand and share his offering of ice cream, cake, lemonade, and orange punch that had been intended only for the "eligible" social elite of Washington.

It was a physical impossibility. Ladies fainted from the press; in the grab for refreshments glasses and china broke, people's clothing got ripped, fights broke out; strong men had to cordon off the frail president to prevent injury by exuberant well-wishers. Jackson escaped by a back door, and some practical person suggested exiting by the windows. Alert servants began carrying tubs of punch onto the lawn to thin the crowd inside the house. The event passed off with nothing worse than mudprints on the furniture (anything to catch a glimpse of Old Hickory) and broken plates and cups. It was not a party anyone would want to repeat, but neither was it the first scene of a social revolution.

Clearly the product of happenstance, of poor planning, the White House party spoke as much of the American people's instinctive good-natured sense of order as it did of their new sense that the White House and the president belonged at last to them. While several aristocratically inclined observers saw the reign of "King Mob" in the inauguration, the *Washington National Intelligencer* commented editorially on the general good order of the crowds:

> What particularly gratifies us, and does credit to the character of our people, is, that, amidst all the excitement and bustle of the occasion, the whole day and night of the Inauguration passed off without the slightest interruption of the public peace and order, that we have heard of. At the mansion of the president, the Sovereign People were a little uproarious, but it was in any thing but a malicious spirit.

A new, but not a revolutionary, political age had begun.

The Election of 1828

The election of 1828 was a landmark in American politics. For the first time in nearly twenty years two vigorous parties contested for the presidency. Responding to this stimulus, the voters turned out in unprecedented numbers to elect Andrew Jackson president of the United States.

The Second Party System. A second two-party system was forming, in which each of the parties would appeal more directly for wide popular support than had the old Federalist and Republican parties and would in time set up extensive local organizations for winning an electorate and holding its loyalty. The new party system rested in part on legal changes that broadened the popular base of government: the gradual removal of qualifications for voting, and the trend among the states toward popular election of public officials and presidential electors in place of the earlier practice of leaving the choice to state legislatures. The new party system was a way of capturing this larger voting public.

In choosing John Quincy Adams over Jackson in 1824, the House of Representatives had unwittingly made for the new era of partisan politics. In the next four years the followers of Adams and Clay, working for federal policies that would actively promote the nation's economy, began to call themselves National Republicans; their opponents kept the name Democratic Republicans (soon shortened to Democrats). Because the House had selected Adams over General Jackson—who had received the greater number of popular votes—under circumstances that suggested to many people the existence of a "corrupt bargain," Jackson became an even stronger political figure than before. He captured the imagination of the public and infused new glamour into national politics.

After his defeat, Jackson allied with Senator Martin Van Buren of New York, a highly skilled political manager, to create the new Democratic Party. At its core were the original Jackson men, those who had supported him in 1824. These included voters in every part of the country except New England, and opportunistic politicians eager to profit from this enthusiasm for the "Old Hero." They were joined after the election by the followers of John C. Calhoun, whose own path to the presidency the alliance between Adams and Clay had blocked. Between 1826 and 1828, Van Buren brought into the party the Southern "Old Republicans," who had formerly supported Crawford. United in their opposition to the Adams and Clay policies that gave the federal government a larger role in organizing the economy, the new coalition worked in Congress to block the administration's programs.

Election of 1828. While the Jacksonians maneuvered in Congress, they also began to build the necessary organization to boost "Old Hickory" into the White House. Most states had adopted the system, still in use today, that gives all the state's electoral votes to the presidential candidate who wins the state's popular vote instead of allotting to other candidates a share of the electoral votes that corresponds to their share of the popular vote. Since a winning of a majority of the popular vote brought so rich a reward, parties wanted a state machinery that could mobilize voters throughout the state. Van Buren thoroughly organized the Democratic Party. He established central committees in Washington and Nashville. The committees worked closely with influential state leaders, who in turn organized "Hickory Clubs" at the local level. A string of newspapers favorable to Jackson appeared across the country. Jackson remained at home in Tennessee, posing as the innocent victim of a "corrupt bargain." Yet he supervised every detail of the campaign. In order to hold together his fragile coalition, he avoided taking a stand on the issues. When asked for his position on the tariff, Jackson replied ambiguously that he favored a "middle and just course." When Van Buren quoted Jackson's comment on the tariff at a New York rally, one man in the audience cheered the remark and then asked his neighbor: "On which side of the tariff question was it?" Meantime, Adams steadfastly refused to electioneer in his own behalf. Too late, his friends tried to erect an organization similar to the Democrats'.

In 1828, as in 1824, more was made of personalities than of issues. The campaign itself was unbelievably dirty. No charge seemed too base. Jackson was portrayed as a frontier ruffian, a gambler, and the son of a prostitute. A "coffin hand-bill" charged the general with the cold-blooded murder of six militiamen during the Creek Campaign of 1814. A rhymester wrote:

All six militia men were shot;
And O! it seems to me
A dreadful deed—a bloody act
of needless cruelty.

Indignant Jacksonians replied that the six were deserters who had been executed after a proper court-martial.

Jackson's wife, Rachel, was not spared. The two had met while Rachel was separated from her first husband. In 1791, believing that her husband had obtained a divorce, she had married Jackson. Not until some time later did the couple learn that the divorce had not become final. The earlier marriage was formally dissolved in September 1793, after which Rachel and Andrew recited their wedding vows a second time. Rumors of this technical adultery circulated for years. During the campaign a Cincinnati newspaper published the story. "Ought a convicted adultress and her paramour husband to be placed in the highest offices of this free and christian land?" fumed the editor. When his beloved Rachel, sick and shamed by the ugly publicity, died suddenly in December 1828, Jackson blamed his political opponents. "May God Almighty forgive her murderers," he cried at her funeral, "as I know she forgave them. I never can."

Jacksonians countered with some mudslinging of their own. It was said that President Adams, while minister to Russia, had procured an American girl for Czar Alexander I. Adams's wife was reported to have had premarital relations with her husband. Stories of the president's "aristocratic" receptions at the White House and his use of public funds to buy "gambling devices" (actually a chess set and a billiard table) circulated widely. The puritanical Adams was so offended by these stories that he refused to attend his successor's inauguration.

Jackson's victory in November 1828 was a

triumph both for the Old Hero and for the Democrats' fresh style of political appeal. Over three times as many voters turned out as in 1824. The general received fifty-six percent of the popular vote, a margin unequaled in any other presidential election during the nineteenth century. As a Southwesterner, a slaveholder, and supposedly an adherent of Jeffersonian doctrines of limitations on the national government, he swept the South and West. Adams carried his native New England along with Delaware and New Jersey, and shared with his rival New York and Maryland, which had not instituted the system of awarding the state's entire electoral vote to the popular winner. Exuberant Jacksonians hailed the election results as a revolution, a triumph of "democracy" over "aristocracy." The following January, after burying his wife, a broken-hearted Andrew Jackson set out for Washington.

The "Rise" of the Common Man

For years history books uncritically accepted the idea that popular democracy arrived with Jackson's election. They pictured him as the champion of frontier democracy, battling the forces of privilege and corruption. During his presidency the common man won the right to vote and took politics out of the hands of the elite. Socially and economically, too, the Jacksonian Era brought greater equality. With Jackson's election, wrote one historian, "a new day dawned in American history. The democratic philosophy of Thomas Jefferson became a reality." Recent studies have substantially modified this view. Historians now realize that the political power of the common man had been increasing for decades. Even in colonial times, the franchise had been quite open in some places. The Revolutionary ideology and the fierce political contests of the Jeffersonian Era had opened still wider the door to popular participation in politics. The new Western states had adopted constitutions that gave the vote to all adult white males and made most public offices elective. Many of the older states, concerned about the loss of population to the West, followed their example. By Jackson's time only two states, Delaware and South Carolina, still left to their legislatures the selection of presidential electors. The Jacksonians shrewdly developed techniques to win this broader electorate. But the most notable political innovation of the Jackson period, the national convention, a democratic way of capturing popular sentiment throughout the nation, was invented not by Democrats but by the Anti-Masonic Party. The Anti-Masons were a short-lived party opposing the fraternal order of Freemasonry, which had aroused suspicion with its secrets and its tight loyalties.

How Much Democracy? Although foreigners like Alexis de Tocqueville considered Jacksonian America remarkably egalitarian, recent historians have painted a less glowing picture. Two million blacks were held as slaves. For most women, free blacks, Irish-Catholic immigrants, and many others, social and economic equality did not exist. Such important economic developments as the rise of the factory system and the transportation revolution were not affected much by Jackson's presidency. The most careful studies of social mobility indicate an increasingly less egalitarian society, with urban elites growing in wealth while industrialism and mass immigration created new lower classes.

And yet people at the time believed that Jackson's eminence was linked to the "rise of the common man." Millions of Americans—for diverse and often conflicting reasons—could readily identify with him. Some saw in him the egalitarian spirit of the nation; he was a child of the frontier, self-made, independent, and democratic. They gloried in his success and hoped to imitate it. Others, looking back romantically to what they thought of as a simpler agrarian society, perceived Jackson as a simple and noble embodiment of that earlier time. As a big loser in the Panic of 1819, he appealed to hard-pressed debtors in the West and South. His opposition to the older entrenched banking system got him support from businessmen who wanted banks that would extend credit more freely.

"Andy" Jackson. Jackson had been born in 1767 in the Waxhaws, a wooded frontier area on the border between North and South Carolina. He had lost both brothers and his widowed mother during the Revolution, in which young Andrew served briefly as a horseman. For a time he seemed destined to be "the most roaring, rollicking, game-cocking, horse-racing, card-playing, mischievous fellow" in the neighborhood until, fired with ambition, he began

***The Verdict of the People*, by George Caleb Bingham. Americans of the 1830s widely linked Andrew Jackson with the rise of the common man, though both the number of voters and the number of elective offices had been increasing for decades.** *(Courtesy, Collection of the Boatmen's National Bank of St. Louis)*

reading law. In 1788, after completing his studies, he moved to Tennessee to take a position of public prosecutor.

This developing country was the ideal place for an eager young attorney. Jackson speculated avidly in land, slaves, and horses. As a public prosecutor, he usually sided with the creditors, executing numerous writs against debtors. In 1796 he was elected to Congress from Tennessee. Albert Gallatin would remember him as "a tall, lanky, uncouth-looking personage . . . [hair] down his back tied with an eel skin. . . . manners of a rough backwoodsman." After three years in Washington he returned to Tennessee, where he served as a superior court judge, once again siding with the land barons. Near Nashville he acquired a fine plantation, the "Hermitage," and many slaves. Although success had polished his rough edges, Jackson never lost his "roaring, rollicking" character; he was wounded three times in duels.

During the War of 1812 Jackson, already an experienced Indian fighter, led a victorious campaign against the Creeks in Alabama. When the theater of war shifted South in 1814, the desperate politicians at Washington called Jackson to save New Orleans. His famous victory over "the conquerors of Europe" electrified the country. He was the nation's savior, its greatest hero since George Washington. His rough handling of the Florida Indians and their British allies in 1818 was wildly popular in rural America.

Jackson lost heavily in the Panic of 1819. In its wake a group of his wealthy friends, alarmed by the growing demand for debtor relief in Tennessee, decided to use Jackson's immense popularity to protect their assets. They began touting him as the "people's candidate" for president—this man who had recently brought suit against 129 people who owed him money. His candidacy caught fire. For what people believed about Jackson was more important than the facts. And no one understood this better than Jackson as he campaigned for the presidency in 1828.

Though Jackson was a large landowner and by some standards an aristocrat, he did have perhaps more democratic sentiments than any previous president. He had a Westerner's inherent distrust of entrenched status and dictatorial government. In his youth he had been of fairly moderate means and could continue to think of himself as a man of the people. And so if Jackson did not come to the presidency with any clearly articulated set of democratic policies, he did have styles and tastes that accorded with popular policies other politicians devised.

The Spoils System. Arriving in Washington, Jackson found the government offices filled with bureaucrats, many of them supporters of the men who had slandered his beloved Rachel. As an astute politician, Jackson recognized the value of rewarding his partisans with government jobs. He agreed with his New York lieutenant, William Marcy, that "to the victors belong the spoils." And Jackson firmly believed that no one had "any more intrinsic right to official station than another." Men who held office too long were "apt to acquire a habit of looking with indifference upon the public interests, and of tolerating conduct from which an unpracticed man would revolt." In his first annual message, Jackson therefore recommended that appointments be limited to four years. Congress balked, but Jackson "rotated" officeholders anyway, insisting: "The duties of all public officers are, or at least admit of being made, so plain and simple that men of intelligence may readily qualify themselves for their performance." In eight years Jackson replaced about twenty percent of the government's employees, sometimes with due cause. Jefferson had removed roughly the same proportion. But it was the Jacksonians, with their spirited defense of the common man, who fixed firmly upon American politics the spoils system and rotation in office.

Van Buren vs. Calhoun

The coalition that elected Andrew Jackson in 1828 was too broad and diverse to be stable. Immediately after the election a struggle broke out between two of its major figures, Martin Van Buren and John C. Calhoun. The clash between these two intensely ambitious men was inevitable.

Usually dressed in black, Calhoun, with his great eyes glowing, looked as though his face were consumed by inner fires. Having already suffered one setback in his quest for the White House, he accepted another vice-presidential term in 1828, with the firm expectation of succeeding Jackson in the presidency.

Calhoun met his equal in Martin Van Buren. This shrewd New Yorker was one of America's first professional politicians. Starting as a lawyer in his hometown of Kinderhook, Van Buren had climbed the political ladder rung by rung: county surrogate, state senator, state attorney general, United States senator. He fashioned a powerful political machine in New York, known as the "Albany Regency," which dispensed patronage, subsidized friendly newspapers, ran campaigns, and set the party line. Van Buren usually worked behind the scenes, trying to mold a consensus toward his own ends. Whenever possible, he avoided controversial commitments. He had managed "to be on circuit" in 1820 when a meeting was called at Albany to endorse the prohibition of slavery in Missouri; he was accompanying "a friend on a visit to the Congressional Cemetery" during a key vote on the tariff in 1827. Enemies considered Van Buren devious, opportunistic, hypocritical; admirers nicknamed him the "Red Fox" and the "Little Magician."

In 1824 Van Buren led William H. Crawford's unsuccessful presidential campaign. Having been burned once, he determined to choose a winner in 1828. He helped to bring the Old Republicans into the Jackson camp and worked tirelessly for the General's election. To assure New York's pivotal vote, Van Buren resigned his Senate seat to run for governor, thus adding his popular name to the Jackson ticket.

Jackson rewarded Van Buren's efforts by making him secretary of state. Otherwise, the new Cabinet was undistinguished. Jackson had no intention of calling on it for advice or of allowing powerful figures like Calhoun to undermine his own power. Instead, he relied on an informal circle of political cronies, who came to be called the "Kitchen Cabinet." Besides old Tennessee

Martin Van Buren of New York was one of the country's first professional politicians. His loyalty to the president won him the chance to succeed Jackson in that office.

friends like Major William B. Lewis, who actually roomed at the White House, this group included several newspaper editors and, before long, Van Buren, who took up horsemanship in order to accompany the president on his morning rides.

The Peggy Eaton Affair. Calhoun fretted over these signs of Van Buren's growing influence. The vice-president had hoped to control the Cabinet appointments, and especially to make a South Carolinian Secretary of War. But Jackson appointed to that position another old Tennessee friend, John H. Eaton. Calhoun was humiliated, and to reassert his power, he set out to force Eaton from the Cabinet. An opportunity soon appeared. The Secretary of War had recently married the notorious Peggy O'Neale Timberlake, a Washington tavern-keeper's daughter with a dubious reputation. Eaton had lived with her while she was married to John Timberlake, a Navy officer, and even "pulled wires to send Timberlake to sea." After Timberlake's death, Eaton married Peggy with Jackson's blessing. Washington society hummed with scandal. An English diplomat described one of Mrs. Eaton's antagonists in the "Ladies' War" as having "worn the enamel off of her teeth by the slander of her tongue." The other Cabinet wives, led by the aristocratic Mrs. Calhoun, refused to receive Peggy socially. All Washington was soon afflicted by this "Eaton malaria," a drawing-room disease.

The president, recalling the slander heaped on his own wife, was sympathetic to the Eatons. "I tell you," roared the Old General, "I had rather have live vermin on my back than the tongue of one of these Washington women on my reputation." Jackson had a tendency to personalize issues, to make them death struggles with a hated foe. Calhoun, he announced, was trying "to weaken me . . . and open the way to his preferment on my ruin." He summoned a special Cabinet meeting to examine the evidence, then pronounced Peggy "chaste as a virgin," and demanded that she be treated with respect. When most of the Cabinet refused, further meetings were suspended. Only Van

John C. Calhoun. As vice-president, Calhoun worked against Jackson, especially during the controversy over a state's right to nullify a federal law that infringed on its sovereignty. *(In the Collection of the Corcoran Galley of Art)*

Buren, long a widower, accepted Mrs. Eaton as a respectable lady.

This petty struggle dragged on into 1831. Finally, to break the deadlock, Van Buren and Eaton offered their resignations. This calculated gesture gave Jackson a chance to reorganize his Cabinet. He asked the other secretaries to resign and replaced them with loyal followers. As a reward, Jackson nominated the faithful Van Buren to be minister to England. In December, when Congress reconvened, Calhoun plotted revenge. A tie vote in the Senate allowed him, as vice-president, to cast the deciding vote, and he gleefully spiked Van Buren's nomination. "It will kill him dead, sir, kill him dead," Calhoun gloated. "He will never kick, sir, never kick." But others agreed with Missouri Senator Thomas Hart Benton, who replied, "You have broken a minister, and elected a vice-president."

Benton was right. The breach between Jackson and Calhoun widened steadily. The president had suspected for some time that it was Calhoun who had urged Monroe's Cabinet in 1818 to censure Jackson's Florida raid. During the Peggy Eaton controversy Calhoun's old enemy, William H. Crawford, provided proof. Hastily, the vice-president published a pamphlet defending his stand and disclosing the feuds within the Administration. When Jackson saw it, his well-known temper flared. "They have cut their own throats," he said of Calhoun and his allies. Van Buren's triumph was complete. He would be Jackson's successor.

Jackson and States' Rights

For years Van Buren had worked to build a political alliance between North and South, stressing principles of laissez-faire and states' rights. He sought particularly to avoid conflicts over the slavery issue, fearing the rise of an antislavery party in the North, and to find a compromise on the tariff, since Pennsylvania Democrats desired a protective tariff—a tariff high enough that it would protect American manufactured goods by pushing the price of imported goods beyond the level at which they could compete—while Southern party voters demanded free trade. (Conscience, or some change in his politics, would later turn Van Buren to the antislavery cause he had once avoided. In 1848 he was the presidential candidate of the Free Soil Party, which urged the banning of slavery from the Western territories.) While Calhoun also advocated states' rights and limited government, he had as much taste for confrontation as did Van Buren for compromise. He wanted to face down the North with Southern demands on slavery and the tariff. The South Carolinian, increasingly the champion of Southern rights, believed that only a party dominated by Southerners could protect the South. During Jackson's first term, he and his followers worked in Congress to create an alliance between South and West based on a program of cheap land for the West and a low tariff for the South. The political maneuvering soon provoked a great national debate on the nature of the federal Union.

Public Lands. Late in 1829 Senator Samuel A. Foote of Connecticut proposed a resolution of inquiry into limiting the sale of public lands. Senator Benton of Missouri promptly denounced Foote's resolution as a plot by Eastern manufacturers to prevent their workers from migrating to the West. Robert Y. Hayne, a debonair young senator from South Carolina, supported Benton and spoke vigorously in favor of a cheap land policy. Continued large revenues from land sales, he warned, would be used to create a powerful and tyrannical government; they would be "a fund for corruption—fatal to the sovereignty and independence of the states. . . ."

Webster vs. Hayne. Daniel Webster of Massachusetts rose to answer both Benton and Hayne. The New Englander was one of the great orators and constitutional lawyers of the day. Deliberately goading Hayne, Webster claimed that the South Carolinian's appeals to state sovereignty were equivalent to preaching disunion. In January 1830 Hayne, with Calhoun's coaching, rose to the challenge. He vigorously defended the right of a state to nullify a federal law that violated "the sovereignty and independence of the states." New Englanders, he reminded Webster pointedly, "were not unwilling to adopt" this same doctrine at Hartford in 1814, "when they believed themselves to be the victims of unconstitutional legislation."

The next day, before a packed gallery, Webster answered Hayne. The people, Webster contended, and not the states, had formed the Constitution. They, and not the individual states, were sovereign. If each of the states could defy the laws of Congress at will, the Union would be a mere "rope of sand." Webster compared the Union to "a copious fountain of national, social, and personal happiness," and urged the individual states and sections to subordinate their selfish interests to the common good. He closed with a moving appeal, later memorized by successive generations of school children: "Liberty *and* Union, now and forever, one and inseparable!"

Jackson vs. Calhoun. Webster had voiced the feelings of a generation of Americans who believed that "while the Union lasts we have high, exciting, gratifying prospects spread out before us—for us and our children." Did Andrew Jackson share this vision? The president's answer came a few weeks later, at a Jefferson Day dinner. The exponents of nullification planned to use the celebration to advertise their views. Jackson, forewarned of their intentions, had prepared his toast in advance. When his turn came the president, glaring at Calhoun, raised his glass and declared: "Our Federal Union—it must be preserved." The boisterous crowd stood in deathly silence. The diminutive Van Buren had climbed onto a chair so as not to miss a moment of his triumph. Calhoun, his hand trembling so "that a little of the amber fluid trickled down the side" of his glass, replied: "The Union—next to our liberties the most dear." But there was no mistaking the president's words; despite his sympathy for states' rights, he would not countenance nullification. Calhoun was further discredited. Most Southerners and Westerners scurried back to the banner of Jackson and Van Buren.

Jackson tried to balance the powers of the federal government and the rights of the states. In 1830, anxious to reassure the strict constructionists in the party, he vetoed a bill providing federal aid for the construction of a turnpike from Maysville to Lexington, Kentucky. This road lay entirely within a single state, and Jackson doubted the constitutionality of federally funding projects of a "purely local character." But well-publicized vetoes like this were the exception; at other times Jackson approved substantial amounts of federal aid for building roads and canals. During his presidency, appropriations for this purpose averaged over $1.3 million annually, nearly double that under Adams.

The Nullification Crisis

South Carolina. South Carolina had once been rich. The mucky swamps of its low country were ideally suited for growing rice. After the invention of Whitney's gin, the Carolina upcountry had become a major cultivator of cotton and for a time the little state had produced half the nation's crop. Flushed with prosperity, South Carolinians shared fully in the nationalistic fervor of the early Republic. Native sons like Pinckney, Calhoun, and Cheves served ably in the nation's councils.

Abruptly in 1819, the state's economic fortunes slid into decline. Falling world prices for cotton, coupled with increased competition from the newer states to the southwest that could produce it more cheaply, wrecked the South Carolina cotton planters' economy. Their worn-out soils could not stand against those in the fertile Black Belt of Alabama and Mississippi. Facing ruin, South Carolinians migrated westward by the thousands.

The Tariff. Those who remained increasingly fixed their frustration and anger on the protective tariff. Only the necessities of national defense had prompted men like Calhoun to accept the tariff of 1816. When Congress began raising duties to protective levels, they objected angrily. Resentful at being deprived of the cheaper prices that foreign manufactured goods would have carried without the tariffs, South Carolinians also warned that foreign governments might retaliate by imposing high tariffs on American exports, such as cotton. In 1830 Congressman George McDuffie of South Carolina charged that higher prices ultimately cost the Southern planter the equivalent of forty out of every one hundred bales of cotton produced. Although McDuffie and others exaggerated the tariff's pernicious effect on their economy, there is no question but that protective duties did contribute to hard times in South Carolina.

In 1824 representatives from the manufactur-

The Nullification Crisis threatened to tear the Union apart. This 1833 cartoon supporting Jackson portrays the South Carolina resolution as leading to civil war and despotism. *(Courtesy, The New York Public Library, Astor, Lenox and Tilden Foundations)*

ing, grain, and wool states pushed through a bill increasing duties on a wide variety of items. Flushed with victory, protectionists held a grand convention at Harrisburg, Pennsylvania, to map out a campaign for still higher duties. In the 1828 session of Congress Northern protectionists resorted to "logrolling." They persuaded members representing Missouri lead miners, Kentucky hemp raisers, Vermont wool growers, and Louisiana sugar planters to support higher rates on manufactured articles in exchange for protective duties on their own constituents' products. To save themselves, Southerners hit upon a scheme that would make the tariff obnoxious to New England manufacturers by increasing the price the New Englanders would have to pay for raw materials. Southerners in Congress would vote with Northern producers to raise the duties on raw materials like wool, flax, and molasses, expecting manufacturing interests to vote with the South against the whole bill. This stratagem was a bit too clever. New England manufacturers, preferring the higher duties on raw materials to no protection at all, accepted the whole bill, saddling the South with the highest tariff rates between the Revolution and the Civil War.

Angry Southerners damned this "Tariff of Abominations" and threatened to boycott goods from the tariff states. Some began dressing in clothes of homespun, scorning Northern broadcloth. Immediately after the tariff bill passed, the South Carolina delegation in Congress met at the home of Senator Robert Y. Hayne to plot resistance. In the fall of 1828 Vice-President John C. Calhoun, bending to the changing opinion in his native state, set to work writing his famous *Exposition and Protest* developing the doctrine of nullification, which held that a state could prevent the exercise of a federal law within its borders.

By now Calhoun was revealing himself to be a relentlessly combative political philosopher, singleminded in his commitment to the doctrine of state sovereignty. In 1835 the British traveler Harriet Martineau would describe the gaunt South Carolinian as "the cast-iron man, who looks as if he had never been born and never could be extinguished. . . . His mind has long since lost all power of communicating with any other. I know of no man who lives in such utter intellectual solitude."

But must South Carolina submit to the federal government? No: and here, rather than on the tariff issue itself, Calhoun's argument had its most ominous implications.

Prior to the formation of the Constitution, Calhoun observed, the states had been independent and sovereign. They had created the federal government and endowed it with strictly limited powers. A state therefore had the "right" to "interpose" its original sovereignty against the "despotism of the many," the sheer weight of a national majority. Thus a state could call a state convention and nullify any act of Congress that exceeded the authority granted by the Constitution.

Under the Constitution, Calhoun argued, Congress might tax for purposes of raising revenue, but not to protect domestic industry against foreign competition. The Tariff of 1828 was therefore "unconstitutional, unequal, and oppressive." It made Southerners "the serfs of the system—out of whose labor is raised, not only the money paid into the Treasury, but the funds out of which are drawn the rich rewards of the manufacturer and his associates in interest."

Racial Fears. In 1828 Calhoun's remedy seemed too drastic for the many Carolinians who still turned hopefully to Jackson. In the meantime, the nullifiers worked to strengthen their cause. They were aided by a deepening of racial fear in South Carolina, a state where in some areas black slaves outnumbered whites by a ratio of eight to one. The decade that began with Denmark Vesey's revolt (1822) and ended with Nat Turner's rebellion in Virginia (1831) left white Carolinians fearful for their property and their very lives. They blamed these unsettling events on the small but noisy antislavery movement. The bitter Missouri Controversy and the Panama debates had awakened slaveholders everywhere to the potential threat that the federal government posed to their peculiar institution. And so even those whites who had not suffered by the fall in cotton prices embraced the doctrine of nullification as offering a constitutional protection against the growing abolitionist movement.

By 1832 nullifiers like George McDuffie were spoiling for a fight. "South Carolina," he told Congress in a typical speech:

> is oppressed (a thump). A tyrant majority sucks her life blood from her (a dreadful thump). Yes sir (a pause), yes, sir, a tyrant (a thump) majority unappeasable (horrid scream), has persecuted and persecutes us (a stamp on the floor). We appeal to them (low and quick), but we appeal in vain (loud and quick). We turn to our brethren of the North (low, with a shaking of the head), and pray them to protect us (a thump), but we t-u-r-n in v-a-i-n (prolonged, and a thump). They heap coals of fire on our heads (with immense rapidity)—they give us burden on burden; they tax us more and more (very rapid, slam-bang, slam—a hideous noise). We turn to our brethren of the South (slow with a solemn, thoughtful air). We work with them; we fight with them; we vote with them; we petition with them (common voice and manner); but the tyrant majority has no ears, no eyes, no form (quick), deaf (long pause), sightless (pause), inexorable (slow, slow). Despairing (a thump), we resort to the rights (a pause) which God (a pause) and nature [have] given us (thump, thump, thump). . . .

The Ordinance of Nullification

After Congress failed to enact significant tariff relief for an entire session, events moved rapidly. Calhoun openly endorsed nullification and resigned as vice-president to accept a seat in the Senate. In October, after a hard-fought contest, the nullification party elected an overwhelming majority to the South Carolina legislature. The governor immediately called the legislature into session, whereupon it authorized a state convention and a special election of delegates. On November 19, 1832, 136 nullifiers and 26 Unionists met at Columbia, the state capital. The convention passed an Ordinance of Nullification declaring the Tariff of 1828 and the recently passed Tariff of 1832 unconstitutional, and null and void in South Carolina. The collection of duties by the federal government after February 1, 1833, was forbidden, unless Congress lowered the tariff to twelve percent. Any attempt by Washington to coerce the state, warned the Ordinance, would be "inconsistent with the longer continuance of South Carolina in the Union." The legislature, at its regular session in December, took steps to implement the Ordinance and appropriated money to buy arms and raise an army.

The nullifiers soon discovered that they had penned themselves in. At home, a determined band of Unionists prepared to resist their fellow Carolinians by force: both sides were soon drilling volunteers in cities and towns across the state. Neighboring slave states sympathized with South Carolina, but condemned her "reckless precipitancy." President Jackson appeared determined to uphold national authority. He reinforced federal installations in Charleston harbor and ordered General Winfield Scott to take charge of military preparations. His famous Nullification Proclamation of December 10, 1832, squarely repudiated nullification. American nationhood, Jackson asserted, had existed before the states; the federal Constitution only made more workable a preexisting Union. Under these circumstances, "to say that any state may at pleasure secede from the Union is to say that the United States is not a nation." The power of nullification was "*incompatible with the existence of the Union, contradicted expressly by the letter of the Constitution, unauthorized by its spirit, inconsistent with every principle on which it was founded, and destructive of the great object for which it was formed.*" Disunion by armed force, Jackson concluded, was "*treason,*" in the face of which he, as president, could not "avoid the performance of his duty."

The Compromise Tariff of 1833. At the same time that he brandished the stick, Jackson held out a carrot to the nullifiers. He urged Congress to lower the tariff, limiting protection to articles essential to the nation's defense. In order to avoid a premature clash of arms, he removed federal troops from the Charleston Citadel to the forts in the harbor. Yet he also secured a "Force Bill" from Congress early in 1833, authorizing the collection of import duties from ships offshore and reaffirming his power to call up the state militias and to use the Army and Navy. Old Hickory had completely outmaneuvered the Carolina radicals. As the "Fatal First" approached, they prudently decided to delay enforcing nullification until Congress completed its deliberations on the tariff. Early in March 1833, Congress passed the Compromise Tariff, which provided that rates on protected articles would be lowered in gradual stages to twenty percent in mid-1842. Even though the new rates were nearly double what the nullification ordinance had demanded, Carolinians accepted the compromise figure with relief. The convention promptly rescinded the Ordinance of Nullification; then, as a symbolic gesture, it declared the "Force Bill" null and void.

South Carolina had lost. The passage of the Compromise Tariff was a signal triumph for nationalism and majority rule. Nullification as a principle had been thoroughly discredited. In the process, Carolinians had learned an unforgettable lesson: successful resistance to Northern "tyranny" demanded the cooperation of the other slave states.

Georgia and Indian Removal

The Indian Removal Act. In one instance, Jackson actually encouraged a state to defy federal authority. He speeded the removal of Indians from lands under settlement by whites by encouraging Georgia to ignore a Supreme Court decision favorable to Indian rights. Since Jefferson's time the government had been forcing the Indian tribes to sell their lands and migrate westward. In 1830 the president urged Congress to set apart "an ample district west of the Mississippi" for their permanent use. Here the "aborigines" might learn "the arts of civilization" and form "an interesting commonwealth, destined to perpetuate the race and to attest the humanity and justice of this government." Senators like Theodore Frelinghuysen of New Jersey courageously defended the Indians' right of "immemorial possession, as the original tenants

***The Trail of Tears*, by Robert Lindneux. Jackson despised Indians and disregarded the Supreme Court ruling that the Cherokees of Georgia had a right to their land. Many perished when they moved west on "the trail of tears."** *(Courtesy, Woolaroc Museum)*

of the soil," but the Indian Removal Act passed anyway. In the following years many Indian nations, recognizing the futility of resistance, signed over their lands and moved west, some of them prodded by the United States Army.

Although disunited and demoralized by defeat, some Indians did not peacefully acquiesce in the march westward. In Illinois portions of the Sac and Fox tribes, led by Chief Black Hawk, refused to leave their rich ancestral lands. Black Hawk initially hoped that, if his people remained peaceful, they would be permitted to keep their farming communities and live alongside the incoming whites. But hunger and incessant military pressure finally forced Black Hawk into war. It was a one-sided fight. In the final battle of the Black Hawk War, the Bad Axe Massacre (1832), United States troops and militiamen killed all but 150 of the original thousand Indian men, women, and children. In the South, the Seminole War (1835-38) was even bloodier. Many Seminole tribesmen, led by Chief Osceola, refused to leave Florida. Accompanied by runaway blacks, they retreated into the swamps. Jackson sent troops, but the Indians conducted a skillful guerrilla war in the impenetrable Everglades. It took several years and $14 million to subdue Osceola's warriors.

Americans had traditionally argued that the white man's "superior" civilization justified dispossessing the wandering "savages" of their ancestral lands. In the case of the Cherokees, Choctaws, and Chickasaws, even this shabby rationalization collapsed. They were all settled peoples, skilled in the ways of agriculture. In spite of this, the government bribed, intimidated, and lied to force the Choctaws and Chickasaws of Mississippi and Alabama to move to the Indian Country (the present state of Oklahoma). Even these tactics failed to move the Cherokees of Georgia. They adopted a written constitution and declared themselves an independent nation. In response the Georgia legislature, ignoring federal treaties recognizing Cherokee nationhood, extended state jurisdiction over them and prepared to seize their lands. Hiring William Wirt, the former federal Attorney General, to represent them, the Cherokees appealed to the Supreme Court for an injunction restraining Georgia from carrying out this seizure. Chief Justice Marshall, in an 1831 decision, *Cherokee Nation v. Georgia*, ruled that the Cherokees were a "domestic dependent nation" possessing unquestioned right to their lands. A year later, in *Worcester v. Georgia*, the Court held that the Cherokee nation was a distinct political community, within which "the laws of Georgia can have no force." The United States, it implied, was duty-bound to keep intruders from the Indian lands.

"The Trail of Tears." Both Jackson and Georgia ignored the Court's ruling. Informed of the *Worcester* opinion, Jackson reputedly said: "John Marshall has made his decision, now let him enforce it." Georgia continued to harass the Cherokees. In 1835 a corrupt faction was bribed into signing a treaty, and General Winfield Scott began the Indians' systematic removal. As usual, the government failed to make adequate preparations for the trip westward; over four thousand of the fifteen thousand Cherokees who made the move perished along "the Trail of Tears." The Choctaws had been forced out of Mississippi in the dead of winter, "thinly clad and without moccasins." In 1838 the government forcibly removed the Pottawattomies from Indiana. They began the trek west "under a blazing noonday sun, amidst clouds of dust, marching in a line, surrounded by soldiers who were hurrying their steps. Next came the baggage wagons, in which numerous invalids, children, and women, too weak to walk, were crammed." Dozens died along this "Trail of Death." The resettlement of these farming Indians west of the Mississippi River created bitter resentment among the Plains tribes who hunted there. The government was soon forced to send troops to the West to separate the warring tribes.

The Second Bank of the United States

Andrew Jackson brought with him to the White House a Westerner's instinctive dislike of monopolies and entrenched privilege, and a vague distrust of banks and paper money. Beyond this, however, he had few ideas about economics; political needs shaped his tariff and internal improvement policies. But in his first message to Congress he sharply criticized the Bank of the United States for its failure to establish "a uniform and sound currency." He urged the lawmakers to consider carefully "the constitutionality and expediency" of renewing the Bank's charter at its expiration in 1836.

Nicholas Biddle. After a shaky start the second Bank of the United States had prospered, especially under its third president, Nicholas Biddle. Born into a wealthy Philadelphia family, Biddle had displayed a precocious versatility from the start. After graduating from Princeton at the age of fifteen, he traveled widely, served in the diplomatic corps, and wrote the classic account of the Lewis and Clark expedition. Impressed with his knowledge of banking, President Monroe appointed him a director of the Bank; four years later, at the age of thirty-seven, he became its president. The choice was a good one. Biddle understood banking and the function of the Bank in the American economy at a time when few others did.

The Bank marketed government securities and performed other Treasury operations. Its loans stimulated business and facilitated the swift exchange of agricultural staples. And one of its most remarkable services was to make possible for the country a reliable paper currency.

During much of the nineteenth century the only money that the nation considered absolutely sound was specie—gold and silver coin. Americans used much paper money, but many thought paper to be money only if it could be taken to a bank and exchanged for its face value in coin. The National Bank was prepared to repay in specie the notes that it issued, and these therefore constituted a currency that was as sound as it was portable. At the same time the bank helped to keep the state banks from issuing reckless amounts of paper currency. This it did by periodically requiring them to redeem in specie their notes that the bank was holding.

Though his direct responsibility was to private stockholders, Biddle's chief concern prior to 1832 seemed always to be the welfare of the country as a whole. He liked to boast that the Bank was "the balance wheel of the banking system."

Biddle's very success proved his undoing. New York bankers chafed at the restraints imposed by a Philadelphia institution. Some people sincerely questioned the constitutionality or

Nicholas Biddle, president of the Second Bank of the United States. *(From,* The National Portrait Gallery of Distinguished Authors)

the wisdom of making an essentially private bank the depository of the public funds. Many still blamed the Bank for the Panic of 1819. "Cheap money" advocates, mainly state bankers and speculators, objected to the Bank because it restrained the state banks from issuing notes as freely as they wished. At the other extreme "hard money" men, believing that specie was the only safe currency, condemned all note-issuing banks as instruments of speculation. Advocates of hard money were now employing the populistic rhetoric, spiced with denunciations of privileged wealth, that more often in American history has been the rhetoric of champions of cheap or paper currency. Banknotes, wrote one critic, formed "the foundation of *artificial* inequality of wealth, and, thereby, of *artificial* inequality of power."

The source of Jackson's hostility to the Bank remains obscure. He did not act in response to popular demand or on behalf of state banks. In spite of his well-known suspicion of banks and paper money, Old Hickory kept his own money in the Bank's Washington and Nashville branches for years. Most likely, his antagonism stemmed from jealousy toward the uncontrolled political power of the Bank. He readily believed the reports that some of the branches had worked against his election in 1828, and reached the conclusion that the Bank was a "hydra of corruption—dangerous to our liberties by its corrupting influence everywhere." He must, he decided, strip the "Monster" of its malign power. Once engaged in the contest, Jackson quickly turned the dispute into another death struggle between himself and a hated foe.

For a time Biddle tried to placate Jackson, but with no success. He then turned to the president's enemies for support. He extended generous loans to Clay, Webster, and other influential politicians and newspaper editors. In 1832 he reluctantly acquiesced in their plan to seek a recharter well in advance of the expiration date. It was an election year, and the Bank's friends reasoned that Jackson would hesitate before vetoing a recharter bill. If he did veto it, they would have a good issue in the presidential campaign.

The Bank War

The bill renewing the Bank's charter cleared Congress in July 1832, with nearly a third of the Democratic representatives voting in favor. Jackson was enraged. "The Bank," he told Martin Van Buren, "is trying to kill me, *but I will kill it!*" He sent the bill back to Congress with a blistering veto message in which he denounced the Bank as "not only unnecessary, but dangerous to the government and country." It enjoyed a virtual "monopoly of foreign and domestic exchange"; it threatened the rights of the states and the liberties of the people; it discriminated against the West. Refusing to be guided by the opinion of the Supreme Court in the *McCulloch* case, Jackson declared the Bank unconstitutional: "The opinion of the judges has no more authority over Congress than the opinion of Congress has over the judges, and on that point the president is independent of both." One-fourth of the Bank's stock was held by foreigners, the veto message observed; the country needed a *"purely American"* institution. Jackson

This cartoon supporting President Jackson's withdrawal of federal deposits from the Bank of the United States shows how successful he was in portraying the Bank and its supporters as tools of the rich.

closed with an impassioned attack on the renewal bill as an attempt by "the rich and powerful" to "bend the acts of government to their selfish purposes" and pledged to resist "the advancement of the few at the expense of the many."

Jackson vs. the Bank. The veto message was superb propaganda but poor economics. A developing country like the United States needed a stable currency to encourage foreign investment, not wildcat banking to drive it away. The Bank was not strictly a monopoly. In 1830 it made about one-fifth of the nation's bank loans and had barely one-third of the total bank deposits and specie reserves held by American banks. In his message Jackson completely ignored the important services the Bank provided and offered no effective substitute for them.

At first, Jackson's enemies rejoiced over the message. Biddle compared the president to "a chained panther biting the bars of his cage" and called the veto "a manifesto of anarchy." But in November 1832 Jackson, with Van Buren as his running mate, overwhelmed the National Republican candidate, Henry Clay, by a margin of five to one in the electoral college.

Jackson took his decisive victory as a mandate to destroy the Bank even before its charter expired. As soon as the Nullification Crisis passed, he set out to remove the government deposits from the bank and place them in selected state banks. By law, it was the secretary of the treasury who had to give the actual order for removing them. When he refused, Jackson "promoted" him to the State Department and named a new treasury secretary. This official, too, refused to do Jackson's bidding, citing the "irresponsible" policies of the state banks. The president then replaced him with Roger B. Taney, formerly the Attorney General. The faithful Taney continued drawing on the government's funds in the Bank to meet current expenses, but he began depositing the incoming receipts in certain state banks. These banks were supposedly chosen for their fiscal soundness, but political considerations were not overlooked. Prior to 1836 over seventy-five percent of the officers in these banks were Democrats. The administration's critics nicknamed them the "pet banks."

As the government's deposits dwindled, Biddle began calling in loans and curtailing the issuing of new notes. In the beginning this contraction was thoroughly justifiable, since the federal deposits had given the notes much of their reliability. But Biddle soon succumbed to baser motives. He continued the contraction into the spring of 1834, in the hope of producing a short recession that would force a recharter of the Bank. "Nothing but the evidence of suffering," he reasoned, would "produce any effect in Congress." As interest rates climbed and credit dried up, the business community begged for relief. All over the country supporters of the Bank organized meetings and flooded Congress with petitions. A Cincinnati man tried a more direct approach: "Damn your—soul," he wrote Jackson, "remove them deposits back again, and recharter the bank or you will certainly be shot in less than two weeks and that by myself!!!"

Old Hickory refused to budge. Told of rumors that a mob threatened to "lay siege to the Capitol until the deposits were restored," he promised to hang the ringleaders "as high as Haman." When a delegation of businessmen visited him seeking relief, he replied coldly: "Go to Nicholas Biddle. . . . Biddle has all the money!" In the end Jackson had his way. Biddle was forced to let credit flow more freely, and the economy quickly recovered.

The chief result of the so-called "Biddle depression" was a marked decrease in the Bank's popularity. In 1836, when the old federal charter expired, the Bank received a new one from the state of Pennsylvania. In 1841, after a series of financial reverses, it closed its doors forever. Biddle died three years later, a broken man.

Jackson had destroyed the Bank in the name of sound money and "those habits of economy and simplicity which are so congenial to the character of republicans." But, in so doing he removed the most effective restraint on "the stock-jobbers, brokers, and gamblers" he professed to despise. Aided by the government deposits, the "pets" flooded the country with paper banknotes. An orgy of speculation and inflation followed. Belatedly, between 1834 and 1836, Jackson tried to drive paper money from circulation. He directed the deposit banks not to issue or receive notes worth less than $10. Land officers were instructed not to take small notes in payment for public lands. Jackson secured a law preventing deposit banks from issuing bills valued at under $20. Finally, in 1836, Jackson issued the Specie Circular, which prohibited the purchase of public lands in anything but coin. He acted too late. In 1837 a "mountain of debt and bad currency" helped to plunge the country into its worst depression to date. Jackson had accused the Second Bank of being beyond federal control, but so were the state banks in which he had deposited federal revenues.

The Democrats in Their Prime

By the end of Andrew Jackson's second term in 1837, the Democratic Party had changed significantly. Gone was the diverse political coalition that had elected the Old Hero in 1828; its leadership now adhered to a fairly definite body of ideas. The accent was on laissez-faire and equality of opportunity. Government, the Jacksonians believed, should restrict its intervention in the economy to eliminating special privilege and monopoly, leaving a fair field for individual competition. Like Adam Smith, whose *Wealth of Nations* (1776) many of them had read, they believed that the power of the marketplace would best regulate the economy and distribute wealth equitably. Watchful that the rich would use the government for personal advantage, the Jacksonians advocated universal political freedom (at least for white men) and majority rule. Although recognizing the supremacy of the Union, Jacksonians respected states' rights, holding that the area of federal authority should be kept within narrow bounds.

The party in the late 1830s was much influenced by the "Locofocos," a powerful Democratic splinter group in New York. These dissidents—who took their name from a type of friction match they had used to light candles when rival Democrats tried to disrupt one of their meetings by turning off the gas lights—opposed monopoly in any form. They denounced banks and corporations, demanding a return to hard money and the abolition of laws allowing limited liability for stockholders. They advocated free trade, labor unions, free public education, and abolition of imprisonment for debt. Although other Democrats rejected many of the more radical Locofoco demands, they never missed a chance to portray the party as the defender of the common man against the forces of wealth and privilege. For the Jacksonian Democratic Party had been designed to capture popular emotions.

Chief Justice Roger Taney. The decisions of the Supreme Court in the late thirties reflected Democratic thinking. During his two terms, Jackson appointed seven associate justices. And when Chief Justice John Marshall died in 1835, the president named Roger B. Taney to succeed him. Under Taney's leadership the Court showed a less rigid respect for private property rights as against the rights of popular majorities, and had more regard for states' rights.

In the *Charles River Bridge* case of 1837 the Court again took up the question posed in the *Dartmouth College* case of whether a state could alter an agreement with a private corporation. The Massachusetts legislature had incorporated the Charles River Bridge Company to operate a toll bridge under a long-term contract. Later it authorized another corporation to erect a toll-free bridge over the Charles River at a point nearby. The first company sought an injunction, contending that the second charter constituted a breach of contract. Taney sided with Massachusetts. The great object of government, he declared, was "to promote the happiness and prosperity of the community." In a collision between the rights of private property and those of the community, the rights of the people came first. The Court could not consent, Taney said, to take away from the states "any portion of that power over their own internal police and improvement, which is so necessary to their well being and prosperity." Although conservatives denounced the decision as a blow to business and the sanctity of contract, the decision was really a liberating one. The young American economy would have been greatly handicapped if established companies had been able to maintain monopolies and choke off competition. Taney's opinion opened the way for a host of developments in industry and transportation.

Two years later, in *Bank of Augusta v. Earle*, the Court enlarged state powers again. Here Taney rejected the claim of a Georgia bank that under the federal Constitution a corporation, like a citizen, could automatically enter another state and engage in business there. Though in the absence of positive legislation a company might do business in another state, said Taney, that state had the power to exclude the corporation if it wished. In the wake of this decision, many states enacted regulatory laws for outside corporations. On the whole, they proved to be socially beneficial, since there was as yet virtually no federal regulation of interstate commerce.

The Democratic appeals for strict economy, equal rights, and the abolition of government favors did appeal to popular sentiments. By the late thirties there was some truth in Jackson's claim that his party represented the "farmers, mechanics, and laborers." It especially attracted people who resented the privileges that established bankers and tariff-protected businessmen seemed to enjoy; people who had been affected adversely by changing patterns of transportation and trade; ordinary people who had been hurt by currency fluctuations and unstable commodity prices. Others supported the Democrats for special reasons. Many Southern planters looked to them to protect slavery and Southern rights from government interference. Businessmen engaged in international trade favored Jackson's call for a lower tariff. The Democratic Party early recognized and encouraged the aspirations of immigrants, particularly Irish Catholics, who flocked to the Democracy. Opponents of evangelical Protestantism, with its righteous moralizing and aggressive crusading, found the rough-and-tumble egalitarianism of the Democrats refreshing. The party attracted free-thinkers and intellectuals. Many Democratic voters just plain liked Jackson.

The Whigs

Yet Jackson's policies and political success provoked growing opposition. Initially, Old Hickory's opponents lacked cohesion, and political alliances were unsettled. In time they would gather into a party that could compete with the Democrats in the tapping of popular emotions.

One of the first of the forces to oppose Jackson was the Anti-Masonic Party, which after 1826 had gained strong support in New England, New York, and Pennsylvania. Originally a protest movement against the supposedly despotic political and economic power of Masonry, it soon turned into a general protest against inequality and immorality. As a powerful religious and democratic movement, it attracted ambitious young politicians—William Seward, Thaddeus Stevens, Horace Greeley, and Millard Fillmore—who welded it into an effective political party. Because Andrew Jackson was a Mason, and because his party was in power, these leaders made the Democrats the chief target of attack. In 1831 the Anti-Masons held the first national nominating convention at Baltimore, choosing William Wirt as their presidential candidate. He won just seven electoral votes in 1832, splitting the anti-Jackson vote with Henry Clay, the National Republican candidate. After that election, leaders of these two groups began organizing an alternative political force to the Democrats.

They were joined by a motley assortment of former Jacksonians. After the Cabinet reshuffle of 1831, two Calhounites, John Branch of North Carolina and John M. Berrien of Georgia, went home to lead movements against the administration. Jackson's firm rebuke to nullification drove many other Southern states' righters into opposition. Then the Bank War caused conservatives everywhere to desert the president. The selection of the New Yorker Martin Van Buren as Jackson's successor awakened hostility in the South and West. Even John C. Calhoun cooperated for a time with nationalists like Clay and Webster in opposing administration measures in Congress.

In 1834 James Watson Webb of the New York *Courier and Enquirer* gave the anti-Jackson coalition the title "Whigs." That name had been in use for earlier British opponents of policies of the monarchy, and for rebel colonists in the period of the American Revolution; it was now supposed to define the opponents of the tyrannical "King Andrew."

Use of the name "Whig" by opponents of Jackson and Jacksonianism became widespread in 1834, but the actual formation of a Whig Party varied in time from state to state. It was organized first in the New England and Mid-Atlantic states, later in the West and South. The lack of an effective national organization and conflicts in ideology among the coalitionists hindered the Whigs in 1836. Unable to agree on a common platform or a single presidential candidate, they adopted the strategy of running strong regional candidates in the hope of throwing the election into the House of Representatives. In the South, the Whigs's choice was Hugh Lawson White, a Tennessean who, like many Southern Jacksonians, distrusted Van Buren on the tariff and slavery. In the East, they ran Daniel Webster. The candidate in the West was General William Henry Harrison of Ohio, a former governor of Indiana Territory and the hero of the Battle of Tippecanoe. Between them the three Whigs piled up 124 electoral votes, but Van Buren, with Jackson's prestige behind him, had 170, enough to win the election.

The Nature of the Growing Whig Party. During the next four years the Whigs slowly gathered strength and developed a more coherent political philosophy. As the Panic of 1837 worsened, people throughout the country flocked to the new banner, convinced that Van Buren's hard-money policies were somehow responsible for their woes. The Whigs's ambitious economic nationalism attracted new adherents in the South, even while it drove Calhoun and the extreme states' righters back to the Democrats.

The Whigs believed that one of the chief functions of government was to promote, actively and positively, the national economy. They advocated internal improvements at federal expense, a national banking system, and a protective tariff for industry. As they saw it, a wise government working alongside capital and labor would harmonize the interests of every class and section. As their taunts at "King Andrew" indicated, the Whigs also believed in a strong congressional voice in government and respect for the opinions of the Supreme Court.

There was also a strong strain of evangelical Protestantism in Whiggery, which gave rise to moral and humanitarian reform. Many Whigs still hoped "to Christianize America through politics." They frequently criticized Jackson's Indian policy; and numbers of northern Whigs opposed slavery. Yet Whigs feared the political power of immigrants and Catholics.

The Whigs attracted a substantial following among all classes of society. Many Northern merchants, bankers, and industrialists found the Whig philosophy appealing; so did large cotton, tobacco, and sugar planters and their urban business associates in the South. Many farmers, hungry for internal improvements, voted Whig. The party was popular among Protestants and native Americans concerned about the influx of immigrants, particularly Irish and German Catholics. Workingmen in industries hurt by foreign imports, or fearful of immigrant competition for jobs, supported the Whig ticket. With broad support throughout the country, the Whigs looked forward eagerly to the election of 1840.

Boom and Bust Again

On March 4, 1837, Andrew Jackson turned over the presidency to Martin Van Buren. As the Old Hero left the Capitol, the crowds cheered him lustily. For once, remarked Thomas Hart Benton, "the rising was eclipsed by the setting sun." In his inaugural message, Van Buren painted a glowing picture of a "great, happy, and flourishing" country. But even as he spoke, the dark clouds of depression were gathering once again.

Since the early 1820s the American economy had grown steadily. Demand for American agricultural products seemed insatiable: exports of cotton alone increased from 92 million pounds in 1818 to 300 million pounds in 1830. Moving these bulky products to market required the expenditure of immense sums on transportation projects of all kinds. Construction of turnpikes and bridges continued in most parts of the country, and steamboat building became an important industry. The success of the Erie Canal brought a time of canal building, even while more than three thousand miles of railroad were completed in the same period. And the construction boom went far beyond internal improvements: the rapid settlement of the West and the growth of urban areas created a great demand for new homes, barns, stores, and public buildings. Manufacturing industries, particularly cotton textiles, iron, and machinery, also grew rapidly.

By the middle thirties healthy growth was giving way to feverish speculation. Investors, most of them British, bought enormous quantities of stock in state-owned canal companies and other public works of increasingly doubtful utility and profitability. With labor and materials in short supply, these new construction projects merely drove up wages and prices. Sales of public land—mainly to speculators—rose from only $2,300,000 in 1830 to almost $25,000,000 in 1836. With speculators snapping up everything in sight, urban land values also soared. A farm near Brooklyn that had gone begging at $20,000 in 1831 was sold in 1835 for $102,000. When Chicago was incorporated in 1833, optimists were already buying and selling lots twenty miles from Lake Michigan. All over the West and South, farmers and planters plunged heavily into debt for land and slaves, sometimes borrowing at rates as high as thirty percent.

The Jackson Administration's monetary policies contributed to this orgy of what contemporaries called "overbanking and overtrading." The demise of the Bank of the United States removed an important check on state banks and their number rose from 330 in 1830 to 788 in 1837. Many were purely speculative ventures, deliberately located "out where the wildcats howled" on the assumption that there they could avoid holders of their notes seeking re-

***Yankee Peddler*, by John Whetton Ehninger. Economic activity was feverish in the 1830s, but too much speculation helped to bring about a depression by the end of the decade.** *(Courtesy, Collection of the Newark Museum)*

demption in specie. Lax state laws permitted these "wildcat banks" to issue banknotes without maintaining adequate specie reserves to back them up. The note circulation of state banks soared from $61 million in 1830 to $149 million in 1837. The shifting of government deposits to the "pet" banks and the decision in 1836 to distribute the surplus federal revenue to the states pushed the inflation further. The series of hard-money policies that the Jackson Administration finally decided to take, culminating in the Specie Circular of 1836, came too late.

In 1837 the boom collapsed. The president's order requiring all payments for public lands in gold or silver led banks in the West to draw heavily on Eastern banks for coin. In the midst of this specie drain a recession in Britain depressed cotton prices and caused British investors to call in their loans. On May 10 New York banks suspended specie payments and other banks followed. Prices fell and credit tightened: for speculators the only question, an observer wrote, "was as to the means of escape, and nearest and best route to Texas." Numerous commercial houses and banks failed. In 1838 the economy revived briefly, as states borrowed heavily for internal improvements, but the revival could not be maintained. Fewer and fewer improvements paid their way: the credit of the states was exhausted: the confidence of foreign investors had evaporated: most improvement projects were halted. It was "national pay day," a contemporary wrote. "The nation has been drawing on the future, and the future dishonors the draft."

Depression. The depression of 1839–1843 was one of the severest in American history. Prices fell by as much as one-half in some places; real estate values and stocks declined even more drastically. The collapse of prices set off a tidal wave of bankruptcies. Under the federal Bankruptcy Act of 1841, some 28,000 debtors freed themselves of nearly a half-billion dollars of debt. Rural areas were hardest hit, but they at least were self-sustaining. In the cities unemployment brought widespread distress. Mobs in New York looted the flour stores in 1837 and similar violence flared elsewhere. Once again municipalities and charitable agencies set up soup kitchens and unemployment offices. Casting about for a more permanent solution to urban unemployment, Horace Greeley advised the unemployed to "go to the Great West, anything rather than remain here." Public land sales had plunged by 1842 to less than six percent of their 1836 peak. With land sales and tariff receipts declining, the federal government, which had been out of debt since 1835 (for the first and only time in its history), began running a new deficit. The states, which had contracted nearly $200 million of debts, were especially hard-pressed. By 1842 eight of them had defaulted, and three had even repudiated part of their debt, thereby ruining American credit with European investors for years to come.

One faction in the Democratic Party favored banks and paper money, wanting the federal government to maintain some active role in managing the economy. Radicals, on the other hand, clung resolutely to hard money and would have the government do little in the economy except discourage banks from issuing paper notes. The "Little Magician" decided to stick with Jackson's policies. He refused to repeal the Specie Circular. Calling Congress into special session, he blamed the depression on "excessive issues of bank paper" and "reckless speculation." Concerned about the growing strain on the federal Treasury, he asked Congress to authorize the borrowing of $10 million for current expenses. And he specifically recommended passage of a law permitting the federal government to keep its receipts in its own Treasury vaults, which would sever all connections with the nation's banks. Beyond this Van Buren refused to go. It was not the place of government, he insisted, to relieve economic distress. The framers of the Constitution had "wisely judged that the less government interfered with private pursuits the better for the general prosperity." Government assistance to one class would mean using "the property of some for the benefit of others," and it was better "to leave every citizen and every interest to reap under its benign protection the rewards of virtue, industry, and prudence." Many of the states made at least some effort to relieve hunger and unemployment.

In spite of Whig protests against "leaving the people to shift for themselves," most of Van Buren's program became law in 1837. The President's opponents concentrated their fire on the Independent Treasury Bill. This proposal would require customs collectors, postmasters, and other government receivers of funds to hold their receipts until ordered to pay them out. It would also direct the Secretary of the Treasury to withdraw the government's deposits from the "pet" banks and to place them in special subtreasuries. Whigs charged that the bill would curtail loans and credit, thereby stifling recovery. Van Buren's supporters countered that it would keep the government independent and the currency safe and check unwise expansion of bank notes. A coalition of Whigs and rebellious Democrats blocked the scheme until 1840, when it finally passed Congress. But the Democratic Party was now the party of depression, and the Whigs, with a presidential election in view, could afford to accept this one legislative defeat gracefully.

The Election of 1840

In 1840 the second national party system came of age. The Democratic organization now faced a Whig Party just as skillfully devised for the winning of a large electorate, and the Whigs had picked as their candidate a military hero. Contesting the election in almost every state, they now proceeded to beat the party of Jackson at its own game.

The Democratic convention had little choice but to renominate Van Buren; but it dropped vice-president Richard M. Johnson, whose private life—he had fathered two daughters by a mulatto mistress—powerfully offended the sensibilities of Southerners. Unable to agree on a substitute, the convention left the choice to the voters. The Democratic platform endorsed the Independent Treasury and condemned federally sponsored internal improvements, a national bank, and protective tariffs.

The early front runner for the Whig nomination was Henry Clay. The veteran Senator from Kentucky had been the chief spokesman for Whiggery and master of the anti-Jackson forces in Congress. The new professional politicians in the Whig Party, however, had a different strategy in mind. Men like Thurlow Weed of New York wanted a candidate with "availability"—someone inoffensive who could appeal to a broad spectrum of the electorate. Clay was too closely identified with the Bank of the United States, and had too many enemies. The Whigs especially wanted a military hero. Their convention passed over Clay and chose William Henry Harrison. In an attempt to balance the ticket geographically, the Whigs selected as Harrison's running mate John Tyler of Virginia, a states' rights strict constructionist. Because there were divergent views within the party on national issues, the Whigs adjourned without drafting a platform.

The Log Cabin Campaign. Born on a Virginia plantation in 1773, the son of a signer of the Declaration of Independence, Harrison began his career in the Old Northwest, first as an army officer, then as governor of Indiana Territory. His rout of Tecumseh's outnumbered Indians at Tippecanoe in 1811 had made him a national hero. As commander in the Northwest during the War of 1812, he won the important Battle of the Thames, finally driving the British and their Indian allies off American soil. After the war, Harrison divided his time between his farm in Ohio, and brief service as a United States Senator and minister to Colombia. Thereafter, however, his career languished and he was serving as a county clerk in 1836 when the Whigs tapped him as one of their presidential candidates. His strong showing at the polls—he

National Convention of Whig Young Men, Baltimore, May 4, 1840. *(Courtesy, The Municipal Museum of the City of Baltimore.)*

got over half the Whig vote—kept him in public view until 1840.

At first, the Democrats professed joy at the Whigs's decision to run "Granny" Harrison (he was sixty-seven) instead of Clay. But when a Democratic newspaper, sneering at Harrison's presumed lack of sophistication, suggested that he would be content with a barrel of hard cider, a log cabin, and a pension of $2000 a year, the Whigs seized on the remark. Mounting an elaborate campaign, they cast Harrison in Jackson's image and portrayed the Whigs as the friends of the people.

In their songs and speeches Whig orators glorified Harrison as a plain, virtuous farmer whose cabin door (he actually owned three thousand acres and lived in a substantial home) was always open to strangers. "Matty" Van Buren, by contrast, was pictured as a bloated aristocrat, squandering the public funds on lavish White House entertainments in the midst of a depression. One Whig song declaimed:

Old Tip he wears a homespun coat,
He has no ruffled shirt-wirt-wirt.
But Mat he has the golden plate,
And he's a little squirt-wirt-wirt.

The Whigs held parades and rallies, with floats, flags, bands, and endless replicas of log cabins. They paraded fake Indians, to remind the voters of Harrison's record of Indian fighting. Another reminder was their catchy campaign slogan, "Tippecanoe and Tyler Too!" Barrels of cider were everywhere, with sweet cider for the drys and hard for the wets. The E.C. Booz Company of Philadelphia packaged its Old Cabin whiskey in cabin-shaped bottles, incidentally giving rise to the word "booze." Wealthy Whigs dressed in homespun and boasted of their humble upbringing. The party distributed a campaign newspaper, the *Log Cabin*, and countless songbooks in the first musical campaign of American history:

Farewell, dear Van,
You're not our man;
To guide the ship,
We'll try old Tip!

Or

Who never did a noble deed?
Who of the people took no heed?
Who is the worst of tyrant's breed?
Van Buren!

The Democrats tried to counter hard cider with hard money, pointing to the newly established Independent Treasury. No one listened. "We could meet the Whigs on the field of argument and beat them without effort," a Democrat lamented. "But when they lay down the weapons of argument and attack us with musical notes, what can we do?" Attracted by the ballyhoo and angry over the depression, nearly eighty percent of the eligible voters went to the polls. Harrison won a clear-cut victory, carrying nineteen out of twenty-six states and fifty-three percent of the two-party vote. Nearly unnoticed in the hullabaloo was the Liberty Party, whose meager 6,225 votes represented an early stirring of antislavery politics in the North.

The election of 1840 established a new pattern in American politics. For the first time a President had been saddled with responsibility for hard times and turned out of office. The carnival atmosphere of the campaign inaugurated a tradition of "shouting and hurrahing" that has persisted in American presidential elections. The public had clearly adopted politics as its favorite spectator sport, and the presidential campaign as its most important national ritual. For the rest of the nineteenth century, Americans in great numbers—usually about eighty percent of the electorate—would cheer for their party and vote for its presidential candidate.

Points To Think About

1. If Andrew Jackson's presidency represented the symbol rather than the substance of democratic rule, the symbol was nonetheless important and has continued to count for much in American politics. Highly successful politicians are, virtually by definition, highly uncommon men and women. Jackson himself is a good example. He was a member of the slaveholding aristocracy. Yet he presented himself as the embodiment of the common folk. And his successors have felt the necessity to do the same. When Jimmy Carter after his inauguration in 1977 walked up Pennsylvania Avenue instead of riding in the pres-

idential limousine, holding hands with his wife and daughter, he was a twentieth-century Jackson. And Jackson, for his part, had been consciously seeking to revive Jefferson's simplicity of manner.

It is ironic that the chief exemplars of the American preference for the "common touch" should have been aristocrats like Jefferson and Jackson. Yet the popular insistence that leaders at least maintain the appearance of being one of them is not to be sneered at. It has saved American politics from endless pretentiousness. And a little hypocrisy seems a small price to pay for such a blessing.

2. Andrew Jackson's grasp of the economic issues associated with the question of rechartering the second Bank of the United States was so uncertain that historians have sometimes wondered whether he had any reasons for attacking it. Perhaps, some have speculated, he opposed it simply because it was there. A variant of this theory is somewhat more plausible. As put forward by Rush Welter in his massive study *The American Mind 1820–1860,* this explanation suggests that Jackson objected to the bank not because it adopted one or another policy but because it had great power.

Jackson was in a number of ways the heir of the Jeffersonian distrust of organized power. Power was, in his mind, antithetical to liberty. So it was not how the bank used its power that Jackson disliked. It was the simple fact that the bank had the power to act decisively. Any bank worthy of the name of course had to have such power. That was the whole reason for having a central bank. And so Jackson took on not merely Biddle's bank, but the whole idea of the central banking system.

Jackson's veto was itself, however, an exercise of power. And historians generally agree that Jackson enormously strengthened the office of the presidency. This left him open to some of the same charges he had leveled at the Bank. The heart of the matter is that Jackson, and Jacksonians, could not conceive of legitimate power even though they recognized that no government could exist without it.

3. It is no small irony that the Whigs who organized themselves in opposition to Jackson did so in Jacksonian terms. They attacked his personal fitness for office, but even more they attacked his style of leadership calling him "King Andrew." Jackson was a very strong president; and he left the office far stronger than it had been when he first assumed it. But Jackson's political style rested on denunciations of power. Thus he left himself open to like denunciations.

The Whigs were happy to turn Jackson's rhetoric against him. Their attack involved questioning the office of the presidency as a potential source of despotism as was, by extension, the national government as a whole. Whigs came to office in 1840 pledged, as Welter puts it, to a "political ethic of self denial." Their political ambitions, expressed in schemes like Henry Clay's American System, made a self-defeating position. They came into power, that is, with grand plans for developing the American economy and with a platform based on denials of governmental power.

Suggested Readings

The Jacksonian Era has inspired broad historical debate. Edward Pessen's *Jacksonian America* (rev. 1978) is a sharp critique of the traditional view of the Old Hero as the representative of an egalitarian society. Pessen finds little to admire in Jackson and writes of a rigidly stratified society with slight opportunity for mobility. Marvin Meyers's *The Jacksonian Persuasion* (1957) examines certain American ideas and attitudes that attended Jacksonian politics, such as the conviction that the nation, having begun as a virtuous republic, needed a politics of renovation that would recover something of that lost republican austerity. Richard P. McCormick describes *The Second Party System* (1966). Robert V. Remini's *Andrew Jackson* (1966) and subsequent works emphasize the man's administrative skill and the importance of his military campaigns and dealings with the Indians. Michael Paul Rogin's *Fathers and Children: Andrew Jackson and the Subjugation of the American Indian* (1975) is intriguing and debatable psychohistory. Lee Benson's *The Concept of Jacksonian Democracy: New York as a Test Case* (1961) remains provocative. The nullification crisis is the subject of William W. Freehling's *Prelude to Civil War* (1966).

FORREST McDONALD

The framers of the Constitution had distrusted democracy as much as monarchy, fearing that the majority could persecute minorities just as monarchies could oppress the people as a whole. They accordingly set up a government in which power was so divided that no majority, so they hoped, would be likely to have its way completely. But despite the efforts of the framers, American politics became more and more democratic. Democratic politics found its expression in the party system—a system that the Constitution had not provided for.

In the first phase of the development of the party system the Republican party of Thomas Jefferson and James Madison formed itself to combat the policies of the Hamilton Federalists. Real differences in principles and programs divided the two parties. Hamiltonians wanted a strong national government that would encourage capitalistic enterprise and thereby stimulate economic growth and progress; Republicans sought to reduce the activities of the national government, leave most decisions to state and local governments, and let the economy go on in its old agricultural way. But then the Republicans, in the wake of the War of 1812, virtually adopted the Hamiltonian program, grafting on to it a more democratic rhetoric; and for a few years they were for practical purposes the only party. Then a second party system developed, which pitted Whigs against Jacksonian Democrats. The new party system—the one Americans have had ever since—differed radically from the original: it was organized not around principles and policies, but around power and personalities.

As reconstituted during the Jacksonian age, American political parties came to exist solely for the purpose of winning elections and handing out the offices and other benefits that victory brings. It is true that the parties were supposed to stand for something, the Whigs being for a national bank, a protective tariff, internal improvements, and other nationalist measures associated with the Hamiltonian tradition, and the Jacksonian Democrats calling for states' rights, low tariffs, a more careful limitation of activities on the part of the federal government, and other positions connected with the Jeffersonian tradition. Yet each party, in Jackson's time and after, accommodated members who held to some or all of the principles for which the other party claimed to stand. What the parties did at election time was carry out a sort of ritual substitute for war, each presenting itself as standing between the nation and the disaster that the other party would bring, each offering candidates who for the moment captured the hopes and dreams of a portion of the American public. And so the two party system has done ever since. This mock warfare has had little or nothing to do with what the candidates have actually proposed to do once they got in office.

The system performed an immensely valuable social function. It provided ordinary Americans with a sense of participation in public affairs; it strengthened their feeling of being part of the nation; and in bringing into the same political camp Americans of differing economic, social, ethnic, and regional identities, it relieved some of the hostilities that arise from these differences. But it also had some grave weaknesses. It kept genuine issues forever out of focus, and thereby prevented Americans from perceiving their fundamental problems and acting on these through government. The triumph of the Jeffersonian and Jacksonian parties had the long-term effect of making Americans identify democracy with local government and distrust the national government as Jeffersonians and Jacksonians distrusted it. And the party system tended to turn democracy and capitalism into uneasy partners if not incompatible opposites. Americans, to be sure, were attached to the proposition that if the individual seeks by any legitimate means to grow as wealthy as possible, society as a whole will be enriched. But the Jeffersonian and Jacksonian tradition preserved a habit of denouncing winners in the pursuit of wealth as enemies of the people and an equally nonsensical habit of regarding economic activity as a "zero sum game" in which, as in poker, if one man wins, another must necessarily lose. Over the years these habits resulted in a succession of stupid, corrupt, and destructive policies; and in modern times they have produced a policy of taking money on a large scale from people who earn it and giving it to people who do not earn it.

What Was the Party System?

EUGENE D. GENOVESE

The party system that Professor McDonald describes probably deserves credit for temporarily keeping under control the quarrels and hostilities that finally resulted in secession and Civil War. Parties did bring together people of different interests and regions. Parties and the factions within them chose leaders, and those leaders could talk things out in Congress and elsewhere—arriving, for example, at the compromises that from moment to moment seemed to calm the slavery question. If in the end compromise failed, it was because the interests and the ideologies that clashed in the slave issue allowed no ultimate reconciliation.

So let us acknowledge that the party system may have kept secession off for a while. That is perhaps the best we can say of it. Professor McDonald has some severe judgments to make of the party system. I think we can still be tougher on it. Providing the occasion for flamboyant political oratory, it spawned speakers and legislators who aroused chauvinistic emotions in themselves and their audiences as they urged the country on its westward march.

During the period of our history that stretched from the era of good feelings to the Civil War and marked the development of the second party system, the United States pushed to the Pacific to round out a continent and perched itself, more or less self-consciously, for the conquest of world power. It pushed southward, too. It annexed Florida and it carried out a long series of thinly disguised aggressions, interventions, and attempted annexations in the Caribbean and Central America. The westward march took in Texas and plunged into a series of dishonorable and hooligan acts that eventually resulted in the dismemberment of Mexico. Citizens of the United States may not wish to dwell on their nation's having seized half of Mexico's territory after provoking a war and having a president lie about it. Mexicans have longer memories.

The westward march, begun long before the appearance of those disagreeable incidents in the Southwest, has provided much of the stuff of American folklore. And indeed the story of the pioneers and settlers who hacked a modern nation out of a wilderness deserves to rank among the wonders of human history. At its best, and its worst, it displayed ingenuity, vision, heroism. Possibly—some would say probably and others would say certainly—the settlers would have had to take the Indians by violence if they intended to win the continent for western civilization. But along the way sober national leaders, especially among the more conservative Whigs, did advance proposals for more humane, or at least less disgusting, solutions. In the event, the United States, the most democratic, freedom-loving nation in the world, simply took land by force, broke treaty after treaty, lied (possibly to itself) about its intentions and policies, cheated people who often made the terrible mistake of trusting the white man's word, and killed. The job could not have been done more savagely.

The party system did not invent the greed that hungered for land, or the swaggering nationalism that shrilled for expansion and power, or the racism that swept the Indians aside. But it did provide the institutions that encouraged the people to send to our state capitals and to Washington politicians prepared to give voice to our worst emotions and desires. And I disagree with Professor McDonald's suggestion that the political system that grew out of those years has recently encouraged "taking" money from those who have "earned" it and giving it to people who have not. What it has encouraged politicians to do is to flatter the angriest and most selfish of popular emotions—emotions that may turn not only against the well-to-do but more often against the helpless poor.

The Erie Canal at Rochester, New York. Cities prospered all along the canal, which extended from Buffalo, on Lake Erie, to Albany, on the Hudson, opening an economical transportation system from the Great Lakes to the Atlantic. *(Courtesy, New-York Historical Society, New York City)*

CHAPTER 10

De Tocqueville's America 1820–1860

THE ERIE CANAL

The idea of an Erie canal caught George Washington's imagination as early as 1783, when he toured the Mohawk Valley and envisioned "the vast inland navigation of these United States." The patriot poet Joel Barlow in his *The Vision of Columbus* (1787) has the explorer predict the building of a canal "From fair Albania" (Albany) to "the far lakes."

Pushed through the New York legislature in 1817 by Governor De Witt Clinton's powerful political machine, the Erie has been called "the most decisive single event in the history of American transportation." Beginning at Albany on the Hudson, the canal wound 363 miles through the Mohawk River Valley to Buffalo, on Lake Erie. Along the way eighty-three locks lifted the boats up and down the 650-foot elevation, and eighteen stone aqueducts carried the canal over rivers and streams.

The Erie Canal was an immediate success. Before its opening, the cost of hauling grain across the Appalachian foothills to New York City had been three times the market value of wheat, six times that of corn, ten times that of oats. Overnight these stifling transportation costs disappeared, as horses pulled hundred-ton barges loaded with freight along "Clinton's Big Ditch" at rates as low as a cent a ton-mile. At the canal's Albany terminus steamboats took over for the swift and economical trip down the Hudson to New York City. By 1825, when the Erie was completed, toll revenues already exceeded a half-million dollars a year. Soon the canal's entire $7-million cost had been recovered, and state officials ordered the canal widened to accommodate the increased traffic. Towns all along the route from Buffalo to New York City prospered, none more than New York, which became the transportation gateway to the West and the nation's largest port.

Once opened in 1825, the Erie became an essential part of a tourist's itinerary: "The canal is in everybody's mouth," one traveler rather awkwardly expressed it. The bustle and activity, the remarkable circumstances of its construction, its overwhelming success and national importance made it an eighth wonder of the world. The Great Western Canal—one of its more formal names—was but four feet deep and forty feet wide (later deepened to seven feet and widened to seventy).

Mule teams on the towpath zipped the fast passenger boats (called packets) along at the canal speed limit of four miles an hour, while freighters made but one and a half to two miles per hour, and log rafts annoyed everyone with their slowness. Yet the trip was not without its excitement. "Commending my soul to God," remarked a first-time rider boarding at Rochester, "and asking His defense from danger, I stepped on board the canalboat and was soon flying towards Utica."

Long trips by water had always been dangerous, and the idea of taking a trip of over 300 miles in complete safety was fascinating. Mock-heroic epics of the dangers of a storm at sea became a standard bit of Erie folklore: the ship pitching, the captain barking orders, the endless verses celebrating each maritime danger.

In a folk song that has survived to the present day, a chorus defines the real danger of a storm on the canal:

Oh, the E-ri-e was a-risin'
And the gin was a-gettin' low,
And I scarce do think we'll get a drink
'Till we get to Buffalo.

But the story ends happily: Buffalo had not run out of gin and the crew got the bawds, the brawls, and the inevitable night in the cooler they had demanded:

Oh the girls are in the Police Gazette,
The crew are all in jail,
And I'm the only living sea cook's son
That's left to tell the tale.

And Buffalo was the "tame" end of the canal. At the other end, in Watervliet near Albany, the notorious "side-cut" area with its twenty-nine saloons in two blocks (with names like The Black Rag and The Tub of Blood), its fights, its large-scale vice, and an occasional body floating in the canal gained the district the title "The Barbary Coast of the East."

The Erie traveler saw a splendid microcosm of young America. The men and women who made the canal work, "part water, part sand, part wind . . . but all canawler," were a colorful lot. The tough Irish workers who had dug the ditch now crewed the boats. The pompous captains, the fierce lockkeepers in endless battle with the crews, the floating showboats, saloons, general stores, and vice dens were famous among travelers, as were the legendary cooks: one "with a bosom like a boxcar," another who "stood six feet in her socks; her hand was like an elephant's ear, her breath would open locks."

These slow boats to Buffalo allowed remarkable freedom for travelers to see the countryside when they were not ducking under the famous low bridges. Even on the packets, a passenger could walk the towpath alongside the boat for exercise. On the slower boats, poor travelers could step ashore and forage for their food, picking berries and hunting rabbits. And the scenes were grand: bustling ports, ingenious locks and romantic swamps, rivers and streams, and magnificent aqueducts; curious bridges of water allowed ships to pass over such picturesque obstacles. Sometimes the canal cut straight through primeval forests with no hint of man's work but the calm swath of canal and towpath. A British visitor, Mrs. Trollope, the most vinegary of travelers, complained that "From the canal nothing is seen to advantage, and very little is seen at all." But another Englishman, the great novelist Charles Dickens, after criticizing the packet's accommodations vividly recalled: "the exquisite beauty of the opening day, when light came glancing off from everything; the gliding on at night so noiselessly, past frowning hills sullen with dark trees and sometimes angry in one red, burning spot high up, where unseen men lay crouching round a fire; the shining out of the bright stars undisturbed by any noise of wheels or steam or any other sound than the limpid rippling of the water as the boat went on; all these were pure delights."

The New Society

When the French nobleman Alexis de Tocqueville began his tour of the United States in 1831, he imagined that he was looking into the very face of the modern democratic future. His *Democracy in America*, published here in translation in the late 1830s, described a nation of exploding energies, of individualists throwing lifetimes of force and work into the pursuit of achievement. At first skeptical about democracy, he nevertheless liked much of what he saw. He was respectfully surprised that American society had managed to enjoy so much liberty amid an equality that he had thought to be an enemy to liberty. And yet he found American individualism flawed. The haste to succeed prevented the slow cultivation of excellence, and the individual American, lacking smaller communities and classes with which to identify, was pitifully submissive to public opinion as a whole.

Tocqueville's analysis of early nineteenth-century American individualism does not take adequate account of powerful elements of community and cooperation, in neighborhoods, in churches, in voluntary associations and activities. And in describing the American mentality as one of submission to public opinion, he was writing too early to see the full flowering of an American literature of private visions and of brooding inquiry into the deeps of the soul. Nathaniel Hawthorne and Edgar Allen Poe were not far into their careers; the works of Herman Melville and still other seers into the secret heart were yet to come. These writers might have revealed to him a side of the American mind that was hauntingly introspective rather than bustlingly aggressive. Tocqueville's portrayal of the energetic American, free to chase after wealth, did not fit the case of Americans condemned to struggle and isolation on farms, or pressed down into the poverty of the growing cities. And of course, as he knew, it did not apply to the black slaves. But Tocqueville offers a starting point for discussion of a society that was, by and large, bursting with energy and hope, and committed to democracy, with its conflicting urges toward freedom and toward conformity.

Economic Developments: The Transportation Revolution

In 1808, when Secretary of the Treasury Albert Gallatin proposed his ambitious system of internal improvements at federal expense, it took a New Yorker three days to travel to Boston, ten days to reach Charleston, and nearly six weeks to journey west to St. Louis. The movement of bulky or heavy goods over long distances by land was prohibitively expensive: it cost more to drag a ton of iron overland a few miles than to bring it across the ocean. Farmers and merchants still depended mainly on waterways to move their crops and merchandise. Coastwise shipping was inexpensive but slow. Inland areas were peculiarly dependent upon river transportation. But this was strictly a one-way affair—downstream. The flatboats that floated down to New Orleans with Western produce had to be broken up for lumber, and the boatmen left to get home as best they could. Sectional jealousies and constitutional squabbles prevented the passage of Gallatin's and Clay's plans for internal improvements. Transportation remained haphazard and wasteful. Nonetheless, the fragmented American republic slowly linked itself up into a connected whole.

Turnpikes. Early American roads were little more than broad, stump-filled paths through the forest. Impassable in wet weather, they were adequate only for local needs. A system of through routes, bringing together the chief commercial centers, was desperately needed. In the 1790s private corporations had begun building turnpikes along the most important routes of travel. These companies financed construction mainly by the sale of stock to investors, and sought profits by collecting tolls from people using the roads. The best turnpikes had a firm stone foundation overlaid with gravel, drainage ditches for run-off, and substantial stone or

Deck Life on the Paragon, **one of Fulton's steamboats.** *(Courtesy, The Metropolitan Museum of Art, Rogers Fund, 1942)*

wooden bridges. The extreme difficulty of moving men and material during the War of 1812 stimulated a boom in turnpike construction. By 1825 these roads crisscrossed New England and the Mid-Atlantic states; Pennsylvania alone had about 2400 miles of toll road. In the West and South, where private capital was scarce, state and local governments often financed the turnpikes. The greatest of them all, the National Road, was built by the federal government. Begun in 1811, it ultimately stretched from Cumberland, Maryland, to Vandalia, Illinois. Travelers on this great western highway encountered an endless stream of people on foot, on horseback, in stagecoaches, on one-horse wagons, and driving lumbering teamster wagons.

Few of these turnpikes ever showed a profit to their owners. Maintenance proved a constant drain. The public devoted considerable ingenuity to outwitting toll collectors: short roads popularly known as "shunpikes" frequently circled around the toll gates. The turnpikes, although popular with travelers, failed to provide economical long-distance freight transportation. Even where tolls were low, it was not profitable for heavy wagons with six- and eight-horse teams to make long hauls over them. Many of the turnpike companies had failed even before the emergence of competition from canals and railroads.

Steamboats. The steamboat provided the first economical inland transportation for both freight and people. Men had been experimenting worldwide for years with the application of steam power to water transportation, but it remained for Robert Fulton, a young American engineer, to perfect an efficient design. His steamboat, equipped with an English-built engine and paddle wheels, averaged five miles per hour on its first voyage up New York's Hudson River in 1807. Spectators on shore watched in astonishment as it overtook the sluggish sailing vessels and "passed them as if they had been at anchor." Fulton and his partner, Robert R. Livingston, tried to keep exclusive control over their invention, but steam navigation was too important to be monopolized. By the time the

Supreme Court, in *Gibbons v. Ogden* (1824), formally annulled the Fulton-Livingston monopoly in New York, steamboats had been introduced on every major river in the country.

The years from 1820 to 1850 were the age of the steamboat. On Eastern rivers, harbors, and bays, steamboats served primarily as passenger vessels. They were designed for speed and comfort, with razor bows, long narrow hulls, giant paddle wheels amidships, and elegantly furnished cabins. Even larger boats plied the Great Lakes, carrying thousands of immigrants west to Detroit and Chicago. But it was in the fertile valley of the Mississippi that steamboats had their greatest importance. Ingenious shipbuilders quickly adapted them to navigate the Western rivers even at low water. Hulls were made broad and shallow, engines and cabins placed on deck, and paddle wheels moved to the stern. Western rivermen boasted that all they needed for successful navigation was a heavy dew. Some of their boats could operate in water as shallow as thirty inches. These floating rafts at last made it economical to ship the bulky exports of the interior to market. Receipts of produce at New Orleans leaped from $12 million in 1820-21 to a peak of $197 million in 1850-51. There larger ships took on the grain and cotton for destinations on the East Coast or in Europe. On their return upstream the steamboats carried consumer goods formerly hauled overland at enormous cost. More than anything else, these ungainly boats brought the West firmly into the national economy.

Canals. Knowing the success of the early English canals, landlocked Americans had talked for years of linking the nation's navigable rivers and lakes with artificial waterways. A major obstacle was the inability of private capital to supply the large sums—$25,000 a mile or more—necessary for canal construction. By 1816 only about a hundred miles of canals had been constructed in the United States, most less than two miles long. None had returned a profit to their owners. Then came the Erie Canal.

The success of the Erie touched off a nationwide boom in canal-building. Several Eastern states, jealous of New York's position, tried to tap the Western market with canals of their own. Pennsylvania's "Main Line" system over the Allegheny Mountains required a portage railroad—a stairstep of inclined planes by which cable cars carried the canal boats up one side of the highest ridges and down the other. In the West, Ohio and Indiana raced to link the waters of Lake Erie and the Ohio River. Indiana's contribution, the Wabash and Erie Canal, was over 450 miles long. By 1840, when the boom collapsed, the American people had constructed over 3300 miles of canals, at a total cost of $125 million. State governments provided most of this huge capitalization, selling bonds against anticipated revenues. Few states or bondholders recovered even a fraction of their investment. Many of the canals were poorly planned and constructed; maintenance costs were high; ice or low water closed them at certain seasons. Nevertheless, these costly ditches greatly stimulated the economy. They offered the first economical means of transferring the bulky products of the West directly eastward.

Railroads. The nation soon had a more satisfactory, cheap, fast, dependable, and profitable overland transportation as Americans took an early interest in another English development, the railroad. Construction of a few small tramways began in the United States during the 1820s, and in 1828 the first major railroad, the Baltimore and Ohio, was chartered. Many early railroads ran only short distances, being designed to serve mainly as feeders into nearby rivers and canals, but major Eastern cities like

Peter Cooper's "Tom Thumb," the first locomotive made in America, racing with a horse-car on the Baltimore-Ohio line, 1830. *(Courtesy, New York Public Library)*

Boston and Baltimore, which lacked adequate water connections, promoted longer lines. Merchants of Charleston, South Carolina, anxious to divert upcountry cotton shipments to their wharves, built a railroad to Hamburg on the lower Savannah River. When completed in 1833, it extended 136 miles and was the longest railroad in the world. In these years ingenious American inventors made a number of important technical improvements in the design of locomotives and roadbeds. By 1840 the nation's total railway mileage equaled that of canals, and many lines were competing successfully with canal companies for business.

Railroads, like other forms of transportation, received public aid. Between 1830 and 1843 the national government lowered tariff duties on railroad iron. State legislatures—once again taking the lead in such public assistance—granted tax incentives, required newly chartered banks to invest in railroad stock, extended large grants, and sometimes operated lines directly. Added to the foreign capital that American railroads attracted, government help provided strong impetus to private companies. Almost 9000 miles of track were laid in the 1840s and 22,000 more in the next decade. At the beginning of the Civil War railroads overshadowed all other forms of long-distance transportation in the country.

Economic Developments: Immigration

The transportation revolution, making the movement of goods vastly easier and cheaper, opened up a large new potential market for manufactured products. But where were the workers to produce these goods? From colonial times, labor had been in short supply in America. Cheap land was so available that people could work their own land instead of hiring out their labor. In 1800 only ten percent of the white labor force were "employees," persons who sold their labor. The rest of the working force were farmers, self-employed artisans and mechanics, and independent tradesmen.

Early manufacturers experimented with various ways of overcoming this acute labor scarcity. One was the "domestic" or "putting-out" system. Entrepreneurs furnished raw materials to people who worked in their own homes, mak-

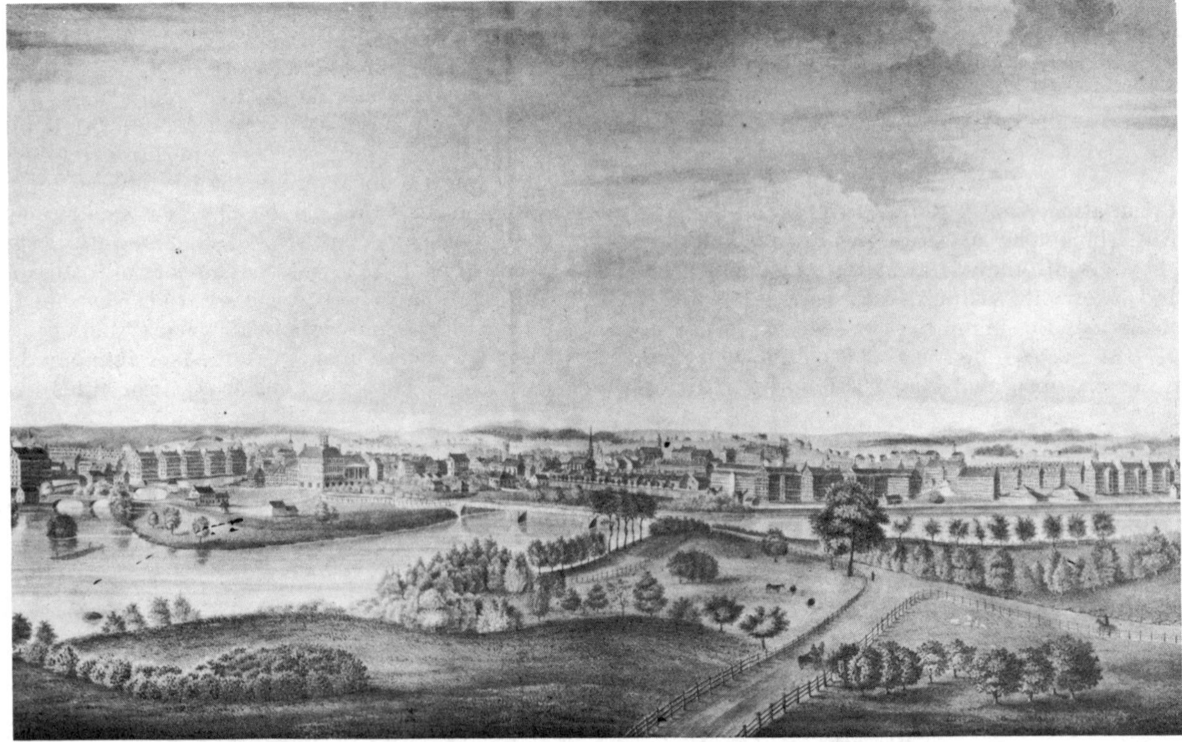

Lowell, Massachusetts, one of the thriving mill towns of New England in the 1830s and 1840s. *(Courtesy, New Stokes Collection, New York Public Library)*

ing cloth, shoes, and wearing apparel; the entrepreneurs then collected and marketed the finished product. In a predominantly agricultural country, where most people lived in rural areas, this system, though cumbersome, allowed manufacturers to tap a tremendous pool of part-time labor, especially women and children. Other businessmen tried to centralize production, hiring whole families whom they housed in tenements adjacent to their mills. But as factories grew larger, requiring a labor force of hundreds, even thousands, factory owners turned increasingly to the Waltham system.

The Waltham System. This system was the brainchild of Francis Cabot Lowell, an early textile manufacturer. Anxious to recruit young women from New England farms to work in his mill at Waltham, Massachusetts, Lowell built dormitories nearby to house them. In order to counteract the widespread reputation of mills as places of loose morals, he placed these dormitories in charge of respectable widows who maintained rigid rules of conduct. The factory girls typically had to be in their rooms by 10 p.m., to attend church regularly, and to save part of their earnings. A few mills sponsored evening classes and libraries for their workers.

Lowell's plan was an immediate success. Young women welcomed the chance to get away from the farm for a few years and to earn a little money of their own. In the 1820s and 1830s they flocked by the thousands to New England mill towns like Lowell, Chicopee, and Manchester. Visitors to the textile factories usually praised the Waltham system. After a tour in 1834, Davy Crockett described Lowell's "mile of gals" as "well-dressed, lively, and genteel" and happy in their work. Many of the female workers were not so enthusiastic. They objected to the length of the work day, the low wages, the overcrowded dormitories, and the close supervision of their lives. Above all, they opposed a series of attempts by the mill owners to increase the amount of work—"speed up" and "stretch out"—and reduce the pay. A group of the more experienced workers founded the Lowell Female Reform Association, which may be viewed as one of the first labor unions in the United States. Ultimately, their two large strikes and their appeal to the Massachusetts State Legislature failed to accomplish their goals. The rapid increase in the immigration of destitute Irish during the 1840s permitted the owners to turn to a new and more dependent supply of labor. The Lowell mill girls had, in their own way,

TIME TABLE OF THE LOWELL MILLS,

Arranged to make the working time throughout the year average 11 hours per day.

TO TAKE EFFECT SEPTEMBER 21st., 1853.

The Standard time being that of the meridian of Lowell, as shown by the Regulator Clock of AMOS SANBORN, Post Office Corner, Central Street.

From March 20th to September 19th, inclusive.

COMMENCE WORK, at 6.30 A. M. LEAVE OFF WORK, at 6.30 P. M., except on Saturday Evenings.
BREAKFAST at 6 A. M. DINNER, at 12 M. Commence Work, after dinner, 12.45 P. M.

From September 20th to March 19th, inclusive.

COMMENCE WORK at 7.00 A. M. LEAVE OFF WORK, at 7.00 P. M., except on Saturday Evenings.
BREAKFAST at 6.30 A. M. DINNER, at 12.30 P.M. Commence Work, after dinner, 1.15 P. M.

BELLS.

From March 20th to September 19th, inclusive.

Morning Bells.	*Dinner Bells.*	*Evening Bells.*
First bell, ... 4.30 A. M.	Ring out, ... 12.00 M.	Ring out, ... 6.30 P. M.
Second, 5.30 A. M.; Third, 6.20.	Ring in, ... 12.35 P. M.	Except on Saturday Evenings.

From September 20th to March 19th, inclusive.

Morning Bells.	*Dinner Bells.*	*Evening Bells.*
First bell, ... 5.00 A. M.	Ring out, ... 12.30 P. M.	Ring out at. . . . . 7.00 P. M.
Second, 6.00 A. M.; Third, 6.50.	Ring in, ... 1.05 P. M.	Except on Saturday Evenings.

SATURDAY EVENING BELLS.

During APRIL, MAY, JUNE, JULY, and AUGUST, Ring Out, at 6.00 P. M.
The remaining Saturday Evenings in the year, ring out as follows:

SEPTEMBER.
First Saturday, ring out 6.00 P. M.
Second " " 5.45 "
Third " " 5.30 "
Fourth " " 5.20 "

OCTOBER.
First Saturday, ring out 5.05 P. M.
Second " " 4.55 "
Third " " 4.45 "
Fourth " " 4.35 "
Fifth " " 4.25 "

NOVEMBER.
First Saturday, ring out 4.15 P. M.
Second " " 4.05 "

NOVEMBER.
Third Saturday ring out 4.00 P. M.
Fourth " " 3.55 "

DECEMBER.
First Saturday, ring out 3.50 P. M.
Second " " 3.55 "
Third " " 3.55 "
Fourth " " 4.00 "
Fifth " " 4.00 "

JANUARY.
First Saturday, ring out 4.10 P. M.
Second " " 4.15 "

JANUARY.
Third Saturday, ring out 4.25 P. M.
Fourth " " 4.35 "

FEBRUARY.
First Saturday, ring out 4.45 P. M.
Second " " 4.55 "
Third " " 5.00 "
Fourth " " 5.10 "

MARCH.
First Saturday, ring out 5.25 P. M.
Second " " 5.30 "
Third " " 5.35 "
Fourth " " 5.45 "

YARD GATES will be opened at the first stroke of the bells for entering or leaving the Mills.

•.• *SPEED GATES commence hoisting three minutes before commencing work.*

Penhallow, Printer, Wyman's Exchange, 28 Merrimack St.

constituted something of an elite labor force. When they struck they claimed the rights of direct heiresses of the Revolution, daughters of the sons of liberty.

European Immigrants. Nothing had prepared the country for the mass immigration that took place in the first half of the nineteenth century. Previously immigrants had come in trickles. After 1815, especially beginning in the mid-1840s, they came in endless waves, fleeing from economic distress or political turmoil in their homelands. Between 1815 and 1860 4,777,000 immigrants entered the country—more than the entire population of the United States in 1790. The largest number, over 2,000,000, came from Ireland, many to work on the construction of the Erie Canal or the railroads. Germany ranked second as a country of origin, with 1.5 million. Another 750,000 arrived from England, Scotland, and Wales; most of the remainder were from Switzerland and Scandinavia.

These immigrants, many of them illiterate, unskilled, without resources, had little in common with those who had come before the War of 1812. Lacking the knowledge and money to undertake farming on the frontier, and anxious to remain near their fellow countrymen, most of the newcomers did not venture far from the ports of arrival. Crowded into cities, they formed an enormous pool of unskilled labor, ripe for exploitation. Some found jobs in the Pennsylvania coal fields and Illinois lead mines. During the 1840s immigrants rapidly began to replace native farmers' daughters in New England textile and shoe factories. The paternalistic spirit of Lowell vanished. "I regard people just as I regard my machinery," a manufacturer explained in 1855:

> So long as they can do my work for what I choose to pay them, I keep them, getting out of them all I can. What they do or how they fare outside my wall I don't know, nor do I consider it my business to know. They must look out for themselves as I do for myself. When my machines get old and useless, I reject them and get new, and these people are part of my machinery.

Neither the factory system nor the great canal and railroad projects of the period could have come into existence so quickly without this foreign labor. Between 1830 and 1850, immigrants supplied nearly half the increase in the free working force. But exploitation brought poverty, disease, and crime.

Economic Developments: Industrialization

Improved transportation unified the national economy; mass immigration provided the necessary labor force. Only one additional ingredient was yet required for the American economy to take off—a native technology capable of sustaining mass production.

Here again, the nation was at first heavily dependent on Britain. When Robert Fulton designed his steamboat, he had the engine made in England, for no one in the United States could produce such a complex piece of machinery.

Inventions. Why did Americans succeed in winning independence from European technology? It has been suggested that Britain's restriction on the export of textile machinery and even on the emigration of skilled mechanics unwittingly forced Americans to become inventive. But this is doubtful. The presence in this country of British machines and artisans might have stimulated American inventiveness. It has also been thought that the chronic shortage of labor compelled Americans to devise labor-saving machinery. This, again, is unconvincing. No matter how much labor is available, a progressive society will contain people of inquisitive mind who will be busy inventing machines to make that labor more effective. But certain facts of American society and culture may explain why technology grew so rapidly here. Freedom from traditional class barriers and the absence of guilds—the associations of craftsmen that in Europe had regulated the conditions and techniques of their trades—allowed Americans to experiment. Perhaps also the nation's natural wealth and the spread of prosperity among its citizens enticed Americans to see how the bounty at their disposal could be made even richer through technology. And the inventiveness that flowered amid this freedom and this promise was not for the sake of material gain alone: intellectual curiosity and an urge to invent were then powerful motives, as they have been in other times of technological and scientific experimentation.

During the first half of the nineteenth century, inventions multiplied. Besides developing the automated grist mill, Oliver Evans pioneered in the design of the high-pressure

McCormick's self-raking reaper was one of the many inventions that transformed American agriculture in the 1800s.

steam engine, a distinct improvement over the British engines of Newcomen and Watt Norbert. Rillieux, a free black, invented a multiple-effect evaporator to process the sugar cane grown in his native Louisiana. The endless fields stimulated significant improvements in farm machinery. Before Cyrus McCormick invented his reaper in 1831 a man with a sickle could cut approximately one acre of wheat in a day; with a reaper he could harvest ten to twelve. In 1837 John Deere perfected a steel plow capable of turning the tough prairie sod of Iowa and Illinois. In 1860 the United States Patent Office issued 4589 new patents, a five hundred percent increase over 1820.

While inventions transformed basic industries and with them much of American life, other ingenious tinkerers sought to increase the comforts of the home: the steam radiator for home heating; an immensely important ice-making machine; condensed milk and concentrated coffee (which came in a cube, light, and with sugar), both invented by Gail Borden in the 1850s; the paper window shade; hundreds of different kinds of new stoves and lamps; thousands of household gadgets. A comfortable, efficient home sheltering a happy and sturdy family was an implicit part of the American democratic ideal, and technology rushed to further it.

Along with new inventions came a specifically American development: mass production employing interchangeable parts. This concept had originated in Europe, but an American, Eli Whitney, first applied it successfully. His unsuccessful fight to get a legal monopoly on his cotton gin had impoverished the inventor. Anxious to recoup his fortunes, Whitney struck upon an idea for producing great numbers of muskets quickly. According to this scheme, a factory making muskets would not make each one separately from parts constructed for it alone, but would make every component part in great quantity and then assemble the parts into identical muskets. In time the spread of interchangeable parts made it possible for owners of damaged objects to send away to a factory for the needed part, confident that the new one would precisely substitute for the old. "In short," Whitney wrote federal officials in 1798, "the tools which I contemplate are similar to an engraving on copper plate from which may be taken a great number of impressions exactly alike."

This was a bold proposal at a time when gunsmiths still made muskets one at a time, filing and fitting the individual pieces to mate them into a working mechanism. The government, then fearful of war with France, and highly respectful of Whitney's talents, accepted his audacious offer to manufacture ten thousand muskets in twenty-eight months. Whitney badly underestimated the difficulties of tooling up for this kind of operation; he was several years late in delivering the promised muskets. Gradually, however, his "uniformity system" gained acceptance, and it was applied in dozens of industries. Americans proved especially adept at designing and building the lathes, borers, and calipers necessary for the precision manufacture of parts for clocks, watches, and sewing machines.

On the eve of the Civil War, industrialization was far advanced in the United States. A modern transportation network had been laid down. A sufficient labor force had been assembled. The factory system had largely displaced household manufacture. Several industries—textiles, carpets, shoes, paper—were thoroughly mechanized. The American economy had begun to assume its now familiar shape.

Manufacturing on a mass scale altered American expectations. From colonial days the material environment had been permanent. People lived in the same houses, used the same furniture, employed the same implements, wore the same clothes, and viewed the same scene from youth to old age. Variety was the privilege of the rich. With the growth of manufactures all this changed. The material surroundings of the average American became diversified in ways undreamed of before. Americans were learning to live in a perpetually changing environment. Their surroundings increasingly taught them that the physical world of buildings, vehicles, implements of work could change over and over, as the older, stable, agricultural environments had once taught people that the world never changes much.

The Land and the People: The Northeast and Mid–Atlantic

Between 1820 and 1860 manufacturing grew rapidly in the New England and Mid-Atlantic states. Both sections boasted readily available capital and labor, and superior transportation. Turnpikes, rivers, the Erie Canal, and safe harbors provided good access to raw materials and markets. Commerce and agriculture, particularly dairy and truck farming, remained important in the region, but southern New England and the Hudson and Delaware river valleys began to resemble the most industrialized areas of Great Britain in their economy and social structure.

Factory Life. The conditions of labor changed fundamentally after 1820, as independent craftsmen, many men, women, and children from farms, and masses of immigrants became wage earners. With the widespread adoption of steam power in the 1840s, factories no longer had to be located in rural areas, close to free-flowing streams, but could be placed near cities. Henceforth workers were completely divorced from the land. With the influx of immigrant labor, wages and working conditions deteriorated in many industries. Most workers had no protection against long hours, occupational hazards, illness, or unemployment. The limited attempts at unionization in this period failed in the face of public hostility and periodic panics that so depressed the economy as to make it impossible for workers to survive in a strike. Not until 1842, in the case of *Commonwealth v. Hunt*, did the Massachusetts Supreme Court uphold the legality of trade unions. White Southerners could be as shocked at the condition of Northern "free" labor as some Northerners were at slavery. Free labor, wrote George Fitzhugh of Virginia, "is more cruel, in leaving the laborer to take care of himself and family out of the pittance which skill or capital have allowed him to retain. When the day's labor is ended, he is free, but he is overburdened with the cares of family and household, which make his freedom an empty and delusive mockery. . . . The Negro slave is free, too, when the labors of the day are over, and free in mind as well as body; for the master provides food, raiment, house, fuel, and everything else necessary for the physical well-being of himself and family."

Cities. Industrialism, immigration, and the expanding transportation system brought a more rapid growth of cities than has occurred at any other time in American history, before or since. In 1820 only 6.1 percent of the population lived in urban areas (that is, places of 2500 or more inhabitants); by 1860 close to twenty percent of the people were city dwellers. On the eve of the Civil War there were fifteen cities (nine of them in the Northeast) with populations in excess of fifty thousand. Philadelphia exceeded 500,000 and New York passed 1,000,000.

The cities were hopelessly ill-equipped to deal with these numbers of people. Municipal water and sewage systems were in their infancy. Pigs roamed the streets in every city, the only effective street cleaners. Housing was always in short supply. Many people lived in tiny apartments; often a whole family, and perhaps a few boarders, were crowded into the same room. The poorest lived in unfinished cellars. In 1849 a Boston doctor found "one cellar . . . occupied nightly as a sleeping-apartment for thirty-nine persons. In another, the tide had risen so high that it was necessary to approach the bedside of a patient by means of a plank which was laid from one stool to another; while the dead body of an infant was actually sailing about the room in its coffin."

Cities festered in filth, overcrowding, and poverty. Cholera epidemics in 1832 and 1849 killed thousands. Fires were an everyday occurrence, sometimes leveling whole sections of cities. Crime, ranging from prostitution to burglary and murder, flourished everywhere, even on Broadway, where according to one contemporary "whores and blackguards made up about two-thirds of the throng." In response the business and middle classes created or expanded such institutions as the police force. Slowly, grudgingly, but inevitably cities ran up debts to finance water and sewer systems, street lights, schools, and parks.

Cities alternately repelled and fascinated Americans. Moralists condemned them as sinful. Native Protestants shuddered at the rapid growth of ethnic ghettos, where immigrants retained their old customs, languages, and Catholic religion. Americans now confronted contrasts between wealth and poverty that their republic in its egalitarian origins had never imagined. Still, people came to the cities in ever-increasing numbers—to visit, to work, to seek their fortunes. For those who could find steady employment, urban life with its shops, newspapers, amusements, and parks had many fascinations. New York's Crystal Palace Exposition of 1853, a visitor observed, reflected on a smaller scale the

New York's Crystal Palace Exhibition of 1853 recorded the accomplishments of Americans and symbolized the vitality of its cities. *(Courtesy, Eno Collection, The New York Public Library)*

essential characteristics of the city as a whole: "What a wilderness of objects! Statues and statuettes, silks and satins, china and glass, furniture of all descriptions, and for all uses. What bright colors! What never ending glitter! What crowds of people!"

The Land and the People: The Northwest

Farming. Between 1820 and 1860 the American economy showed a growing regional specialization. While manufacturing expanded in the Northeast and the South continued to cultivate staple crops for agriculture, the Northwest turned increasingly to commercial agriculture. The growth of industry, and the resulting rise of cities in the Northeast and in Europe, created a steadily expanding market for farm products. The upper Mississippi and Ohio valleys, with their fertile soil and vast tracts of public land, were in an ideal position to meet this need, especially after canals and railroads made it possible to ship large quantities of meat and grain directly eastward. The Northwest became the nation's breadbasket, supplying food for Northern cities and Southern plantations.

With every decade the centers of production for wheat, corn, cattle, hogs, and sheep shifted westward, as settlers opened the prairies to cultivation. Many of these newcomers had abandoned the thin soils of New England for places like Indiana and Michigan, where wheat yields were several times greater per acre. Farmers from the upper South flocked into the southern counties of Ohio, Illinois, and Indiana, giving that region a distinctively Southern character. Sizable numbers of English, German, and Scandinavian immigrants migrated west, fanning out through the rich farmlands of Iowa, Illinois, Minnesota, and Wisconsin. On the eve of the Civil War the population of the Northwest, which had numbered less than one million in 1820, exceeded nine million.

Farms in the Northwest tended to be small—about 200 acres on the average. Most farmers owned their own land, relying on their families, on hired help, and increasingly on machines for labor. Wheat, always in demand, was the cash crop; and mechanical drills, harvesters, and threshers permitted an enormous increase in production throughout the period.

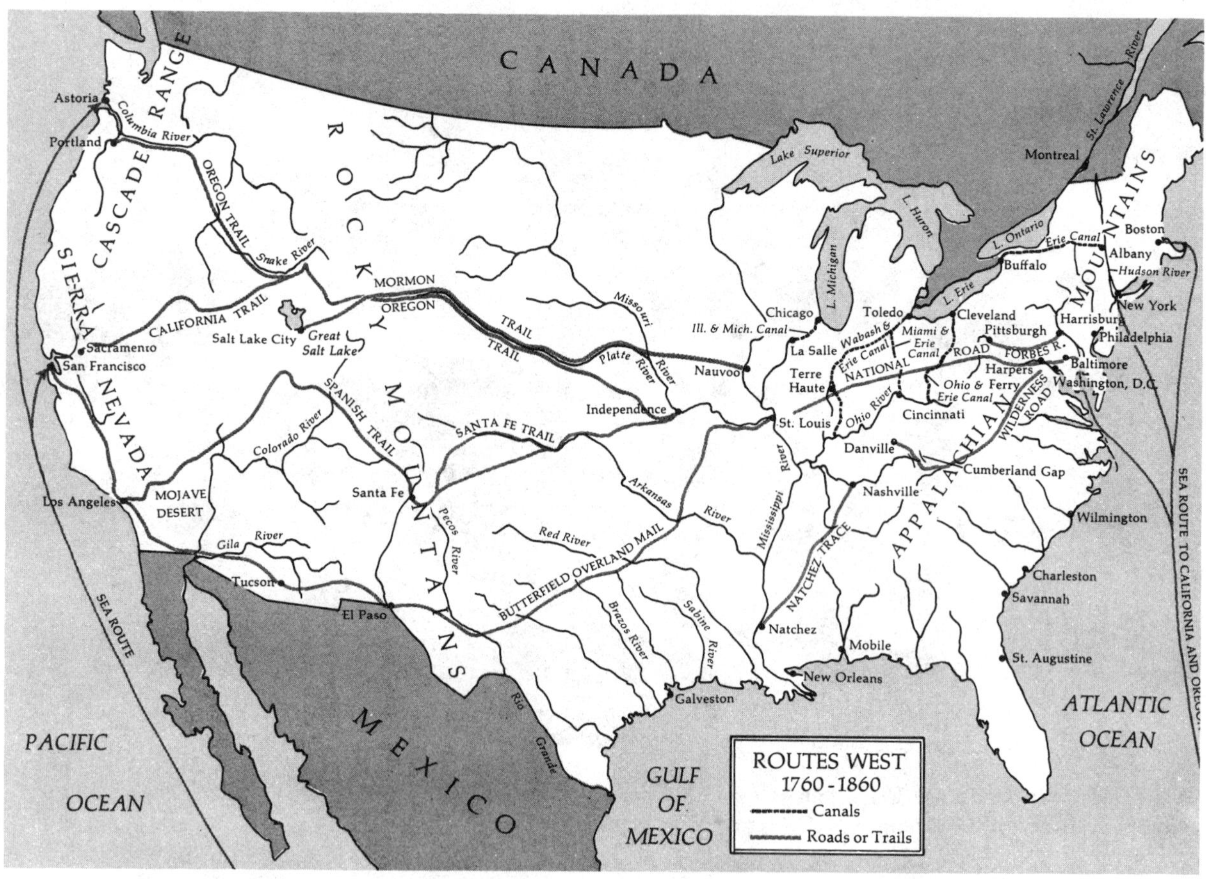

In the 1840s and 1850s wheat dominated farming in the upper Mississippi Valley almost as completely as cotton dominated agriculture in the lower South. Wheat and flour became important export items in the fifties, undermining slightly the dominant position of cotton in American foreign trade. Western farmers also grew much corn and oats, but primarily as feed for livestock. The demands of Eastern cities and Southern planters assured a ready market and good prices for the beef, pork, and mutton of the prairies. Before railroads penetrated the Ohio Valley, cattle were driven overland to market; most hogs were slaughtered and packed locally. Frequently they were "stuck," or cut in the throat—often the pioneer woman's job. Then women and children took out and washed the various innards, saving the bladder to inflate and use as a football. So much pork was processed at Cincinnati that the city became known for a time as "Porkopolis." Later, increasing numbers of livestock were shipped east by rail to city markets for slaughter.

Cities. While the Northwest remained primarily agrarian, the region's cities grew swiftly. Older communities like St. Louis, Cincinnati, and Louisville all expanded rapidly in this period. Even more spectacular was the progress of new cities like Milwaukee, Indianapolis, and especially Chicago. The Windy City had barely 17,000 people when Cyrus McCormick moved his reaper factory there in 1847: thirteen years later the population numbered 109,000. Yet the city remained a raw and uncomfortable place. Its mud was the subject for endless tales. Signs read "No Bottom," "Road to China," or "Man Lost." A story was told of a man who saw a hat in the mud; picking it up, he saw a man's face underneath. "Say, stranger, you're stuck in the mud! Can I give you a hand to pull you out?" "Oh, no, thanks," replied the face, "I'm riding a good horse. He's got me out of the worst spots." These Western cities served principally as extensions of the rural economy, processing, shipping, and marketing agricultural products. Their mills and packinghouses led the country in 1850 in the production of lumber, flour and meal, liquor and meat. The cities were also the site of the growing farm-machinery industry.

The expansion of urban markets had a dramatic effect on sectional alignments. Between

1820 and 1860, Western farmers came increasingly to depend on Eastern cities to purchase their produce, while the industrial Northeast, in turn, found a growing market for its manufactures in the Western states. An economic bond was being forged between the two sections that would undermine the old alliance between the West and the South.

The Land and the People: The South

The antebellum Southern economy was surprisingly diverse. Cotton was "King," but corn was actually the South's most widely grown crop. Many planters in Virginia and Maryland, their soil exhausted after prolonged tobacco cultivation, shifted to raising wheat or cattle. Rice grew in the swampy low country of South Carolina and Georgia. Southern Louisiana produced another exotic crop, sugar. Cotton, the South's major cash crop, was cultivated throughout the lower South. The center of cotton production moved steadily westward after 1820—the inevitable result of overplanting and soil exhaustion. Just before the Civil War over a fourth of the 4.3 million bales grown in the United States came from west of the Mississippi River. Southern industry was limited primarily to the processing of locally grown timber, tobacco, and grain, but a start had been made in the manufacture of cotton goods, machinery, and iron. A number of important cities—Baltimore, Richmond, New Orleans, St. Louis, Charleston, Mobile—dotted the South's navigable perimeter.

The South was not inhabited solely by rich planters, impoverished "white trash," and enslaved blacks. In 1860 the bulk of the South's five and one-half million whites lived on small farms not unlike those in the North. Most farmers owned their land, cultivating it with their own hands or the help of a few slaves. With the exception of rice and sugar, these yeoman farmers raised the same crops as did the planters. Many of them also grazed cattle. Outside of the older states of Virginia and the Carolinas, small farmers frequently moved upward into the planter class. They had little in common with poor whites—the "crackers" or "white trash"—who eked out a meager existence in the sterile sand hills or pine barrens. These unfortunate people existed under miserable living conditions and suffered the ravages of malaria, hookworm and pellagra.

The Planters. The actual number of planters was small. The federal census of 1860—defining a planter as a person owning at least twenty slaves—counted 46,274. Most of these were "small" planters owning up to fifty slaves and 500 to 800 acres. They were hardworking businessmen with field work to supervise, laborers to oversee, books to balance. And their wives seldom conformed to the Southern-belle stereotype. Managing a large household required energy and intelligence, as well as graceful manners. Home was more likely to be a modest frame cottage than a Tara or a Mount Vernon. At the apex of Southern society were the large planters. Although few in number—only 1700 people owned as many as a hundred slaves in 1850—these planter aristocrats cast a giant shadow over the region. Their wealth gave them considerable social and political influence. Living in palatial mansions or elegant townhouses, surrounded by vast fields and liveried servants, they represented the ideal to which other white Southerners aspired before the Civil War.

In spite of this diversity, the South possessed a distinctive flavor. The great majority of Southern whites were Protestant and Anglo-Saxon or Scots-Irish. The economy was colonial: Southerners raised staple crops for export and imported finished goods. Before the Revolution they had traded mainly with England, but in the first half of the nineteenth century Southern trade, because of the lack of local capital to finance merchant shipping, came increasingly under the control of Northerners, and particularly under the dominance of the port of New York. Above all, there was slavery, a uniquely Southern institution that exerted a powerful influence over the region. In 1850 only one white person in four had a vested interest in slavery. But the presence of millions of blacks gave whites of all classes something in common—a determination to keep the South a white man's country. Race consciousness helped to unify the South.

The Slaves. Slaves worked everywhere in the antebellum South: as common laborers, skilled craftsmen, and servants; in factories, mines, and foundries; on riverboats, wharves, and railroads; in hotels, stores, and private homes. A Charleston census of 1848 listed forty-six occupations that employed slaves. Most, of course, worked as field hands. Over half belonged to planters owning twenty or more slaves. These large units were especially common in the newer states of the lower South, where the work was harder and the conditions more brutal than in the older slave states.

On farms of less than ten slaves, the slaves usually worked alongside their masters, who directly supervised their labor. Male slaves frequently performed the same tasks as the farmer and female slaves the same tasks as his wife, though in the busiest seasons all slaves were likely to work in the fields together. On plantations slaves were organized in two ways. Rice planters preferred the task system, allotting individual slaves a particular task for the day. Cotton and tobacco planters favored the gang system, dividing the slaves into work parties under the supervision of an overseer or trusted Negro driver. The plantation routine followed the seasons in a monotonous cycle. Both men and women worked in the fields, plowing and planting in the spring, weeding in the summer, harvesting in the fall. In winter and in slack times, they dug ditches, repaired fences, and sawed wood. Although masters of large plantations usually worked their female slaves as hard as their male slaves, and to assign them to most tasks in the fields, they frequently observed gender distinctions in the organization of labor. Above all, they were likely to organize male and female slaves into work gangs according to gender so that female field hands would work with other female field hands, frequently under the supervision of a male slave. Masters rarely assigned supervisory positions in field work to female slaves. The young and the elderly tended livestock or cared for the small children. Field hands labored from sunrise to sunset, with a rest at midday. They usually had Sunday off and received a week's vacation at Christmas. For many slaves these holidays, with their occasional feasts, dances, and visits to neighboring plantations, provided the only relief from the hardship of their daily lives.

Most slaves lived in rude cabins. Some masters encouraged their bondsmen to marry and live as families; others left the matter to the slaves or assigned them arbitrarily to a mate. The owner provided food, clothing, and medical care. The typical slave's ration consisted of cornmeal, fatback, and molasses; but many slaves varied this boring and unhealthful diet by raising their own vegetables or fishing.

Household servants and city slaves enjoyed a somewhat easier life than field hands. And many slaveholders hired out their bondsmen as servants, laborers, and mechanics, sometimes for extended periods. This practice of "hiring out" was especially common in the upper South and in the cities, where there was frequently a surplus of slaves. Many hired slaves became quasi-free, though the practice of hiring-out normally brought more advantages to male than to female

Slaves who worked the fields labored from sunrise to sunset. The lives of household servants and city slaves was somewhat less rigorous.

slaves. Although female slaves might be hired out as house servants, especially as cooks, their position did not give them much excuse for free movement in the society. Slave women, much like free white women, tended to be confined within households. Masters almost never offered slave women training in such skilled crafts as carpentry or blacksmithing. But the slave men who held those positions received an unusual opportunity to learn to read, to accumulate some money of their own, and, above all, to have an excuse to circulate fairly freely in society. The pool of slave craftsmen provided runaways and participants in revolts in disproportion to its numbers. Women, who did not belong to that pool, were less likely than men to run away or to engage directly in revolts.

Slaves had little motivation to work hard. Although some worked willingly for kindly masters, others delighted in "first-rate tricks to dodge work." Planters combined close supervision with a system of incentives—praise, additional rations, extra holidays—in an attempt to make their slaves work efficiently; but often they found it necessary to resort to whipping, deprivation of privileges, and other punishments to keep them in line. "The only principle that can maintain slavery," slaveholders reluctantly admitted, "tis the principle of fear." Masters who maintained a rigid discipline had the least trouble in the long run. Those who found employing a lash distasteful—and there were many—often saw their plantation go to ruin. Yet punishment too severe could bring the injury or loss of a prime male or fertile female, and no owner would want that. And of course there were cases of affection or respect. Some owners allowed their slaves to acquire property or taught them to read and write.

Slave men lacked many of the powers that free men could draw upon to maintain their control of women, notably the legal powers assigned to husbands and property. Yet slave women, as women, remained vulnerable to particular hardships such as the sexual exploitation of white men and being separated from their children. Slave women's reproductive capacities also afforded them some marginal advantages. Since masters were eager to increase the numbers of their slaves through reproduction—and the slaves of the United States were the only self-reproducing slave population in the New World—they were likely to accord women who claimed to be pregnant some release from work. But overall, slave women did not benefit from the idealization of womanhood that whites cultivated for themselves.

Was slavery profitable to the planters? Although all the evidence is not in, the answer appears to be "yes." Investments in new plantations in the lower South consistently yielded a return upon capital sufficient to attract outside funds, an indication that a well-managed cotton plantation on good soil was at least as profitable as alternative forms of investment. Slaveholders in the less productive regions of the upper South exported their surplus slaves profitably to the Cotton Belt. For the South as a whole slavery was probably less economically beneficial. Four million blacks were kept in the strictest poverty, when as free property owners they could have provided a rich market for the products of Southern agriculture and industry, and as free workers they could have constituted a versatile and energetic work force. Slavery caused white Southerners to concentrate their resources in staple agriculture at the expense of industry and transportation. The human effects of slavery were, of course, horrible; it stifled the intellectual and creative energies of generations of black Americans.

Race Control. Slavery was more than a labor system; it was also a means of race control. The Southern states enacted elaborate slave codes touching virtually all of black life. Slave marriages and divorces had no legal validity. Slaves were forbidden to leave their plantations without a pass, to be out after curfew, to congregate in groups unless a white man was present, to carry arms, or to strike a white person. They could not own property or testify in court against whites. Punishment for most crimes was left to the master, who was given immunity from prosecution should a slave die under "moderate" correction. Death was the penalty for rebellion or plotting to rebel. To enforce these codes, the white males mounted regular patrols, which traveled the neighborhood at night in search of arms or runaways. Members were chosen at militia muster and all members of the community—slaveholders and non-slaveholders alike—were supposed to take their turn.

Enslaved blacks faced the constant task of adjusting to the condition of bondage. Rebellion was rare; outright resistance was suicidal. When Nat Turner, a slave preacher, led a band of armed followers on a bloody rampage through Southampton County, Virginia, in 1831, killing sixty men, women, and children, terrified whites retaliated by slaughtering at least one hundred blacks. The South was on edge for months afterward. No one knew when this black fury, like some smothered volcano, would erupt again. In-

$200 Reward.

RANAWAY from the subscriber, on the night of Thursday, the 30th of Sepember,

FIVE NEGRO SLAVES,

To-wit: one Negro man, his wife, and three children.

The man is a black negro, full height, very erect, his face a little thin. He is about forty years of age, and calls himself *Washington Reed*, and is known by the name of Washington. He is probably well dressed, possibly takes with him an ivory headed cane, and is of good address. Several of his teeth are gone.

Mary, his wife, is about thirty years of age, a bright mulatto woman, and quite stout and strong.

The oldest of the children is a boy, of the name of FIELDING, twelve years of age, a dark mulatto, with heavy eyelids. He probably wore a new cloth cap.

MATILDA, the second child, is a girl, six years of age, rather a dark mulatto, but a bright and smart looking child.

MALCOLM, the youngest, is a boy, four years old, a lighter mulatto than the last, and about equally as bright. He probably also wore a cloth cap. If examined, he will be found to have a swelling at the navel.

Washington and Mary have lived at or near St. Louis, with the subscriber, for about 15 years.

It is supposed that they are making their way to Chicago, and that a white man accompanies them, that they will travel chiefly at night, and most probably in a covered wagon.

A reward of $150 will be paid for their apprehension, so that I can get them, if taken within one hundred miles of St. Louis, and $200 if taken beyond that, and secured so that I can get them, and other reasonable additional charges, if delivered to the subscriber, or to THOMAS ALLEN, Esq., at St. Louis, Mo. The above negroes, for the last few years, have been in possession of Thomas Allen, Esq., of St. Louis.

WM. RUSSELL.

ST. LOUIS, Oct. 1, 1847.

dividual acts of resistance, such as arson, running away, or even suicide, were not uncommon. Instead of confronting their masters directly, blacks developed various stratagems of accommodation and subtle resistance. They became particularly adept at malingering, breaking tools, and otherwise obstructing the workings of a system in which they were not free participants.

The black family may have been a more cohesive unit than historians and sociologists once believed. If plantation records contain instances of families being broken up, these same sources reveal many more in which they remained intact over several generations. And even when spouses and children were sent to other areas, black people retained a powerful sense of family. After emancipation, thousands of blacks wandered across the South in search of relatives and loved ones.

A treasury of folklore demonstrates the extent to which slaves retained a sense of identity. Slaves blended African and New World materials into their own culture. Black spirituals were a form of religious music unique in sound and feeling but expressive of profoundly Christian themes of sorrow and hope. Spirituals could also be a commentary on the system in which the slave was imprisoned. One song, ostensibly about Biblical Samson, expressed the wish that "if I had my way, I'd tear this building down." Field hollers and work songs combated the boredom of mindless field labor and provided the coordination and timing essential to people working under close and difficult conditions:

> Massa in the great house, counting out
>   his money,
> Oh, shuck that corn and throw it in the barn.
> Mistis in the parlor, eating bread and honey.
> Oh, shuck that corn and throw it in the barn.

And in their quarters, conducting prayer meetings of their own, often in defiance of the law, the slaves created forms of preaching, of worship, of social union that would give structure to black society not only under slavery but in the dangerous century of freedom that followed emancipation.

Points To Think About

1. Colonial Americans were justifiably proud of their reputation for being skillful and versatile workmen. The shortage of skilled craftsmen and the relative isolation of many farming settlements meant that

the average American needed to be a jack-of-all-trades. He had to know some carpentry, some masonry, something about shoe making, and so forth. But he was aided by the fact that he did not have to master any of the trades completely. Colonial America lived by the rule of the thumb. Virtually nothing the average American needed to do required precise measurement or exact work.

As Elting Morison points out in his *From Know How To No Where,* the canals were the first projects that required modern engineering skills. Canals called for a very high level of workmanship. If their walls were not of a precise thickness, for example, they would leak; the water level would fall; and the boats would be unable to move. This is, in fact, what happened with most of America's early canals.

The Erie presented enormous technical challenges. Gratings had to be measured exactly, new kinds of locks designed and built, and all had to be constructed to last for generations. The rule of thumb would not suffice. So the first generation of American engineers learned their profession on the job. For the next thirty years, America's canals, railroads, and machines would be built by the graduates of the Erie Canal.

In this sense the Erie had an enormous impact on American economic development quite apart from the improvement in transportation and shipping it brought. The Erie not only opened up the West but also provided the opportunity for Americans to learn the skills which rapid industrialization would require. In the long run, this may have been as important as the link between the Great Lakes and the Atlantic.

2. Historians, until recently, thought of slavery as an institution which, on the one hand, destroyed the African culture the slaves brought with them, and, on the other, prevented them from fully assimilating the white American culture (slaves were not permitted to marry or learn to read, for example). The rise of black consciousness in the 1960s prompted historians to reexamine the question. And their research now supports a sharply different view. Slaves did manage to hold on to at least some of their African heritage, and, more importantly, managed to build a distinctive Afro-American culture of their own despite the many obstacles the institution of slavery put in their way. Slaves formed stable families, developed their own religious institutions, produced a rich musical tradition, and invented their own language—a colorful and expressive variant of standard English that employed a number of African expressions and rhythms of speech.

One prominent black historian, John Blassingame, has developed a typology of male slave personality types which can help us understand how blacks adapted to life on the plantations. The plantation, Blassingame reminds us, was more than just a big house, where the planter and his family lived, and cotton fields. It also included a slaves' quarters where blacks lived without any continuous white supervision. Black culture developed in the quarters. And it was developed by the kind of typical slave Blassingame nicknames "Jack." Unlike the shuffling, grinning "Sambo" who continually abased himself before whites and the rebellious "Nat" (named after Nat Turner) who either ran away or revolted, "Jack" accepted slavery as something he could not change but insisted on a measure of human dignity. "Jack" was normally quiet and obedient, but he expected the slave owner to treat him decently. He refused to accept cruel treatment or uncalled for punishment. And he demanded that his family rights be respected. Blassingame's work is part of a continuing effort by black scholars to demonstrate that, terrible as the institution was, even slavery did not crush the blacks' human spirit.

Suggested Readings

The classic work on the United States of the 1830s is Alexis de Tocqueville's *Democracy in America* (1832). Although a French nobleman, Tocqueville is prepared to view the growth of popular institutions sympathetically. He defined a clash between free and strong individuality, which he believed was nurtured in a civilization of class distinctions, and a democratic tendency to submerge individuality within mass public opinion. He found that special conditions in this country made for a reconciliation of liberty and democracy.

Good studies of economic development are Stuart Bruchey's *Roots of Economic Growth, 1607–1861: An Essay in Social Causation* (1968), Thomas C. Cochran's *200 Years of American Business* (1977), and George Rogers Taylor's *The Transportation Revolution, 1815–1860 (1951).* The emergence of a market economy is discussed in W. Elliot Brownlee, *Dynamics of Ascent* (1974). The economic changes under way in the pre-Civil War era are covered in Cochran's *Frontiers of Change: Early Industrialism in America* (1981) and Paul Gates's *The Farmer's Age: Agriculture, 1815–1860* (1960). Ronald E. Shaw studied the Erie Canal in *Erie Water West* (1966). Anthony Wallace's *Rockdale* (1978) is an important study of an early textile community near Philadelphia, while Hannah Josephson treats both employer and employees in *Golden Threads: New England Mill Girls and Magnates* (1949).

FORREST McDONALD

The United States did not merely survive in the early nineteenth century; it thrived. By 1840 its territory, swelled with the acquisition of Louisiana and Florida, was double what it had been in 1790, and some of its citizens were looking hungrily toward California, Oregon, and Texas. Its population had grown even faster, from less than four million to more than seventeen million. Its economic growth was greater yet, its annual exports increasing nearly sevenfold, from $20 million to $132 million. Attending this phenomenal growth were a pair of institutions, capitalism and democracy, which made the young republic a beacon light for the world.

Capitalism was largely a matter of casting off shackles that had restrained economic endeavors from early times. Ancient religion had taught the nonsense that the love of money is the route of all evil, and for many dreary centuries a government-ridden, tradition-ridden, and priest-ridden western civilization was in paralysis and poverty because law and institutional inflexibility had discouraged and hampered the ambitious or flatly prohibited them from winning a profit. The American commitment to capitalism was based on an understanding that the desire for private profit quickens effort and inventiveness and can therefore be the wellspring of great public good. The principle was as simple as it was profound: that the free exchange of goods for private profit can better serve the material needs of society than can government planning, community spirit, or love of mankind. Into the bargain, Americans embraced a new, broadened concept of freedom: that people should be free to sell their time, their talents, and their labor as they alone see fit, and in exchange should take their chances on survival.

But all of this describes for the most part only the North, and only portions of the Northern population. The Southerners continued to follow the life patterns of their Scots, Irish, and Welsh ancestors as adapted in America. The vast majority of white Southerners owned no slaves, did a little farming, and raised animals for cash. The minority who were slaveholders lived well or moderately so on the yields of their plantations. What the two major elements of white society had in common was disinclination for a life given over to work and money. They had no prejudice against work if they could force slaves or animals to do it for them, but they were not disposed to do it themselves. The herdsmen simply let their animals roam the woods—anybody's woods, for the open range system that prevailed throughout the South prevented landowners from fencing any land except that with crops growing on it—and rounded them up for slaughter from time to time. Planters exploited the labor of the slaves—though even the slaves did not usually work especially hard, and their material standards of living were higher than those of most agricultural workers in Europe, Asia or Africa. Southerners, like Yankees, sought the material things of this world, but for use and enjoyment, not for Yankee-style accumulation. They preferred a leisure ethic as opposed to the Yankees' work ethic. They were generally indolent unless roused to war (which they loved) or to some other form of violent amusement. Even their religion—the doctrine of Arminianism, which contrasted sharply with the Yankees' perfectionism—offered a lazy man's way to heaven. Arminianism, which Southerners embraced during and after the Second Great Awakening (1801–06), taught that eternal salvation required only confessing and repenting sin and accepting Jesus Christ as Savior.

Not all Americans were either Yankees or Southerners, of course. Most people in the middle tier of states from New York and Pennsylvania westward avoided the two extremes, as did many in the West. Together, people in those areas constituted nearly half the total population. As long as they remained neutral between the extremes, the United States could remain a house divided yet not divided against itself, and the nation could continue to thrive and grow. If the middle should embrace either side, and if enough loud and shrill voices began to cry that the house must be all one or all the other, the vibrant young republic would be torn asunder. In 1840, however, such a sinister prospect seemed remote.

American Capitalism: A Beacon? ☆ ☆ ☆ ☆ ☆

EUGENE D. GENOVESE

Many commentators at home and abroad looked to a brilliant future for the new republic. Its tough, free, enterprising people, its extraordinary natural resources, the sheer size of its open spaces gave reason to expect that its history would be a happy one. Yet a country so short of capital and labor would surely take several centuries to develop into an important power. Probably few if any of the nation's optimistic observers would have predicted as fast a growth of the economy of the United States as actually happened. What was the place of capitalism in that growth?

It is the freedom that the modern world has given to the desire for profit, Professor McDonald suggests, that is the reason for the productivity and wealth of modern times; and capitalism, of course, worships profit. But in fact much more than the profit motive has found expression in recent centuries and moved populations to work and invent in such a way as to add to the world's wealth. Scientific curiosity, an inventor's delight in designing a new machine, even a simple dedication to work itself: all these, by themselves or mixed in with an ambition for personal gain, have made an increase in production. And the profit motive, by itself, has no interest in getting out a good product if it can make a flimsy one for greater margin of profit. The best motives for good workmanship operate in socialist nations as well as capitalistic ones. What the modern age has provided in the service of industrialism is not greed—which Professor McDonald quite correctly associates with capitalism—but a new way of looking at the world as not fixed but changeable in response to inventive effort. And it is that perception of the world, and not capitalism, that was the most creative component of nineteenth-century American civilization and provided a beacon for the world.

There was one fact about the remarkable expansion in the American economy that should have been an embarrassment to capitalism and to democracy both. The economic miracle arose on the strength of an export crop. Without that crop the American economy would have moved forward much more slowly. The crop was cotton. Its producers were hundreds of thousands, then millions, of laborers who did not enjoy the political rights that democracy demands, and did not possess that liberty to sell their labor-power on the market that capitalism proclaims. These laborers were black slaves. They or their forebears had been part of the massive forced migration from Africa—part of the millions who had been shipped into the plantation colonies by a greedy European capitalism. What they might have had to say about the American system of free enterprise, if anyone had thought to ask them, we must leave to our imaginations.

What did the slave plantations contribute to the American economy? The sale of cotton to Britain and Europe gave to Americans the financial credit with which to buy the industrial commodities and technology the country had to have for a modern economy. Southern cotton constituted the raw material for the northern textile industry. Northern factories profited from orders from the South for clothing and for agricultural implements. Farmers migrated to the Northwest, which was supplying the South as well as the Northeast with food. An impressive meat-packing industry rose in Cincinnati, and before long the Northwest had a far-flung warehousing and shipping network and was demanding a national transportation system, the building of which would be another great industrial project. Since the South itself, like other plantation societies, did not develop its own financial and commercial facilities at as great a rate as that of its agricultural growth, northern bankers, insurance agents, and assorted middlemen did a splendid business; they thereby siphoned off much of the profits of the cotton trade to the advantage of the northern free states. Meanwhile, European capital was flowing into the country, attracted by the robust young economy and nourishing it further.

Elizabeth Cady Stanton. *(Courtesy, American Antiquarian Society)*

Lucretia Mott. *(Courtesy, Library of Congress)*

Stanton and Amelia Bloomer shown wearing the daring loose "bloomers"—long full Turkish trousers of black broadcloth with a short skirt and Spanish cloak. *(Seneca Falls Lily)*

CHAPTER 11

The Logic of Democracy 1820–1860

THE WOMEN'S DECLARATION: SENECA FALLS, NEW YORK, JULY 19-20, 1848

The World Anti-Slavery Convention, held in London in 1840, was an even more important event in the women's rights movement than in the antislavery movement. American women, who had gained their first access to public platforms in antislavery activity, were horrified when their idols, the heroes of Great Britain's successful abolition of slavery in the empire, and particularly the many clergymen present, refused to allow them their seats as delegates to the conference. Lucretia Mott, who had long exercised a public role both in Quaker and in antislavery affairs, was particularly incensed. Her straightforward anger, her willingness to argue with the men, and especially her preaching in a Unitarian Church in London "opened to me a new world of thoughts," Elizabeth Cady Stanton would recall. One of Stanton's thoughts was of organizing for women's rights. "As Mrs. Mott and I walked away arm in arm, commenting on the incidents of the day, we resolved to hold a convention as soon as we returned home, and form a society to advocate the rights of women."

Eight years elapsed before this resolve bore fruit in the Seneca Falls Women's Rights Convention. The barriers had been many. Elizabeth Cady Stanton was newly married in 1840, and in the subsequent eight years she settled in three different locations, bore three children, and assumed all the other cares of a busy middle-class household. She needed further maturation and confidence to move on to a public stage. Lucretia Mott was unusual in having had so many opportunities, largely because of her Quaker environment, to speak in public and organize meetings. Stanton cautiously worked for a New York State law that would give married women control of their inherited wealth, but she remained quite timid, fearing the social disapproval that befell women who spoke in public on any subject, no less women's rights. Finally in 1848, with Lucretia Mott planning a visit to relatives in the Seneca Falls area, the two women made a last minute decision to hold a small local convention, which they advertised only in the Seneca Falls newspapers.

The results were a surprise to the organizers, the participants, and particularly to the press and pulpit whose subsequent attacks gave the conference much of its historical importance. Three hundred people—including forty men—attended this meeting. Overwhelmed by the response, the women had Lucretia's husband James preside. In two days of orderly meetings, the Convention heard a series of well-prepared speeches, adopted a Declaration of Sentiments and a set of resolutions, and planned a set of further meetings that flowered into one of the major reform movements of American history.

What made the Seneca Falls Convention more than simply a historic "first" was its Declaration of Sentiments. Written by Elizabeth Cady Stanton and modeled after Jefferson's Declaration of Independence, the document aligned women's rights with American ideology, posing a clear challenge to national tradition. It also avoided the thicket of religious arguments about the role of women which had bedeviled the World Anti-Slavery Convention and was a major part of the anti-feminist argument then as now. The Declaration (reprinted here) is both a good summary of the sources of the women's rights movement and is still capable of provoking at least some of the controversy that it stirred in the years before the Civil War.

Declaration of Sentiments

When, in the course of human events, it becomes necessary for one portion of the family of man to assume among the people of the earth a position different from that which they have hitherto occupied, but one to which the laws of nature and of nature's God entitle them, a decent respect to the opinions of mankind requires that they should declare the causes that impel them to such a course.

We hold these truths to be self-evident: that all men and women are created equal; that they are endowed by their Creator with certain inalienable rights; that among these are life, liberty, and the pursuit of happiness; that to secure these rights governments are instituted, deriving their just powers from the consent of the governed. Whenever any form of government becomes destructive of these ends, it is the right of those who suffer from it to refuse allegiance to it, and to insist upon the institution of a new government, laying its foundation on such principles, and organizing its powers in such form, as to them shall seem most likely to effect their happiness. Prudence, indeed, will dictate that governments long established should not be changed for light and transient causes; and accordingly all experience hath shown that mankind are more disposed to suffer, while evils are sufferable, than to right themselves by abolishing the forms to which they were accustomed. But when a long train of abuses and usurpations, pursuing invariably the same object evinces a design to reduce them under absolute despotism, it is their duty to throw off such government, and to provide new guards for their future security. Such has been the patient sufferance of the women under this government, and such is now the necessity which constrains them to demand the equal station to which they are entitled.

The history of mankind is a history of repeated injuries and usurpations on the part of man toward woman, having in direct object the establishment of an absolute tyranny over her. To prove this, let facts be submitted to a candid world.

He has compelled her to submit to laws, in the formation of which she had no voice.

He has withheld from her rights which are given to the most ignorant and degraded men—both natives and foreigners.

Having deprived her of this first right of a citizen, the elective franchise, thereby leaving her without representation in the halls of legislation, he has oppressed her on all sides.

He had made her, if married, in the eye of the law, civilly dead.

He has taken from her all right in property, even to the wages she earns.

He has made her, morally, an irresponsible being, as she can commit many crimes with impunity, provided they be done in the presence of her husband. In the covenant of marriage, she is compelled to promise obedience to her husband, he becoming, to all intents and purposes, her master—the law giving him power to deprive her of her liberty, and to administer chastisement.

He has so framed the laws of divorce, as to what shall be the proper causes, and in case of separation, to whom the guardianship of the children shall be given, as to be wholly regardless of the happiness of women—the law, in all cases, going upon a false supposition of the supremacy of man, and giving all power into his hands.

After depriving her of all rights as a married woman, if single, and the owner of property, he has taxed her to support a government which recognizes her only when her property can be made profitable to it.

He has monopolized nearly all the profitable employments, and from those she is permitted to follow, she receives but a scanty remuneration. He closes against her all the avenues to wealth and distinction which he considers most honorable to himself. As a teacher of theology, medicine, or law, she is not known.

He has denied her the facilities for obtaining a thorough education, all colleges being closed against her.

He allows her in Church, as well as State, but a subordinate position, claiming Apostolic authority for her exclusion from the ministry, and, with some exceptions, from any public participation in the affairs of the Church.

He has created a false public sentiment by giving to the world a different code of morals for men and women, by which moral delinquencies which exclude women from society, are not only tolerated, but deemed of little account in man.

He has usurped the prerogative of Jehovah himself, claiming it as his right to assign for her a sphere of action, when that belongs to her conscience and to her God.

He has endeavored, in every way that he could, to destroy her confidence in her own powers, to lessen her self-respect, and to make her willing to lead a dependent and abject life.

A Reforming Spirit: Political and Economic Radicalism

During the first half of the nineteenth century, new social forces broke in upon the American villages, farms, and regions that had once existed in near isolation, practicing slow, traditional ways of work and life. Poverty, disease, and illiteracy became more concentrated and apparent as cities grew. The transportation revolution broke down barriers of distance and isolation, uprooting established communities and existing markets. Increasing reliance on machines turned independent craftsmen and sturdy farmers into wage earners. A few Americans questioned the very foundations of capitalism. Some turned to religious or social experiments designed to reform society. A large number, however, aimed at correcting specific problems. Reformers disagreed on goals and methods. But they shared frustration at disorder in society, apprehension about loss of consensus and community, and fear that morality was declining. Above all, they shared a faith in the ultimate perfectibility of American society. A vigorous and many-sided movement for reform gained energy in the 1830s and continued to the Civil War.

The Early Labor Movement. The American labor movement had its origins in the economic upheavals of the Jacksonian Era. In dozens of cities, craftsmen and artisans organized associations and sponsored strikes for better hours and wages. A few citywide federated unions and one national federation—the National Trades' Union—existed until hostile judges and the economic cataclysm of 1837 dragged them under. Labor also entered politics. In the early 1830s, for example, New York City workingmen organized politically to seek improved working conditions, free public education, abolition of imprisonment for debt, and an end to chartered banks and other monopolies. Most of their demands were eminently practical; some of their leaders were not.

Frances Wright and Robert Dale Owen attracted a considerable following in New York. "Fanny" Wright's avowals of atheism and her intemperate attacks on organized religion caused one conservative newspaper to brand her "the great Red Harlot of Infidelity"; Owen advocated birth-control measures to alleviate the miseries of the poor. Their chief remedy for society's ills, however, was to make the state guardian of all children, providing them with food, clothing, board, and education. Only then could they enter a highly competitive world on an equal footing. Opponents immediately denounced state guardianship as an infringement on parental rights and a covert attack on marriage. The question of endorsing it split the ranks of New York workingmen.

George Henry Evans had another remedy for unemployment and poverty: "Let us . . . emancipate the white laborer, *by restoring his natural right to the soil.*" As early as 1834, Evans advocated free land grants to actual settlers and a limitation on the holdings of any one person. Adopting the motto "Vote yourself a farm," he tried for years to convince Eastern workingmen that their happiness and independence could be found only in agriculture. In 1862, six years after Evans's death, Congress passed the Homestead Act, offering free grants of Western land. Workingmen did not have the capital, the knowledge, or the desire to go west and take up farming; and so the Homestead Act did not succeed in making independence and prosperity available to the whole nation. But the Act, an important component of the Republican scheme for nurturing the economy under governmental leadership, was a nineteenth-century foreshadowing of more daring twentieth-century social reforms.

A Reforming Spirit: Religious Movements

The Second Great Awakening. During the first half of the nineteenth century, America experienced a second "Great Awakening" of religious enthusiasm. Relying on the excitement of revival meetings, a wide variety of evangelical sects sought to turn the masses toward spiritual regeneration. Evangelists like Charles G. Finney rejected the harsh traditional Calvinist view of original sin and predestination and preached that any good Christian could attain eternal salvation. Their teachings generally involved a literal interpretation of the Bible. Many emphasized the Second Coming of Christ and believed that God's Kingdom would establish itself on earth. This religious resurgence reflected distinctly American values and attitudes. Its intensely democratic message stressed individual free will and immediate salvation; it breathed optimism; it brought religion to the people in language they could understand. Like the first Great Awakening of a century before, the new evangelicalism was more than a religious movement. For ordinary people caught up in social and economic change, it restored a sense of orderliness and coherence to their daily lives. In isolated frontier areas the churches served as socializing and civilizing agencies.

The Second Great Awakening has been called "a women's awakening." Although men certainly responded to the religious enthusiasm, women far outnumbered them among converts and played a decisive role in leading men either back to established churches, or into new ones. Historians have shown that male conversions frequently followed the conversion of one or more female members of the family. Mothers often proved especially influential in converting their sons and husbands. But the most characteristic converts were adolescent girls. An affirmation, or reaffirmation, of religious belief and commitment seems to have offered young women a powerful sense of identity and purpose at a time in which their brothers and male peers could look forward to identifying themselves with jobs or careers, while women were expected to prepare for a life of secluded domesticity.

Religious enthusiasm rapidly increased the membership of most Protestant denominations, with Methodists and Baptists increasing the fastest. But new sects also arose. Each new prophet, interpreter, or mystic found followers willing to join in anticipating the literal fulfillment of even the most outlandish prophecies. For a time the poor farming district of upstate New York burned with religious emotions. "Enthusiastic" sects, sects cultivating emotion—among them Adventists and Universalists—flourished in this "burned-over district," as it was called, perhaps because it was seared by so many fires of religious enthusiasm.

Some of the fervent young religious movements of the early 1800s encouraged believers to join together in exclusive communities of the faithful. The more distinctive the tenets of their faith, leaders reasoned, the more necessary the

Shaker Society Meeting. During worship members were sometimes "seized with a mighty trembling, with violent agitations of the body, running and walking on the floor, with singing, shouting, and leaping for joy." *(Courtesy, American Antiquarian Society)*

intensive instruction and supervision that community living made possible. This often led to communal property-holding and cooperative economic enterprise. Many of the religious communities barely survived the death of their founders; others, such as the Shaker Society, lasted a century or more.

The Shakers and the Mormons. Ann Lee had led the Shakers to America in 1774. The community received its name from one of its most distinctive practices, a sacred dance during which the members "shook" their bodies free of sin through their fingertips. "Mother Ann," as she was called, believed that she had received direct revelations from God and, since she preached millennialism—that is, the imminent coming of the millennium, the period of Christ's rule on earth—she saw no need for the Shakers to have children. The members therefore practiced celibacy. After reaching a membership of some six thousand in the 1830s, the Shakers gradually died out. Their furniture and housing arrangements, which were simplicity itself, are their best-remembered achievements.

By far the most important of the religious communitarians were the Mormons. Mormonism strikingly elaborated the new theology of free will, direct revelation, universal salvation, the expectation of Christ's imminent return, and the establishment of a millennial Kingdom.

In 1830, at the age of twenty-five, Joseph Smith of Palmyra, New York, published the *Book of Mormon.* He had transcribed it, he claimed, from gold plates that had lain undisturbed in a nearby hillside for more than a thousand years. The angel Moroni had directed him to the spot where the plates were buried. Using two magic "seeing stones" fixed in silver bows, Smith translated the ancient script into a readable text. The book was a curious mixture of Old Testament theology, popular history, and social beliefs of the times.

Although Mormonism borrowed freely from the convictions and practices of evangelical Protestantism, it offered a simple alternative to the

Mormons on Mosquito Creek, Iowa, 1846, during their long journey westward to establish a new Zion. *(Courtesy, Church of Christ of Latter Day Saint, Salt Lake City)*

confusing proliferation of Christian sects. By extending salvation to all adherents and clerical status to each adult white male, and by stressing the sanctity of secular accomplishments and the need for a community of "saints" (the church's official name was and is "The Church of Jesus Christ of Latter-Day Saints"), the new faith tapped the energies and talents of the unsuccessful and the neglected. In Joseph Smith, a prophet at the top of the church hierarchy who received instructions or "revelations" directly from God, Mormonism provided theological truths and authoritarian leadership to those who craved practical and spiritual guidance.

After converting a small group of relatives and friends, Smith moved his flock to Ohio and then to Missouri in an attempt to establish a commonwealth of believers. In each place, nonbelievers persecuted the Mormons and drove them from their lands. In 1839 Smith led his followers to Illinois. After securing political authority from state officials, he founded a city, called Nauvoo, which became a self-sufficient religious community. The success of Nauvoo, which grew to fifteen thousand inhabitants by 1844, as well as its voting power in state elections, brought the envy and hostility of outsiders. Smith's increasingly eccentric behavior (he declared himself a candidate for president in 1844) also generated unfavorable publicity. When a disgruntled Mormon confirmed that Smith and other members of the church's elite practiced polygamy, state officials arrested Smith and his brother. Soon after their confinement at Carthage, a mob of disbanded militia murdered them both.

When the harassment and violence continued, Brigham Young, Smith's successor as president of the church, led the Mormons on the long difficult exodus from Illinois to uninhabited Mexican territory beyond the Rocky Mountains. Under Young's stern but effective leadership, the Mormons established a thriving agricultural community near the Great Salt Lake. Believers recall a miracle that saved that first band. After a desperate winter, the Mormons had planted a small crop and irrigated it by hand, a backbreaking task. Then, just as harvest time approached, a hoard of locusts swept down upon the fields. Near despair as they watched the insects devouring the only food available for the next winter, the Mormons suddenly heard the calls of hundreds of seagulls. The mysterious visitors, a thousand miles away from any ocean, ate the locusts and saved the community. The event freshened the vision of a new Zion. By 1877, the year of Young's death, the commonwealth numbered some 350 settlements with a total population of 140,000.

Organized like a medieval kingdom, the church collected an annual tithe in goods, labor, or money, from each individual and channeled this surplus into projects that benefited everyone. Banning or discouraging the use of tea, coffee, tobacco, liquor, fashionable clothing, and elegant furniture, the church curtailed wasteful spending and assured the development of industrious community. This mixture of collectivism and private enterprise saved the community from the worst evils of uncontrolled capitalism and prevented Utah from becoming dependent on imports from the industrial East.

Although the Mormons wished to be self-sufficient and independent, they also considered themselves Americans and asked for Utah's admission to the Union. Congress, however, balked at the Mormon practice of polygamy. In fact, only a small percentage of the community participated in this patriarchal institution; but most of the American public thought that Brigham Young's twenty-seven wives and fifty-six children were typical, and they considered polygamy to be a form of "Oriental" debauchery. In 1890 the church formally renounced polygamy. Mormonism was retreating from the attempt to establish a society operating in entire accordance with religious principles and communal ideals. The Mormon faith was shortly reduced to a religion of the spirit that did not interfere conspicuously with the American way of life. Congress admitted Utah to the Union in 1896.

Millennialism. Not content with establishing an earthly paradise, some Americans looked to the fulfillment in their own time of the New Testament prophecy of Christ's Second Coming. The foremost exponent of millennialism was William Miller, a hard-working farmer in upstate New York who became caught up in a revival shortly after the War of 1812 and spent the rest of his life pondering religious questions. A literal interpretation of the Bible led him to a graphic belief in the Second Coming (or Advent), which he calculated would occur in about 1843. Aided by the widespread economic distress of the late 1830s, Miller made crowds of converts throughout New England with his vivid sermons depicting the glory of the Advent, the joy of those who would be saved, the suffering of the unrepentant. In a single year he gave 627 hour-and-a-half lectures before eager audiences, often of a thousand or more. Ministerial disciples with a knack for publicity spread Miller's views over an even wider area.

Miller hesitated to give his frantic followers a definite date, promising only that deliverance would come soon, in God's appointed time. As 1843—the Last Year—passed, March of 1844 came to be accepted as the crucial month. (A little girl told her mother, "I want to die this summer—I don't want to live next year and *be burnt up*.") Finally, when nothing happened, a weary and discouraged Miller frankly admitted his mistake, explaining that he had done his best. But his lieutenants were not yet ready to quit. They chose October 22, 1844, as the new "Advent Day" and talked Miller into accepting it. Excitement mounted higher than before as extensive preparations were made to enter God's Kingdom. The faithful made themselves white "ascension robes" and neglected nearly all secular business. Voting in the fall elections was very light in some districts. Crowds blocked the streets near Boston's Millennial Tabernacle, forcing the mayor to close the building.

On the night of October 21, Millerites gathered on hilltops to meet the new world together. No provisions were made for eating or sleeping, and many suffered as the night and the next day and then another night passed; in some places severe thunderstorms added to their terror. Some claimed to have seen a jeweled crown in the sky. In western New York, an earthquake intensified the expectation. A few Adventists committed suicide—one man leaped over Niagara Falls. The day of the "Great Delusion" effectively ended the Adventist movement, although isolated Adventist sects continued to flourish.

The Fox Sisters. Various forms of spiritualism, or attempts to contact the spirit world, were another manifestation of the desire to break down all barriers between this world and the next. Mesmerism, electro-biology, clairvoyance, phrenology, magnetism—each had its following. New York farmer John Fox had two remarkable young daughters, Maggie and Katie. Wherever they went in their home, mysterious rapping sounds were heard. Eventually the girls and their mother worked out a system of communication with the presumably otherworldly source of the rappings. Soon the neighbors flocked in to observe these conversations with the spirit world. The Fox home in this year 1848 set off a mania of spiritualist excitement. With an older sister acting as manager, the Fox girls began holding exhibitions—at the insistence of the spirits, of course—and quickly developed into professional fee-charging mediums.

With the wide publicity given the Fox sisters, mediums rapidly appeared all over the country, and spiritualist circles developed in nearly every town and village. These mediums refined their techniques as they went along; the Foxes' managing sister, for instance, discovered that total darkness could produce many more manifestations of the spirits' presence. Table-moving, spirit-writing, and cold, ghostly hands soon supplemented the mystic rappings, and within a few years all the now-familiar paraphernalia of spiritualism were in use. The spiritualist excitement filled for thousands of people a need to become more comfortable with the mysteries of death and immortality. A number of intellectuals saw in spiritualism a replacement for traditional Christianity—a proof of the existence of a supernatural world for a scientific age which could not accept revelation resting only on faith. Even when the Fox sisters some years later admitted that their whole career had been a fraud (the rappings had from the first been produced by the joints of their toes), many spiritualists remained undeterred.

Methodism. The most powerful evangelical movement, more orthodox than these other religions of excitement, had begun in the eighteenth century. John Wesley had led within the Church of England a revival movement that produced a separate denomination, the Methodist church. Methodists believed in free will. In its early days especially, Methodism had a strong element of emotional revivalism; but it also preached a rigorous piety and a morality of self-discipline, industry, thrift, and good works. Methodism was powerfully attractive, in Great Britain to the working classes and to the poor, and in this country to people on the frontier. It is said that in both nations it had something to do with the bringing of an ordered moral life to previously disordered sections of society. While the Methodist church did have an organization, in its first period it did not stress the role of bishops or of a highly trained ministry. That made it possible for Methodism here to develop a distinctive and effective system in which preachers, many with little, if any, formal religious education, would travel about on the frontier, bringing a sustaining Methodism to the families and communities at which they stopped Each preacher worked a "circuit" or route that covered a particular area. Francis Asbury, who had come to this country in 1771 and was influential in the beginnings of Methodism here, was an early and influential traveling preacher. The typical circuit rider went by horseback, depended on friendly settlers for food and shelter, and was much a part of the frontier environment: Peter Cartwright could thrash a rowdy who tried to disrupt a Methodist meeting. The Methodists divided their territory into regions, each holding an annual conference that heard reports, appointed new preachers, and assigned circuits. As the frontier became heavily populated, large circuits—some had been hundreds of miles long—were replaced by smaller ones, and by about the middle of the nineteenth century these had given way to settled parishes. By that time the Methodist church had become the largest Protestant denomination in the country.

A Reforming Spirit: Secular Communitarianism

Many Americans believed that small communitarian groups, isolated from society, could develop social principles that would purify the whole nation. Dozens of experimental communities built upon a trust in human perfectibility sprouted up in the nineteenth century, some of them later succumbing to selfishness, quarrels, or loss of interest.

New Harmony. Robert Owen, a famous English socialist whose model factory town at New Lanark, Scotland, inspired so many American utopians, organized his own communal experiment at New Harmony, Indiana. Owen believed that the American West provided the unspoiled and egalitarian location that a new social system required, and in 1825 he collected a mixed group of followers whom he intended to transform into a prosperous, self-governing community. Stressing cooperation and common ownership of property, Owen hoped to eliminate selfishness and want. He soon discovered that it

***A Philadelphia Anabaptist Immersion During a Storm*, by Pavel Svinin.** *(Courtesy, Metropolitan Museum of Art, Rogers Fund, 1942)*

"was premature to unite a number of strangers to operate for their common interest, and live together as a common family." Quarrels and dissatisfaction finally forced Owen to abandon his misnamed experiment. Such experiments, his son Robert Dale Owen later concluded, were bound to fail in a country where cheap land and high wages fostered individualism and discouraged cooperative action.

Brook Farm. Brook Farm, a New England community, existed for a few years in the 1840s. Most of its members, such as Margaret Fuller, Nathaniel Hawthorne, and its founder George Ripley, were New England intellectuals; and it was influenced by transcendentalism, a moral and spiritual doctrine to which numbers of New England writers and social critics adhered. Transcendentalism was an American variant of the idealist philosophy that teaches that the world of material objects as we see them is really no more than an expression of mind or consciousness. Transcendentalists believed that since it is mind rather than the objective and physical world that is the ultimate reality, the mind can draw into itself and cultivate its own powers. Transcendentalist intellectuals opposed slavery and other institutions that they perceived as getting in the way of individual and collective perfection. Brook Farm aimed at combining manual and intellectual work; this, its members hoped, would develop and enrich the inner self. Brook Farm—much of it destroyed by a major fire—is remembered for the high and not always practical intellectuality of its life, though residents did operate a successful experimental school.

The Oneida Community. John Humphrey Noyes, whose social ideas rested on a creed known as perfectionism, founded a community at Oneida in upstate New York. Residents operated thriving manufactures, but the community was better known for its sexual arrangements. Wishing to substitute cooperativeness for competitive individualism, Noyes prohibited "special love" and instead established "complex marriage," a system in which every member resident was considered married to every other of the opposite sex. Behavior was not promiscuous but strictly regulated. Women had sexual equality with the men and shared in the work; the entire community had responsibility for the children. The community had a prosperous and successful existence. Later in the century it abandoned complex marriage in the face of attacks from moral critics.

A Reforming Spirit: Social Reform

Communities like these—there were many others and have been many since—implicitly held a double relationship to society as a whole. In part they were withdrawn from that society and existed to provide for their own residents. Yet they could want also to provide examples for the rest of humankind, and such communitarians as Robert Owen and the Brook Farm people spent lives of reformist activity outside the experimental communities as well. The United States during the Jacksonian era and afterward was thick with reformers who gave themselves not to communitarian experiments but to efforts to improve society in general. Such organizations as the Bible Society, the American Tract Society, and the Home Missionary Society worked to instill religious principles in the population or portions of it; meanwhile, revivalists like Charles G. Finney preached to crowds. Other reformers worked for education, women's rights, improvement of prisons, care of the insane, temperance in drinking, total abstinence from drink, or the abolition of war. The best known of the reform movements, of course, were those opposed to slavery. Some opponents of slavery wished to colonize former slaves in Africa; some wanted to keep slavery from being permitted in the Western territory; others, the most militant, called for abolition of slavery in the South. For all its varieties and conflicts of objectives, much of the reformist activity in the United States was of a single mind in its restless morality, its conviction that the world can be improved and that we are under obligation to set ourselves to improving it.

Personal experience motivated such reformers as Southern abolitionists Angelina and Sarah Grimké and the black abolitionist Frederick Douglass. Others, especially those associated with the Bible societies and the American Tract Society, came from an elite. Fearing that social disorder would grow worse unless the masses were inculcated with "proper values," they took it upon themselves to serve as the moral stew-

Temperance. This song about drinking gives an idea of what worried the reformers.

If the ocean was whisky,
And I was a duck,
I'd dive to the bottom
And never come up.

But the ocean ain't whisky
And I ain't a duck,
So we'll round up the cattle
And then we'll get drunk.

I'll drink my own whisky,
I'll drink my own wine;
Some ten thousand bottles
I've killed in my time.

I've no wife to quarrel
No babies to bawl;
The best way of living
Is no wife at all.

Beefsteak when I'm hungry,
Red liquor when I'm dry,
Greenbacks when I'm hard up,
And religion when I die.

An 1826 caricature depicting the evils of drink. *(Courtesy, The New-York Historical Society, New York City)*

ards of the nation. "The gospel is the most economical police on earth," said a leader of the Home Missionary Society. The religious enthusiasm of the 1830s inspired such men as the antislavery activist Theodore Dwight Weld and the temperance advocate Neal Dow. And the prevalent belief in moral perfectionism sharpened the conviction of many reformers. The abolitionist editor William Lloyd Garrison, for example, became so obsessed with the need to maintain moral purity that he publicly burned a copy of the Constitution, symbolically dissociating himself from a document contaminated by slavery.

Temperance. From colonial days Americans had been heavy drinkers. When Thomas Jefferson returned from France in 1789, he brought back over three hundred bottles of wine. Less affluent New Englanders settled for rum, which the Puritans distilled from West Indian molasses. Before the advent of canals and railroads, farmers often sent their corn to market distilled in a jug: whiskey cost less than corn to ship over long distances and found a ready market. In many places it was safer to drink than water. An early nineteenth-century traveler in Ohio found the use of ardent spirits near universal: "A house could not be raised, a field of wheat cut down, nor could there be a log rolling, a husking, a quilting, a wedding, a sheepwashing, or a funeral without the aid of alcohol." Concerned particularly over the harm that drink could do to the family, reformers mounted a determined attack on "Demon Rum."

The temperance crusade seemed, superficially at least, to be one of the most successful reforms. Using techniques borrowed from religious revivals and mass politics, temperance workers distributed leaflets, held "cold water parades," and organized lecture circuits of reformed drunkards who made emotional appeals for converts to sign "temperance pledges." In the late 1830s a million people belonged to temperance societies. Timothy Shay Arthur's lurid account of the evils of drink, *Ten Nights in a Bar-room, and What I Saw There* (1854), ranked just behind *Uncle Tom's Cabin* as the bestseller of the 1850s. A book of etiquette of the period instructed a lady to write to a young man fond of liquor: "Under ordinary circumstances, I would be delighted to go to the opera with you. I regret to add, however, that I have undoubted evidence that you are becoming addicted to the use of the wine-cup. With an earnest prayer for your reformation, ere it be too late, I beg you to consider our intimacy at an end."

Yet, in spite of the impressive numbers of pledges obtained, moral suasion had obvious limitations. Pledges of abstinence did not affect hard-core drinkers who did not care to sign, and the pledges represented no more than the good intentions of those who did. The fervent converts of one day could be staggering out of the taverns the next.

As growing numbers of immigrants entered the country, the Germans bringing their tradition of beer and the Irish their taste for hard liquor, temperance crusaders grew more fearful. Many women's rights activists also joined the cause. Feminists argued that women, as the victims of the behavior of drunken men, were the chief sufferers. Amelia Bloomer answered the claim that women had no business speaking out on this matter:

> None of woman's business, when she is subject to poverty and degradation and made an outcast from respectable society! None of woman's business, when her starving naked babes are compelled to suffer the horrors of the winter's blast! . . . In the name of all that is sacred, what is woman's business if this be no concern of hers?

Slowly, moral appeals gave way to political action. Under the leadership of Neal Dow, Maine in 1851 passed the nation's first statewide prohibition statute—the celebrated "Maine Law." In the next decade over a dozen states followed Maine's lead, although not all of these measures remained on the books.

Public Schools. Like temperance, educational reform appealed to Americans who believed that dangerous influences and moral decay were spreading throughout the land. Horace Mann, the first Massachusetts superintendent of education and a crusader for state-financed education, warned that "the unrestrained passions of men are not only homicidal, but suicidal; and a community without a conscience would soon extinguish itself." How could individuals and society be saved? Universal education—entailing moral guidance and firm discipline—must become the responsibility of the state. Mann and his supporters in the common school movement also argued that leaving education in the hands of families, or preserving it as a luxury of the elite, threatened the nation's political and economic stability. Public schools would encourage social mobility and lessen class differences by providing rich and poor with a common educational background as a basis for the pursuit of future careers. The schools would also prepare Americans for the exercise of intelligent, informed citizenship. "In a republic," Mann wrote, "ignorance is a crime":

> If we do not prepare children to become good citizens—if we do not develop their capacities, if we do not enrich their minds with knowledge, imbue their hearts with the love of truth and duty, and a reverence for all things sacred and holy, then our republic must go down to destruction, as others have gone before it; and mankind must sweep through another vast cycle of sin and suffering, before the dawn of a better era. . . .

Coupled with the growing civic interest in free schools, these arguments produced results.

In 1800 there were no public school systems outside New England; by 1850 every state had at least some public elementary and secondary schools, although Northern states surpassed Southern in the percentage of white children enrolled. Several states made appropriations for schools to educate the deaf and the blind. Public schools required a new, more practical curriculum, in place of the traditional, classical one designed for an elite. The study of Greek and Latin or of classical authors would be of limited value for future generations of farmers and mechanics. McGuffey's *Reader* and Webster's *Speller*, whose short lessons simultaneously taught useful skills and proper moral habits, became standard classroom texts, and teachers added exercises in geography, United States history, and science. Gradually, the look of the classroom changed—maps, globes, and blackboards all made their appearance.

Institutions of higher education also proliferated. New kinds of schools opened: technical schools such as Rensselaer Polytechnic Institute in New York; state universities in most Western states; hundreds of denominational colleges, and some "colleges"—more correctly, advanced academies and seminaries—for women. Women's education presented a special problem and challenge to the reform movement; since the end of the eighteenth century there had been a growing sentiment among both men and women in favor of education for women. But few of those who sought to educate women wanted to train them for the professions or otherwise give them a schooling identical to men's. Women were to be educated for enlightened, republican motherhood, and as suitable companions to educated husbands. Female educators such as Emma Willard, who founded the Troy Seminary, and Mary Lyon, who founded Mount Holyoke Seminary, justified women's schooling with the claim that educated women would enhance the home. But increasingly, some female educators, notably Catharine Beecher—daughter of Lyman Beecher and sister of Harriet Beecher Stowe—also stressed the importance of educating women as primary school teachers, especially single women who would have to earn their livings. The teaching profession, which was distinctly moving toward feminization by the middle of the century, was viewed as an appropriate extension of women's primary domestic role.

Throughout higher education the content of schooling changed. Older universities modified their curricula, reducing the heavy dose of theology and the classics in favor of modern languages, "political economy," and the sciences. Several added professional programs in law, medicine, and engineering. A number of Western colleges adopted the unusual concept of student self-help through manual labor. Founded by radical reformers, these schools, such as Oberlin in Ohio (also the first to be coeducational) and Knox in Illinois, became centers of both educational experimentation and antislavery activism.

In taking over from the family the primary obligation for schooling, the state was doing what it was coming to do also for other dependent members of society. Formerly, responsibility for them, too, had also been left to the family or to local authorities; but as an increasing density of population intensified social problems, reformers began seeking better solutions. To the Christian cult of perfectionism these humanitarians added a growing belief in the power of environment to shape human character. The result, in the words of one historian, was "the discovery of the asylum."

Reform of Prisons and Asylums. At the urging of reformers, most states rewrote their colonial penal codes, abolishing imprisonment for debt and restricting the application of the death penalty to murderers. For lesser offenses, imprisonment took the place of such brutal corporal punishments as whipping, dunking, and branding. To house and rehabilitate prisoners,

In response to the prison reform movement of the 1820s and 1830s, states began to build modern facilities like "Sing Sing" Prison in Ossining, New York. *(Courtesy, The New York Public Library)*

the states began to build modern prisons. (Connecticut had formerly housed felons in an abandoned copper mine.) New York, with the construction of its prison at Auburn (1821), inaugurated the system of individual confinement by night and group labor by day. Under the theory that isolation would promote moral reflection (in fact it often promoted suicide), Pennsylvania's new penitentiary (1829) provided for strict solitary confinement of prisoners at all times. Alexis de Tocqueville concluded that, while the Pennsylvania system made "the deepest impression on the soul of the convict," the Auburn system was "more conformable to the habits of man in society, and on this account effects a greater number of reformations." States also created special correctional facilities for juveniles, and for minor criminals such as drunks and vagrants.

Before 1840, victims of mental illness had been cared for privately—in locked rooms, cages, or outhouses—or else confined to jails and poorhouses. Appalled, a Massachusetts schoolteacher, Dorothea Dix, undertook an investigation of the problem in her native state. Armed with the facts, she prepared a memorial to the legislature. Pledging to "tell what I have seen," she described graphically "the *present* state of insane persons confined within the Commonwealth, in *cages, closets, cellars, stalls, pens! chained, naked, beaten with rods, and lashed into obedience!*" Shocked by her descriptions, the lawmakers voted funds in 1843 to enlarge the state hospital for the insane. During the next decade Miss Dix traveled over thirty thousand miles in behalf of her cause. As a result, nearly every state made some provision for the care and treatment of the indigent insane.

Women's Rights. The career of Dorothea Dix illustrates nicely the general plight of women in the mid-nineteenth century. Intelligent, educated, and an expert in her field, she was obliged, in the interests of maintaining a "womanly dignity," to work mainly behind the scenes, rarely speaking in public herself. The only professions open to upper-class and middle-class women at that time were those of teacher, missionary, and writer; women of other classes worked in factories or as laundresses, seamstresses, or servants.

Yet throughout the nineteenth century, reform movements increasingly would come to draw the energies of women, even in an era that seemed in many ways to be relegating them to a life of privacy and domesticity. From the beginning of the nineteenth century, but especially following 1820 and particularly in the Northeast, home was becoming separate from income-earning work. A major reason was that the development of commerce and cities, followed by the development of modern industry, created workplaces—physically as well as socially distant from dwellings. Men went out to work; women, or a large proportion of them, stayed home. This separation of home from "work"—a word that is often confined to efforts that earn money—reinforced the nineteenth-century ideals of domesticity and true womanhood, which suggested that human life is divided into a public male sphere based on competitive values and a private female sphere of nurture and morality. Women were expected to concentrate on housekeeping and child-rearing, leaving public affairs to men. A woman, wrote one (male) observer, "cannot too studiously shun the gaze of the multitude. The strife and tumults of the senate-house and the platform are too much even for her eye to rest upon, much more for her voice to mingle in. Her chastity is her tower of strength, her modesty and gentleness are her charm, and her ability to meet the high claims of her family and dependents, the noblest power she can exhibit to the admiration of the world." Public opinion and economic circumstance were embodied in the law, which regarded women as perpetual minors. Married women had no rights over their property or children; they could not sue in their own name. They could not even sign contracts.

All this could have encouraged women to stay away from reform movements, which aggressively entered the public sphere that sentimentality claimed to be the domain of males; and many women undoubtedly drew that lesson. Nevertheless, they gradually became more and more important in attempting to introduce "their" moral values into public life. Women engaged in a long struggle to assert their right to speak in public, to organize, and eventually to vote on behalf of moral issues. They made slow but solid progress. In their effort they relied particularly upon the bonds and networks that they had established with other women—the "bonds of sisterhood." These female networks supported a wide variety of female associations providing charity to the needy, raising funds for the education of ministers, combating slavery, working for various moral reforms that included temperance and the elimination of prostitution, and giving support to mothers seeking to set their children on the right path. Although many

I'll Be No Submissive Wife. This song of the 1840s went into many editions.

I'll be no submissive wife
No, not I; not I.
I'll not be a slave for life
No, not I; no, not I.

Think you on a wedding day
That I said, as others say
Love and honor and obey
Love and honor and obey?
No no no no no no no
No no no, not I.

I to dullness don't incline
No, not I; no, not I.
Go to bed at half-past nine
No, not I; no, not I.

Should a humdrum husband say
That at home I ought to stay
Do you think that I'll obey,
Do you think that I'll obey?
No no no no no no
No no no, not I.

reform associations, such as those contributing to the abolitionist and the temperance movements, remained firmly under male leadership throughout the first half of the nineteenth century, female reformers supplied much of the dedication.

The cause of women's rights soon became a movement in itself. Lucy Stone, an antislavery and women's-rights activist who retained her maiden name after marriage, refused to pay taxes since she was not represented in the government. Some women even rejected their long, immobilizing skirts in favor of the less-constricting "Bloomer" costume. Today, the Bloomer costume seems tame indeed, and rather constricting compared to contemporary women's clothing. It consisted of a tunic that fell to mid-calf worn over a pair of ample bloomers that covered the legs and were gathered tightly at the ankle. But in its time and place, it earned the women who wore it ridicule, hostility, and a showering of rotten eggs and tomatoes. Even those most determined advocates of women's rights, Susan B. Anthony and Elizabeth Cady Stanton, eventually gave it up with heartfelt relief. Women reformers proved especially active in defense of the personal rights of other women whom they perceived as oppressed or exploited by the familial and sexual demands of men. Susan B. Anthony helped a woman kidnap her child from her husband's custody—idealization of motherhood notwithstanding, fathers regularly got custody of children. Other women worked for temperance to protect women from the beatings and domestic violence of drunken husbands. A group of women in New York—objecting to the double standard that allowed men to have sex outside marriage while denying it to women—started a society to reform the city's prostitutes.

Dorothea Dix's crusade on behalf of victims of mental illness led most states to make provisions for the indigent insane. *(Courtesy, Library of Congress)*

Numbers of middle-class women who took up feminist causes had begun by becoming involved in other social reforms. As women extended their interests outside the home, met together, assumed leadership, and became adept at public speaking, they soon came to recognize the status in which women were kept. "In striving to strike the [black man's] irons off, we found most surely, that *we* were manacled ourselves," wrote Abby Kelley, a women's rights leader. But if the antislavery cause helped launch the women's rights movement, it also contributed to its temporary demise. Even many sympathetic men abandoned feminist causes when they threatened to divert or divide the antislavery crusade. Led by Lucretia Mott, Elizabeth Cady Stanton, and Susan B. Anthony, women held conventions (the Seneca Falls, New York, meeting in 1848, had been the first) and brought their concerns before the public. They asked for full rights to hold property and leave bequests, for educational and economic opportunities, and for the right to vote. But despite the feminists' energy and intelligence, fundamental changes in popular attitudes, occupational choice, legal status, and political participation came slowly. The "cult of true womanhood," emphasizing the frailty and purity of women, remained strong.

Anti-Catholicism. The conviction that American society has special democratic and moral traditions to preserve and perfect has led more than once to movements to rid the country of something or somebody. Before 1830 American Catholics had been too few in number to attract much attention. Over the next thirty years, mass immigration swelled the Catholic population of the United States from barely two to ten percent of the national total. Many native Protestants were convinced that these newcomers, with their strange customs and peculiar faith, posed a threat to America's Protestant heritage and democratic institutions. One woman recounted the "poor fellows, strung along the canal, stupid from drink . . . they are for the most part covered with mud, where they have rolled when drunk." Such prominent men as Lyman Beecher and Samuel F. B. Morse warned against "papal puppets" working to "inflame and divide the nation, break the bond of our union, and throw down our free institutions." Militant Protestants formed societies aimed at converting "Papists to Christianity," stoutly resisted all suggestions of public aid to parochial schools, and demanded curbs on immigration. Zealots composed and circulated fictitious stories of convent life replete with sex orgies. Maria Monk wrote her *Awful Disclosures* (1836) of life in a Montreal nunnery where, she claimed, priests and nuns had used trapdoors and secret passageways to engage in licentious practices: "I can form only a rough conjecture," she wrote, "of the number of infants born, and murdered of course. . . ." This agitation culminated in outbreaks of violence in the 1830s and 1840s, during which Catholic convents and churches were burned in New York City, Boston, and Philadelphia.

The Arts

During the Age of Jackson America at last achieved cultural independence of Europe. Architects launched a Greek revival that filled the country with handsome public buildings and pretentious temple-fronted houses. A nationalistic school of nature painters won acclaim. American authors like Nathaniel Hawthorne and Edgar Allan Poe attracted international attention. The newly popular lyceums and public lectures furnished native talent with an audience. In 1860 knowledgeable Europeans would no longer ask, as one English literary wit had in 1820, "In the four quarters of the globe, who reads an American book? Or goes to an American play? Or looks at an American picture or statue?"

Speaking at Harvard in 1837, the philosopher Ralph Waldo Emerson attacked "the timid, imitative, and tame" in American creative life. Americans, he asserted, must learn to work with their own hands and speak with their own minds. And they were doing so.

American painters abandoned the formal, classical style of the eighteenth century. Influenced by the romantic movement and nationalism, they experimented with more individualistic, democratic, emotional styles of painting. Genre painters like William Sidney Mount and George Caleb Bingham took their studios outdoors to capture revealing incidents of American life. Bingham's "Stump Speaker" and "Country Elections" are miniature essays on Jacksonian politics. Nature painters like Thomas Cole glorified the spectacular qualities of the American landscape. Cole was a leader of the so-called Hudson River School, those painters who captured especially the magnificent Hudson River Valley with its deep woods, its jagged rocks, its sweeping vistas.

American architects also turned from eighteenth-century styles of European origin. Their search for a pure, simple, democratic architecture led naturally to the Greek Revival, inspired by the buildings of ancient Greece. Among the best examples of this style are Benjamin Latrobe's Bank of the United States at Philadelphia and Robert Mills's Treasury Building at Washington. Responding to the individualistic and romantic impulses of the age, American architects later adopted a variety of styles. By 1850 Philadelphia had an Egyptian jail, a Greek bank, medieval cottages, and Moorish churches, while New York boasted a Jewish synagogue with a Gothic tower.

American Literature. American writers and poets were also influenced by the forces of nationalism. Breaking with the rigid neoclassical writing of the eighteenth century, they sought a literature that was expressive, imaginative, intuitive—one filled with "the animating spirit of democracy." The poet, Walt Whitman proclaimed, became one with the spirit of his times and with his country's culture, incarnating its "geography and national life and rivers and lakes." Whitman's *Leaves of Grass* (1855) used

Nathaniel Hawthorne. He and the other writers of the period—Poe, Emerson, Melville, Whitman, Thoreau—created a literature that was uniquely American and attracted international attention. *(Courtesy, Essex Institute, Salem, Massachusetts)*

free verse and slang words and borrowed freely from music, religion, and politics for its imagery and metaphors. *Leaves of Grass* was American.

Edgar Allan Poe became the master of the short story. Each tale was "a complete . . . moment of emotional tension." Nathaniel Hawthorne brought intensity, depth, and craftsmanship to the American novel. In works like *The Scarlet Letter* (1850) and *The House of the Seven Gables* (1851) he moved from fact to symbol, probing the souls of American Puritans and Quakers. Hawthorne looked into dark motives and somber emotions, but looked as well for the innocence and freshness that human nature could contain. Herman Melville aspired to be a "thought-diver." His *Moby Dick* (1851), with its driven Captain Ahab searching for the great white whale, symbolized the human quest for the mysterious forces of the universe.

Then, as now, the mass of Americans preferred a different sort of literature. With the development of more efficient printing techniques, inexpensive books and newspapers circulated widely. The most prolific type of fiction was the sentimental domestic novel. Filled with scenes of domestic joy and sorrow, these novels preached conventional morality and pictured church, home, and family as anchors against life's trials. Novels like Mrs. E. D. E. N. Southworth's *Retribution* and Mary Jane Holmes's *Tempest and Sunshine* were bestsellers for years. Another form of popular culture was the humorous essay, which dated from Benjamin Franklin's *Poor Richard*. It gained new popularity in the 1830s with Seba Smith's *Jack Downing Papers*. Downing was a "crackerbox philosopher" who commented on current events and poked gentle fun at American foibles. Smith soon had dozens of imitators, among them James Russell Lowell's Hosea Biglow, Charles F. Browne's Artemus Ward, and Johnson Hooper's Simon Slugs. Plays, minstrel shows, lectures, and public speaking also provided entertainment and education.

The cult of patriotism grew in the early nineteenth century. Holidays were increasingly devoted to skyrocketing oratory, parades, and patriotic enthusiasms. Monuments and statues appeared by the hundreds, and biographies of American heroes sold by the tens of thousands. And along with the cult of patriotism flourished a variety of popular symbols.

Americans adopted a native bird, the eagle. For holidays they chose Washington's Birthday and the Fourth of July. "Uncle Sam," a creation of the War of 1812, soon displaced "Yankee Doodle" as the national prototype. Although not adopted officially as the national anthem until

1913, Francis Scott Key's "Star-Spangled Banner" gradually replaced "My Country 'Tis of Thee." No token of nationalism became more important than the American flag. Originally created in 1777, the stars and stripes had remained chiefly a naval flag until 1834, when the army adopted it as well.

Along with symbols, Americans needed heroes. They turned to the Revolutionary War for material. By Jackson's day the important figures in the War—Francis "Swamp Fox" Marion, Ethan Allen and his "Green Mountain Boys," John Paul Jones, the martyred Nathan Hale—were celebrated in song and prose. Jackson himself became an instant hero after the Battle of New Orleans that followed the War of 1812. Above all other national heroes was George Washington. Even before his death Washington had attained in the estimation of his countrymen a place above politics and above criticism. Much of the responsibility should go to Mason Locke Weems. In 1800 this itinerant book salesman and evangelist published his *Life of Washington.* Although partly fabricated (the cherry tree story started here), the book fulfilled the American public's need for heroes.

Americans were swept up in the outpouring of nationalism. "We were taught every day and in every way," recalled one contemporary, "that ours was the freest, the happiest, and soon to be the greatest and most powerful country in the world. . . . We read it in our books and newspapers, heard it in sermons, speeches, and orations, thanked God for it, in our prayers, and devoutly believed it always." Not even the cult of patriotism, however, would forever quiet the disruptive effects of the slavery question, which burst on the country again in the 1840s.

Points To Think About

1. Historians, long preoccupied with politics, have characterized the period between the "era of good feelings" and the onset of the Civil War as the Age of Jackson. An equally strong case can be made for calling it the Age of Finney—after the leading revivalist of the day, Charles G. Finney. Finney was the George Whitefield of the nineteenth century. His revivals had the same spectacular success. And he used methods which were equally controversial. Finney, for example, often prayed for sinners by name.

Finney's revivals reflected many of the contradictory strains in American culture. On the one hand, he called on his hearers to acknowledge their abject dependence upon the process of conversion. Salvation was his work. And a revival was a gift from on high. Yet Finney also insisted that he could start a revival with the same likelihood of success that a farmer had when he planted his crops. In fact, Finney published a handbook on revivals, in which he spelled out in detail just what a successful preacher should do. Man, Finney preached in defiance of the old Puritan beliefs, could help himself. He could be saved by wanting to be saved. Finney's preaching also reflected the general concern for order. Like the upper-class builders of the benevolent empire, who generously supported his work, he saw religion as a bulwark of the social order. And he encouraged his converts to join established churches. Yet Finney also preached the primacy of the individual conscience. He told his listeners that conversion would mark a radical change in their lives. They should, he urged, reexamine the whole pattern of their lives. Finney always left it for his converts to determine the direction of their new lives for themselves. He did not, that is, attempt to channel the enthusiasm he unleashed.

And so Finney's revivals, despite the conservative cast of much of his preaching, often produced unpredictable results. Theodore Dwight Weld became a radical abolitionist. John Humphrey Noyes became the leading utopian socialist of the period.

Conscience is a form of individualism. And Finney faithfully reflected the duality of nineteenth-century American culture in his hope that social order could arise out of appeals to individuals freely to choose their own lives.

2. A revival, Finney used to lament, presupposes a declension (that is, a falling away from religious fervor). Revivals, he believed, should not be necessary. Converts should have been able to maintain the intensity of their first enthusiasm. But of course they did not. Too many were "backsliders" who needed periodically to be recalled to a higher standard.

Finney's complaint went to the heart of American evangelicalism. It had produced a kind of cyclical religion. American Protestants, that is, oscillated between intense fervor and indifference. Finney, like most ministers, wanted instead a steady religiosity. The question was how to produce it. Clearly the revival did not. Although Finney never admitted as much, one reason was that the revival produced such intense experiences that they were impossible to sustain. Something else was needed.

Finney thought he had found the answer in the theological doctrine of perfectionism. Its basis was the New Testament injunction by Christ to the disciples to be "perfect even as your heavenly Father is perfect." Religious thinkers had commonly interpreted this passage to mean that Jesus wished his followers to try to be perfect. No one could reach such a goal, they had agreed, but believers had an obligation to try. Finney thought differently. Jesus would not, he argued, have obliged the disciples to attempt something unless he had also offered them the grace (that is, the supernatural assistance) to achieve it. It followed, he thought, that actual spiritual perfection was possible. There was, he concluded, a spiritual state even higher than salvation, an experience beyond even conversion. And he told his converts that they could reach it.

Perfectionism, seems, in retrospect, a doctrine which could only have achieved prominence in nineteenth-century America. Nowhere else were people so ready to believe that anything was possible. Perfectionism mirrors perfectly the tendency in America to believe, at one and the same time, that things are going to hell in a handbasket and that they can be dramatically improved in a single stroke. It mirrors, that is, the curious mixture of pessimism and optimism that so much of American life displays. Recall, for a moment, that the same conservative reformers who bemoaned the social chaos of democracy also thought that they had in the asylum a means of ending crime, mental illness, and poverty.

This same combination of pessimism about the present and boundless confidence in the future would also mark, as you will see, the utopian socialists. Their experiments in communal living grew out of their deep dissatisfaction with American society on the one hand, and on the other their faith that they had discovered the blueprint for a perfect tomorrow.

3. Communitarians, Arthur Bestor has observed in a classic article, shared with other Americans a "Patent Office Model of Society." Americans through the first half of the nineteenth century were intensely aware of how new their society was. It was being, in a word, invented, and this sense that a whole nation was being invented encouraged some people to go farther and try to invent perfect societies.

The patent office model is an apt designation. Communitarians, like other inventors, sat down with pencil in hand and designed new social forms. This seemed shockingly naive to European conservatives. They believed that forms like the family or the community were slow historical growths that reflected, in Edmund Burke's phrase, the "accumulated wisdom of the race." The idea of inventing a society seemed preposterous. And, to judge from the eventual failure of the communitarian experiments, they were right.

Yet if European conservatives could see the hopeless innocence of drawing up blueprints for a better family, American conservatives could not. They, in fact, shared the very same patent office approach. They were the ones, we should recall, who drew up the blueprints for the penitentiary and insane asylum. They, too, were inventors, and that means that they were not classical conservatives, who did not invent but preserve.

The communitarian experiments failed, and that was an end to them. But while the penitentiaries and other asylums also failed (they did not, that is, rehabilitate the criminal or cure the insane), they were nevertheless widely copied. For all of their shortcomings, they did serve as real models. The reason, according to David Rothman in his *The Discovery of the Asylum*, was that they did succeed in one important respect. They did quarantine the socially undesirable. Rehabilitation may have failed, but custody remained. And so the asylum was adopted widely.

Suggested Readings

R.G. Walters's *American Reformers, 1815–1860* (1978) is a good introduction to the period while Rowland Berthoff's *An Unsettled People: Social Order and Disorder in American History* (1971) is a stimulating general study. On feminism a good book to begin with is Barbara J. Berg, *The Remembered Gates: Origins of Feminism—Women and the City, 1800–1860* (1977). Other new books also tell some of the story of women in this era: Ellen Carol DuBois's *Feminism and Suffrage* (1979), Nancy Cott's *The Bonds of Womanhood: "Women's Sphere in New England," 1780–1835* (1977), and G.J. Barker-Benfield's *The Horrors of the Half-Known Life: Male Attitudes Toward Women and Sexuality in Nineteenth-Century America* (1976). Lewis Perry's *Childhood, Marriage, and Reform* (1980), is thought-provoking.

Rush Welter's *The Mind of America, 1820–1860* (1975), is a good treatment of intellectual history. In *The Discovery of the Asylum: Social Order and Disorder in the New Republic* (1971), David S. Rothman argues that people believed the "asylum"—the orphanage, the penitentiary, the poorhouse—would rehabilitate the individual and provide a model of social organization. On religion see William G. McLoughlin, *Revivals, Awakenings, and Reform* (1978) and *Modern Revivalism: Charles Grandison Finney to Billy Graham* (1959), Paul E. Johnson, *A Shopkeeper's Millennium: Society and Revivals in Rochester, New York, 1815–1837* (1978), and John Boles, *The Great Revival in the South* (1972). Herbert Hovenkamp, *Science and Religion in America, 1800–1860* (1978) is a useful survey of the relation of religious to scientific thought in the early republic.

DEBATE

FORREST McDONALD

"Idle hands," according to the Victorian aphorism, "are the devil's workshop." The saying was conventionally used as a justification for keeping the poor toiling away in factories from dawn to dusk and even longer, but in fact it was the well-to-do who were apt to have leisure to commit mischief. During the 1830s and the 1850s, especially, prosperity was sufficiently widespread in America that a goodly number of such people, mainly in cities and towns, could live fairly comfortably without working; and they confirmed the wisdom of the aphorism. Old maids of both sexes, having made thorough botches of their own lives, busily turned their idle hands to silly schemes for remaking other people's lives. So much for the "reforming spirit."

But leisure also makes possible a blossoming of arts and letters, if a people have it in them. Americans had neither taste nor talent for most of the arts. Of painters, sculptors, and architects the nation had none of consequence. No good serious music was to be heard, even in the larger cities, until German immigrants began to arrive in quantity in the 1850s, and opera did not begin to flourish until large scale Italian immigration commenced later in the century. The one creative art in which Americans did excel was the one in which English-speaking people had ever excelled, the composition of prose literature.

This is not to claim that what American authors wrote was uniformly original or uniformly of high quality. Much of the fruits of the so-called Flowering of New England—the work of such writers as Emerson, Thoreau, and Holmes—was drivel. Much of the fiction written by American authors was both flimsy and imitative. But when Hawthorne, and Melville, and Poe explored in their work the darker recesses of the soul, the results were novels of depth and power comparable to those of Dostoevski and Dickens.

The impressive thing about American literature during the middle years of the nineteenth century, however, is not so much what Americans wrote but that so many of them read. From the beginning of American nationhood, it had been an unquestioned tenet that the republic could flourish only if the citizenry were literate and informed, and the Northwest Ordinance as well as the state constitutions had committed government to support general public education. The crusade of Horace Mann was a reaffirmation and a revitalization of that early commitment. The yield was by far the highest literacy rate in the world—over ninety percent of the adult white population. And Americans not only could but did read. Newspapers, of course, were their most common fare: there were about 3,000 newspapers by 1860 (three or four times the number in England or France), some having circulations in the scores of thousands. But the newspapers contained more than just news. The New York *Weekly Tribune*, for instance, treated its 200,000 subscribers to full reports of lectures, to serialized novels by Dickens and lesser English writers, to condensations of other books, to poems long and short, and to book reviews. In addition, sales of books were often large and sometimes (as with *Uncle Tom's Cabin*) utterly stupefying. And the impact of Harriet Beecher Stowe's melodrama indicated that the written word could be powerful.

In sum, while the emergence of democracy and capitalism in America regrettably brought with it the demise of the classical and civic humanist traditions, it also brought about what Jose Ortega y Gasset called "a rise in the historic level." The great masses of the country's ordinary people had achieved not only a large measure of economic security and abundance but also something more precious, free access to information and to the world of ideas. That was unprecedented in human history.

Reform and the Arts: A Link?

EUGENE D. GENOVESE

Reformers can be humorless and unpleasant. Their business is to mind other people's business. It is not so much that they quit smoking, for example, as that, once they do so, they expect everyone else to follow. They are, in short, easy to make fun of. We could have great sport with the persistent efforts of antebellum reformers to bring God's Kingdom to earth—whether or not their neighbors, not to mention God, would have it so. Among their least attractive qualities was the firm conviction that they had special knowledge of God's will and were His chosen instruments.

For all that, this country would have been much worse off without them. The greatest of their antebellum projects was antislavery, and, it is largely through their intransigent struggle that the slumbering conscience of the nation was finally aroused against the greatest evil of the nineteenth century. In pursuing their object of abolishing slavery, they displayed, among other splendid qualities, the physical and moral courage to face down lynchings, imprisonment, beatings, and constant assaults on their meetings. If men like Thomas Wentworth Higginson, not to mention John Brown, and women like the Grimké sisters qualify as "old maids of both sexes," then let's hear it for the old maids. And I assume that even Professor McDonald would not snear so at the gallant efforts of the black abolitionists like Frederick Douglass and Sojourner Truth to free their people.

Among the other campaigns for reform that marked the period feminism, as it would come to be called, ranked high. The abolitionists, or rather a solid proportion of them, joined the effort to secure rights for women. Northern conservatives, like Southern slaveholders, were shocked to learn that women dared to address abolitionist meetings and that they were often well received by "old maid" men who fought side by side with them in the cause of black freedom. The historical verdict has gone not to those shocked but to those who did the shocking. Honor to them.

A sizable number of these reformers were "intellectuals," broadly defined. By no means were all Northern intellectuals reformers. Hawthorne, for example, opposed the abolitionists as readily as Emerson supported them. The intellectual life of the period, like so much else, demonstrated the deepening chasm between the sections. The literary giants, as Professor McDonald says, were largely Northerners, but even in New England the best literary men—and women like Emily Dickinson, the greatest American poet of her time—appealed to small "highbrow" audiences, while others made money on trashy novels. And the South also had its claims to a thriving literary culture of sorts.

Political writing, including work in political economy and what by the 1850s was coming to be called "sociology," aroused substantial interest. The more philosophical discourses of John C. Calhoun, as well as his more direct political speeches and essays, displayed considerable power. The South boasted the finest political economists in the United States in Jacob N. Cardozo, a luminary of the Jewish community in Charleston, and George Tucker of Virginia, who wrote widely on moral philosophy, the arts, and other subjects besides economics. During the 1820s and 1830s Thomas Cooper, who settled in South Carolina late in life, and Thomas R. Dew of Virginia, had set a high standard in history and political science as well as economics. But to one extent or another, they, as well as other writers like the learned clergymen William Stringfellow and James. H. Thornwell, applied their talent to the defense of slavery, not as a "necessary evil" or a profitable labor system, but as the foundation of a healthy social order. And the South welcomed their ringing defense of slavery. Southern "reformers" had been dispatched—driven out or silenced. The South was not much troubled by "silly" campaigns for reform. Too bad. It would, in a short time, pay dearly for its immunity to the disease of radicalism.

The Battle at the Alamo, 1836. The Mexican "victory" cost Santa Anna 1600 of his best troops and helped Texas win its war of independence.

CHAPTER 12

Expansion and Division: The 1840s

THE ALAMO

In nineteenth-century America, no place had a larger reputation for wild living than Texas. Men tired of society could move to the frontier; if the frontier offered too little excitement, room, danger, opportunity, they could go to Texas. The history of Texas justified this reputation. For nearly three centuries Texas had belonged to Spain, but throughout that long period, the Spanish system of colonization—missions, soldiers, conversion of Indians, entrance of white settlers—had failed. Hundreds of miles of deserts and mountains separated Texas from the other Spanish lands, and the Indians of the region—Karankawas, Comanches, Apaches—preferred to race their swift horses across the plains than to settle with the friars. This land, which Mexico inherited with its independence, remained ungovernable.

The Alamo was an apt symbol of this history. The mission at San Antonio opened in 1718; construction on the now-familiar stone building began in 1757, and it acquired its historic name soon after. Three-quarters of a century's work by the friars and the Spanish army created the largest settlement in Texas—about seventeen hundred people living in filth, poverty, and irreligion. When the friars left in 1793 in search of more fertile ground for their work, there were only about forty converts. The mission itself was then in decay, housing a few squalid Indians and half-breeds. In 1802 Spanish troops evicted these unfortunates, and the Alamo became a fort. By that time the Spaniards needed all the forts they could man. Not only had they failed to defeat the Texas Indians; they now faced rebellion from the Mexicans and—after 1803, when the United States acquired Louisiana—new and dangerous neighbors to their east.

When Mexico became independent in 1821, Texas was joined to the state of Coahuila, with a promise that when its population was large enough, it would become a separate Mexican state. The newly established Mexican government planned to turn a profit from the territory and to end Indian power by allowing immigrants from the United States to develop agricultural settlements, provided they became at least nominal Catholics and Mexican citizens. The plan worked, perhaps too well. With immigrants pouring in—many of them unruly frontiersmen—and the United States government making clumsy overtures to "buy" Texas, the Mexicans could easily envision this potentially rich province slipping from them. They forbade further immigration, raised tariffs, set trade restrictions, and reinforced their military presence. The situation was further complicated by internal revolution in Mexico. Antonio Lopez de Santa Anna, Mexico's most brilliant general, was in conflict with his own government. When war came in Texas it was by no means a straightforward battle for independence on the part of the immigrants from the North. But once Santa Anna took control in Mexico City and then moved to garrison his northern province, the Texans fought to defeat his army. Independence would be an outcome of the war, not its initial objective.

The Texans, by and large, were fighters, not soldiers. Skilled marksmen, deadly with knives and fists, they loved a good scrap. The slow, boring routine of soldiering was another story. The Texans picked up an army—or several armies—but enlistments were for very short periods, many for as little as sixty days, and volunteers, answerable to no one, often outnumbered the loosely disciplined regulars. Men who would risk their lives in a moment would then refuse to carry out such mundane tasks as building fortifications, gouging gun slits in the Alamo's walls, or erecting fences.

The rebels managed to defeat Mexican detachments in several small battles. But then their amateurism began to tell: their general took a vacation; the men began drifting off to their farms or to the *cantinas* and *señoritas* in the town. Sam Houston, struggling to put together a military strategy and an army to carry it out, doubted that the Alamo could be held with so small a detachment. He sent a man he trusted to the Alamo to decide whether to destroy the fort and retreat or to hold it. The man was Jim Bowie, a legendary figure of the tough Southwest frontier. Houston must have known what his man would choose. Bowie, who had recently turned from land speculation, gambling, and personal fights with his famous eight-and-one-half-inch-long knife, and taken to battling the Mexican army, encountered a discouraging situation. It would have required a thousand men to defend the Alamo adequately, not the 104 unpaid and discouraged soldiers he found there. But Bowie decided: "We will rather die in these ditches than give them up to the enemy."

The Alamo needed reinforcements. It got a few, powerful in legend but not in number. William Barret Travis, a militant advocate of war and independence and now a regular officer in the rag-tag Texas army, was ordered there with all the troops he could muster. He arrived with thirty men. When Bowie contracted pneumonia, it was the able Travis who took command of the beleaguered fort. Davy Crockett arrived from Tennessee with twelve men. Then as now, he was the epitome of the American frontiersman, the teller and subject of tall tales. Following his legend right into the West, by some instinct he arrived (having had no previous connection with the Texas revolution) at the place that would transform his essentially comic career into real and towering heroism. Eventually another thirty-odd men arrived. And so it was that, all told, about 180 men garrisoned the old mission, when on February 23, 1836, Santa Anna's army of thousands began its siege.

With Mexican guns tightly ringing the fort, the Alamo's defenders abandoned their hopes for further reinforcements. Travis called the men together, so the story goes, explained why it was essential to hold the fort, and indicated their probable fate. At the conclusion of his speech, in a gesture duplicating Pizarro's centuries before, he drew a line in the dust with his sword, stepped across it, and asked who would join him and who would leave. All but one man—who got through the Mexican lines and lived to tell the tale—crossed the line. Bowie, from his sickbed, asked to be carried across. Travis wrote his final letter, correctly predicting that "The victory will cost the enemy so dear that it will be worse for him than defeat." The next morning revealed Mexican cannon virtually under the wall. In one more day the cannonade finally blasted a sizable hole in the old mission's wall. The final assault had begun.

Santa Anna knew he would take huge losses in the assault; the Texans had already picked off hundreds of his soldiers. Some of his commanders counseled continuing to pound the walls with cannon until they could wipe out the garrison with grapeshot. But the general knew what this siege was costing him. Bowie was right to defend the Alamo. The long and brave defense of the fort kept Santa Anna from sweeping the main Texas army off the field before it could have fully mobilized.

Before dawn on March 6, the Mexicans—four thousand strong—attacked, almost catching the exhausted defenders by surprise. The first assault with scaling ladders was repulsed with dreadful carnage. A second wave was more successful, actually getting ladders onto the walls, only to have the men driven off by rifle butts, tomahawks, and Bowie knives. Then came the third assault, and there were simply not enough Texans, enough cannon, or enough wall left. Taking incredible losses—one battalion lost 670 of 800 men—the Mexican soldiers poured in with a courage to match that of their adversaries. Abandoning the central plaza of the Alamo, the defenders retreated to the smaller rooms, to kill and then to die in hand-to-hand battle. Crockett and two of his men were found after the battle under a heap of seventeen dead Mexicans. (Another version has Crockett begging that his life be spared.) Jim Bowie, confined to a sickbed in the chapel, was one of the last to die. The first two soldiers that burst into the room he dispatched with his brace of singleshot pistols; then he was helpless, too weak to wield his famous knife. One of the few survivors, the wife of an officer, deliberately spared to spread the news of Texan defeat, remembered seeing his body being tossed on the bayonets of a dozen soldiers when the battle ended and the wanton mutilations began. By 9:00 a.m. on March 6, 1836, the siege had ended with all the Alamo's defenders dead.

No question at all: Santa Anna's "victory" in this battle cost him the war. He had lost sixteen hundred of his best troops, with many more wounded. He had lost not only the weeks it took to besiege the fortress, but the weeks his army needed afterward to recover. The Texans, sobered and inspired, declared their independence, settled their quarrels, and gave Sam Houston a chance to build an army.

Santa Anna chased Houston and caught up with him at San Jacinto, an elbow formed by the confluence of a river and a bayou. Houston burned his bridges behind him so that neither his army nor Santa Anna's could retreat. The Texans, shouting as their battlecry "Remember the Alamo!" destroyed the Mexican army in an afternoon. Texas was an independent nation, the Lone Star Republic, until 1846, when it became part of the United States.

The Fall of the Alamo **by T. Genlitz.** *(Courtesy, Library of Congress)*

America in 1840

In 1840 the future of the young American Republic seemed rich with promise. In fifty years the population had increased by over four hundred percent, while the land area had more than doubled. As each region found what it could best manufacture or grow and as transportation improved, the different sections became more interdependent in the making of a richer economy. With two national parties competing for office in every part of the country, the political system worked to bind the country together. The vast majority of Americans remained English in speech, Protestant in religion, lower middle-class in social status, agricultural in occupation; this common social ground, together with the experience of two wars against Britain, made for a shared national loyalty. Each July 4, Americans in every part of the country gathered for elaborate ceremonies glorifying the Union. Alexis de Tocqueville was deeply impressed by one such celebration at Albany, with its dramatic reading of the Declaration of Independence and its parade of Revolutionary veterans "preserved like precious relics, and whom all the citizens honor. . . ."

And yet, even as patriotism and economic interdependence strengthened the Union, one issue threatened the country with disruption. In the 1830s a crusade against slavery arose in the North. During the next decade the slavery question became entangled with the issue of territorial expansion, and that combination gradually eclipsed all other issues. Unable to settle the question peacefully, Americans resorted in 1861 to arms.

The Antislavery Crusade

The roots of the antislavery movement in the United States stretched back to the eighteenth century. Confronted by the powerful forces of rationalism and revolution, many Americans had condemned slavery as incompatible with the egalitarianism of the Declaration of Independence. In 1787 Congress excluded slavery from the area it was organizing north of the Ohio River as the Northwest Territory. That same year the delegates to the Constitutional Convention agreed to a compromise permitting, though not requiring, Congress to abolish the African slave trade in 1808. In the meantime, a number of Northern states abolished slavery within their own borders, and abolition societies multiplied even in a few Southern states.

Most Americans, although opposed to slavery, rejected the idea of its immediate eradication in the South—a course fraught with serious constitutional, economic, and social difficulties. Many favored a policy of gradual emancipation, to be followed by deportation. With the support of such influential men as Henry Clay and John Marshall, these gradualists in 1817 founded the American Colonization Society. The Society worked to resettle emancipated American blacks in Africa. Free blacks themselves objected to colonization. "We are *natives* of this country," one protested; "we only ask that we be treated as well as *foreigners*." Their opposition gradually undermined the Society's efforts.

The Abolition Movement. During the early 1830s a small but vocal band of activists began calling for the total and immediate abolition of slavery. Abolitionism became an integral part of the reform ferment of the Jackson Era. Slavery, abolitionists believed, was both a national and an individual sin; Americans could not wait for time or circumstance to eradicate it. These abolitionists viewed gradual emancipation and colonization as dead ends. Any large-scale deportation of blacks would have raised both enormous practical obstacles and grave moral difficulties. And Southern opposition to gradual emancipation, which stiffened after the invention of the cotton gin, indicated that the opponents of slavery had little to lose by adopting a more radical stance. The victory of the British abolitionist movement in 1833 gave new hope to advocates of immediate emancipation in the United States. The president of Harvard, Edward Everett, registered the intensity of these militants' feelings when he responded to criticism of his having allowed a Negro to take the entrance test: "If this boy passes the examination he will be admitted; and if the white students choose to withdraw, all the income of the college will be devoted to his education."

Everett was a good representative of the Eastern intellectual wing of the antislavery movement. Most abolitionists were of a different character, drawing their inspiration from revi-

Illustrations of the American Anti-Slavery Almanac for 1840.

"*Our* Peculiar *Domestic Institutions.*"

Northern Hospitality—New-York nine months law. [The Slave steps out of the Slave State, and his chains fall. A Free State, with another chain, stands ready to re-enslave him.]

Burning of McIntosh at St. Louis, in April, 1836.

Showing how slavery improves the condition of the female sex.

The Negro Pew, or "Free" Seats for black *Christians.* | *Mayor of New-York refusing a Carman's license to a colored Man.*

Servility of the Northern States in arresting and returning fugitive Slaves.

Selling a Mother from her Child.

Hunting Slaves with dogs and guns. A Slave drowned by the dogs.

"*Poor things, 'they can't take care of themselves.'* "

Mothers with young Children at work in the field.

A Woman chained to a Girl, and a Man in irons at work in the field.

Branding Slaves.

Cutting up a Slave in Kentucky.

Paid. *Unpaid.*

The abolition movement was an integral part of the reform sentiment that began in the 1830s. It emphasized moral suasion rather than legal coercion. *(Courtesy, Library of Congress)* valistic religion, with its doctrine of "perfectionism." Perfectionists argued that all people, through an act of conversion, could cleanse themselves of sin (defined as voluntary selfishness) and live in harmony with divine law. When enough individuals embraced God's way, the larger society could be purged of evils such as slavery. Slaveholders had only to recognize their complicity in sin and renounce it. It was by using the techniques of moral suasion—appealing to the American conscience rather than employing legal coercion—that abolitionists would end human bondage in the United States.

Garrison and Weld. One person led to abolitionism by perfectionist beliefs was the young William Lloyd Garrison. He had embraced a number of reform causes in the 1820s and worked with the famous Quaker abolitionist Benjamin Lundy before establishing his own antislavery newspaper, the *Liberator*, at Boston in 1831. In unequivocal, though bombastic, language, Garrison preached the cause of immediate abolition with no compensation to slaveholders: "I *will be* as harsh as truth, and as uncompromising as justice. . . . I will not equivocate—I will not excuse—I will not retreat a single inch—AND I WILL BE HEARD." In his obsessive moral purity, he denounced the churches as "cages of unclean birds" for tolerating slavery and burned copies of the Constitution because it recognized slavery. Northerners at first dismissed Garrison as a fanatic; only eleven people accepted his invitation to form the New England Antislavery Society. But the Nat Turner revolt of 1831 made his name familiar throughout the nation, as nervous slaveholders connected the "incendiary publications" of Garrison and others with the bloody events in Southampton County, Virginia. The Georgia Senate offered a $1000 reward for his arrest and conviction. Newspapers throughout the country began reprinting Garrison's fiery editorials, and the stern Massachusetts editor soon became the very personification of abolition.

Abolitionism had other leaders, and much of the movement was outside of New England. Some of Garrison's contemporaries, and a few later historians, considered Theodore Dwight Weld an even more important figure. Like Gar-

---

ESSAY ON CIVIL DISOBEDIENCE *by Henry David Thoreau*
Thoreau was ardently opposed to slavery.

How does it become a man to behave toward this American government to-day? I answer, that he cannot without disgrace be associated with it. I cannot for an instant recognize that political organization as *my* government which is the *slave's* government also.

All men recognize the right of revolution: that is, the right to refuse allegiance to, and to resist, the government, when its tyranny or its inefficiency are great and unendurable. But almost all say that such is not the case now. But such was the case, they think, in the Revolution of '75. If one were to tell me that this was a bad government because it taxed certain foreign commodities brought to its ports, it is most probable that I should not make an ado about it, for I can do without them. When a sixth of the population of a nation which has undertaken to be the refuge of liberty are slaves, and a whole country is unjustly overrun and conquered by a foreign army, and subjected to military law, I think that it is not too soon for honest men to rebel and revolutionize. What makes this duty the more urgent is the fact that the country so overrun is not our own, but ours is the invading army.

If the injustice is part of the necessary friction of the machine of government, let it go, let it go: perchance it will wear smooth,—certainly the machine will wear out. If the injustice has a spring, or a pulley, or a rope, or a crank, exclusively for itself, then perhaps you may consider whether the remedy will not be worse than the evil; but if it is of such a nature that it requires you to be the agent of injustice to another, then, I say, break the law. Let your life be a counter friction to stop the machine. What I have to do is to see, at any rate, that I do not lend myself to the wrong which I condemn.

rison, Weld had entered the movement because of intense religious convictions about the evils of slavery. After being converted by the famous evangelist Charles G. Finney, he devoted his life to the cause of moral reform. In 1834, while a student at Cincinnati's Lane Theological Seminary, he organized debates on the slavery question. After eighteen nights of discussion, the students endorsed immediatism—immediate abolition—and rejected colonization. When their antislavery activities aroused opposition among Lane's trustees, Weld and forty others left to attend Oberlin College near Cleveland. Securing funds from two wealthy New York City reformers, Arthur and Lewis Tappan, the Lane rebels made Oberlin a center of abolitionist activity. By employing the techniques and rhetoric of the religious revival, they converted to abolitionism thousands throughout the Old Northwest and nearby areas of New York and Pennsylvania. Weld also joined with his Southern wife, Angelina, and her sister, Sarah Grimké, to write *Slavery as It Is* (1839). This popular tract, a compilation of Southern newspaper accounts revealing the cruelties of slavery, offered documentary evidence to support the abolitionists' moral outrage. "Slaves," they wrote, "are often hunted with bloodhounds and shot down like beasts, or torn in pieces by dogs . . . they are often suspended by the arms and whipped and beaten till they faint, . . . and sometimes till they die; . . . they are maimed, mutilated and burned to death over slow fires. All these things, and more, and worse, we shall PROVE."

Initially, the abolitionists' demands for emancipation and an end to racial discrimination angered many people in the North, and during the mid-1830s anti-abolitionist mobs harassed and assaulted prominent abolitionists. A Boston mob dragged Garrison through the streets with a rope around his neck in 1835; two years later a crowd at Alton, Illinois, killed the abolitionist editor Elijah Lovejoy. Often leading citizens—lawyers, doctors, bankers, merchants—directed these actions; they, like many other Americans in the Jackson Era, considered mob violence a legitimate means of protecting society, not itself a threat to law and order. Abolitionists, thought these "gentlemen of property and standing," were troublemaking outsiders who bypassed traditional local elites and pitched their radical message directly to the mass of citizens by means of printed propaganda and traveling speakers.

Southern Counterattack

The rise of militant abolitionism, coupled with the Nat Turner uprising, stimulated another round of soul-searching among Southern whites. In 1831-32 the Virginia House of Delegates began a lengthy debate on a plan for the gradual emancipation and deportation of all slaves. The proposal was at last defeated, and this defeat marked a turning point. Thereafter, few Southerners would deny that slavery was sanctioned by the Bible and the laws of nature, provided a harmonious solution to the South's racial dilemma, and offered beneficent schooling to the black race. A scientific apologist, Dr. Josiah Nott, of Mobile, Alabama, published his *Types of Mankind* in 1854, concluding on the basis of head size that blacks were a separate and permanently inferior species fit only for slavery. Other writers contrasted the "security" that slaves enjoyed with the brutal exploitation suffered by Northern workingmen.

To shore up their "peculiar institution," Southern legislatures enacted tougher slave codes and further curtailed the liberties of free blacks. The repression touched whites as well. Slave-state lawmakers forbade the publication or distribution of antislavery propaganda—sometimes under penalty of death. Public pressure silenced other critics of slavery: several prominent university professors left the South. The antislavery societies that had existed throughout the region quickly disappeared.

The "Gag" Rule. Southerners also sought to stifle criticism from without. Backed by a war chest of over $30,000, abolitionists embarked in 1835 on their "great postal campaign," an attempt to send hundreds of thousands of antislavery pamphlets to all parts of the country. A mob of South Carolinians seized the materials from the Charleston post office and in a huge bonfire burned them, along with effigies of Arthur Tappan and Garrison. Afterward, Postmaster General Amos Kendall, with President Jackson's approval, authorized Southern postmasters to censor the mails and stop the flow of antislavery material into the South. Southern politicians urged the House of Representatives not to receive petitions demanding the abolition of slavery in the states or the District of Columbia. Formerly Congress had accepted such memorials and then rejected the request as "inexpedient." Following angry debate, the House now approved a modified "gag" rule; henceforth it would receive antislavery petitions but automatically table them without formal consideration.

Repressive tactics rebounded against slaveholders. "Gag" rules, mob attacks, the censorship of mails, and other violations of civil liberties created a reaction that broadened the antislavery movement's appeal. Sounding a note that would grow loud by the 1850s, abolitionists charged that a vast "slavepower" conspiracy was threatening the liberty of Northern whites as well as Southern blacks. Slaveholders and their Northern allies, those "gentlemen of property and standing," stood ready to destroy the freedom of all Americans in order to safeguard slavery.

Antislavery Disunity

As they struggled to influence popular opinion, abolitionists promoted one broad organization: the American Antislavery Society, founded in 1833. Garrison, Weld, the Tappan brothers, and the Grimké sisters all belonged to the Society, which claimed as many as thirteen hundred local chapters. Under Weld's direction, the Society's members bombarded Congress with petitions opposing slavery in the District of Columbia and urging an end to the interstate slave trade. The petition campaign attracted widespread support after Southern Congressmen obtained their "gag" rule. Former President John Quincy Adams led the battle to vindicate the historic right of petition. Year after year "Old Man Eloquent," though never an advocate of immediatism, fought to get petitions discussed before the House of Representatives, winning thousands to the antislavery cause in the process. In 1844 Adams finally secured repeal of the "gag" rule. American abolitionists also sought closer ties with British reformers, and in 1840 many had attended the World Antislavery Convention in London. Yet the antislavery movement had deep internal divisions. Personality clashes, doctrinal conflicts among different religious denominations, and fundamental differences over strategy splintered the movement.

Tactical Disagreements. The split over strategy and tactics involved conflicting interpretations of American society and the role of abolitionism in American life. Shocked by antiabolition mob violence, Garrisonians concluded that American society was sick. Slavery was one of the symptoms of moral decay, but there were others—militarism, expansionism, the oppression of women and the poor. Only a total reformation of the nation's ethical values would suffice. Abolitionists, Garrison maintained, must "revolutionize the public sentiment" by an expanded campaign of moral suasion; having done this, they would accomplish the overthrow of slavery. Garrison's opponents in the antislavery movement possessed a broader faith in the possibilities of American society and a narrower vision of reform. When they surveyed the events of the 1830s, they concluded that abolitionism had made considerable progress. Efforts to link the movement too closely with other causes, they felt, risked alienating people who had been converted by the campaign against postal censorship or angered by Southern violations of the civil liberties of whites. "Garrisonian fanaticism," so they feared, only endangered the future of abolitionism.

Involvement in the antislavery movement fostered female abolitionists' demands for the equality of their own sex. When Garrison's New England Antislavery Society voted to accept women on equal terms with men, several important male leaders promptly resigned. When female abolitionists found themselves segregated in the gallery at the London World Antislavery Convention of 1840, Garrison and other sympathetic men joined them there. The Garrisonians' active support for the women's cause angered many antislavery activists who charged that feminism would only sidetrack the crusade against slavery.

The Liberty Party. The question of involvement in politics proved even more divisive. The "Log Cabin and Hard Cider" campaign of 1840 expressed the nation's new fascination with mass politics, and many antislavery leaders wanted to get involved. The success of the petition drives and other quasi-political activities offered some hope that electoral politics and antislavery would be joined. Over the strident objections of Garrison, a group of abolitionists formed the Liberty Party in 1840; as their presidential candidate, they selected James G. Birney, a slaveholder turned abolitionist, and they framed a platform calling for the abolition of slavery in America. Lost in the hoopla of the contest between the Whig Harrison and the Democrat Van Buren, the Liberty Party attracted little at-

William Lloyd Garrison, one of the earliest abolitionists and a key organizer of antislavery societies.

tention. Birney, in London for the World Antislavery Convention, did not even campaign. But in the next presidential election Birney polled almost 65,000 votes. Although an improvement over 1840, this still represented only 32 out of every 1,000 votes cast in the North. Garrison and his followers consistently opposed the Liberty Party experiment. Political organizations, they argued, implied acceptance of the legitimacy of the existing system, which for them was morally diseased at its root. Retaining his faith in perfectionism, Garrison refused even to vote.

But abolitionists, including even Garrison, were more than simple idealists or frustrated politicians. Most were hard-headed reformers who recognized the need for many types of nonviolent action. They tried, unsuccessfully, to organize a boycott of slave-produced products; they worked to impel churches to denounce slavery; a few helped slaves escape Southern bondage on the celebrated "underground railroad" that has enjoyed a legend beyond its reality; many courageously demanded equal rights for blacks in the North.

Northern Blacks. By 1850 the quarter of a million blacks who lived in the free states were free in name only. In most places they could not vote, hold office, or testify in court. They were confined to menial jobs and wretched housing. Everywhere law and public opinion combined to exclude or segregate them: in railroad coaches, schools, restaurants, theaters, churches, even cemeteries. Most Northerners, including some who condemned slavery, viewed this not as a departure from democratic principles, but as a natural and legitimate response to the presence of the Negro.

Excluded from the dominant political and social institutions, Northern blacks found in the abolitionist crusade their first opportunity to play a major role in American public life. Their subscriptions kept Garrison's newspaper alive, and Boston blacks protected him from violence. David Walker, a free black who had migrated from North Carolina to Boston, electrified the country in 1831 with his *Appeal,* a pamphlet urging militant resistance to slavery. Escaped slaves like Frederick Douglass lectured and wrote of their experiences. Harriet Tubman, an escapee who made nineteen trips into slave country to bring out runaways, had a price of $40,000 on her head. Initially the protégés of white abolitionists, blacks gradually asserted their independence. They founded newspapers and civil-rights organizations of their own and established vigilance committees in Northern cities that protected black fugitives from slavecatchers. "Should any wretch enter my dwelling, any pale-faced spectre among ye, to execute this fugitive slave law on me or mine," a black abolitionist warned defiantly in 1850, "I'll seek his life, I'll shed his blood."

Slavery in the Territories

In 1840, the antislavery movement was still struggling for a foothold in American politics. Abolitionist sentiment was vague, sporadic, and moralistic; the slavery interest was concentrated, practical, and testily defensive. Moral suasion had utterly failed to convert Southerners, who feared not only a loss of property but a loss of racial mastery. Most Northerners scorned the abolition movement as radical and disruptive. Since the North was also a white-supremacist society, the vast majority of whites there discriminated against free blacks and were content to leave slavery alone where it existed. Northerners may have opposed slavery in the abstract, but few favored actual emancipation unless it was accompanied by colonization, fearing that the free states would be overrun with emancipated blacks. Slavery also had powerful allies among Northern businessmen dependent on the success of Southern crops.

The United States Constitution itself discouraged abolitionists. Both sides in the slavery controversy recognized that the Constitution perceived slaves as property and that the federal government could not abolish slavery in the states. This was a decision for the people of the states themselves to make. The Southern states were happy to uphold a Constitution and a Union that protected slavery. Abiding by the Missouri Compromise, both Whigs and Democrats shunned the potentially divisive slavery issue in order to preserve harmony between their Northern and Southern wings.

There was one area, however, where the federal government did hold power over slavery. The Constitution authorized the Congress to make "all needful rules and regulations" respecting the territories.

For decades Americans had agreed to an informal division of territory into free and slave soil. The Northwest Ordinance of 1787 had prohibited slavery north of the Ohio River. South of the Ohio, North Carolina and Georgia had ceded Western lands to the national government on the specific condition that slavery should be permitted in the states that would eventually be formed from these lands—Tennessee, Alabama, and Mississippi. The Missouri Compromise line of 1820 divided the vast Louisiana Purchase into slave and free soil. These arrangements covered all the existing United States territory, leaving nothing after 1820 for argument in Congress. Abolitionists were left to battle over such narrow issues as the status of slavery in the District of Columbia, where Congress had undisputed authority.

Suddenly in the late 1840s the issue of slavery in the territories came alive. For Congress now had to deal with slavery in the regions acquired after the Mexican War. The antislavery movement now had a practical political issue to which it could attach itself. Since the government could determine the status of slavery in the territories, abolitionists could make concrete demands on Congress. And because many Northerners had some thought of moving to the fresh land in the territories and did not want those lands dominated by slaveholders, abolitionists could appeal to self-interest as well as to conscience. Beginning in the late 1840s the antislavery movement fixed upon the territorial issue, and for the next fifteen years this question dominated national politics as no issue before or since.

Manifest Destiny

The Whig Party. In March 1841 jubilant Whigs flooded Washington, hungry for government offices. The crush of office-seekers proved tiring for the elderly and infirm William Henry Harrison. A cold contracted while he was doing the White House grocery-shopping soon developed into pneumonia, and on April 4—just a month after the inauguration—he died. Two days later Vice-President John Tyler, summoned hastily from his Virginia plantation, took the presidential oath. Since Harrison was the first president to die in office, questions arose over whether Tyler was actually president or merely the vice-president assuming the duties and responsibilities of the presidency. Tyler insisted that he had become president in every sense of the word. His conduct in support of this claim set an important precedent.

Lean and hawk-nosed, with a Virginian's pride and a streak of obstinacy, the fifty-one-year-old Tyler entered the White House with a distinguished career in Virginia politics behind him. He had started in politics as a states' rights Democrat and he and the Whigs were mismatched from the start. The new president resisted domination by Henry Clay and Daniel Webster, the acknowledged leaders of the party. He had no sympathy for the Whigs's economic nationalism. In September, when he vetoed Clay's bill to reestablish a national bank, the entire Harrison Cabinet resigned except Secretary of State Daniel Webster. He stayed on to conduct negotiations with Great Britain over various outstanding problems, especially the disputed northeastern boundary between Maine and New Brunswick. In 1842, he concluded the Webster-Ashburton Treaty, which settled the Maine boundary and other problems by compromise, and set an example for the friendly resolution of future disputes between Britain and the United States and between this country and Canada. Shortly after the treaty was signed, Webster too left the Cabinet. That resignation completed the break between Tyler and the Whigs, who henceforth referred to the President as "His Accidency."

Tyler appointed a new Cabinet heavy with Southern Democrats, and began searching for issues that would win him reelection. For the North he signed the Tariff of 1842, restoring protective duties to roughly the level of 1832. To soothe Southern resentment over the tariff, Tyler offered a daring proposal—the annexation of Texas.

Spanish Settlement. In the early nineteenth century American interest had grown in lands that existed mainly as lonely outposts on the edge of Northern Mexico. These lands, stretching from present-day Texas to California and north to the Great Salt Lake, already had a long history of cultural contact between the Indians and the Hispanics. Conquistadores had led the early Spanish activity in these areas, leaving one settlement at Santa Fé in 1598, established by Juan de Onate, who became the first governor of the province of New Mexico. Sante Fé became the provincial capital in 1610, and is generally recognized as the oldest seat of government in what is now the United States.

Soon, however, Spanish church and civil authorities quarreled among themselves and with the Indians. The friars established schools for the Indians and attempted to convert them, while the civil government enslaved the Pueblos in a forced labor system. In 1680 the Pueblos drove the Spanish eastward to present-day El Paso, Texas, killing 400 and destroying all traces of the church. But the Indians found their power broken by 1692, and the Spanish returned with their missions.

In the more usual pattern of Spanish settlement, the missionaries preceded the military. Spanish friars, representing the various Catholic orders (Dominican, Franciscan, or Jesuit), typically established mission settlements after investigating favorable locations. The friars then gathered some of their fellows, along with some soldiers and Christianized Indians, and moved them to the settlement, where they sought to convert local Indians while building communities. These missions gradually established themselves as relatively self-sufficient islands, far from the centers of New Spain and linked to the local Indian economies. They survived by cultivating grain, raising cattle, and developing such local crafts as blacksmithing and milling, using local adobe to build their churches and Indian dyes to decorate them. After the friars succeeded in converting a sufficient number of the local Indians, each mission served as a stepping stone for the establishment of further missions, often no more than a day's walk away. Eventually these missions strung from Texas to California.

The progress of Spanish settlement was slow. In 1718 San Antonio became the center of Spanish government in Texas, but by 1793, after a hundred years of missionary effort, the Spanish settlers in Texas numbered only around 7,000. The first Spanish settlement in Arizona was established at the Tubac presidio (military post) in 1752 and another at Tucson in 1776. Although missions had long before been started in lower California (Baja), the main Spanish missionary effort began only in 1769 when the Franciscans moved a settlement of friars, Indians, and soldiers from Arizona to San Diego Bay. Fearing Russian outposts to the north, the Spanish, over the next fifty years, established twenty missions from San Diego to Sonoma, north of San Francisco. These missions were accompanied by two presidios and may have included as many as 13,000 California Indians.

After Mexico won its independence from Spain in 1821, the mission era ended and many of the holdings were taken by large landholders who established *ranchos,* often encompassing thousands of acres. These estates produced a lively cattle-raising economy controlled by men of Spanish descent. Their *vaqueros* began cowboy traditions in the Southwest, many of which would later be adopted by the incoming white settlers. Their chaps, bandannas, and rodeos would become American traditions. The distinctive architecture of the Spanish missions, with their red-tiled roofs, whitewashed adobe walls, courtyards, and fountains graced the landscape from San Antonio to San Francisco. The patio barbecue descended from a Spanish custom. The Southwest would retain many Spanish laws regarding water and mining, along with techniques for irrigation, sheep ranching, and orchard planting. Even Spanish laws and customs concerning the disposition of property within families prevailed long after these areas became part of the United States.

The independence of Mexico from Spain did not eliminate the isolation of the Spanish outposts to the north. Isolation gave these settlements much self-sufficiency, but they were receptive to the manufactures that American traders were able to furnish. By 1824 wagons and pack animals were hauling tools, textiles,

Texas land titles were freely issued to colonists, here by Stephen Austin and Baron de Bastrop, representing the Mexican government. *(Courtesy, Southern Pacific Company)*

and weapons over the Santa Fé Trail, forged by William Becknell in the early 1820s. In the 1830s English-speaking Americans and even Europeans began to drift into California. Some traversed the California trail and competed as successful ranchers alongside the Spanish. The Swiss John Sutter, who would discover gold in California in 1849, settled in Monterey. Other Americans came to California, having sailed around the Southern tip of South America, and established trading enterprises in San Diego and elsewhere. Some of these newcomers married into Spanish families and adopted their religion.

In all these areas, relations with the Mexican government deteriorated. In the wake of a rebellion among California's Mexicans, the influence of the Mexican republic was weakening even among its own California citizens. In New Mexico, Mexicans and Indians rebelled in 1837 against the government, executing the governor and seizing his palace.

Annexation of Texas. The broad plains stretching west and south of the Sabine River had long attracted Americans. In the 1820s, immigrants such as Moses and Stephen Austin obtained Mexican land grants in Texas and began colonizing there. Lured by the cheap land, several thousand settlers followed. Mexican law required them to become nominal Catholics as well as Mexican citizens; otherwise the colonists enjoyed considerable autonomy and retained their national character. Stephen Austin advised them to "play the turtle, head and feet within your own shell," but differences soon arose between the Texans and the Mexican government. Alarmed by these signs of independence, and by the rapid increase in the number of Americans in Texas (30,000 in 1835), the Mexican government tightened its control and prohibited further immigration. After several armed uprisings, the Texans declared their independence in 1836. The ruthless treatment of the defenders of the Alamo—designed to intimidate the rebels—only united them behind General Sam Houston, and led to the rout of the Mexican army at San Jacinto, and the capture of General Santa Anna.

The United States had adopted a distinctly unneutral attitude during the Texan war of independence. Money was raised for supplies, and many volunteers swelled the ranks of the Texan army. After independence, the public on both sides of the United States border strongly favored annexation. But since Mexico refused to acknowledge Texan independence, annexation might provoke war. Politicians also feared that incorporating new slave territory into the Union would aggravate the rising antislavery sentiment in the North. President Jackson waited until his last day in office before recognizing the new Texan republic. His successor, Martin Van Buren, carefully avoided the question of annexation. Texas drifted for several years, developing ever closer ties with Great Britain.

The movement for annexation revived in 1842. Texas President Sam Houston, facing an empty treasury and renewed hostilities with Mexico, made overtures to Washington and found an enthusiastic ally in John Tyler. Annexation was politically expedient, and, like other slaveholders, Tyler was convinced that continued expansion was vital to the slave economy and the Southern way of life. After the unsympathetic Webster resigned as secretary of state, Tyler appointed a fellow Virginian, Abel P. Upshur, and ordered him to seek a treaty of annexation.

The move was well timed: Americans dreamed anew of continental empire. Southerners feared that Britain was working to abolish slavery in Texas. Northern commercial interests sought American control of valuable Pacific coast ports as trading centers, and annexation of Texas would shorten the distance to the Pacific. It was the nation's "manifest destiny," orators told Americans, to overspread and civilize the continent. Secretary Upshur, confident that the Senate would approve a treaty, negotiated with Texan representatives. After Upshur's death the new secretary of state, John C. Calhoun, completed the arrangements for annexation and submitted the treaty to the Senate.

James Polk: Expansionist. The Senate, however, delayed action until after the 1844 party nominating conventions, at which Texas suddenly emerged as a major political issue. Both leading candidates, Henry Clay and Martin Van Buren, came out against annexation. The Whigs, passing over Tyler, nominated Clay, but the Democrats bypassed Van Buren in favor of an avowed expansionist, James Knox Polk. This po-

President James K. Polk. His aggressive actions against New Mexico and California brought about the Mexican War.

litical maneuvering and Calhoun's defense of annexation as a proslavery measure doomed the treaty. A combination of Whigs and disappointed Van Buren Democrats killed it. Tyler refused to surrender; he sent a message to the House of Representatives three days later proposing to annex Texas by other means.

Tyler had forced the issue of expansion to the center of American politics. Democratic politicians hoped to preserve sectional harmony within their party with a platform promising both the "re-annexation" of Texas and the "re-occupation" of Oregon all the way to 54° 40′ latitude. Too late, Clay sensed the public mood and endorsed annexation "upon just and fair terms." That November, Polk won a narrow victory in the presidential election, and Tyler interpreted this as a mandate for annexation of Texas. Just before he left office in March 1845, the president obtained a joint congressional resolution (which required only a majority vote in each house, while a treaty would have required approval by two-thirds of the Senate) admitting Texas to the Union. When Polk entered the White House, annexation was a settled question.

Another of Polk's major objectives was the solution of the Oregon boundary question. Formidable mountain barriers had retarded American settlement in the Pacific Northwest until the 1830s, when traders and missionaries began publicizing the area. By 1845 five thousand Americans had migrated there, settling mainly in the fertile Willamette Valley in Oregon. Throughout his campaign, Polk had promised to assert American control over all the Oregon Territory, which the United States and Great Britain had occupied jointly since 1818. Once in power, however, Polk began a search for compromise with Britain.

The British government at first rejected the American idea of putting the line at the 49th

"Red Buttes, where the Oregon Trail leaves the Platte for Sweetwater." The Trail, which stretched from Independence, Missouri, to Oregon, carried hundreds of emigrant wagon trains across the continent to "Manifest Destiny."

parallel, which would place the Columbia River wholly in American hands. Polk then called upon Congress for authority to give the required one year's notice terminating joint occupation. The United States, he announced, would look John Bull "straight in the eye." Congress consented. Polk served the expected notice in April 1846; on both sides of the Atlantic, people talked of war.

Neither side really wanted a fight. Britain had all but abandoned the area between the Columbia River and the 49th parallel to the advancing wave of American settlers. Polk, anticipating war with Mexico at any moment, could no longer afford a quarrel with Britain. He therefore welcomed a British offer to divide Oregon at the 49th parallel. The Senate approved this arrangement, despite angry protests from Northwestern Democrats, who charged that Polk and his Southern Democratic allies, having acquired Texas, had reneged on their promise to acquire "all of Oregon or none." Their residual bitterness combined with abolitionist sentiment to hamper Polk's conduct of the Mexican War.

The Mexican War

Polk's other objective, acquiring California, was not so easily accomplished. Mexico had no intention of selling the province. The proud Latin republic had broken diplomatic relations with the United States in March 1845, in protest over the American decision to annex Texas. And a controversy had arisen over the question of just what had been annexed. Texans asserted that their republic stretched as far south as the Rio Grande; Mexico insisted that the province's boundary stopped at the Nueces River. Mexico probably had the better case. Polk nevertheless claimed all the disputed area for the United States and used the American demands on the Texas boundary to press Mexico to a settlement on California.

The Drift Toward War. In July 1845, Polk ordered General Zachary Taylor, with nearly four thousand troops, to take up a position south of the Nueces. Taylor halted at Corpus Christi, where he remained for several months. At about the same time, the president issued secret orders to naval officers in the Pacific to occupy the California ports in the event of war with Mexico. He worked actively to encourage a Texas-style revolution among settlers. Just in case the dissatisfied settlers from the United States needed any help, the president sent Colonel John C. Frémont and a party of heavily armed engineers on a "scientific expedition" to California.

His weapons now primed and ready, Polk sent John Slidell, a Louisiana politician, to Mexico in November 1845 to negotiate. The president, refusing to compromise on the Rio Grande boundary, offered only to assume payment of American claims against the Mexican government in return for its acquiescence. He also authorized Slidell to purchase all or part of Upper California and New Mexico. When two successive Mexican governments refused to risk public disfavor by receiving him, Slidell withdrew. "Be assured," he wrote to the Secretary of State, "that nothing is to be done with these people until they shall have been chastised." Polk had reached the same conclusion. In January 1846 he sent General Taylor's army to the Rio Grande. Taylor took up a fortified position opposite the Mexican City of Matamoros; naval units then blockaded the mouth of the river. For several months, nothing happened.

Polk decided to ask Congress for a declaration of war against Mexico for failing to pay the claims due citizens of the United States and refusing to receive Slidell. News arrived that very evening of a skirmish with Mexican forces on the north bank of the Rio Grande. Polk at once revised his war message. Mexico, he told Congress, had "invaded our territory and shed American blood upon American soil." Congress, not fully aware of the president's maneuvering, voted overwhelmingly for war. Thousands of volunteers enthusiastically answered the call.

Polk and his Cabinet agreed at the outset that the United States must acquire both New Mexico and Upper California (the present state, as distinct from Lower California, still part of Mexico) and secure the Rio Grande boundary. New Mexico and California took but six months to conquer. During the summer of 1846 Colonel Stephen W. Kearny's "Army of the West" (actually just sixteen hundred men) marched from Fort Leavenworth, Kansas, to Santa Fé, and occupied it without opposition. Kearny then proceeded with part of his force to aid the Navy in the conquest of California. A column of Missouri volunteers under Colonel A. W. Doniphan descended the Rio Grande to El Paso, marched from there into the interior, and in March 1847 occupied Chihuahua.

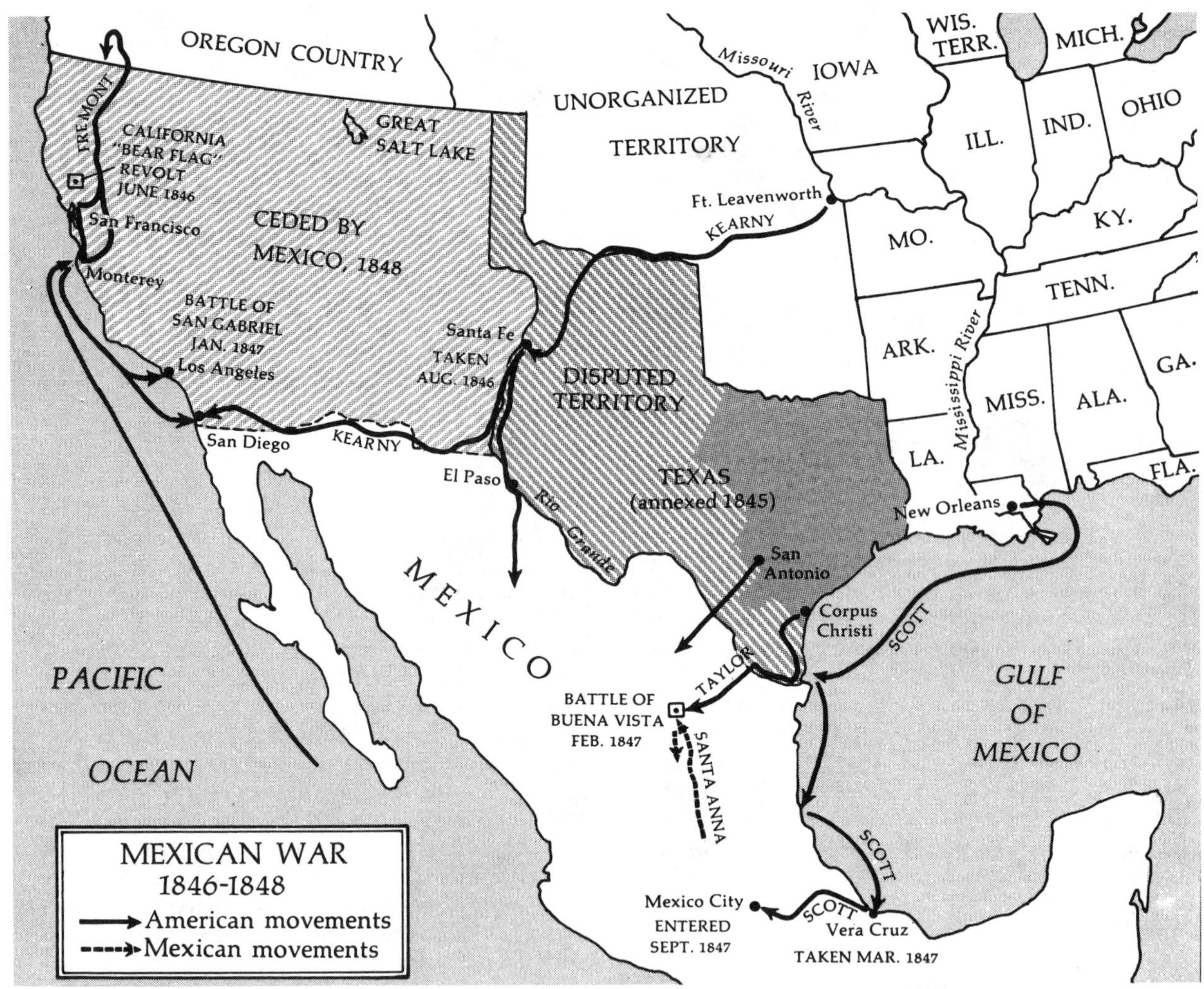

Polk's objectives in Mexico were unclear. Apparently he hoped that an advance into Mexico would force General Santa Anna into a quick settlement.

Taylor at once pushed the Mexicans back across the Rio Grande and occupied Matamoros. The enthusiasm of the volunteers waned as the summer advanced. From a camp on the Rio Grande, one reported: "The water here unless well-qualified with brandy has a very peculiar effect on one. . . . it opens the bowels. . . . Gen. Scott came to see us the other day. He complimented Major Sumner very warmly on our improvement and especially on the extraordinary vigilance of our scouts—who, as he said, were peering at him from behind every bush as he approached the camp. To those aware of the disease prevalent here, the mistake of the General is ludicrous." In September, nevertheless, Taylor captured the Mexican stronghold of Monterrey and moved on to Saltillo and Victoria. The following February he repulsed Santa Anna at Buena Vista. "Old Rough and Ready's" victories and Doniphan's occupation of Chihuahua secured northern Mexico and California from further attack.

In the meantime, Polk had decided to bring the stubborn Santa Anna to terms with a strike at Mexico City itself. Polk, hating the Whigs even more than the Mexicans, picked General Winfield Scott to lead the campaign instead of Zachary Taylor, who was already being pushed as a Whig presidential candidate. Landing at Vera Cruz in March 1847, Scott pushed inland through the mountains, routing Santa Anna at the pass of Cerro Gordo, after a party of engineers under Captain Robert E. Lee had hacked a path through ravines and underbrush to sur-

An early daguerrotype of Thomas Wood, a member of Zachary Taylor's staff, leading American troops through the streets of Saltillo, capital of Coahuila province in northern Mexico. *(Courtesy, Yale University Library)*

round the Mexicans. On September 13, Scott's army stormed the fortress of Chapultepec guarding Mexico City. The capital fell the next day.

Treaty of Guadalupe Hidalgo (1848). Polk was by now desperate to end the fighting, and the intense domestic opposition to "Mr. Polk's War." Whig politicians—among them a young Illinois congressman named Abraham Lincoln—charged him with provoking Mexico into war as an excuse for expansion. Antislavery spokesmen like James Russell Lowell accused the President of wanting "bigger pens to cram with slaves." The American Peace Society grew in membership, and Henry David Thoreau counseled civil disobedience. Some critics of the war even longed for American defeat. As Scott's army approached Mexico City, William Lloyd Garrison thundered in the *Liberator:* "We only hope that, if blood has had to flow, that it has been that of the Americans, and that the next news we shall hear will be that General Scott and his army are in the hands of the Mexicans. . . ." At the same time "Continental Democrats," party members of extreme expansionist persuasion, were urging the President to take all of Mexico. Polk had previously dispatched Nicholas P. Trist to Mexico as a peace negotiator, and although in late 1847 he called Trist home, the emissary ignored Polk's order and stayed to sign the Treaty of Guadalupe Hidalgo on February 2, 1848. The United States gained the Rio Grande boundary, New Mexico, and California in return for an agreement to assume the claims of its citizens against the Mexican government, and to pay $15 million to Mexico.

With the Treaty of Guadalupe Hidalgo, in 1853, the United States annexed approximately 80,000 Mexicans whose citizenship, property rights, and religious freedom the treaty supposedly guaranteed. Mexican Americans residing within the United States gradually saw their property and influence dwindle as they faced increasing pressure from the flood of Anglo-Americans. The California Land Law of 1851 required that they submit proof of their land ownership. The cost of doing so in taxes, legal fees, and battles with "squatters," in combination with the rainfall conditions that made incomes uncertain, gradually took away their land. Violence broke out in Northern California in the 1850s and 1860s, and some Mexican Americans, called *Californios*, resorted to banditry. *Bandidos* who roamed the California area spawned legends. In Southern California, in the 1870s and 1880s, the *Californios* lost more land to the railroads which, nonetheless, provided jobs for Hispanics. In New Mexico, the *ricos*, wealthy Mexican American landowners and merchants, played an important role in the creation of the territorial government. While remaining separate from the Anglo-Americans, they retained substantial influence into the post-Civil War era. In Texas, the Spanish and Anglo cultures blended after the war into the familiar cowboy traditions of that area as the cattle industry grew phenomenally in response to growing demands for beef.

The war was over. Writing in 1848, a Mexican historian observed: "To explain then in a few words the true origin of the war, it is sufficient to say that the insatiable ambition of the United States, favored by our weakness, caused it." For an apparently small price the United States had rounded out its continental domain, acquiring the present states of California, Nevada, Utah, New Mexico, and Arizona. Eventually, however, the cost would prove enormous: the problem of organizing this vast new territory reopened the explosive issue of slavery expansion, ultimately splitting in two the new transcontinental republic.

Manifest Destiny Again

A new president, Franklin Pierce, would call for further expansion in his inaugural address. "My administration," he boldly proclaimed in 1849, "will not be controlled by any timid forebodings of evil from expansion." True to his word, Pierce dispatched James Gadsden of South Carolina to Mexico with instructions to purchase additional territory. At the very least, Gadsden was to acquire the Gila River region, which lay along the proposed Southern railroad route to the Pacific. In addition, he might offer up to $50 million for the northern provinces of Mexico. The Mexican government refused to sell anything more than the Gila River region. Even this small triumph for Gadsden was too much for the Senate. Northern Senators, suspecting a Southern plot to expand the domain of slavery, accepted the Gadsden Treaty only after 9,000 square miles, one-sixth of the total, had been cut from the purchase. For the first time in its history, the United States had refused to accept land ceded to it. Despite this minor setback, the hapless Pierce embarked upon a new imperialist venture. This time the object was Spanish-owned Cuba.

Southerners had long desired to acquire Cuba, with its large and valuable slave population. It would compensate the South for the admission of California as a free state and prevent England from intervening in the island and eliminating slavery. President Polk had tried without success to purchase Cuba from Spain. During 1853 the Pierce Administration lent support to John A. Quitman of Mississippi and others who proposed to "liberate" Cuba by force. When Quitman backed off, Pierce instructed the American Minister in Madrid, Pierre Soulé, to offer Spain as much as $130 million for Cuba. Spain indignantly rejected the American offer. Soulé then arranged a meeting at Ostend, Belgium, in October 1854, with the American ministers to London and Paris, to consider further action regarding Cuba. Their recommendations to Washington, known as the "Ostend Manifesto," soon found their way into print, to the great embarrassment of the Pierce Administration. Particularly damaging was the statement that, should Spain refuse renewed offers to purchase Cuba, the United States would "by every law, human and Divine, be . . . justified in wresting it from Spain." Both American and European critics branded the Manifesto "a robber doctrine," "a highwayman's plea." The administration promptly repudiated the Manifesto, whereupon Soulé resigned amidst bitter recriminations. Manifest Destiny had suffered by its association with slavery. Renewed expansion would have to await the return of sectional peace.

The Costs of Manifest Destiny. Barely three months after the start of the Mexican War, the question of slavery in the territories had erupted in Congress. During debate on a military appropriations bill in August 1846, Representative David Wilmot, a Pennsylvania Democrat, introduced an amendment that would prohibit slavery forever in any territory acquired from Mexico. On the question of adopting Wilmot's amendment, the roll call produced an ominous division. Congress was splitting not between Whigs and Democrats, but between Northerners and Southerners. The House of Representatives passed Wilmot's Proviso; the Senate, dominated by Southerners, refused to accept it. Congress adjourned without further action.

Upon reassembling, the national legislature deadlocked on the question of arranging new territorial governments. Every time a bill was introduced in Congress to organize the New Mexico and California territories, Northerners in the House voted to add Wilmot's Proviso. Southerners, who controlled the Senate, just as promptly voted to strike it out. The slavery question soon crowded out all others in Congress. Senator Thomas Hart Benton compared it to the Biblical plague of the frogs: "You could not look upon the table but there were frogs, you could not sit down at the banquet but there were frogs, you could not go to the bridal couch and lift the sheets but there were frogs!" So it was with this slavery question, "forever on the table, on the nuptial couch, everywhere!"

With each new debate, tempers sharpened on both sides. "We will establish a cordon of free states that shall surround you," Columbus Delano of Ohio warned Southerners, "and then we will light up the fires of liberty on every side until they melt your present chains and render all your people free." Southerners responded by threatening to break up the Union if slavery were barred from the territories. Moderates on both sides sought to break the impasse by removing from Congress the decision over slavery in New Mexico and California. President Polk had recommended dividing the Western territories into slave and free soil by an extension of the Missouri Compromise line to the Pacific. Senator Lewis Cass of Michigan advocated "popular sovereignty"—leaving the question of slavery or non-slavery to the people of each territory. These compromises satisfied neither Northern "free soilers," who upheld the absolute authority of the federal government over slavery in the territories, nor Southern states' righters, who now denied that the federal government had any authority to restrict slavery in the common territories.

The Free Soil Party. The divisiveness of the slavery question entered into the 1848 presidential election. Both major parties turned to military men in hopes of diverting attention from slavery. The Democrats nominated Senator Lewis Cass, a hero of the War of 1812 and an ardent expansionist as well as an advocate of popular sovereignty in the territories. Just to play safe, the Democrats circulated one campaign biography of Cass in the North and another in the South. The Whigs picked General Zachary Taylor, hero of the Mexican War, who had never so much as voted in an election before. The Whig convention then adjourned without adopting a platform. During the campaign Taylor was pictured in the South as a friend of slavery (he owned over one hundred slaves), and in the North as a friend of the Wilmot Proviso. A third party, the Free Soil Party, was formed out of a coalition of three elements—the abolitionist Liberty Party, "conscience" or antislavery Whigs, and Northern Democrats alienated by Polk's rejection of internal improvement and a protective tariff. The Free Soilers made opposition to slavery expansion their main plank. For president they chose Martin Van Buren.

Although these heterogeneous elements in the Free Soil Party could barely stifle their differences long enough for a campaign, theirs was a broadly based antislavery party, the first. In November 1848 the Free Soilers failed to carry a single state; yet the party captured an impressive ten percent of the popular vote. By cutting heavily into the Democratic vote in New York, Massachusetts, and Vermont, Van Buren made possible Taylor's victory.

The Compromise of 1850

It was a warring Congress that met in December 1849. It took three weeks and fifty-nine ballots to elect a Speaker of the House. Californians, tired of waiting for Congress, had held a convention at Monterey and drafted a state constitution prohibiting slavery: some of them simply did not want whites to have to compete with black labor. Without waiting for congressional approval,

California chose a governor and legislature. Only one obstacle—formal admission to statehood—remained.

On this Congress could not agree. The new president, Zachary Taylor, decided to intervene in the imbroglio. Although a defender of slavery, Taylor did not regard expansion as necessary for its protection. Like Polk, he considered California and the Southwest as unsuitable for slavery. The president therefore recommended to Congress that California and New Mexico be admitted directly to statehood, bypassing the territorial stage. The residents could then decide the slavery question for themselves, and thereby without embarrassment to Congress. Southerners, seeing that California had already prohibited slavery and expecting New Mexico to do the same, realized that Taylor's plan was as effective as Wilmot's Proviso in keeping slavery out of this area. When they protested, the old soldier drew a firm line, threatening to use force if necessary to preserve the Union.

Taylor, Southerners decided, had betrayed them. California would be the first in what they feared would be a flood of new "free" states admitted to the Union. Free and slave states had been equal in number, and therefore North and South had enjoyed equal representation in the Senate. Now the South would lose that precarious equality. Northerners would make war upon slavery—an institution, Southern spokesmen insisted, "upon which is staked our property, our social organization and our peace and safety." When a call went out in October 1849 for the Southern states to send delegates to a convention at Nashville the following June to consider secession, most of these states accepted.

Daniel Webster. His plea to both North and South to show tolerance over slavery brought about a fragile but temporary truce.

Clay, Calhoun, and Webster. At this moment, with disunion threatening, an aged Senator Henry Clay offered a compromise that he hoped would settle for good the territorial crisis and other disputed issues between the sections. Clay's plan, introduced in Congress in January 1850, contained five key provisions: immediate admission of free California; organization of the rest of the area acquired from Mexico into two territories (Utah and New Mexico) without restriction on slavery; assumption of the Texan national debt by the federal government; abolition of the slave trade in the District of Columbia; and a tough new fugitive slave law.

The debate on Clay's compromise was the grand twilight for the generation of statesmen who had guided America's destinies since 1812. Twice before, in 1820 and 1833, stirring appeals to love of Union, flag, and Constitution had soothed sectional tensions. During the winter and spring of 1850, Senate veterans tried to revive this tested formula. Day after day, packed galleries followed their speeches.

Clay took the floor first, urging the North not to demand the principle of the Wilmot Proviso—nature would as effectively exclude slavery—and to honor the constitutional obligation to return fugitive slaves. He reminded the South of the many benefits she enjoyed in the Union. The "Great Pacificator" closed his two-day oration with an appeal to both sides to pause at the edge of the cliff, before leaping "into the yawning abyss below." Clay expressed the hope that, should disunion occur, he would not live to see it.

Clay's compromises did not go far enough to satisfy John C. Calhoun. The old Nullifier, his body wracked by tuberculosis, sat defiantly while his speech was read for him. The North, he charged, had taken advantage of tariffs and other federal favors to outstrip the South in population and power. He demanded that the North must not only grant slaveholders equal rights in the territories but pass constitutional guarantees giving the South equal power in the government. The only alternative for the South was secession.

Daniel Webster spoke on March 7, displaying an eloquence reminiscent of his brilliant reply to Hayne two decades before. He pleaded with both sections to show tolerance for the sake of Union. He criticized the abolitionists' ethical absolutism and deplored the agitation over slavery in the territories. The law of nature precluded a slave economy there, he asserted, and no legislation was needed to reenact God's will. He took sharp issue with Calhoun's talk of "peaceable secession": "There can be no such thing as a peaceable secession. Peaceable secession is an utter impossibility." A thousand physical and social ties bound the sections together. Disunion, Webster warned the South pointedly, "must produce such a war as I will not describe, *in its twofold character*"—a hint at the prospect of slave revolts. Much to the anger of abolitionists, who criticized it savagely, Webster's Seventh of March speech did much to rally Northern support for compromise.

For all his skill, Clay had miscalculated. Patriotic appeals for Union could not overcome sectional bitterness in 1850. When Clay's package of compromise measures (known as the "Omnibus" bill) came to a vote in July, opponents of the individual measures ganged up to defeat it. With his bill and his health in ruins, Clay withdrew into retirement.

Stephen A. Douglas. Thirty-four-year-old Stephen A. Douglas assumed his place in steering the compromise through Congress. Only five feet four, nicknamed "the Little Giant" and "a steam engine in britches," this brash, hard-driving Senator from Illinois devised a new compromise strategy. He introduced Clay's measures separately, relying on sectional blocs and a few "swing" votes to form majorities for each. The individual bills, one senator remarked, resembled "cats and dogs that had been tied together by their tails for months, scratching and biting." Upon being released "every one of them ran off to his own hole and was quiet."

Douglas's strategy worked. The North won admission of free California and a ban on the slave trade in Washington. The South had a more stringent fugitive slave law and a promise that there would be no congressional prohibition of slavery in the New Mexico and Utah territories. The federal government assumed the Texas debt. Two events immeasurably aided Douglas's efforts that hot summer. The first was the death on July 9 of President Taylor, who had obstinately opposed any compromise plan but his own; his successor, Millard Fillmore, supported the Clay-Douglas measures. The second was the lobbying of Texas bondholders, who stood to gain handsomely if the federal government purchased their depreciated securities.

The Compromise of 1850 received an enthusiastic welcome. Celebrations were held in many cities. In Washington, word went out that it was the duty of every patriot to get drunk. Before the next morning dawned, many citizens, including Senators Foote, Douglas, and Webster, had amply proved their patriotism. To many Americans, it now seemed that the slavery question had at last been settled.

Events soon revealed that the Compromise had settled nothing at all. Deliberate ambiguities embedded in it raised questions rather than comfortably obscuring them. The Utah and New Mexico territories had been organized without congressional restriction on slavery. The Compromise said only that they would be admitted to statehood with or without slavery, as their constitutions prescribed "at the time of their admission." But could the people of these territo-

As Senator from Illinois, Stephen A. Douglas skillfully engineered the Compromise of 1850.

San Francisco, 1849—a year after gold was discovered in California and one year before it was admitted as a free state. *(Courtesy, Stokes Collection, The New York Public Library)*

ries now restrict slavery as long as the new lands remained in a territorial status? Northerners were left to believe that popular sovereignty applied, while Southerners assumed an unrestricted right to hold slaves in these territories. The critical question of slavery in the territories had merely been evaded. There had been no compromise in 1850, only a fragile truce.

Points To Think About

1. The Missouri Compromise of 1820 temporarily removed the slavery issue from national politics, but it did not settle the issue permanently. There were many reasons for this, including the world-wide reaction against slavery that characterized the nineteenth century. Closer to home there was the relentless push west. As Americans asserted their "Manifest Destiny" to control the continent, they repeatedly resurrected the slavery question. Each new territorial acquisition threatened to upset the delicate balance of power the compromise had established.

In this way the issue of slavery continuously came up against one of the strongest forces in nineteenth-century America—nationalism. The balance between slave and free states might have been maintained indefinitely in a country of stable dimensions. But America's "destiny" was to grow, and growth involved ceaseless changes for both slave and free states. Over the long run these changes favored the free states. And, as time passed, the Missouri Compromise became obsolete. The Wilmot Proviso merely signaled this key fact.

2. The label of conservative does not closely fit the Whigs, who have been assigned it. To the extent that the Whigs shared a coherent ideology—and American political parties have never prized ideological consistency—it was a commitment to the efficient and rapid development of the country. If a label must be attached, modernizer may be more accurate than conservative. It captures the unconservative Whig commitment to promoting change.

The Whig faith was that the rapid development of the country could be combined with social stability. It was, like the Jacksonian faith in growth without planning, a naive vision.

3. Abolitionism was a remarkably dangerous trade. Elijah Lovejoy had his printing press thrown in a river, and subsequently lost his life as a mob sought to seize a second. Other abolitionists also confronted angry mobs. Most escaped with their lives, but not until suffering harrowing ordeals. Terrifying as they were, some abolitionists seemed to court these dangers. Theodore Dwight Weld, the author with his wife of *Slavery As It Is,* was wont to ride into hostile towns, announce an abolitionist meeting, and then attempt to convert to his view the angry crowd who would collect.

This seeking of danger has led some historians to suspect that many abolitionists suffered from a martyr complex. They were heroic because they were unhinged. This explanation may hold for one or another individual. But it is hazardous to psychoanalyze historical figures. Psychoanalysis normally involves an intensive exploration of an individual's emotional life. The historian cannot put subjects on the couch and ask about the details of their childhoods. Psychoanalytic categories, moreover, reflect the personal values of an era in which they are developed. These change over time, and it is unwise to attempt to fit the lives of people long dead into today's classifications. And psychoanalysis deals with the individual psyche. It is misleading to speak of whole groups such as the abolitionists as if they shared a single mental life.

We still need to explain the extraordinary fortitude of the abolitionists. One explanation, first offered in Gilbert H. Barnes's *The Anti-Slavery Impulse,* focuses upon the ties between antislavery activism and the revival. Weld was a Finney convert, as were many other abolitionists. They adopted the movement against slavery as a vocation, a form of ministry; it was their calling, the work they were intended to do. And, like the early Christians they so often modeled themselves after, they were even willing to suffer martyrdom.

Not all abolitionists, of course, were evangelical converts; some, like William Lloyd Garrison, had no formal connection with any church. Yet Garrison too was an intensely religious person. He too regarded slavery as a sin. There is, in brief, much evidence to suggest that abolitionism is better understood as a religious movement than as a psychic aberration.

Suggested Readings

Eugene D. Genovese's *Roll, Jordan, Roll: The World the Slaves Made* (1974) is a literary study of slave life before the war. The author discusses the slave family, the black work ethic, slave resistance, miscegenation, and slave language, all within the larger themes of the paternalistic ideology of the Southern planter and the accommodation between master and slave. Genovese's *The World the Slaveholders Made* (1969) elaborates on the class structure of Southern society. Herbert G. Gutman, in *The Black Family in Slavery and Freedom, 1750-1925* (1976), challenges theories that speak of the disorganization of the black slave family—and the lasting effect of that disorganization on black life; instead, he argues, the black family was resilient and adaptive. It is impossible to escape the debate over a two-volume study by Robert Fogel and Stanley Engerman, *Time on the Cross* (1974). This book by two economists quantifies the Southern slave economy to conclude that slaves were productive and efficient, well fed, rarely abused, and enjoying a variety of incentives. Excellent critiques of this argument include Paul A. David et al., *Reckoning with Slavery: A Critical Study in the Quantitative History of American Negro Slavery* (1976) and Herbert G. Gutman, *Slavery and the Numbers Game: A Critique of 'Time on the Cross'* (1978). George M. Fredrickson examines the sources of racist ideas in *The Black Image in the White Mind* (1971). John Blassingame collected *Slave Testimony* (1977) about the slave experience. Vincent Harding's *There Is a River* (1981) examines the black community. In *Slavery and the Annexation of Texas* (1972), Frederick W. Merk studies the Mexican imbroglio from the standpoint of slavery. His *Manifest Destiny and Mission in American History* (1965) is standard. K. Jack Bauer's *The Mexican-American War* (1974) is a recent account while Gene M. Brack's *Mexico Views Manifest Destiny, 1821–1846* (1975) presents the Mexican viewpoint. The politics of sectionalism is the subject of William Brock's *Parties and Political Conscience: American Dilemmas, 1840–1850* (1979).

FORREST McDONALD

For the most part the expansion of the United States across the continent requires neither explanation nor apology. Doing so, as the politicians said, was the nation's manifest destiny: to extend from sea to sea was the logic of a great nation in the making. An enormous expanse of virtually unoccupied land (there was roughly one native for every five square miles) awaited the taking; and the Americans, a restless, energetic, and adventuresome people, simply took it.

But that bald statement of the facts, though accurate, may be misleading: it suggests that the expansion was motivated by the desire for material gain and national pride. As Henry Adams pointed out a century ago, materialism and idealism were inseparable in America, and if this were properly understood, the American was the most idealistic man on earth. Other people looked upon the world as a vale of misery and resigned themselves to it. The American looked at the savage wilderness and saw boundless acres of grain and magnificent cities, in a future world that he and his would make—and he set out to make it. Impelled by this dream, even the humblest immigrant was caught up in the American spirit, "for every stroke of the axe and the hoe made him a capitalist, and made gentlemen of his children."

The other respect in which expansionism was nonmaterialistic had to do with American ideas about the quality of life. Most Americans shared the belief that living on the land was the most desirable kind of existence, breeding independence and strength of character. Most also viewed with horror the prospect that some day America, like Europe, might be plagued with huge industrial centers with their foul air and teeming multitudes of impoverished laborers. Since the time of Jefferson's presidency it had been the policy of the United States government to stave off "progress" toward that kind of world by regularly acquiring new territory. Jefferson bespoke this attitude when he declared, upon receiving news of the Louisiana Purchase, that the acquisition would make it possible for the United States to remain a nation of farmers for a thousand years. (It was a part of the same policy, however, to share America's bounty with those who fled from Europe's sorrows. During the 1840s scores of thousands of refugees from Ireland's potato famine were finding their way to America, and they would soon be followed by political refugees from the abortive European revolutions of 1848.)

As for the Mexican War, several points may be briefly made. It was the annexation of Texas that led to the conflict. Texas had won its independence from Mexico, even as Mexico, a short time earlier, had won its freedom from Spain; if Mexico's independence was legitimate, so was that of Texas. Again, the United States offered to buy all disputed territory, but Mexico scornfully turned down the prewar offer on the ground that any nation that preferred to purchase rather than fight for what it wanted was too cowardly to win it in a fight. After the war, when the United States compensated Mexico for the territory it had taken, Mexico was not too proud to accept the settlement. And who, in the long term, gained and who lost as a result of the transfer of the great southwest from Mexico to the United States? The lucky ones were those who thereby became Americans. The unlucky were those who had to remain under Mexican rule. No further proof should be needed, I think, than the silent testimony of the millions of immigrants, legal and illegal, who have moved from Mexico to the United States over the course of the years.

How Manifest a Destiny? 

EUGENE D. GENOVESE

Professor McDonald, to my great surprise, neglected to call upon the authority of a leading theorist of genius who proclaimed that the conquest of Mexico by the progressive, enterprising Americans would be a great favor to the backward, slothful Mexicans. But then, conservatives do not like to quote Karl Marx. With due respect to Marx and to Professor McDonald, I think I detect a trace of Eurocentric racial presumption in this version of "I am doing this to you for your own good."

The primary difference between, say, the *mafia* and gangster nations is that *mafiosi* normally know and admit that they are stealing and murdering. With at least a speck of concern for their immortal souls, they prefer not to commit the sin of lying or, worse, of self-deception. If indeed superior American energy, economic and technological advancement, and political and military prowess justify the American annexation of Texas and then half of Mexico, then the Soviets should have been encouraged to enter Afghanistan a long time ago. And why all the fuss about the Libyan invasion of Chad or the Somalian invasion of the sparsely populated Ogaden region of Ethiopia? The United States is today rich and Mexico poor. The reasons are complex, as I am sure Professor McDonald would agree. Here I only wish to note that if the Mexicans had held on to California and developed those gold mines, as they certainly would have, Mexico might have done a good deal better.

Very well. Let us be blunt in answering the question of the origins of national boundaries. All of northern Mexico, from California to Texas, was ripe for the taking, and we took it. As a conservative United States senator from California said about the Panama Canal during the debates of the 1970s, "We stole it fair and square." The Mexicans fought for their country, and their soldiers and armed civilians showed great courage under superior fire. It is no disgrace for a people to get speedily crushed by a vastly superior military machine.

Americans combined high idealism with the most vulgar material greed in an ideology of expansion that had fateful consequences for the world, and the first consequence descended upon the Americans themselves. Mexico was our nation's forbidden fruit. Even before the annexation of half of our neighbor's territory, northern and southern bandits—capitalists and slaveholders—began to compete for the spoils. The "territorial question"—should the acquired territories be opened to slavery or preserved for Northern economic interests—brought to a climax the long-building confrontation between North and South. As the inhabitants of the United States fell on one another during the ghastly war of 1861–1865, the Mexicans were too busy with their own troubles to take much solace. But St. Paul in his Epistle to the Galatians says of God's justice: "Be not deceived. God is not mocked. For whatsoever a man soweth, that he shall also reap." Nineteenth-century Christian Americans had much to reflect on as their country, having torn Mexico apart, now tore at itself.

135,000 SETS, 270,000 VOLUMES SOLD.

UNCLE TOM'S CABIN

FOR SALE HERE.

AN EDITION FOR THE MILLION, COMPLETE IN 1 Vol., PRICE 37 1-2 CENTS.
" " IN GERMAN, IN 1 Vol., PRICE 50 CENTS.
" " IN 2 Vols., CLOTH, 6 PLATES, PRICE $1.50.
SUPERB ILLUSTRATED EDITION, IN 1 Vol., WITH 153 ENGRAVINGS,
PRICES FROM $2.50 TO $5.00.

The Greatest Book of the Age.

CHAPTER 13

Distant Thunder: The 1850s

UNCLE TOM'S CABIN (1852)

In 1826, when Harriet Beecher was fifteen years old, she had already read much of her father's theological library. She would recall with fondness her "non-resistant" childhood in Massachusetts and Cincinnati and her admiration for her "God-like" father, Lyman Beecher. In Harriet's youth her father became president of Lane Theological Seminary, and she married a young teacher there, Calvin Stowe. Stowe encouraged his wife's first writings for literary magazines, and she supported him during his long encounter with hallucinations and an inability to work. In 1850, Bowdoin College offered Calvin Stowe a professorship. Within a few months of Harriet's arrival in Maine she began to turn her moral attention to matters of a worldly nature. After a chance reading of a Southern slave-dealing newspaper, American black slavery arrested her with "an icy hand." Mrs. Stowe began a considerable research into the institution of chattel labor, reading Southern defenses of slavery as well as the attacks on it by Theodore Weld and Frederick Douglass, himself an ex-slave.

The Fugitive Slave Law of 1850 angered her into action, and she wrote *Uncle Tom's Cabin* in serial form in 1852. Mrs. Stowe later described the novel as having been "dictated" to her from a source outside of herself. One measure of the novel's power was the number of imitations it generated. More than fifty novels about slavery appeared after 1852, thirty of which were intent on portraying the institution as beneficial. None of these captured Mrs. Stowe's great audience. Sales in book form set publishing records: 300,000 copies the first year, a million in seven years. Adapted for the stage, the story quickly became America's most popular play. By 1861, millions of Northerners had thrilled over Eliza's dramatic escape and wept for Tom's fortitude under the lash.

Avoiding abolitionist stereotypes of saint-like slaves and vicious slaveholders, Mrs. Stowe cut right to the heart of the matter: it was not fundamentally people who were evil, but the system under which they lived. Given absolute power over their slaves, few masters could resist the temptation to use it. Slavery often dragged down even "good" masters when circumstances occurred beyond their control. At its worst (Simon Legree's plantation) the "peculiar institution" brutalized everyone—black and white. It is difficult to measure the exact impact of *Uncle Tom's Cabin*, but after its appearance the Northern attitude toward slavery was never quite the same. There was truth in the remark with which President Lincoln allegedly greeted Mrs. Stowe when she visited the White House during the Civil War: "So you're the little lady who wrote the book that made the great war."

Mrs. Stowe was not pursuing slavery with a bludgeon. Her instrument was as delicate as a surgeon's knife, and she operated on the national psyche. The slave was commercial property, and the business of slavery passed through Northern as well as Southern hands. The trade in human beings tore against the fabric of a society whose warp was the family and whose woof was Christianity and the morality it supports. Mrs. Stowe possessed a firm sense of the uneasiness that many Americans felt over the disrupting tendencies of commerce. Instead of making the slaveowning South a direct contrast with the "free" society of the North, she made it a grotesque extension and intensification of that world. Men "alive to nothing but trade and profit—cool, and unhesitating, and unrelenting as death and the grave roamed the American earth, building things and disrupting and destroying lives." Under slavery, men of commerce could take their avarice to its final meaning: trade in human flesh. Mrs. Stowe originally and correctly subtitled her book *The Man That Was a Thing*, a commodity to be traded on the market. Northerners understood her picture of slavery because it reached the guilt they felt about their own society. Southerners knew this too: their many replies to *Uncle Tom's Cabin* aimed ineffectual blows at Northern commercial society. No wonder Southerners were so furious.

Scenes from *Uncle Tom's Cabin*. *(Courtesy, The New-York Historical Society, New York City)*

The Fugitive Slave Law

President Fillmore had barely signed the Compromise of 1850 into law before the slavery controversy flared anew. It was the Comromise itself that rekindled the quarrel. Among its several provisions was one designed to assist slaveholders in recovering their runaway property. This Fugitive Slave Law had been passed in response to Southern complaints that the original law of 1793 was weak and ineffectual, putting slaveholders to great personal expense and failing to provide for assistance from federal officers. The new law of 1850 remedied these defects, and did more. It created special commissioners to deal with fugitive-slave cases. These commissioners had only to be convinced of a fugitive slave's identity before granting the owner authority to seize the runaway. They were empowered to call on federal marshals to enforce the law, and to compensate slaveholders who had incurred undue expense. Anyone who aided fugitives or obstructed their arrest was subject to fine and imprisonment. Here was a slaveholder's dream. But to many Northerners it was an outrage. Especially offensive were the sections denying fugitive slaves the right to a jury trial, or even to testify in their own behalf.

Here was not a complicated, constitutional issue pitting federal against state sovereignty in the territories. Here was concrete oppression on Northern soil before Northern eyes. Northerners had before them the spectacle of fugitive slaves, handcuffed and guarded, and read of cases of mistaken identity in the kidnapping of free blacks. The fugitive slave question drew together the splintered antislavery movement. Garrisonians, free-soilers, Whigs, Democrats, blacks: all could agree on it.

Enforcement of the Fugitive Slave Law sparked several well-publicized acts of resistance. In 1851 a mob of blacks in Boston burst into a courtroom during the extradition hearing of a fugitive slave named Shadrach. While the crowd struggled with the police, two husky blacks grabbed the startled Shadrach and carried him out of the building. Shadrach was soon spirited off to Canada. Later that same year, black and white abolitionists successfully resisted enforcement of the law at Syracuse, New York, and Christiana, Pennsylvania.

In over eighty percent of the cases brought under the law, slaveholders successfully recovered their property. But spectacular rescues like that of Shadrach confirmed Southerners in their conviction that the Fugitive Slave Law could not be enforced north of the Mason-Dixon Line. As a result, few Southerners made use of the new law. Instead the South nursed its feeling that the North had failed to fulfill an essential part of the compromise.

FUGITIVE

SLAVE BILL!

HON. HENRY WILSON

Will address the citizens on

Thursday Evening, April 3,

At the

At 7 o'clock, on the all-engrossing topics of the day—the FUGITIVE SLAVE BILL, the pro-slavery action of the National Government and the general aspect of the Slavery question.

Let every man and woman, without distinction of sect or party, attend the meeting and bear a testimony against the system which fills the prisons of a free republic with men whose only crime is a love of freedom—which strikes down the habeas corpus and trial by jury, and converts the free soil of Massachusetts into hunting ground for the Southern kidnappers.

Ashby, March 29, 1851.

White & Potter's Steam Press—4000 Impressions per hour—Spring Lane, Boston.

Harriet Tubman

> We have had the greatest heroine of the age here, Harriet Tubman, a black woman, and a fugitive slave, who had been back eight times secretly and brought out in all sixty slaves with her, including all her own family, besides aiding many more in other ways to escape. Her tales of adventure are beyond anything in fiction and her ingenuity and generalship are extraordinary. . . . The Slaves call her Moses. She has had a reward of twelve thousand dollars offered for her in Maryland and will probably be burned alive whenever she is caught, which she probably will be, first or last, as she is going again.

They never caught Harriet Tubman. She lived fifty-four years after the famous abolitionist Thomas Wentworth Higginson wrote these

Harriet Tubman. After she fled to the North and gained her freedom in 1849, Tubman returned to the South to lead others to freedom and became part of the legendary "Underground Railroad."

words in 1859. Other accounts credit her with the escape of two to three hundred slaves and clothe her with various achievements that suggest a figure out of folklore rather than history, a black Paul Bunyan or a female John Henry. The legends identifying her as "Black Moses" or "Chief Conductor on the Underground Railroad" merely extend a real history that is already heroic enough.

No one recorded the birthday of Harriet Ross, one of eleven children born to a slave family on the eastern shore of Maryland. But the child who would become Harriet Tubman was probably born in 1820 or 1821. She never spent a day in school and never learned to read or write. Her childhood in any sense that we would understand the term ended at the age of five or six. Then her master attempted unsuccessfully to apprentice her to a weaver. Various efforts to make her useful about the master's house also proved unsuccessful, and Harriet became a runaway for the first time at age seven. She stayed away four days, hiding in a pigsty and scrapping with the pigs for garbage to eat, until hunger drove her back to the inevitable whipping. Eventually she was sent to the fields where she became a powerful worker, a match for most of the men. A serious head injury in the early teens left her with a permanent injury which caused her to fall asleep involuntarily for brief periods, even at the height of danger. Her rebellious temperament, combined with this odd malady, set her apart from others in her youth, and she absorbed a brand of millennial slave Christianity. Marriage to a free black, John Tubman, further aroused her questionings about slavery and freedom, but the difficulty of escape and concern for her parents and husband held her back until 1849, when the death of her owner led her to fear being sold into the deep South. Harriet headed north, traveling by night, and with help from some sympathetic whites made her way to Pennsylvania.

"I had crossed the line," Harriet Tubman recalled. "I was *free;* but there was no one to welcome me to the land of freedom. . . . My home, after all, was down in Maryland; because my father, my mother, my brothers, my sisters, and friends were there. But I was free and *they should be free!* I would make a home in the North and bring them there!" And so she did: earning money as best she could to finance such desperate ventures. Joining with the loose network of free blacks and Quakers—out of whose limited activities post-Civil War legend created the "Underground Railroad," complete with "switching station," "conductors," and "brakemen"—and traveling without benefit of maps or signs, she brought back from Maryland first her relatives, then other slaves, and finally her aged parents. Even in December 1860, with political turmoil over slavery at its height, Harriet made her last trip south before the war, returning with seven slaves, one of them an infant child who had to be drugged with paregoric to keep its cries from giving away their hiding places.

Harriet headed south again during wartime, now to serve as a nurse, a scout, and even as a spy for the Union army in South Carolina. Although most of her activities were in caring for runaway slaves and black troops, she seems to have taken an active part in several guerrilla raids behind southern lines: "And then we saw the lightning," she reported, "and that was the guns; and then we heard the thunder, and that was the big guns; and then we heard the rain falling, and that was the drops of blood falling; and when we came to get in the crops, it was dead men that we reaped."

Harriet Tubman outlived the entire generation of antislavery heroes with whom she had worked, becoming a legendary reminder of the age of runaway slaves and abolitionists. Her home in Auburn, New York, became a place of pilgrimage. Black leaders like Booker T. Washington would visit Harriet and then view John Brown's grave in the Adirondacks. Women suffrage leaders came as well; this had become one of her causes in the postwar years. She founded a Home for the Aged and Indigent in Auburn on land abutting her house, moving to it herself in 1911 when she became too infirm to live alone. She died in 1913 and received, fittingly enough, a soldier's burial, with the local post of the Union army veterans' association, the Grand Army of the Republic, presenting the honors.

The Kansas-Nebraska Act

The settlement of the Oregon boundary controversy and the acquisition of California made the United States a Pacific power. American commerce quickly expanded across the great ocean. In 1844 Caleb Cushing, the first American Minister to China, negotiated a treaty granting Americans special trade privileges in that country. A decade later, Commodore Matthew Perry gained a diplomatic and commercial toehold in Japan. The United States sought unsuccessfully in 1854 to annex the Hawaiian Islands, already a cultural outpost of the United States. Forward-looking Americans proclaimed the dawn of a great commercial era in the Pacific.

For shortening the route from Atlantic ports to the Orient and improving communications between the two American coasts, the United States began considering a canal that would link the two oceans. An 1846 treaty with Colombia granted Americans the right of transit across the Isthmus of Panama, in return for American recognition of Colombian sovereignty there. American efforts to control the alternative canal route through Nicaragua aroused protests from Britain, which had bases of its own in the vicinity. In 1850 the two sides compromised their differences in the Clayton-Bulwer Treaty. Each party agreed not to seek exclusive control over the proposed isthmian canal or to colonize the surrounding area. In spite of this official enthusiasm, American capitalists showed little interest in the idea of building a canal. Travel across the isthmus remained a primitive affair until 1855, when a railroad replaced muleback and coach as the chief means of transportation.

More attractive was the idea of a trans-continental railroad. Asa Whitney, a New York merchant who had made a fortune in the China trade, labored throughout the 1840s to persuade Congress to finance construction of a railroad from Lake Michigan to the mouth of the Columbia River. This route, although mountainous, had the advantage of passing north of Mexican California. The Treaty of Guadalupe-Hidalgo brought California into the United States, but a new obstacle—sectional rivalry—soon appeared. The South favored a Southern route for the railroad, running from New Orleans to California via Texas and the Gila River Valley. The North preferred either Whitney's Northern route or a central route, extending from Chicago or St. Louis by way of South Pass to San Francisco. Unable to agree on any one route, Congress in 1853 authorized surveys of all three.

This delay was intolerable to Stephen A. Douglas of Illinois, the foremost advocate of a central route. As chairman of the Senate Committee on Territories, Douglas had pioneered in opening the Mississippi Valley to settlement. A Pacific railroad would help his "Great West" become a reality. Personal considerations also motivated Douglas. His home town of Chicago, where he had heavy real estate investments, would be the probable eastern terminus of a central railroad. But the land west of Iowa and Missouri—known as Nebraska—was still unorganized Indian country. Until the region had territorial government, it could not be surveyed and opened for settlement. In this respect, advocates of a Southern route had a real advantage: all the area along their route had already been made into states or territories.

Douglas late in 1853 had to find some way to induce Southerners in Congress to vote for a bill organizing Nebraska. Southerners had no motive to support a measure that cleared the path for a rival railroad route to the Pacific. And they had absolutely no reason to vote to create what would become another free territory. As part of the Louisiana Purchase, Nebraska had been made "forever" free by the Missouri Compromise of 1820. Senator David Atchinson of Missouri spoke for many Southerners when he vowed that he would "sink in hell" before hand-

Samuel Clemens (Mark Twain).

ing Nebraska over to the free-soilers. Douglas therefore decided that he would have to make a concession to the South.

Popular Sovereignty. The Illinois Senator offered the repeal of the Missouri Compromise line excluding slavery north of 36° 30′ latitude. His territorial bill, introduced in Congress in January 1854, would create two territories—Kansas and Nebraska. It would specifically repeal the Missouri Compromise restriction on slavery. In its place, Douglas substituted the principle of popular sovereignty. The people of these territories were free "to form and regulate their domestic institutions in their own way." Thus, to enlist Southern support for his railroad, Douglas held out the bait of making Kansas and Nebraska slave states by the operation of popular sovereignty.

As Douglas himself had predicted, the idea of repealing the Missouri Compromise line raised "a hell of a storm." Most Northerners regarded the Act of 1820 as an inviolable pledge of freedom. Repeal was part of a slaveholder's plot to make free territory into "a dreary region of despotism, inhabited by masters and slaves." In Congress, many Northern Democrats joined their Whig colleagues in opposition. Objections came not only from abolitionists but from moderates who had accepted the Compromise of 1850 but had now lost all confidence in the good faith of the South. Douglas and his co-conspirators, wrote Horace Greeley in the *New York Tribune,* had made "more abolitionists than Garrison . . . could have made in half a century." Slavery, Douglas insisted in response, was an outmoded institution, unsuited by climate and geography to the plains of Kansas. Popular sovereignty would just as effectively bar slavery as would exclusion. After three months of fierce debate Douglas, with the support of President Franklin Pierce, carried his bill.

Passage of the Kansas-Nebraska Act shredded what little had remained of the uneasy truce of 1850. It turned Kansas into a battleground and ruptured the Democratic Party. By using the scheme of popular sovereignty to open free soil to slavery, Douglas discredited what until then had been an effective instrument for compromise. Rarely in American history had so much been risked for so little. The next year—1855—when Douglas introduced his long-awaited Pacific Railroad bill in Congress, his enemies had their revenge by killing it. At Douglas's death in 1861 his great Pacific railroad, on which he had expended so much energy and prestige, was still bottled up in Congress, a victim of the sectional conflict he had helped to revive.

Huckleberry Finn *by Samuel Clemens*

. . . I about made up my mind to pray, and see if I couldn't try to quit being the kind of a boy I was and be better. So I kneeled down. But the words wouldn't come. Why wouldn't they? . . . I was trying to make my mouth say I would do the right thing and the clean thing, and go and write to that nigger's owner and tell where he was; but deep down in me I knowed it was a lie, and He knowed it. You can't pray a lie—I found out.

So I was full of trouble, full as I could be; and didn't know what to do. At last I had an idea; and I says, I'll go and write the letter—and then see if I can pray. Why, it was astonishing, the way I felt as light as a feather right straight off, and my troubles all gone. So I got a piece of paper and a pencil, all glad and excited, and set down and wrote:

Miss Watson, your runaway nigger Jim is down here two mile below Pikesville, and Mr. Phelps had got him and he will give him up for the reward if you send.

I felt good and all washed clean of sin for the first time I had ever felt so in my life, and I knowed I could pray now. But I didn't do it straight off, but laid the paper down and set there thinking—thinking how good it was all this happened so, and how near I come to being lost and going to hell. And went on thinking. And got to thinking over our trip down the river; and I see Jim before me all the time: in the day and in the night-time, sometimes moonlight, sometimes storms, and we a-floating along, talking and singing and laughing. But somehow I couldn't seem to strike no places to harden me against him, but only the other kind. I'd see him standing my watch on top of his'n, 'stead of calling me, so I could go on sleeping; . . . and at last I struck the time I saved him by telling the men we had small-pox aboard, and he was so grateful, and said I was the best friend old Jim ever had in the world, and the only one he's got now; and then I happened to look around and see that paper.

It was a close place. I took it up, and held it in my hand. I was a-trembling, because I's got to decide, forever, betwixt two things, and I knowed it. I studied a minute, sort of holding my breath, and then says to myself:

"All right, then, I'll go to hell"—and tore it up.

"Bleeding Kansas"

With the passage of the Kansas-Nebraska Act, the slavery contest moved from the halls of Congress to the plains of Kansas. Both sections attached great importance to the decision over slavery there. Southerners hoped to make Kansas a slave state and thereby to restore to the South the equality of representation in the Senate that the region had lost when California was admitted as a free state. Slavery expansion also had great symbolic importance to Southerners. By denying the South's right to expand, the North seemed to be denying Southern equality. Southerners reasoned that if they could not take their slaves into the common territories, they would no longer be the equal of Northern citizens. Opponents of slavery of course wished to prevent its extension into Kansas. The expansion of slavery also had a more unsavory side. Many Northerners, especially in the Midwest, were determined to preserve the rich prairie soils for the white race. Here, said David Wilmot, "the sons of toil, of my own race and color, can live without the disgrace which association with Negro slavery brings upon free labor." These same racial prejudices applied to free blacks in the North. Such attitudes increasingly dominated the antislavery movement, and conditioned the public views even of moral opponents of slavery like Abraham Lincoln. The demand for free soil, then, greatly broadened the antislavery movement's appeal at the same time that it diluted the morality of the movement.

Border War. From the beginning, the contest in Kansas over slavery was mainly the work of outsiders. In the North, groups like the New England Emigrant Aid Company, founded in 1854, subsidized the migration of free-state settlers to Kansas. To protect them, the Company sent new breech-loading rifles known popularly as "Beecher's Bibles," after Harriet's ministerial brother, Henry Ward Beecher, who proclaimed them a greater moral agency in Kansas than the Bible. Bands of Missouri "border ruffians" regularly crossed into neighboring Kansas to aid the proslavery cause. In March 1855, at the first election for a territorial legislature, their votes helped to give the proslavery party a majority. This assembly immediately enacted a slave code for the territory. Free-state settlers, refusing to recognize this legislature, elected one of their own. By late 1855, Kansas had two rival governments, neither of which would recognize the other's laws or participate in its elections.

Orderly government was impossible, and militants on both sides of the slavery question carried on a private war of their own. After proslavery men raided the free-state stronghold of Lawrence, the fanatical John Brown and seven followers (four of them his sons) retaliated at Pottawatomie Creek by rounding up five sympathizers with slavery and hacking them to death with broadswords. Many settlers had to take sides in self-defense.

The recently established telegraph system, which now made possible swift reports of faraway events, brought the warfare in Kansas extensive press coverage. The antislavery press pictured the sack of Lawrence as an orgy of destruction and killing. In reality, it was a rather tame affair; only one person was killed, and he a proslavery man struck on the head by a falling brick.

Early in 1857 federal troops restored order to Kansas, and the free- and slave-state parties each promptly fell to internal quarreling. Before the year was out, a visitor to Kansas reported

***John Brown*, by John Steuart Curry. Following a raid against the free-state stronghold of Lawrence, Kansas, by proslavery men, Brown and his followers murdered five slavery sympathizers at Pottawatomie Creek.**
(Courtesy, Kansas Industrial Development Commission, Topeka, Kansas)

that "speculations run high [here], politics seldom named, *money* now seems to be the question." Nevertheless, the territory remained deeply divided, with each side retaining its own government.

The struggle in Kansas forced the slavery issue back into Congress. (The intent of instituting popular sovereignty had been to get the slavery question out of that body.) In 1856 the House of Representatives sent a fact-finding committee to Kansas. Meantime, Congress endlessly debated the Kansas question amid steadily rising tempers. Passion spilled into violence on the floor of the Senate. Senator Charles Sumner of Massachusetts delivered a violent antislavery speech entitled "The Crime Against Kansas." In it he made several personal references to Senator Andrew P. Butler of South Carolina. Butler's nephew, Representative Preston S. Brooks of South Carolina, decided to avenge these insults to an elderly kinsman. Brooks stole up behind Sumner at his Senate desk during a recess and beat him severely over the head with a cane.

The attack, Northerners believed, was another example of the domineering insolence of slaveholders. The injured Sumner became a martyr of the antislavery cause. Southerners, although many privately disapproved, publicly applauded Brooks's action and showered him with canes inscribed with slogans like "Use Knockdown Arguments." When Brooks resigned from Congress, his Carolina constituents reelected him. This incident, and the controversy over Bleeding Kansas, further polarized a country already divided.

Political Upheaval

Before 1850 the country's political system had been a strong bond of union. In both the Whig and the Democratic parties, strong Northern and Southern wings had worked together in their mutual interest, especially in presidential elections. The dependence of each wing on the other served to override the potentially divisive effect of issues like slavery. Party loyalty was intense. William Pitt Fessenden, a Whig stalwart, declared that he "would vote for a dog, if he was the candidate of my party." The Compromise of 1850 and the Kansas-Nebraska Act drastically altered the system, destroyed one party, disrupted another, and created a new one. A once unifying political system had become sectionalized.

The Decline of the Whig Party. It was the Whigs who felt the strain of slavery first. They had never been as strong organizationally as the Democrats, and moreover drew their strength in the North from Yankee Protestants whose sense of moral stewardship made them especially sympathetic to the antislavery cause. The abolitionist and Free Soil movements made many converts among these "conscience" Whigs. At the 1852 Whig Convention the dispute over slavery broke wide open. The two sides even disagreed over the choice of a minister to lead the opening prayer. President Fillmore, the favorite of Southern Whigs, had supported the Compromise of 1850, and so Northern Whigs opposed him. The Northerners backed instead another Mexican War hero, the Virginian General Winfield Scott, and Scott was finally chosen after fifty-three ballots. In retaliation, Southern Whigs rammed through a platform endorsing the Compromise, including the Fugitive Slave Law.

Saddled with a candidate unpopular in the South and a platform unpopular in the North, the Whigs lost disastrously in 1852. Franklin Pierce of New Hampshire, the Democratic candidate, carried twenty-seven of thirty-one states—the most lopsided election victory since 1820. Surveying the ruins, antislavery Whigs began to seek a new alliance.

Not long afterward, it was the Democrats whom the slavery issue divided. The Kansas-Nebraska Act bitterly antagonized Northern antislavery Democrats, and their frustration found expression in the "Appeal of the Independent Democrats," composed in 1854 by Charles Sumner, Salmon P. Chase, and other antislavery Democratic congressmen. The appeal invited all opponents of slavery expansion to form a common front "to rescue the country from the domination of slavery."

This rebellion among antislavery Democrats made for a dramatic restructuring of Northern politics. Antislavery politicians—former Whigs, breakaway Democrats, some of the more moderate abolitionists—struggled to create the coalition called for in the appeal. The new organization came formally into existence at a convention held in Ripon, Wisconsin, in February 1854; the delegates adopted a statement of principles proclaiming their opposition to the exten-

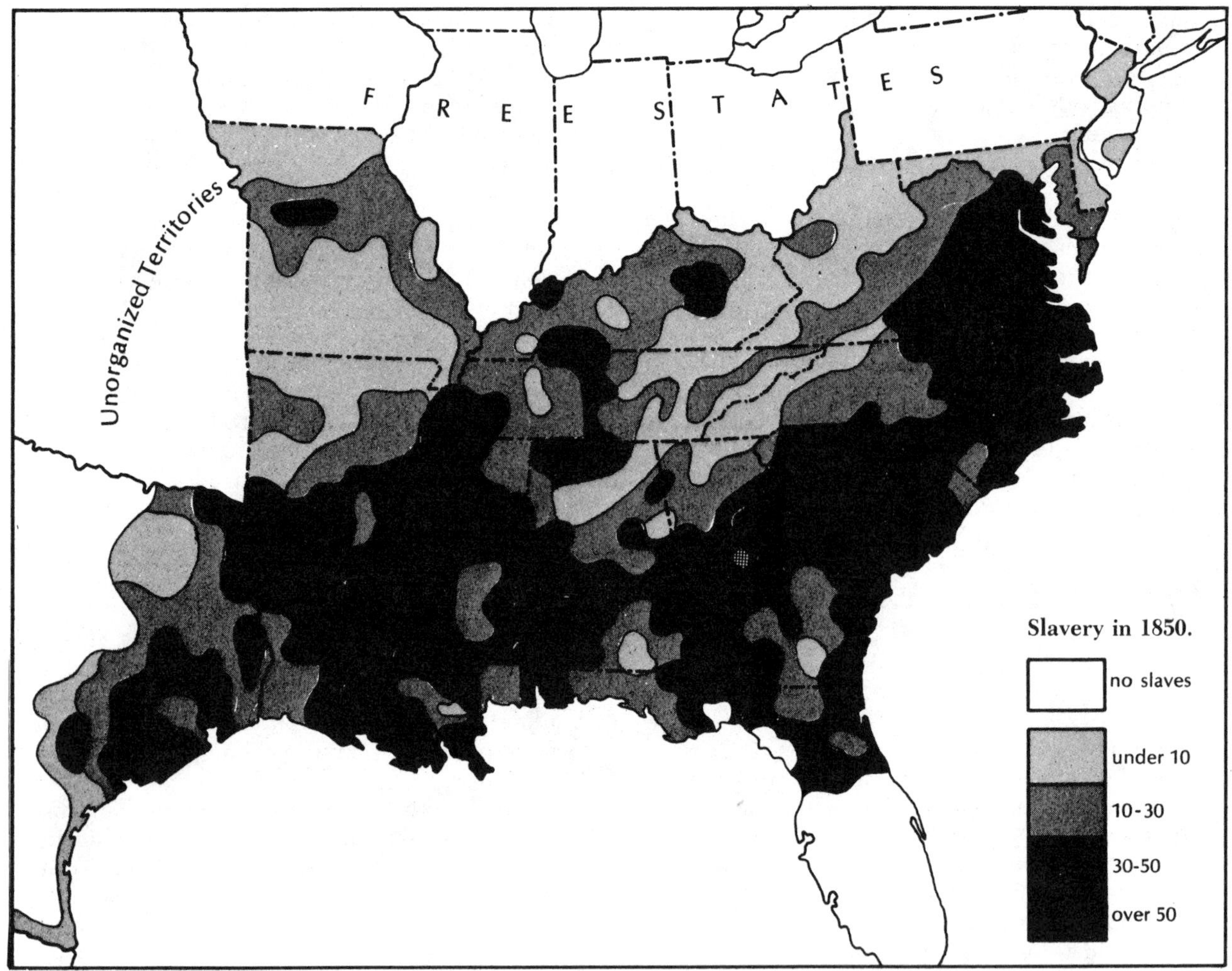

sion of slavery in the territories. The new party officially adopted the name "Republican" a few months later.

The "Know-Nothing" Party. For a time another party, the "Know-Nothings," was also in the field. The flood of Irish and German immigrants after 1840 had alarmed old-stock Protestants, who feared that this predominantly Catholic immigration would undermine republican institutions. Those "governed by a head in a foreign land," exclaimed one nativist editor, and where "*no genuine liberty, either civil or religious*" exists, must not "control the American Ballot Box." The newcomers were also charged with corrupting the nation's morals. According to another nativist, they brought "grog shops like the frogs of Egypt upon us." The visit of a special papal envoy to the United States in 1853 triggered a series of riots in Cincinnati, Pittsburgh, and elsewhere. A mob in Charlestown, Massachusetts, burned a Catholic convent to the ground. In 1849 Charles B. Allen of New York had formed a secret "patriotic" society, the Order of the Star-Spangled Banner, anti-Catholic and anti-foreign. Members, when questioned by outsiders, customarily answered, "I know nothing." For a few years the society remained an obscure local organization, but in 1854, hoping to capitalize on the breakup of the old party alignments, nativists went political and formed the American, or "Know-Nothing" party.

For a time the Know-Nothings demonstrated much political strength, capturing several state governorships and seventy-five seats in Congress. They were strongest in the Northeast and the border states. The Know-Nothings soon discovered, however, that as a bisectional party, they enjoyed no more immunity from the disruptive influence of the slavery question than the other parties. After a quarrel at the 1855 national convention, the party disintegrated. Most Northern Know-Nothings went into the new Republican Party, which had been actively soliciting the nativists with pledges of "No Popery and Slavery."

The Republican Party. The 1856 Republican Convention resembled a revival meeting. "There is but a slight quantity of liquor consumed," a journalist reported, "very little profane swearing is heard, and everything is managed with excessive and intense propriety." The platform condemned slavery as a "relic of barbarism" and reaffirmed the "right and duty" of Congress to prohibit it in the territories. For president the Republicans nominated John C. Frémont, the dashing "Pathfinder" of Western exploration. The Democrats bypassed President Pierce and Stephen A. Douglas, who were too closely identified with the Kansas-Nebraska Act, in favor of James Buchanan of Pennsylvania. Buchanan was a veteran politician and diplomat who, happily, had been out of the country during the Kansas-Nebraska struggle. A third candidate, ex-President Millard Fillmore, was nominated by the still-existing Southern wing of the Know-Nothing Party.

The election itself was not a three-cornered affair, but rather two separate contests—one between Buchanan and Frémont in the North, the other between Buchanan and Fillmore in the South. As the only really national candidate, Buchanan benefited from the fear that a clear-cut sectional victory would split the Union. In November he won, carrying all the slave states but one, and gaining Pennsylvania, New Jersey, Indiana, Illinois, and California. In the other eleven free states, Frémont made a clean sweep—an impressive showing for a new party. The real winner in 1856 was sectionalism: with the exception of Ohio, all eleven Frémont states were farther north than any of the twenty Buchanan states. No longer was the national political system a bond of union. Another of the cords holding the country together had snapped.

The Triumph of Sectional Politics

Dred Scott. After 1848 the slavery question, like some evil curse, transformed everything it touched. It divided churches, shattered political parties, turned Congress into a battleground, and ruined presidential careers. Only one institution—the Supreme Court—had remained unchanged. Pressure had been building on the Court for a definitive judgment regarding slavery in the territories. In 1857, in the case of *Dred Scott v. Sanford,* the Court's majority, sympathetic to the South, abandoned judicial impartiality in the hope of settling this nagging question once and for all. The justices assumed that respect for the Court would insure acceptance of its decision by all sides. Rarely had American public figures so misgauged the popular temper: rather than settling the slavery question, the *Dred Scott* decision pushed the country forward on the road to civil war.

The case involved a Missouri slave, Dred Scott, who had sojourned with his master for several years in Illinois and in Minnesota Territory. Upon returning to Missouri, Scott sued for his freedom, contending that he was emancipated by virtue of his residence on free soil. Chief Justice Roger B. Taney, speaking for a majority of the Supreme Court, rejected his claim on three grounds: as a Negro he could not be a citizen, and therefore had no right to bring suit in the federal courts; as a resident of Missouri he did not fall within the law of Illinois prohibiting slavery; and his sojourn in Minnesota Territory had not emancipated him, for the provision of the Missouri Compromise prohibiting slavery north of 36° 30′ was unconstitutional. Congress, Taney declared, had no right to deprive citizens of their property—human or otherwise—in the territories without "due process of law."

On nearly every point the Chief Justice's opinion was either plainly wrong or open to serious dispute. To declare that Negroes in general, and hence even free blacks, were non-citizens who, as Taney said, had "no rights [that whites] were bound to respect" defied American history. Free blacks had always been recognized as citizens in at least some Northern states, and therefore did have the right to sue in the federal courts. In rejecting the principle that the status one state granted to an individual held for that person in another state, Taney ignored several earlier decisions in which Missouri courts had recognized the claim to freedom of slaves who had sojourned in free territory. The supreme authority of Congress over the territories had previously been upheld no less than three times by the Taney Court itself.

Taney's pronouncement that it was unconsti-

Dred Scott. The Supreme Court's decision in the Scott case—denying both the right of a slave to sue for freedom and the right of a territory to exclude slavery within its boundaries—further inflamed the antislavery factions. *(Courtesy, The Missouri Historical Society)*

tutional for Congress to exclude slavery in the territories provoked a storm of criticism in the North. Republicans dismissed the decision as part of the "slavepower conspiracy." According to Horace Greeley's *New York Tribune*, it was entitled "to just so much moral weight as would be the judgment of a majority of those congregated in any Washington bar-room." The decision also embarrassed Northern Democrats such as Stephen A. Douglas. They had fixed their hopes on the doctrine of popular sovereignty. But if Congress could not exclude slavery in the territories, then neither could it bestow on the people of a territory the authority to do so. Southerners, of course, hailed the *Dred Scott* decision as a vindication of their claim that slavery could not be excluded from the territories prior to statehood. By striking down popular sovereignty, the Supreme Court had destroyed just about the last device for sectional compromise. Meanwhile, events in Kansas deepened sectional division still further.

The Lecompton Constitution. In 1857 the proslavery faction in Kansas held a convention at Lecompton, drafted a constitution recognizing slavery, and applied for statehood. Although a clear majority of the territory's residents opposed the Lecompton Constitution, President Buchanan accepted it and asked Congress to admit Kansas to statehood. The President took this fateful step out of fear that a rejection of Lecompton would antagonize Southern Democrats.

Buchanan's action outraged Stephen Douglas, who had proposed popular sovereignty as a democratic solution to the question of slavery in Kansas. Bucking the administration, he denounced the "Lecompton fraud" as a travesty on popular sovereignty and joined with Republican congressmen in opposing it. Douglas's opposition to Lecompton offended Southerners and probably ruined his presidential prospects. After a struggle, Congress in 1858 sent the Lecompton Constitution back to the people of Kansas to be voted on again. This time a fair election was held, and Kansas rejected the "Lecompton fraud" by a margin of 11,300 to 1,788. Kansas remained a territory until after the Civil War had begun.

Buchanan's attempt to ram the Lecompton Constitution through Congress, coming so soon after the Kansas-Nebraska Act, broke the Northern wing of the Democratic Party. Few Northern Democrats who supported him on Kansas survived the 1858 mid-term elections. From this point on the Democratic Party was the party of the South.

The Republicans were now just as surely the party of the North. Within the party antislavery sentiment was coalescing with Northern economic nationalism.

Numbers of American statesmen, among them Hamilton, John Quincy Adams, and Henry Clay, had wished to make the national government an active partner in the shaping and strengthening of a unified American economy. But economic nationalist programs differed in detail. Adams would have kept a high price on public lands in the West and applied the revenues to his ambitious governmental programs for the enriching of the economy and culture. For a time, Northeastern business interests also had wanted the price of public lands to remain high, for they had feared that cheap land would drain away Eastern labor to the West. But now industrialists could think differently: immigration was supplying labor for Northern industry and a prosperous West could be a customer for

Northeastern manufactured goods. So Northerners of varying economic condition, land-hungry farmers along with ambitious businessmen, could unite behind a nationalist program that would have the government nurture Northern industry, turn government land over to Western settlers, and finance transportation connecting the Northeast to the West.

This economic nationalism had much common ground with the antislavery movement. Northerners wishing to settle in the West did not want the new lands dominated by the slave powers. Northern industrialists were at war politically with Southern slaveholders who opposed protective tariffs. The Republican conviction that Congress had the authority to prohibit slavery in the territories blended with a larger belief in strong federal government, the kind that could legislate an active and continental economic program. Perhaps Northerners who championed a vigorous program of economic development could even detect a cultural identity between their economic and their antislavery convictions, believing that industriousness and progress were the way of the free-labor North while indolence was the way of the Southern slaveholding class.

In any event, Republicans sponsored legislation in Congress favoring free homesteads for settlers, agricultural colleges financed by grants of land, government-aided internal improvements, and a protective tariff. Southern Democrats blocked each of these measures. By obstructing the dynamic economic forces then at work in the North and Midwest, the South pressed these two sections to work together.

Northern politics, like the Northern economy, was now moving along an east-west axis. And the Republican program for the economy, like the Republican opposition to slavery, had the more generous view of how the republic could conduct its life, for the party was really looking beyond the localism of states' rights and proposing a cooperative commonwealth in which the resources of the entire nation would be put to the common welfare.

The Emergence of Lincoln

The Lincoln-Douglas Debates. The earliest principal contender for the Republican nomination in 1860 was William Seward. After four years as governor of New York and twelve in the Senate, he enjoyed a national reputation. But suddenly, in 1858, a new potential candidate appeared. Throughout that summer, newspapers carried reports of a series of debates between Stephen A. Douglas and a little-known Illinois lawyer and former congressman named Abraham Lincoln. The occasion was the contest for Douglas's seat in the Senate. When it was over, Lincoln had lost the election but had become a figure to be reckoned with in the Republican Party. "You are like Byron," a friend wrote, "who woke up one morning and found himself famous."

The Supreme Court's *Dred Scott* decision, which in effect denied to the people of a territory the right to exclude slavery within its boundaries, had placed Douglas in a difficult situation. The "Little Giant" was the foremost advocate of popular sovereignty. If he accepted the Court's decision, he would probably lose the election in Illinois, where free-soil sentiment was strong. But if he reaffirmed the right of settlers to decide the slavery question for themselves, he would lose the support of Southerners, which he desperately needed if he hoped to

Abraham Lincoln lost the 1858 election for senator of Illinois to Stephen S. Douglas, but beat Douglas and two other candidates to become president of the increasingly divided nation in 1860.

win the Democratic presidential nomination in 1860.

According to legend, Lincoln took advantage of Douglas's predicament to further his own political ends. At Freeport he asked Douglas whether, in light of Taney's opinion, the people could still exclude slavery from a territory. Douglas replied that they could, merely by withholding the police regulations and local laws that slavery needed in order to exist. The Freeport formula, summed up in the phrase "unfriendly legislation," supposedly assured Douglas's reelection to the Senate, but would cost him the support of Southerners in 1860. Lincoln, so the legend goes, had thus with superhuman foresight sacrificed the short-run of a Senate seat in the interests of winning the big prize in 1860.

This story, like so many pieces of Lincoln lore, is more fiction than fact. In reality Douglas had announced his doctrine of "unfriendly legislation" months before the Freeport debate. And by the time of his confrontation with Lincoln, popular sovereignty was no longer a major issue. The real issue between the two men—and the one Lincoln strove to develop—was the ultimate one of the morality of slavery. Here Lincoln and Douglas differed fundamentally.

Douglas did not regard the question of slavery in the territories as a moral issue. He believed that blacks, whatever their status, would never achieve equality with whites. Whether they were subordinated as slaves, therefore, or merely as second-class citizens was not a matter of great concern for him, certainly not an issue worth breaking up the country over. Douglas disliked slavery; but what to do about it, he thought, should remain a local decision. Southerners had chosen to keep it. Northerners had decided to get rid of it. In the territories Douglas would let the local residents decide by popular sovereignty. He would never try to impose a single national policy on the slavery question.

For Lincoln slavery was a profound moral wrong. Although political considerations and respect for constitutional guarantees to slaveholders often impelled Lincoln to compromise his moral views in public, he never deserted them. Lincoln could never say, as Douglas said, that he did not care whether slavery was "voted up or voted down."

Lincoln differed from Douglas on another point: he insisted that slavery, as a national problem, required a national policy. Lincoln would not interfere with slavery where it existed; but he would not allow it to expand. Lincoln believed that the Founding Fathers, recognizing slavery as a wrong, had placed restrictions on it designed to produce its eventual extinction. Douglas and the Democrats, by refusing to recognize the moral wrong, had provided constitutional sanctions for slavery and made possible its expansion.

In 1858, Douglas narrowly won reelection to the Senate. But it was Lincoln who had sensed and shared the growing moral and emotional concern over the slavery issue in the North. This would prove critical in the election of 1860.

The Election of 1860

As the election year approached, North and South ceased even to pretend to any interest in compromise. In 1859 Senator Jefferson Davis of Mississippi introduced resolutions in Congress designed to get the Democratic Party to support the extreme Southern position on slavery in the territories. These upheld the constitutional right of slaveholders to go into territories and called for the creation of a federal slave code for those areas. Senate Democrats finally adopted the Davis resolutions, over the vigorous objections of Stephen Douglas. At about the same time some Southerners launched a movement to revive the African slave trade. This proposal had no chance of success, even among Southerners; its main purpose, successfully achieved, was to irritate Northern sensibilities. During the 1850s several Northern state legislatures had defied the Fugitive Slave Act by passing "personal liberty" laws. Most of these prohibited state officers from aiding federal officials in their efforts to reclaim fugitives. In 1854 the Wisconsin supreme court had carried defiance of the federal government a step farther by declaring the Fugitive Slave Act of 1850 unconstitutional. Eventually the United States Supreme Court overturned this judgment, whereupon the Wisconsin legislature, taking a line from the Kentucky Resolves of 1798, declared the Court's action to be "an act of undelegated power, void, and of no

This cartoon employs a setting from the new game of baseball to argue that Lincoln won the 1860 election because he stood for equal rights and free territory. *(Courtesy, The New-York Historical Society, New York City)*

force." But going beyond these acts of North and South in prefiguring sectional war was John Brown's raid at Harpers Ferry, Virginia (see introduction to the next chapter).

The Democrats Meet in Charleston. Four months after John Brown's execution, the Democrats began their national convention at Charleston, South Carolina. The choice of the convention site was unfortunate; Charleston was a tinderbox of Southern radicalism. For the Democrats, 1860 was the climax of the intraparty struggle between the dominant Southern faction and the Northerners, whose spokesman was Stephen Douglas. Ever since the split over Lecompton, both sides had been spoiling for a confrontation over the question of slavery in the territories. Most Southern delegates came to Charleston pledged to the adoption of the Davis Resolutions. When the convention rejected their inclusion on the platform, delegates from eight Southern states left. The convention then adjourned for several weeks, reassembling at Baltimore on June 18, where the fight immediately resumed. This time delegates from eleven Southern states (all the future states of the Confederacy) walked out. The remaining delegates nominated Douglas for president on a platform endorsing popular sovereignty. The bolters met in another hall and nominated John Breckinridge of Kentucky for president. Their platform upheld the Davis Resolutions. The split between the Democrats was complete.

A number of factors brought this fatal action by the Southern Democrats, which virtually assured a Republican victory in November. A few hotheads sought deliberately to split the party, precisely in order to produce the Republican victory that would, they anticipated, precipitate secession. Some delegates hoped merely to force the election into the House of Representatives. The Democrats had met amidst extreme excitement, and many delegates were simply swept away by the violent speeches of "fire-eaters" like William Yancey of Alabama. They bolted without fully considering the consequences. Right up to November, many of the bolters assumed that somehow the party would come back together.

Between the two Democratic conventions another party had met at Baltimore. This was the Constitutional Union Party, composed mainly of old Whigs from both sections and of Southern Know-Nothings. These conservatives joined in their general concern for the safety of the Union. For president, they nominated John Bell of Tennessee, a Whig and a large slaveholder, although not an extreme advocate of Southern rights. As their platform, the Constitutional Unionists settled for a vague pledge to uphold the Constitution and the Union.

The Republicans Convene in Chicago. The Republican convention opened at Chicago on May 16. The Republican strategy in 1860 was simple: to win the White House the party had only to win the same states Frémont had carried in 1856, plus just 34 additional electoral votes. This meant carrying Pennsylvania (27 votes) and either Illinois (11), Indiana (13), or New Jersey (7). All these states adjoined the South and were less hostile to slavery than was the upper North. And each of these four states had special concerns such as the tariff or internal improvements.

The Republican platform had these states in mind. It treated the slavery question cautiously. The delegates reaffirmed Republican opposition to the expansion of slavery, but promised to leave slavery alone where it existed. The platform pledged support for a protective tariff, a Pacific railroad, and a homestead law.

This same concern for the swing states governed the choice of a candidate. William Seward was considered extreme on the slavery question, and the party's congressional and local candidates in the states in question did not want to run with him. After reviewing the other contenders, the party pros settled on Abraham Lincoln as the man most "available": he resided in the important state of Illinois, was a moderate on slavery, had never been identified with nativism, and had made fewer enemies than his rivals. Lincoln also benefited from the shrewd tactics of his managers, who packed the galleries at the convention hall by distributing counterfeit tickets, and stationed men around the floor to begin noisy demonstrations on a prearranged signal.

In 1860 the national political system effectively failed to operate. There were two campaigns that year. In the North the contest was between Lincoln and Douglas: Bell and Breckinridge were also on the ballot, but neither had much support. In the South Breckinridge divided votes with Bell, though Douglas was also on the ballot. Lincoln, Bell, and Breckinridge adhered to the tradition of staying close to home and letting their respective supporters do the campaigning. On the real issue of the campaign—the possible dissolution of the Union—Lincoln and Breckinridge remained silent. Stephen Douglas campaigned hard and heroically throughout the country—at some risk to his personal safety in the South—in an attempt to break down the barriers between the two sections.

On election day each of the hard line candidates won in his own section. Lincoln carried all the Northern states except New Jersey; Breckinridge captured eleven slave states. Douglas ran well in the North, but carried only Missouri and three electoral votes in New Jersey. Bell, whose popular vote was the smallest, took Virginia, Kentucky, and Tennessee. In the country as a whole Lincoln won only 39 per cent of the popular vote, but his votes were concentrated in the populous North. As a result, he had a clear victory in the electoral college—180 votes against a total of 112 for his three opponents. Lincoln carried all but three of the Northern states by majorities. He would have won even if the opposition to him had been united. The Republican victory in November might not alone have ruptured the Union. Conservatives within the Republican Party hoped to appease the upper South with a policy of popular sovereignty instead of outright opposition to admission of any of the territories as slave states. But a single event of 1859 stuck in the craw of Southerners, the act of a madman or a saint—John Brown's nightmare attack at Harpers Ferry.

Points To Think About

1. As the late Edmund Wilson argued in *Patriotic Gore, Uncle Tom's Cabin* is a far better novel than it is credited with being. The book is filled with melodramatic episodes and sentimental death-bed scenes—both likely to strike present day readers as excessive. But the novel is also blessed with a remarkable cast of characters. Harriet Beecher Stowe created evil slaveholders and saintly slaves. Yet she also portrayed kind, well-intentioned masters and rascally slaves. She created a whole range of human types. Even Uncle Tom himself is believable, because Mrs. Stowe insists that he was not a typical slave but an extraordinarily heroic and saintly man. Mrs. Stowe continually emphasized the distinction between slaveholders and the institution of slavery. There were, she insisted, good masters. There were even contented slaves. But slavery, as an institution, often forced even kind masters to be cruel. The novel opens with such a master forced to sell his slaves to meet his debts. He had been used to thinking of them as people, but they were also his property. The novel's greatest source of strength, perhaps, was evangelical pietism. Mrs. Stowe was the daughter of Lyman Beecher, who—next to Finney—was the most famous preacher of his day. Her husband was also a minister, as were several brothers. Her Uncle Tom stands, throughout the whole novel, as the embodiment of true piety. He is neither servile nor cringing, as the present day use of the term might suggest. He is gentle and always willing to turn the other cheek because that is his Christian duty. And the novel of which he is the central figure is a moving reflection on sin and redemption.

2. The politics of the 1850s had both a highly moral and amoral character. Most public issues, such as internal improvements, concern questions that are serious enough, but do not raise questions of good or evil. Slavery, however, did raise questions of good and evil. And so the politics of the 1850s forced contemporaries to make moral judgments about public issues. And historians have had to make similar judgments. So it is disconcerting to find that the Republican Party, so good in its opposition to slavery, also harbored much hostility to immigrants. And the same Democratic Party that welcomed immigrants and defended their rights also contained many defenders of slavery.

The key to the Republican mentality, many historians believe, lies in evangelical Christianity. Republicans brought a fervent Protestant conscience to politics. It made them deeply suspicious of Irish and German Catholic immigrants, whose aptitude for self-government they doubted. And it made them deeply susceptible to moral arguments against the sin of slavery. Hence their approach to these issues is less contradictory than it may have first seemed.

Suggested Readings

The politics of the 1850s is increasingly well covered. Notably, see Michael F. Holt, *The Political Crisis of the 1850s* (1976), David M. Potter, *The Impending Crisis: 1848-1861* (1976), Gerald W. Wolf, *The Kansas-Nebraska Bill: Party, Section, and the Coming of the Civil War* (1977), Don E. Fehrenbacher, *The Dred Scott Case* (1978), and Eric Foner, *Free Soil, Free Labor, Free Men: The Ideology of the Republican Party Before the Civil War* (1970). Holt argues that voters could not discern substantial differences between the old parties in the fifties (the "second American party system" of the Whigs and Democrats), and that as a result there was a crisis in confidence in political institutions. Roger Brown, *Modernization* (1976), demonstrates that the North did, and the South did not, "modernize" by the mid-nineteenth century. Other important studies are George B. Forgie, *Patricide in the House Divided: A Psychological Interpretation of Lincoln and His Age* (1979), and Drew Gilpin Faust, *A Sacred Circle: The Dilemma of the Intellectual in the Old South, 1840-1860* (1978). Stephen B. Oates's biography of John Brown is entitled *To Purge This Land With Blood* (1970).

The best discussion of *Uncle Tom's Cabin* appears in the opening pages of Edmund Wilson's *Patriotic Gore* (1961). Milton Rugoff's family history is entitled *The Beechers* (1981).

FORREST McDONALD

Scholars have argued endlessly about the causes of the Civil War, but the argument usually ignores the longer-range course of history. It fails to consider that the Americans' ancestors in Great Britain had been at war with one another, off and on, from ancient times through the eighteenth century, even though none of the supposed causes of the American Civil War had then been present. It also fails to consider that every modern nation-state had at least one civil war, and most had several, before diverse peoples could be brought to give their allegiance to a single government: civil war is part of the price of nationhood. It is better, therefore, to view the coming of the Civil War as part of an ongoing process rather than as a departure requiring special explanation.

Culturally, Yankees and Southerners remained worlds apart, as they had been since the arrival of the first colonists. Yankees were dedicated to work and achievement; Southerners preferred to have others work for them, or else let it go undone. Yankees were realistic, Southerners romantic. Yankees were shrewdly calculating: they schemed, bargained, negotiated, put success ahead of scruple. Southerners were hot-blooded: they dreamed, bragged, fought, put honor ahead of money. Yankee life was oriented toward the community and the marketplace, Southern toward the family and the land. Perhaps most importantly, eternal salvation was, to the Yankee, a community matter, whereas to the Southerner it was intensely personal.

The political issues were complex. As a constitutional matter, to be sure, the question was clear: it was whether the Constitution had established a political union of the American people and a national government superior to the state governments, as the North maintained, or a compact among states that retained final authority, as the South insisted. But people on each side had taken each position more than once in the past, responding according to whether it was they or their enemies who controlled the government, and people on both sides had more than once flirted with nullification and secession. What was genuinely at stake, therefore, was not the nature of the federal Union but the uses to which the powers of the federal government were to be put. And on that crucial question the positions of the two societies had come to be polarized during the three decades since Andrew Jackson became president.

The South advocated a system of free trade among nations and a domestic policy that did not invite much governmental interference in the economy; and through its dominance of the Democratic party, it largely succeeded in creating such a system and establishing such a policy during the 1840s and 1850s. Meanwhile, ever-larger portions of the North, and ultimately almost all of it, advocated high tariffs and active governmental interference to promote economic development; and though the North lacked the political clout until 1858 to enact such a program on the federal level, it increasingly employed the power of state governments toward that end. The surge of the Republican party to power in the House elections of 1858 and its victory in the elections of 1860 indicated the triumph on the federal level of the Northern system of political economy.

Most portentously, what was at issue was whether social relations should be fixed or free. The South was defending a way of life in which birth, law, custom, and a stable social structure determined relations among people. The North was defending the idea that a man's status and wealth, his place and his privileges, should be determined by what he did on this earth, and not by what his ancestors had done before him. The Southern way was as old as man, and was in fact all that man had ever known. The Northern was a radical experiment, not yet a century old, but one that had already wrought astonishing changes. The Southern cause was supported by the record of history, the Northern by the promise of the future.

The Civil War: Causes? ☆ 

EUGENE D. GENOVESE

Professor McDonald presents the conflict between North and South as a conflict of cultures. It was that. But it was also a conflict of ideologies, and, as Professor McDonald demonstrates, a conflict of economies. What I do not perceive in his analysis is any perception of the absolute centrality of slavery to all that divided the two sections.

The South was not just another society that tolerated slavery; it was a slave society. The distinctive features of southern culture were the products of slavery—more precisely, of the relationship between master and slave. The slaveholders were very much a breed apart, with contradictory qualities rooted in the condition of being outright owners of human flesh. They had their virtues, which even some of their harshest critics admired: graciousness, generosity, tolerance of human foibles, physical courage, a strong sense of personal and family honor. These were the proud virtues of people who, as masters, could afford and were expected to show a certain confident kindness toward others, and as masters shunned any conduct suggestive of weakness or smallness. And the slaveholders had their vices, which their warmest admirers conceded: hot tempers, a frightening penchant for violence, an inability to allow contradiction on any matter that touched their honor, and a fearful habit of defining their honor to include everything and anything. These were the proud vices of masters. If slaveholders despised the virtues northern culture admired and practiced, it was precisely because they were slaveholders. The diligent money-making of the North seemed to them mean, beneath the dignity of masters.

It is true that the majority of southern whites owned no slaves; the South was nonetheless a slave society. A much smaller percentage of citizens of the United States today owns capital; yet few if any would argue that the United States is therefore not capitalist. Capitalism, like slavery and all other systems in which one class dominates another, defines itself by its ruling class. And the slaveholders did face constant challenge from the small white farmers and the middle classes. There was always the danger that white southerners without slaves would begin to look on slavery as giving too much wealth and power to the planter class at the expense of the rest of the South. The slaveholders' push for secession from the Union was at least partially the result of their fear of political opposition, an opposition that could even turn against slavery itself. For the moment, though, white Southerners who owned no slaves were loyal enough to the planters' regime: they raised no powerful anti-slavery movement before the war came and, with significant exceptions, fought bravely for the Confederacy during the war.

One reason that nonslaveholders supported, or at least did not actually oppose, the slaveowners' regime was their fear of the black population, and of what it might do if it were ever free. But this fear, while important, has been much exaggerated. That small farmers in the plantation areas were related to slaveholders by blood was additional reason for their goodwill toward the slave system. Then, too, they suffered no direct exploitation by the slaveholders, and only the most knowledgeable could glimpse the ways in which slavery as a whole oppressed them. Their small surpluses of food or cotton had to be sold to the wealthy planters or marketed through them: the planters were able to offer friendship and services. These and other relationships strengthened the ties between planters and other whites and lessened the antagonisms. Probably, too, nonslaveholders shared a little of the pride of the planters: if they were not masters, they could at least see themselves as participating in the masters' domination of the slaves.

Harper's Ferry, Virginia, the site of John Brown's raid. *(Courtesy, Stokes Collection, The New York Public Library)*

CHAPTER 14

Civil War and Reconstruction

JOHN BROWN'S RAID

In the summer of 1859, the nation seemed still capable of veering off the collision course on which its sections were hurtling. Then John Brown, his bloody work in Kansas still fresh in the minds of millions, shocked the country with a bold desperate stroke in western Virginia.

Brown, whom William Lloyd Garrison described as a "tall, spare, farmer-like man, with head disproportionately small, and that inflexible mouth," had gone in July 1859, to Harpers Ferry, about sixty miles northwest of Washington, D.C., at the confluence of the Potomac and Shenandoah rivers. Renting a farm near the town and using funds supplied by several abolitionists, he accumulated 198 rifles, a load of pistols he could not use because he had purchased the wrong firing caps for them, and 950 pikes with which to arm slaves. He had gathered an army of sixteen whites and five blacks. His plan—to seize the nearby United States Arsenal and to arm the slaves—was known to at least eighty people. One had actually written to the Secretary of War, who had ignored the letter. On the evening of October 16, his little band set out to capture the town, the federal properties, and the arms. No slaves voluntarily joined them, and the townspeople, militia from the county, and then United States Marines led by Robert E. Lee besieged them. Within thirty-six hours, Brown and his army were captured. Ten of them died, including two of Brown's own sons. That was all there was to the raid, a total failure and, had people accepted it as a failure, a demonstration of the impossibility of starting a vast slave insurrection.

That was all there was to the raid, but not all there was to John Brown. "He is the gamest man I ever saw," admitted the governor of Virginia, who came to question the wounded captive. Brown replied to every questioner at his interrogation and at his trial with crisp assurance borne of clarity of purpose. His many letters after his conviction breathed saintly dedication to the biblical injunction to remember them that are in bonds as bound with them. Brown never wavered, showed no fear, no vindictiveness toward his captors, no selfish purposes at all. He awed his enemies and captured the respect of much of the North for a deed that few would actually have condoned. He transparently but consistently lied about his purposes in making the raid, just as he was evasive to the point of dishonesty about his role in the Pottawatomie Massacre in 1856, when in retaliation against a proslavery group, Brown and a small band had murdered five proslavery settlers near Pottawatomie Creek, Kansas. The man whose tiny army had accumulated rifles and pikes to distribute to slaves nonetheless asserted: "I never did intend murder, or treason, or the destruction of property, or to excite slaves to rebellion, or to make insurrection." "It was all so thin," Robert Penn Warren observed of Brown's argument before the court, "that it should not have deceived a child, but it deceived a generation." A generation, trapped between its idealism about liberty and the intractability of the slavery issue, would forgive a great deal for the certitude obtained of John Brown. Henry Ward Beecher said it in a sermon delivered during Brown's trial: "His soul was noble; his work miserable. But a cord and a gibbet would redeem all that, and round up Brown's failure with a heroic success." "Good," wrote Brown on a newspaper copy of the sermon.

John Brown's favorite saying was that "without the shedding of blood there is no remission of sin." When his eldest son, John, Jr., was less than ten years old, he had kept a record of the son's sins in an account book:

For disobeying mother .... 8 lashes
For unfaithfulness at work .... 3 lashes
For telling a lie .... 8 lashes

Eventually Brown declared his son "bankrupt" and collected one-third of the debt "reckoned in strokes from a nicely-prepared blue-beech switch." Then the elder Brown removed his own shirt, handed the boy the whip and ordered him to "lay it on." "I dared not refuse to obey," John, Jr., would remember, "but at first I did not strike hard. 'Harder!' he said, 'harder, harder!' until he *received the balance of the account*." The son would also remember the "drops of blood showing on his back."

It was only years later that John, Jr., began to think that he understood this bizarre event. It was, he decided, a "practical illustration" of the doctrine of atonement. "I was then too obtuse to perceive how Justice could be satisfied by inflicting penalty upon the back of the innocent instead of the guilty." In 1856 on Pottawatomie Creek in Kansas, and in 1859 at Harpers Ferry, John Brown offered an entire nation a "practical illustration" of the doctrine of atonement which he had derived from his family heritage and from "the ponderous volumes of Jonathan Edwards' sermons which father owned." John Brown, a lifelong failure, a bankrupt, sometimes a thief, eccentric, fanatic, a liar, perhaps insane, would take upon his own back the nation's giant sin, would remove the debt that a society gone morally and politically bankrupt with slavery could not discharge. Brown actually believed that the shedding of his own blood and the blood of other innocents (for Brown appears to have felt no guilt over either the Pottawatomie Massacre or the deaths at Harpers Ferry) could save the nation.

Brown's acts struck terror in the South, aroused many fears and uncertainties in the North, yet played upon the deepest chords of the Puritan conscience. Brown's behavior facing execution, which impressed even his captors, caught the imagination of Americans who accepted the doctrine of atonement, voiced most eloquently in Lincoln's Second Inaugural Address.

There is something blasphemous in Brown's practical theology; the Son of God, not the son of Owen Brown, atones for mankind's sins. His last words, sent out to the world as he mounted the wagon that would carry him to the gallows, burn both with prophecy and with his disappointment at the realization that his own killings had not been enough.

> I John Brown am now quite *certain* that the crimes of this *guilty land: will* never be purged *away;* but with Blood. I had *as I now think: vainly* flattered myself that without *very much* bloodshed; it might be done.

Yet many Northerners could easily link Brown with Christ. Ralph Waldo Emerson predicted that Brown "will make the gallows as glorious as the cross." Julia Ward Howe (whose husband, Samuel Gridley Howe, was one of the "Secret Six" supplying Brown with arms and money) wrote *The Battle Hymn of the Republic.* One stanza—the one about Christ—reads:

> In the beauty of the lilies Christ was born across the sea,
> With a glory in his bosom that transfigures you and me,
> As he died to make men holy, let us die to make men free,
> While God is marching on.

But Union troops marching to the melody sang:

> John Brown's body lies a moldering in the grave.
> John Brown's body lies a moldering in the grave.
> John Brown's body lies a moldering in the grave.
> His truth is marching on.

John Brown being hanged for treason on December 2, 1859. His defiant last words helped make him a martyr to many Northerners.

Secession

Appropriately, South Carolina led the way toward secession. As soon as Lincoln's election was certain, the South Carolina legislature called for a state convention. On December 20, 1860, the convention met at Charleston and unanimously declared "that the Union now subsisting between South Carolina and other States of America is hereby dissolved." Similar declarations followed in rapid succession in Alabama, Georgia, Florida, Mississippi, and Louisiana. The smooth course of secession was upset only in Texas, where crusty old Governor Sam Houston, a staunch Unionist, refused to summon a special session of the legislature. The lawmakers met anyway, and called an election of delegates and a convention without Houston's authorization.

Up to this point, the secession process had moved forward with electrifying speed. In the space of forty-two days, seven states, stretching from South Carolina to Texas, had seceded from the Union. On February 4, 1861, however, the secessionist tide broke momentarily when the voters of Virginia elected a majority of convention delegates opposed to immediate secession. Subsequently the electorate in four other upper South states—Tennessee, North Carolina, Arkansas, and Missouri—voted in effect against secession. The three remaining slave states—Kentucky, Maryland, and Delaware—did not even call conventions. Having stronger ties to the North and smaller ratios of blacks in its population, the upper South was hesitant to secede. For the moment, the lower South was isolated.

Nonetheless, at Montgomery, Alabama, on February 7, 1861, delegates from the seven states proceeded to adopt a provisional constitution for the Confederate States of America. It was modeled closely on the United States Constitution, but several modifications safeguarded state sovereignty and slavery. The Confederate Constitution reserved to the states the power of amendment and even permitted them to impeach Confederate officials under certain circumstances. It guaranteed the property rights of slaveholders both in the existing states and in any future territory the Confederacy might acquire. To lead the new government the delegates chose Jefferson Davis of Mississippi as provisional president and Alexander H. Stephens of Georgia as vice-president.

A Compact of States. The reasons for secession were spelled out in declarations issued by the various state conventions. South Carolina's was typical. The United States Constitution, the declaration began, was a compact among sovereign states for the purpose of establishing "a government with defined objects and powers." Like all compacts, this one bound the contracting parties to certain mutual obligations. The failure of one of the parties to perform these obligations, in whole or in part, released the other from its bond. The Northern states, continued the South Carolina declaration, had refused to fulfill their constitutional obligation to return fugitive slaves. They had denounced slavery as "sinful" and tolerated abolition societies "designed to disturb the peace and steal the property of the citizens of other states." They had encouraged "servile insurrection"—a reference to John Brown. At last, a sectional party "hostile to slavery" had captured control of the federal government. This party was dedicated not merely to excluding slavery from the "common territory," but to slavery's ultimate extinction. The actions of Brown and the writings of Harriet Beecher Stowe and others incorrectly convinced many Southerners that abolitionists had triumphed in the North.

We can now see that even on their own terms Southerners were wrong: slavery would have remained far safer in the Union than out of it. Democrats and Southerners still had a majority in both houses of Congress. Lincoln could not have acted without their approval. Even had the South eventually lost all control of the government, important constitutional guarantees protected slavery in the states where it existed and Republicans had pledged themselves not to interfere with it there. Lincoln even expressed his willingness early in 1861 to support a constitutional amendment to that effect. If the Southern states had remained in the Union, the Republicans could never have put through a constitutional amendment abolishing slavery. This could only have been done by act of war. Secession united a North previously divided on the question of slavery and doomed the peculiar institution.

Secession as the founders of the Confederacy viewed it was not an act of revolution but a defense of a traditional order. It was, they argued, a return to the system of independent states out of which the Constitution had come, a resumption by individual states of the exercise of a sovereignty they had never surrendered to the United States. The object was to preserve a so-

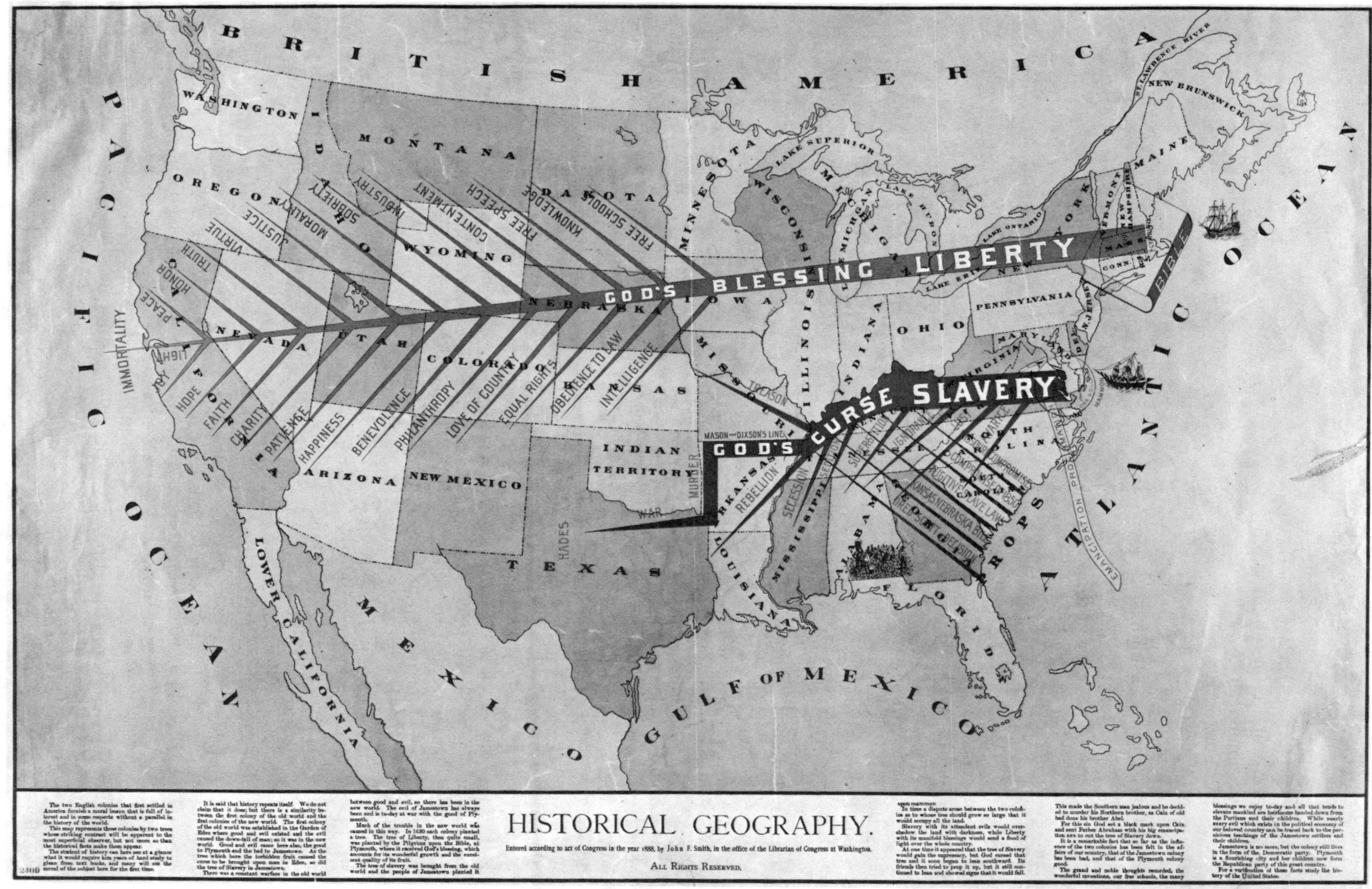

A textbook map depicting the tree of Slavery (God's curse) branching out below the Mason-Dixon line and into Missouri, and the tree of Liberty (God's blessing) branching out across the rest of the nation.

cial system and to protect a form of property, the holding of slaves. Yet secessionists would not have described themselves as repudiating the modern world. Their society, so they thought, was one of freedom—for white people—and of enlightened republican government.

Southerners of this sort would associate the case for slavery with the case for secession, claiming that both slaveholding and states' rights were old institutions strongly founded in law. But the two issues were in fact quite separate. In previous years Northern opponents of slavery had proposed that free states refuse cooperation with a national government that protected slavery; and in 1860 some sympathizers with slavery were also supporters of the Union. Earlier in the century political and constitutional quarrels had taken place over whether it was the Union or the states that possessed sovereignty. The argument looked back to the process of ratification, in which each state had held a convention to decide whether that state should adhere to the Constitution. Nineteenth-century champions of state sovereignty concluded from this that ratification had been by individual states, each state retaining sovereignty and the right of independence. They believed that sovereignty belonged also to the states formed after ratification.

President and Mrs. Jefferson Davis. In February 1861, the seven Confederate States of America elected Davis as President. *(Courtesy, Confederate Museum, Richmond, Virginia)*

Northern Reactions. Advocates of the authority of the federal government held that ratification had been by the American people as a whole, acting for mere convenience in separate state conventions, and that the states were subordinate to the unified American people and to the Constitution. In 1860 and 1861 reasoning of that kind, in this age that took seriously such philosophical inquiries, must have been in the minds of unionists, and even a citizen convinced of the legal right of secession might be a unionist out of patriotism toward the Union or a recognition of its economic and strategic benefits. In their appeals to Southerners to stay by the United States, unionists could keep away from the slavery issue, on which they could not have made converts, and instead could make use of the self-interest, the patriotism, or the constitutional arguments that might even draw slaveholders to the Union.

By early winter 1861 when Lincoln was on his way to Washington, the seven states of the deep South had seceded and formed themselves into the Confederate States of America, with Montgomery, Alabama, as their capital. The crisis was the greatest since the Revolution. Washington was astir with worry and excitement.

The nation's capital, tucked between the slave states of Virginia and Maryland, was a largely Southern city. For decades Southern politicians, or "northern men with southern principles," had dominated the political, business, and social life of the capital. The city still had hundreds of slaves in its population, although since the 1850 Compromise the slave pens and auction blocks had gone. Now, in the country's greatest crisis, the Southern sympathies of Washingtonians were visible everywhere. At the city's many bars the imbibers of "toddies" and "flips" announced that Lincoln would never be inaugurated: proud "southrons" would not allow it. At the government executive departments young clerks wore "secession cockades" much as we wear campaign buttons in presidential election years.

Unionists who found themselves in the capital during the secession winter were apprehensive. The young Henry Adams, who had come to Washington as private secretary to his father, Congressman Charles Francis Adams of Massachusetts, thought the Southerners "demented."

Confident of independence, they were already cultivating the good will of their future Yankee customers. Senator Stephen Douglas, waiting for Congress to begin its session, talked darkly of the "slave power" conspiracy that had connived at defeating him for president and was now intent on breaking up the Union. Other unionists were charging that the conspirators could be found in President Buchanan's cabinet itself. Cabinet members Howell Cobb of Georgia, Jacob Thompson of Mississippi, and John B. Floyd of Virginia, they said, were providing the Confederacy with guns and ammunition from federal arsenals and threatening the weak-willed Buchanan that if he tried to move against the secessionists he would be either assassinated or impeached.

Indeed, from the unionist view it looked at first as if the seventy-year-old James Buchanan had been terrified into inaction. The Democratic president had proclaimed secession illegal and declared the Union "perpetual." But he denied that the federal government had any constitutional authority to force the return of seceded states, and he feared that any attempt at coercion would make the situation worse. Buchanan attributed the whole trouble to fanatical abolitionists and to the menace the free-soil movement posed for the South. The president hoped for some new compromise that would still the issue of slavery as had the arrangements of 1820 and 1850.

Efforts at compromise were not wanting. The issue needing resolution was that of whether or to what extent the territories should be open to slavery. Early in 1861 the Washington Peace Convention, a gathering of statesmen under the chairmanship of former President John Tyler, looked for a solution. Congress also debated. A plan pressed by Senator John J. Crittenden of Kentucky would extend the Missouri Compromise line to the Pacific and add a constitutional amendment protecting slavery wherever it existed. But the extremists dominating politics in the cotton states would probably have turned down the plan, and the Republican party could not have abandoned its principle of "free soil," the opposition to slavery in the territories.

While attempts at compromise were unsuccessful, neither secession nor war appeared anything like a certainty. Republican and Democratic upholders of the sovereignty of the United States perceived secession as an impulsive and irrational act that the South could decide to reverse. War, or at any rate a prolonged one, must have been almost unthinkable. While many, and perhaps almost all, Northern statesmen along with some Southerners would have agreed that secession was unconstitutional, it was not clear that the federal government had the constitutional means to prevent it by force: President Buchanan denied that the government did. Nor could supporters of the Union have any confidence that the Northern people could summon the will to march against the seceded states. For President-elect Lincoln and prospective members of his cabinet, the problem was to find a political solution to the crisis.

The Problem of the Forts

Lincoln in his inaugural address told the South that he would enforce the Fugitive Slave Law and support a constitutional amendment protecting slavery where it already existed. But he did not modify his position on free soil; and he condemned secession, pledging to "hold, occupy and possess" all Union property within the regions that had announced their secession.

By February 1861 the issue was largely symbolic, but not the less critical for that. Throughout the lower South federal forts, customs houses, and post offices had fallen into the hands of the Confederate or state authorities soon after secession. But two key posts held out, Fort Pickens at Pensacola, Florida, and Fort Sumter in Charleston harbor. For the Confederates to concede these to the United States meant accepting the intolerable presence of a "foreign" power in the new Southern nation's territory. For the Union to surrender them would be acquiescence in Southern independence. The Pickens problem was not acute, since in Florida authorities were for the moment willing to tolerate the presence of the forces of the United States. Fiery Charleston was a different story.

Fort Sumter. As the citizens of the Southern port went about their business, they were aware of the drama at their doorsteps. Across the harbor they could see the stars and stripes flying defiantly over Sumter, while on Confederate-held Morris Island and at the city's main fortifications uniformed men rushed here and there moving big guns, ammunition, and powder.

For weeks South Carolina officials had been negotiating with both the Washington authorities and Major Robert Anderson, the garrison commander, for evacuation of the fort. Anderson had holed up at Sumter when he concluded that his small force was inadequate to occupy all three federal strong points in the harbor, but from that grim, gray bastion he refused to depart. Soon after the new year Buchanan, his resolve stiffened by four new unionist cabinet members, dispatched the *Star of the West*, an unarmed steamer, to reinforce Anderson with men and supplies. The Charleston authorities ordered their guns to let loose at the vessel. Anderson came within an eyelash of returning the fire to protect the ship, but before he could, it turned back.

Lincoln inherited the Sumter problem from his predecessor. He sought advice from his cabinet members and other statesmen. William Seward of New York, his Secretary of State, startled him with the suggestion that the administration bring the country together by getting into a war with Europe. On April 4, 1861, the president announced the sending of a squadron for the relief of Fort Sumter. The ships would carry only food. If the secessionists allowed them through, the federal government would make no attempt to send men or ammunitions to Anderson.

News of Lincoln's intentions infuriated the Confederate authorities in Montgomery, who believed that the Republican president had assured them he would evacuate Sumter. Convinced that they could not avoid a clash without seeming to be weak, they reluctantly ordered that Sumter be reduced by attack before the promised reinforcement could arrive.

The hotheads at Charleston, the moral and intellectual capital of "Secessia," rejoiced. Happiest of all, perhaps, was the venerable Edmund Ruffin. Now a silver-haired man of sixty-seven, Ruffin had been among the staunchest defenders of Southern rights and had long advocated secession. When his own state of Virginia proved slow to take up the Northern challenge he had come to fire-eating Charleston and, despite his age, had joined the Palmetto Guard of the South Carolina infantry. When the order to attack Sumter was given early on the morning of April 12, the elderly gentleman was positioned at the great Columbiad cannon pointing at the federal fort. Later Ruffin would insist that he had fired the first shot of the war. In reality his shot was preceded by a mortar barrage. But it was to him that the symbolic honor went.

The bombardment lasted for ten hours, a respectable period for the outnumbered Union force. Then Anderson, his food and gunpowder low, sent word that he was ready to surrender. The next day the flag of the Union was lowered and the Palmetto banner of South Carolina raised. By seceding and by firing the first shot, the Confederacy brought together in defense of the Union a North that might not have chosen to fight the South on the question of slavery alone.

The War Strategies

The attack on the fort began the Civil War. In the absence of Congress, President Lincoln issued a proclamation requesting 75,000 volunteers for the suppressing of "combinations too powerful to be suppressed by the ordinary course of judicial proceedings." Upon its reassembling that summer, Congress gave legality to this proclamation along with other actions that Lincoln had taken in the military emergency.

Lincoln's call for troops confronted the upper South states with an unwelcome choice: to fight against the South or to fight against the Union. Virginia, North Carolina. Tennessee, and Arkansas joined the Confederacy. In the remaining slave states—Delaware, Maryland, Kentucky, and Missouri—opinion was divided. Only Delaware remained peaceably in the Union. President Lincoln used force to aid the Union cause in strategic Maryland. When a mob favoring the South attacked federal soldiers in Baltimore and cut the rail line between that city and Washington, he sent troops to subdue the disorder and arrest potential secessionists. Kentucky, birthplace of both Lincoln and Jefferson Davis, declared its neutrality, but within months Union and Confederate troops had entered the state. It and Missouri became the scene of guerrilla warfare, as supporters of both sides fought for control of the state government. Although the Confederacy claimed these two states, both remained in the old nation. Later in the Civil War, the government arranged to make into a separate state West Virginia, the Northwestern region of Virginia where slaves were few and Unionist sentiment was strong.

Two basic facts dictated the North's military strategy: restoring the Union required subduing the South; and a war of conquest required vast material and human resources. These the North possessed in abundance. Its population in 1860 numbered twenty million, while the South had barely nine million, one third of whom were slaves. Nine-tenths of the country's manufacturing capacity was situated in the North, which also had two-thirds of the railroad mileage. Most of the nation's merchant shipping and financial resources were in Northern hands.

Recognizing these advantages, General Winfield Scott mapped out the basic Northern strategy right after Sumter's fall. He proposed starving the South by a blockade of her ports; driving down the Mississippi River, which would divide the Confederacy in two; sending in armies of invasion that would break the Southern nation into bits. Northerners expected a short war, but once the reality of a long war sank in, they closely followed Scott's strategy.

The Confederacy's crucial disadvantage was economic, though it also suffered from a deep moral isolation from a world struggling to end slavery. Having few mills, factories, and foundries, the South began the war with a stockpile of captured or imported equipment. In spite of heroic efforts toward industrial self-sufficiency, the South could never replace equipment as rapidly as it wore out. With imports cut off, the Confederacy would gradually die of economic starvation.

Yet the South at the beginning of the war was not in a weak position. For while the Confederacy could not have won a head-on conflict with the North, it did not have to. Against the North's enormous task of conquering a vast territory, the rebels needed to do no more than demonstrate to the Northern people and to Europe, by one military strategy or another, that the old Union was no longer a single, workable nation. A few decisive Southern victories might have done that. Instead the South fought a mostly defensive war, keeping the Confederate armies close to home base. That revealed itself ultimately as a losing strategy because it made for a long war that expended the South's limited supplies and troops.

The South made other mistakes. Unwilling to see their black slaves as men, Southerners never effectively used this vast source of manpower. Only in the closing months of the war would the Confederate Congress at last authorize using slaves in the army—too late to affect the outcome. Equally damaging to the South's cause was its naive faith in the power of "King Cotton." Convinced that Britain could not long do without Southern cotton, the new Confederate government in 1861 forbade all exports of this, the South's only major source of foreign credit. Starving British textile makers, Richmond thought, would force Britain to intervene in the Confederacy's behalf. But British manufacturers, expecting war in America, had stockpiled cotton. By the time the South realized its error, the Northern blockade had closed tight. For the rest of the war the South's "white gold" rotted on the wharves while Southerners starved.

Classic War in the East; Decisive War in the West

The American Civil War, like other wars, was shaped as much by geography as by generals. The placing of the Confederate capital at Richmond, only one hundred miles from Washington, focused the fighting in the East in a narrow theater between the capitals. Here in northern Virginia rival armies marched and countermarched for four years, as each side sought to protect its capital and threaten its rival. The dramatic battles fought here—such as Chancellorsville and Gettysburg—constitute the classic war so celebrated in Civil War legend. It is often overlooked that after four years of bloodshed neither side had accomplished its objective—destruction of the enemy's capital.

Robert E. Lee, who led the Confederacy's northern Virginia troops and would become the South's most prominent general, had been no enthusiast for secession. Family tradition opposed it: his father, "Lighthorse Harry" Lee, had been a Revolutionary War hero, and his mother's family had also played an honorable role in the founding of the United States. His wife was the great granddaughter of Martha Washington, and Lee had grown up in Alexandria, Virginia, surrounded by mementos of George Washington, upon whom he modeled his life. Lee received his education at West Point and had served all his adult life in the United States Army, distinguishing himself in the Mexican War, serving as the superintendent of West Point, and achieving some eminence as an army engineer. When secession came, the Lincoln administration sounded him out about taking command of the Union army. Lee, who had only days before accepted promotion to colonel, saw no choice but to resign his commission rather than to face the responsibility of

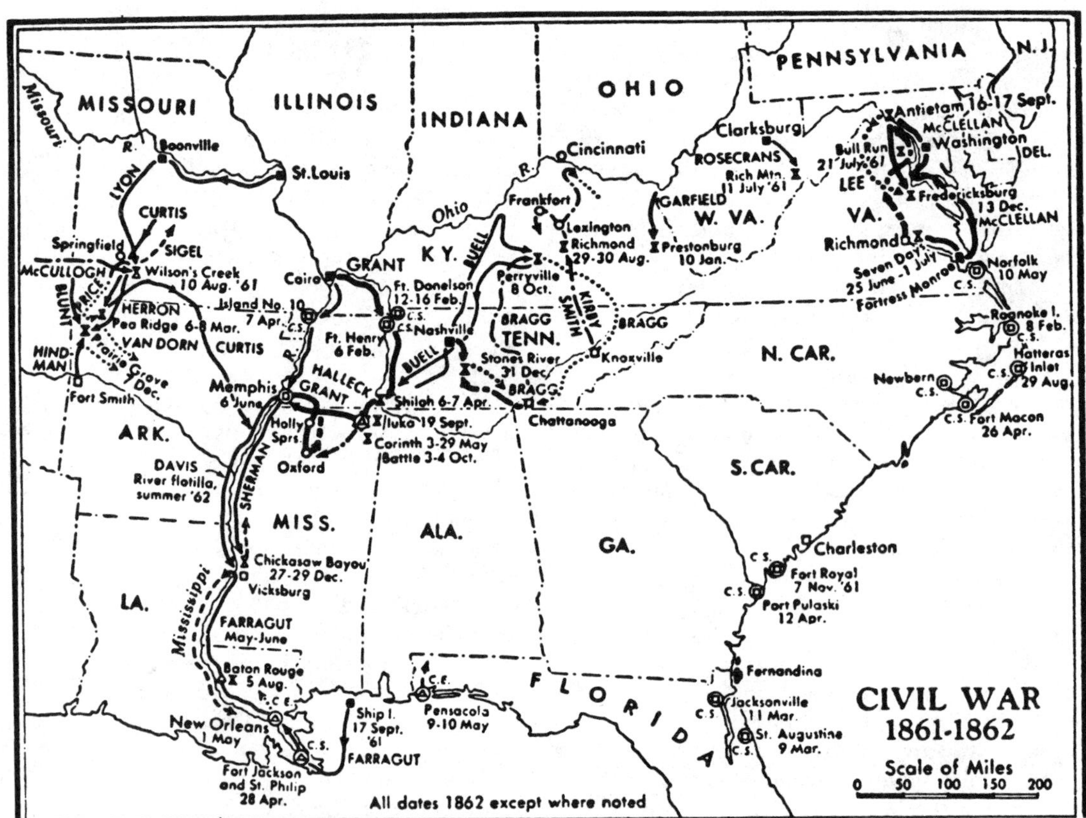

leading troops against his native state. In the end he was a Virginian. When after 1865 the Confederacy was no more, he found it relatively easy to resume his loyalty to the Union and to urge other Southerners to follow his lead. Perhaps he was never a Southern nativist, only a Virginian in a bad season.

The decisive theater of the Civil War was in the West. Here nature had formed a series of southerly flowing rivers—the Cumberland, the Tennessee, the Mississippi—that thrust into the heart of the Confederacy. Union strategists recognized early the value of these rivers for rapid movement of men and supplies, and acted to secure control of them. It was here, and in Sherman's later invasion of the deep South from the West, that the North won and the South lost the Civil War.

Both governments were totally unprepared for war in April 1861. Guns and ammunition were in short supply. Few officers on either side had commanded large bodies of men. The hastily formed volunteer regiments lacked even the rudiments of military training. Each wore gaudy, impractical uniforms and adopted flamboyant names.

These amateur armies had their first taste of war in July 1861. Pressured by public cries of "Forward to Richmond," Union General Irvin McDowell led his ill-trained army into northern Virginia, followed by carriages full of Washingtonians out to see the show. At Bull Run (or Manassas Junction), the Union troops met an equally ill-prepared army under General P.G.T. Beauregard. For some time the two armies fought with a courage beyond their experience. After early reverses, Confederates rallied behind General Thomas Jackson—"Stonewall," as he would soon be known because his soldiers held firm on this day—and broke the Union advance. Retreat became chaos as green troops struggled with panic-stricken civilians along the roads to Washington. McDowell's army simply fell apart; soldiers threw down their guns and ran. The Confederate soldiers, nearly as disorganized, did not pursue, although Jackson boasted that with 5000 men he could have finished the job.

Bull Run awakened the North to reality. Lincoln gave the command to General George B. McClellan, a cautious soldier but brilliant organizer, who set about shaping the Army of the Potomac into a real fighting machine. As McClellan trained his troops, critical events were taking place in the West. Union attention here focused on the rivers, where Confederate strong points barred an advance southward.

Western Campaigns. In February 1862 an army under General Ulysses S. Grant, supported by a fleet of iron-clad gunboats, pushed up the Tennessee River and captured Fort Henry. Union forces crossed over immediately and besieged Fort Donelson on the Cumberland. Grant took this fort, too, and fired the North's imagination with his demand for "immediate and unconditional surrender."

Confederate troops struck back hard at Grant's army in April at Shiloh, on the Tennessee River near the northern border of Mississippi. Catching Grant off guard, they nearly pushed his troops back into the river. All day long the battle raged. "From right to left, everywhere," an Illinois soldier was to write, "it was one never ending, terrible roar, with no prospect of stopping." At nightfall Union reinforcements turned the battle. The human cost at Shiloh was appalling—nearly 23,000 casualties—but the results were decisive. The Confederacy had lost its supreme bid to regain western Tennessee. Other Union forces opened the upper Mississippi as far as Memphis. That same April of 1862 the Confederacy suffered one of its greatest losses when Admiral David Farragut captured New Orleans, the South's biggest seaport. By midsummer the South's hold on the Mississippi was limited to a narrow stretch of river between Vicksburg, Mississippi, and Port Hudson, Louisiana.

Blockade. While the North was pressing in on the Confederacy in the West, it was also pushing in from the sea. The blockade included the stopping of foreign merchant ships and the confiscation of nonmilitary goods that they were carrying to the Confederacy. In a regular war between independent countries such seizures would have been contrary to international law, and the United States faced complaints from Europe. But the South, the federal government responded in effect, was not an independent nation at war, to which citizens from neutral

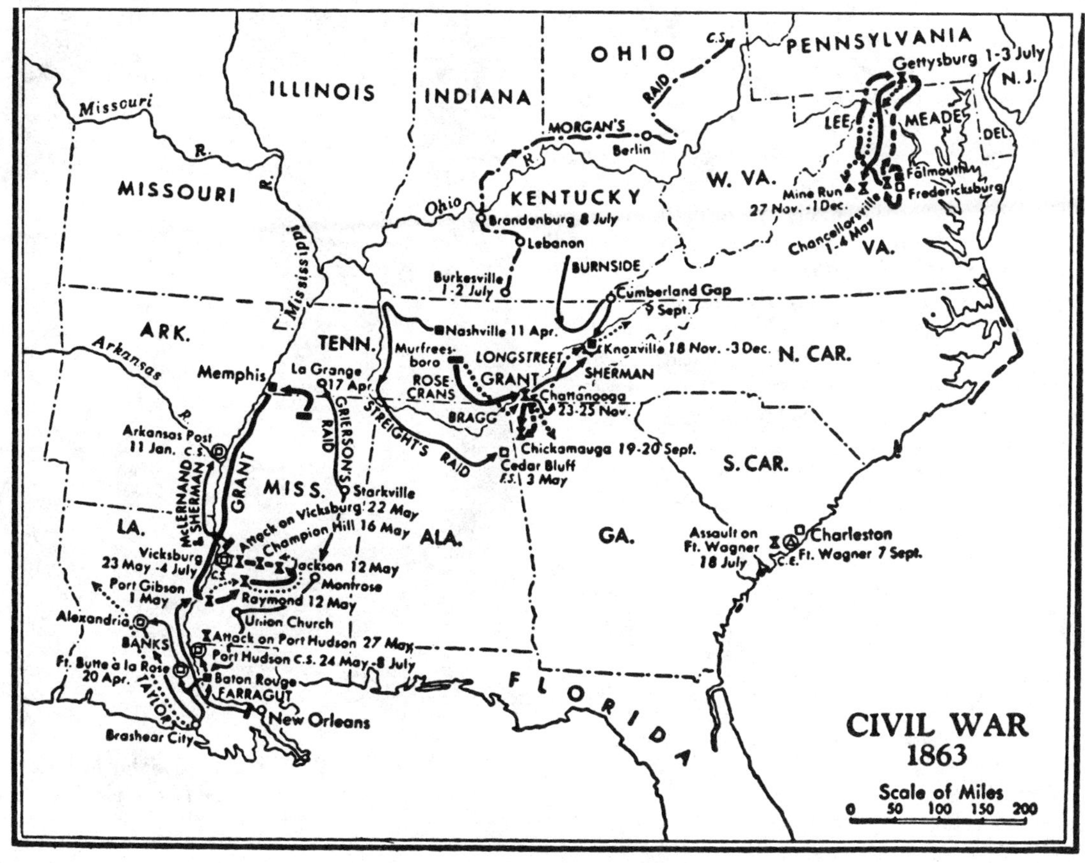

countries could have the right to ship nonmilitary provisions. It was instead a rebellious part of the United States, and the national government therefore had the authority to exclude commerce from Southern ports. For a time the Union had to face the possibility that Great Britain or France, not displeased at a weakening of the United States and eager to resume full trade with the cotton South, might recognize the Confederacy as a separate nation. British recognition would give a tremendous lift to Southern morale and injure that of the North. And in recognizing the Confederacy as an independent country the British would have grounds for challenging the federal blockade for not following the rules that international law dictated in war between sovereign nations. France might recognize the Confederacy in return for Southern support of Napoleon III's plan to install a French puppet, Austrian Archduke Maximilian, on a specially created Mexican throne. But when federal troops in September 1862 stopped a rebel invasion at the Battle of Antietam (or Sharpsburg, as the Southerners called it), Great Britain decided to put off recognition of the Confederacy. The blockade was safe from direct foreign interference.

The Southern navy could not successfully take on the Union fleet. For one day in 1862 in a battle off Hampton Roads, Virginia, the Confederate vessel *Merrimac* did much damage to Union naval forces. In a great technological innovation, the ship had been covered with iron plates, and against them Northern naval guns had little effect. The next day the North set its own ironclad *Monitor* against the *Merrimac*, rendering it harmless. Later in the war Northern commerce suffered from the raids of the Confederate ship *Alabama*, built in Britain by a private company. Charles Francis Adams, the American minister to that nation, protested to the British government for its failure to stop the construction and after the war the United States would win compensation from Britain for losses the ship had inflicted. The Union navy finally sank the *Alabama*. Confederate privateers could attack merchant ships, but were no threat to the Northern navy. While the blockade could not keep the Confederacy from the sea trade, it was effective enough to deprive Confederate society of much that it needed for smooth functioning.

Eastern Campaigns. In the East, General McClellan in 1862 drilled his Army of the Potomac for months, all the while ignoring the public clamor for action. (An exasperated Lincoln once said he would like to borrow McClellan's army if the general did not intend to use it.) Prodded by the president, he finally proposed in the spring of 1862 a bold plan to take Richmond from the rear. Instead of fighting his way overland, McClellan would make an amphibious landing on the James River Peninsula; from there he could march up the Peninsula and seize the confederate capital. Lincoln approved, provided McClellan left enough men behind to protect Washington.

McClellan embarked in March 1862, without leaving the promised covering force. When Lincoln discovered this, he recalled part of the Army of the Potomac. This nearly immobilized the cautious McClellan, who consistently overestimated Confederate strength (he in fact still had 90,000 men to the enemy's 70,000). The

Robert E. Lee, native son of Virginia, brilliant military strategist, and leader of the Confederate forces. *(Courtesy, Library of Congress)*

slowness of his progress up the Peninsula gave the Confederate troops, commanded by Lee, time to organize. In a series of battles known as the Seven Days, Lee hammered at McClellan's army and threw it back. In August McClellan began a slow withdrawal from the Peninsula. Command of the Army of the Potomac passed to General John Pope.

Sensing an opportunity to strike before the federal army could regroup, Lee took the offensive. On August 30 he smashed Pope's army at the second battle of Bull Run, then swung north into Maryland. But a copy of his battle plans fell into the hands of McClellan, whom Lincoln had hurriedly recalled to command. On September 17, McClellan engaged the invading Confederates at Antietam Creek. After the bloodiest single day's battle of the entire war—24,000 dead and wounded—Lee withdrew unpursued. Tactically the battle had been a draw, but measured against Confederate expectations it was a crushing defeat.

Although Lee had failed at Antietam, he was still unbeatable on his home ground. Twice during the winter of 1862-63, federal generals renewed the offensive against Richmond, each time with disastrous results. In December General Ambrose Burnside, a handsome West Pointer remembered for his legendary growth of side whiskers, was soundly defeated at Fredericksburg. In a series of hopeless frontal assaults against Lee's entrenched army at Chancellorsville in the spring of 1863, Lee and Jackson caught the army of Burnside's successor, General Joseph Hooker, straddling the Rappahannock River and cut it to pieces. Lee paid a fearful price—"Stonewall" Jackson was mortally wounded, shot down by his own men in the confusion of battle. After two years the Northern drive on Richmond was back where it had started—on the Potomac.

In Ulysses S. Grant, Lincoln finally found a general who would pursue Lee's outnumbered forces relentlessly, a strategy that ended the war.
(Courtesy, Library of Congress)

Vicksburg and Gettysburg. At this point, in the summer of 1863, two battles put the North on the way to final victory in the war. Ulysses S. Grant struck in the West. For months his troops had besieged Vicksburg, the last Confederate stronghold on the Mississippi River. Situated high on a hill above the river, with bayous on both flanks, the city seemed impregnable. After repeated failures to dislodge the Confederate defenders, Grant hit on a bold plan. Abandoning his supply base, he slipped around the city on the Louisiana side, marched downstream, and crossed below Vicksburg. With dazzling speed, he moved inland to Jackson, cutting Vicksburg's rail link with the Confederacy, then turned west to lock up the city from the land side. Cut off, Vicksburg surrendered on July 4, 1863. Grant had reopened the Mississippi and split the Confederacy in two, leaving the trans-Mississippi region isolated. And in the East, just a day before, the Union army at Gettysburg had won what was to become the most famous battle of the war.

Gettsyburg was the devastating outcome of a daring Confederate attempt that had begun in June, when Lee marched his army north again in search of a decisive victory. The South needed one. It was in trouble in the West, and the Union blockade was withering the Southern economy.

Lee's army moved quickly out of the Blue

Ridge Mountains into Maryland. Hooker followed, keeping to the east in order to protect Washington. As Lee drove into Pennsylvania, a nervous Lincoln replaced the timid Hooker with George G. Meade. Respectful of General Meade's abilities, Lee concentrated his forces at Gettysburg. Rushing forward, Meade collided with him at that Pennsylvania town, and on July 1, 2, and 3 they fought the greatest single battle of the war.

Lee struck first, before Meade could concentrate his army, and on July 1 nearly drove the Federals from the field. During the night Union troops arrived in strength and dug in. On the next two days Lee attacked at both flanks and the center of the Union line in an all-out effort to crush the Army of the Potomac. Nothing quite worked. The climax came on July 3 when 15,000 Confederate troops under General George Pickett made a gallant frontal assault on the Union center on—appropriately—Cemetery Ridge. On Pickett's men came, "an ocean of armed men . . . magnificent, grim, irresistible," as Union gunners fired triple loads of canister (iron shot) into their ranks. A few Confederate soldiers reached the Ridge; then suddenly Union reinforcements poured into the breach. The surviving Confederate troops retreated, leaving half their number dead. The battle was over. On July 4, while a rainstorm washed the blood from the grass, the Confederate army withdrew. Meade, as paralyzed as his predecessors, did not pursue. Lee had lost 20,000 men—a third of his army. The Confederacy's offensive power was broken forever.

Grant Takes Command. In 1864 the Union organized for final victory. Lincoln called Grant

The blood-soaked battlefield at Gettysburg after the fighting of July 1, 1863.

to Washington and put him in overall command of federal armies. Grant outlined a coordinated Union campaign. In the East he would lead the Army of the Potomac against Lee. From the West William T. Sherman, a trusted subordinate, would press into Georgia.

Grant pushed south in May. In a region of Virginia known as the Wilderness, his army, larger than Lee's, drove relentlessly forward. Repeatedly Lee checked Grant's advance, but the Army of the Potomac did not retreat. After each battle Grant slipped around the Confederate right flank and continued south, never giving Lee the initiative. The brilliant Virginian had no chance to organize one of those counterstrokes that had disrupted previous federal offensives. By the end of June the Confederate troops were bottled up around Richmond. There followed months of siege warfare suggestive of World War I, as Grant gradually squeezed Lee's Army of Northern Virginia.

Simultaneously with Grant's offensive, Sherman began an advance from Tennessee into Georgia. Joseph E. Johnston conducted a skillful retreat, and the invaders did not reach Atlanta until September. At this point Sherman changed the rules. Leaving sufficient troops behind to deal with Johnston, he marched off across Georgia, allowing his men to burn and loot as they went. By marching a federal army unmolested through the heart of the Confederacy, living off the land as it went, he aimed to demonstrate to Southerners the futility of continued resistance. Sherman's army reached Savannah in December, leaving a fifty-mile-wide path of destruction in its wake. From there, Sherman slashed northward through the Carolinas, while Johnston tailed him, powerless to intervene.

The Confederacy's end came swiftly in the spring of 1865. With his last supply line threatened, Lee abandoned Richmond. Grant caught up with him at Appomattox Court House, and on April 9 Lee surrendered his proud but exhausted Army of Northern Virginia. Johnston surrendered to Sherman a few days later and the war was over.

Life in the Confederacy

During the rush of enthusiasm following Sumter many Southerners rejoiced at the prospect of glory and independence. "I feel as tho' I could live poetry," exclaimed Mrs. Catherine Edmonston, mistress of a North Carolina plantation. But among the South's white population thousands wondered whether their section had not made a colossal mistake. Even slaveholders had their doubts. One Mississippi planter anticipated the defeat of the Confederacy and saw the time "when the northern soldier would tread her cotton fields, when the slave should be made *free* and the proud Southerner stricken to the dust in his presence."

Still more skeptical were large groups of people who owned no slaves. In the mountain backbone that split the older from the newer South, unionist sentiment smoldered. Virginia's Western counties would carry their dissent so far as to secede from "Secessia" and form the state of West Virginia. In eastern Tennessee, and western North Carolina, and Kentucky—that state never seceded anyway—thousands of young men joined the Union army. Dissent from the rebellion was not confined to the Appalachian plateau. Wherever small farmers tilled their acres with the sole help of their families or a few hired hands, the Union found favor. In places like northern Louisiana, Alabama, and Mississippi, however, unionist sentiment was more difficult to act on than in the mountains.

For many years after the Civil War Southerners with a nostalgic affection for the Confederacy would speak of how loyal slaves had been to their Southern masters. When Southern white men were off fighting Yankees and blacks had a chance to revolt, they remained at their jobs, providing the Confederacy with its food and manufactured goods. This romantic image of contented and loyal slaves is only partly accurate. The experience of the Pryor family of Georgia furnishes an example. In 1861 Shepard G. Pryor went off to fight, leaving his wife in charge of his farm and his thirteen slaves. Mrs. Pryor chose as her overseer a white man who had no control over the slaves. Eventually she made a crucial decision to appoint one of her slaves, Will, as overseer. The choice was fateful for the Pryors' corner of the slave system. For a while Will performed as his mistress wished, and he successfully managed the 1862 crop harvest. But soon Will was hiding slave runaways and in general refusing to cooperate with the slave system. The authorities finally arrested him for sheltering slave fugitives. By late 1863 the slave system was disintegrating in many parts of the South. Nowhere was there a major slave uprising, but black people were helping to

Slaves planting sweet potatoes on James Hopkinson's plantation, Edisto Island, South Carolina, 1862. Though there were no major uprisings, the old slave system began to disintegrate by late 1863 as blacks refused to work for their old masters or simply left the plantations. *(Courtesy, The New-York Historical Society, New York City)*

pull the system apart in other ways. Whenever rumors spread of Yankee troops nearby the slaves of the neighborhood would desert the plantations in droves. Many of those who remained became disobedient and refused to work.

Economic Problems. Life in the Confederacy after the early months of enthusiasm was difficult for everybody. The Southern economy was not suited for swift adaptation to war production. Most Southern railroads were short lines; the rail system consisted of eleven different gauges, which meant that a railroad car fitted for one gauge would have to confine itself to some portion of the tracks; and there was not enough railway equipment. The South in 1861 did only a fifth of the whole nation's manufacturing, and it lacked the knowledge and technology necessary for quick growth. By the award of generous contracts, the Confederate and state governments gave their encouragement to industries such as textiles and iron, and by the end of the war Atlanta had become a considerable industrial center. But some manufacturers had to be satisfied with makeshifts, such as lard in place of grease and cloths soaked in linseed oil as a substitute for machine belts. The Confederacy had to import much of its arms and civilian goods, slipping a large portion of them through the Union blockade. To support itself the Confederate government turned to "tithing in kind," collecting from farmers one-tenth of their produce in certain crops, and printed great amounts of paper money that worsened inflation. Shortages and, by the last years of the war, invasion and the sense of defeat were the lot of the rebel population.

The price of flour in Richmond more than doubled in the first year of the war. Soap, made from scarce animal fat, went up a thousand percent in price. Imported coffee, selling for twelve cents a pound before the war, went to five dollars by 1863. In late December 1863 some Richmond prices in Confederate money were: apples, $65 to $75 a barrel; onions, $30 a barrel; Irish potatoes, $6 to $9 a bushel; sugar, $3.50 a pound; and eggs, $3 a dozen. Worst of all to one young soldier stationed at the Confederate capital was the price of whiskey. "It would cost about fifty Dollars to get tight here," he wrote his family in 1863.

At times essential commodities were unavailable at any price. Shortages were more common in the cities, swollen with war refugees and soldiers, than in the countryside. In the spring of 1863, three hundred Richmond women, some brandishing revolvers and others bowie knives, attacked the city's business district demanding affordable food. The riot soon got out of hand and the women looted the jewelry and clothing stores before they were stopped. And even in the country districts food and clothing shortages provoked direct action. In 1863 fourteen women armed with "guns, pistols, knives, and tongues" attacked a mill near Thomasville, Georgia, and seized a large supply of flour.

War transformed the lives of Southern white women. They were often fiery Confederate patriots. It has been said that young Southern belles, by favoring army volunteers and shunning young men who avoided the war, were the most effective recruiters for the Confederate army. Southern women of the middle and upper classes had always managed large households. As the war progressed, their administrative skills were put to running the plantations and businesses their husbands had left behind. Wives of ordinary farmers, too, took over managerial duties. The Confederate Treasury hired hundreds of women clerks. Women found jobs in the South's factories or worked in Confederate hospitals. Few of these gains lasted beyond the war, but they demonstrated what women were capable of and foreshadowed expanded opportunities in later generations.

States' rights, the doctrine upon which the Confederacy had been founded, was no help in wartime. Several governors, notably Joseph E. Brown of Georgia and Zebulon Vance of North Carolina, showed a narrow jealousy of every exercise of Confederate power. They developed revenue programs of their own and obstructed Confederate tax collections in their states. They retained control of state troops and even prevented them from leaving the state. In Georgia, men who wished to escape Confederate service could do so by enlisting in the state militia. Governor Vance hoarded food and supplies for North Carolina troops that Lee's starving army at Richmond desperately needed.

Ultimately the Confederate government resorted to measures of centralization that amounted to a revolution within a revolution. Davis declared martial law in "disloyal" areas. The Confederate Congress authorized the first thorough military draft on the North American continent. Richmond took an increasingly active role in the Southern economy, impressing food supplies from farmers, building factories to produce critical war materials, commandeering space on blockade runners for essential imports. In 1865 the Confederate government reached the ultimate measure of centralization when it got authority to take black men into the army.

Life in the Union

Initially the Northern economy faltered as businessmen, fearful of disruption and disorder, sought to call in debts. In many Northern cities, especially New York, Chicago, and Cincinnati, the loss of Southern customers disrupted the economy. Some economic historians claim that on the whole the Civil War slowed economic growth. Yet the newspapers of the day suggest that, after the middle of 1862, the Union experienced an economic boom. The draining of men into the military left shortages of labor. On some farms women filled in. The North, however, had more machines than the South with which to replace manpower; during the years from 1860 to 1865 the McCormick Reaper Company received more orders for its harvesting machines than it could fill. The continuing influx of immigrants, almost half a million during the war years, relieved labor shortages in the cities. The demand for war supplies invigorated the Northern economy, already fitted for manufacturing. Factories hummed and wages rose. Farmers benefited from the increase in demand in food. The effect of the war on the economy of the North was quite the opposite from the effect in the South, where invasion unsettled the normal pattern of production and trade and the blockade broke commerce with Europe.

Still, the Union had an inflation rate only slightly less staggering than that of the Confederacy. The policy of financing the war by a combination of heavy borrowing and paper money was a cause; so was the scarcity of labor that machines and immigrants only partially offset. And the wartime prosperity bestowed itself unevenly. While consumer prices had risen by 1865 between seventy-five and a hundred percent, the wages of skilled workers went up during the same period about sixty percent, and those of common laborers rose just under fifty percent. Meanwhile the business and professional classes crowded Broadway in New York, Michigan Avenue in Chicago and Pennsylvania Avenue in Cincinnati, buying at the fashionable shops, attending the theaters, and dining at the fancy restaurants. Some of these people were profiteers who had made a good thing out of the swelling orders from the War and Navy Departments and the flow of greenback currency. Charging the government high prices for desperately needed supplies, some profiteers also provided uniforms and shoes that disintegrated at the first heavy rain, powder that would not explode, and beef, pork, and flour that were inedible.

In the Army

The Civil War sorely tested the American traditions of individualism and provincialism. In the beginning men on both sides enlisted in local regiments raised by the state governors. Each regiment wore its own uniform and many elected their own officers, a practice that discouraged strict discipline. Gradually all this changed. The national governments took over many duties of recruitment and the appointment of officers. Standardized uniforms were introduced. Drill and discipline tightened. The sons of a rawboned democracy slowly adjusted to become cogs in a larger machine. At the same time they accustomed themselves to a world beyond their own communities. Their care and feeding became increasingly the responsibility of central governments or national organizations like the United States Sanitary Commission (a forerunner of the Red Cross). Along with the Union victory, the experience of army life could contribute to the nationalist element in American civilization that has struggled to maintain itself against the pull of loyalty to region, state, or locality.

At the same time that the armies were taking American farmboys and town dwellers away from their familiar surroundings, they were also pulling in thousands of immigrants. The Union army especially spoke with many tongues, and in that sense represented what American cities were and would increasingly become in the years after the victory of the Union.

Patriotic Gore. Of about two million federal troops, 360,000 died. Among the more than one million who at some time served in the Confederate military, about 250,000 never came back. Only one in three of these died of battle wounds; the others succumbed to disease or accident. There were also about a half million wounded, many of them severely maimed.

The Civil War was more dangerous for participants than many wars that had preceded and most that followed. During the 1860s infantry weapons became highly destructive while infantry tactics continued to follow older concepts. Many soldiers carried rifles rather than smoothbore muskets. These hurled a lead ball for hundreds of yards with deadly accuracy. Yet until the very end of the war commanders on both sides frequently ordered their men to charge the enemy across open fields as if the older, less accurate musket opposed them. Toward the end of the war attackers had to face the fast-firing breech-loaders with which more and more soldiers were being equipped.

If a man were wounded his chance for survival was not very good. Nothing was known about infectious bacteria, and military surgeons performed operations without sanitary precautions. Soldiers contracted gangrene and other deadly infections. Though anesthetics were known, doctors did not always have them on hand, and shock, followed by death, was often the consequence of major surgery. Long delays occurred in getting the casualties to medical aid stations or hospitals. Following the battle of Seven Pines in mid-1862, wounded federal soldiers were carried to the rear for shipment to the hospitals around Washington. The trains were slow to arrive, a sensitive observer noted, and the men "lay by the hundreds on either side of the railway track . . . exposed to the drenching rain . . . shivering from the cold, calling for water,

***Prisoners from the Front*, by Winslow Homer. Union and Confederate soldiers respected each other's fighting abilities, but prison conditions for those captured were brutal.** *(Courtesy, The Metropolitan Museum of Art. Gift of Mrs. Frank B. Porter, 1922.)*

food, and dressings . . . the most heart-rending spectacle. Many died from exposure, others prayed for death to release them from their anguish."

In every part of the battlefront were mosquitoes, lice, and biting flies, which helps to explain the high incidence of malaria and other diseases. Heat in the deep South and cold, particularly in the mountain areas and the upper South, afflicted the soldiers. Wool uniforms were standard year-round issue and soldiers of both armies simply shed as much as they could during the summer. If Northern troops were often overdressed, rebels were often half naked. As the Union blockade took hold and internal transport broke down, Confederate soldiers found it difficult to get replacements for worn or torn uniforms. Many ended up wearing home-made garments sent by relatives and friends. Others relied on captured Yankee shoes and other clothes. Especially serious was the shortage of boots and shoes. In the last winter of the war the troops accompanying General J. B. Hood on his campaign through Tennessee often marched barefoot through snow and sleet. The path of Hood's army, it was said, was marked by a trail of blood.

Few Union soldiers went hungry, but the diet of salt pork, bread, and coffee undermined health. The Confederate soldier's standard diet consisted of bacon, cornmeal, and coffee—when he could get them. Coffee, an imported item that had run the Union blockade, went quickly; the bacon lasted longer, but it, too, was often in short supply and Southern troops supplemented their meat rations with cuts of mule, horse, racoon, and bear. Sometimes Confederates were reduced to consuming little more than parched corn. Chewing the grains, reported one Southern soldier, was "hard work"; it made "the jaws ache and the gums so sore as to cause unendurable pain."

During the Civil War, as during the Revolution, both sides required the mobilization of society as a whole in the service of the war effort. But the Civil War reflected social and economic changes that would also influence the nature of the civilian contribution. The nursing of soldiers acquired a far more organized and professional character. Under the auspices of the United States Sanitary Commission, Dorothea Dix organized nursing services for the Union side. In the early months of the war, Ladies Aid Societies sprang up throughout the North to provide volunteer services for soldiers, including sewing, assembling food, clothing, and supplies, and providing communication between soldiers and their families. These societies eventually joined in a unified national institution. In the South, comparable societies remained local, volunteer efforts. Southern women volunteered their services to nurse the wounded soldiers of the Confederacy in what were frequently makeshift hospitals. The growing professionalization of the federal government during the war years resulted in the hiring of the first female government clerks.

At the beginning of the war, North and South had relied on volunteers and militia. In time, both sides resorted to a draft. The Union conscription law permitted a draftee to find a substitute. He could also make a payment in place of service; that feature drew charges that the law favored the wealthy. In neither North nor South was conscription popular. In 1863 an antidraft riot broke out among the Irish in New York City. The rioters lynched several blacks and burned a black orphanage, and federal troops had to be called. But volunteers continued to come in; the large bounty the Union offered was an inducement, as was the threat of the draft.

While it was not until the South was badly in need of additional troops at almost the end of the war that the Confederacy contemplated the recruitment of blacks, the Union was accepting them as early as 1862. Earlier Lincoln's government had held back, fearing that the presence of black soldiers would seem to indicate that the war was not only for restoration of the Union but for the abolition of slavery. The acceptance of black volunteers came at the urging of black leaders and white abolitionists, and by the end of the war, blacks composed about a tenth of the army and a fourth of the navy. For most of the war, black privates got three dollars a month less than whites. Some were relegated to labor units. Some Confederate commanders declared a policy of putting black prisoners into slavery or of killing them. But in combat the black soldiers won the respect of their officers and helped to discredit further the remnants of the slave system.

The War and Civil Liberties

In the extraordinary danger that the nation faced at the time of the war, free civil institutions continued in the North and for the most part in the border states. Lincoln's government did not attempt in any major and consistent way to put those institutions aside. But it was conscious that disruption or demoralization among the people in the regions loyal to the Union could bring to the Confederates the victory that they were not far from achieving.

Lincoln suspended the writ of *habeas corpus*—the power of a court to have a prisoner brought before it—in cases in which an individual was suspected of illegal disruptions of the war effort. The suspension meant that the federal government could hold people for long periods without trial. Despite protests, Lincoln in the autumn of 1862 issued a proclamation subjecting to martial law and to trial in military tribunals anyone who discouraged others from enlisting or committed any disloyal act. The War Department in the course of the conflict arrested at least thirteen thousand people, most of whom never came to trial.

The chief Northern political opponents of the conduct of the war were the Peace Democrats, or Copperheads, as supporters of the war called them. The most prominent of the Peace Democrats was Clement Vallandigham of Ohio, who insisted that the war was strengthening the central government at the expense of civil liberties. Vallandigham called for "the Constitution as it is, the Union as it was." In 1862 he was defeated for reelection to Congress. He continued his attacks on the war and after General Ambrose Burnside arrested him in 1863, a military tribunal sentenced him to prison for its duration. The affair was an assault on the constitutional right of free speech; protest was widespread, and the situation was a political danger to the administration. To deflect the issue, Lincoln, by use of his executive power, banished Vallandigham to the Confederacy. But the Ohioan returned to the North and kept up his criticisms. The administration now left him alone. When Vallandigham tried to get the Supreme Court to consider his claim that the government had acted unconstitutionally, the Court in 1864 ruled in *ex parte Vallandigham* that it had no jurisdiction over the proceedings of military tribunals. In 1866, however, the Supreme Court did find the methods of the war administration to have been unconstitutional. In *ex parte Milligan* the Court held that martial law and the subjection of civilians to military trials were illegal when the civil courts were open and in full operation.

Emancipation

At the beginning of the war the federal government was careful to insist that it was fighting only to preserve the Union and not to free the slaves. The war, said a resolution adopted by Congress, was not for "overthrowing or interfering with the rights or established institutions" of the seceded states. The government wanted to convince those proslavery Southerners who were prepared to be sympathetic to the Unionist cause that the institution of slavery was not in danger. But it is reasonable to suppose that something beyond mere political strategy lay behind the caution of the president and Congress about interfering with slavery. Neither Lincoln nor most of the national legislators had been abolitionists; and however distasteful slavery may have been to much of the government, the slave system had been so firmly established, and so hedged with legal protections, that even opponents might have had doubts about the sudden military abolition of slavery. Politicians and statesmen, like the rest of humankind, are hesitant to imagine any workable society that is far different from whatever one they are accustomed to. It took time and the events of the war to make the government see the tangible possibility of wiping out slavery at a stroke.

General John C. Frémont issued a military order freeing the slaves in Missouri, but Lincoln modified Frémont's order. He did, however, ask Congress in 1862 to grant federal funds to any state adopting a scheme of emancipation. Though Congress did not respond, it declared in the Second Confiscation Act of 1862 that wherever the Union army was in control, all slaves owned by rebels would be free. The Act was both a substantial measure and a somewhat limited one. It did not apply to slaves held by Southern unionists. But the Second Confiscation Act did something toward breaking Union politicians of their timidity about abolishing slavery, and the very existence of the Act must have provided a certain momentum toward abolition. Abolitionists meanwhile were urging a wider policy of emancipation. Such a policy, moreover, could have desirable diplomatic effects. The apparent success of the South in maintaining its independence, and the advantage that European countries might gain from a dividing of the United States, raised the danger that they might recognize the Confederacy as a sovereign nation, which would greatly weaken the Union effort. Lincoln believed that if European nations could see the war as a struggle not merely between Union and secession but between freedom and slavery, they would be less likely to recognize the slave republic. And while Lincoln had not been an abolitionist, he had been a free soiler and a moral opponent of slavery. Surely his conscience welcomed the decision toward which political considerations were pushing him.

The Emancipation Proclamation. The Union victory of Antietam gave Lincoln the opportunity to issue in September 1862 a preliminary Emancipation Proclamation, announcing that as of January 1, 1863, all slaves in those regions still in rebellion on that date would be free. Lincoln was offering to secessionists an alternative to loss of their slaves: they could voluntarily bring their communities back into the Union. The Emancipation Proclamation itself, issued on January 1, carried out the terms of the preliminary proclamation: it declared that all slaves in areas still in rebellion were "then, thenceforward, and forever free." Lincoln was drawing on the power he possessed as Commander in Chief; the Proclamation was essentially a military order, on somewhat the same principle as the instructions an officer might give his troops for the treatment of citizens and property. The Emancipation Proclamation, like the Second Confiscation Act, was of sharply limited scope; it freed no slaves immediately because it did not apply to the border states or to regions already under Union control. But it was understood at the time, as it has been understood ever since, as the great symbolic moral action of the war, a public statement, in however confined a form, that the war was now for freedom. After the preliminary Proclamation the military had begun seriously taking in black volunteers. It was a logical consequence of the events of the Civil War that in 1865 the nation adopted the Thirteenth Amendment outlawing slavery.

Congress contained a variety of opinions on racial matters. At one extreme were several Democrats reluctant to make changes in existing institutions. At the other extreme, as the war progressed, was a small but important group of Republicans who wanted the strongest possible policy of abolition and of protection for the rights of the freed slaves. Within this faction ideas emerged for going beyond emancipation and bringing about changes in the social and economic condition of black Americans. Congress in the course of the war repealed a law prohibiting blacks from carrying the mail and a ban on testimony of black witnesses in federal court, outlawed slavery in the territories, and established a scheme for emancipation in the District of Columbia that would provide compensation to the slaveholders. Blacks were allowed in places from which they had once been excluded: the congressional visitors gallery, lectures at the Smithsonian Institution. Some states got rid of a number of discriminating laws. The country was taking some halting steps beyond emancipation and toward equality or at least a concept of justice.

Politics and Economics

The successful waging of the war required that Lincoln have as much popular support as he could get. In his 1864 reelection campaign he ran not as a Republican but as the candidate of a coalition of Republicans and Democratic supporters of the war, which called itself the Union Party. The vice-presidential candidate of the party was Andrew Johnson, a Tennessee Democrat who had remained loyal to the Union. The presidential candidate of the regular Democratic party was General McClellan. McClellan, who had been commander of the Union armies, was loyal to the war effort, and in effect he rejected his party's pronouncement that the war was a failure. By the time of the campaign and election the war had been going so successfully for the North that Lincoln's victory was assured.

While the winning of the war was the most important objective for the Republicans, they were committed also to an entire political, social and economic policy within which the emancipation of the slaves and the preservation of the Union were elements. Before the Civil War much of the antislavery movement had also wanted a more vigorous national government working for the achievement of an advanced industrial and agricultural economy. Some Americans had possessed a vision of what a powerful American economy and society might be: an industrialized Northeast trading its manufactured goods for the produce of a great agricultural West. The federal government, these people believed, should stimulate Eastern manufactures through a protective tariff, populate the agrarian West by giving government lands to settlers, and tie together the two regions by a railroad system built with federal aid. Northern politicians who thought this way could wish to exclude slavery from the territories not only because they genuinely disliked slavery on moral grounds but also because they desired that the Western lands be reserved for free American farmers. And in the years before the Civil War they clashed with the South on other political issues: the Southern cotton interest opposed a protective tariff, wanting instead to bring manufactured goods more cheaply from Europe, and resisted the construction of a Northern railroad from East to West, holding out for a Southern route. It is fitting that political circumstances put the Republicans in command of the war for the saving of the Union; for the Union came to mean strong central government presiding over a vast and economically progressive nation, while secession would have broken the country into weaker republics. It is fitting also that the Republicans became the champions of federally enforced emancipation.

Wartime Legislation. In 1861, just before Lincoln's inauguration, Congress passed the Morrill Tariff, a protectionist measure putting duties to the levels they had been at in 1846; and later the national legislature raised duties higher. The war put a strain on the system of banking and currency. In response, Congress reformed the system in a way that agreed with the Republican concept of strong government in the service of a national economy. The National Banking Acts of 1863 and 1864 provided that, in return for investing one-third of their capital in federal banks, private banks could issue national bank notes that would serve as paper money: these could be in amounts up to ninety percent of the market value of the securities the banks had purchased from the government. The notes of state banks, which had circulated as a form of money, were unstable and injured the economy; in order to suppress them, Congress later placed a ten percent tax on the notes of all institutions that did not take part in the national bank system.

The Republican idea of supplying federal lands for settlers triumphed in the Homestead Act of 1862. A settler who filed a claim to a quarter-section of one hundred and sixty acres of federal land and lived on it for five years would get ownership of it after payment of a small fee. The act permitted single women as well as men to file a claim. In practice, women alone, or even women with children, had great difficulty in sustaining their claims. Men needed the assistance of a woman as much as women needed the assistance of a man, but when men and women settled together in a family unit, the man invariably held title to the claim and officially directed its operation. Nor did the law permit married couples to file claims. Later in the century considerable amounts of the land went to timber and mining companies that had employees put in claims for homesteads. But at the time of the adoption of the act, there was some expectation that it would pull labor from the East to the free lands; and in face of the labor shortage that the war was bringing about, Congress authorized immigration of contract workers from Europe and the Orient, permitting employers who paid the laborers' passage to deduct that cost from the pay.

Congress made another use of federal lands. The Morrill Land Grant Act of 1862 offered lands to states that in return would finance colleges offering schooling in agriculture, engineering, and military science. It was a less dramatic measure than others of these wartime years, but a significant one: it made the national government a partner to modern technical education.

The absence of legislators from the deep South made it easier for Congress during the war to adopt a scheme for a transcontinental railway running through the middle of the country, from Omaha to California. Southerners would have fought for a more Southern road. During the 1860s the national legislature granted to railroad developers thirty million acres of federal land and made them large loans. It was one of the first of many extensive projects in which the government has joined with business.

Early Reconstruction Plans

Wherever travelers went in the months following Appomattox they saw abandoned fields, twisted rails, and burned structures. People in creaking wagons drove their gaunt mules for miles to find fords across bridgeless streams. The defeat of the Confederacy had also wiped out millions of dollars of bank capital and made all Confederate money worthless. For decades to come, men hobbling on one leg or with empty sleeves would be common sights throughout Dixie. In 1866 the state of Mississippi would spend a fifth of its revenues on artificial arms and legs for Confederate veterans. But most unsettling of all the changes the war had brought was the end of slavery. For generations it had been the foundation on which the entire Southern economy rested. Now that it was gone, what would take its place?

Many former slaves remained on farms and plantations, but others had departed. Some had gone to the towns where life seemed more interesting than in the sleepy countryside. Others took to the road to test their new freedom. Even more went traveling to seek out lost relatives and friends separated years ago by the migration of white masters or by the domestic slave trade. The tide of wandering freedmen in the immediate postwar months attests to the strong ties of kinship among them. Eventually most would return to the land somewhere in the South.

Reorganizing the Union. The Confederate surrender opened a difficult constitutional question about the status of the defeated states. Did the former rebel states have the right, as members of the Union, to come straight back to Congress and resume their old political life under the Constitution? Would the government have no authority to set conditions that they would have to meet before they resumed their seats in the House and Senate? If so, Congress would lack the power to force on the South whatever reforms might be necessary for the protection of the freed slaves and the prevention of any future disloyalty. Republicans who favored a coercive policy toward the South argued that by the act of secession the Confederate states had forfeited their status of statehood and reverted to the condition of territories. If they were no longer states, they were not entitled to the rights of states and could be subject to the will of the federal government.

Charleston, South Carolina. At the war's end, much of the South lay in ruins. *(Courtesy, Library of Congress)*

The Union victory might actually give the South a stronger presence in the House of Representatives than the region had enjoyed before the war. The Constitution had provided that in counting the population of a state for determining how many members it was to have in the House, three-fifths of the slaves in the state were to be counted in. But if slavery no longer existed and the blacks were legally free, the whole black population rather than three-fifths of it would be counted within the population of the state, and the South would gain about twenty seats in the House of Representatives. And if former Confederate states should succeed in finding methods denying full freedom for the black populace, the South would be getting extra seats without even having to give up its oppression of the black race.

Overshadowing all these issues was the question of the future place of the black people. By eradicating slavery, the country unwittingly confronted long-delayed questions regarding the civil and political status of blacks. Would the ballot and citizenship be conferred on them? Could the federal government confer these privileges if the Southern states refused to put them into effect?

All these questions had to be worked out amid a legacy of bitterness and frustration created by the war. White Southerners found themselves in the unique position of being the only Americans to know defeat in wartime, their region burned and bare, their economy a shambles. The abolition of slavery also threatened white racial domination. The North had not suffered the physical and economic devastation experienced by the South. Even its human losses were proportionally less. But Northerners had sacrificed to preserve the Union. They needed to know that their expenditures had gone for something, that their principles had been vindicated. They expected a measure of symbolic satisfaction from the South as well as physical surrender.

In the efforts during the war to settle on some scheme for restoration of the rebel states to the Union, President Lincoln generally favored policies that would make few demands on the South. He had originally hoped for a speedy end to the war and a rapid resumption of antebellum political ties. Although the prolonged struggle on the battlefield made that impossible, the president continued to advocate a moderate postwar Reconstruction. Lincoln had not been an advocate of black equality. He always approached racial issues cautiously. He had hoped that the process of emancipation would be gradual and under the direction of officials of the former slave states. Believing that the colonization of blacks outside the United States was the ideal solution, Lincoln's Administration sponsored efforts to resettle blacks in the Caribbean and Central America. And Lincoln was a cagey politician. An ex-Whig himself, he may have had it in mind that moderate policies attractive to Southern former Whigs might draw them to the Republican Party.

In December 1863 Lincoln outlined a formal plan for Confederate areas coming under Union control. It clearly contemplated swift restoration, with no penalties for ex-rebels beyond loss of their slaves. It did not anticipate black participation in Reconstruction. Under Lincoln's "ten percent plan," whenever a total of whites equal to one-tenth the number who had voted in 1860 took an oath of future loyalty to the United States and its laws—which included the abolition of slavery—they could form a new state government. Before the war ended Lincoln had recognized "ten percent" governments in Arkansas, Tennessee, Virginia, and Louisiana. But Congress refused to admit representatives from these states, and their votes were not counted in the 1864 presidential election. Lincoln agreed that Congress should take some role in the reconciliation process, but he always sought to keep restoration under presidential leadership.

The national legislators were looking for a plan more firmly insuring that the new Southern governments would remain loyal. The Wade-Davis Bill of 1864 required that, before a formerly seceded state could form a government, fifty percent of the adult white males in that state would have to take an oath of loyalty to the Union. The state could then hold a constitutional convention to make a new government for itself. But voting for delegates to that convention would be limited to people who had taken an oath that they had never supported the secession. The state must outlaw slavery. The plan was not to go into effect until the war had ended. Thinking the Wade-Davis Bill too severe and an invasion of presidential responsibility for reconstruction, Lincoln vetoed it. Supporters of the bill responded with a manifesto calling Lincoln's veto an "outrage on the legislative authority."

Neither Lincoln's plan nor that of the Wade-Davis Bill provided for blacks to be given the vote. But some Republicans in Congress wished for a program of reconstruction that would grant a wide range of rights to the freedmen and guarantee protection of these rights. Legislators of this kind wanted the national government to have strong control over former rebel states, so that their legal and social systems could be thoroughly reshaped and white Southerners would not get the chance to bring back the old slavery system in a new form.

During the final year of the war President Lincoln appeared to be moving somewhat toward a more active and progressive solution to the race question. In March 1864 he came out in favor of granting the vote to "very intelligent" black people and black Union soldiers. He vigorously supported the Thirteenth Amendment outlawing slavery. A month before his death Lincoln signed the bill creating a Freedmen's Bureau to aid the ex-slaves in their transition to freedom.

Reconstruction was to be in hands other than Lincoln's. But at the beginning of the spring of 1865 the president and the Union public did have a few days to savor victory.

Lincoln's Last Days. On April 4 Lincoln went to Richmond to view the Confederate capital now evacuated by the government of Jefferson Davis. Accompanied by his son and a military escort, he walked up Main Street to the Confederate executive mansion. Black men and women crowded around the presidential party and sang and shouted. When he entered the Confederate president's house and took a seat in Davis's chair, the Union troops, black and white, cheered. Later the president toured the captured city that for four bloody years had been the supreme goal of Union armies. Like many other large Southern towns Richmond was in ruins: it was blackened by a fire set accidentally by the Confederate authorities before they withdrew.

Lincoln returned to Washington on April 9, the day Lee surrendered to Grant at Appomattox Court House. The news reached Washington the next day and the government declared a holiday for its employees. On the tenth throngs gathered on the streets of the capital. The crowds eventually converged on the White House, where Lincoln was working at his desk. They interrupted him several times by their shouts for a speech until he finally made an appearance. He would deliver some appropriate remarks the following evening, he said, but for the moment he would just order the bands to play "Dixie." The Confederate anthem, he noted, was now the lawful property of the Union.

The next evening the president came to the upper window of the White House as he had promised and made some graceful remarks. "We meet this evening . . . in gladness of heart" he began, and then went on to deliver a thoughtful address, his last, on the problems to come. If the crowd had wanted a rousing cock-crow of triumph, it was disappointed. At least one man in the audience, however, the actor John Wilkes Booth, found himself deeply moved, but to rage and anger. A Marylander from a distinguished acting family, he felt deeply for the South and its defeat had sent him into despair.

On the evening of April 14 the president, accompanied by his wife and several friends, went to see the comedy *Our American Cousin* at Ford's Theater. The president's party arrived late but quickly settled down to enjoy the story of a shrewd comic American visiting his English relatives. During the third act the sounds of a muffled shot and a scuffle came from the president's box. Suddenly a tall figure leaped from the box to the stage and shouted *Sic semper tyrannis*! (thus ever to tyrants), the motto of Virginia. Before he could be stopped Booth escaped into the night.

They carried the unconscious president to a house nearby and placed him on a bed. While high officials and family members gathered around, the doctors examined him. The bullet had entered the rear of his head and lodged near his eye. Nothing could be done. He died at 7:22 A.M.

Andrew Johnson

Like most vice-presidents in American history, Andrew Johnson was selected without much consideration that he might become president. A self-educated tailor from East Tennessee and a strong Jacksonian Democrat, Johnson had been in 1861 the only Southern senator to support the Union. After Tennessee fell to Union troops, Lincoln made him war governor, a task he performed with vigor and courage. In 1864 the Republican Party, seeking to broaden itself into a Union party, turned naturally to Johnson, an ex-Democrat and Southern unionist, to be Lincoln's running mate. Then suddenly, on April 14, 1865, he was the president.

Johnson, a president without a party, had to deal with a Republican Congress. And Johnson was a Southern white supremacist, willing and perhaps happy to accept emancipation and some rights for black Americans but cooperative with Southerners who wished to place strict controls over the black population. This brought him into conflict not only with the increasingly strong band of radical Republicans in Congress but with moderates as well. Courageous and stubborn but belligerent and lacking in political tact, Johnson both endured and to an extent brought on himself one of the most troubled presidential administrations in American history.

Johnson wanted an easy restoration of the seceded states. There was not yet any clearly defined program that would instruct a rebel state in how it must go about reorganizing itself so as to be accepted back into the Union, and Johnson did not wait for Congress to reconvene (it was out of session until December) before dealing with the problem. He announced at

Andrew Johnson's attempt to assume primary responsibility for Reconstruction after Lincoln's death alienated Congress while his leniency toward the South increasingly angered Northern voters.

once a program of restoration similar to Lincoln's. He too offered pardon to ex-rebels pledging future loyalty. He asked only that the reorganized state governments nullify their ordinances of secession, repudiate their Confederate debts, and ratify the Thirteenth Amendment.

Johnson's assumption of primary responsibility for Reconstruction policy was bound to alienate Republicans in Congress. His leniency toward the South angered radicals. Southerners, moreover, took a course that aroused Northern resentment. They elected to state office and to Congress prominent ex-Confederates, including vice-president Alexander Stephens and numerous generals. Some of the reorganized state governments refused to repudiate their Confederate debts or nullify their secession ordinances. A number of them passed "black codes" defining the rights of emancipated slaves in ways that severely restricted their freedom. A typical code might bar blacks from jury duty and from testifying in court against whites; it might forbid them to take up any occupation except agriculture or to rent land on their own; some subjected unemployed blacks to arrest and forced labor. The character of the "restored" governments and the "black codes" seemed to indicate that Southerners remained rebels at heart.

Congressional Reconstruction

When Congress met in December 1865, it refused to seat newly elected Southern representatives, but disagreed on what to do next. Radicals demanded a thoroughgoing political and economic shakeup of the South. Moderate Republicans wanted only minimal guarantees of legal protection for the ex-slaves. "To have refused the Negroes the simplest rights granted to every other inhabitant, native or foreigner, would be outrageous," declared Senator John Sherman of Ohio, a moderate leader. The emancipated slave, warned another Senator, would "be tyrannized over, abused, and virtually reenslaved without some legislation by the nation for his protection."

At this point moderates still dominated Republican policy. But they too wanted to insure the civil rights of black Southerners. In 1866 Congress passed a bill giving to a Freedmen's Bureau the power to try by military commission anyone charged with depriving freedmen of their civil rights. It also put through a bill that gave the freedmen citizenship and civil rights. Johnson vetoed both bills as unconstitutional extensions of federal power. Congress thereupon enacted the civil rights measure over his veto, passed a revised bill for a Freedmen's Bureau, and overrode Johnson's veto of it.

Congress's establishment of the Freedmen's Bureau departed from normal government policy by addressing various aspects of people's lives that had normally been left to private initiative. The bureau was essentially responsible for protecting blacks against reenslavement in the unsettled conditions of the southern states. Its activities were directed toward both men and women, who were acknowledged as important in reconstructing social, family, and economic life in the South. But the policies of the bureau reflected a deep commitment to northeastern attitudes toward the importance of domesticity. The records of the bureau, which provide the best available evidence of the attitudes of the ex-slaves, demonstrate that they themselves placed a high value on legitimating the unions between men and women as "proper" marriages. And they would go to great lengths to be reunited with spouses and children in order to reconstruct their family life.

The Fourteenth Amendment. The national legislature soon offered Johnson and the South another chance. It framed an elaborate Fourteenth Amendment covering a range of issues and gave each of the state governments favored by Johnson the opportunity to return to Congress if it should ratify.

The Fourteenth Amendment declared "all persons"—the lawmakers were thinking particularly of black Americans—"born or naturalized in the United States, and subject to the jurisdiction thereof, are citizens of the United States and of the State wherein they reside." The Amendment prohibited the states from violating the "privileges or immunities of citizens of the United States," depriving "any person of life, liberty, or property, without due process of law," or denying "to any person within its jurisdiction the equal protection of the laws." It barred from public office anyone who, having taken a federal or state oath of office to protect the Constitution of the United States, afterward engaged in rebellion against the nation. The provision was aimed at high-ranking confederate officials who before the Civil War had served in federal or state office. A two-thirds vote of the Senate and the House of Representatives could relieve any individual of that disability. The Amendment prohibited the states and the nation from paying any debt incurred in rebellion against the country. The Amendment did not directly extend the right to vote. It attempted instead to entice the states to give the vote to blacks. It provided that a state would lose seats in the House of Representatives insofar as it denied to some of its adult male population the right to vote for federal and state officials.

A state ratifying the Amendment could expect to be granted readmission without further reform. Implicit in the offer was penalty for rejection: restoration would begin anew, with Congress dictating terms. Had it not been for Johnson, the South might have ratified. But Johnson refused to bend. On his advice all the Southern states except his Tennessee rejected the amendment. Tennessee ratified and was readmitted to the Union. The other ten, said James A. Garfield, had "flung back into our teeth the magnanimous offer of a generous nation."

The break between the president and Congress was now complete. In the fall of 1866 Johnson stumped the North encouraging the defeat at the polls of leading Republican Congressmen. The tour was a disaster for the president personally and politically. Forgetting that he was no longer a Tennessee stump-speaker, Johnson engaged in undignified arguments with hecklers and even suggested hanging leading radicals. In November the Republicans swept the elections, winning over a two-thirds majority in both houses of Congress. Reconstruction would begin anew, under the leadership of such radicals as the Massachusetts Senator Charles Sumner and Representative Thaddeus Stevens of Pennsylvania.

Radical Reconstruction

The situation when Congress met in December 1866 was very different from that a year earlier. Events during 1866 had conspired to bring together moderate and radical Republicans, at least temporarily. A majority in Congress now agreed on the necessity of creating new Southern state governments on the basis of black suffrage and excluding ex-Confederates. Arming blacks with the ballot, Republicans hoped, would give them a weapon against white Democratic oppression and build up a strong Republican Party in the South.

The Military Reconstruction Act of 1867 set the terms of the Congressional program. It divided the South into five military districts. Military governors in each were to register voters, including blacks but not whites who had held public office before the Civil War and then supported the Confederacy. The governors would thereupon call elections for new constitutional conventions. These conventions had to write black suffrage into the new state constitutions. Once the voters had approved these constitutions and the Fourteenth Amendment, the states might apply to Congress for readmission. If the constitution met approval, the state would be readmitted to the Union and its representatives seated. Three other Reconstruction Acts followed the first.

Reconstruction had something in common

Massachusetts Senator Charles Sumner and Pennsylvania Representative Thaddeus Stevens, leaders of Radical Reconstruction. *(Courtesy, Library of Congress)*

with the economic policy of the Republican Party and with the party's defense of the Union during the Civil War. It represented that commitment to strong and active central government toward which Republicans tended. In the enforcement of civil rights, the legal establishment of universal male suffrage, and the work of the Freedmen's Bureau, the federal government for the first time in its history was lending its resources, or some of them, to a political and social revolution.

To Southern whites haunted by a two-century-old fear of slave insurrection, radical reconstruction seemed a nightmare come true. With their traditional leaders barred from office and illiterate ex-slaves enfranchised, they predicted a grim era of black rule. This image has persisted, even among historians.

Changing Interpretations of Reconstruction. The earliest critics of Reconstruction condemned it as a cynical and brutal rape of Southern society. Political opportunism and hatred of the South motivated the radical Republican policies: military rule; black suffrage; and violation of the spirit, if not the letter, of the Constitution. Accounts sympathetic to the white South stressed the corruption of Reconstruction state regimes, the unruliness—by which some of them may have meant the "uppityness"—of former slaves, the greed of Northern "carpetbaggers," and the treachery of Southern "scalawags." Reconstruction was a "blackout of honest government." In this view, the lifting of radical rule by the white "redeemers" represented a return to constitutional government and to proper racial relations in the South.

By the 1930s historians were becoming increasingly interested in explaining events by economic causes. That brought a new way of interpreting Reconstruction. Now writers looked back to the days before the Civil War when Southerners had opposed such measures favorable to Northern business as the protective tariff, which would force the South to buy its manufactured goods from the North rather than at cheaper European prices. Scholars now perceived the radical Republicans as representatives of Northeastern business interests. These interests had feared that a speedily reconstructed South might regain its political power and overturn the control of the national government that Northern business had gained during the war years, when Southern seats in Congress were empty. Idealistic rhetoric had masked the sordid economic motives of the business-dominated Republican party exploitation of the South and advancement of industrial over agrarian interests.

Yet even in the years when historians were attributing Reconstruction to the ambitions of business interests, scholarship was beginning to find much good in it. More recently, a generation influenced by the civil rights struggles of the 1950s and 1960s has taken up these findings and begun describing Reconstruction as another phase in the black American search for justice. Radical Republicans, this analysis insists, represented the last moment of abolitionist idealism; the radicals tried to provide national protection for the rights of the freed people and to extend some measure of social and economic assistance. Not particularly vindictive and not the tools of a capitalist conspiracy, congressional Republicans, moderates as well as radicals, undertook their actions only after they realized the extent of white Southern stubbornness and presidential obstructionism. And their measures were not especially severe, particularly when compared to the postwar policies of other victorious nations. The national government committed only a small number of troops to military Reconstruction, and the whole process lasted only a few years in most states. This recent idea of Reconstruction would hold that if any fault is to be found with the policy, it is not for being too severe toward the defeated South but for not being thorough enough to win the black race full and permanent equality and justice.

Reconstruction and the South

The Road to Freedom? Reconstruction did attempt to achieve a degree of racial equality for blacks. Two important additions to the Constitution, the Fourteenth and Fifteenth Amendments, laid the basis for greater federal protection of civil and political rights.

The Fourteenth Amendment, ratified in 1868, offered a definition of national citizenship that included black people and prohibited the states from denying the privileges of citizenship. Although during the late nineteenth and early twentieth centuries the Supreme Court would use the Fourteenth Amendment to shield business corporations from state regulation, there is little evidence to suggest a business conspiracy behind the amendment. Its framers saw it as a constitutional bulwark not only for newly freed blacks but for all citizens.

Two years later Congress brought the right to vote under federal control. The Fifteenth Amendment declared that a citizen's right to vote "shall not be denied or abridged . . . on account of race, color, or previous condition of servitude." The Amendment applied to black males in the North—much of the North had not allowed black Americans to vote—as well as to former slaves in the South. Most of the black vote went to Republicans, and some Northern supporters of the Amendment may have been mainly concerned with strengthening the Republican Party. But others risked a white backlash to guarantee suffrage to the black man.

The vote that was granted to black males was denied to both black and white females. White women leaders of the movement for women's rights were incensed. Before the war, they had worked within the abolitionist movement and then supported the Republican cause. In 1866, Susan B. Anthony, Elizabeth Cady Stanton, Lucy Stone, and Lucretia Mott organized the American Equal Rights Association (AERA) to support suffrage for both white women and blacks. The refusal to grant women the vote angered them, and some even asserted that white women were better fitted to vote than black men. In the ensuing dispute about priorities, the AERA split into two groups. Lucy Stone and Henry Blackwell formed the American Woman Suffrage Association, which accepted the refusal to grant women the vote in order not to jeopardize the vote for black men. Susan B. Anthony and Elizabeth Cady Stanton organized the more militant National Woman Suffrage Association. Bitter about what they took to be the betrayal by male Republican leaders, they warned that women could not trust men, refused to support the freedmen's right to the vote, and even used racist arguments to defend the greater importance of giving the vote to white women than to black men. Although their racism declined after the passage of the Fifteenth Amendment, it left a disturbing legacy to the women's movement.

In most Southern states, Reconstruction lasted for only a few years. In states with large white majorities, conservatives regained political control rather quickly. Virginia was "redeemed" in 1869, Tennessee and North Carolina in 1870. Georgia fell under conservative rule in 1872, Al-

Louisiana was one of five Southern states to have a majority of black voters after the Civil War. A total of 133 black legislators served in the state from 1868 to 1896. *(Courtesy, Louisiana State Museum)*

abama, Texas, and Arkansas in 1874, and Mississippi in 1876. In only three states—Louisiana, Florida and South Carolina—did radical Republican government last a full decade, and they were all "redeemed" in 1877. Congress hastened the process of redemption through a generous policy of restoring the right to hold public office to former rebels deprived of it under terms of the Fourteenth Amendment. And a look at Reconstruction in action reveals something quite different from the dreadful years of corruption, disorder, and tyranny that postwar Southern lamentings and subsequent legend have described.

Even in those states where blacks made up a majority of the voters, they did not dominate the reconstructed state governments. They formed a majority in one state constitutional convention, that of South Carolina, exactly one half the membership in the Louisiana convention, and a minority in eight others. After the new governments were formed, blacks never held a majority in both houses of a state legislature. No state had an elected black governor; only two black senators and fourteen black representatives were elected to the national Congress. At the local level, blacks never enjoyed a proportionate share of offices. In the constitutional conventions and in legislatures, blacks rarely pressed for equal access to public facilities.

Nor were the Reconstruction governments particularly incompetent or corrupt. Much of the leadership of Republican regimes fell to native whites or to Northerners who had resettled in the South after the war. Most of the local whites—known derisively as "scalawags"—were ex-Whigs seeking to reenter the political arena.

Store for freedmen, Beaufort, South Carolina. The Freedmen's Bureau coordinated relief efforts and tried to ease the transition from slavery to freedom. *(Courtesy, National Archives)*

The Northerners—nicknamed "carpetbaggers"—defy easy characterization. Many were former Union soldiers attracted by the South's climate and cheap land. Some undoubtedly were profiteers; others, like Governor Adelbert Ames of Mississippi and Governor Daniel Chamberlain of South Carolina, were idealists. Any discussion of corruption must be measured against the records of previous white Southern administrations and against the sorry performance of several Northern governments during this era. On the whole, Reconstruction governments made substantial progress toward postwar recovery and social reform. They drafted progressive new constitutions, reapportioned legislatures to give back-country districts equitable representation, expanded social services, improved roads, encouraged railroad construction, and established the South's first public school system. Much of the so-called extravagance of Reconstruction legislatures merely represented expenditures for public services that previous regimes had neglected.

Humanitarian Efforts. During the Reconstruction years, the national government provided some assistance to the freed people in the South. The Freedmen's Bureau coordinated relief activities and tried to ease the difficult transition from slavery to freedom. The Bureau found employment opportunities, supervised labor contracts, and attempted to safeguard the legal rights of black people. Critics at the time generally indicted the Bureau for doing too much to assist blacks. Later historians have found quite the opposite. Many well-meaning officials were overly paternalistic; others displayed outright prejudice toward black people; some encouraged freedmen to enter into exploitive labor contracts; most did too little to enlarge opportunities for the former slaves. Yet the Bureau represented a notable though mild and temporary expansion of the social role of the federal government.

Private philanthropic and religious groups also tried to aid freed people. Various churches, especially the Congregationalists and the Quakers, sent both money and volunteers to the South. Educational institutions related to the churches gave many black children and adults their first opportunity to learn to read and write. Blacks rushed to make use of the new schools, where Northern female schoolteachers played an especially important role. Teachers like Laura Towne left poignant records of their experiences in the South during Reconstruction. Their devotion to the people they were teaching mingled with their commitment to inculcating them with Northern, middle-class values. Church groups also helped establish black colleges and industrial schools, and the Freedmen's Bureau extended some financial assistance to missionary schools, including Howard University in Washington, D.C.

Many Northern black churchmen and educators journeyed south to spread the gospel and the primer among the ex-slaves. Former slaves themselves put up school houses and paid for teachers, established churches, organized conventions to lobby for equal rights and the ballot, and opened savings banks. A black convention in New Orleans in 1865 explained:

> If we are men—as our friends contend we are—we are able to attend to our own business. There is no man in the world so perfectly identified with our own interest as to understand it better than we do ourselves. . . . We need friends, it is true; but we do not need tutors. The age of guardianship is past forever. We now think for ourselves, and we shall act for ourselves.

The Land Question

The blacks were legally free and had the vote. But they lacked the one essential basis of independence and equality: land or an equivalent property. Both races in the postwar South recognized the importance of the land question. "The way we can best take care of ourselves is to have land and turn it and till it by our labor," contended a delegation of freed people in 1865. This is exactly what former slaveholders feared most, and they determined early on to prevent blacks from owning land. Without access to employment except on white-owned land, all the ballots and education in the world would be worthless. "They who own the real estate of a country control its vote," warned one observer. It is this as much as anything else that explains the successful overthrow of Reconstruction in the South.

A few antislavery activists had wanted to provide land for emancipated slaves. As early as 1862 Congress passed legislation confiscating plantations of Confederate sympathizers, and it was proposed to resettle blacks on them. But the Lincoln Administration showed little interest. In 1865 General William T. Sherman temporarily allotted small tracts of confiscated land along the South Atlantic coast to thousands of homeless ex-slaves. After the war Representative Thaddeus Stevens of Pennsylvania advocated breaking up the large Southern plantations and allocating them in forty acre tracts to freed people. "Forty acres and a mule" became a byword among landless ex-slaves.

This was as close as anyone came to providing a new life for the blacks to move into when they moved out of slavery. Andrew Johnson restored confiscated lands to their previous owners and evicted the black tenants. Few Northerners supported Stevens's plan to confiscate private property, even from slaveholders. Congress soundly defeated his watered-down confiscation plan in 1866, though it did set aside certain public lands in the South for purchase by freed people. This scheme failed badly, however, because the land available was inferior, and because few ex-slaves had the capital to buy land and farm equipment.

In many areas, the first system to develop in the absence of slavery was that of wage labor. Guided and prodded by agents of the Freedmen's Bureau, blacks signed contracts to work for so much a month and were provided with cabins, often in the former plantation slave quarters, and sometimes with food. Yet work in the fields at the white man's bidding, on the white man's land, under the immediate supervision of a white overseer seemed far too much like old slavery in a new guise. Many blacks would have none of it and sabotaged the arrangement. One way was to collect wages during the planting and cultivating months and then decamp just before the crucial harvest, which left the owner with the problem of gathering in the cotton or tobacco without a work force.

Sharecropping. The land and labor system finally devised in the postwar South was sharecropping. In this form of tenancy the black worker contributed labor and perhaps the use of some tools and a mule, and received from the landlord some land to farm. At harvest time the cropper got to keep from one-half to two-thirds of the crop, the remaining portion going to the landowner.

The system had some advantages. Blacks now had some personal freedom; there was no overseer to supervise their work. Instead of living in the old slave quarters, moreover, each black family could reside apart on its own rented piece of land. Some blacks simply raised the slave cabin from the old quarters and removed it to their own farm. Blacks could now decide how to spend their money. And they could arrange their own family division of labor. Almost immediately, some black women abandoned field work and began to confine themselves to the roles of mothers and wives like white women.

The conflict between ex-masters and ex-slaves proved especially intense over the role of ex-slave women. The evidence suggests that both male and female ex-slaves were strongly committed to women remaining at home and working only for their own families. Husbands did not want their wives working in the households of white masters or, for that matter, in their fields. The poverty of the ex-slaves dictated that women would work, but where and for whom was taken to be an important indicator of the integrity of the ex-slaves' families and communities. Just as the ex-slaves strongly resisted the gang labor that reminded them too much of slavery, so too did they resist any hint that whites, and especially white men, might have any control over the labor or persons of black women. One of the great tragedies of Reconstruction was that black women *were* forced back into field labor, domestic service, and laundry work because their men could not alone earn enough to support their families, and because they did not control enough property to become independent farmers.

The sharecropper system was a poor substitute for landowning. Sharecroppers, like other tenants, had little incentive to improve the land they farmed. Since they did not own it, they could not expect to be the beneficiaries. The credit system that grew up alongside sharecropping was its worst element. Tenants often could not wait until harvest to buy the things they needed during the year. Storekeepers sold them cloth, tools, knick-knacks, and even food on credit, taking out a lien, a kind of mortgage, on the crop as security until harvest time in the fall. Then, when the crop was sold, the storekeeper subtracted the debt from the cropper's share. Those caught in this crop-lien process might not ever see any cash once the storekeeper and the landlord had taken their shares. Goods bought on credit were far more expensive than those bought with cash. The system also allowed many opportunities for fraud. Storekeepers, themselves under considerable economic pressure, kept the accounts and sometimes juggled the books to make sure that the sharecropper remained permanently in debt. Such a tenant remained tied to the storekeeper as a perpetual customer, unable legally to deal with any other storekeeper until the debt was discharged. Some scholars have seen this "debt peonage" as the virtual reenslavement of the South's black population. It certainly destroyed any chance that sharecropping could become a way-station to land ownership for any sizable number of former slaves.

Impeachment of President Johnson

Although his policies had clearly been rejected, President Johnson continued to resist Radical Reconstruction by every possible means. Using the authority he possessed as commander-in-chief, he issued orders curtailing the powers of the military commanders in the South. He also removed from office people friendly to radical policies. Congress responded in 1867-68 by trying to trim the president's powers so as to reduce his capacity for harm. In particular it passed the Tenure of Office Act, which forbade him to dismiss federal officials without the consent of the Senate. Another law required him to issue all orders to the army through its commanding general, U. S. Grant.

There had been talk among radicals for some time of removing Johnson from office. Under the Constitution a president could be removed only for "treason, bribery, or other high crimes and misdemeanors." Johnson had committed none of these. His only real offense was to refuse to cooperate in legislative policies that Congress and the public had approved. This might indicate bad political judgment, but it was not a crime.

Then Johnson, always his own worst enemy, blundered. In August 1867 he suspended Secretary of War Edwin M. Stanton, a close ally of the radicals. There followed a comic opera in which Stanton barricaded himself in his office while his successor stood outside begging him to vacate. Outraged at Johnson's defiance, and convinced that he intended to destroy Radical Reconstruction, the House of Representatives in February 1868 impeached the president—that is, charged him with misconduct. Johnson stood accused of a number of doubtful offenses such as delivering "inflammatory and scandalous" speeches, but especially for dismissing Stanton. Impeachment meant that Johnson now had to go on trial before the Senate, which would decide whether to remove him from the presidency.

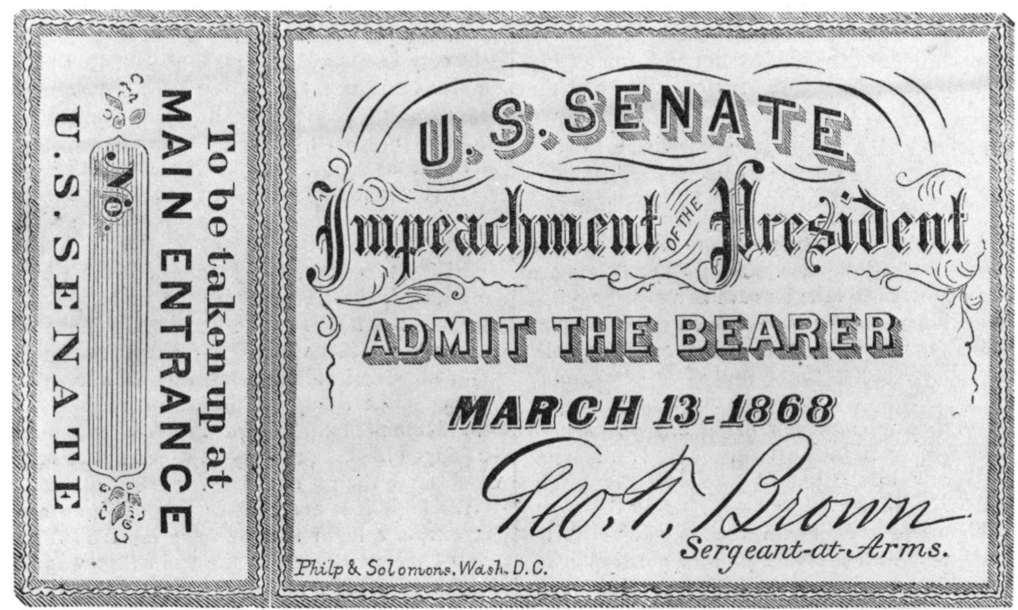

Facsimile of a ticket to Andrew Johnson's impeachment trial. Though Johnson was guilty of no crime other than continued resistance to Radical Reconstruction, a switch of a single Senate vote would have removed him from office. *(Courtesy, Library of Congress)*

For three months the Senate sat as a court, listening to arguments from attorneys for both sides. Johnson's lawyers argued that a president could be impeached only for violation of criminal law; counsel for the House contended that Johnson had exceeded his presidential authority and therefore provided adequate grounds for impeachment. Suspense mounted as it became clear that Republican senators were divided over the question of Johnson's guilt. In the end, seven Republicans broke with their colleagues and voted with Democrats against impeachment. As a result the Senate fell one vote short of the required two-thirds needed to remove the president from office.

Johnson's impeachment and trial were the product of nerves stretched to the limit after three years of feuding. So convinced were many Northerners that Johnson had joined with unrepentant rebels to undo the results of the war that they sanctioned any means to drive him from office. With hindsight we can see that Johnson's conviction—especially on such flimsy grounds—might have damaged permanently the role of the president in the American political system.

The End of Reconstruction

Reconstruction remained, at least in fragments, into the 1870s. After white organizations, among them the Ku Klux Klan, had begun threatening and committing violence on black citizens for exercising their newly acquired rights, the national legislature in the early 1870s put through several Force Acts that aimed at restraining the terrorist groups. The administration of Ulysses S. Grant, elected president in 1868 as the candidate of the Republican Party, broke the Klan by the end of 1871. In 1875 Congress passed a Civil Rights Act—which in 1883 the Supreme Court would find unconstitutional—that required states to provide equality to blacks in public places and prohibited the exclusion of blacks from jury duty. For a while into the 1870s, some Southern states had Reconstruction governments that represented black as well as white voters. And in 1876 there were still a few federal soldiers in the South whose object was to defend the rights of the black community. But by that year American politics had been turning away from Reconstruction for some time.

In 1868 Grant, as a war hero, had won a solid victory over Democratic presidential candidate Horatio Seymour of New York. In the next years Democrats made politically effective attacks on Reconstruction policy, winning voters unsure of the wisdom of Radical Reconstruction or unfriendly to the rights black people were gaining. Some Republicans were also challenging the party's Southern programs. In 1872 Democrats and a faction of Republicans put up newspaperman Horace Greeley as a presidential candidate. Grant won reelection, but his administration suffered from a number of political scandals that suggested widespread corruption. In the elections of 1874 the Democratic Party won control of the House of Representatives and cut into Republican strength in the Senate.

The Reconstruction governments in the South were facing both political opposition and violence from citizens who wanted whites to be in control of Southern society. White Democrats formed terrorist organizations, disrupted Republican gatherings, and threatened blacks. The federal government, tiring of Reconstruction, did little to stop all this.

The Compromise of 1877. Finally, in the events that followed the presidential contest of 1876 between Republican candidate Rutherford B. Hayes of Ohio and Democrat Samuel J. Tilden of New York, the Republican party ended Reconstruction and abandoned black Southerners and their rights. After the general election, which chose the presidential electors who were to cast the actual vote for president, charges of irregularities had arisen concerning procedures in three Southern states, South Carolina, Florida, and Louisiana. There the election boards that had counted the popular presidential vote, giving it in each case to the Republicans, were under the control of Republican Reconstruction forces; Democrats suggested that the vote in each state had actually gone for the Democrats. They also challenged the legitimacy of one Republican elector in Oregon. Unless the Republican claims could stand in each of the four states, the majority in the whole electoral college would be Democratic and Tilden would be the next president. Democrats and Republicans worked out a scheme for a commission that was to decide among the disputed electors; it was supposed to be balanced between Democratic and Republican members, with one other member who would be independent of either party in his decisions. When it came to appear that this member, a justice on the Supreme Court, was going to decide in all cases in favor of the Republicans, Democrats believed that they were about to have the election taken away from them. After the dispute had lasted for months, during which there was talk of civil war, the parties came to a solution. In return for a Democratic agreement not to oppose the selection of Hayes electors, Republicans agreed that a Republican presidential administration would not only remove the remaining federal troops from the South but also give political patronage to white Southerners and be friendly to economic legislation beneficial to Southern states. Hayes, who had expressed concern for the rights of black Southerners, presided over the end of a policy that by 1877 no longer had political support. The Republican effort to protect civil rights in the South in a major way had ceased.

Points To Think About

1. Who was John Brown? And what did he hope to accomplish? According to Brown's own account, the raid was designed to demonstrate to the South the necessity of emancipation. He and his small band would seize the arsenal. They would arm nearby slaves and lead them into the hills. From there they would stage periodic raids. Slaveholders would be forced to recognize that they could not crush Brown's guerrillas and so could not protect their slave property. They would be forced to turn to emancipation. That was the idea. It explains Brown's famous remark that he once fancied slavery could be ended without the shedding of "very much" blood. Once Brown took the arsenal, however, he made no move to put the rest of his plan into effect. He simply stayed at Harpers Ferry. It was as if he were waiting to be captured. When Virginian forces arrived, Brown fought as if he were eager to die in battle. Instead he was wounded, captured, and held for trial. His remarkable composure during and after his trial also suggested to some that he was seeking death. What did motivate this unusual man?

We do know that Brown was intensely religious, that he had learned from his father to shoulder heavy responsibilities and that, until the Panic of 1837, he had been a moderately successful businessman as well as the conscientious father of a large family. Brown went bankrupt in the panic and never again managed to succeed in business. For fifteen years he struggled through one unhappy enterprise after another. Meanwhile he had to feed his family. Brown's first wife died, and one of his children accidentally scalded another to death. Brown's life during these years, in fact, reads like the Book of Job.

It may be that Brown found in antislavery militancy a sense of redemption. It certainly redeemed him from having to continue his unavailing efforts to reestablish himself in business. And it released him from the terrible responsibilities of caring for his family. Brown had taken these responsibilities very seriously and the frustration of being unable to meet them for so long a time might have been more than he could bear.

However all of that may be, it is striking that once embarked upon his abolitionist activities Brown was downright reckless with the lives of his sons and sons-in-law. In the failure of his raid on Harpers Ferry he found a success so vast that it made up for all his other failures. His manner of death made him a martyr in the North. And this did what all of his years of business activity could not. It moved wealthy supporters to step forward and guarantee the decent living for his family.

John Brown may have been both madman and saint. And he may also have been a victim of the American competitive system, who found in religious fanaticism a way of escaping from the rat-race.

2. Did states have a right to secede? The South, of course, claimed and the federal government denied that right.

The two positions, though irreconcilable, were at least clear. They remained clear through the first several years of the fighting. The North had sought to impose a total blockade on all shipping entering or leaving Southern ports—an act contrary to international law if the South was a separate nation, but permissible if it was only a rebellious province. Hence the Lincoln Administration continued to argue that secession was not possible under the Constitution and that the Southern states were still legally part of the Union. Southerners, for their part, continued to argue the opposite.

Yet, as the prospects of a Northern victory grew brighter, the constitutional waters grew muddier. The North intended to exact certain concessions from the Southern states before letting them back into the Union. But if, as the North argued, the South had never legally left the Union, there was no need to readmit it. Nor was there a legal basis for demanding concession.

Northern politicians devised doctrines that would

describe what the Southern states had done and would entitle the North to reconstruct them as the price of their readmission. Plainly, the North wished to treat the Confederate states as if they had seceded. Southerners were quick to seize upon the obvious contradictions between these new formulations and the North's original view.

Lincoln, for his part, avoided elaborate constitutional theorizing. The Southern states, he held, had disrupted the "normal" relations between themselves and the Union. The task was to "restore" those normal relations.

The legal issues never were sorted out. Instead the nation adopted the thirteenth, fourteenth, and fifteenth amendments. They at least make it clear that secession would be unconstitutional in the future.

3. Lee's strategy of defending Virginia before all else was one of the fatal flaws in the Confederate military strategy. The South could have fought a defensive, guerrilla-style war of attrition of the sort Washington had waged against the British. But Washington's strategy, which was designed not to defeat the British in open battle but to prevent them from gaining secure control of the countryside, required him to sacrifice a good deal of territory including such prizes as New York and, for a time, Philadelphia. In the Civil War a similar strategy would have involved sacrificing much of Virginia including, in all probability, Richmond. It would, in fact, have run against the very reason people like Lee supported the Confederacy in the first place. His goal, after all, was the preservation of Virginia, and it led him to try to defend every inch of her soil. Despite Lee's tactical brilliance, it was a strategy doomed to defeat in the long run because it involved too many open battles with the stronger Union forces.

Lee's strategy, moreover, faithfully reflected the spirit of secession; its failure mirrored the failure of the Confederacy as a whole. The secessionists were dedicated to their individual states. The resulting states' rights philosophy made it impossible for them to make the kinds of national decisions waging a successful war requires. So one can say that the very ideas which led to secession also led, in the long run, to a Northern victory.

4. The predominant public image of Lincoln is that of the "Great Emancipator." Ironically, the Emancipation Proclamation did not free the slaves. The Thirteenth Amendment did that. What the Proclamation did was provide the states still in rebellion (portions of several had been recaptured) with one hundred days to return peacefully to the Union. The penalty was that those which remained in the Confederacy would suffer the loss of their slaves. But first the Union armies had to reconquer the territory. So it is accurate to say that the Proclamation did not really free anyone although it meant that all would be free in the event of a Union victory.

Lincoln's Proclamation also signaled a crucial change in the Union's war aims. It had begun the war with the simple intent of putting down the rebellion (as it saw secession). Lincoln made it clear he would respect the "peculiar institution" wherever it legally existed. But as the war dragged on, and the toll of dead and wounded rose ever higher, Lincoln—and the Union—came to think of the war as a great moral crusade. By the time of his second inaugural address (one of the few masterpieces by an American president), Lincoln had come to view the terrible suffering of the war as a punishment from God for the national sin of slavery. The war was no longer simply to restore the union. Now it was also to free the slaves. The Emancipation Proclamation was a turning point in this process.

5. Historians have long speculated over how Lincoln would have approached the problem of postwar reconstruction. And in so doing they are merely following the lead of his contemporaries, most of whom claimed their own proposals reflected Lincoln's plans. The real question, however, may be: did Lincoln have any plans?

It seems probable that he did, but Lincoln confided them to no one. In this matter, as in most others, he kept his own counsel. The result is that, following the assassination, people have tried to infer his postwar plans from his wartime programs. This is a very dubious enterprise. The reason is that Lincoln sought throughout the war to shorten it by enticing the seceding states back into the Union. The generous terms he offered were contingent on their willingness to lay down their arms. And so they should be seen as the carrot Lincoln used alongside the military stick. That they should not be seen as likely precedents for his postwar plans is suggested by this logic. Leniency was held out as a reward for voluntarily returning to the Union. None of the Confederate states earned that reward. We also have Lincoln's reaction to the Wade-Davis Bill to go by. He objected not so much to its rigor as that it would tie his hands in advance. Lincoln wanted to be free to deal with a defeated South as circumstances might suggest.

All in all it seems that we will never know what Lincoln would have proposed. But the disastrous course of Johnson's attempts at reconstruction will always tempt us to speculate on what Lincoln might have done had he lived.

6. Reconstruction has, until recently, been almost universally seen as a tragic failure. And it is certainly true that it left many vital problems unresolved. After more than a century blacks are still second-class citizens. They still are denied equal opportunity. They still suffer discrimination. The obvious question is: what went wrong?

The obvious answer is: plenty! After the war President Johnson decided not to summon a special session of Congress. This was a disastrous mistake because Congress would be highly critical of plans adopted in its absence, no matter how wise. It was a mistake too because Johnson, as a Southerner himself, could not give even the appearance of leniency without creating the suspicion on the part of Northerners that they were being cheated of the fruits of victory. And it was a mistake because it gave the South the false impression that, if it followed Johnson's lead, all would be well.

By the time Congress met, in December of 1865, Northern public opinion was convinced: Johnson had betrayed them by issuing wholesale pardons; the South was trying to reinstitute slavery by passing the notorious black codes; and only the Congress could be trusted to safeguard the rights of the slave and preserve the fruits of victory. Southern opinion, meanwhile, was convinced that the Southern states had already met every reasonable demand and should be readmitted as quickly as possible. Under these circumstances, Congressional Reconstruction began. There were two further handicaps. Republicans in Congress were unwilling to break up the plantation system because respect for property rights was too basic to their ideology. And Northerners, while determined to give the former slaves some protection, were themselves racist. The limits of their sympathies for black people were quickly reached.

All things considered we might better marvel that Reconstruction accomplished so much instead of so little. The race question ran too deep to be resolved in so short a time. The South's economy was in a shambles. The task would perhaps have been impossible under the best circumstances. The schools and roads built, the hundreds and thousands fed, the protection given to life and property were not negligible achievements.

Suggested Readings

The standard work on the era is James G. Randall and David Donald, *The Civil War and Reconstruction* (revised 1973). James McPherson also presents an excellent guide to the period in *Ordeal by Fire: The Civil War and Reconstruction* (1982) while all of Bruce Catton's books make beautiful reading. Emory L. Thomas analyzes *The Confederate Nation* (1979). For biographies of the Union and Confederate leaders, see Stephen B. Oates's *With Malice Toward None* (1978) and Clement Eaton's *Jefferson Davis* (1977). Two major books on the response of intellectuals to the war are George Fredrickson, *The Inner Civil War: Northern Intellectuals and the Crisis of the Union* (1965) and Daniel Aaron, *The Unwritten War: American Writers and the Civil War* (1973). Robert Manson Myers, ed., *The Children of Pride: A True Story of Georgia and the Civil War* (1972), presents history in the first person; this collection of the letters of a Georgia planter's family gives us its religious sentiments and attitudes toward human property, the day-to-day demands of running a plantation, and the dissolution of a way of life.

Kenneth Stampp's *The Era of Reconstruction, 1865–1877* (1965) is thorough on the Reconstruction years. An important study of the consequences of freedom for blacks is Leon F. Litwack's *Been in the Storm so Long: The Aftermath of Slavery* (1979). Michael Les Benedict, *The Impeachment and Trial of Andrew Johnson* (1973) is a superior analysis of the divisions and alignments within the Reconstruction Congress and its relationships with the President, whom the author depicts unfavorably. C. Vann Woodward's *Reunion and Reaction* (1951) is a collection of essays that takes as its theme the South's distinctive heritage. See also John Hope Franklin, *Reconstruction After the Civil War* (1961), William Gillette, *Retreat from Reconstruction* (1980), Eric McKitrick, *Andrew Johnson and Reconstruction* (1965), and Allen W. Trelease, *White Terror: The Ku Klux Klan Conspiracy and Southern Reconstruction* (1971).

On the Freedmen's Bureau see George R. Bentley, *A History of the Freedmen's Bureau* (1955) and William S. McFeely, *Yankee Step-Father: General O. O. Howard and the Freedmen's Bureau* (1968). A good state study is Joe Gray Taylor's *Louisiana Reconstructed, 1863–1877* (1974).

FORREST McDONALD

The economic consequences of the Civil War and Reconstruction were enormous, most of them flowing from policies of government. Congress increased the tariff from a modest seventeen percent to a highly protective forty-seven percent, and thereby gave a large stimulus to manufacturing; it granted tens of millions of acres of federal land to subsidize the building of railroads; it granted more lands for "land-grant colleges" to provide agricultural and mechanical training and offer extension services as well. What was most significant was a dramatic change in the pattern of capital accumulation in the United States. Southern capital had been concentrated almost exclusively in slavery and land; and when slavery was abolished, wiping out more than $2 billion of capital in human form, nearly that amount of capital in the form of plantations was also flushed down the drain.

In the North capital was created on a scale that matched its destruction in the South. This took the form of Greenback currency and United States government bonds, which represented obligations of the government but also represented an unprecedented concentration of purely liquid capital in private hands. As a result of these various developments, the ultimate triumph of urban capitalism was assured. Rural, agricultural America was not dead, but it did not own the future. The future belonged to the city—which meant merchants, industrialists, and financiers, and if they could win a share, the urban workingmen.

Constitutionally, the results were likewise significant, though they were not nearly so profound as they might have been had the Radicals not slackened. State sovereignty as a doctrine was discredited, and the government in Washington increased greatly in authority and in the scope of its powers. The most significant long-range change was the emergence of the Supreme Court as the final arbiter of what the states could and could not do—and, after Congressional Radicalism had run its course, as the most energetic branch of the federal government. In the entire period before the war the Court had declared only two acts of Congress unconstitutional, and on both occasions the decisions aroused powerful opposition that threatened the very existence of the Court. During the first decade after the war the Court struck down more than a dozen congressional acts and many state laws, and it virtually nullified the Fourteenth and Fifteenth Amendments, yet almost no one protested.

The ideologues who brought about most important result of all, the abolition of slavery, failed to understand and accommodate in the polity of emancipation a basic conservative principle. The greatest burden the freedmen had to bear was psychological: they had been enculturated into a mentality of dependence and were suddenly thrust into a position of responsibility for their own welfare. In ancient times the Lord Jehovah had required the Children of Israel to wander the desert for forty years, until none was alive among them who could remember slavery, before He delivered them unto the Promised Land. In 1865 the government of the United States delivered unto an accursed land a people who could remember nothing but slavery; and the efforts of the Freedmen's Bureau to help them learn to cope with the awesome responsibilities of freedom were pathetically inadequate.

That was not all. Instead of encouraging blacks to fill the millions of jobs created by the technological revolution that was just getting under way, Congress continued an unrestricted immigration policy and even passed a contract labor law, under which industrialists could recruit cheap European labor. Moreover, the government compounded the great economic damage done in the South. Within a generation the vast majority of people in the region, black and white alike, had fallen into the peonage of sharecropping.

Lincoln was right: the nation could not continue to exist half slave and half free, and slavery had to be abolished. But the cost was enormous, and the scars were indelible.

The Civil War: Results? ☆ 

EUGENE D. GENOVESE

By the Civil War the Northern hostility to slavery had made its broadest connections with the other beliefs and habits that characterized the Northern culture Professor McDonald speaks of. Slavery came to be identified with economic backwardness, political reaction, and social disorder—with all that was slow and untidy and offensive to the Yankee morality that demanded work and progress. The ideology of the marketplace had a vision of boundless expansion—of enterprise and riches, of liberty and democracy, of free land and booming manufacturers, of a continent to be filled with farms and factories. Few Northerners outside the abolitionist ranks wanted to interfere with slavery in the South, but countless others could not tolerate the expansion of slavery into the West, where it could monopolize land that ought to go to free working farmers and where it could increase the political power of the slaveholders who opposed the ways and values of the North. Two alternative social systems—systems of relationships among classes—had coexisted in the Union, one founded in slavery and the other in freedom. They could coexist no longer.

The economic consequences of the Civil War that Professor McDonald speaks of would bring social conditions of a needless brutality that he will not acknowledge. On the more immediate social results of the war he is right on one particular: that the efforts of the Freedman's Bureau were inadequate to protect the liberated blacks and bring them fully into the technological future that was being prepared. He does not tell why or in what ways the Bureau acted inadequately. The United States, as daring for the time as it had been in freeing the slaves, had no satisfactory vision of what to do next. It was too racist to make a central project of the integration of blacks into the rest of society. And its notions of the rights of property and the limits of government restrained it from undertaking a program large enough to bring political, economic, and social justice to the Freedmen. It recoiled, for example, from any major redistribution of land of the former slaveholders into the hands of the slaves who had worked it; and that hesitancy meant a failure to make more widespread the propertyholding that the nation so revered. Neither the Freedmen's Bureau nor the rest of the Northern establishment was able to see how vigorous a social existence the black Americans had developed under slavery, an existence that with government aid could have been made the basis for full social equality.

During the last decade or two many historians have told us much about that antebellum black society. Among the oppressed peoples of modern times none has surpassed in courage and resourcefulness the blacks who struggled for survival during and after slavery. Despite laws that denied them the right to marry and have legitimate families, despite every attempt to impose upon them a religion that taught submission to the will of their masters, despite the whip and separation from loved ones, despite countless abuses and indignities, they created a powerful religious and family life of their own, which sustained their sense of humanity, justice, and deliverance—which kept alive their determination to be free. In the 1860s they became free, or free according to law, but soon afterwards their liberators became interested in other things, abandoned them to the nation's powerful white racist majority, and therein blighted the promise that even as slaves blacks had implicitly, perhaps unconsciously, made to themselves to live as a free community.

Appendixes

The Declaration of Independence

When in the Course of human events, it becomes necessary for one people to dissolve the political bands which have connected them with another, and to assume among the Powers of the earth, the separate and equal station to which the Laws of Nature and of Nature's God entitle them, a decent respect to the opinions of mankind requires that they should declare the causes which impel them to the separation.

We hold these truths to be self-evident, that all men are created equal, that they are endowed by their Creator with certain unalienable Rights, that among these are Life, Liberty and the pursuit of Happiness. That to secure these rights, Governments are instituted among Men, deriving their just powers from the consent of the governed, That whenever any Form of Government becomes destructive of these ends, it is the Right of the People to alter or to abolish it, and to institute new Government, laying its foundation on such principles and organizing its powers in such form, as to them shall seem most likely to effect their Safety and Happiness. Prudence, indeed, will dictate that Governments long established should not be changed for light and transient causes; and accordingly all experience hath shown, that mankind are more disposed to suffer, while evils are sufferable, than to right themselves by abolishing the forms to which they are accustomed. When a long train of abuses and usurpations, pursuing invariably the same Object evinces a design to reduce them under absolute Despotism, it is their right, it is their duty, to throw off such Government, and to provide new Guards for their future security.—Such has been the patient sufferance of these Colonies; and such is now the necessity which constrains them to alter their former Systems of Government. The history of the present King of Great Britain is a history of repeated injuries and usurpations, all having in direct object the establishment of an absolute Tyranny over these States. To prove this, let Facts be submitted to a candid world.

He has refused his Assent to Laws, the most wholesome and necessary for the public good.

He has forbidden his Governors to pass Laws of immediate and pressing importance, unless suspended in their operation till his Assent should be obtained; and when so suspended, he has utterly neglected to attend to them.

He has refused to pass other Laws for the accommodation of large districts of people, unless those people would relinquish the right of Representation in the Legislature, a right inestimable to them and formidable to tyrants only.

He has dissolved Representative Houses repeatedly, for opposing with manly firmness his invasions on the rights of the people.

He has refused for a long time, after such dissolutions, to cause others to be elected; whereby the Legislative Powers, incapable of Annihilation, have returned to the People at large for their exercise; the State remaining in the mean time exposed to all the dangers of invasion from without, and convulsions within.

He has endeavoured to prevent the population of these States; for that purpose obstructing the Laws of Naturalization of Foreigners; refusing to pass others to encourage their migration hither, and raising the conditions of new Appropriations of Lands.

He has obstructed the Administration of Justice, by refusing his Assent to Laws for establishing Judiciary Powers.

He has made Judges dependent on his Will alone, for the tenure of their offices, and the amount and payment of their salaries.

He has erected a multitude of New Offices, and sent hither swarms of Officers to harass our People, and eat out their substance.

He has kept among us, in times of peace, Standing Armies without the Consent of our legislature.

He has affected to render the Military independent of and superior to the Civil Power.

He has combined with others to subject us to a jurisdiction foreign to our constitution, and unacknowledged by our laws; giving his Assent to their acts of pretended legislation:

For quartering large bodies of armed troops among us:

For protecting them, by a mock Trial, from Punishment for any Murders which they should commit on the Inhabitants of these States:

For cutting off our Trade with all parts of the world:

For imposing taxes on us without our Consent:

For depriving us in many cases, of the benefits of Trial by Jury:

For transporting us beyond Seas to be tried for pretended offences:

For abolishing the free System of English Laws in a neighbouring Province, establishing therein an Arbitrary government, and enlarging its Boundaries so as to render it at once an example and fit instrument for introducing the same absolute rule into these Colonies:

For taking away our Charters, abolishing our most valuable Laws, and altering fundamentally the Forms of our Governments:

For suspending our own Legislature, and declaring themselves invested with Power to legislate for us in all cases whatsoever.

He has abdicated Government here, by declaring us out of his Protection and waging War against us.

He has plundered our seas, ravaged our Coasts, burnt our towns, and destroyed the lives of our people.

He is at this time transporting large armies of foreign mercenaries to compleat the works of death, desolation and tyranny, already begun with circumstances of Cruelty & perfidy scarcely paralleled in the most barbarous ages, and totally unworthy the Head of a civilized nation.

He has constrained our fellow Citizens taken Captive on the high Seas to bear Arms against their Country, to become the executioners of their friends and Brethren, or to fall themselves by their Hands.

He has excited domestic insurrections amongst us, and has endeavoured to bring on the inhabitants of our frontiers, the merciless Indian Savages, whose known rule of warfare, is an undistinguished destruction of all ages, sexes and conditions.

In every stage of these Oppressions We have Petitioned for Redress in the most humble terms: Our repeated Petitions have been answered only by repeated injury. A Prince, whose character is thus marked by every act which may define a Tyrant, is unfit to be the ruler of a free People.

Nor have We been wanting in attention to our British brethren. We have warned them from time to time of attempts by their legislature to extend an unwarrantable jurisdiction over us. We have reminded them of the circumstances of our emigration and settlement here. We have appealed to their native justice and magnanimity, and we have conjured them by the ties of our common kindred to disavow these usurpations, which, would inevitably interrupt our connections and correspondence. They too have been deaf to the voice of justice and of consanguinity. We must, therefore, acquiesce in the necessity, which denounces our Separation, and hold them, as we hold the rest of mankind, Enemies in War, in Peace Friends.

We, therefore, the Representatives of the United States of America, in General Congress, Assembled, appealing to the Supreme Judge of the world for the rectitude of our intentions, do, in the Name, and by Authority of the good People of these Colonies, solemnly publish and declare, That these United Colonies are, and of Right ought to be Free and Independent States; that they are Absolved from all Allegiance to the British Crown, and that all political connection between them and the State of Great Britain, is and ought to be totally dissolved; and that as Free and Independent States, they have full Power to levy War, conclude Peace, contract Alliances, establish Commerce, and to do all other Acts and Things which Independent States may of right do. And for the support of this Declaration, with a firm reliance on the Protection of Divine Providence, we mutually pledge to each other our Lives, our Fortunes and our sacred Honor.

The Constitution of the United States

We the people of the United States, in Order to form a more perfect Union, establish Justice, insure domestic Tranquility, provide for the common defense, promote the general Welfare, and secure the Blessings of Liberty to ourselves and our Posterity, do ordain and establish this CONSTITUTION for the United States of America.

ARTICLE 1

Section 1. All legislative Powers herein granted shall be vested in a Congress of the United States which shall consist of a Senate and House of Representatives.

Section 2. The House of Representatives shall be composed of Members chosen every second Year by the People of the several States, and the Electors in each State shall have the Qualifications requisite for Electors of the most numerous Branch of the State Legislature.

No Person shall be a Representative who shall not have attained to the Age of twenty-five Years, and been seven Years a Citizen of the United States, and who shall not, when elected, be an inhabitant of that State in which he shall be chosen.

Representatives and direct Taxes shall be apportioned among the several States which may be included within this Union, according to their respective Numbers, which shall be determined by adding to the whole Number of free Persons, including those bound to Service for a Term of Years and excluding Indians not taxed, three fifths of all other Persons. The actual Enumeration shall be made within three Years after the first Meeting of the Congress of the United States, and within every subsequent Term of ten Years, in such Manner as they shall by Law direct. The Number of Representatives shall not exceed one for every thirty Thousand, but each State shall have at Least one Representative; and until such enumeration shall be made, the State of New Hampshire shall be entitled to chuse three, Massachusetts eight, Rhode-Island and Providence Plantations one, Connecticut five, New-York six, New Jersey four, Pennsylvania eight, Delaware one, Maryland six, Virginia ten, North Carolina five, South Carolina five, and Georgia three.

When vacancies happen in the Representation from any State, the Executive Authority thereof shall issue Writs of Election to fill such Vacancies.

The House of Representatives shall chuse their Speaker and other Officers; and shall have the sole Power of Impeachment.

Section 3. The Senate of the United States shall be composed of two Senators from each State, chosen by the Legislature thereof, for six Years; and each Senator shall have one Vote.

Immediately after they shall be assembled in Consequence of the first Election, they shall be divided as equally as may be into three Classes. The Seats of the Senators of the first Class shall be vacated at the Expiration of the second Year, of the second Class at the Expiration of the fourth Year, and of the third Class at the Expiration of the sixth Year, so that one-third may be chosen every second Year; and if Vacancies happen by Resignation, or otherwise, during the Recess of the Legislature of any State, the Executive thereof may make temporary Appointments until the next Meeting of the Legislature, which shall then fill such Vacancies.

No Person shall be a Senator who shall not have attained to the Age of thirty Years, and been nine Years a Citizen of the United States, and who shall not, when elected, be an Inhabitant of that State in which he shall be chosen.

The Vice President of the United States shall be President of the Senate, but shall have no vote, unless they be equally divided.

The Senate shall chuse their other Officers, and also a President pro tempore, in the absence of the Vice President, or when he shall exercise the Office of the President of the United States.

The Senate shall have the sole Power to try all Impeachments. When sitting for that purpose, they shall be on Oath or Affirmation. When the President of the United States is tried, the Chief Justice shall preside: And no person shall be convicted without the Concurrence of two thirds of the Members present.

Judgment in Cases of Impeachment shall not extend further than to removal from Office, and disqualification to hold and enjoy an Office of honor, Trust, or Profit under the United States: but the Party convicted shall nevertheless be liable and subject to Indictment, Trial, Judgment, and Punishment, according to Law.

Section 4. The Times, Places and Manner of holding Elections for Senators and Representatives, shall be prescribed in each state by the Legislature thereof; but the Congress may at any time by Law make or alter such Regulations, except as to the Places of Chusing Senators.

The Congress shall assemble at least once in every Year, and such Meeting shall be on the first Monday in December, unless they shall by Law appoint a different Day.

Section 5. Each House shall be the Judge of the Elections, Returns and Qualifications of its own Members, and a Majority of each shall constitute a Quorum to do Business from day to day, and may be authorized to compel the Attendance of absent Members, in such Manner, and under such Penalties, as each House may provide.

Each House may determine the Rules of its Proceedings, punish its Members for disorderly Behavior, and, with the Concurrence of two thirds, expel a Member.

Each House shall keep a Journal of its Proceedings, and from time to time publish the same, excepting such Parts as may in their Judgment require Secrecy; and the Yeas and Nays of the Members of either House on any question shall, at the Desire of one fifth of those Present, be entered on the Journal.

Neither House, during the Session of Congress, shall, without the Consent of the other, adjourn for more than three days, nor to any other Place than that in which the two Houses shall be sitting.

Section 6. The Senators and Representatives shall receive a Compensation for their Services, to be ascertained by Law, and paid out of the Treasury of the United States. They shall in all Cases, except Treason, Felony, and Breach of the Peace, be privileged from Arrest during their Attendance at the Session of their respective Houses, and in going to and returning from the same; and for any Speech or Debate in either House, they shall not be questioned in any other Place.

No Senator or Representative shall, during the Time for which he was elected, be appointed to any civil Office under the Authority of the United States, which shall have been created, or the Emoluments whereof shall have been increased, during such time; and no Person holding any Office under the United States shall be a Member of either House during his continuance in Office.

Section 7. All Bills for raising Revenue shall originate in the House of Representatives; but the Senate may propose or concur with Amendments as on other bills.

Every Bill which shall have passed the House of Representatives and the Senate, shall, before it become a Law, be presented to the President of the United States. If he approve he shall sign it, but if not he shall return it, with his Objections, to that House in which it shall have originated, who shall enter the Objections at large on their Journal, and proceed to reconsider it. If after such Reconsideration two thirds of that House shall agree to pass the bill, it shall be sent, together with the objections, to the other House, by which it shall likewise be reconsidered, and if approved by two thirds of that House, it shall become a Law. But in all such Cases the Votes of both Houses shall be determined by Yeas and Nays, and the Names of the Persons voting for and against the Bill shall be entered on the Journal of each House respectively. If any Bill shall not be returned by the President within ten Days (Sundays excepted) after it shall have been presented to him, the Same shall be a Law, in like Manner as if he had signed it, unless the Congress by their Adjournment prevent its Return, in which Case it shall not be a Law.

Every Order, Resolution, or Vote to which the Concurrence of the Senate and House of Representatives may be necessary (except on a question of Adjournment) shall be presented to the President of the United States; and before the Same shall take Effect, shall be approved by him, or being disapproved by him, shall be repassed by two thirds of the Senate and House of Representatives, according to the Rules and Limitations prescribed in the Case of a Bill.

Section 8. The Congress shall have Power To lay and collect Taxes, Duties, Imposts and Excises, to pay the Debts and provide for the common Defence and general Welfare of the United States; but all Duties, Imposts and Excises shall be uniform throughout the United States;

To borrow money on the credit of the United States;

To regulate Commerce with foreign Nations, and among the several States, and with the Indian Tribes;

To establish an uniform Rule of Naturalization, and uniform Laws on the subject of Bankruptcies throughout the United States;

To coin Money, regulate the Value thereof, and of foreign Coin, and fix the Standard of Weights and Measures;

To provide for the Punishment of counterfeiting the Securities and current Coin of the United States;

To establish Post Offices and post Roads;

To promote the Progress of Science and useful Arts, by securing for limited Times to Authors and Inventors the exclusive Right to their respective Writings and Discoveries;

To constitute Tribunals inferior to the Supreme Court;

To define and punish Piracies and Felonies committed on the high Seas, and Offences against the Law of Nations;

To declare War, grant Letters of Marque and Reprisal, and make Rules concerning Captures on Land and Water;

To raise and support Armies, but no Appropriation of Money to that Use shall be for a longer Term than two Years;

To provide and maintain a Navy;

To make Rules for the Government and Regulation of the land and naval forces;

To provide for calling forth the Militia to execute the Laws of the Union, suppress Insurrections and repel Invasions;

To provide for organizing, arming, and disciplining the Militia, and for governing such Part of them as may be employed in the Service of the United States, reserving to the States respectively, the Appointment of the Officers, and the Authority of training the Militia according to the discipline prescribed by Congress;

To exercise exclusive Legislation in all Cases whatsoever, over such District (not exceeding ten Miles square) as may, by Cession of particular States, and the acceptance of Congress, become the Seat of Government of the United States, and to exercise like Authority over all Places purchased by the Consent of the Legislature of the States in which the Same shall be, for the Erection of Forts, Magazines, Arsenals, dock-Yards, and other needful Buildings;—And

To make all Laws which shall be necessary and proper for carrying into Execution the foregoing Powers, and all other Powers vested by this Constitution in the Government of the United States, or in any Department or Officer thereof.

Section 9. The Migration or Importation of such Persons as any of the States now existing shall think proper to admit, shall not be prohibited by the Congress prior to the Year one thousand eight hundred and eight, but a tax or duty may be imposed on such Importation, not exceeding ten dollars for each Person.

The privilege of the Writ of Habeas Corpus shall not be suspended, unless when in Cases of Rebellion or Invasion the public Safety may require it.

No Bill of Attainder or ex post facto Law shall be passed.

No capitation, or other direct, Tax shall be laid unless in Proportion to the Census or Enumeration herein before directed to be taken.

No Tax or Duty shall be laid on Articles exported from any State.

No Preference shall be given by any Regulation of Revenue to the Ports of one State over those of another: nor shall Vessels bound to, or from, one State, be obliged to enter, clear, or pay Duties in another.

No Money shall be drawn from the Treasury, but in Consequence of Appropriations made by Law; and a regular Statement and Account of the Receipts and Expenditures of all public Money shall be published from time to time.

No Title of Nobility shall be granted by the United States: And no Person holding any Office of Profit or Trust under them, shall, without the Consent of the Congress, accept of any present, Emolument, Office, or Title, of any kind whatever, from any King, Prince, or foreign State.

Section 10. No State shall enter any Treaty, alliance, or Confederation; grant Letters of Marque and Reprisal; coin Money; emit Bills of Credit; make any Thing but gold and silver Coin a Tender in Payment of Debts; pass any Bill of Attainder, ex post facto Law, or Law impairing the Obligation of Contracts, or grant any Title of Nobility.

No State shall, without the Consent of the Congress, lay any Imposts or Duties on Imports or Exports, except what may be absolutely necessary for executing its inspection Laws: and the net Produce of all Duties and Imposts, laid by any State on Imports or Exports, shall be for the Use of the Treasury of the United States; and all such Laws shall be subject to the Revision and Control of the Congress.

No State shall, without the Consent of Congress, lay any duty of Tonnage, keep Troops, or Ships of War in time of Peace, enter into any Agreement or Compact with another State, or with a foreign Power, or engage in War, unless actually invaded, or in such imminent Danger as will not admit of delay.

ARTICLE II

Section 1. The executive Power shall be vested in a President of the United States of America. He shall hold his Office during the Term of four years, and, together with the Vice-President, chosen for the same Term, be elected, as follows:

Each State shall appoint, in such Manner as the Legislature thereof may direct, a Number of Electors, equal to the whole Number of Senators and Representatives to which the State may be entitled in the Congress; but no Senator or Representative, or Person holding an Office of Trust or Profit under the United States, shall be appointed an Elector.

The Electors shall meet in their respective States, and vote by Ballot for two persons, of whom one at least shall not be an Inhabitant of the same State with themselves. And they shall make a List of all the Persons voted for, and of the Number of Votes for each; which List they shall sign and certify, and transmit sealed to the Seat of the Government of the United States, directed to the President of the Senate. The President of the Senate shall, in the Presence of the Senate and House of Representatives, open all the Certificates, and the Votes shall then be counted. The Person having the greatest Number of Votes shall be the President, if such Number be a Majority of the whole Number of Electors appointed; and if there be more than one who have such Majority, and have an equal Number of Votes, then the House of Representatives shall immediately chuse by Ballot one of them for President; and if no Person have a Majority, then from the five highest on the List the said House shall in like Manner chuse the President. But in chusing the President, the Votes shall be taken by States, the Representation from each State having one Vote; a quorum for this Purpose shall consist of a Member or Members from two-thirds of the States, and a Majority of all the States shall be necessary to a Choice. In every Case, after the Choice of the President, the Person having the greatest Number of Votes of the Electors shall be the Vice President. But if there should remain two or more who have equal votes, the Senate shall chuse from them by Ballot the Vice-President.

The Congress may determine the Time of chusing the Electors, and the Day on which they shall give their Votes; which Day shall be the same throughout the United States.

No person except a natural-born Citizen, or a Citizen of the United States, at the time of the Adoption of this Constitution, shall be eligible to the Office of President; neither shall any Person be eligible to that Office who shall not have attained to the Age of thirty-five years, and been fourteen Years a Resident within the United States.

In Case of the Removal of the President from Office, or of his Death, Resignation, or Inability to discharge the Powers and Duties of the said Office, the same shall devolve on the Vice-President, and the Congress may by Law provide for the Case of Removal, Death, Resignation, or Inability, both of the President and Vice-President, declaring what Officer shall then act as President, and such Officer shall act accordingly, until the disability be removed, or a President shall be elected.

The President shall, at stated Times, receive for his Services a Compensation, which shall neither be increased nor diminished during the Period for which he shall have been elected, and he shall not receive within that Period any other Emolument from the United States, or any of them.

Before he enter on the execution of his Office, he shall take the following Oath or Affirmation:—"I do solemnly swear (or affirm) that I will faithfully execute the Office of President of the United States, and will, to the best of my Ability, preserve, protect, and defend the Constitution of the United States."

Section 2. The President shall be Commander in Chief of the Army and Navy of the United States, and of the Militia of the several States, when called into the actual Service of the United States; he may require the Opinion, in writing, of the principal Officer in each of the executive Departments, upon any subject relating to the Duties of their respective Offices, and he shall have Power to Grant Reprieves and Pardons for Offences against the United States, except in Cases of Impeachment.

He shall have Power, by and with the Advice and Consent of the Senate, to make Treaties, provided two thirds of the Senators present concur; and he shall nominate, and by and with the Advice and Consent of the Senate, shall appoint Ambassadors, other public Ministers and Counsuls, Judges of the Supreme Court, and all other Officers of the United States, whose Appointments are herein otherwise provided for, and which shall be established by Law: but the Congress may by Law vest the Appointments of such inferior Officers, as they think proper, in the President alone, in the Courts of Law, or in the Heads of Departments.

The President shall have Power to fill up all Vacancies that may happen during the Recess of the Senate, by granting Commissions which shall expire at the End of their next Session.

Section 3. He shall from time to time give to the Congress Information of the State of the Union, and recommend to their Consideration such Measures as he shall judge necessary and expedient; he may, on extraordinary occasions, convene both Houses, or either of them, and in Case of Disagreement between them, with respect to the Time of Adjournment, he may adjourn them to such Time as he shall think proper; he shall receive Ambassadors and other public Ministers; he shall take Care that the Laws be faithfully executed, and shall Commission all the Officers of the United States

Section 4. The President, Vice President and all civil Officers of the United States, shall be removed from Office on Impeachment for, and Conviction of, Treason, Bribery, or other high Crimes and Misdemeanors.

ARTICLE III

Section 1. The judicial Power of the United States, shall be vested in one supreme Court, and in such inferior Courts as the Congress may from time to time ordain and establish. The Judges, both of the supreme and inferior Courts, shall hold their Offices during good Behaviour, and shall, at stated Times, receive for their Services, a compensation, which shall not be diminished during their Continuance in Office.

Section 2. The judicial Power shall extend to all Cases, in Law and Equity, arising under this constitution, the Laws of the United States, and treaties made, or which shall be made, under their Authority;—to all Cases affecting ambassadors, other public ministers and consuls;—to all cases of admiralty and maritime Jurisdiction;—to Controversies to which the United States shall be a Party;—to Controversies between two or more States;—between a State and Citizens of another State;—between Citizens of different States,—between Citizens of the same State claiming Lands under Grants of different States, and between a State, or the Citizens thereof, and foreign States, Citizens or Subjects.

In all Cases affecting Ambassadors, other public Ministers and Consuls, and those in which a State shall be Party, the supreme Court shall have original Jurisdiction. In all the other Cases before mentioned, the supreme Court shall have appellate Jurisdiction, both as to Law and Fact, with such Exception, and under such Regulations as the Congress shall make.

The trial of all Crimes, except in Cases of Impeachment, shall be by Jury; and such Trial shall be held in the State where the said Crimes shall have been committed; but when not committed within any State, the Trial shall be at such Place or Places as the Congress may by Law have directed.

Section 3. Treason against the United States, shall consist only in levying War against them, or in adhering to their Enemies, giving them Aid and Comfort. No Person shall be convicted of Treason unless on the Testimony of two Witnesses to the same overt Act, or on Confession in open Court.

The Congress shall have power to declare the Punishment of Treason, but no Attainder of Treason shall work Corruption of Blood, or Forfeiture except during the Life of the Person attainted.

ARTICLE IV

Section 1. Full Faith and Credit shall be given in each State to the public Acts, Records, and judicial Proceedings of every other State. And the Congress may by general laws prescribe the Manner in which such Acts, Records and Proceedings shall be proved, and the Effect thereof.

Section 2. The Citizens of each State shall be entitled to all Privileges and Immunities of Citizens in the several States.

A Person charged in any State with Treason, Felony, or other Crime, who shall flee from Justice, and be found in another State, shall on demand of the executive Authority of the State from which he fled, be delivered up, to be removed to the State having Jurisdiction of the crime.

No Person held to Service or Labour in one State, under the Laws thereof, escaping into another, shall, in Consequence of any Law or Regulation therein, be discharged from such Service or Labour, but shall be delivered up on Claim of the Party to whom such Service or Labour may be due.

Section 3. New States may be admitted by the Congress into this Union; but no new State shall be formed or erected within the Jurisdiction of any other State; nor any State be formed by the Junction of two or more States, or parts of States, without the Consent of the Legislatures of the States concerned as well as of the Congress.

The Congress shall have Power to dispose of and make all needful Rules and Regulations respecting the Territory or other Property belonging to the United States; and nothing in this constitution shall be so construed as to Prejudice any Claims of the United States, or of any particular State.

Section 4. The United States shall guarantee to every State in this Union a Republican Form of Government, and shall protect each of them against Invasion; and on Application of the Legislature, or the Executive (when the Legislature cannot be convened) against domestic Violence.

ARTICLE V

The Congress, whenever two-thirds of both Houses shall deem it necessary, shall propose Amendments to this Constitution, or, on the Application of the Legislatures of two-thirds of the several States, shall call a Convention for proposing Amendments, which, in either Case, shall be valid to all Intents and Purposes, as part of this Constitution, when ratified by the Legislatures of three-fourths of the several States, or by Conventions in three-fourths thereof, as the one or the other Mode of Ratification may be proposed by the Congress; Provided that no Amendment which may be made prior to the Year One thousand eight hundred and eight shall in any Manner affect the first and fourth Clauses in the Ninth Section of the first Article; and that no State, without its Consent, shall be deprived of its equal Suffrage in the Senate.

ARTICLE VI

All Debts contracted and Engagements entered into, before the Adoption of this Constitution, shall be as valid against the United States under this Constitution, as under the Confederation.

This Constitution, and the Laws of the United States which shall be made in Pursuance thereof; and the Treaties made, or which shall be made, under the Authority of the United States, shall be the supreme Law of the Land; and the Judges in every State shall be bound thereby, any Thing in the Constitution of Laws of any State to the Contrary notwithstanding.

The Senators and Representatives before mentioned, and the Members of the several State Legislatures, and all executive and judicial Officers, both of the United States and of the several States, shall be bound by Oath or Affirmation to support this Constitution; but no religious Test shall ever be required as a qualification to any Office or public Trust under the United States.

ARTICLE VII

The Ratification of the Conventions of nine States shall be sufficient for the Establishment of this Constitution between the States so ratifying the same.

Done in Convention by the Unanimous Consent of the States present the Seventeenth Day of September in the Year of our Lord one thousand seven hundred and Eighty seven, and of the Independence of the United States of America the Twelfth. In Witness whereof We have hereunto subscribed our names.

Articles in Addition to, and Amendment of, the Constitution of the United States of America. Proposed by Congress, and Ratified by the Legislatures of the Several States, Pursuant to the Fifth Article of the Original Constitution.

AMENDMENT I [1791]

Congress shall make no law respecting an establishment of religion, or prohibiting the free exercise thereof; or abridging the freedom of speech, or of the press; or the right of the people peaceably to assemble, and to petition the Government for a redress of grievances.

AMENDMENT II [1791]

A well regulated Militia, being necessary to the security of a free State, the right of the people to keep and bear Arms shall not be infringed.

AMENDMENT III [1791]

No Soldier shall, in time of peace, be quartered in any house, without the consent of the Owner, nor in time of war, but in a manner to be prescribed by law.

AMENDMENT IV [1791]

The right of the people to be secure in their persons, houses, papers, and effects, against unreasonable searches and seizures, shall not be violated, and no Warrants shall issue, but upon probable cause, supported by Oath or affirmation, and particularly describing the place to be searched, and the persons or things to be seized.

AMENDMENT V [1791]

No person shall be held to answer for a capital or otherwise infamous crime, unless on a presentment or indictment of a Grand Jury, except in cases arising in the land or naval forces, or in the Militia, when in actual service in time of war or public danger; nor shall any person be subject for the same offence to be twice put in jeopardy of life or limb; nor shall be compelled in any criminal case to be a witness against himself, nor be deprived of life, liberty, or property, without due process of law; nor shall private property be taken for public use, without just compensation.

AMENDMENT VI [1791]

In all criminal prosecutions, the accused shall enjoy the right to a speedy and public trial, by an impartial jury of the State and district wherein the crime shall have been committed, which district shall have been previously ascertained by law, and to be informed of the nature and cause of the accusation; to be confronted with the witnesses against him; to have compulsory process for obtaining witnesses in his favor, and to have the Assistance of Counsel for his defence.

AMENDMENT VII [1791]

In suits at common law, where the value in controversy shall exceed twenty dollars, the right of trial by jury shall be preserved, and no fact tried by a jury, shall be otherwise reexamined in any Court of the United States, than according to the rules of the common law.

AMENDMENT VIII [1791]

Excessive bail shall not be required, nor excessive fines imposed, nor cruel and unusual punishments inflicted.

AMENDMENT IX [1791]

The enumeration in the Constitution, of certain rights, shall not be construed to deny or disparage others retained by the people.

AMENDMENT X [1791]

The powers not delegated to the United States by the Constitution, nor prohibited by it to the States, are reserved to the States respectively, or to the people.

AMENDMENT XI [1798]

The Judicial power of the United States shall not be construed to extend to any suit in law or equity, commenced or prosecuted against one of the United States by Citizens of another State, or by Citizens or Subjects of any Foreign State.

AMENDMENT XII [1804]

The Electors shall meet in their respective States and vote by ballot for President and Vice-President, one of whom, at least, shall not be an inhabitant of the same State with themselves; they shall name in their ballots the person voted for as President, and in distinct ballots the person voted for as Vice-President, and they shall make distinct lists of all persons voted for as President, and of all persons voted for as Vice-President, and of the number of votes for each, which lists they shall sign and certify, and transmit sealed to the seat of the government of the United States, directed to the President of the Senate;—The President of the Senate shall, in the presence of the Senate and House of Representatives, open all the certificates and the votes shall then be counted;—The person having the greatest number of votes for President, shall be the President, if such number by a majority of the whole number of Electors appointed; and if no person have such majority, then from the persons having the highest numbers not exceeding three on the list of those voted for as President, the House of Representatives shall choose immediately, by ballot, the President. But in choosing the President, the votes shall be taken by states, the representation from each state having one vote; a quorum for this purpose shall consist of a member or members from two-thirds of the states, and a majority of all the states shall be necessary to a choice. And if the House of Representatives shall not choose a President whenever the right of choice shall devolve upon them, before the fourth day of March next following, then the Vice-President shall act as President, as in the case of the death or other constitutional disability of the President.—The person having the greatest number of votes as Vice-President, shall be the Vice-President, if such number be a majority of the whole number of Electors appointed, and if no person have a majority, then from the two highest numbers on the list, the Senate shall choose the Vice-President; a quorum for the purpose shall consist of two-thirds of the whole number of Senators, and a majority of the whole number shall be necessary to a choice. But no person constitutionally ineligible to the office of President shall be eligible to that of Vice-President of the United States.

AMENDMENT XIII [1865]

Section 1. Neither slavery nor involuntary servitude, except as a punishment for crime whereof the party shall have been duly convicted, shall exist within the United States, or any place subject to their jurisdiction.

Section 2. Congress shall have power to enforce this article by appropriate legislation.

AMENDMENT XIV [1868]

Section 1. All persons born or naturalized in the United States, and subject to the jurisdiction thereof, are citizens of the United States and of the State wherein they reside. No State shall make or enforce any law which shall abridge the privileges or immunities of citizens of the United States; nor shall any State deprive any person of life, liberty, or property, without due process of law; nor deny to any person within its jurisdiction the equal protection of the laws.

Section 2. Representatives shall be apportioned among the several States according to their respective numbers, counting the whole number of persons in each State, excluding Indians not taxed. But when the right to vote at any election for the choice of electors for President and Vice-President of the United States, Representatives in Congress, the Executive and Judicial officers of a State, or the members of the Legislature thereof, is denied to any of the male inhabitants of such State, being twenty-one years of age, and citizens of the United States, or in any way abridged, except for participation in rebellion, or other crime, the basis of representation therein shall be reduced in the proportion which the number of such male citizens shall bear to the whole number of male citizens twenty-one years of age in such State.

Section 3. No person shall be a Senator or Representative in Congress, or elector of President and Vice-President, or hold any office, civil or military, under the United States, or under any State, who, having previously taken an oath, as a member of Congress, or as an officer of the United States, or as a member of any State legislature, or as an executive or judicial officer of any State, to support the Constitution of the United States, shall have engaged in insurrection or rebellion against the same, or given aid or comfort to the enemies thereof. But Congress may by a vote of two-thirds of each House, remove such disability.

Section 4. The validity of the public debt of the United States, authorized by law, including debts incurred for payment of pensions and bounties for services in suppressing insurrection or rebellion, shall not be questioned. But neither the United States nor any State shall assume or pay any debt or obligation incurred in aid of insurrection or rebellion against the United States or any claim for the loss or emancipation of any slave; but all such debts, obligations, and claims shall be held illegal and void.

Section 5. The Congress shall have the power to enforce, by appropriate legislation, the provisions of this article.

AMENDMENT XV [1870]

Section 1. The right of citizens of the United States to vote shall not be denied or abridged by the United States or by any State on account of race, color, or previous condition of servitude—

Section 2. The Congress shall have power to enforce this article by appropriate legislation.

AMENDMENT XVI [1913]

The Congress shall have power to lay and collect taxes on incomes, from whatever source derived, without apportionment among the several States, and without regard to any census or enumeration.

AMENDMENT XVII [1913]

The Senate of the United States shall be composed of two Senators from each State, elected by the people thereof, for six years; and each Senator shall have one vote. The electors in each State shall have the qualifications requisite for electors of the most numerous branch of the State legislatures.

When vacancies happen in the representation of any State in the Senate, the executive authority of such State shall issue writs of election to fill such vacancies: *Provided,* That the legislature of any State may empower the executive thereof to make temporary appointments until the people fill the vacancies by election as the legislature may direct.

This amendment shall not be so construed as to affect the election or term of any Senator chosen before it becomes valid as part of the Constitution.

AMENDMENT XVIII [1919]

Section 1. After one year from the ratification of this article the manufacture, sale, or transportation of intoxicating liquors within, the importation thereof into, or the exportation thereof from the United States and all territory subject to the jurisdiction thereof for beverage purposes is hereby prohibited.

Section 2. The Congress and the several States shall have concurrent power to enforce this article by appropriate legislation.

Section 3. This article shall be inoperative unless it shall have been ratified as an amendment to the Constitution by the legislatures of the several States, as provided in the Constitution, within seven years from the date of the submission hereof to the States by the Congress.

AMENDMENT XIX [1920]

The right of citizens of the United States to vote shall not be denied or abridged by the United States or by any State on account of sex.

Congress shall have power to enforce this article by appropriate legislation.

AMENDMENT XX [1933]

Section 1. The terms of the President and Vice-President shall end at noon on the 20th day of January, and the terms of Senators and Representatives at noon on the 3d day of January, of the years in which such terms would have ended if this article had not been ratified; and the terms of their successors shall then begin.

Section 2. The Congress shall assemble at least once in every year, and such meeting shall begin at noon on the 3d day of January, unless they shall by law appoint a different day.

Section 3. If, at the time fixed for the beginning of the term of the President, the President elect shall have died, the Vice-President elect shall become President. If a President shall not have been chosen before the time fixed for the beginning of his term, or if the President elect shall have failed to qualify, then the Vice-President until a President shall have qualified; and the Congress may by law provide for the case wherein neither a President elect nor a Vice-President elect shall have qualified, declaring who shall then act as President, or the manner in which one who is to act shall be selected, and such person shall act accordingly until a President or Vice-President shall have qualified.

Section 4. The Congress may by law provide for the case of the death of any of the persons from whom the House of Representatives may choose a President whenever the right of choice shall have devolved upon them, and for the case of the death of any of the persons from whom the Senate may choose a Vice-President whenever the right of choice shall have devolved upon them.

Section 5. Sections 1 and 2 shall take effect on the 15th day of October following the ratification of this article.

Section 6. This article shall be inoperative unless it shall have been ratified as an amendment to the Constitution by the legislatures of three-fourths of the several States within seven years from the date of its submission.

AMENDMENT XXI [1933]

Section 1. The eighteenth article of amendment to the Constitution of the United States is hereby repealed.

Section 2. The transportation or importation into any State, Territory, or possession of the United States for delivery or use therein of intoxicating liquors, in violation of the laws thereof, is hereby prohibited.

Section 3. This article shall be inoperative unless it shall have been ratified as an amendment to the Constitution by conventions in the several States, as provided in the Constitution, within seven years from the date of the submission hereof to the States by the Congress.

AMENDMENT XXII [1951]

No person shall be elected to the office of the President more than twice, and no person who has held the office of President, or acted as President, for more than two years of a term to which some other person was elected President shall be elected to the office of the President more than once.

But this Article shall not apply to any person holding the office of President when this Article was proposed by the Congress, and shall not prevent any person who may be holding the office of President, or acting as President, during the term within which this Article becomes operative from holding the office of President or acting as President during the remainder of such term.

AMENDMENT XXIII [1961]

Section 1. The District constituting the seat of Government of the United States shall appoint in such manner as the Congress may direct:

A number of electors of President and Vice President equal to the whole number of Senators and Representatives in Congress to which the District would be entitled if it were a State, but in no event more than the least populous State; they shall be in addition to those appointed by the States, but they shall be considered, for the purposes of the election of President and Vice President, to be electors appointed by a State; and they shall meet in the District and perform such duties as provided by the twelfth article of amendment.

Section 2. The Congress shall have power to enforce this article by appropriate legislation.

AMENDMENT XXIV [1964]

Section 1. The right of citizens of the United States to vote in any primary or other election for President or Vice President, for electors for President or Vice President, or for Senator or Representative in Congress, shall not be denied or abridged by the United States or any State by reason of failure to pay any poll tax or other tax.

Section 2. The Congress shall have the power to enforce this article by appropriate legislation.

AMENDMENT XXV [1967]

Section 1. In case of the removal of the President from office or his death or resignation, the Vice President shall become President.

Section 2. Whenever there is a vacancy in the office of the Vice President, the President shall nominate a Vice President who shall take the office upon confirmation by a majority vote of both houses of Congress.

Section 3. Whenever the President transmits to the President pro tempore of the Senate and the Speaker of the House of Representatives his written declaration that he is unable to discharge the powers and duties of his office, and until he transmits to them a written declaration to the contrary, such powers and duties shall be discharged by the Vice President as Acting President.

Section 4. Whenever the Vice President and a majority of either the principal officers of the executive departments, or of such other body as Congress may by law provide, transmit to the President pro tempore of the Senate and the Speaker of the House of Representatives their written declaration that the President is unable to discharge the powers and duties of his office, the Vice President shall immediately assume the powers and duties of the office as Acting President.

Thereafter, when the President transmits to the President pro tempore of the Senate and the Speaker of the House of Representatives his written declaration that no inability exists, he shall resume the powers and duties of his office unless the Vice President and a majority of either the principal officers of the executive departments, or of such other body as Congress may by law provide, transmit within four days to the President pro tempore of the Senate and the Speaker of the House of Representatives their written declaration that the President is unable to discharge the powers and duties of his office. Thereupon Congress shall decide the issue, assembling within 48 hours for that purpose if not in session. If the Congress, within 21 days after receipt of the latter written declaration, or, if Congress is not in session, within 21 days after Congress is required to assemble, determines by two-thirds vote of both houses that the President is unable to discharge the powers and duties of his office, the Vice President shall continue to discharge the same as Acting President; otherwise, the President shall resume the powers and duties of his office.

Admission of States to the Union

1	Delaware	Dec. 7, 1787	26	Michigan	Jan. 26, 1837
2	Pennsylvania	Dec. 12, 1787	27	Florida	Mar. 3, 1845
3	New Jersey	Dec. 18, 1787	28	Texas	Dec. 29, 1845
4	Georgia	Jan. 2, 1788	29	Iowa	Dec. 28, 1846
5	Connecticut	Jan. 9, 1788	30	Wisconsin	May 29, 1848
6	Massachusetts	Feb. 6, 1788	31	California	Sept. 9, 1850
7	Maryland	Apr. 28, 1788	32	Minnesota	May 11, 1858
8	South Carolina	May 23, 1788	33	Oregon	Feb. 14, 1859
9	New Hampshire	June 21, 1788	34	Kansas	Jan. 29, 1861
10	Virginia	June 25, 1788	35	West Virginia	June 19, 1863
11	New York	July 26, 1788	36	Nevada	Oct. 31, 1864
12	North Carolina	Nov. 21, 1789	37	Nebraska	Mar. 1, 1867
13	Rhode Island	May 29, 1790	38	Colorado	Aug. 1, 1876
14	Vermont	Mar. 4, 1791	39	North Dakota	Nov. 2, 1889
15	Kentucky	June 1, 1792	40	South Dakota	Nov. 2, 1889
16	Tennessee	June 1, 1796	41	Montana	Nov. 8, 1889
17	Ohio	Mar. 1, 1803	42	Washington	Nov. 11, 1889
18	Louisiana	Apr. 30, 1812	43	Idaho	July 3, 1890
19	Indiana	Dec. 11, 1816	44	Wyoming	July 10, 1890
20	Mississippi	Dec. 10, 1817	45	Utah	Jan. 4, 1896
21	Illinois	Dec. 3, 1818	46	Oklahoma	Nov. 16, 1907
22	Alabama	Dec. 14, 1819	47	New Mexico	Jan. 6, 1912
23	Maine	Mar. 15, 1820	48	Arizona	Feb. 14, 1912
24	Missouri	Aug. 10, 1821	49	Alaska	Jan. 3, 1959
25	Arkansas	June 15, 1836	50	Hawaii	Aug. 21, 1959

Population of the United States, 1790–1980

YEAR	NUMBER OF STATES	POPULATION	PERCENT INCREASE
1790	13	3,929,214	
1800	16	5,308,483	35.1
1810	17	7,239,881	36.4
1820	23	9,638,453	33.1
1830	24	12,866,020	33.5
1840	26	17,069,453	32.7
1850	31	23,191,876	35.9
1860	33	31,443,321	35.6
1870	37	39,818,449	26.6
1880	38	50,155,783	26.0
1890	44	62,947,714	25.5
1900	45	75,994,575	20.7
1910	46	91,972,266	21.0
1920	48	105,710,620	14.9
1930	48	122,775,046	16.1
1940	48	131,669,275	7.2
1950	48	150,697,361	14.5
1960	50	179,323,175	19.0
1970	50	203,235,298	13.3
1980	50	226,504,825	11.4

The Vice Presidents and the Cabinet

SECRETARY OF STATE (1789–)

Thomas Jefferson	1789
Edmund Randolph	1794
Timothy Pickering	1795
John Marshall	1800
James Madison	1801
Robert Smith	1809
James Monroe	1811
John Q. Adams	1817
Henry Clay	1825
Martin Van Buren	1829
Edward Livingston	1831
Louis McLane	1833
John Forsyth	1834
Daniel Webster	1841
Hugh S. Legaré	1843
Abel P. Upshur	1843
John C. Calhoun	1844
James Buchanan	1845
John M. Clayton	1849
Daniel Webster	1850
Edward Everett	1852
William L. Marcy	1853
Lewis Cass	1857
Jeremiah S. Black	1860
William H. Seward	1861
E. B. Washburne	1869
Hamilton Fish	1869
William M. Evarts	1877
James G. Blaine	1881
F. T. Frelinghuysen	1881
Thomas F. Bayard	1885
James G. Blaine	1889
John W. Foster	1892
Walter Q. Gresham	1893
Richard Olney	1895
John Sherman	1897
William R. Day	1897
John Hay	1898
Elihu Root	1905
Robert Bacon	1909
Philander C. Knox	1909
William J. Bryan	1913
Robert Lansing	1915
Bainbridge Colby	1920
Charles E. Hughes	1921
Frank B. Kellogg	1925
Henry L. Stimson	1929
Cordell Hull	1933
E. R. Stettinius, Jr.	1944
James F. Byrnes	1945
George C. Marshall	1947
Dean Acheson	1949
John Foster Dulles	1953
Christian A. Herter	1959
Dean Rusk	1961
William P. Rogers	1969
Henry A. Kissinger	1973
Cyrus Vance	1977
Edmund Muskie	1979
Alexander M. Haig, Jr.	1981
George Shultz	1982

SECRETARY OF THE TREASURY (1789–)

Alexander Hamilton	1789
Oliver Wolcott	1795
Samuel Dexter	1801
Albert Gallatin	1801
G. W. Campbell	1814
A. J. Dallas	1814
William H. Crawford	1816
Richard Rush	1825
Samuel D. Ingham	1829
Louis McLane	1831
William J. Duane	1833
Roger B. Taney	1833
Levi Woodbury	1834
Thomas Ewing	1841
Walter Forward	1841
John C. Spencer	1843
George M. Bibb	1844
Robert J. Walker	1845
William M. Meredith	1849
Thomas Corwin	1850
James Guthrie	1853
Howell Cobb	1857
Philip F. Thomas	1860
John A. Dix	1861
Salmon P. Chase	1861
Wm. P. Fessenden	1864
Hugh McCulloch	1865
George S. Boutwell	1869
William A. Richardson	1873
Benjamin H. Bristow	1874
Lot M. Morrill	1876
John Sherman	1877
William Windom	1881
Charles J. Folger	1881
Walter Q. Gresham	1884
Hugh McCulloch	1884
Daniel Manning	1885
Charles S. Fairchild	1887
William Windom	1889
Charles Foster	1891
John G. Carlisle	1893
Lyman J. Gage	1897
Leslie M. Shaw	1902
George B. Cortelyou	1907
Franklin MacVeagh	1909
William G. McAdoo	1913
Carter Glass	1919
David F. Houston	1919
Andrew W. Mellon	1921
Ogden L. Mills	1932
William H. Woodin	1933
Henry Morgenthau, Jr.	1934
Fred M. Vinson	1945
John W. Snyder	1946
George M. Humphrey	1953
Robert B. Anderson	1957
C. Douglas Dillon	1961
Henry H. Fowler	1965
David M. Kennedy	1969
John B. Connally	1970
George P. Shultz	1972
William E. Simon	1974
Michael W. Blumenthal	1977
G. William Miller	1979
Donald T. Regan	1981

SECRETARY OF WAR (1789–1947)

Henry Knox	1789
Timothy Pickering	1795
James McHenry	1796
John Marshall	1800
Samuel Dexter	1800
Roger Griswold	1801
Henry Dearborn	1801
William Eustis	1809
John Armstrong	1813
James Monroe	1814
William H. Crawford	1815
Isaac Shelby	1817
George Graham	1817
John C. Calhoun	1817
James Barbour	1825
Peter B. Porter	1828
John H. Eaton	1829
Lewis Cass	1831
Benjamin F. Butler	1837
Joel R. Poinsett	1837
John Bell	1841
John McLean	1841

John C. Spencer	1841
James M. Porter	1843
William Wilkins	1844
William L. Marcy	1845
George W. Crawford	1849
Charles M. Conrad	1850
Jefferson Davis	1853
John B. Floyd	1857
Joseph Holt	1861
Simon Cameron	1861
Edwin M. Stanton	1862
Ulysses S. Grant	1867
Lorenzo Thomas	1868
John M. Schofield	1868
John A. Rawlins	1869
William T. Sherman	1869
William W. Belknap	1869
Alphonso Taft	1876
James D. Cameron	1876
George W. McCrary	1877
Alexander Ramsey	1879
Robert T. Lincoln	1881
William C. Endicott	1885
Redfield Proctor	1889
Stephen B. Elkins	1891
Daniel S. Lamont	1893
Russell A. Alger	1897
Elihu Root	1899
William H. Taft	1904
Luke E. Wright	1908
J. M. Dickinson	1909
Henry L. Stimson	1911
L. M. Garrison	1913
Newton D. Baker	1916
John W. Weeks	1921
Dwight F. Davis	1925
James W. Good	1929
Patrick J. Hurley	1929
George H. Dern	1933
H. A. Woodring	1936
Henry L. Stimson	1940
Robert P. Patterson	1945
Kenneth C. Royall	1947

SECRETARY OF THE NAVY (1798–1947)

Benjamin Stoddert	1798
Robert Smith	1801
Paul Hamilton	1809
William Jones	1813
B. W. Crowninshield	1814
Smith Thompson	1818
S. L. Southard	1823
John Branch	1829
Levi Woodbury	1831
Mahlon Dickerson	1834
James K. Paulding	1838
George E. Badger	1841
Abel P. Upshur	1841
David Henshaw	1843
Thomas W. Gilmer	1844
John Y. Mason	1844
George Bancroft	1845
John Y. Mason	1846
William B. Preston	1849
William A. Graham	1850
John P. Kennedy	1852
James C. Dobbin	1853
Isaac Toucey	1857
Gideon Welles	1861
Adolph E. Borie	1869
George M. Robeson	1869
R. W. Thompson	1877
Nathan Goff, Jr.	1881
William H. Hunt	1881
William E. Chandler	1881
William C. Whitney	1885
Benjamin F. Tracy	1889
Hilary A. Herbert	1893
John D. Long	1897
William H. Moody	1902
Paul Morton	1904
Charles J. Bonaparte	1905
Victor H. Metcalf	1907
T. H. Newberry	1908
George von L. Meyer	1909
Josephus Daniels	1913
Edwin Denby	1921
Curtis D. Wilbur	1924
Charles F. Adams	1929
Claude A. Swanson	1933
Charles Edison	1940
Frank Knox	1940
James V. Forrestal	1945

SECRETARY OF DEFENSE (1947–)

James V. Forrestal	1947
Louis A. Johnson	1949
George C. Marshall	1950
Robert A. Lovett	1951
Charles E. Wilson	1953
Neil H. McElroy	1957
Thomas S. Gates, Jr.	1959
Robert S. McNamara	1961
Clark M. Clifford	1968
Melvin R. Laird	1969
Elliot L. Richardson	1973
James R. Schlesinger	1973
Donald Rumsfeld	1974
Harold Brown	1977
Caspar Weinberger	1981

POSTMASTER GENERAL (1789–1970)

Samuel Osgood	1789
Timothy Pickering	1791
Joseph Habersham	1795
Gideon Granger	1801
Return J. Meigs, Jr.	1814
John McLean	1823
William T. Barry	1829
Amos Kendall	1835
John M. Niles	1840
Francis Granger	1841
Charles A. Wickliffe	1841
Cave Johnson	1845
Jacob Collamer	1849
Nathan K. Hall	1850
Samuel D. Hubbard	1852
James Campbell	1853
Aaron V. Brown	1857
Joseph Holt	1859
Horatio King	1861
Montgomery Blair	1861
William Dennison	1864
Alexander W. Randall	1866
John A. J. Creswell	1869
James W. Marshall	1874
Marshall Jewell	1874
James N. Tyner	1876
David M. Key	1877
Horace Maynard	1880
Thomas L. James	1881
Timothy O. Howe	1881
Walter Q. Gresham	1883
Frank Hatton	1884
William F. Vilas	1885
Don M. Dickinson	1888
John Wanamaker	1889
Wilson S. Bissel	1893
William L. Wilson	1895
James A. Gary	1897
Charles E. Smith	1898
Henry C. Payne	1902
Robert J. Wynne	1904
George B. Cortelyou	1905
George von L. Meyer	1907
F. H. Hitchcock	1909
Albert S. Burleson	1913
Will H. Hays	1921
Hubert Work	1922

Harry S. New	1923
Walter F. Brown	1929
James A. Farley	1933
Frank C. Walker	1940
Robert E. Hannegan	1945
J. M. Donaldson	1947
A. E. Summerfield	1953
J. Edward Day	1961
John A. Gronouski	1963
Lawrence F. O'Brien	1965
W. Marvin Watson	1968
Winton M. Blount	1969

ATTORNEY GENERAL (1789–)

Edmund Randolph	1789
William Bradford	1794
Charles Lee	1795
Theophilus Parsons	1801
Levi Lincoln	1801
Robert Smith	1805
John Breckinridge	1805
Caesar A. Rodney	1807
William Pinkney	1811
Richard Rush	1814
William Wirt	1817
John M. Berrien	1829
Roger B. Taney	1831
Benjamin F. Butler	1833
Felix Grundy	1838
Henry D. Gilpin	1840
John J. Crittenden	1841
Hugh S. Legare	1841
John Nelson	1843
John Y. Mason	1845
Nathan Clifford	1846
Isaac Toucey	1848
Reverdy Johnson	1849
John J. Crittenden	1850
Caleb Cushing	1853
Jeremiah S. Black	1857
Edwin M. Stanton	1860
Edward Bates	1861
Titian J. Coffey	1863
James Speed	1864
Henry Stanbery	1866
William M. Evarts	1868
Ebenezer R. Hoar	1869
Amos T. Ackerman	1870
George H. Williams	1871
Edward Pierrepont	1875
Alphonso Taft	1876
Charles Devens	1877
Wayne MacVeagh	1881
Benjamin H. Brewster	1881
A. H. Garland	1885
William H. H. Miller	1889
Richard Olney	1893
Judson Harmon	1895
Joseph McKenna	1897
John W. Griggs	1897
Philander C. Knox	1901
William H. Moody	1904
Charles J. Bonaparte	1907
G. W. Wickersham	1909
J. C. McReynolds	1913
Thomas W. Gregory	1914
A. Mitchell Palmer	1919
H. M. Daugherty	1921
Harlan F. Stone	1924
John G. Sargent	1925
William D. Mitchell	1929
H. S. Cummings	1933
Frank Murphy	1939
Robert H. Jackson	1940
Francis Biddle	1941
Tom C. Clark	1945
J. H. McGrath	1949
J. P. McGranery	1952
H. Brownell, Jr.	1953
William P. Rogers	1957
Robert F. Kennedy	1961
Nicholas Katzenback	1964
Ramsey Clark	1967
John N. Mitchell	1969
Richard G. Kleindienst	1972
Elliot L. Richardson	1973
William Saxbe	1974
Edward H. Levi	1974
Griffin B. Bell	1977
Benjamin R. Civiletti	1979
William French Smith	1981

SECRETARY OF THE INTERIOR (1849–)

Thomas Ewing	1849
T. M. T. McKennan	1850
Alexander H. H. Stuart	1850
Robert McClelland	1853
Jacob Thompson	1857
Caleb B. Smith	1861
John P. Usher	1863
James Harlan	1865
O. H. Browning	1866
Jacob D. Cox	1869
Columbus Delano	1870
Zachariah Chandler	1875
Carl Schurz	1877
Samuel J. Kirkwood	1881
Henry M. Teller	1881
L. Q. C. Lamar	1885
William F. Vilas	1888
John W. Noble	1889
Hoke Smith	1893
David R. Francis	1896
Cornelius N. Bliss	1897
E. A. Hitchcock	1899
James R. Garfield	1907
R. A. Ballinger	1909
Walter L. Fisher	1911
Franklin K. Lane	1913
John B. Payne	1920
Albert B. Fall	1921
Hubert Work	1923
Roy O. West	1928
Ray L. Wilbur	1929
Harold L. Ickes	1933
Julius A. Krug	1946
Oscar L. Chapman	1949
Douglas McKay	1953
Fred A. Seaton	1956
Steward L. Udall	1961
Walter J. Hickel	1969
Rogers C. B. Morton	1971
Thomas S. Kleppe	1975
Cecil D. Andrus	1977
James G. Watt	1981
William Ruckelshaus	1983

SECRETARY OF AGRICULTURE (1889–)

Norman J. Colman	1889
Jeremiah M. Rusk	1889
J. Sterling Morton	1893
James Wilson	1897
David F. Houston	1913
Edward T. Meredith	1920
Henry C. Wallace	1921
Howard M. Gore	1924
William M. Jardine	1925
Arthur M. Hyde	1929
Henry A. Wallace	1933
Claude R. Wickard	1940
Clinton P. Anderson	1945
Charles F. Brannan	1948
Ezra Taft Benson	1953
Orville L. Freeman	1961
Clifford M. Hardin	1969
Earl L. Butz	1971
John A. Knebel	1976
Bob Bergland	1977
John R. Block	1981

SECRETARY OF COMMERCE AND LABOR (1903–1913)

George B. Cortelyou	1903
Victor H. Metcalf	1904
Oscar S. Straus	1906
Charles Nagel	1909

SECRETARY OF COMMERCE (1913–)

William C. Redfield	1913
Joshua W. Alexander	1919
Herbert Hoover	1921
William F. Whiting	1928
Robert P. Lamont	1929
Roy D. Chapin	1932
Daniel C. Roper	1933
Henry L. Hopkins	1939
Jesse Jones	1940
Henry A. Wallace	1945
W. A. Harriman	1946
Charles Sawyer	1948
Sinclair Weeks	1953
Lewis L. Strauss	1958
F. H. Mueller	1959
Luther Hodges	1961
John T. Connor	1965
A. B. Trowbridge	1967
C. R. Smith	1968
Maurice H. Stans	1969
Peter G. Peterson	1972
Frederick B. Dent	1973
Elliot L. Richardson	1974
Juanita M. Kreps	1977
Philip M. Klutznick	1979
Malcolm Baldridge	1981

SECRETARY OF LABOR (1913–)

William B. Wilson	1913
James J. Davis	1921
William N. Doak	1930
Frances Perkins	1933
L. B. Schwellenbach	1945
Maurice J. Tobin	1948
Martin P. Durkin	1953
James P. Mitchell	1953
Arthur J. Goldberg	1961
W. Willard Wirtz	1962
George P. Shultz	1969
James D. Hodgson	1970
Peter J. Brennan	1973
W. J. Usery, Jr.	1974
Ray Marshall	1977
Raymond J. Donovan	1981

SECRETARY OF HEALTH, EDUCATION, AND WELFARE (1953–1979)

Oveta Culp Hobby	1953
Marion B. Folsom	1955
Arthur S. Flemming	1958
Abraham A. Ribicoff	1961
Anthony J. Celebrezze	1962
John W. Gardner	1965
Wilbur J. Cohen	1968
Robert H. Finch	1969
Elliot L. Richardson	1970
Caspar W. Weinberger	1973
David Matthews	1974
Joseph A. Califano, Jr.	1977

SECRETARY OF HEALTH AND HUMAN SERVICES (1979–)

Patricia R. Harris	1979
Richard S. Schweiker	1981
Margaret Heckler	1983

SECRETARY OF HOUSING AND URBAN DEVELOPMENT (1966–)

Robert C. Weaver	1966
George W. Romney	1969
James T. Lynn	1973
Carla Anderson Hills	1974
Patricia Harris	1977
Moon Landrieu	1979
Samuel R. Pierce, Jr.	1981

SECRETARY OF TRANSPORTATION (1967–)

Alan S. Boyd	1967
John A. Volpe	1969
Claude S. Brinegar	1973
William T. Coleman	1974
Brock Adams	1977
Neil E. Goldschmidt	1979
Andrew L. Lewis, Jr.	1981
Elizabeth Dole	1983

SECRETARY OF ENERGY (1977–)

James R. Schlesinger	1977
Charles W. Duncan, Jr.	1979
James B. Edwards	1981
Donald Hodel	1982

SECRETARY OF EDUCATION (1979–)

Shirley M. Hufstedter	1979
Terrel Bell	1981

VICE PRESIDENT

John Adams	1789–97
Thomas Jefferson	1797–1801
Aaron Burr	1801–05
George Clinton	1805–13
Elbridge Gerry	1813–17
Daniel D. Tompkins	1817–25
John C. Calhoun	1825–33
Martin Van Buren	1833–37
Richard M. Johnson	1837–41
John Tyler	1841
George M. Dallas	1845–49
Millard Fillmore	1849–50
William R. King	1853–57
John C. Breckinridge	1857–61
Hannibal Hamlin	1861–65
Andrew Johnson	1865
Schuyler Colfax	1869–73
Henry Wilson	1873–77
William A. Wheeler	1877–81
Chester A. Arthur	1881
Thomas A. Hendricks	1885–89
Levi P. Morton	1889–93
Adlai E. Stevenson	1893–97
Garret A. Hobart	1897–1901
Theodore Roosevelt	1901
Charles W. Fairbanks	1905–09
James S. Sherman	1909–13
Thomas R. Marshall	1913–21
Calvin Coolidge	1921–23
Charles G. Dawes	1925–29
Charles Curtis	1929–33
John Nance Garner	1933–41
Henry A. Wallace	1941–45
Harry S Truman	1945
Alben W. Barkley	1949–53
Richard M. Nixon	1953–61
Lyndon B. Johnson	1961–63
Hubert H. Humphrey	1965–69
Spiro T. Agnew	1969–73
Gerald R. Ford	1973–74
Nelson W. Rockefeller	1974–77
Walter F. Mondale	1977–81
George Bush	1981–

Presidential Elections, 1789–1980

Year	Candidates	Party	Popular Vote	Electoral Vote
1789	**George Washington**			69
	John Adams			34
	Others			35
1792	**George Washington**			132
	John Adams			77
	George Clinton			50
	Others			5
1796	**John Adams**	Federalist		71
	Thomas Jefferson	Democratic-Republican		68
	Thomas Pinckney	Federalist		59
	Aaron Burr	Democratic-Republican		30
	Others			48
1800	**Thomas Jefferson**	Democratic-Republican		73
	Aaron Burr	Democratic-Republican		73
	John Adams	Federalist		65
	Charles C. Pinckney	Federalist		64
1804	**Thomas Jefferson**	Democratic-Republican		162
	Charles C. Pinckney	Federalist		14
1808	**James Madison**	Democratic-Republican		122
	Charles C. Pinckney	Federalist		47
	George Clinton	Independent-Republican		6
1812	**James Madison**	Democratic-Republican		128
	DeWitt Clinton	Federalist		89
1816	**James Monroe**	Democratic-Republican		183
	Rufus King	Federalist		34
1820	**James Monroe**	Democratic-Republican		231
	John Quincy Adams	Independent-Republican		1
1824	**John Quincy Adams**	Democratic-Republican	113,122 (30.9%)	84
	Andrew Jackson	Democratic-Republican	151,271 (41.3%)	99
	Henry Clay	Democratic-Republican	47,531 (12.9%)	37
	William H. Crawford	Democratic Republican	40,856 (11.1%)	41
1828	**Andrew Jackson**	Democratic	642,553 (55.9%)	178
	John Quincy Adams	National Republican	500,897 (43.6%)	83
1832	**Andrew Jackson**	Democratic	701,780 (54.2%)	219
	Henry Clay	National Republican	484,205 (37.4%)	49
	William Wirt	Anti-Masonic	100,715 (7.7%)	7
1836	**Martin Van Buren**	Democratic	763,176 (50.8%)	170
	William H. Harrison	Whig	550,816 (36.6%)	73
	Hugh L. White	Whig	146,107 (9.7%)	26
	Daniel Webster	Whig	41,201 (2.7%)	14
1840	**William H. Harrison** (**John Tyler,** 1841)	Whig	1,275,390 (52.8%)	234
	Martin Van Buren	Democratic	1,128,854 (46.8%)	60

Year	Candidates	Party	Popular Vote	Electoral Vote
1844	**James K. Polk**	Democratic	1,339,494 (49.5%)	170
	Henry Clay	Whig	1,300,004 (48.0%)	105
	James G. Birney	Liberty	62,103 (2.3%)	
1848	**Zachary Taylor**	Whig	1,361,393 (47.2%)	163
	(**Millard Fillmore**, 1850)			
	Lewis Cass	Democratic	1,223,460 (42.4%)	127
	Martin Van Buren	Free Soil	291,501 (10.1%)	
1852	**Franklin Pierce**	Democratic	1,607,510 (50.8%)	254
	Winfield Scott	Whig	1,386,942 (43.8%)	42
1856	**James Buchanan**	Democratic	1,836,072 (45.2%)	174
	John C. Frémont	Republican	1,342,345 (33.1%)	114
	Millard Fillmore	American	873,053 (21.5%)	8
1860	**Abraham Lincoln**	Republican	1,865,908 (39.8%)	180
	Stephen A. Douglas	Democratic	1,382,202 (29.4%)	12
	John C. Breckinridge	Democratic	848,019 (18.0%)	72
	John Bell	Constitutional Union	591,901 (12.6%)	39
1864	**Abraham Lincoln**	Republican	2,218,388 (55.0%)	212
	(**Andrew Johnson**, 1865)			
	George B. McClellan	Democratic	1,812,807 (44.9%)	21
1868	**Ulysses S. Grant**	Republican	3,013,650 (52.6%)	214
	Horatio Seymour	Democratic	2,708,744 (47.3%)	80
1872	**Ulysses S. Grant**	Republican	3,598,235 (55.6%)	286
	Horace Greeley	Democratic	2,834,761 (43.8%)	66
1876	**Rutherford B. Hayes**	Republican	4,034,311 (47.9%)	185
	Samuel J. Tilden	Democratic	4,288,546 (50.0%)	184
1880	**James A. Garfield**	Republican	4,446,158 (48.2%)	214
	(**Chester A. Arthur**, 1881)			
	Winfield S. Hancock	Democratic	4,444,260 (48.2%)	155
	James B. Weaver	Greenback-Labor	305,997 (3.3%)	
1884	**Grover Cleveland**	Democratic	4,874,621 (48.5%)	219
	James G. Blaine	Republican	4,848,936 (48.2%)	182
	Benjamin F. Butler	Greenback-Labor	175,096 (1.7%)	
1888	**Benjamin Harrison**	Republican	5,443,892 (47.8%)	233
	Grover Cleveland	Democratic	5,534,488 (48.6%)	168
1892	**Grover Cleveland**	Democratic	5,551,883 (46.0%)	277
	Benjamin Harrison	Republican	5,179,244 (42.9%)	145
	James B. Weaver	People's	1,024,280 (8.5%)	22
1896	**William McKinley**	Republican	7,108,480 (51.0%)	271
	William J. Bryan	Democratic; Populist	6,511,495 (46.7%)	176
1900	**William McKinley**	Republican	7,218,039 (51.6%)	292
	(**Theodore Roosevelt**, 1901)			
	William J. Bryan	Democratic; Populist	6,358,345 (45.5%)	155
1904	**Theodore Roosevelt**	Republican	7,626,593 (56.4%)	336
	Alton B. Parker	Democratic	5,082,898 (37.6%)	140
	Eugene V. Debs	Socialist	402,489 (2.9%)	

Year	Candidates	Party	Popular Vote	Electoral Vote
1908	**William H. Taft**	Republican	7,676,258 (51.5%)	321
	William J. Bryan	Democratic	6,406,801 (43.0%)	162
	Eugene V. Debs	Socialist	420,380 (2.8%)	
1912	**Woodrow Wilson**	Democratic	6,293,152 (41.8%)	435
	Theodore Roosevelt	Progressive	4,119,207 (27.3%)	88
	William H. Taft	Republican	3,486,383 (23.1%)	8
	Eugene V. Debs	Socialist	900,369 (5.9%)	
1916	**Woodrow Wilson**	Democratic	9,126,300 (49.2%)	277
	Charles E. Hughes	Republican	8,546,789 (46.1%)	254
1920	**Warren G. Harding**	Republican	16,133,314 (60.3%)	404
	(**Calvin Coolidge,** 1923)			
	James M. Cox	Democratic	9,140,884 (34.1%)	127
	Eugene V. Debs	Socialist	913,664 (3.4%)	
1924	**Calvin Coolidge**	Republican	15,717,553 (54.0%)	382
	John W. Davis	Democratic	8,386,169 (28.8%)	136
	Robert M. La Follette	Progressive	4,814,050 (16.5%)	13
1928	**Herbert C. Hoover**	Republican	21,411,991 (58.2%)	444
	Alfred E. Smith	Democratic	15,000,185 (40.7%)	87
1932	**Franklin D. Roosevelt**	Democratic	22,825,016 (57.4%)	472
	Herbert C. Hoover	Republican	15,758,397 (39.6%)	59
	Norman Thomas	Socialist	883,990 (2.2%)	
1936	**Franklin D. Roosevelt**	Democratic	27,747,636 (60.7%)	523
	Alfred M. Landon	Republican	16,679,543 (36.5%)	8
	William Lemke	Union	892,492 (1.9%)	
1940	**Franklin D. Roosevelt**	Democratic	27,263,448 (54.7%)	449
	Wendell L. Wilkie	Republican	22,336,260 (44.8%)	82
1944	**Franklin D. Roosevelt**	Democratic	25,611,936 (53.3%)	432
	(**Harry S Truman,** 1945)			
	Thomas E. Dewey	Republican	22,013,372 (45.8%)	99
1948	**Harry S Truman**	Democratic	24,105,587 (49.5%)	303
	Thomas E. Dewey	Republican	21,970,017 (45.1%)	189
	J. Strom Thurmond	States' Rights	1,169,134 (2.4%)	39
	Henry A. Wallace	Progressive	1,157,057 (2.3%)	
1952	**Dwight D. Eisenhower**	Republican	33,936,137 (55.1%)	442
	Adlai E. Stevenson	Democratic	27,314,649 (44.3%)	89
1956	**Dwight D. Eisenhower**	Republican	35,585,245 (57.3%)	457
	Adlai E. Stevenson	Democratic	26,030,172 (41.9%)	73
1960	**John F. Kennedy**	Democratic	34,221,344 (49.7%)	303
	(**Lyndon B. Johnson,** 1963)			
	Richard M. Nixon	Republican	34,106,671 (49.5%)	219
1964	**Lyndon B. Johnson**	Democratic	43,126,584 (61.0%)	486
	Barry M. Goldwater	Republican	27,177,838 (38.4%)	52
1968	**Richard M. Nixon**	Republican	31,783,148 (43.4%)	301
	Hubert H. Humphrey	Democratic	31,274,503 (42.7%)	191
	George C. Wallace	Amer. Independent	9,901,151 (13.5%)	46

Year	Candidates	Party	Popular Vote	Electoral Vote
1972	**Richard M. Nixon**	Republican	47,170,179 (60.6%)	520
	George S. McGovern	Democratic	29,171,791 (37.5%)	17
1974	**Gerald R. Ford**	Republican	Appointed on August 9, 1974, as President after the resignation of Richard M. Nixon.	
1976	**Jimmy Carter**	Democratic	40,828,587 (50.1%)	297
	Gerald R. Ford	Republican	39,147,613 (48.0%)	240
1980	**Ronald Reagan**	Republican	43,899,248 (50.7%)	489
	Jimmy Carter	Democratic	35,481,435 (41.0%)	49
	John Anderson	Independent	5,719,437 (6.6%)	

Index